PROFESSIONAL ANDROID®, FOURTH EDITION

PROFESSIONAL

Android®

Fourth Edition

PROFESSIONAL

Android®

Fourth Edition

Reto Meier
Ian Lake

A Wiley Brand

Professional Android®, Fourth Edition

Published by
John Wiley & Sons, Inc.
10475 Crosspoint Boulevard
Indianapolis, IN 46256
www.wiley.com

Copyright © 2018 by John Wiley & Sons, Inc., Indianapolis, Indiana

Published simultaneously in Canada

ISBN: 978-1-118-94952-8
ISBN: 978-1-118-94954-2 (ebk)
ISBN: 978-1-118-94953-5 (ebk)

Manufactured in the United States of America

C10003525_081518

Library of Congress Control Number: 2018951986

To Kris.

—Reto

To Andrea and Hannah.

—Ian

ABOUT THE AUTHORS

RETO MEIER has been working to help Android developers create the best applications possible for their users since the initial Android release in 2007. Reto grew up in Perth, Western Australia, and then spent "the next 18 months" in London for a total of 6 years, before settling in the San Francisco Bay Area with his wife in 2011.

Reto has spent 10 years as a Developer Advocate at Google, contributing articles, online training, conference talks, and YouTube videos to the developer community.

Before smartphones were invented, Reto spent over 10 years as a software developer in various industries, including offshore oil and gas and finance.

You can learn more about Reto's thoughts on Android development, ask him questions, and see pictures of his cats on Twitter at `www.twitter.com/retomeier`, where he shares more than he probably should, and read longer thoughts on Medium at `medium.com/@retomeier`.

IAN LAKE has lived in nine states across the United States before settling in the San Francisco Bay Area in 2013.

Ian is a member of the Android Toolkit team at Google, focused on providing the libraries and APIs needed for modern Android development. His prior experience includes that as an Android Developer Advocate, Android app developer, and enterprise application developer back when Android wasn't even an option.

You can connect with Ian on Google+ (`plus.google.com/+IanLake`) or Twitter (`www.twitter.com/ianhlake`) to learn more about his wonderful family, hobbies (mostly Android development), and interests.

While Reto and Ian work at Google, the views and opinions expressed in this book are theirs alone and do not necessarily represent those of their employer.

ABOUT THE TECHNICAL EDITORS

DANIEL ULERY is a Senior Software Engineer who lives near Lewiston, Idaho. His experience includes software engineering projects using technologies such as Java Enterprise, C# WinForms, SQL Server, Raspberry Pi, and Android. Dan received his Bachelor of Science in Computer Science from the University of Idaho in 2004. When he's not working on software projects, he's likely working on one of many DIY projects.

ED WOODWARD is a Senior Development Manager and Android Developer for OpenStax at Rice University. He currently manages the Devops team and is tech lead on the Business Intelligence team along with developing OpenStax's Android app. Prior to joining OpenStax, Ed was a Vice President/Application Architect at JPMorganChase. Ed was a Band Director at the high school and middle school level for several years before transitioning to programming.

CHAIM KRAUSE is an expert computer programmer with more than 30 years of experience to prove it. He has worked as a lead tech support engineer for ISPs as early as 1995, as a senior developer support engineer with Borland for Delphi, and has worked in Silicon Valley for over a decade in various roles, including technical support engineer and developer support engineer. He is currently a military simulation specialist for the US Army's Command and General Staff College, working on projects such as developing serious games for use in training exercises. He has also authored several video training courses on Linux topics, and has been a technical reviewer for over 20 books, including *Amazon Web Services for Mobile Developers* (Sybex, 2017) and *Professional Swift* (Wrox, 2015). It seems only natural then that he would be an avid gamer and have his own electronics lab and server room in his basement. He currently resides in Leavenworth, Kansas, with his beautiful partner Ivana and a menagerie of four-legged companions: their two dogs, Dasher and Minnie, and their three cats, Pudems, Talyn, and Alaska.

MURAT YENER is a code geek, open source committer, Java Champion, and ex-Google Developer Expert on Android, who is working at Google. He is the author of *Expert Android Studio* (Wiley, 2016) and *Professional Java EE Design Patterns* (Wiley, 2015). He has extensive experience with developing Android, Java, web, JavaEE, and OSGi applications, in addition to teaching courses and mentoring. Murat was an Eclipse committer and one of the initial committers of the Eclipse Libra project. Murat had been a user group leader at GDG Istanbul and in GDG San Francisco, organizing, participating, and speaking at events. He is also a regular speaker at major conferences, such as DroidCon, JavaOne, and Devoxx.

CREDITS

PROJECT EDITOR
John Sleeva

TECHNICAL EDITORS
Daniel Ulery
Ed Woodward
Chaim Krause
Murat Yener

PRODUCTION EDITOR
Barath Kumar Rajasekaran

COPY EDITOR
Kimberly A. Cofer

PRODUCTION MANAGER
Kathleen Wisor

CONTENT ENABLEMENT AND OPERATIONS MANAGER
Pete Gaughan

MARKETING MANAGER
Christie Hilbrich

EXECUTIVE EDITOR
Jim Minatel

PROJECT COORDINATOR, COVER
Brent Savage

PROOFREADER
Nancy Bell

INDEXER
Johnna VanHoose Dinse

COVER DESIGNER
Wiley

COVER IMAGE
© 1971yes/iStock.com

ACKNOWLEDGMENTS

FIRST, I'D LIKE TO THANK MY WIFE KRISTY, whose love and support makes everything I do possible.

A big thank you to my friends and colleagues at Google, particularly all the amazing people in the Android team, without whom I'd have nothing to write about, and the developer relations team who inspire me every day.

I also thank our army of technical editors, including Dan Ulery, Ed Woodward, Chaim Krause, Murat Yener, James Harmon, and Chad Darby, without whom this book would contain far more errors than it does. Those that remain are entirely my fault. Thank you to the whole team at Wrox, especially John Sleeva and Jim Minatel, whose patience and support in getting this book completed was non-trivial.

An extra big thank you goes out to the incredible Android community, made up of passionate, generous, and hard working developers who seem to spend as much time helping each other as they do building amazing apps. Your efforts have been critical in making Android the huge success that it is. Thank you.

—Reto

MY FAMILY, ANDREA AND HANNAH, are what make everything worth it. Without their support, I wouldn't be able to do much of anything, much less write this book.

I'd like to echo Reto's thanks for everyone involved in publishing and making this book a reality, the Android team for giving us plenty to talk about, and the Android developer community for sharing our passion around building better apps.

—Ian

CONTENTS

INTRODUCTION

For many people, smartphones have become an extension of themselves. Now running on over 2 billion monthly-active devices, Android is the most common smartphone operating system in use world-wide, with users installing an average of 50 apps each, resulting in over 94 billion apps downloaded from the Play app store in 2017 alone.

Ubiquitous and indispensable, smartphones are so advanced and personal that studies have shown people become anxious if they misplace their device, lose connectivity, or run low on battery.

In the 10 years since launching in 2008, Android has expanded beyond mobile phones to become a development platform for a wide range of hardware, with 24,000 devices from over 1,300 brands, including everything from tablets to televisions, watches, cars, and Internet of Things (IoT) devices. Over the same period, there have been 28 platform and SDK releases.

These innovations, combined with the size of the ecosystem, provide unparalleled opportunities for developers to create innovative new applications for a global audience of users.

Android offers an open platform for mobile application development. Without artificial barriers, Android developers are free to write apps that take full advantage of an incredible range of devices. Using Google Play for distribution, developers can distribute free and paid applications to compatible Android devices globally.

This book is a hands-on guide to building Android applications for all Android devices. It's written based on version 8.1 of the Android SDK, using Android Studio 3.1. Chapter by chapter, it takes you through a series of sample projects, each introducing new features and techniques to get the most out of Android. It covers all the basic functionality to get started, as well as the information for experienced mobile developers to take full advantage of the features of Android, to enhance existing products or create innovative new ones.

The Android team releases a new major platform every year, a new version of Android Studio every few months, and incremental changes to Jetpack, such as the support library and Android Architecture Components, many times each year. With such rapid release cycles, there are regular changes, additions, and improvements to the tools, platform APIs, and development libraries you'll use—and which are described in this book. To minimize the impact of these changes, the Android engineering team works hard to ensure backward compatibility.

However, future releases will date some of the information provided in this book, and not all active Android devices will be running the latest platform release. To mitigate this, wherever possible, we have used backward-compatible support libraries, and included details on which platform releases support the functionality described—and which alternatives may exist to provide support for users of devices running earlier platforms.

Further, the explanations and examples included will give you the grounding and knowledge needed to write compelling mobile applications using the current SDK, along with the flexibility to quickly adapt to future enhancements.

WHO THIS BOOK IS FOR

This book is for anyone interested in creating applications for the Android platform. It includes information that will be valuable, whether you're an experienced mobile developer on other platforms, making your first foray into writing mobile apps, and if you have some Android development experience.

It will help if you've used a smartphone (particularly an Android device), but it's not necessary, nor is prior experience in mobile application development.

It's expected that you'll have experience in software development and be familiar with basic object-oriented paradigms. An understanding of Java syntax is expected, though not a strict necessity.

Chapters 1 and 2 introduce mobile development and the Android development platform, and contain instructions to get you started. Beyond that, there's no requirement to read the chapters in order, although a good understanding of the core components described in Chapters 3–7 is important before you venture into the remaining chapters. Chapter 11 covers important details on how to ensure your apps are responsive and efficient, while Chapters 12–14 describe how to provide a rich and consistent user experience. The remaining chapters cover a variety of functionality whose relevance will vary based on your application, and can be read in whatever order interest or need dictates.

WHAT THIS BOOK COVERS

Chapter 1 introduces Android, including what it is and how it fits into the mobile development ecosystem. What Android offers as a development platform and why it's an exciting opportunity for creating mobile phone applications are then examined in greater detail.

Chapter 2 covers some best practices for mobile development and explains how to download and install Android Studio and the Android SDK. It then introduces some of the tools and features included with Android Studio, and demonstrates how they can be used to create and debug new applications.

Chapters 3–7 take an in-depth look at the fundamental Android application components—starting by examining the components that make up an Android application, and then moving on to "Activities" and "Fragments," and their associated lifetimes and lifecycles.

You'll then be introduced to the application manifest and the Gradle build system, before learning more about the external resource framework used to support devices used in different counties, with different languages, and in a variety of shapes and sizes.

You'll learn how to create basic user interfaces with layouts, Views, and Fragments, before being introduced to the Intent and Broadcast Receiver mechanisms used to perform actions and send messages between application components. Accessing Internet resources is then covered, followed by a detailed look at data storage, retrieval, and sharing. You'll start with the preference-saving mechanism and then move on to file handling, databases, and Content Providers—including accessing data from the native databases.

This section finishes with an examination of how to ensure your app is always responsive, and is efficient in its use of battery when running in the background. You'll be introduced to threading APIs that enable asynchronous execution, and mechanisms that support efficient scheduling of background work. You'll also learn how to create and display interactive Notifications.

Chapters 12–14 build on the UI framework introduced in Chapter 5. You'll learn to enhance the user experience through the principles of material design and to make your applications accessible and optimized for a variety of screen sizes and resolutions. You'll further improve the user experience by understanding the variety of navigation options available, adding movement through animations, and the use of Toolbars and Menus.

Chapters 15–19 look at more advanced topics. You'll learn how to use Google Play services to add interactive maps, find the user's location, and how to create geo- and awareness-fences. Using movement and environmental Sensors—including the compass, accelerometers, and the barometer— you'll make your applications react to their environment.

After looking at how to play and record multimedia, as well as how to use the camera to take pictures and record video, you'll be introduced to Android's communication capabilities, including Bluetooth, NFC, and Wi-Fi Direct. Next, you'll learn how your applications can interact with users directly from the home screen using dynamic Widgets, Live Wallpaper, and the Application Shortcuts.

Chapter 20 discusses several advanced development topics, including security, using the fingerprint sensor, and Strict Mode, followed by the telephony APIs and the APIs used to send and receive SMS messages.

Finally, Chapter 21 examines the process for building, releasing, monitoring, and monetizing your applications. In particular, it includes details for publishing and distributing your applications within Google Play.

HOW THIS BOOK IS STRUCTURED

This book is structured in a logical sequence to help readers of different development backgrounds learn how to write advanced Android applications. There's no requirement to read each chapter sequentially, but several of the sample projects are developed over the course of multiple chapters, adding new functionality and other enhancements at each stage.

Experienced mobile developers who have already installed Android Studio, and those with a working knowledge of Android development, can skim the first two chapters—which are an introduction to mobile development and instructions for creating your development environment—and then dive in at Chapters 3–7. These chapters cover the fundamentals of Android development, so it's important to have a solid understanding of the concepts they describe.

With this covered, you can move on to the remaining chapters, which look at material design, maps, location-based services, background applications, and more advanced topics, such as hardware interaction and networking.

WHAT YOU NEED TO USE THIS BOOK

To use the code samples in this book, you will need to create an Android development environment by downloading Android Studio and the Android SDK. It's also possible to use other IDEs, or even to build your apps from the command-line. We'll assume, however, you're using Android Studio.

Android development is supported on Windows, macOS, and Linux, with Android Studio and the SDK available from the Android website.

You do not need an Android device to use this book or develop Android applications—though it can be useful, particularly when testing.

> **NOTE** *Chapter 2 outlines these requirements in more detail and describes where to download and how to install each component.*

CONVENTIONS

To help you get the most from the text and keep track of what's happening, we've used a number of conventions throughout the book.

> **NOTE** *Notes, tips, hints, tricks, and asides to the current discussion are offset and placed in italics like this.*

> **WARNING** *Boxes like this one hold important, not-to-be forgotten information that is directly relevant to the surrounding text.*

As for styles in the text:

➤ We show file names, URLs, and code within the text like so: `persistence.properties`.

➤ To help readability, class names in text are often represented using a regular font but capitalized like so: Content Provider.

➤ We present code in two different ways:

```
We use a monofont type with no highlighting for most code examples.
```

We use bold to indicate changes or additions from a similar previous code snippet.

➤ In some code samples, you'll see lines marked as follows:

```
[... Existing code ...]
```

or

```
[... Implement something here ...]
```

These represent instructions to replace the entire line (including the square brackets) with actual code, either from a previous code snippet (in the former case) or with your own implementation (in the latter).

➤ To keep the code samples reasonably concise, we have not always included every `package` definition or `import` statement required in the code snippets. The downloadable code samples described below include all the required `import` statements. Additionally, if you are developing using Android Studio, you can enable auto-import or use the keyboard shortcut Ctrl+Space (Cmd+Space) to add the required `import` statements.

SOURCE CODE

As you work through the examples in this book, you may choose either to type in all the code manually, or to use the source code files that accompany the book. All the source code used in this book is available for download at www.wrox.com. When at the site, simply locate the book's title (use the Search box or one of the title lists) and click the Download Code link on the book's detail page to obtain all the source code for the book.

Once you download the code, just decompress it with your favorite compression tool. Alternately, you can go to the main Wrox code download page at www.wrox.com/dynamic/books/download.aspx to see the code available for this book and all other Wrox books.

ERRATA

We make every effort to ensure that there are no errors in the text or in the code. However, no one is perfect, and mistakes do occur. If you find an error in one of our books, like a spelling mistake or faulty piece of code, we would be very grateful for your feedback. By sending in errata, you may save another reader hours of frustration, and at the same time, you will be helping us provide even higher quality information.

To find the errata page for this book, go to www.wrox.com and locate the title using the Search box or one of the title lists. Then, on the book details page, click the Book Errata link. On this page, you can view all errata that has been submitted for this book and posted by Wrox editors. A complete book list, including links to each book's errata, is also available at `www.wrox.com/misc-pages/booklist.shtml`.

If you don't spot "your" error on the Book Errata page, go to `www.wrox.com/contact/techsupport.shtml` and complete the form there to send us the error you have found. We'll check the information and, if appropriate, post a message to the book's errata page and fix the problem in subsequent editions of the book.

PROFESSIONAL

Android®

Fourth Edition

1

Hello, Android

WHAT'S IN THIS CHAPTER?

- ➤ A background of mobile application development
- ➤ What is Android?
- ➤ Which devices Android runs on
- ➤ Why you should develop for mobile and Android
- ➤ An introduction to the Android SDK and development framework

ANDROID APPLICATION DEVELOPMENT

Whether you're an experienced mobile engineer, a desktop or web developer, or a complete programming novice, Android represents an exciting opportunity to write applications for an audience of over two billion Android device users.

You're probably already familiar with Android, the most common software powering mobile phones. If not, and you purchased this book in the hope that Android development would help you create an unstoppable army of emotionless robot warriors on a relentless quest to cleanse the earth of the scourge of humanity, you should reconsider this book purchase (and your life choices.)

When announcing Android at its launch in 2007, Andy Rubin described it as follows:

> *The first truly open and comprehensive platform for mobile devices. It includes an operating system, user-interface and applications—all of the*

software to run a mobile phone but without the proprietary obstacles that have hindered mobile innovation.

—Where's My Gphone?

(http://googleblog.blogspot.com/2007/11/wheres-my-gphone.html)

Since then, Android has expanded beyond mobile phones to provide a development platform for an increasingly wide range of hardware, including tablets, televisions, watches, cars, and Internet-of-Things (IoT) devices.

Android is an open source software stack that includes an operating system, middleware, and key applications for mobile and embedded devices.

Critically, for us as developers, it also includes a rich set of API libraries that make it possible to write applications that can shape the look, feel, and function of the Android devices on which they run.

In Android, system, bundled, and all third-party applications are written with the same APIs and executed on the same run time. These APIs feature hardware access, video recording, location-based services, support for background services, maps, notifications, sensors, relational databases, inter-application communication, Bluetooth, NFC, and 2D and 3D graphics.

This book describes how to use these APIs to create your own Android applications. In this chapter you learn some guidelines for mobile and embedded hardware development, and are introduced to some of the platform features available to Android developers.

Android has powerful APIs, a huge and diverse ecosystem of users, excellent documentation, a thriving developer community, and has no required costs for development or distribution. As the Android device ecosystem continues to grow, you have the opportunity to create innovative applications for users, no matter what your development experience.

A LITTLE BACKGROUND

In the days before Instagram, Snapchat, and Pokémon Go, when Google was still a twinkle in its founders' eyes and dinosaurs roamed the earth, mobile phones were just that—portable phones small enough to fit inside a briefcase, featuring batteries that could last up to several hours. They did, however, offer the freedom to make calls without being physically connected to a landline.

In the 10 years since the first Android device was launched, smart phones have become ubiquitous and indispensable. Hardware advancements have made devices more powerful, featuring bigger, brighter screens and featuring advanced hardware including accelerometers, fingerprint scanners, and ultra-high-resolution cameras.

These same advances have more recently resulted in a proliferation of additional form factors for Android devices, including a large variety of smart-phones, tablets, watches, and televisions.

These hardware innovations offer fertile ground for software development, providing many opportunities to create innovative new applications.

The Not-So-Distant Past

In the early days of native phone application development, developers, generally coding in low-level C or C++, needed to understand the specific hardware they were coding for, typically a single device or possibly a range of devices from a single manufacturer. The complexity inherent in this approach meant the applications written for these devices often lagged behind their hardware counterparts. As hardware technology and mobile Internet access have advanced, this closed approach has become outmoded.

The next significant advancement in mobile phone application development was the introduction of Java-hosted MIDlets. MIDlets were executed on a Java virtual machine (JVM), a process that abstracted the underlying hardware and let developers create applications that ran on many devices that supported the Java run time.

Unfortunately, this convenience came at the price of more heavily restricted access to the device hardware. Similarly, it was considered normal for third-party applications to receive different hardware access and execution rights from those given to native applications written by the phone manufacturers, with MIDlets often receiving few of either.

The introduction of Java MIDlets expanded developers' audiences, but the lack of low-level hardware access and sandboxed execution meant that most mobile applications were regular desktop programs or websites designed to render on a smaller screen, and didn't take advantage of the inherent mobility of the handheld platform.

Living in the Future

At its introduction, Android was part of a new wave of modern mobile operating systems designed specifically to support application development on increasingly powerful mobile hardware.

Android offers an open development platform built on an open source Linux kernel. Hardware access is available to all applications through a series of API libraries, and application interaction, while carefully controlled, is fully supported.

In Android, all applications have equal standing. Third-party and native Android applications are written with the same APIs and are executed on the same run time. Users can replace most system application with a third-party developer's alternative; indeed, even the dialer and home screens can be replaced.

THE ANDROID ECOSYSTEM

The Android ecosystem is made up of a combination of three components:

> ➤ A free, open source operating system for embedded devices

> ➤ An open source development platform for creating applications

> ➤ Devices that run the Android operating system (and the applications created for it)

More specifically, Android is made up of several necessary and dependent parts, including the following:

➤ A Compatibility Definition Document (CDD) and Compatibility Test Suite (CTS) that describe the capabilities required for a device to support the Android software stack.

➤ A Linux operating system kernel that provides a low-level interface with the hardware, memory management, and process control, all optimized for mobile and embedded devices.

➤ Open source libraries for application development, including SQLite, WebKit, OpenGL, and a media manager.

➤ A run time used to execute and host Android applications, including the Android Run Time (ART) and the core libraries that provide Android-specific functionality. The run time is designed to be small and efficient for use on embedded devices.

➤ An application framework that agnostically exposes system services to the application layer, including the Window Manager and Location Manager, databases, telephony, and sensors.

➤ A user interface framework used to host and launch applications.

➤ A set of core preinstalled applications.

➤ A software development kit (SDK) used to create applications, including the related tools, IDE, sample code, and documentation.

What really makes Android compelling is its open philosophy, which ensures that you can fix any deficiencies in user interface or native application design by writing an extension or replacement. Android provides you, as a developer, with the opportunity to create applications designed to look, feel, and function exactly as you imagine them.

With more than 2 billion monthly active users of devices running the Android operating system, installing over 82 billion apps and games in from Google Play in 2016 alone, the Android ecosystem represents an unparalleled chance to create apps that can affect and improve billions of people's lives.

PRE-INSTALLED ANDROID APPLICATIONS

Android devices typically come with a suite of preinstalled applications that users expect. On smart phones these typically include:

➤ A phone dialer

➤ An SMS management application

➤ A web browser

➤ An e-mail client

➤ A calendar

➤ A contacts list

➤ A music player and picture gallery

➤ A camera and video recording application

➤ A calculator

➤ A home screen

➤ An alarm clock

In many cases Android devices also ship with the following proprietary Google mobile applications:

➤ The Google Play Store for downloading third-party Android applications

➤ The Google Maps application, including StreetView, driving directions, and turn-by-turn navigation, satellite views, and traffic conditions

➤ The Gmail email client

➤ The YouTube video player

➤ The Google Chrome browser

➤ The Google home screen and Google Assistant

The data stored and used by many of these native applications—such as contact details—are also available to third-party applications.

The exact makeup of the applications available on new Android devices is likely to vary based on the hardware manufacturer, the carrier or distributor, and the type of device.

The open source nature of Android means that carriers and OEMs can customize the user interface and the applications bundled with each Android device.

It's important to note that for compatible devices, the underlying platform and SDK remains consistent across OEM and carrier variations. The look and feel of the user interface may vary, but your applications will function in the same way across all compatible Android devices.

ANDROID SDK FEATURES

For us developers, the true appeal of Android lies in its APIs.

As an application-neutral platform, Android gives you the opportunity to create applications that are as much a part of the phone as anything provided out-of-the-box. The following list highlights some of the most noteworthy Android features:

➤ Transparent access to telephony and Internet resources through GSM, EDGE, 3G, 4G, LTE, and Wi-Fi network support, enabling your app to send and retrieve data across mobile and Wi-Fi networks

➤ Comprehensive APIs for location-based services such as GPS and network-based location detection

➤ Full support for integrating maps within the user interface

➤ Full multimedia hardware control, including playback and recording with the camera and microphone

➤ Media libraries for playing and recording a variety of audio/video or still-image formats

➤ APIs for using sensor hardware, including accelerometers, compasses, barometers, and finger-print sensors

➤ Libraries for using Wi-Fi, Bluetooth, and NFC hardware

➤ Shared data stores and APIs for contacts, calendar, and multi-media

➤ Background services and an advanced notification system

➤ An integrated web browser

➤ Mobile-optimized, hardware-accelerated graphics, including a path-based 2D graphics library and support for 3D graphics using OpenGL ES 2.0

➤ Localization through a dynamic resource framework

WHAT DOES ANDROID RUN ON?

The first Android mobile handset, the T-Mobile G1, was released in the United States in October 2008. By the end of 2017 there are more than 2 billion monthly active Android devices globally, making it the most common smart phone operating system in use world-wide.

Rather than being a mobile OS created for a single hardware implementation, Android is designed to support a large variety of hardware platforms, from smart phones to tablets, televisions, watches, and IoT devices.

With no licensing fees or proprietary software, the cost to handset manufacturers for providing Android devices is comparatively low, which, combined with a massive ecosystem of powerful applications, has encouraged device manufacturers to produce increasingly diverse and tailored hardware.

As a result, hundreds of manufacturers, including Samsung, LG, HTC, and Motorola, are creating Android devices. These devices are distributed to users via hundreds of carriers world-wide.

WHY DEVELOP FOR MOBILE?

Smart phones have become so advanced and personal to us that for many people they've become an extension of themselves. Studies have shown that many mobile phone users become anxious if they misplace their device, lose connectivity, or their battery runs out.

The ubiquity of mobile phones, and our attachment to them, makes them a fundamentally different platform for development from PCs. With a microphone, camera, touchscreen, location detection, and environmental sensors, a phone can effectively become an extra-sensory perception device.

Smart phone ownership easily surpasses computer ownership in many countries, with more than 3 billion mobile phone users worldwide. 2009 marked the year that more people accessed the Internet for the first time from a mobile phone rather than a PC.

The increasing popularity of smart phones, combined with the increasing availability of high-speed mobile data and Wi-Fi hotspots, has created a huge opportunity for advanced mobile applications.

Smartphone applications have changed the way people use their phones. This gives you, the application developer, a unique opportunity to create dynamic, compelling new applications that become a vital part of people's lives.

WHY DEVELOP FOR ANDROID?

In addition to providing access to the largest ecosystem of smart phone users, Android represents a dynamic framework for app development based on the reality of modern mobile devices designed by developers, for developers.

With a simple, powerful, and open SDK, no licensing fees, excellent documentation, a diverse range of devices and form-factors, and a thriving developer community, Android represents an opportunity to create software that can change people's lives.

The barrier to entry for new Android developers is minimal:

➤ No certification is required to become an Android developer.

➤ The Google Play Store provides free, up-front purchase, in-app billing, and subscription options for distribution and monetization of your applications.

➤ There is no approval process for application distribution.

➤ Developers have total control over their brands.

From a commercial perspective, Android represents the most common smart phone operating system, and provides access to over 2 billion monthly active Android devices globally, offering unparalleled reach to make your applications available to users around the world.

INTRODUCING THE DEVELOPMENT FRAMEWORK

Android applications normally are written using the Java or Kotlin programming languages, and are executed by means of the Android Run Time (ART).

> **NOTE** *Historically, Android apps were written primarily using Java language syntax. More recently, Android Studio 3.0 introduced full support for Kotlin as an official first class language for application development. Kotlin is a JVM language, which is interoperable with existing Android languages and the Android Run Time, allowing you to use both Java and Kotlin syntax within the same applications.*

Each Android application runs in a separate process, relinquishing all responsibility for memory and process management to the Android Run Time, which stops and kills processes as necessary to manage resources.

ART sits on top of a Linux kernel that handles low-level hardware interaction, including drivers and memory management, while a set of APIs provides access to all the underlying services, features, and hardware.

What Comes in the Box

The Android SDK includes everything you need to start developing, testing, and debugging Android applications:

➤ **The Android API Libraries**—The core of the SDK is the Android API libraries that provide developer access to the Android stack. These are the same libraries that Google uses to create native Android applications.

➤ **Development tools**—The SDK includes the Android Studio IDE and several other development tools that let you compile and debug your applications to turn Android source code into executable applications. You learn more about the developer tools in Chapter 2, "Getting Started."

➤ **The Android Virtual Device Manager and Emulator**—The Android Emulator is a fully interactive mobile device emulator featuring several alternative skins. The Emulator runs within an Android Virtual Device (AVD) that simulates a device hardware configuration. Using the Emulator you can see how your applications will look and behave on a real Android device. All Android applications run within ART, so the software emulator is an excellent development environment—in fact, because it's hardware-neutral, it provides a better independent test environment than any single hardware implementation.

➤ **Full documentation**—The SDK includes extensive code-level reference information detailing exactly what's included in each package and class and how to use them. In addition to the code documentation, Android's reference documentation and developer guides explain how to get started, give detailed explanations of the fundamentals behind Android development, highlight best practices, and provide deep-dives into framework topics.

➤ **Sample code**—The Android SDK includes a selection of sample applications that demonstrate some of the possibilities available with Android, as well as simple programs that highlight how to use individual API features.

➤ **Online support**—Android has vibrant developer communities on most online social networks, Slack, and many developer forums. Stack Overflow (www.stackoverflow.com/questions/tagged/android) is a hugely popular destination for Android questions and a great place to find answers to beginner questions. Many Android engineers from Google are active on Stack Overflow and Twitter.

Understanding the Android Software Stack

The Android software stack is a Linux kernel and a collection of C/C++ libraries exposed through an application framework that provides services for, and management of, the run time and applications, as shown in Figure 1-1.

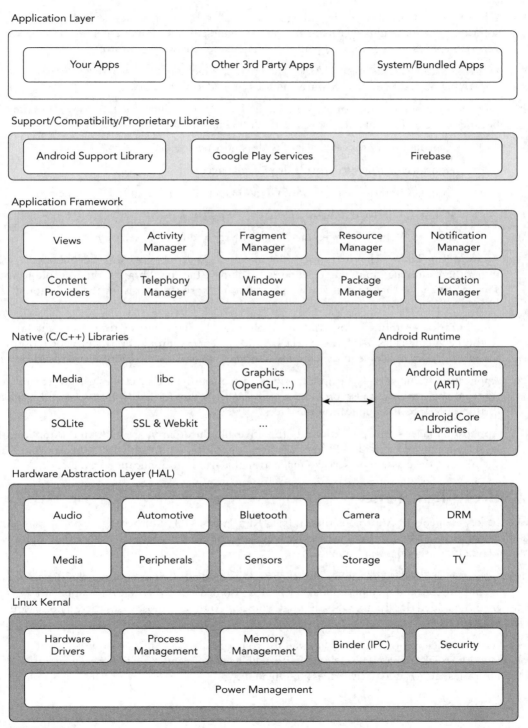

FIGURE 1-1

➤ **Linux kernel**—Core services (including hardware drivers, process and memory management, security, network, and power management) are handled by a Linux kernel (the specific kernel version depends on the Android platform version and hardware platform).

➤ **Hardware Application Layer (HAL)**—The HAL provides an abstraction layer between the underlying physical device hardware and the remainder of the stack.

➤ **Libraries**—Running on top of the kernel and HAL, Android includes various C/C++ core libraries such as libc and SSL, as well as the following:

   ➤ A media library for playback of audio and video media

   ➤ A surface manager to provide display management

   ➤ Graphics libraries that include SGL and OpenGL for 2D and 3D graphics

   ➤ SQLite for native database support

   ➤ SSL and WebKit for integrated web browser and Internet security

➤ **Android Run Time**—The run time is what makes an Android phone an Android phone rather than a mobile Linux implementation. Including the core libraries, the Android Run Time is the engine that powers your applications and forms the basis for the application framework.

➤ **Core libraries**—Although most Android application development is written using the Java or Kotlin JVM languages, ART is not a Java VM. The core Android libraries provide most of the functionality available in the core Java libraries, as well as the Android-specific libraries.

➤ **Application framework**—The application framework provides the classes used to create Android applications. It also provides a generic abstraction for hardware access and manages the user interface and application resources.

➤ **Application layer**—All applications, both native and third-party, are built on the application layer by means of the same API libraries. The application layer runs within the Android Run Time, using the classes and services made available from the application framework.

The Android Run Time

One of the key elements of Android is the Android Run Time (ART). Rather than using a traditional Java VM such as Java ME, Android uses its own custom run time designed to ensure that multiple instances run efficiently on a single device.

ART uses the device's underlying Linux kernel to handle low-level functionality, including security, threading, and process and memory management. It's also possible to write C/C++ applications that run closer to the underlying Linux OS. Although you *can* do this, in most cases there's no reason you should need to.

If the speed and efficiency of C/C++ is required for your application, Android provides a native development kit (NDK). The NDK is designed to enable you to create C++ libraries using the libc and libm libraries, along with native access to OpenGL.

> **NOTE** *This book focuses exclusively on writing applications that run within ART using the SDK; NDK development is not within the scope of this book. If your inclinations run toward NDK development, exploring the Linux kernel and C/C++ underbelly of Android, modifying ART, or otherwise tinkering with things under the hood, check out the Android Open Source Project at* `source.android.com`.

All Android hardware and system service access is managed using ART as a middle tier. By using this run time to host application execution, developers have an abstraction layer that ensures they should never have to worry about a particular hardware implementation.

ART executes Dalvik executable files (`.dex`)—named after an earlier virtual machine implementation named "Dalvik"—a format optimized to ensure minimal memory footprint. You create `.dex` executables by transforming Java or Kotlin language compiled classes using the tools supplied within the SDK.

> **NOTE** *You learn more about how to create Dalvik executables in Chapter 2.*

Android Application Architecture

Android's architecture encourages component reuse, enabling you to publish and share Activities, Services, and data with other applications, with access managed by the security restrictions you define.

The same mechanism that enables you to produce a replacement contact manager or phone dialer can let you expose your application's components in order to let other developers build on them by creating new UI front ends or functionality extensions.

The following application services are the architectural cornerstones of all Android applications, providing the framework you'll be using for your own software:

➤ **Activity Manager and Fragment Manager**—Activities and Fragments are used to define the user interface of your apps. The Activity and Fragment Managers control the life cycle of your Activities and Fragments, respectively, including management of the Activity stack (described in Chapters 3 and 5).

➤ **Views**—Used to construct the user interfaces controls within your Activities and Fragments, as described in Chapter 5.

➤ **Notification Manager**—Provides a consistent and nonintrusive mechanism for signaling your users, as described in Chapter 11.

➤ **Content Providers**—Lets your applications share data, as described in Chapter 10.

➤ **Resource Manager**—Enables non-code resources, such as strings and graphics, to be externalized, as shown in Chapter 4.

➤ **Intents**—Provides a mechanism for transferring data between applications and their components, as described in Chapter 6.

Android Libraries

Android offers a number of APIs for developing your applications. Rather than list them all here, check out the documentation at `developer.android.com/reference/packages.html`, which gives a complete list of packages included in the Android SDK.

Android is intended to target a wide range of mobile hardware, so be aware that the suitability and implementation of some of the advanced or optional APIs may vary depending on the host device.

2

Getting Started

WHAT'S IN THIS CHAPTER?

➤ Installing the Android SDK and Android Studio development environment

➤ Creating and debugging your projects

➤ Writing Android apps using Kotlin

➤ Using the Android Support Library

➤ Understanding mobile design considerations

➤ The importance of optimizing for speed and efficiency

➤ Designing for small screens and mobile data connections

➤ Introducing Android Virtual Devices and the Emulator

➤ Tips for using Android Studio and improving build performance

➤ Understanding app performance using the Android Profiler

➤ Introducing Gradle builds and app testing

WROX.COM CODE DOWNLOADS FOR THIS CHAPTER

The downloads for this chapter are found at www.wrox.com. The code for this chapter is divided into the following major examples:

➤ Snippets_ch2.zip

➤ HelloWorld.zip

GETTING STARTED DEVELOPING ANDROID APPS

All you need to start writing your own Android applications is a copy of the Android SDK and a Java Development Kit (JDK). Unless you're a masochist, you'll also want to use an integrated development environment (IDE)—we strongly recommend using Android Studio, Google's officially supported IDE for Android app development that includes an integrated JDK and manages the installation of the Android SDK and associated tools.

Android Studio, the Android SDK, and a JDK are each available for Windows, MacOS, and Linux, so you can explore Android from the comfort of whatever operating system (OS) you favor. Android applications themselves are run within the ART managed runtime, optimized for resource-constrained mobile devices, so there's no advantage to developing on any particular OS.

Traditionally, Android code is written using Java language syntax—until 2017 Android app development required the use of Java. Android Studio 3.0 added Kotlin as a fully supported language alternative, allowing you to write Android app in part, or entirely, using Kotlin.

Kotlin is a statically typed language that is fully interoperable with Java source files and the Android runtime. It's considered expressive and concise and introduces improvements including reduced language verbosity, null-pointer safety, extension functions, and infix notation.

> **NOTE** *At the time of writing this book Java was still the default for new projects, and most existing Android projects were written predominantly using Java syntax. Accordingly, we've used Java syntax for the code snippets and sample projects featured within this book.*
>
> *Given the advantages of Kotlin, we expect its use to increase quickly, and highly recommend you familiarize yourself with the Kotlin language for writing Android apps. More details on using Kotlin for your Android Apps are available in the aptly named section, "Getting Started Writing Android Apps Using Kotlin."*

The core Android libraries include most of the features from the core Java APIs in addition to the rich suite of Android-specific APIs. You can access all these libraries using either Java or Kotlin when writing your apps.

Although it's possible to download and install the Android SDK and JDK separately, installing and using Android Studio simplifies the process of getting started. Android Studio includes an integrated OpenJDK and manages the installation of the Android SDK components and tools using the integrated Android SDK Manager.

The SDK Manager is used to download Android framework SDK libraries and optional add-ons (including the Google APIs and support libraries). It also includes the platform and development tools you will use to write and debug your applications, such as the Android Emulator to run your projects and the Android Profiler to profile CPU, memory, and network use. All these tools are integrated directly into Android Studio for your convenience.

By the end of this chapter, you'll have installed Android Studio, the Android SDK and its add-ons, and the development tools. You'll have set up your development environment, built your first Hello World application in Java and Kotlin, and run and debugged it using the DDMS and Emulator running on an Android Virtual Device (AVD).

If you've developed for mobile devices before, you already know that their small form factor, limited battery life, and restricted processing power and memory create some unique design challenges. Even if you're new to the game, it's obvious that some of the things you can take for granted on the desktop, web, or server—such as always-on Internet and power—aren't applicable when writing apps for mobile or embedded devices.

The user environment brings its own challenges in addition to those introduced by hardware limitations. Many Android devices are used on the move and are often a distraction rather than the focus of attention, so your application needs to be fast, responsive, and easy to learn. Even if your application is designed for devices more conducive to an immersive experience, such as tablets or televisions, the same design principles can be critical for delivering a high-quality user experience.

DEVELOPING FOR ANDROID

The Android SDK includes all the tools and APIs you need to write compelling and powerful mobile applications. The biggest challenge with Android, as with any new development toolkit, is learning the features and limitations of those APIs.

Since Android Studio 3.0, it's possible to write Android apps using Java, Kotlin, or a combination of both languages. If you have experience in Java or Kotlin development, you'll find that the syntax and grammar you've been using will translate directly into Android. If you don't have experience with Java, but have used other object-oriented languages (such as C#), you should find the transition to either Java or Kotlin syntax straightforward.

The power of Android comes from its APIs, not the language being used, so being unfamiliar with Java or Kotlin syntax and/or Java-specific classes won't present a meaningful disadvantage.

There's no cost to download or use the SDK, and Google doesn't require your application to pass a review to distribute your finished apps on the Google Play Store. Although Google Play requires a small one-time fee to publish applications, if you choose not to distribute via the Google Play Store, you can do so at no cost.

What You Need to Begin

Because Android applications run within the Android Run Time, you can write them on any platform that supports the developer tools. Throughout this book we'll be using Android Studio, which currently supports:

➤ Microsoft Windows 7/8/10 (32- or 64-bit)

➤ Mac OS X 10.8.5 or later

➤ GNOME or KDE Linux desktop (including GNU C Library 2.11 or later)

On all platforms, Android Studio requires at least 2 GB of RAM (with 8 GB strongly recommended), and 1280 x 800 minimum screen resolution.

> **NOTE** *Android development requires Java Development Kit (JDK) 8 to be installed. Android Studio has integrated the latest version of the OpenJDK since Android Studio 2.2; if you don't plan to use Android Studio, you'll need to download and install a compatible JDK.*

Developing with Android Studio

The examples and step-by-step instructions in this book are targeted at developers using Android Studio. Android Studio is Android's official IDE, built on top of IntelliJ IDEA, a popular IDE for Java development that also supports Android development using Kotlin.

Android Studio is purpose-built by the Android team at Google to accelerate your development and help you build high-quality apps. It supports all Android form factors including phones, tablets, TV, Wear, and Auto—and offers tools tailored specifically for Android developers, including rich code editing, debugging, testing, and profiling.

Some of Android Studio's features include:

➤ Intelligent code editing with advanced code completion, refactoring, and code analysis.

➤ Version control integration including GitHub and Subversion.

➤ Robust static analysis framework with over 280 different Lint checks along with quick fixes.

➤ Extensive testing tools and frameworks including JUnit 4 and functional UI tests. You can run your tests on a device, an emulator, a continuous integration environment, or in the Firebase Test Lab.

In addition to these IDE features, using Android Studio for your Android development offers some significant advantages through the tight integration of many of the Android build and debug tools, as well as ensured support for the latest Android platform releases.

Android Studio includes the following features:

➤ The Android Project Wizard, which simplifies creating new projects and includes several application and Activity templates

➤ Editors to help create, edit, and validate your XML resources

➤ Automated building of Android projects, conversion to Android executables (`.dex`), packaging to package files (`.apk`), and installation of packages onto Android Run Times (running both within the Emulator or on physical devices)

➤ The Android Virtual Device manager, which lets you create and manage virtual devices to host Emulators that run a specific release of the Android OS and with set hardware and memory constraints

➤ The Android Emulator, including the ability to control the Emulator's appearance and network connection settings, and the ability to simulate incoming calls, SMS messages, and sensor values

➤ The Android Profiler, which lets you monitor CPU, memory, and network performance

➤ Access to the device or Emulator's filesystem, enabling you to navigate the folder tree and transfer files

➤ Runtime debugging, which enables you to set breakpoints and view call stacks

➤ All Android logging and console outputs

> **NOTE** *Android Studio replaces the Android Development Tools (ADT) plug-in for Eclipse, which was deprecated in 2014 and sunsetted after the release of Android Studio 2.2 in 2016. Though it remains possible to develop for Android using Eclipse or other IDEs, the use of Android Studio is highly recommended.*

Installing Android Studio and the Android SDK

You can download the latest version of Android Studio for your chosen development platform from the Android Studio homepage at `developer.android.com/studio`.

> **NOTE** *Unless otherwise noted, the version of Android Studio used for writing this book was Android Studio 3.0.1.*

When you have initiated the download for your platform, you will be shown detailed installation instructions that can be summarized as follows:

➤ **Windows**—Run the downloaded installation executable. The Windows installer download includes OpenJDK and the Android SDK.

➤ **MacOS**—Open the downloaded Android Studio DMG file, and then drag Android Studio into your "Applications" folder. Double-click to open Android Studio, and the Setup Wizard will guide you through the rest of the setup, which includes downloading the Android SDK.

➤ **Linux**—Unzip the downloaded `.zip` file to an appropriate location for your applications, such as within `/usr/local/` for your user profile, or `/opt/` for shared users. Open a terminal, navigate to the `android-studio/bin/` directory, and execute `studio.sh`. The Setup Wizard will then guide you through the rest of the setup, which includes downloading the Android SDK.

Since Android Studio 2.2, OpenJDK has been integrated with Android Studio, ensuring you don't need to download and install the JDK separately.

Once the installation wizard is completed, the latest Android platform SDK; SDK, platform, and build tools; and support library will have been downloaded and installed.

You can download older platform versions, as well as additional SDK components using the SDK Manager as described in the following section.

> **NOTE** *As an open source platform, the Android SDK source is also available for you to download and compile from* source.android.com.

Installing Additional Android SDK Components Using the SDK Manager

The SDK Manager (Figure 2-1) is available through a shortcut on the toolbar, the Android SDK settings option, or from within the Tools ➪ Android ➪ SDK Manager menu item. It offers tabs for SDK Platforms, SDK Tools, and SDK Update Sites.

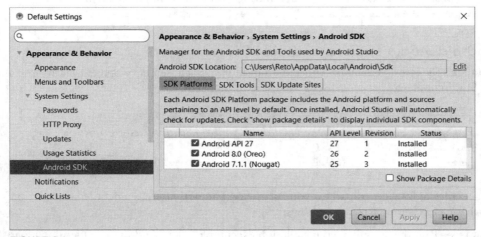

FIGURE 2-1

The SDK Platforms tab shows which platform SDKs you have downloaded. By default, this will include the newest Android platform SDK—in this case, Android 8.1 Oreo (API Level 27).

The SDK Tools tab shows which tools and support libraries you have installed, including the SDK, platform, and build tools—as well as the support repository, which is required to use the Android Support Library (described later in this chapter.)

By selecting the Show Package Contents Details checkbox, you can find additional details on which versions each tool have been installed.

Downloading and Installing Updates to Android Studio, the Android SDK, and Tools

Android Studio receives frequent updates that improve stability and add new features. You will be prompted with an alert tip when a new version of Android Studio is available for download, as shown in Figure 2-2.

FIGURE 2-2

You will similarly be prompted when new revisions of the Android SDK, developer tools, support library, Kotlin, and other SDK packages become available.

You can force a check for a new version of Android Studio by opening the Settings dialog box and navigating to Settings ⇨ Updates and clicking the "Check Now" button, as shown in Figure 2-3, or by selecting the Help ⇨ Check For Updates menu item.

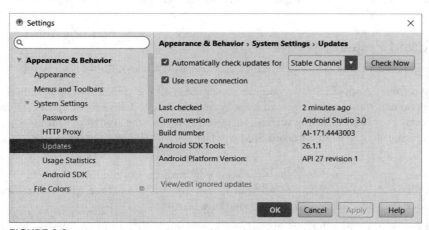

FIGURE 2-3

> **NOTE** *In addition to the official "stable" release available from the Android Developer site, the Android Studio team also makes preview releases of the next version available to developers who like to live on the edge. If you too like to live dangerously, you can change the channel to which your installation of Android Studio is subscribed by selecting Canary or Beta from the drop-down menu in the Updates screen shown in Figure 2-3.*
>
> *Canary represents the bleeding edge, released approximately weekly. These are early previews released in order to obtain real-world feedback during development.*
>
> *Beta represents release candidates based on stable Canary builds, released and updated to obtain feedback prior to the stable release.*
>
> *You can learn more about each release channel, including details on how to install parallel installations of Android Studio, at* `developer.android.com/studio/preview`.

Creating Your First Android Application

With Android Studio installed and the SDK downloaded you're ready to start developing apps for Android. You'll begin by creating a new Android project, configuring the Android Emulator, and setting up your Android Studio *run* and *debug* configurations, as described in the following sections.

Creating a New Android Project

To create a new Android project using Android Studio's New Project Wizard, do the following:

1. The first time you start Android Studio you are presented with the welcome screen shown in Figure 2-4. You can return to this screen by selecting the File ➪ Close menu item to close any open projects. From the welcome screen, select the "Start a new Android Studio project" option. Alternatively, within Android Studio select the File ➪ New ➪ New Project... menu item.

2. In the wizard that appears, enter the details for your new project. On the first page (Figure 2-5) enter an Application Name and your Company Domain. These will be combined to create a unique Package Name as displayed on the wizard.

   Each Android application must have a unique package name, so it's good practice to use a domain you own to minimize the chance of a collision. That said, owning the domain you use isn't required or enforced, so you can use almost any domain you want provided the resulting package name is unique.

   Finally, select the directory location to which your project will be saved.

FIGURE 2-4

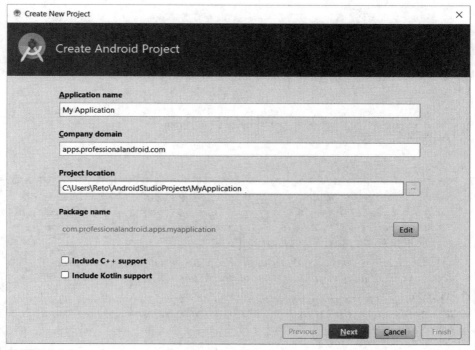

FIGURE 2-5

3. The next page (Figure 2-6) lets you select the form factors you wish to support within this project, as well as the minimum Android platform version on which your application will run. To get started, we'll target just phones and tablets and use the default minimum SDK.

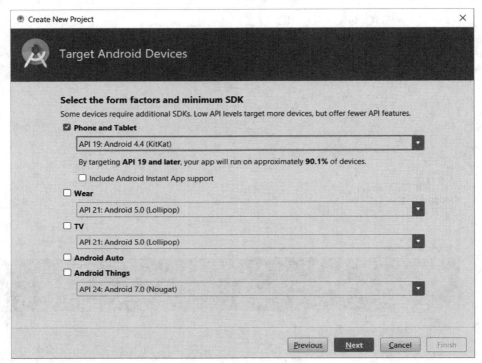

FIGURE 2-6

> **NOTE** *Selecting the minimum SDK version allows you to choose the level of backward compatibility you're willing to support. The lower this SDK version, the more devices will be able to run your app, but this will also make it more challenging to support newer platform features.*
>
> *Selecting each minimum SDK from the drop down will display the proportion of active Android devices running that platform version.*
>
> *At the time of this writing, more than 90% of Android devices were running at least Android 4.4 KitKat (API Level 19), while the latest release was Android 8.1 (API Level 27).*

4. The next page (Figure 2-7) lets you select a template for your app's main Activity (user interface screen). Select the Empty Activity.

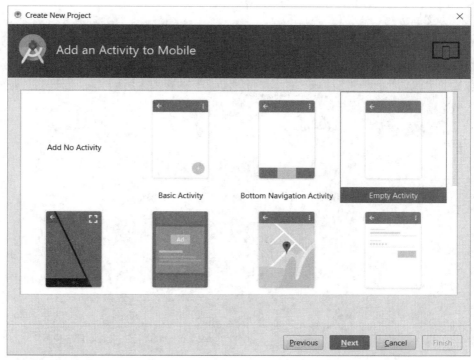

FIGURE 2-7

5. The final page (Figure 2-8) allows you to specify the class name for your initial Activity, and specify the name for the XML file that will be used to provide the Activity's UI layout. In the case of the empty Activity template, you can also choose if you wish the wizard to generate a layout file at all. You also have the option to make your Activity backward compatible by selecting the Backwards Compatibility check box, which is highly recommended. Marking this box checked will result in the new Activity inheriting from the Android Support Library's `AppCompatActivity` class rather than the framework's `Activity` class, which will allow your Activity to take advantage of new API features in a way that's backward compatible.

6. When you've entered these details, click Finish.

Android Studio will now create a new project that includes a class that extends `AppCompatActivity`. Rather than being completely empty, the default template implements "Hello World."

Before modifying the project, take this opportunity to create an Android Virtual Device, enable debugging on a physical device, and run our new Hello World project.

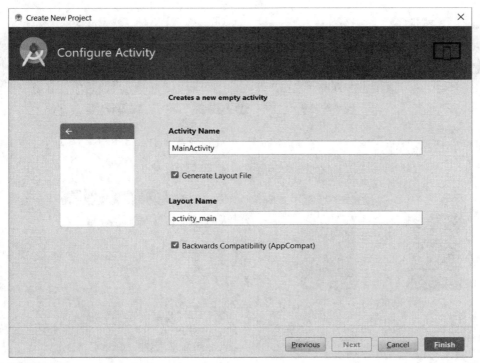

FIGURE 2-8

Creating an Android Virtual Device

Android Virtual Devices (AVDs) are used to simulate the hardware and software configurations of physical Android devices. The Android Emulator runs within AVDs, allowing you test your applications on a variety of different hardware and software platforms.

There are no prebuilt AVDs included in the Android Studio or Android SDK downloads so, if you don't have a physical device, you'll need to create at least one before you can run and debug your applications:

1. Select Tools ⇨ Android ⇨ AVD Manager (or select the AVD Manager icon on the Android Studio toolbar).

2. Click the "Create Virtual Device…" button.

    The resulting Virtual Device Configuration dialog box (Figure 2-9) allows you to select a device definition from a list of Pixel and Nexus hardware and standard device configurations—each with its own physical size, resolution, and pixel density.

3. You'll then be asked to select a device system image corresponding to a particular Android platform release, as shown in Figure 2-10. If you have not already done so, you will need to download the desired system image before it can be used.

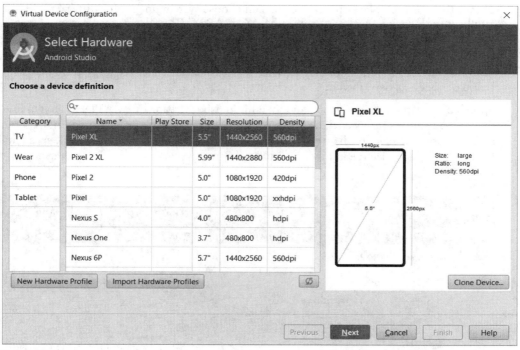

FIGURE 2-9

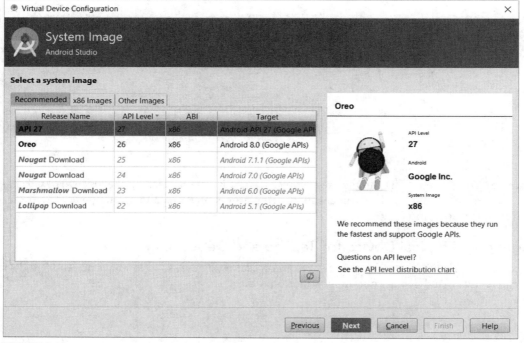

FIGURE 2-10

Notice that for each platform release you can choose system images for different ABIs (application binary interfaces)—typically x86 or ARM. Consider using a system image using the same architecture as your host computer to maximize Emulator performance.

You can also decide if you want a system image that includes the Google APIs. These are necessary if your app includes Google Play Services features such as maps and Location Based Services, as described in Chapter 15.

4. Specify a descriptive device name, and then hit Finish to create a new AVD, as shown in Figure 2-11. Note that by clicking Show Advanced Settings you can reveal additional options to assign your webcam to the front or rear camera, adjust the emulated network speed and latency, and customize the number of emulated cores, system memory, and storage.

FIGURE 2-11

5. Starting a new AVD can take some time, so start it now by clicking the green arrow in the right-most column. This will ensure the emulator is prepared and running when you're ready to run your app on it.

Configuring a Physical Device for Testing and Debugging

There's nothing quite like making software run on real hardware, so if you have an Android device, it's simple to run and debug your applications on it directly:

1. Start by enabling developer mode on your device. Open the phone's Settings and find and select System ⇨ "About phone." Scroll to the bottom of the resulting list until "Build number" is visible, as shown in Figure 2-12.

FIGURE 2-12

2. Touch "Build number" seven times, until a message is displayed congratulating you on becoming a developer. If you embarked on your journey to become an Android developer to win a bet, you can now safely collect. Congratulations!

3. If not, navigate back, and you'll find a new settings category labeled "Developer options." Select it, and scroll until you see the option for "USB debugging," as shown in Figure 2-13.

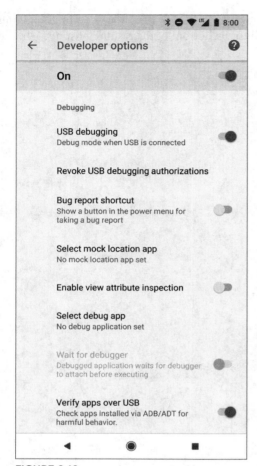

FIGURE 2-13

4. Enable "USB debugging."

5. Now connect your device to your development host computer using a USB cable. Your device will display the dialog box shown in Figure 2-14, asking if you wish to allow USB debugging when connected to the current computer. Select OK.

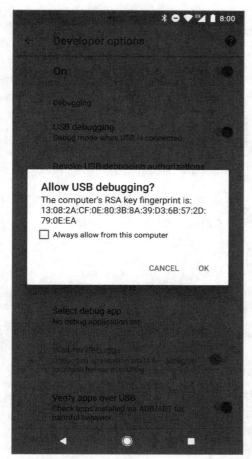

FIGURE 2-14

6. When connected, this device will now be available as a target when launching your app for running or debugging within Android Studio.

Running and Debugging Your Android Application

You've created your first project and created an Android Virtual Device (or connected a physical device) on which to run it. Before making any changes, let's try running and debugging the Hello World project.

From the Run menu, select "Run app" (or "Debug app"). If you haven't already selected a default, you'll be presented with the dialog box shown in Figure 2-15, asking you to select your deployment target—a connected device, a running AVD, or a defined (but not yet running) AVD.

FIGURE 2-15

Running or debugging your application does the following behind the scenes:

➤ Compiles the current project source to bytecode, and converts that to an Android executable (`.dex`)

➤ Packages the executable and your project's resources and manifest into an Android package (`.apk`)

➤ Starts the virtual device (if you've targeted one and it's not already running)

➤ Deploys your APK to the target device and installs it

➤ Starts your application

If you're debugging, the Android Studio debugger will then be attached, allowing you to set break-points and debug your code.

If everything is working correctly, you'll see a new Activity running on the device or in the Emulator, as shown in Figure 2-16.

Understanding Hello World

Take a step back and have a look at the source code for your first Android application, starting with the `MainActivity.java` file.

In Android, `Activity` is the base class for the visual, interactive screens within your application; it is roughly equivalent to a Form in traditional desktop development (and is described in detail in Chapter 3, "Applications and Activities and Fragments, Oh My!").

`AppCompatActivity` is a variation of the `Activity` class supplied by the Android Support Library, which provides backward compatibility. Using `AppCompatActivity` in preference to the `Activity` class is considered best practice, and we'll be doing so throughout this book. Note that by conven-tion we still refer to classes that extend `AppCompatActivity` as *Activities*.

FIGURE 2-16

Listing 2-1 shows the skeleton code for an Activity; note that it extends `AppCompatActivity` and overrides the `onCreate` method.

LISTING 2-1: Hello World

```
package com.professionalandroid.apps.helloworld;

import android.support.v7.app.AppCompatActivity;
import android.os.Bundle;

public class MainActivity extends AppCompatActivity {

  @Override
  protected void onCreate(Bundle savedInstanceState) {
    super.onCreate(savedInstanceState);
    setContentView(R.layout.activity_main);
  }
}
```

Visual components within Activities are called *Views*, which are similar to controls or widgets in traditional desktop and web development. The Hello World template created by the wizard overrides the `onCreate` method to call `setContentView`, which lays out the UI by inflating a layout resource, as highlighted in bold in the following snippet:

```
@Override
protected void onCreate(Bundle savedInstanceState) {
  super.onCreate(savedInstanceState);
  setContentView(R.layout.activity_main);
}
```

The resources for an Android project are stored in the `res` folder of your project hierarchy, which includes `layout`, `values`, `drawable`, and `mipmap` subfolders. Android Studio interprets these resources and provides design-time access to them through the `R` variable, as described in Chapter 4.

Listing 2-2 shows the UI layout as defined in the `activity_main.xml` file, created by the Android project template and stored in the project's `res/layout` folder.

LISTING 2-2: Hello World layout resource

```
<?xml version="1.0" encoding="utf-8"?>
<android.support.constraint.ConstraintLayout
  xmlns:android="http://schemas.android.com/apk/res/android"
  xmlns:app="http://schemas.android.com/apk/res-auto"
  xmlns:tools="http://schemas.android.com/tools"
  android:layout_width="match_parent"
  android:layout_height="match_parent"
  tools:context="com.professionalandroid.apps.myapplication.MainActivity">
  <TextView
    android:layout_width="wrap_content"
    android:layout_height="wrap_content"
    android:text="Hello World!"
    app:layout_constraintBottom_toBottomOf="parent"
    app:layout_constraintLeft_toLeftOf="parent"
    app:layout_constraintRight_toRightOf="parent"
    app:layout_constraintTop_toTopOf="parent"/>
</android.support.constraint.ConstraintLayout>
```

> **NOTE** *The specific layout created as part of the Android Project Wizard may change over time, so your layout may look slightly different to the XML shown here, though the resulting UI should appear very similar.*

Defining your UI in XML and inflating it is the preferred way of implementing your user interfaces (UIs), because it neatly decouples your application logic from your UI design.

To get access to your UI elements in code, you can add identifier attributes to them in the XML definition:

```
<TextView
  android:id="@+id/myTextView"
  android:layout_width="wrap_content"
  android:layout_height="wrap_content"
```

```
    android:text="Hello World!"
    app:layout_constraintBottom_toBottomOf="parent"
    app:layout_constraintLeft_toLeftOf="parent"
    app:layout_constraintRight_toRightOf="parent"
    app:layout_constraintTop_toTopOf="parent"/>
```

You can then use the `findViewById` method to return a reference to each named item at run time:

```
TextView myTextView = findViewById(R.id.myTextView);
```

Alternatively (although it's not generally considered good practice), you can create your layout directly in code, as shown in Listing 2-3.

LISTING 2-3: Creating layouts in code

```
public void onCreate(Bundle savedInstanceState) {
    super.onCreate(savedInstanceState);

    RelativeLayout.LayoutParams lp;
    lp =
        new RelativeLayout.LayoutParams(LinearLayout.LayoutParams.MATCH_PARENT,
                                        LinearLayout.LayoutParams.MATCH_PARENT);

    RelativeLayout.LayoutParams textViewLP;
    textViewLP = new RelativeLayout.LayoutParams(
        RelativeLayout.LayoutParams.WRAP_CONTENT,
        RelativeLayout.LayoutParams.WRAP_CONTENT);

    Resources res = getResources();
    int hpad = res.getDimensionPixelSize(R.dimen.activity_horizontal_margin);
    int vpad = res.getDimensionPixelSize(R.dimen.activity_vertical_margin);

    RelativeLayout rl = new RelativeLayout(this);
    rl.setPadding(hpad, vpad, hpad, vpad);

    TextView myTextView = new TextView(this);
    myTextView.setText("Hello World!");

    rl.addView(myTextView, textViewLP);

    addContentView(rl, lp);
}
```

Note that all the properties available in code can also be set with attributes in the XML layout.

More generally, keeping the visual design decoupled from the application code helps keep the code concise. With Android available on hundreds of different devices of varying screen sizes, defining your layouts as XML resources makes it easier for you to include multiple layouts optimized for different screens.

You learn how to build your user interface by creating layouts and building your own custom Views in Chapter 5, "Building User Interfaces."

Opening Android Sample Projects

Android includes a number of well-documented sample projects that are an excellent source for full, working examples of applications written for Android. When you finish setting up your development environment, it's worth going through some of them.

The Android sample projects are stored on GitHub, and Android Studio provides a simple mechanism for cloning them:

1. From within Android Studio, select File ➪ New ➪ Import Sample… to open the Import Sample Wizard, as shown in Figure 2-17. You can also select "Import an Android code sample" from the Welcome to Android Studio Wizard if you have no projects currently open.

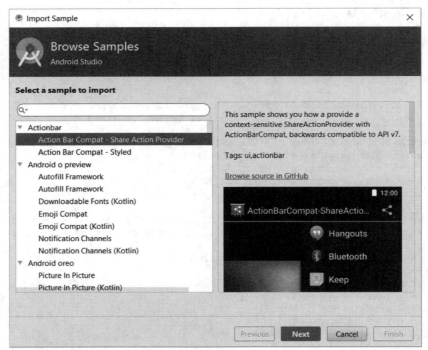

FIGURE 2-17

2. Select the sample you wish to import and click Next.
3. Specify an application name and location on your host machine and click Finish to download and open the sample.

The selected sample project will be cloned from GitHub and be opened as a new Android Studio project.

> **NOTE** *To view all of the Android code samples available for import into Android Studio, see the Google Samples page on GitHub at* `github.com/googlesamples/`.

Getting Started Writing Android Apps Using Kotlin

Until 2017, Android app development required the use of the Java language syntax. Android Studio 3.0 added Kotlin as a fully supported language alternative.

Kotlin is a statically typed language that is fully interoperable with the existing Java language syntax and runtime used with Android. It's considered expressive and concise, and introduces improvements including reduced language verbosity, null-pointer safety, extension functions, and infix notation.

Since Android Studio 3.0, Kotlin is an officially supported Android development language; however, at the time of this book's writing, Java was still the default for new projects—and most existing Android projects were still written predominantly using Java syntax. It's also very easy to convert Java syntax into Kotlin, simply by pasting Java syntax into a Kotlin source file. As a result, we have used Java syntax within the code snippets and sample projects featured within this book.

Given the advantages of Kotlin in terms of improved development time and code readability, we expect the proportion of apps written primarily in Kotlin to increase quickly, and we highly recommend that you familiarize yourself with the Kotlin language for writing Android apps. To assist, each of the code snippets and sample projects are also available in Kotlin, downloadable from the Wrox site alongside the Java syntax versions.

Your Android projects can be written from scratch in Kotlin, can include interoperable Kotlin and Java source files, or can be converted from Java source files to Kotlin during development.

To begin a new project in Kotlin, select the File ⇨ New ⇨ New Project... menu item, as previously described, but on the first page of the wizard, select the "Include Kotlin support" checkbox, as shown in Figure 2-18.

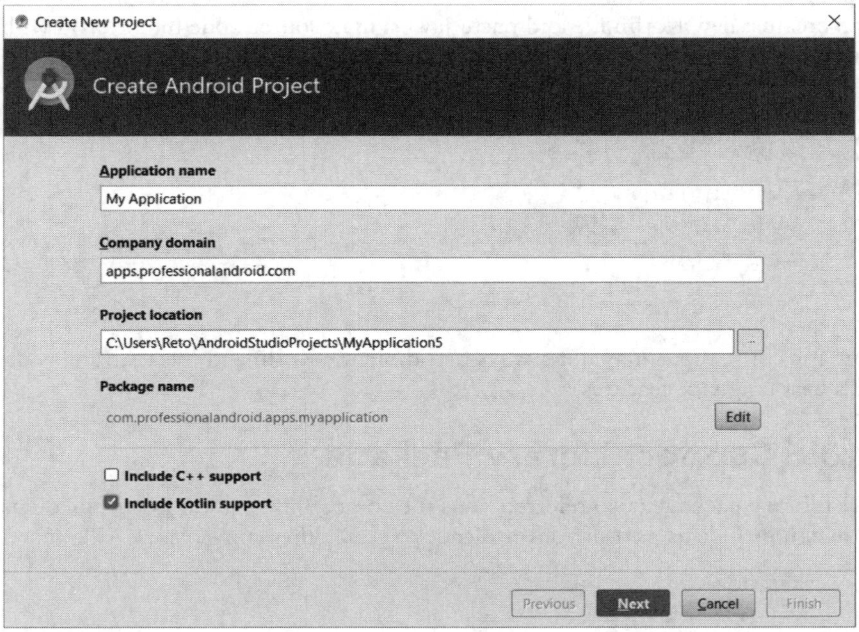

FIGURE 2-18

Proceed through the wizard as described in the earlier section. When complete, take a look at the Kotlin source code for your Activity in the `MainActivity.kt` file. Kotlin files are stored alongside Java source files and can be found in the Java folder when using the Android project view:

```
package com.professionalandroid.apps.myapplication

import android.support.v7.app.AppCompatActivity
import android.os.Bundle

class MainActivity : AppCompatActivity() {

  override fun onCreate(savedInstanceState: Bundle?) {
    super.onCreate(savedInstanceState)
    setContentView(R.layout.activity_main)
  }
}
```

Note that while the code is somewhat more concise, the syntactic changes at this point are minimal. The package and import statements are the same, the `MainActivity` class still extends `AppCompatActivity`, and the override of the `onCreate` method remains the same.

To add a new Kotlin file to your project, select Kotlin from the Source Language dropdown list when adding a new application component from the File ⇨ New menu. Alternatively, you can select the File ⇨ New ⇨ Kotlin File/Class menu item to create a basic file.

Because Kotlin and Java files can coexist in the same project, it's possible to add Kotlin source files to a project you started without ticking the Kotlin support checkbox or to add Java source files to a project started with Kotlin support.

It's also possible to convert existing Java syntax source files into Kotlin. You can do this by opening an existing Java source file and selecting the Code ⇨ Convert Java File to Kotlin File menu item. Alternatively, you can create a new Kotlin file and paste Java syntax source code into it. You will be prompted to convert the pasted code into Kotlin, as shown in Figure 2-19.

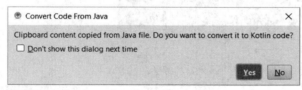

FIGURE 2-19

Note that these automatic conversions may not always use idiomatic Kotlin, so the resulting code might not use Kotlin's best language features.

Using the Android Support Library Package

The Android Support Library package (also referred to as the compatibility library or AppCompat) is a set of libraries you can include as part of your projects, to gain either convenience APIs that aren't packaged as part of the framework (such as the View Pager), or useful APIs that are not available on all platform releases (such as Fragments).

The Support Library enables you to use framework API features that were introduced in newer Android platform releases on devices running earlier platform versions. This helps you provide a consistent user experience and greatly simplifies your development process by reducing the burden of supporting older platform versions, while taking advantage of newer features.

> **NOTE** *It's good practice to use the Support Library rather than the framework APIs when you want to support devices running earlier platform releases, and where the Support Library offers all the functionality you require.*
>
> *Accordingly, the examples in this book will target Android 8.1 (API Level 27) and use the support library APIs where available, in preference to the framework, while highlighting specific areas where the Support Library may not be a suitable alternative.*

The Android Support Library package contains several individual libraries, each of which offers support for a specific range of Android platform versions and features.

We will introduce new libraries as required in the following chapters. To begin with, it's good practice to include the v7 appcompat library in all new projects because it supports a wide range of Android versions—back to Android 2.3 Gingerbread (API Level 9)—and provides APIs for many recommended user interface patterns.

The application templates provided by Android Studio—including the Hello World example we created earlier—include a dependency on the v7 appcompat library by default.

To incorporate an Android Support Library package into your project, perform the following steps:

1. Use the SDK Manager to ensure you have downloaded the Android Support Repository.

2. Add a dependency to your Gradle build for the desired library, either by:

2.1 Opening your `module:app build.gradle` file and adding a reference to the library name and version you wish to include, within the dependency node:

```
dependencies {
  [... Existing dependencies ...]
  implementation 'com.android.support:appcompat-v7:27.1.1'
}
```

2.2 Or using Android Studio's Project Structure UI, as shown in Figure 2-20. Select the File ⇨ Project Structure..., menu item and then select your app module from the list on the left before choosing the Dependencies tab. Add a new library by selecting the green "plus" symbol on the right-side toolbar and selecting the desired library.

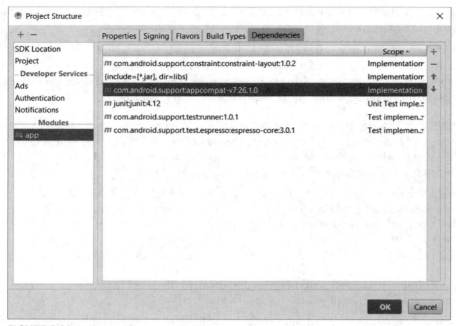

FIGURE 2-20

Notice that we're adding a dependency to a specific version of the support library. By design, the Android Support Library package will be updated more regularly than the Android framework SDK. By downloading new versions of the Support Libraries, and updating your dependencies to reference the newest releases, you can continue to incorporate bug fixes and improvements to your app as the Support Libraries are updated.

> **NOTE** *The Support Library classes mirror the names of their framework counterparts. In most cases the Support Library class is postfixed with* compat *(for example,* NotificationCompat*); however, some earlier Support Library classes use the same names as their framework equivalents. As a result, there's a significant risk that the code completion and automatic import-management tools in Android Studio (and other IDEs) will select the wrong library—particularly when you're building against newer versions of the SDK.*
>
> *It's good practice to set your project build target to the minimum platform version you plan to support, and to ensure the import statements are using the compatibility library for classes that also exist in the target framework.*

DEVELOPING FOR MOBILE AND EMBEDDED DEVICES

Android does a lot to simplify mobile- or embedded-device software development, but to build high-quality apps you need to understand the reasons behind the conventions. You have several factors to consider when writing software for mobile and embedded devices, and when developing for Android in particular.

> **NOTE** *In this chapter you learn some of the techniques and best practices for writing efficient Android code. In later chapters, these best practices are sometimes compromised for clarity and brevity when new Android concepts or functionality are introduced. In the best tradition of "Do as I say, not as I do," some examples will show the simplest (or easiest-to-understand) way of doing something, not necessarily the best way of doing it in production.*

Hardware-Imposed Design Considerations

Small and portable, mobile devices offer exciting opportunities for software development. Their limited screen size and reduced memory, storage, and processor power are far less exciting, and instead present some unique challenges.

Compared to desktop or notebook computers, mobile devices have relatively:

➤ Low processing power

➤ Limited RAM

➤ Limited storage capacity

➤ Small screens

➤ High costs associated with data transfers

➤ Intermittent connectivity, slow data transfer rates, and high latency

➤ Limited battery life

Each new generation of devices improves on many of these restrictions, but the device ecosystem also caters for a wide variety of prices—which results in significant variety in hardware capabilities. This is amplified by the huge growth in smart phone adoption in emerging markets, which are significantly more price sensitive, and that in turn results in large numbers of new devices with lower specification hardware.

The expansion of Android into an increasingly diverse variety of form factors—including tablets, TVs, automotive head-units, and wearable devices further expands the range of devices on which your application may be running.

In some cases you may find your app running on hardware significantly more powerful than you expected; however it's always good practice to design to accommodate the worst-case scenario to ensure you're providing a great user experience to all users, no matter what their hardware platform.

Performance Matters

Manufacturers of embedded devices, particularly mobile devices, often value thinner form factors and bigger (and higher resolution) screens over significant improvements to processor speeds. For us as developers, that means losing the head start traditionally afforded thanks to Moore's law (the doubling of the number of transistors placed on an integrated circuit every two years). In desktop and server hardware, Moore's Law typically results directly in processor performance improvements; for mobile devices, it instead means thinner devices, with brighter, higher-resolution screens. By comparison, improvements in processor power take a back seat.

In practice, this means that you always need to optimize your code so that it runs quickly and responsively, assuming that hardware improvements over the lifetime of your software are unlikely to do you any favors.

Code efficiency is a big topic in software engineering, so I'm not going to try to cover it extensively here. Later in this chapter you learn some Android-specific efficiency tips, but for now note that efficiency is particularly important for resource-constrained platforms.

Expect Limited Storage Capacity

Advances in flash memory and solid-state disks have led to a dramatic increase in mobile-device storage capacities. Although devices with 64, 128, or even 256 GB of storage are no longer uncommon, many popular lower-end devices have significantly less available space. Given that most of the available storage on a mobile device is likely to be used to store photos, music, and movies, users are likely to uninstall apps that are taking a disproportionate amount of storage space relative to their perceived value.

As a result, the install size of your application is an important consideration, though even more important is ensuring that your application is polite in its use of system resources—so you must carefully consider how you store your application data.

To make life easier, you can use the Android databases to persist, reuse, and share large quantities of data, as described in Chapter 9, "Creating and Using Databases." For files, preferences, and state information, Android provides optimized frameworks, as described in Chapter 8, "Files, Saving State, and User Preferences."

Part of being polite is cleaning up after yourself. Techniques such as caching, pre-fetching, and lazy loading are useful for limiting repetitive network lookups and improving application responsiveness, but don't leave files on the filesystem or records in a database when they're no longer needed.

Design for Different Screens and Form Factors

The small size and portability of mobiles are challenge for creating good interfaces, particularly when users are demanding an increasingly striking and information-rich graphical user experience.

Combined with the wide range of screen sizes that make up the Android device ecosystem, creating consistent, intuitive, and delightful user interfaces can be a significant challenge.

Write your applications knowing that users will often only glance at the screen. Make your applications intuitive and easy to use by reducing the number of controls and putting the most important information front and center.

Graphical controls, such as the ones you'll create in Chapter 5, are an excellent means of displaying a lot of information in a way that's easy to understand. Rather than a screen full of text with a lot of buttons and text-entry boxes, use colors, shapes, and graphics to convey information.

You'll also need to consider how touch input is going to affect your interface design, and how you can support accessibility and non–touch screen devices such as TVs.

Android devices are now available in a huge variety of screen sizes, resolutions, and input mechanisms. With multi-window support included in Android 7.0, the screen size for your app may even change while running on a single device.

To ensure that your application looks good and behaves well on all the possible host devices, you need to create responsive designs and test your application on a variety of screens, optimizing for small screens and tablets, while also ensuring that your UIs scale well.

You learn some techniques for optimizing your UI for different screen sizes in Chapters 4 and 5.

Expect Low Speeds, High Latency

The ability to connect to the Internet is a big part of what has made smart phones smart, and ubiquitous. Unfortunately, mobile Internet connectivity isn't as fast, reliable, cheap, or readily available as we would like; when you're developing your Internet-based applications, it's best to assume that the network connection will be slow, intermittent, expensive, and unreliable.

This is especially true in emerging markets where relative data prices are significantly higher. By designing for the worst case you can ensure that you always deliver a high-standard user experience. This also means making sure that your applications can handle losing (or not finding) a data connection.

The Android Emulator enables you to control the speed and latency of your network connection. Figure 2-21 shows the Emulator's network connection speed and signal strength, simulating a distinctly suboptimal EDGE connection.

Experiment to ensure seamlessness and responsiveness no matter what the speed, latency, and availability of network access. Some techniques include limiting the functionality of your application, or reducing network lookups to cached bursts, when the available network connection supports only limited data transfer capabilities.

In Chapter 7, "Using Internet Resources," you learn how to use Internet resources in your applications.

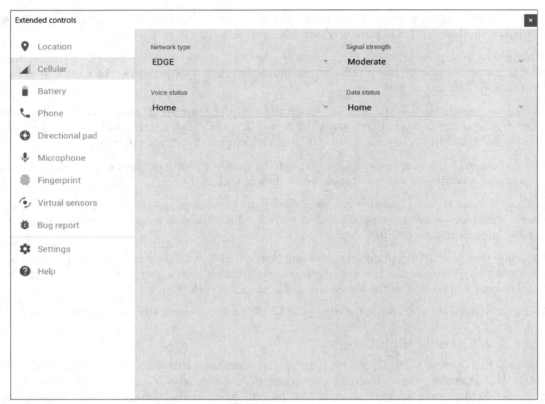

FIGURE 2-21

Save Battery Life

The more useful the apps on a device, the more that device is used—and the more quickly its battery is depleted. Combine this with larger, higher-resolution screens and thinner device form factors, and battery life quickly becomes a significant issue for device owners.

There's no more effective way to have users uninstall your app than to have it quickly deplete the battery. You should always endeavor to create apps that limit their impact on battery life.

One of the most dramatic influencers of how your app affects battery life is its use of network data transfers—particularly when your app isn't currently in the foreground. For your app to be a good citizen on the device, you must carefully consider if, and when, you choose to transfer data.

Android offers a number of APIs to help you minimize your impact on battery life, including Doze, App Standby, and Job Scheduler—each of which is designed to help you ensure your app adheres to best practices in conserving battery life when performing network transfers and operating in the background.

We explore these and other battery-saving best practices in Chapter 11.

Considering the User's Environment

Sadly, you can't assume that your users will consider your application the most important feature of their device.

In the case of smart phones, they are typically first and foremost a communications device, secondly a camera, thirdly a music and video player, and fourthly a games platform. The applications you write will most likely be in the fifth category of "useful stuff."

That's not a bad thing—they'll be in good company with others, including Google Maps and the web browser. That said, each user's usage model will be different; some people will never use their device to listen to music, some devices don't support telephony, and some don't include cameras— but the multitasking principle inherent in a device as ubiquitous as it is indispensable is an important consideration for usability design.

It's also important to consider when and how your users will use your application. People use their mobiles all the time—on the train, walking down the street, or even while driving. You can't make people use their phones appropriately, but you can make sure that your applications don't distract them any more than necessary.

What does this mean in terms of software design? Make sure that your application:

➤ **Is predictable and well behaved**—There's a fine line between a delightful moment and an unpleasant surprise. The outcome of any user interaction should be predictable and reversible, making it easy for new users to understand how to perform tasks, and minimizing any risk from experimenting.

➤ **Switches seamlessly from the background to the foreground**—With the multitasking nature of mobile devices, it's likely that your applications will regularly move into and out of the background. It's important that they "come to life" quickly and seamlessly. Unless users have explicitly closed your app, they shouldn't notice a difference between restarting and resuming it; switching should be seamless, with users being shown the UI and application state they last saw.

➤ **Is polite**—Never steal focus or interrupt a user's current Activity. Use Notifications (detailed in Chapter 11) to request user attention, when and as appropriate, when your application isn't in the foreground.

➤ **Presents an attractive and intuitive UI**—Spend the time and resources necessary to produce a UI that is as attractive as it is functional, and don't force users to interpret and relearn your application every time they open it. Using your app should be simple, easy, obvious, and delightful.

➤ **Is responsive**—Responsiveness is one of the most critical design considerations on a mobile device. You've no doubt experienced the frustration of a "frozen" piece of software; the multifunctional nature of mobile devices makes this even more annoying. With the possibility of delays caused by slow and unreliable data connections, it's important that your application always remains responsive.

Developing for Android

In addition to the preceding general guidelines, the Android design philosophy demands that high-quality applications be designed for:

➤ Performance

➤ Responsiveness

➤ Freshness

➤ Security

➤ Seamlessness

➤ Accessibility

Being Performant

One of the keys to writing efficient Android code is not to carry over assumptions from desktop and server environments into embedded devices. A lot of what you already know about writing efficient code will be applicable to Android, but the limitations of embedded systems and the use of the Android Run Time mean you can't take things for granted.

There are two basic rules for writing efficient code:

➤ Don't do work that you don't need to do.

➤ Don't allocate memory if you can avoid it.

System memory is a scarce commodity, so you need to take special care to use it efficiently. This means thinking about how you use the stack and heap, limiting object creation, and being aware of how variable scope affects memory use.

The Android team has published specific and detailed guidance on writing efficient code for Android, so rather than rehashing it here, visit `d.android.com/training/articles/perf-tips .html` for suggestions.

Being Responsive

Generally, 100 to 200ms is the threshold at which users perceive a delay or "jank" in an application, so you should always endeavor to respond to user input within that timeframe.

The Android Activity Manager and Window Manager also enforce a time limit beyond which the application is considered unresponsive, and the user will be given the opportunity to force-close the app. If either service detects an unresponsive application, it will display an "[Application] isn't responding" (ANR) dialog box, as shown in Figure 2-22.

FIGURE 2-22

Android monitors two conditions to determine responsiveness:

➤ An application must respond to any user action, such as a key press or screen touch, within 5 seconds.

➤ A Broadcast Receiver must return from its onReceive handler within 10 seconds.

The ANR dialog box is a last resort of usability; the generous five-second limit is a worst-case scenario, not a target. You can ensure that your application doesn't trigger an ANR, and is as responsive as possible, in a number of ways:

➤ Lengthy tasks such as network or database lookups, complex processing (such as calculating game moves), and file I/O should all be moved off the main UI thread and run asynchronously.

➤ Show progress within your UI if there are long-running tasks happening in the background.

➤ If your application has a time-consuming initial setup phase, render the main view as quickly as possible, indicate that loading is in progress, and fill the information asynchronously. You could also consider showing a splash screen—but in either case, indicate that progress is being made, to avoid the user perception that the application has frozen.

Ensuring Data Freshness

From a usability perspective, the right time to update your application is immediately before the user looks at it—in practice, you need to weigh the update frequency against its effect on battery life and data usage.

When designing your application, it's critical that you consider how often you will update its data. You need to minimize the time users are waiting for refreshes or updates, while limiting the effect of these background updates on the battery life. You are introduced to the Job Scheduler to update your application in the background in Chapter 11.

Developing Secure Applications

Android applications have access to networks and hardware, can be distributed independently, and are built on an open source platform featuring open communication, so it shouldn't be surprising that security is a significant consideration.

The Android security model sandboxes each application and restricts access to services and functionality by requiring applications to declare the permissions they require, and allowing users to accept or reject those requests.

The framework also includes robust implementations of security functionality including cryptography and secure IPC, as well as technologies like ASLR, NX, ProPolice, safe_iop, OpenBSD dlmalloc, OpenBSD calloc, and Linux mmap_min_addr to mitigate risks associated with common memory management errors.

This doesn't get you off the hook. You not only need to make sure your application is secure for its own sake, but you also need to ensure that it doesn't "leak" permissions, data, and hardware access to compromise the device or user data. You can use several techniques to help maintain device security, and they are covered in more detail as you learn the technologies involved. In particular, you should do the following:

➤ Be security conscious when storing or transmitting data. By default, files that you create on internal storage are accessible only to your app, but you must be particularly careful if your app shares files or data with other applications—for example, through shared Services, Content Providers, or broadcast Intents. If you have access to user data and can avoid storing or transmitting the information, do not store or transmit the data. Take special care to ensure you aren't sharing or transmitting sensitive information, such as PII (personally identifiable information) or location data.

➤ Always perform input validation. Insufficient input validation is one of the most common security problems affecting applications, regardless of what platform they run on. Take special care when accepting input to your application from user input or external sources, such as the Internet, Bluetooth, NFC, SMS messages, or instant messaging (IM).

➤ Be cautious when your application may expose access to lower-level hardware to third-party applications.

➤ Minimize the data your application uses and which permissions it requires.

> **NOTE** *You can learn more about Android's security model in Chapter 20,* *"Advanced Android Development," and at* `developer.android.com/train-ing/articles/security-tips.html`.

Ensuring a Seamless User Experience

The idea of a seamless user experience is an important, if somewhat nebulous, concept. What do we mean by *seamless*? The goal is a consistent user experience in which applications start, stop, and transition instantly and without perceptible delays or jarring transitions.

The speed and responsiveness of a mobile device shouldn't degrade the longer it's used. Android's process management helps by acting as a silent assassin, killing background applications to free resources as required. Knowing this, your applications should always present a consistent interface, regardless of whether they're being restarted or resumed.

Start by ensuring that your Activities are properly suspended when they're not in the foreground. Android fires event handlers when your Activity is paused and resumed, so you can pause UI updates and network lookups when your application isn't visible—and resume them as soon as it is.

Persist data between sessions, and when the application isn't visible, suspend tasks that use processor cycles, network bandwidth, or battery life.

When your application is brought back to the front, or restarted, it should seamlessly return to its last visible state. As far as your users are concerned, each application should be sitting silently, ready to be used but just out of sight.

Use a consistent and intuitive approach to usability. You can create applications that are revolutionary and unfamiliar, but even these should integrate cleanly with the wider Android environment.

Use a consistent design language within your app—ideally following the material design principles discussed in more detail in Chapter 12 and at `material.io/guidelines/`.

You can use many other techniques to ensure a seamless user experience, and you'll be introduced to some of them as you discover more of the possibilities available in Android in the upcoming chapters.

Providing Accessibility

When designing and developing your applications, it's important not to assume that every user will be exactly like you. This has implications for internationalization and usability but is critical for providing accessible support for users with disabilities that require them to interact with their Android devices in different ways.

Android provides facilities to help these users navigate their devices more easily using text-to-speech, haptic feedback, and trackball or D-pad navigation.

To provide a good user experience for everyone—including people with visual, physical, or age-related disabilities that prevent them from fully using or seeing a touch screen—you can leverage Android's accessibility features.

> **NOTE** *Best practices for making your application accessible are covered in detail in Chapter 14, "Advanced Customization of Your User Interface."*

As a bonus, the same steps required to help make your touch screen applications useful for users with disabilities will also make your applications easier to use on non–touch screen devices, such as TVs.

ANDROID DEVELOPMENT TOOLS

The Android SDK includes several tools and utilities to help you create, test, and debug your projects. We explore several of these in more detail throughout the remainder of this book, though a detailed examination of each developer tool is outside our scope. However, it is worth reviewing what's available, and for additional details, check out the Android Studio documentation at `developer.android.com/studio`.

As mentioned earlier, Android Studio conveniently incorporates all of these tools, including the following:

➤ **The Android Virtual Device Manager and Emulator**—The AVD Manager is used to create and manage AVDs, virtual hardware that hosts an Emulator running a particular build of Android. Each AVD can specify a particular screen size and resolution, memory and storage capacities, and available hardware capabilities (such as touch screens and GPS). The Android Emulator is an implementation of the Android Run Time designed to run within an AVD on your host development computer.

➤ **The Android SDK Manager**—Used to download SDK packages including Android platform SDKs, support libraries, and the Google Play Services SDK.

➤ **Android Profiler**—Visualize the behavior and performance of your app. The Android Profiler can track memory and CPU use in real time, as well as analyze network traffic.

➤ **Lint**—A static analysis tool that analyzes your application and its resources to suggest improvements and optimizations.

➤ **Gradle**—An advanced build system and toolkit that manages the compilation, packaging, and deployment of your applications.

➤ **Vector Asset Studio**—Generates bitmap files for each screen density to support older versions of Android that don't support the Android vector drawable format.

➤ **APK Analyzer**—Provides insight into the composition of your built APK files.

The following additional tools are also available:

➤ **Android Debug Bridge (ADB)**—A client-server application that provides a link between your host computer and virtual and physical Android devices. It lets you copy files, install compiled application packages (`.apk`), and run shell commands.

➤ **Logcat**—A utility used to view and filter the output of the Android logging system.

➤ **Android Asset Packaging Tool (AAPT)**—Constructs the distributable Android package files (`.apk`).

➤ **SQLite3**—A database tool that you can use to access the SQLite database files created and used by Android.

➤ **Hprof-conv**—A tool that converts HPROF profiling output files into a standard format to view in your preferred profiling tool.

➤ **Dx**—Converts Java `.class` bytecode into Android `.dex` bytecode.

➤ **Draw9patch**—A handy utility to simplify the creation of NinePatch graphics using a WYSIWYG editor.

➤ **Monkey and Monkey Runner**—Monkey runs within the Android Run Time, generating pseudorandom user and system events. Monkey Runner provides an API for writing programs to control the VM from outside your application.

➤ **ProGuard**—A tool to shrink and obfuscate your code by replacing class, variable, and method names with semantically meaningless alternatives. This is useful to make your code more difficult to reverse engineer.

Android Studio

As a developer, the Android Studio IDE is where you'll be spending the majority of your time, so it pays to understand some of its nuances. The following sections introduce some tips for reducing build times—specifically through the use of Instant Run—as well as some shortcuts and advanced features you can use while writing and debugging your code.

Improving Build Performance

The simplest way to improve build performance is by ensuring you have allocated enough RAM to the build process. You can modify the amount of RAM allocated to the build system (the Gradle Daemon VM) by editing the `gradle.properties` file within your project.

For good performance, it's recommended that you allocate a minimum of 2Gb, using the `org.gradle.jvmargs` property:

```
org.gradle.jvmargs=-Xmx2048m
```

The ideal value for each system will vary based on different hardware, so you should experiment to see what works best for you.

Additionally, if you're on Windows, Windows Defender Real-Time Protection might cause build slowdowns. You can avoid this by adding your project folder to the list of Windows Defender exclusions.

Using Instant Run

Instant Run is an Android Studio feature that significantly reduces the build and deploy times for incremental code changes during your coding, testing, and debugging life cycles.

The first time you hit Run or Debug, the Gradle build system will compile your source code into bytecode and convert that to Android .dex files. Those are combined with your application's manifest and resources into an APK, which is deployed to your target device where the app is installed and launched.

When Instant Run is enabled, the build process will inject some additional instrumentation and an App Server into your debug APK to support Instant Run.

From then on, a small yellow lightning bolt icon is available, indicating that Instant Run is active. Each time you make a change and hit Instant Run, Android Studio will attempt to improve the build and deploy speed by "swapping" code and resource changes directly into your running debug app process.

The nature of the improvements varies based on the changes you make as follows:

➤ **Hot Swap**—Incremental code changes are applied and reflected in the app without needing to relaunch the app or even restart the current Activity. Can be used for most simple changes within method implementations.

➤ **Warm Swap**—The Activity needs to be restarted before changes can be seen and used. Typically required for changes to resources.

➤ **Cold Swap**—The app is restarted (but still not reinstalled). Required for any structural changes such as to inheritance or method signatures.

Instant Run is enabled by default, and is controlled by Android Studio, so only start/restart your debug instance from the IDE—don't start/restart your app from the device or command line.

Tips for Using Android Studio

Hundreds of tips and tricks can make your Android Studio experience faster and more productive. The following are a small sampling of some not immediately obvious, but very helpful shortcuts to help you make every keystroke count.

Quick Search

The most useful shortcut to remember in Android Studio is action search, triggered by pressing Ctrl+Shift+A (Cmd+Shift+A on MacOS). After pressing that shortcut, you can start typing keywords, and any available actions or options containing those words will be available for your selection.

To specifically search for files within a project, you can press Shift twice to display the Search Everywhere dialog.

Alternatively, wherever there's a long list—such as files in the project hierarchy or menu options in a large menu such as Refactor This..., just start typing and it'll start filtering results.

Using Tab to Autocomplete Selections

Pressing Tab (instead of Enter) when selecting an autocomplete option replaces any existing methods and values, rather than inserting the new selection in front of it.

Postfix Code Completion

Postfix code completion lets you transform a simple, already typed, value or expression into a more complex one.

For example, you can create a for-loop over a List variable by typing `.fori` after the variable name, or turn a Boolean expression into an if statement by postfixing `.if` (or `.else`). You can see all the valid postfixes available for a given context by typing Ctrl+J (Cmd+J on MacOS).

Live Templates

Live Templates let you use shortcuts that are available as autocompletion options to insert templatized snippets into your code.

Dozens of generic and Android-specific Live Templates are available, including a selection of logging shortcuts—or you can create your own to simplify best-practice patterns or boilerplate within your own code. You can view the existing Live Templates (and create your own) by opening the settings window and navigating to Editor ⇨ Live Templates.

The Android Virtual Device Manager

The Android Virtual Device Manager is used to create and manage the virtual hardware devices that will host instances of the Emulator.

AVDs are used to simulate the hardware configurations of different physical devices. This lets you test your application on a variety of hardware platforms without needing to buy a variety of phones.

> **NOTE** *The Android SDK doesn't include any prebuilt virtual devices, so you will need to create at least one device before you can run your applications within an Emulator.*

Each virtual device is configured with a name, physical device type, Android system image, screen size and resolution, ABI/CPU, memory and storage capacities, and hardware capabilities including camera and network speeds.

Different hardware settings and screen resolutions will present alternative UI skins to represent the different hardware configurations. This simulates a variety of device types including different phones and tablets, as well as TVs and Android Wear devices.

The Android Emulator

The Emulator runs within an AVD, and is available for testing and debugging your applications as an alternative to using a physical device.

The Emulator is an implementation of the Android Run Time, making it as valid a platform for running Android applications as any Android phone. Because it's decoupled from any particular hardware, it's an excellent baseline to use for testing your applications.

Full network connectivity is provided along with the ability to tweak the Internet connection speed and latency while debugging your applications. You can also simulate placing and receiving voice calls and SMS messages.

Android Studio integrates the Emulator so that it's launched automatically within the selected AVD when you run or debug your projects.

Once running, you can use the toolbar shown in Figure 2-23 to emulate pressing the hardware power and volume buttons, software home, back, and recents buttons, rotate the display, or take screen shots. Pressing the "…" button opens the extended controls, which are also shown in Figure 2-23, and that allow you to:

➤ Set the current GPS location, and simulate GPS track playback.

➤ Modify the simulated cellular network connectivity, including signal strength, speed, and data connection type.

➤ Set battery health, level, and charging status.

➤ Simulate incoming phone calls and SMS messages.

➤ Simulate the fingerprint sensor.

➤ Provide mock sensor data including results for accelerometer, ambient temperature, and magnetic field sensor.

Android Profiler

The Emulator enables you to see how your application will look, behave, and interact, but to actually see what's happening under the surface, you need the Android Profiler.

The Android Profiler displays real-time profiling data for the CPU, memory, and network activity related to your app. You can perform sample-based method tracing to time your code execution, capture heap dumps, view memory allocations, and inspect the details of network-transmitted files.

To open the Android Profiler, click the Android Profiler icon in the toolbar, or navigate to the View ➪ Tool Windows ➪ Android Profiler menu item. The shared timeline window will be displayed, as shown in Figure 2-24.

The Profiler window displays real-time graphs for CPU, memory, and network usage, as well as an event timeline that indicates changes in Activity state, user inputs, and screen rotations.

To access the detailed profiling tools for CPU, memory, or network use, click the associated graph. Depending on the resource being profiled, each detail view will allow you to do one of the following:

➤ Inspect CPU activity and method traces.

➤ Inspect the Java heap and memory allocations.

➤ Inspect incoming and outgoing network traffic.

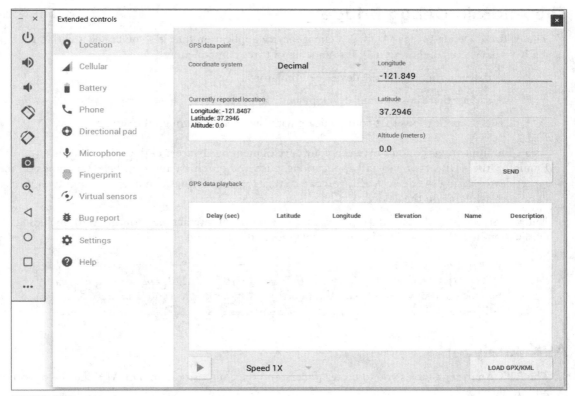

FIGURE 2-23

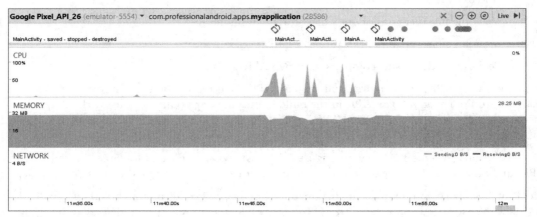

FIGURE 2-24

The Android Debug Bridge

The Android Debug Bridge (ADB) is a client-service application that lets you connect with an Android device (virtual or actual). It's made up of three components:

➤ A daemon running on the device or Emulator

➤ A service that runs on your development computer

➤ Client applications that communicate with the daemon through the service

As a communications conduit between your development hardware and the Android device/Emulator, the ADB lets you install applications, push and pull files, and run shell commands on the target device. Using the device shell, you can change logging settings and query or modify SQLite databases available on the device.

Android Studio automates and simplifies a lot of your usual interaction with the ADB, including application installation and updating, file logging, and debugging.

> **NOTE** *To learn more about what you can do with the ADB,* check out the documentation at `developer.android.com/studio/command-line/adb.html`.

APK Analyzer

The APK Analyzer enables you to better understand the composition of your APK files by providing an interface to:

➤ View the absolute and relative size of files stored within the APK, including .DEX and resource files.

➤ View the final versions of .DEX files stored within the APK.

➤ View the final version of the AndroidManifest.xml file.

➤ Perform a side-by-side comparison of two APKs.

To analyze your APK, you can drag and drop an APK file directly into the editor window of Android Studio, navigate to an APK in the build ➪ output ➪ apks directory using the Project perspective and double-click the desired APK, or click the Build ➪ Analyze APK menu item and select an APK.

The APK Analyzer window, shown in Figure 2-25, displays each file and folder stored within the APK, and allows you to navigate within each folder or to display additional details on each file.

The Raw File Size column represents the uncompressed size of each entity, while the Download Size indicates the estimated compressed size of the entity when delivered by Google Play.

By selecting the application manifest, you can view the XML form of the final manifest file packaged within your APK.

For more details on how to use the APK Analyzer, refer to `developer.android.com/studio/ build/apk-analyzer.html`.

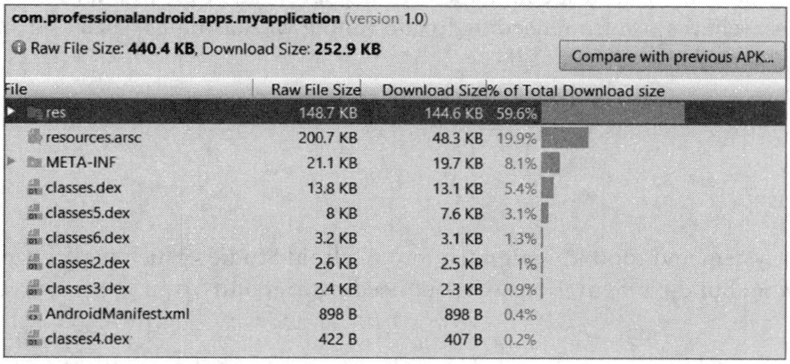

com.professionalandroid.apps.myapplication (version 1.0)

ⓘ Raw File Size: **440.4 KB**, Download Size: **252.9 KB**

File	Raw File Size	Download Size	% of Total Download size
▶ ▇ res	148.7 KB	144.6 KB	59.6%
resources.arsc	200.7 KB	48.3 KB	19.9%
▶ META-INF	21.1 KB	19.7 KB	8.1%
classes.dex	13.8 KB	13.1 KB	5.4%
classes5.dex	8 KB	7.6 KB	3.1%
classes6.dex	3.2 KB	3.1 KB	1.3%
classes2.dex	2.6 KB	2.5 KB	1%
classes3.dex	2.4 KB	2.3 KB	0.9%
AndroidManifest.xml	898 B	898 B	0.4%
classes4.dex	422 B	407 B	0.2%

FIGURE 2-25

The Lint Tool

Android Studio provides a static code analysis tool called Lint, which helps identify and correct structural quality issues within your code, without having to run the app or write those specific tests.

The configured Lint and IDE inspections run automatically whenever you build your app, checking your source code and resource files for potential bugs and optimization improvements, including correctness, security, performance, usability, accessibility, and internationalization.

Potential problems are highlighted within the IDE with a description, severity level, and where possible a suggested remedy.

Using Lint to identify and rectify potential structural issues within your code can dramatically improve the readability, reliability, and efficiency of your code. It's best practice to ensure all Lint warnings are dealt with as part of your development process.

Monkey, Monkey Runner, and Espresso UI Testing

UI testing helps to ensure that users don't encounter unexpected results when interacting with your app. Android Studio includes a number of tools to assist you in creating user interface/user interaction tests.

Monkey works from within the ADB shell, sending a stream of pseudorandom, but repeatable, system and UI events to your application. It's particularly useful to stress-test your applications to investigate edge cases you might not have anticipated through unconventional use of the UI.

Alternatively, Monkey Runner is a Python scripting API that lets you send specific UI commands to control an Emulator or device from outside the application. It's extremely useful for performing UI, functional, and unit tests in a predictable, repeatable fashion.

The Espresso testing framework, provided through the Android Testing Support Library, provides APIs for writing UI tests to simulate specific user interactions for a specific app. Espresso detects when the main thread is idle, and runs your test commands at the appropriate time to improve test reliability. This capability also relieves you from needing to add timing workarounds, such as a sleep period, into your test code.

You can learn more about Espresso testing at `developer.android.com/training/testing/espresso`.

Gradle

Gradle is an advanced build system and toolkit, integrated into Android Studio, which makes it possible for you to perform custom build configurations without needing to modify your app's source files.

The use of Gradle as Android's build system is intended to make it easier to configure, extend and customize the build process, simplify code and resource reuse, and to more easily create multiple build variants of an application.

Gradle is plug-in–based, so integration with Android Studio is managed through the Android Plugin for Gradle, which works with the build toolkit to provide a UI within Android Studio for processes and configurable settings that are specific to building and testing Android applications.

Gradle itself, and the Android Plugin, are integrated with—but ultimately independent of—Android Studio. As a result, you can build your Android apps from within Android Studio, the command line on your machine, or on machines where Android Studio is not installed (such as continuous integration servers). The output of the build is the same whether you are building a project from the command line, on a remote machine, or using Android Studio.

Within this book, we will be building our applications within Android Studio using the Android Plugin for Gradle to manage our interactions with the build system. Full coverage of Gradle, custom builds, and Gradle build scripts is beyond the scope of this book, but you can learn more details at `developer.android.com/studio/build/`.

> **NOTE** *Because Gradle and the Android Plugin for Gradle are independent from Android Studio, you will be prompted to update your build tools separately from Android Studio, similarly to how SDK updates are performed.*

3

Applications and Activities and Fragments, Oh My!

WHAT'S IN THIS CHAPTER?

- ➤ Introducing the Android application
- ➤ Understanding the Android application life cycle
- ➤ Recognizing your application's priority
- ➤ Creating new Activities
- ➤ Understanding an Activity's state transitions and life cycle
- ➤ Responding to system memory pressure
- ➤ Creating and using Fragments

WROX.COM CODE DOWNLOADS FOR THIS CHAPTER

The code downloads for this chapter are found at www.wrox.com. The code for this chapter is divided into the following major examples:

- ➤ Snippets_ch3.zip
- ➤ Earthquake_ch3.zip

APPLICATIONS, ACTIVITIES, AND FRAGMENTS

Android applications (or simply "apps") are software programs that are installed and run natively on Android devices. To write high-quality applications, it's important to understand the components they consist of, and how those components work together. This chapter introduces each of the application components, with special attention paid to Activities and Fragments—the visual components of your application.

In Chapter 2, "Getting Started," you learned that each Android application runs in a separate process, in its own instance of the Android Run Time. In this chapter, you learn how the Android Run Time manages your application, and the impact this has on the application life cycle. An application's state determines its priority that, in turn, affects the likelihood of its being terminated when the system requires more resources. You are also introduced to the Activity and Fragment states, state transitions, and event handlers.

The `Activity` class forms the basis for all your user interface (UI) screens. You'll learn how to create Activities and gain an understanding of their life cycles and how they affect the application lifetime and priority.

The range of screen sizes and display resolutions for the devices on which your application will be used has expanded with the range of Android devices now available. The Fragment API provides support for creating dynamic layouts that can be optimized for all devices including tablets and smartphones.

You'll learn how to use Fragments to encapsulate state within your UI components, and to create layouts that scale and adapt to accommodate a variety of device types, screen sizes, and resolutions.

THE COMPONENTS OF AN ANDROID APPLICATION

Android applications consist of loosely coupled components, bound by an application manifest that describes each component and how they interact. The following components comprise the building blocks for all your Android applications:

➤ **Activities**—Your application's presentation layer. The UI of your application is built around one or more extensions of the `Activity` class. Activities use Fragments and Views to lay out and display information, and to respond to user actions. Compared to desktop development, Activities are equivalent to Forms. You learn more about Activities later in this chapter.

➤ **Services**—Service components run without a UI, updating your data sources, triggering Notifications, and broadcasting Intents. They're used to perform long-running tasks, or those that require no user interaction (such as tasks that need to continue even when your application's Activities aren't active or visible). You learn more about how to create and use Services in Chapter 11, "Working in the Background."

➤ **Intents**—A powerful inter-application message-passing framework; Intents are used extensively throughout Android. You will use Intents to start and stop Activities and Services, to broadcast messages system-wide or to a specific Activity, Service, or Broadcast Receiver—or to request an action be performed on a particular piece of data. Explicit, implicit, and broadcast Intents are explored in more detail in Chapter 6, "Intents and Broadcast Receivers."

➤ **Broadcast Receivers**—Broadcast Receivers (or just "Receivers") are used to receive broadcast Intents, enabling your application to listen for Intents that match the criteria you specify. Broadcast Receivers start your application to react to any received Intent, making them perfect for creating event-driven applications. Broadcast Receivers are covered alongside Intents in Chapter 6.

➤ **Content Providers**—Content Providers are the preferred means to share data across application boundaries. You can configure your application's Content Providers to allow access from other applications, and you can access the Content Providers exposed by others. Android devices include several native Content Providers that expose useful databases such as the media store and contacts. You learn how to create and use Content Providers in Chapter 10, "Content Providers and Search."

➤ **Notifications**—Notifications enable you to alert users to application events without stealing focus or interrupting their current Activity. They're the preferred technique for getting a user's attention when your application is not visible or active, typically triggered from within a Service or Broadcast Receiver. For example, when a device receives a text message or an e-mail, the messaging and Gmail applications use Notifications to alert you. You can trigger these notifications from your applications, as discussed in Chapter 11.

By decoupling the dependencies between application components, you can share and use individual Content Providers, Services, and even Activities with other applications—both your own and those of third parties.

THE ANDROID APPLICATION LIFE CYCLE, PRIORITY, AND PROCESS STATES

Unlike many traditional application platforms, Android applications have limited control over their own life cycles. Instead, application components must listen for changes in the application state and react accordingly, taking particular care to be prepared for untimely termination.

By default, each Android application runs in its own process, each of which is running a separate instance of the Android Run Time (ART). Memory and process management is handled exclusively by the run time.

> **NOTE** *You can force application components within the same application to run in different processes or to have multiple applications share the same process using the* android:process *attribute on the affected component nodes within the manifest.*

Android aggressively manages its resources, doing whatever is necessary to ensure a smooth and stable user experience. In practice, that means processes (and therefore applications) will be killed, in some cases without warning, to free resources if higher-priority applications require them.

The order in which processes are killed to reclaim resources is determined by the priority of their hosted applications. An application's priority is equal to that of its highest-priority component.

If two applications have the same priority, the process that has been at that priority longest will typically be killed first. Process priority is also affected by interprocess dependencies; if an application has a dependency on a Service or Content Provider supplied by a second application, the secondary application is assigned at least as high a priority as the application it supports.

It's important to structure your application to ensure that its priority is appropriate for the work it's doing. If you don't, your application could be killed while it's in the middle of something important, or it could remain running when it could safely be terminated to free resources and maintain a smooth user experience.

Figure 3-1 shows the priority tree used to determine the order of application termination.

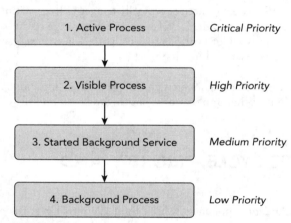

FIGURE 3-1

The following list details each of the application states shown in Figure 3-1, explaining how the state is determined by the application components of which it comprises:

➤ **Active processes (Top Priority)**—Active (foreground) processes have application components the user is interacting with. These are the processes Android tries to keep running smoothly and responsively by reclaiming resources from other applications. There are generally very few of these processes.

Active processes include one or more of the following components:

➤ Activities in an active state—that is, those in the foreground responding to user events. You explore Activity states in greater detail later in this chapter.

➤ Broadcast Receivers executing onReceive event handlers as described in Chapter 6.

➤ Services executing onStart, onCreate, or onDestroy event handlers as described in Chapter 11.

➤ **Visible processes (High Priority)**—Visible but inactive processes are those hosting "visible" Activities or foreground Services. As the name suggests, visible Activities are visible but they aren't in the foreground or responding to user input. This happens when an Activity is only partially obscured (by a non–full-screen or transparent Activity), or the non-active window in a multi-window environment. There are generally very few visible processes, and they'll be killed only under extreme circumstances to allow active processes to continue. Since Android 6.0 Marshmallow (API Level 23), running Services that have been flagged to run in the foreground have a slightly lower priority than active processes, making it possible—though unlikely—for a foreground Service to be killed to allow an active Activity with significant memory requirements to continue running.

➤ **Started background Service processes (Medium Priority)**—Processes hosting background Services that have been started. Because these Services don't interact directly with the user, they receive a slightly lower priority than visible Activities or foreground Services. You learn more about Services in Chapter 11.

➤ **Background processes (Low Priority)**—Processes hosting Activities that aren't visible and that don't have any running Services. Every time you switch between applications by pressing the home key, or using the "recent apps" selector, the previously active application goes to the background. There will generally be a large number of background apps that Android will kill using a last-seen-first-killed pattern, giving some consideration to prioritize killing applications consuming more memory, in order to obtain resources for foreground processes.

INTRODUCING THE ANDROID APPLICATION CLASS

Your application's `Application` object remains instantiated whenever your application is running—unlike Activities, the Application is not restarted as a result of configuration changes.

Extending the `Application` class with your own implementation enables you to respond to application-level events broadcast by the Android run time (such as low memory conditions.)

When your `Application` implementation is registered in the manifest, it will be instantiated when your application process is created. As a result, if you choose to create a custom `Application` class implementation, it is by nature a singleton and should be implemented as such.

A CLOSER LOOK AT ANDROID ACTIVITIES

Each Activity represents a screen that an application can present to your users. The more complicated your application, the more screens you are likely to need.

Typically, this includes at least a "main Activity"—the primary interface screen—that handles the main UI functionality of your application. This primary interface is generally supported by a set of secondary Activities. To move between screens, you start a new Activity (or return from one).

Creating Activities

To create a new Activity, extend the `Activity` class—or one of its subclasses (most commonly the `AppCompatActivity`, as described in the next section). Within your new class you must assign a UI and implement your functionality. Listing 3-1 shows the basic skeleton code for a new `Activity`.

LISTING 3-1: Activity skeleton code

```
package com.professionalandroid.apps.helloworld;

import android.app.Activity;
import android.os.Bundle;

public class MyActivity extends Activity {

  /** Called when the activity is first created. */
  @Override
  public void onCreate(Bundle savedInstanceState) {
    super.onCreate(savedInstanceState);
  }
}
```

The base `Activity` class presents an empty screen that encapsulates the window display handling. An empty `Activity` isn't particularly useful, so the first thing you'll want to do is create the UI using Fragments, layouts, and Views.

Views are the UI widgets/controls that display data and provide user interaction. Android provides several layout classes, called *View Groups*, which can contain multiple Views to help you lay out your UI. Fragments—discussed later in this chapter—are also available to encapsulate segments of your UI, making it simple to create dynamic interfaces that can be rearranged to optimize your layouts for different screen sizes and orientations.

> **NOTE** *Chapter 5 discusses Views, View Groups, and layouts in detail, examining what's available, how to use them, and how to create your own.*

To assign a UI to an Activity, call `setContentView` from the `onCreate` method. In this next snippet, an instance of a `TextView` is used as the Activity's UI:

```
@Override
public void onCreate(Bundle savedInstanceState) {
  super.onCreate(savedInstanceState);
  TextView textView = new TextView(this);
  setContentView(textView);
}
```

There's a good chance you'll want to use a slightly more complex UI design. You can create a layout in code using layout View Groups, or you can use the standard Android convention of passing a resource ID for a layout defined in an external resource, as shown in the following snippet:

```
@Override
public void onCreate(Bundle savedInstanceState) {
  super.onCreate(savedInstanceState);
  setContentView(R.layout.main);
}
```

To use an Activity in your application, you need to register it in the manifest. Add a new `activity` tag within the `application` node of the manifest; the `activity` tag includes attributes for meta-data, such as the label, icon, required permissions, and themes used by the `Activity`.

```
<activity android:label="@string/app_name"
          android:name=".MyActivity">
</activity>
```

An Activity without a corresponding `activity` tag can't be used—attempting to start it will result in a runtime exception:

Within the `activity` tag you can add `intent-filter` nodes that specify the Intents that can be used to start your Activity. Each Intent Filter defines one or more actions and categories that your `Activity` supports. Intents and Intent Filters are covered in depth in Chapter 6, but it's worth noting that for an `Activity` to be available from the application launcher, it must include an Intent Filter listening for the MAIN action and the LAUNCHER category, as highlighted in Listing 3-2.

LISTING 3-2: Main Application Activity definition

```
<activity android:label="@string/app_name"
          android:name=".MyActivity">
  <intent-filter>
    <action android:name="android.intent.action.MAIN" />
    <category android:name="android.intent.category.LAUNCHER" />
  </intent-filter>
</activity>
```

Using the AppCompatActivity

As mentioned in Chapter 2, the `AppCompatActivity` class is an `Activity` subclass available from the Android Support Library. It provides ongoing, backward compatibility for features added to the `Activity` class in each new platform release.

As such, it's considered best practice to use the `AppCompatActivity` in preference to the `Activity` class, and we'll continue to do so throughout this book, generally referring to classes that extend `AppCompatActivity` as Activities.

Listing 3-3 updates the code from Listing 3-1 showing the skeleton code for a new Activity that extends `AppCompatActivity`.

LISTING 3-3: AppCompatActivity Activity skeleton code

```
package com.professionalandroid.apps.helloworld;

import android.support.v7.app.AppCompatActivity;
import android.os.Bundle;

public class MyActivity extends AppCompatActivity {

  /** Called when the activity is first created. */
  @Override
  public void onCreate(Bundle savedInstanceState) {
    super.onCreate(savedInstanceState);
  }
}
```

The Activity Life Cycle

A good understanding of the Activity life cycle is vital to ensure that your application provides a seamless user experience and properly manages its resources.

As explained earlier, Android applications do not control their own process lifetimes; the Android Run Time manages the process of each application, and by extension that of each Activity within it.

Although the run time handles the termination and management of an Activity's process, the Activity's state helps determine the priority of its parent application. The application priority, in turn, influences the likelihood that the run time will terminate it and the Activities running within it.

Activity Stacks and the Least-Recently Used (LRU) List

The state of each Activity is determined by its position on the Activity stack (or "back stack"), a last-in–first-out collection of all the currently running Activities. When a new Activity starts, it becomes active and is moved to the top of the stack. If the user navigates back using the Back button, or the foreground Activity is otherwise closed, the next Activity down on the stack moves up and becomes active. Figure 3-2 illustrates this process.

As described previously in this chapter, an application's priority is influenced by its highest-priority Activity. When the Android memory manager is deciding which application to terminate to free resources, it uses this Activity stack to determine the priority of applications.

When none of an application's Activities are visible, the application itself moves onto the least-recently used (LRU) list, which is used to determine the order in which applications will be terminated to free resources as described earlier.

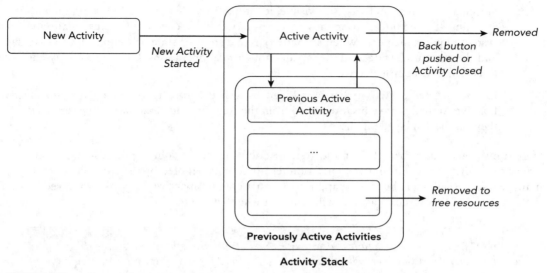

FIGURE 3-2

Activity States

Throughout an application's life cycle, its Activities move in and out of the Activity stack, as shown in Figure 3-2. As they do so, they transition through four possible states:

➤ **Active**—When an Activity is at the top of the stack it is the visible, focused, foreground Activity that is receiving user input. Android will attempt to keep it alive at all costs, killing applications that own Activities further down the stack as needed, to ensure this Activity has the resources it needs. When another Activity becomes active, this one will be paused—and when it is no longer visible, it will be stopped, as described in the following points.

➤ **Paused**—In some cases your Activity will be visible but will not have focus; at this point it's paused. This state may also be reached in which your application is being used in a multi-window environment—where multiple applications may be visible, but only the Activity with which the user last interacted is considered active. Similarly, if your Activity has a transparent or non–full-screen Activity active in front of it, it will remain in a paused state. When paused, an Activity is treated as if it were active; however, it doesn't receive user input events. In extreme cases Android will kill a paused Activity to recover resources for the active Activity. When an Activity becomes totally obscured, it is stopped; all Activities transition through the paused state before becoming stopped.

➤ **Stopped**—When an Activity isn't visible, it "stops." The Activity will remain in memory, retaining all state information; however, it is now a likely candidate for termination when the system requires memory. When an Activity is in a stopped state, it's important to save data and the current UI state, and to stop any non-critical operations. Once an Activity has exited or closed, it becomes inactive.

➤ **Inactive**—After an Activity has been killed, as well as before it's been launched, it's inactive. Inactive Activities have been removed from the Activity stack and need to be restarted before they can be displayed and used.

State transitions occur through user and system actions, meaning your application has no control over when they happen. Similarly, application termination is handled by the Android memory manager, which will start by closing applications that contain inactive Activities, followed by those that are stopped. In extreme cases, it will remove those that are paused.

> **NOTE** *To ensure a seamless user experience, transitions between states should be invisible to the user. There should be no difference in an Activity moving from a paused, stopped, or inactive state back to active, so it's important to save all UI state and persist all data when an Activity is stopped.*
>
> *It's best practice to perform any time-consuming state persistence operations (such as database transactions or network transfers) when the Activity transitions to the stopped state (within the onStop handler, as described later in this chapter), rather than during the transition to the paused state (within onPause).*
>
> *Activities may transition between active and paused states frequently and rapidly—particularly when used in a multi-window environment—so it's important that this transition execute as quickly as possible. Once an Activity does become active, it should restore those saved values.*
>
> *Similarly, apart from changes to the Activity's priority, transitions between the active, paused, and stopped states have little direct impact on the Activity itself. It's up to you to use these signals to pause and stop your Activities accordingly, and to be prepared for termination at any time.*

Understanding Activity Lifetimes

To ensure that Activities can react to state changes, Android provides a series of event handlers that are fired as an Activity transitions through its full, visible, and active lifetimes. Figure 3-3 summarizes these lifetimes in terms of the Activity states described in the previous section.

Within an Activity's full lifetime, between creation and destruction, it goes through one or more iterations of the active and visible lifetimes. Each transition triggers the method handlers previously described. The following sections provide a closer look at each of these lifetimes and the events that bracket them.

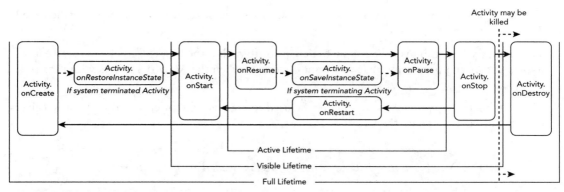

FIGURE 3-3

The Full Lifetime

The full lifetime of your Activity occurs between the first call to onCreate and when it is destroyed. It's not uncommon for an Activity's process to be terminated *without* the corresponding onDestroy handler being called.

Use the onCreate method to initialize your Activity: inflate the user interface, get references to Fragments, allocate references to class variables, bind data to controls, and start Services. If the Activity was terminated unexpectedly by the run time, the onCreate method is passed a Bundle object containing the state saved in the last call to onSaveInstanceState. You should use this Bundle to restore the UI to its previous state, either within the onCreate method or onRestoreInstanceState.

Override onDestroy to clean up any resources created in onCreate, and ensure that all external connections, such as network or database links, are closed.

As part of Android's guidelines for writing efficient code, it's recommended that you avoid repeated creation of short-term objects. The rapid creation and destruction of objects forces additional garbage collection, a process that can have a direct negative impact on the user experience. If your Activity creates the same set of objects regularly, consider creating them in the onCreate method, as it's called only once during the Activity's lifetime.

The Visible Lifetime

An Activity's visible lifetimes are bounded between calls to onStart and onStop. Between these calls your Activity will be visible to the user, although it may not have focus and may be partially obscured. Activities are likely to go through several visible lifetimes during their full lifetime as they move between the foreground and background. Since Android 3.0 Honeycomb (API Level 11), you can safely assume onStop will be called before your application process is terminated.

The onStop method should be used to pause or stop animations, threads, Sensor listeners, GPS lookups, Timers, Services, or other processes that are used exclusively to update the UI. There's little value in consuming resources (such as memory, CPU cycles, or network bandwidth) to update the

UI when it isn't visible. Use the `onStart` method to resume or restart these processes when the UI is visible again.

The `onRestart` method is called immediately prior to all but the first call to `onStart`. Use it to implement special processing that you want done only when the Activity restarts within its full lifetime.

The `onStart`/`onStop` methods should also be used to register and unregister Broadcast Receivers used exclusively to update the UI.

> **NOTE** *You learn more about using Broadcast Receivers in Chapter 6.*

The Active Lifetime

The active lifetime starts with a call to `onResume` and ends with a corresponding call to `onPause`.

An active Activity is in the foreground and is receiving user input events. Your Activity is likely to go through many active lifetimes before it's destroyed, as the active lifetime will end when a new Activity is displayed, the device goes to sleep, or the Activity loses focus. Try to keep code in the `onPause` and `onResume` methods fast and lightweight to ensure that your application remains responsive when moving in and out of the foreground. You can safely assume that during the active lifetime `onPause` will be called before the process is terminated.

> **NOTE** *If the system determines that this Activity state may need to be resumed, then immediately before* `onPause` *a call is made to* `onSaveInstanceState`. *This method provides an opportunity to save the Activity's UI state in a* `Bundle` *that may be passed to the* `onCreate` *and* `onRestoreInstanceState` *methods.*
>
> *Use* `onSaveInstanceState` *to save the UI state to ensure that the Activity can present the same UI when it next becomes active. The* `onSaveInstanceState` *handler will not be called if the system determines that the current state will not be resumed—for example, if the Activity is closed by pressing the Back button.*

Since Android 3.0 Honeycomb (API Level 11), the completion of the `onStop` handler marks the point beyond which an Activity may be killed without warning. This allows you to move all time-consuming operations required to save state into `onStop`, keeping your `onPause` lightweight and focused on suspending memory- or CPU-intensive operations while the Activity isn't active. Depending on your application architecture, that may include suspending threads, processes, or Broadcast Receivers while your Activity is not in the foreground.

The corresponding `onResume` method should also be lightweight. You do not need to reload the UI state here, because this should handled by the `onCreate` and `onRestoreInstanceState` methods as required. Use `onResume` to reverse actions performed within `onPause`—such as allocating released resources, initializing or registering removed or unregistered components, and resuming any suspended behavior.

Monitoring State Changes

The skeleton code in Listing 3-4 shows the stubs for the state change method handlers available in an Activity as described in the previous section. Comments within each stub describe the actions you should consider taking on each state change event.

LISTING 3-4: Activity state event handlers

```java
public class StateChangeMonitoringActivity extends AppCompatActivity {

  // Called at the start of the full lifetime.
  @Override
  public void onCreate(Bundle savedInstanceState) {
    super.onCreate(savedInstanceState);

    // Initialize Activity and inflate the UI.
  }

  // Called before subsequent visible lifetimes
  // for an Activity process. That is, before an Activity
  // returns to being visible having previously been hidden.
  @Override
  public void onRestart() {
    super.onRestart();

    // Load changes knowing that the Activity has already
    // been visible within this process.
  }

  // Called at the start of the visible lifetime.
  @Override
  public void onStart() {
    super.onStart();

    // Apply any required UI change now that the Activity is visible.
    // This is where you'd typically start any processes that
    // are required to ensure your UI is appropriately populated and
    // updated.
  }

  // Called after onStart has finished, in cases where an Activity is
  // started after having last been destroyed by the runtime rather than
  // through user or programmatic action (such as the user hitting back or
  // your app calling finish().
  @Override
  public void onRestoreInstanceState(Bundle savedInstanceState) {
    super.onRestoreInstanceState(savedInstanceState);

    // Restore UI state from the savedInstanceState.
    // This bundle has also been passed to onCreate.
    // Will only be called if the Activity has been
    // killed by the system since it was last visible.
  }
```

```java
// Called at the start of the active lifetime.
@Override
public void onResume() {
  super.onResume();

  // Resume any paused UI updates, threads, or processes required
  // by the Activity but suspended when it becomes inactive.
  // At this stage, your Activity is active and receiving input
  // from users actions.
}

// Called at the end of the active lifetime.
@Override
public void onPause() {
  super.onPause();

  // Suspend UI updates, threads, or CPU intensive processes
  // that don't need to be updated when the Activity isn't
  // the active foreground Activity. Note that in multi-screen
  // mode, paused Activities may still be visible, and as such
  // should continue performing required UI updates.
}

// Called when appropriate to save UI state changes at the
// end of the active lifecycle.
@Override
public void onSaveInstanceState(Bundle savedInstanceState) {
  super.onSaveInstanceState(savedInstanceState);

  // Save UI state changes to the savedInstanceState.
  // This bundle will be passed to onCreate and
  // onRestoreInstanceState if the process is
  // killed and restarted by the run time. Note that
  // this handler may not be called if the runtime determines
  // that the Activity is being "permanently" terminated.
}

// Called at the end of the visible lifetime.
@Override
public void onStop() {
  super.onStop();

  // Suspend remaining UI updates, threads, or processing
  // that aren't required when the Activity isn't visible.
  // Persist all edits or state changes as your Activity
  // may be killed at any time after onStop has
  // completed.
}

// Sometimes called at the end of the full lifetime.
@Override
public void onDestroy() {
  super.onDestroy();

  // Clean up any resources including ending threads,
  // closing database connections etc.
}
```

As shown in the preceding code, you should always call back to the superclass when overriding these event handlers.

Responding to Memory Pressure

The Android system will terminate applications without warning in order to free resources required by any active and visible applications.

To provide the best possible user experience, Android must find a balance between killing applications to free resources and provide a responsive system, and retaining as many background apps as possible to improve the experience of switching between apps.

You can help by overriding the onTrimMemory handler, to respond to system requests that you reduce your memory usage. When killing application processes, the system will begin with empty processes before moving on to background applications—those hosting Activities that aren't visible and that don't have any running Services. In extreme cases, applications with visible Activities, or even foreground Services, may be terminated to free resources for the application hosting the active Activity.

The order in which applications are terminated is generally determined by the least-recently used (LRU) list—where the applications that have been unused the longest are the first killed. However, the run time does also consider the amount of memory potentially freed by killing each application, and is more likely to kill those that offer higher gains. So the less memory you consume, the less likely it is that your application will be terminated, and the better the overall system performance.

The onTrimMemory handler is available within each application component, including Activities and Services. It provides an opportunity for well-behaved applications to free additional memory when the system is running low on resources.

You should implement onTrimMemory to incrementally release memory based on current system constraints using the level parameter that provides context for the request. Note that the levels passed into onTrimMemory don't represent a simple linear progression, but rather a series of contextual clues to help you decide how best to reduce overall system memory pressure:

TRIM_MEMORY_RUNNING_MODERATE—Your application is running and not being considered for termination, but the system is beginning to feel memory pressure.

TRIM_MEMORY_RUNNING_LOW—Your application is running and not being considered for termination, but the system is beginning to run significantly low on memory. Releasing memory now will improve system (and therefore your application's) performance.

TRIM_MEMORY_RUNNING_CRITICAL—Your application is running and not being considered for termination, but the system is running extremely low on memory. The system will now begin killing background processes if apps don't free resources, so by releasing non-critical resources now you can prevent performance degradation and reduce the chance of other apps being terminated.

TRIM_MEMORY_UI_HIDDEN—Your application is no longer displaying a visible UI. This is a good opportunity to release large resources that are used only by your UI. It's considered good practice to do this here, rather than within your onStop handler, as it will avoid purging/reloading UI resources if your UI quickly switches from hidden to visible.

TRIM_MEMORY_BACKGROUND—Your application is no longer visible and has been added to the least-recently used (LRU) list—and is therefore a low-risk candidate for termination. However, the system is running low on memory and may already be killing other apps on the LRU list. Release resources that are easy to recover now, to reduce system pressure and make your application less likely to be terminated.

TRIM_MEMORY_MODERATE—Your application is in the middle of the LRU list and the system is running low on memory. If the system becomes further constrained for memory, there's a good chance your process will be killed.

TRIM_MEMORY_COMPLETE—Your application is one of the, if not *the*, most likely candidates for termination if the system does not recover memory immediately. You should release absolutely everything that's not critical to resuming your application state.

Rather than compare the current level to these exact values, you should check if the level value is greater or equal to a level you are interested in, allowing for future intermediate state, as shown in Listing 3-5.

LISTING 3-5: Memory trim request event handlers

```
@Override
public void onTrimMemory(int level) {
  super.onTrimMemory(level);

  // Application is a candidate for termination.
  if (level >= TRIM_MEMORY_COMPLETE) {
    // Release all possible resources to avoid immediate termination.
  } else if (level >= TRIM_MEMORY_MODERATE) {
    // Releasing resources now will and make your app less likely
    // to be terminated.
  } else if (level >= TRIM_MEMORY_BACKGROUND) {
    // Release resources that are easy to recover now.
  }

  // Application is no longer visible.
  else if (level >= TRIM_MEMORY_UI_HIDDEN) {
    // Your application no longer has any visible UI. Free any resources
    // associated with maintaining your UI.
  }

  // Application is running and not a candidate for termination.
  else if (level >= TRIM_MEMORY_RUNNING_CRITICAL) {
    // The system will now begin killing background processes.
    // Release non-critical resources now to prevent performance degradation
    // and reduce the chance of other apps being terminated.
  } else if (level >= TRIM_MEMORY_RUNNING_MODERATE) {
    // Release resources here to alleviate system memory pressure and
    // improve overall system performance.
  } else if (level >= TRIM_MEMORY_RUNNING_LOW) {
    // The system is beginning to feel memory pressure.
  }
}
```

> **NOTE** *You can retrieve your application process's current trim level at any point using the static* `getMyMemoryState` *method from the* `ActivityManager`, *which will return the result via the passed in* `RunningAppProcessInfo` *parameter. Additionally, to support API levels lower than 14, you can use the* `onLowMemory` *handler as a fallback that's roughly equivalent to the* `TRIM_MEMORY_COMPLETE` *level.*

INTRODUCING FRAGMENTS

Fragments enable you to divide your Activities into fully encapsulated reusable components, each with its own life cycle and state.

Each Fragment is an independent module that is loosely coupled but tightly bound to the Activity into which it is added. Fragments can either contain a UI or not, and can be used within multiple Activities. Fragments that encapsulate a UI can be laid out in a variety of combinations to suit multi-pane UIs, and also added to, removed from, and exchanged within a running Activity to help build dynamic user interfaces.

Although it is not necessary to divide your Activities (and their corresponding layouts) into Fragments, doing so can drastically improve the flexibility of your UI and make it easier for you to adapt your user experience for new device configurations.

> **NOTE** *Fragments were introduced to Android as part of the Android 3.0 Honeycomb (API Level 11) release. They are now also available as part of the Android Support Library, including through the use of the* `AppCompatActivity`, *as we are using.*
>
> *If you are using the compatibility library, it's critical that you ensure that all your Fragment-related imports and class references are using only the Support Library classes. The native and Support Library set of Fragment packages are closely related, but their classes are not interchangeable.*

Creating New Fragments

Extend the `Fragment` class to create a new Fragment, (optionally) defining the UI and implementing the functionality it encapsulates.

In most circumstances you'll want to assign a UI to your Fragment. It is possible to create a Fragment that *doesn't* include a UI but instead provides background behavior for an Activity. This is explored in more detail later in this chapter.

If your Fragment does require a UI, override the `onCreateView` handler to inflate and return the required View hierarchy, as shown in the Fragment skeleton code in Listing 3-6.

LISTING 3-6: Fragment skeleton code

```java
import android.content.Context;
import android.net.Uri;
import android.os.Bundle;
import android.support.v4.app.Fragment;
import android.view.LayoutInflater;
import android.view.View;
import android.view.ViewGroup;

public class MySkeletonFragment extends Fragment {

  public MySkeletonFragment() {
    // Required empty public constructor
  }

  @Override
  public View onCreateView(LayoutInflater inflater, ViewGroup container,
                           Bundle savedInstanceState) {
    // Inflate the layout for this fragment
    return inflater.inflate(R.layout.my_skeleton_fragment_layout,
                            container, false);
  }
}
```

You can create a layout in code using layout View Groups; however, as with Activities, the preferred way to design Fragment UI layouts is by inflating an XML resource.

Unlike Activities, Fragments don't need to be registered in your manifest. This is because Fragments can exist only when embedded into an Activity, with their life cycles dependent on that of the Activity to which they've been added.

The Fragment Life Cycle

The life cycle events of a Fragment mirror those of its parent Activity; however, after the containing Activity is in its active—resumed—state, adding or removing a Fragment will affect its life cycle independently.

Fragments include a series of event handlers that mirror those in the Activity class. They are triggered as the Fragment is created, started, resumed, paused, stopped, and destroyed. Fragments also include a number of additional callbacks that indicate attaching and detaching the Fragment to and from its parent's Context, creation (and destruction) of the Fragment's View hierarchy, and the completion of the creation of the parent Activity.

Figure 3-4 summarizes the Fragment life cycle.

The skeleton code in Listing 3-7 shows the stubs for the life-cycle handlers available in a Fragment. Comments within each stub describe the actions you should consider taking on each state change event.

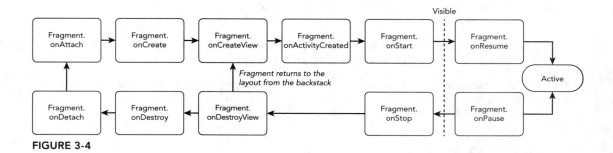

FIGURE 3-4

> **NOTE** *You must call back to the superclass when overriding most of these event handlers.*

LISTING 3-7: Fragment life cycle event handlers

```java
public class MySkeletonFragment extends Fragment {

  // Required empty public constructor
  public MySkeletonFragment() {}

  // Called when the Fragment is attached to its parent Activity.
  @Override
  public void onAttach(Context context) {
    super.onAttach(context);
    // Get a reference to a Context representing
    // the parent component.
  }

  // Called to do the initial creation of the Fragment.
  @Override
  public void onCreate(Bundle savedInstanceState) {
    super.onCreate(savedInstanceState);
    // Initialize the Fragment.
  }

  // Called once the Fragment has been created in order for it to
  // create its user interface.
  @Override
  public View onCreateView(LayoutInflater inflater,
                           ViewGroup container,
                           Bundle savedInstanceState) {
    // Create, or inflate the Fragment's UI, and return it.
    // If this Fragment has no UI then return null.
    return inflater.inflate(R.layout.my_skeleton_fragment_layout,
                            container, false);
  }
```

```java
// Called once the parent Activity and the Fragment's UI have
// been created.
@Override
public void onActivityCreated(Bundle savedInstanceState) {
  super.onActivityCreated(savedInstanceState);

  // Complete the Fragment initialization - particularly anything
  // that requires the parent Activity to be initialized or the
  // Fragment's view to be fully inflated.
}

// Called at the start of the visible lifetime.
@Override
public void onStart() {
  super.onStart();

  // Apply any required UI change now that the Fragment is visible.
}

// Called at the start of the active lifetime.
@Override
public void onResume() {
  super.onResume();

  // Resume any paused UI updates, threads, or processes required
  // by the Fragment but suspended when it became inactive.
}

// Called at the end of the active lifetime.
@Override
public void onPause() {
  super.onPause();

  // Suspend UI updates, threads, or CPU intensive processes
  // that don't need to be updated when the Activity isn't
  // the active foreground activity.
  // Persist all edits or state changes
  // as after this call the process is likely to be killed.
}

// Called to save UI state changes at the
// end of the active lifecycle.
@Override
public void onSaveInstanceState(Bundle savedInstanceState) {
  super.onSaveInstanceState(savedInstanceState);

  // Save UI state changes to the savedInstanceState.
  // This bundle will be passed to onCreate, onCreateView, and
  // onCreateView if the parent Activity is killed and restarted.
}

// Called at the end of the visible lifetime.
@Override
public void onStop() {
  super.onStop();
```

```
    // Suspend remaining UI updates, threads, or processing
    // that aren't required when the Fragment isn't visible.
  }

  // Called when the Fragment's View has been detached.
  @Override
  public void onDestroyView() {
    super.onDestroyView();

    // Clean up resources related to the View.
  }

  // Called at the end of the full lifetime.
  @Override
  public void onDestroy() {
    super.onDestroy();

    // Clean up any resources including ending threads,
    // closing database connections etc.
  }

  // Called when the Fragment has been detached from its parent Activity.
  @Override
  public void onDetach() {
    super.onDetach();

    // Clean up any references to the parent Activity
    // including references to its Views or classes. Typically setting
    // those references to null.
  }
}
```

Fragment-Specific Life-Cycle Events

Most of the Fragment life-cycle events correspond to their equivalents in the Activity class, which were covered in detail earlier in this chapter. Those that remain are specific to Fragments and the way in which they're added to their parent Activity.

Attaching and Detaching Fragments from the Parent Context

The full lifetime of your Fragment begins when it's bound to its parent's Context and ends when it's been detached. These events are represented by the calls to onAttach and onDetach, respectively.

The onAttach event is triggered before the Fragment's UI has been created, before the Fragment itself or its parent have finished their initialization. Typically, the onAttach event is used to gain a reference to the parent component's Context in preparation for further initialization tasks.

The onDetach handler will be called if you remove a Fragment from its parents, as well as if the component containing your Fragment is destroyed. As with any handler called after a Fragment/ Activity has become paused, it's possible that onDetach will not be called if the parent component's process is terminated *before* completing its full life cycle.

Creating and Destroying Fragments

The created lifetime of your Fragment occurs between the first call to onCreate and the final call to onDestroy. It's not uncommon for an Activity's process to be terminated *without* the corresponding onDestroy method being called, so a Fragment can't rely on its onDestroy handler being triggered.

As with Activities, you should use the onCreate method to initialize your Fragment. It's good practice to create any class-scoped objects here to ensure they're created only once in the Fragment's lifetime.

Note that unlike Activities, the Fragment UI is *not* inflated within the onCreate handler.

Creating and Destroying User Interfaces

A Fragment's UI is initialized (and destroyed) within a new set of event handlers: onCreateView and onDestroyView, respectively.

Use the onCreateView method to initialize your Fragment: inflate the UI and get references (and bind data to) the Views it contains.

Once you have inflated your View hierarchy, it should be returned from the handler:

```
return inflater.inflate(R.layout.my_skeleton_fragment_layout,
                        container, false);
```

If your Fragment needs to interact with the UI of a parent Activity, wait until the onActivity-Created event has been triggered. This signifies that the containing Activity has completed its initialization and its UI has been fully constructed.

Fragment States

The fate of a Fragment is inextricably bound to that of the component to which it belongs. As a result, Fragment state transitions are closely related to the corresponding Activity state transitions.

Like Activities, Fragments are "active" when they belong to an Activity that is focused and in the foreground. When an Activity is paused or stopped, the Fragments it contains are also paused and stopped, and the Fragments contained by an inactive Activity are also inactive. When an Activity is finally destroyed, each Fragment it contains is likewise destroyed.

As the Android memory manager regularly closes applications to free resources, the Fragments within those Activities are also destroyed.

While Activities and their Fragments are tightly bound, one of the advantages of using Fragments to compose your Activity's UI is the flexibility to dynamically add or remove Fragments from an Activity. As a result, each Fragment can progress through its full, visible, and active life cycle several times within the active lifetime of its parent Activity.

Whatever the trigger for a Fragment's transition through its life cycle, managing its state transitions is critical in ensuring a seamless user experience. There should be no difference in a Fragment moving from a detached, paused, stopped, or inactive state back to active, so it's important to save all UI state and persist all data when a Fragment is paused or stopped. Like an Activity, when a Fragment becomes active again, it should restore that saved state.

Introducing the Fragment Manager

Each Activity includes a Fragment Manager to manage the Fragments it contains. As we're using the support library, we'll access the Fragment Manager using the getSupportFragmentManager method:

```
FragmentManager fragmentManager = getSupportFragmentManager();
```

The Fragment Manager provides the methods used to access the Fragments currently added to the Activity, and to perform Fragment Transactions to add, remove, and replace Fragments.

Adding Fragments to Activities

The simplest way to add a Fragment to an Activity is by including it within the Activity's layout using the fragment tag, as shown in Listing 3-8.

LISTING 3-8: Adding Fragments to Activities using XML layouts

```xml
<?xml version="1.0" encoding="utf-8"?>
<LinearLayout xmlns:android="http://schemas.android.com/apk/res/android"
  android:orientation="horizontal"
  android:layout_width="match_parent"
  android:layout_height="match_parent">
  <fragment android:name="com.professionalandroid.apps.MyListFragment"
    android:id="@+id/my_list_fragment"
    android:layout_width="wrap_content"
    android:layout_height="match_parent"
    android:layout_weight="1"
  />
  <fragment android:name="com.professionalandroid.apps.DetailFragment"
    android:id="@+id/details_fragment"
    android:layout_width="wrap_content"
    android:layout_height="match_parent"
    android:layout_weight="3"
  />
</LinearLayout>
```

Once the Fragment has been inflated, it becomes a View Group within the view hierarchy, laying out and managing its UI within the Activity.

This technique works well when you use Fragments to define a set of static layouts based on various screen sizes. If you plan to dynamically modify your layouts by adding, removing, and replacing Fragments at run time, a better approach is to create layouts that use container Views into which Fragments can be placed at run time, based on the current application state.

Listing 3-9 shows an XML snippet that you could use to support this approach.

LISTING 3-9: Specifying Fragment layouts using container views

```xml
<?xml version="1.0" encoding="utf-8"?>
<LinearLayout xmlns:android="http://schemas.android.com/apk/res/android"
  android:orientation="horizontal"
  android:layout_width="match_parent"
  android:layout_height="match_parent">
  <FrameLayout
    android:id="@+id/list_container"
    android:layout_width="wrap_content"
    android:layout_height="match_parent"
    android:layout_weight="1"
  />
  <FrameLayout
    android:id="@+id/details_container"
    android:layout_width="wrap_content"
    android:layout_height="match_parent"
    android:layout_weight="3"
   />
</LinearLayout>
```

You then need to create and add the corresponding Fragments to their appropriate parent containers within your Activity using Fragment Transactions, as described in the next section.

Using Fragment Transactions

Fragment Transactions are used to add, remove, and replace Fragments within an Activity at run time. Using Fragment Transactions, you can make your layouts dynamic—that is, they will adapt and change based on user interactions and application state.

Each Fragment Transaction can include any combination of supported actions, including adding, removing, or replacing Fragments. They also support the specification of the transition animations to display and whether to add a Transaction to the back stack.

A new Fragment Transaction is created using the `beginTransaction` method from the Fragment Manager. Modify the layout using the `add`, `remove`, and `replace` methods, as required, before setting the animations to display, and setting the appropriate back-stack behavior. When you are ready to execute the change, call `commit` to add the transaction to the UI queue asynchronously, or `commitNow` to block until the transaction is fully complete:

```java
FragmentTransaction fragmentTransaction = fragmentManager.beginTransaction();

// Add, remove, and/or replace Fragments.
// Specify animations.
// Add to back stack if required.

fragmentTransaction.commitNow();
```

Using `commitNow` is the preferred alternative, but is only available if the current transaction is *not* being added to the back stack. This option, as well as each transaction type and related options, is explored in the following sections.

Adding, Removing, and Replacing Fragments

When adding a new UI Fragment, begin by creating it and pass the new Fragment instance, along with the container View into which the Fragment will be placed, to the add method of your Fragment Transaction. Optionally, you can specify a tag that can later be used to find the Fragment when using the findFragmentByTag method:

```
final static String MY_FRAGMENT_TAG = "detail_fragment";
```

With the tag defined, you can use the add method as follows:

```
FragmentTransaction fragmentTransaction = fragmentManager.beginTransaction();
fragmentTransaction.add(R.id.details_container, new DetailFragment(),
                MY_FRAGMENT_TAG);
fragmentTransaction.commitNow();
```

To remove a Fragment, you first need to find a reference to it, usually using either the Fragment Manager's findFragmentById or findFragmentByTag methods. Then pass the found Fragment instance as a parameter to the remove method of a Fragment Transaction:

```
FragmentTransaction fragmentTransaction = fragmentManager.beginTransaction();
Fragment fragment = fragmentManager.findFragmentByTag(MY_FRAGMENT_TAG);
fragmentTransaction.remove(fragment);
fragmentTransaction.commitNow();
```

You can also replace one Fragment with another. Using the replace method, specify the container ID containing the Fragment to be replaced, the Fragment with which to replace it, and (optionally) a tag to identify the newly inserted Fragment:

```
FragmentTransaction fragmentTransaction = fragmentManager.beginTransaction();
fragmentTransaction.replace(R.id.details_container,
                    new DetailFragment(selected_index),
                    MY_FRAGMENT_TAG);
fragmentTransaction.commitNow();
```

Fragments and Configuration Changes

In order to maintain a consistent UI state between configuration changes, all the Fragments added to your UI will automatically be restored when an Activity is re-created following an orientation change or unexpected termination.

This is particularly important if you are populating your Activity layout with Fragments within the onCreate handler—in which case you must check if the Fragments have already been added to avoid creating multiple copies.

You can do this either by checking for Fragments before adding them, or if this is an Activity restart by checking if the savedInstanceState is null:

```
protected void onCreate(Bundle savedInstanceState) {
    super.onCreate(savedInstanceState);
    setContentView(R.layout.activity_main);

    if (savedInstanceState == null) {
```

```
      // Create and add your Fragments.
    } else {
      // Get references to Fragments that have already been restored.
    }
  }
}
```

Using the Fragment Manager to Find Fragments

To find Fragments within your Activity, use the Fragment Manager's `findFragmentById` method. If you have added your Fragment to the Activity layout in XML, you can use the Fragment's resource identifier:

```
MyFragment myFragment =
  (MyFragment)fragmentManager.findFragmentById(R.id.MyFragment);
```

If you've added a Fragment using a Fragment Transaction, you can instead specify the resource identifier of the container View to which you added the Fragment you want to find:

```
DetailFragment detailFragment =
  (DetailFragment)fragmentManager.findFragmentById(R.id.details_container);
```

Alternatively, you can use the `findFragmentByTag` method to search for the Fragment using the tag you specified in the Fragment Transaction:

```
DetailFragment detailFragment =
  (DetailFragment)fragmentManager.findFragmentByTag(MY_FRAGMENT_TAG);
```

Later in this chapter you are introduced to Fragments that don't include a UI. The `findFragment-ByTag` method is essential for interacting with these Fragments. Because they're not part of the Activity's View hierarchy, they don't have a resource identifier or a container resource identifier to pass in to the `findFragmentById` method.

Populating Dynamic Activity Layouts with Fragments

If you're dynamically changing the composition and layout of your Fragments at run time, it's good practice to define only the parent containers within your XML layout and populate it exclusively using Fragment Transactions at run time to ensure consistency when configuration changes (such as screen rotations) cause the UI to be re-created, as described earlier.

Listing 3-10 shows the skeleton code used to populate an Activity's layout with Fragments at run time; in this case we test for the existence of a Fragment before creating and adding a new one.

LISTING 3-10: Populating Fragment layouts using container views

```
public void onCreate(Bundle savedInstanceState) {
  super.onCreate(savedInstanceState);

  // Inflate the layout containing the Fragment containers
  setContentView(R.layout.fragment_container_layout);

  FragmentManager fragmentManager = getSupportFragmentManager();
```

```
// Check to see if the Fragment containers have been populated
// with Fragment instances. If not, create and populate the layout.
DetailFragment detailsFragment =
    (DetailFragment) fragmentManager.findFragmentById(R.id.details_container);

if (detailsFragment == null) {
    FragmentTransaction ft = fragmentManager.beginTransaction();
    ft.add(R.id.details_container, new DetailFragment());
    ft.add(R.id.list_container, new MyListFragment());
    ft.commitNow();
    }
}
```

To ensure a consistent user experience, Android persists the Fragment layout and associated back stack when an Activity is restarted due to a configuration change.

For the same reason, when creating alternative layouts for run time configuration changes, it's considered good practice to include any view containers involved in any transactions in all the layout variations. Failing to do so may result in the Fragment Manager attempting to restore Fragments to containers that don't exist in the new layout.

To remove a Fragment container in a given orientation layout, simply mark its visibility attribute as gone in your layout definition, as shown in Listing 3-11.

LISTING 3-11: Hiding Fragments in layout variations

```xml
<?xml version="1.0" encoding="utf-8"?>
<LinearLayout xmlns:android="http://schemas.android.com/apk/res/android"
  android:orientation="horizontal"
  android:layout_width="match_parent"
  android:layout_height="match_parent">
  <FrameLayout
    android:id="@+id/list_container"
    android:layout_width="wrap_content"
    android:layout_height="match_parent"
    android:layout_weight="1"
  />
  <FrameLayout
    android:id="@+id/details_container"
    android:layout_width="wrap_content"
    android:layout_height="match_parent"
    android:layout_weight="3"
    android:visibility="gone"
  />
</LinearLayout>
```

Fragments and the Back Stack

Earlier in this chapter we described the concept of Activity stacks—the logical stacking of Activities that are no longer visible—which allow users to navigate back to previous screens using the Back button.

Fragments enable you to create dynamic Activity layouts that can be modified to present significant changes in the UIs. In some cases these changes could be considered a new screen—in which case a user may reasonably expect the Back button to return to the previous layout. This involves reversing previously executed Fragment Transactions.

Android provides a convenient technique for providing this functionality. To add the Fragment Transaction to the back stack, call `addToBackStack` on a Fragment Transaction before calling `commit`. It's important to note that `commitNow` cannot be used when applying Fragment Transactions that are added to the back stack.

In the following code snippet, we have a layout that displays either the list or the detail view. This transaction will remove the list Fragment and add the detail Fragment, and adds the change to the back stack:

```
FragmentTransaction fragmentTransaction = fragmentManager.beginTransaction();

// Find and remove the list Fragment
Fragment fragment = fragmentManager.findFragmentById(R.id.ui_container);
fragmentTransaction.remove(fragment);

// Create and add the detail Fragment
fragmentTransaction.add(R.id.ui_container, new DetailFragment());

// Add the Fragment Transaction to the backstack and commit the change.
fragmentTransaction.addToBackStack(BACKSTACK_TAG);
fragmentTransaction.commit();
```

Pressing the Back button will then reverse the previous Fragment Transaction and return the UI to the earlier layout.

When the preceding Fragment Transaction is committed, the List Fragment is stopped, detached, and moved to the back stack, rather than simply destroyed. If the Transaction is reversed, the Detail Fragment is destroyed, and the List Fragment is restarted and reattached to the Activity.

Animating Fragment Transactions

To apply one of the default transition animations, use the `setTransition` method on any Fragment Transaction, passing in one of the `FragmentTransaction.TRANSIT_FRAGMENT_*` constants:

```
fragementTransaction.setTransition(FragmentTransaction.TRANSIT_FRAGMENT_OPEN);
```

You can also apply custom animations to Fragment Transactions by using the `setCustomAnimations` method, before calling the `add` or `remove` methods in your Fragment Transaction.

This method accepts two Object Animator XML resources: one for Fragments that are being added to the layout, and another for Fragments being removed:

```
fragmentTransaction.setCustomAnimations(android.R.anim.fade_in,
                                        android.R.anim.fade_out);
```

This is a particularly useful way to add seamless dynamic transitions when you are replacing Fragments within your layout. You can find more details on creating custom Animator and Animation resources in Chapter 14, "Advanced Customization of Your User Interface."

Communicating Between Fragments and Activities

When your Fragment needs to share events with its host Activity (such as signaling UI selections), it's good practice to create a callback interface within the Fragment that a host Activity must implement.

Listing 3-12 shows a code snippet from within a Fragment class that defines a public event listener interface. The onAttach handler is overridden to obtain a reference to the host Activity, confirming that it implements the required interface. The onDetach handler sets our reference to null, and the onButtonPressed method is used as a placeholder example that calls the interface method on our parent Activity.

LISTING 3-12: Defining Fragment event callback interfaces

```java
public class MySkeletonFragment extends Fragment {

    public interface OnFragmentInteractionListener {
        // TODO Update argument type and name
        void onFragmentInteraction(Uri uri);
    }

    private OnFragmentInteractionListener mListener;

    public MySkeletonFragment() {}

    @Override
    public View onCreateView(LayoutInflater inflater, ViewGroup container,
                             Bundle savedInstanceState) {
        // Inflate the layout for this fragment
        return inflater.inflate(R.layout.my_skeleton_fragment_layout,
                                container, false);
    }

    @Override
    public void onAttach(Context context) {
        super.onAttach(context);
        if (context instanceof OnFragmentInteractionListener) {
            mListener = (OnFragmentInteractionListener) context;
        } else {
            throw new RuntimeException(context.toString()
                    + " must implement OnFragmentInteractionListener");
        }
    }

    @Override
    public void onDetach() {
        super.onDetach();
        mListener = null;
    }
```

```
    public void onButtonPressed(Uri uri) {
      if (mListener != null) {
        mListener.onFragmentInteraction(uri);
      }
    }
  }
```

You can also use the getContext method within any Fragment to return a reference to the Context of the component within which it's embedded.

Although it's possible for Fragments to communicate with each other using the host Activity's Fragment Manager, it's generally considered better practice to use the Activity as an intermediary. This allows the Fragments to be as independent and loosely coupled as possible, with the responsibility for deciding how an event in one Fragment should affect the overall UI falling to the host Activity.

Fragments Without User Interfaces

In most circumstances, Fragments are used to encapsulate modular components of the UI; however, you can also create a Fragment without a UI to provide background behavior that persists across Activity restarts caused by configuration changes.

You can choose to have an active Fragment retain its current instance when its parent Activity is re-created using the setRetainInstance method. After you call this method, the Fragment's life cycle will change.

Rather than being destroyed and re-created with its parent Activity, the same Fragment instance is retained when the Activity restarts. It will receive the onDetach event when the parent Activity is destroyed, followed by the onAttach, onCreateView, and onActivityCreated events as the new parent Activity is instantiated.

The following snippet shows the skeleton code for a Fragment without a UI:

```
public class WorkerFragment extends Fragment {

  public final static String MY_FRAGMENT_TAG = "my_fragment";

  @Override
  public void onAttach(Context context) {
    super.onAttach(context);

    // Get a type-safe reference to the parent context.
  }

  @Override
  public void onCreate(Bundle savedInstanceState) {
    super.onCreate(savedInstanceState);

    // Create ongoing threads and tasks.
  }
```

```
  @Override
  public void onActivityCreated(Bundle savedInstanceState) {
    super.onActivityCreated(savedInstanceState);

    // Initiate worker threads and tasks.
  }
}
```

To add this Fragment to your Activity, create a new Fragment Transaction, specifying a tag to use to identify it. Because the Fragment has no UI, it should not be associated with a container View and must not be added to the back stack:

```
FragmentTransaction fragmentTransaction = fragmentManager.beginTransaction();

fragmentTransaction.add(new WorkerFragment(), WorkerFragment.MY_FRAGMENT_TAG);

fragmentTransaction.commitNow();
```

Use the `findFragmentByTag` from the Fragment Manager to find a reference to it later:

```
WorkerFragment workerFragment
  = (WorkerFragment)fragmentManager
    .findFragmentByTag(WorkerFragment.MY_FRAGMENT_TAG);
```

BUILDING AN EARTHQUAKE VIEWER APPLICATION

In the following example you'll start to create an app that will use a feed of earthquake data from the United States Geological Survey (USGS) to display a list (and eventually a map) of recent earthquakes.

In this chapter we'll begin by creating the Activity UI for this application using Activities, layouts, and Fragments; you will return to this earthquake application several times in the following chapters, gradually adding more features and functionality.

Figure 3-5 shows the basic application architecture that we'll construct using the following steps.

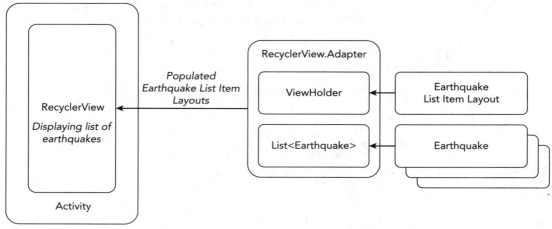

FIGURE 3-5

> **NOTE** *To simplify readability, each of these examples excludes the import statements. If you are using Android Studio, you can enable "automatically add unambiguous imports on the fly" within the Settings dialog under Editor ⇨ General ⇨ Auto Import, as shown in Figure 3-6, to populate the import statements required to support the classes used in your code as you type. Alternatively, you can press Alt+Enter on each unresolved class name as required.*

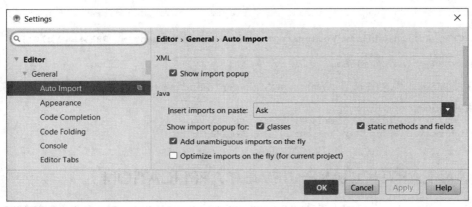

FIGURE 3-6

1. Start by creating a new Earthquake project. It should support phones and tablets, with a minimum SDK of API 16. When prompted, name the primary Activity EarthquakeMainActivity using the Empty Activity template. It should also use the App Compatibility library, which is enabled by selecting the Backwards Compatibility (AppCompat) checkbox.

2. Create a new public `Earthquake` class. This class will be used to store the details (id, date, details, location, magnitude, and link) of each earthquake. Override the `toString` method to provide the string that will be used to represent each earthquake in the earthquake list:

```java
import java.util.Date;
import java.text.SimpleDateFormat;
import java.util.Locale;

import android.location.Location;

public class Earthquake {
  private String mId;
  private Date mDate;
  private String mDetails;
  private Location mLocation;
  private double mMagnitude;
  private String mLink;

  public String getId() { return mId; }
  public Date getDate() { return mDate; }
  public String getDetails() { return mDetails; }
```

```
        public Location getLocation() { return mLocation; }
        public double getMagnitude() { return mMagnitude; }
        public String getLink() { return mLink; }

        public Earthquake(String id, Date date, String details,
                          Location location,
                          double magnitude, String link) {
          mId = id;
          mDate = date;
          mDetails = details;
          mLocation = location;
          mMagnitude = magnitude;
          mLink = link;
        }

        @Override
        public String toString() {
          SimpleDateFormat sdf = new  SimpleDateFormat("HH.mm", Locale.US);
          String dateString = sdf.format(mDate);
          return dateString + ": " + mMagnitude + " " + mDetails;
        }

      @Override
        public boolean equals(Object obj) {
          if (obj instanceof Earthquake)
            return (((Earthquake)obj).getId().contentEquals(mId));
          else
            return false;
        }
      }
```

3. Create a new `dimens.xml` XML resource file in the `res/values` folder to store dimension resource values. Create new dimensions for screen margins based on the 16dp recommended by the Android design guidelines.

```xml
<?xml version="1.0" encoding="utf-8"?>
<resources>
  <!-- Default screen margins, per the Android Design guidelines. -->
  <dimen name="activity_horizontal_margin">16dp</dimen>
  <dimen name="activity_vertical_margin">16dp</dimen>
  <dimen name="text_margin">16dp</dimen>
</resources>
```

4. Now create a new `list_item_earthquake.xml` layout resource in the `res/layout` folder. This will be used to display each earthquake in the list. For now, use a simple `TextView` that displays a single line of text using the margin from Step 3, and the Android framework's list item text appearance. We'll return to this in Chapter 5 to create a richer, more complex layout:

```xml
<?xml version="1.0" encoding="utf-8"?>
<FrameLayout xmlns:android="http://schemas.android.com/apk/res/android"
  android:layout_width="match_parent"
  android:layout_height="wrap_content">
  <TextView
    android:id="@+id/list_item_earthquake_details"
    android:layout_width="match_parent"
```

```
        android:layout_height="wrap_content"
        android:layout_margin="@dimen/text_margin"
        android:textAppearance="?attr/textAppearanceListItem"/>
</FrameLayout>
```

5. Create a new `EarthquakeListFragment` class that extends Fragment and stores an array of Earthquakes:

```
public class EarthquakeListFragment extends Fragment {

  private ArrayList<Earthquake> mEarthquakes =
    new ArrayList<Earthquake>();

  public EarthquakeListFragment() {
  }

  @Override
  public void onCreate(Bundle savedInstanceState) {
    super.onCreate(savedInstanceState);
  }
}
```

6. Our list of Earthquakes will be displayed using a `RecyclerView` within the Fragment created in Step 5. A Recycler View is a visual component that displays a scrolling list of items, we explore the Recycler View in more detail in Chapter 5. To begin, add a dependency to the Recycler View library in the app module `build.gradle` file:

```
dependencies {
  [... Existing dependencies ...]
  implementation 'com.android.support:recyclerview-v7:27.1.1'
}
```

7. Now create a new `fragment_earthquake_list.xml` layout file in the `res/layout` folder, which defines the layout for the Fragment class created in Step 5; it should include a single `RecyclerView` element:

```
<?xml version="1.0" encoding="utf-8"?>
<android.support.v7.widget.RecyclerView
  xmlns:android="http://schemas.android.com/apk/res/android"
  xmlns:app="http://schemas.android.com/apk/res-auto"
  android:id="@+id/list"
  android:layout_width="match_parent"
  android:layout_height="match_parent"
  android:layout_marginLeft="16dp"
  android:layout_marginRight="16dp"
  app:layoutManager="LinearLayoutManager"
/>
```

8. Return to the Earthquake List Fragment class and override the `onCreateView` method to inflate the layout from Step 7:

```
@Override
public View onCreateView(LayoutInflater inflater, ViewGroup container,
                         Bundle savedInstanceState) {
  View view = inflater.inflate(R.layout.fragment_earthquake_list,
                               container, false);
  return view;
}
```

9. Modify the `activity_earthquake_main.xml`, replacing the default layout with a `FrameLayout` that will be used as the container for the Fragment you created in Step 5. Be sure to give it an ID so that you can reference it from the Activity code:

```xml
<?xml version="1.0" encoding="utf-8"?>
<FrameLayout xmlns:android="http://schemas.android.com/apk/res/android"
  android:layout_width="match_parent"
  android:layout_height="match_parent"
  android:id="@+id/main_activity_frame">
</FrameLayout>
```

10. Return to the Earthquake Main Activity, and update the `onCreate` method to use the Fragment Manager to add the Earthquake List Fragment from Step 5, to the Frame Layout we defined in Step 9. Note that if your Activity is re-created due to a device configuration change, any Fragments added using the Fragment Manager will automatically be re-added. As a result, we only add a new Fragment if this is not a configuration-change restart; otherwise, we can find it using its tag:

```java
private static final String TAG_LIST_FRAGMENT = "TAG_LIST_FRAGMENT";

EarthquakeListFragment mEarthquakeListFragment;

@Override
protected void onCreate(Bundle savedInstanceState) {
  super.onCreate(savedInstanceState);
  setContentView(R.layout.activity_earthquake_main);

  FragmentManager fm = getSupportFragmentManager();

  // Android will automatically re-add any Fragments that
  // have previously been added after a configuration change,
  // so only add it if this isn't an automatic restart.
  if (savedInstanceState == null) {
    FragmentTransaction ft = fm.beginTransaction();

    mEarthquakeListFragment = new EarthquakeListFragment();
    ft.add(R.id.main_activity_frame,
           mEarthquakeListFragment, TAG_LIST_FRAGMENT);

    ft.commitNow();
  } else {
    mEarthquakeListFragment =
      (EarthquakeListFragment)fm.findFragmentByTag(TAG_LIST_FRAGMENT);
  }
}
```

11. Now create a new `EarthquakeRecyclerViewAdapter` class that extends `RecyclerView` `.Adapter`, and within it create a new `ViewHolder` class that extends `RecyclerView`

`.ViewHolder`. The View Holder will be used to hold a reference to each View from the Earthquake item layout definition in Step 4, when you bind the earthquake values to it in the `onBindViewHolder` method of the Earthquake Recycler View Adapter. The role of the Earthquake Recycler View Adapter is to provide populated View layouts based on the list of Earthquakes it maintains. We'll look at the Recycler View and its adapter in more detail in Chapter 5.

```java
public class EarthquakeRecyclerViewAdapter extends

RecyclerView.Adapter<EarthquakeRecyclerViewAdapter.ViewHolder> {

  private final List<Earthquake> mEarthquakes;

  public EarthquakeRecyclerViewAdapter(List<Earthquake> earthquakes ) {
    mEarthquakes = earthquakes;
  }

  @Override
  public ViewHolder onCreateViewHolder(ViewGroup parent, int viewType) {
    View view = LayoutInflater.from(parent.getContext())
                .inflate(R.layout.list_item_earthquake,
                         parent, false);
    return new ViewHolder(view);
  }

  @Override
  public void onBindViewHolder(final ViewHolder holder, int position) {
    holder.earthquake = mEarthquakes.get(position);
    holder.detailsView.setText(mEarthquakes.get(position).toString());
  }

  @Override
  public int getItemCount() {
    return mEarthquakes.size();
  }

  public class ViewHolder extends RecyclerView.ViewHolder {
    public final View parentView;
    public final TextView detailsView;
    public Earthquake earthquake;

    public ViewHolder(View view) {
      super(view);
      parentView = view;
      detailsView = (TextView)
                    view.findViewById(R.id.list_item_earthquake_details);
    }

    @Override
    public String toString() {
      return super.toString() + " '" + detailsView.getText() + "'";
    }
  }
}
```

12. Return to the Earthquake List Fragment and update `onCreateView` to get a reference to the Recycler View, and override the `onViewCreated` method to assign the `EarthquakeRecyclerViewAdapter` from Step 11 to the Recycler View:

```
private RecyclerView mRecyclerView;
private EarthquakeRecyclerViewAdapter mEarthquakeAdapter =
  new EarthquakeRecyclerViewAdapter(mEarthquakes);

@Override
public View onCreateView(LayoutInflater inflater, ViewGroup container,
                         Bundle savedInstanceState) {
  View view = inflater.inflate(R.layout.fragment_earthquake_list,
                               container, false);

  mRecyclerView = (RecyclerView) view.findViewById(R.id.list);

  return view;
}

@Override
public void onViewCreated(View view, Bundle savedInstanceState) {
  super.onViewCreated(view, savedInstanceState);

  // Set the Recycler View adapter
  Context context = view.getContext();
  mRecyclerView.setLayoutManager(new LinearLayoutManager(context));
  mRecyclerView.setAdapter(mEarthquakeAdapter);
}
```

13. Still within the Earthquake List Fragment, add a `setEarthquakes` method that takes a List of Earthquakes, checks for duplicates, and then adds each new Earthquake to the Array List. It should also notify the Recycler View Adapter that a new item has been inserted:

```
public void setEarthquakes(List<Earthquake> earthquakes) {
  for (Earthquake earthquake: earthquakes) {
    if (!mEarthquakes.contains(earthquake)) {
      mEarthquakes.add(earthquake);
      mEarthquakeAdapter
        .notifyItemInserted(mEarthquakes.indexOf(earthquake));
    }
  }
}
```

14. In Chapter 7 you'll learn how to download and parse the USGS feed for earthquakes, but to confirm that your application is working, update your `onCreate` method of the Earthquake Main Activity to create some dummy Earthquakes—ensuring that you're importing the `java.util.Date` and `java.util.Calendar` libraries for the date/time functions. Once created, pass the new Earthquakes to your Earthquake List Fragment using its `setEarthquakes` method:

```
@Override
protected void onCreate(Bundle savedInstanceState) {
  super.onCreate(savedInstanceState);
  setContentView(R.layout.activity_earthquake_main);
```

```
FragmentManager fm = getSupportFragmentManager();
if (savedInstanceState == null) {
  FragmentTransaction ft = fm.beginTransaction();
  mEarthquakeListFragment = new EarthquakeListFragment();
  ft.add(R.id.main_activity_frame, mEarthquakeListFragment,
      TAG_LIST_FRAGMENT);
  ft.commitNow();
} else {
  mEarthquakeListFragment =
    (EarthquakeListFragment)fm.findFragmentByTag(TAG_LIST_FRAGMENT);
}

Date now = Calendar.getInstance().getTime();
List<Earthquake> dummyQuakes = new ArrayList<Earthquake>(0);
dummyQuakes.add(new Earthquake("0", now, "San Jose", null, 7.3, null));
dummyQuakes.add(new Earthquake("1", now, "LA", null, 6.5, null));

mEarthquakeListFragment.setEarthquakes(dummyQuakes);
}
```

15. When you run your project, you should see a Recycler View that features the two dummy earthquakes, as shown in Figure 3-7.

FIGURE 3-7

Defining the Android Manifest and Gradle Build Files, and Externalizing Resources

WROX.COM CODE DOWNLOADS FOR THIS CHAPTER

The code download for this chapter is found at www.wrox.com:

➤ Snippets_ch4.zip

THE MANIFEST, BUILD FILES, AND RESOURCES

Each Android project includes a manifest file that defines the structure and metadata of your application, its components, and its requirements.

In this chapter you learn how to configure your application manifest, as well as understand how to modify the Gradle build configuration files. These Gradle build files are used to define required dependencies, and define parameters when compiling and building your apps.

You should always provide the best possible experience for users, no matter which country they're in or which of the wide variety of Android device types, form factors, and screen sizes they're using. In this chapter, you learn how to externalize resources, and use the resource framework to provide optimized resources to ensure your applications run seamlessly on different hardware (particularly different screen resolutions and pixel densities), in different countries, and supporting multiple languages.

INTRODUCING THE ANDROID MANIFEST

Each Android project includes a manifest file, `AndroidManifest.xml`. Within Android Studio, you can access the application manifest from the `app/manifests` folder as shown in Figure 4-1.

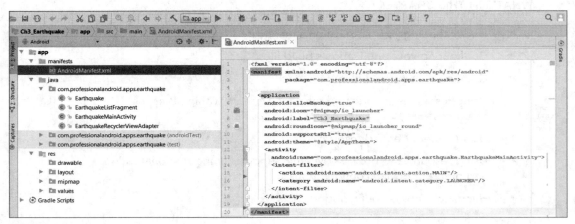

FIGURE 4-1

The manifest defines the structure and metadata of your application, its components, and its requirements.

Your manifest includes nodes for each of the Activities, Services, Content Providers, and Broadcast Receivers that make up your application and, using Intent Filters and Permissions, determines how they interact with each other and with other applications.

The manifest is made up of a root `manifest` tag with a `package` attribute set to the project's unique package name. It should also include an `xmlns:android` attribute that supplies several system attributes required within the file.

The following XML snippet shows a typical manifest root node:

```
<manifest xmlns:android="http://schemas.android.com/apk/res/android"
          package="com.professionalandroid.apps.helloworld" >
  [ ... manifest nodes ... ]
</manifest>
```

The manifest specifies application metadata (such as its icon and theme) within the top-level `application` node. Additional top-level nodes can specify any required permissions, unit tests, and define hardware, screen, or platform requirements (as described in the following section).

The following list gives a summary of some of the available `manifest` sub-node tags and provides an XML snippet demonstrating how each tag is used:

➤ `uses-feature`—Android is available on a wide variety of hardware platforms, you can use `uses-feature` nodes to specify hardware and software features your application *requires* in order to properly function.

Note that this will prevent your application from being installed on a device that does not include a specified feature, such as NFC hardware in the following snippet:

```
<uses-feature android:name="android.hardware.nfc" />
```

Use this node only if you want to prevent your application being installed on devices that don't include certain features. Currently, supported required features include the following categories:

➤ **Audio**—For applications that require a low-latency or pro-level audio pipeline, or require microphone input.

➤ **Bluetooth**—Where a Bluetooth or BTLE radio is required.

➤ **Camera**—For applications that require a camera. You can also require (or set as optional) front- or rear-facing, autofocus, manual post-processing, manual sensor, flash, or RAW support.

➤ **Device Hardware UI**—Where the application is designed for a specific device user interface: such as automotive or watch.

➤ **Fingerprint**—Requires biometric hardware capable of reading fingerprints.

➤ **Gamepad**—For games (or apps) that require game controller input, either from the device itself or from a connected gamepad.

➤ **Infrared**—Indicates a requirement for infrared (IR) capabilities (typically to communicate with other consumer IR devices).

➤ **Location**—If you require location-based services. You can also specify either network or GPS support explicitly.

➤ **NFC**—Requires NFC (near-field communications) support.

➤ **OpenGL ES hardware**—The application requires the OpenGL ES Android Extension Pack installed on the device.

➤ **Sensors**—Enables you to specify a requirement for any of the potentially available hardware sensors, including a accelerometer, barometer, compass, gyroscope, sensors to detect ambient temperature, heart rate, light, proximity, humidity, and a step counter and step detector.

➤ **Telephony**—To specify that either telephony in general, or a specific telephony radio (GSM or CDMA) is required.

➤ **Touchscreen**—To specify the type of touch screen your application requires, including how many distinct input touches can be detected and tracked.

➤ **USB**—For applications that require either USB host or accessory mode support.

➤ **Wi-Fi**—Where Wi-Fi networking support is required.

➤ **Communication software**—The application requires support for Session Initiation Protocol (SIP) services or Voice Over Internet Protocol (VoIP) services.

➤ **Device management software**—Use these optional software features to specify that your application requires the device support device management features including backup service, device policy enforcement, managed users, user removal, and verified boot.

➤ **Media software**—If your application requires MIDI support, printing, a "lean back" (television) UI, live TV, or homescreen widgets.

As the variety of platforms on which Android is available increases, so too will the optional hardware and software. You can find a full list of `uses-feature` hardware at `developer.android.com/guide/topics/manifest/uses-feature-element .html#features-reference`.

To ensure compatibility, specifying the requirement of some permissions, implies a feature requirement. Specifically, requesting permission to access Bluetooth, the camera, any of the location service permissions, audio recording, Wi-Fi, and telephony-related permissions implies the corresponding hardware feature. You can override these implied requirements by adding a `required` attribute and setting it to `false`—for example, a note-taking application that supports (but does not require) recording an audio note may choose to make the microphone hardware optional:

```
<uses-feature android:name="android.hardware.microphone"
              android:required="false" />
```

The camera hardware also represents a special case. For compatibility reasons, requesting permission to use the camera, or adding a `uses-feature` node requiring it, implies a requirement for the camera to support autofocus. You can specify it as optional as necessary:

```
<uses-feature android:name="android.hardware.camera" />
<uses-feature android:name="android.hardware.camera.autofocus"
              android:required="false" />
<uses-feature android:name="android.hardware.camera.flash"
              android:required="false" />
```

➤ supports-screens—With the proliferation of hundreds of different screen sizes, resolutions, and densities—and the introduction of multi-window mode, you should create responsive UI designs for your application that provide a good experience for all users. While it is technically possible to use the supports-screen node to limit your application's availability to a subset of supported screen resolutions, this is considered bad practice and should be avoided.

➤ supports-gl-texture—Declares that the application is capable of providing texture assets that are compressed using a particular GL texture compression format. You must use multiple supports-gl-texture elements if your application is capable of supporting multiple texture compression formats. You can find the most up-to-date list of supported GL texture compression format values at developer.android.com/guide/topics/manifest/supports-gl-texture-element.html.

```
<supports-gl-texture android:name="GL_OES_compressed_ETC1_RGB8_texture" />
```

➤ uses-permission—As part of the security model, uses-permission tags declare the user permissions your application requires. Each permission you specify will be presented to the user either before the application is installed (on devices running Android 5.1 or lower), or while the application is running (on devices running Android 6.0 and higher). Permissions are required for many APIs and method calls, generally those with an associated cost or security implication (such as dialing, receiving SMS, or using the location-based services). We introduce these throughout the rest of this book as required.

```
<uses-permission android:name="android.permission.ACCESS_FINE_LOCATION"/>
```

➤ permission—Your shared application components can also create permissions to restrict access to them from other application components. You can use the existing platform permissions for this purpose, or define your own permissions in the manifest. To do this, use the permission tag to create a permission definition.

You can specify the level of access the permission permits (normal, dangerous, signature, signatureOrSystem), a label, and an external resource containing the description that explains the risks of granting the specified permission. You can find more details on creating and using your own permissions in Chapter 20, "Advanced Android Development."

```
<permission android:name="com.professionalandroid.perm.DETONATE_DEVICE"
            android:protectionLevel="dangerous"
            android:label="Self Destruct"
            android:description="@string/detonate_description">
</permission>
```

➤ application—A manifest can contain only one application node. It uses attributes to specify the metadata for your application including its name, icon, and theme. You can also indicate if you will allow data to be backed up automatically using Android Auto Backup (as described in Chapter 8), and if you support right-to-left UI layouts.

If you are using a custom application class, you must specify it here using the android:name attribute.

The `application` node also acts as a container for the Activity, Service, Content Provider, and Broadcast Receiver nodes that specify the application components.

```
<application
  android:label="@string/app_name"
  android:icon="@mipmap/ic_launcher"
  android:theme="@style/AppTheme"
  android:allowBackup="true"
  android:supportsRtl="true"
  android:name=".MyApplicationClass">
  [ ... application component nodes ... ]
</application>
```

➤   `activity`—An `activity` tag is required for every Activity within your application. Use the `android:name` attribute to indicate the `Activity` class name. You must include the main launch Activity and any other Activity that may be displayed. Trying to start an Activity that's not included in the manifest will throw a runtime exception. Each Activity node supports `intent-filter` child tags that define the Intents that can be used to start the Activity.

Note that a period is used as shorthand for the application's package name when specifying the Activity's class name:

```
<activity android:name=".MyActivity">
  <intent-filter>
    <action android:name="android.intent.action.MAIN" />
    <category android:name="android.intent.category.LAUNCHER" />
  </intent-filter>
</activity>
```

➤   `service`—As with the `activity` tag, add a `service` tag for each `Service` class (described in Chapter 11) used in your application.

```
<service android:name=".MyService"/>
```

➤   `provider`—Provider tags specify each of your application's Content Providers. Content Providers are used to manage database access and sharing as described in Chapter 10.

```
<provider
  android:name=".MyContentProvider"
  android:authorities="com.professionalandroid.myapp.MyContentProvider"
/>
```

➤   `receiver`—By adding a `receiver` tag, you can register a Broadcast Receiver without having to launch your application first. As you'll see in Chapter 6, Broadcast Receivers are like global event listeners that, when registered, will execute whenever a matching Intent is broadcast by the system. By registering a Broadcast Receiver in your manifest, you can make this process entirely autonomous.

```
<receiver android:name=".MyIntentReceiver">
</receiver>
```

> **NOTE** *You can find a more detailed description of the manifest and each of these nodes at* `developer.android.com/guide/topics/manifest/manifest-intro.html`.

The Android Studio New Project Wizard automatically creates a new manifest file when it creates a new project. You'll return to the manifest as each of the application components is introduced and explored throughout this book.

CONFIGURING THE GRADLE BUILD

Each project contains a series of Gradle files used to define your build configuration, consisting of a:

➤ Project-scoped `settings.gradle` file that defines which modules should be included when building your application.

➤ Project-scoped `build.gradle` file in which the repositories and dependencies for Gradle itself are specified, as well as any repositories and dependencies common to all your modules.

➤ Module-scoped `build.gradle` file(s) used to configure build settings for your application, including dependencies, minimum and targeted platform versions, your application's version information, and multiple build types and product flavors.

For most applications the default settings and project-scoped build Gradle files won't need to be changed. The default settings file specifies a single module (your application). The top-level Gradle build file includes JCenter and Google as repositories for Gradle to search for dependencies and includes the Android Plugin for Gradle as a project dependency.

In contrast, you will likely need to make ongoing changes to the module-level Gradle build file, which lets you define one or more build configurations for your application including dependencies on new support libraries, changes in version numbers, and which platform and SDK versions you support.

Gradle Settings File

The `settings.gradle` file is located in your project's root folder and is used to tell Gradle which modules it should include when building your application. By default, your single application module is included:

```
include ':app'
```

If your project expands to use multiple modules, you would need to add them here.

Project Gradle Build File

The top-level project-scoped `build.gradle` file is located in the root project directory. It allows you to specify dependencies—and the repositories Gradle uses to search for and then download those dependencies—that apply to the project and all its modules.

The `buildscript` node is used to indicate the repositories and dependencies that are used by Gradle itself—not for your application.

For example, the default `dependencies` block includes the Android Plugin for Gradle, because that's necessary for Gradle to build Android application modules, and the `repositories` block pre-configures JCenter and Google as repositories Gradle should use to look for it:

```
buildscript {
  repositories {
    google()
    jcenter()
  }
  dependencies {
    classpath 'com.android.tools.build:gradle:3.1.3'
  }
}
```

Note that this is not where you indicate your application dependencies; they belong in the relevant module `build.gradle` file for your application module, as described in the next section.

Use the `allprojects` block to specify repositories and dependencies used by all modules in your project, though for projects with a single module it's common practice to include its dependencies in the module-level `build.gradle` file.

For new projects, Android Studio adds JCenter and Google as default repositories.

```
allprojects {
  repositories {
    google()
    jcenter()
  }
}
```

Android Studio also defines a new project task—`clean`—that deletes the contents of your project's build folder:

```
task clean(type: Delete) {
  delete rootProject.buildDir
}
```

Module Gradle Build Files

The module-level `build.gradle` file, located in each of your project's module directories, is used to configure build settings for the corresponding module, including required dependencies, minimum and targeted platform versions, your application's version information, and different build types and product flavors.

The first line in the build configuration applies the Android Plugin for Gradle to this build, which makes it possible to use the `android` block to specify Android-specific build options:

```
apply plugin: 'com.android.application'
```

Within the top level of the `android` block you specify the Android application configuration options, such as the version of the SDK with which to compile your application. Be sure to update these values when you download a new SDK release:

```
android {
  compileSdkVersion 27

  defaultConfig {...}
  buildTypes {...}
  productFlavors {...}
  splits {...}
}
```

Default Configuration

The `defaultConfig` block (within the `android` block) specifies default settings that will be shared across all your different product flavors:

```
defaultConfig {
  applicationId 'com.professionalandroid.apps.helloworld'

  minSdkVersion 16
  targetSdkVersion 27

  versionCode 1
  versionName "1.0"
}
```

As shown in the preceding code, you should specify the:

> `applicationId`—To provide a unique "package name" that will be used to identify the built APK for publishing and distribution. By default, and requirement, this should use the same package name as defined within your manifest, and you application classes.

> `minSdkVersion`—To set the lowest version of the Android platform your application is compatible with. This lets you indicate the earliest Android platform release on which your application can be installed and run—the Android framework will prevent users from installing your application if the system's API level is lower than this value. If you fail to specify a minimum version, it defaults to 1 and will be available on all devices, resulting in crashes if unavailable APIs are called.

> `targetSdkVersion`—To specify the Android platform version against which you did your development and testing. Setting a target SDK tells the system that there is no need to apply any forward- or backward-compatibility changes to support that particular platform. To take advantage of the newest platform UI improvements, it's considered good practice to update the target SDK of your application to the latest platform release after you confirm it behaves as expected, even if you aren't making use of any new APIs.

> `versionCode`—To define the current application version as an integer that increases with each version iteration you release.

`versionName`—To specify a public version identifier that will be displayed to users.

`testInstrumentationRunner`—To specify a test runner to use. By default, the Android support library AndroidJUnitRunner instrumentation will be included, and allows you to run JUnit3 and JUnit4 tests against your application.

> **NOTE** *Some of these build configuration values can also be specified within the Android manifest. When your application is built, Gradle merges these values with those provided by your manifest—with the Gradle build values taking precedence. To avoid confusion it's best practice to only specify these values within the Gradle build files.*
>
> *One special case is your application's package name. You must still include a package attribute at the root element of your manifest file. The package name defined there also serves a secondary purpose as the package name used for your application's classes, including the* R *resource class.*
>
> *As you see later, Gradle makes it possible to easily build multiple variations (or "flavors") of your application (for example "free" and "pro" or "alpha," "beta," and "release" variants). Each flavor must have a different package name, but to use a single codebase, the package name for your classes must be consistent.*
>
> *As a result, the package name used in your manifest is used for your* R *class, and to resolve any other class name ambiguities within your application, but the application ID indicated in your Gradle build files are used as the package names when building their associated APKs.*

Build Types

The `buildTypes` block is used to define multiple different build types—typically debug and release. When you create a new module, Android Studio automatically creates a release build type for you, and in most cases you won't need to change it.

Note that the debug build type doesn't need to be explicitly included in the Gradle build file, but by default Android Studio will configure your debug builds with `debuggable true`. As a result, these builds are signed with the debug keystore, and you can debug them on locked and signed Android devices.

The default release build type (shown in the following code) applies Proguard settings to shrink and obfuscate the compiled code, and does not use a default signing key:

```
buildTypes {
  release {
    minifyEnabled true
    proguardFiles getDefaultProguardFile('proguard-android.txt'),
                               'proguard-rules.pro'
  }
}
```

Product Flavors and Flavor Dimensions

The `flavorDimensions` and `productFlavors` blocks are optional nodes, not included by default, which allows you to override any of the values you defined in the `defaultConfig` block to support different versions (flavors) of your application using the same codebase. Each product flavor should specify its own unique application ID so that each can be distributed and installed independently:

```
productFlavors {
  freeversion {
    applicationId 'com.professionalandroid.apps.helloworld.free'
    versionName "1.0 Free"
  }

  paidversion {
    applicationId 'com.professionalandroid.apps.helloworld.paid'
    versionName "1.0 Full"
  }
}
```

Flavor dimensions allow you to create groups of product flavors that can be combined to create a final build variant. This allows you to specify build changes along multiple dimensions—for example, changes based on free versus paid builds—as well as changes based on minimum API level:

```
flavorDimensions "apilevel", "paylevel"

productFlavors {
    freeversion {
      applicationId 'com.professionalandroid.apps.helloworld.free'
      versionName "1.0 Free"
      dimension "paylevel"
    }

    paidversion {
applicationId 'com.professionalandroid.apps.helloworld.paid'
      versionName "1.0 Full"
      dimension "paylevel"
    }

    minApi24 {
      dimension "apilevel"
      minSdkVersion 24
      versionCode 24000 + android.defaultConfig.versionCode
      versionNameSuffix "-minApi24"
    }

    minApi23 {
      dimension "apilevel"
      minSdkVersion 16
      versionCode 16000  + android.defaultConfig.versionCode
      versionNameSuffix "-minApi23"
    }
  }
}
```

When building your application, Gradle will combine the product flavors along each dimension, along with a build type configuration, to create the final build variant. Gradle does not combine product flavors that belong to the same flavor dimension.

Note that Gradle determines the priority of flavor dimensions based on the order in which they are specified, where the first dimension will override values assigned along the second dimension and so on.

Since Gradle 3.0.0, in order to define flavors, you must define at least one product dimension. Each flavor must have an associated product dimension, though if you have only one dimension defined, it will be used by default by each flavor.

You can detect the current product flavor at run time, and modify your product behavior accordingly, using this code snippet:

```
if (BuildConfig.FLAVOR == "orangesherbert") {
  // Do groovy things
} else {
  // Enable paid features
}
```

Alternatively, you can create a new set of classes and resources—a new source-set—for your application to use for each flavor, by creating an additional directory structure parallel to the default "main" source path.

For classes, you'll need to create the folders manually, whereas for resources, you can choose the source-set a new resource should belong to, as shown in the New Resource File dialog box in Figure 4-2.

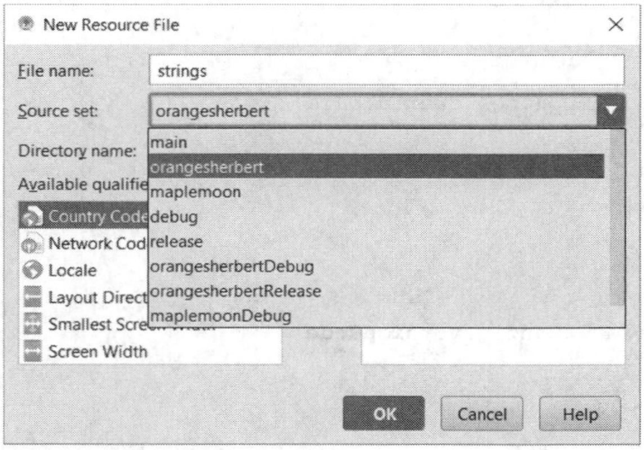

FIGURE 4-2

> **NOTE** *When building your application, Gradle will merge the Java source and resources from your flavor source-set with the "main" source-set using the same package name (as defined in your manifest). As a result, you can't use a class name in a flavor that duplicates a class name in the main source-set.*

Within Android Studio, you can select the build you wish to build and run using the Build ⇨ Select Build Variant menu item and selecting it from the drop-down displayed in the Build Variant window.

Splits

You can use the optional `splits` block to configure different APK builds that contain only the code and resources for each supported screen density or ABI.

It's generally best practice to create and distribute a single APK to support all your target devices, but in some cases (particularly games) this might result in a prohibitively large APK size.

Creating and distributing split APKs is outside the scope of this book, but you can find more details on configuring APK splits at `developer.android.com/studio/build/configure-apk-splits .html`.

Dependencies

The `dependencies` block specifies the dependencies required to build your application.

By default, a new project will include a local binary dependency that tells Gradle to include all JAR files located in the `apps/libs` folder, remote binary dependencies on the Android Support Library and JUnit, and a dependency on the Android Espresso testing library:

```
dependencies {
    implementation fileTree(dir: 'libs', include: ['*.jar'])
    implementation 'com.android.support:appcompat-v7:27.1.1'
    implementation 'com.android.support.constraint:constraint-layout:1.1.2'
    testImplementation 'junit:junit:4.12'
    androidTestImplementation 'com.android.support.test:runner:1.0.2'
    androidTestImplementation 'com.android.support.test.espresso:espresso-core:3.0.2'
}
```

We'll return to the dependency block throughout the book as new library dependencies are required.

EXTERNALIZING RESOURCES

It's always good practice to keep non-code resources, such as images and string constants, external to your code. Android supports the externalization of resources, ranging from simple values such as strings and colors to more complex resources such as images, animations, themes, and UI layouts.

By externalizing resources, you make them easier to maintain, update, and manage. This also lets you create alternative resource values to support internationalization, and to include different resources to support variations in hardware—particularly screen size and resolution.

When an application starts, Android automatically selects the correct resources from the available alternatives without you having to write a line of code. Later in this section you see how Android dynamically selects resources from resource trees that contain different values for alternative hardware configurations, languages, and locations.

Among other things, this lets you change the layout based on the screen size and orientation, images based on screen density, and customize text based on a user's language and country.

Creating Resources

Application resources are stored under the `res` folder in your project hierarchy. Each of the available resource types is stored in subfolders, grouped by resource type.

If you create a new project using the Android Studio New Project Wizard, it creates a `res` folder that contains subfolders for the `values`, `mipmap`, and `layout` resources that contain the default values for string, dimensions, color, and style resource, as well as an application icon and the default layout, as shown in Figure 4-3.

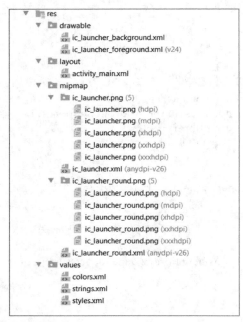

FIGURE 4-3

> **NOTE** *Note that the `mipmap` resource folder contains five different application icons for different density displays. You learn more about supplying different resource values for hardware variations later in this chapter.*

When your application is built, these resources will be compressed as efficiently as possible and packaged into your APK.

The build process also generates an R class file that contains references to each of the resources included in your project. This enables you to reference resources from your code, with the advantage of design-time syntax checking.

The following sections describe many of the specific resource types available and how to create them for your applications.

In all cases, the resource filenames should contain only lowercase letters, numbers, and the period (.) and underscore (_) symbols.

Simple Values

Supported simple values include strings, colors, dimensions, styles, Boolean or integer values, and string or typed arrays. All simple values are stored within XML files in the res/values folder.

Each values XML file allows you to describe multiple resources. You indicate the type of value being stored using tags, as shown in the sample XML file in Listing 4-1.

LISTING 4-1: Simple values XML

```xml
<?xml version="1.0" encoding="utf-8"?>
<resources>
  <string name="app_name">To Do List</string>
  <plurals name="androidPlural">
    <item quantity="one">One android</item>
    <item quantity="other">%d androids</item>
  </plurals>
  <color name="app_background">#FF0000FF</color>
  <dimen name="default_border">5px</dimen>
  <integer name="book_ignition_temp">451</integer>
  <bool name="is_a_trap">true</bool>
  <string-array name="string_array">
    <item>Item 1</item>
    <item>Item 2</item>
    <item>Item 3</item>
  </string-array>
  <integer-array name="integer_array">
    <item>3</item>
    <item>2</item>
    <item>1</item>
  </integer-array>
  <array name="color_typed_array">
    <item>#FF0000FF</item>
    <item>#00FFFF00</item>
    <item>#FF00FF00</item>
  </array>
  <style name="AppTheme" parent="Theme.AppCompat.Light.DarkActionBar">
    <item name="colorPrimary">@color/colorPrimary</item>
  </style>
</resources>
```

This example includes many different simple value types. By convention, for clarity and readability, resources are typically stored in separate files, one for each type; for example, `res/values/strings.xml` would contain only string resources.

The following sections detail the options for defining some common simple resources.

Strings

Externalizing your strings helps maintain consistency within your application and makes it much easier to internationalize them.

String resources are specified with the `string` tag, as shown in the following XML snippet:

```
<string name="stop_message">Stop.</string>
```

Apostrophes (') , double-quotes ("), and backslashes (\) must be escaped using a backslash, like this:

```
<string name="quoting_myself">
Escape \"Apostrophes (\') and double-quotes (\") with a backslash (\\)\"
</string>
```

Android supports simple text styling, so you can use the HTML tags `<b>`, `<i>`, and `<u>` to apply bold, italics, or underlining, respectively, to parts of your text strings, as shown in the following example:

```
<string name="stop_message"><b>Stop.</b></string>
```

You can also use resource strings as input parameters for the `String.format` method. However, `String.format` does not support the text styling previously described. To apply styling to a format string, you have to escape the HTML tags when creating your resource, as shown in the following snippet:

```
<string name="stop_message">&lt;b>Stop&lt;/b>. %1$s</string>
```

Within your code, use the `Html.fromHtml` method to convert this back into a styled character sequence:

```
String rString = getString(R.string.stop_message);
String fString = String.format(rString, "Collaborate and listen.");
CharSequence styledString = Html.fromHtml(fString, FROM_HTML_MODE_LEGACY);
```

> **NOTE** *Android 6.0 Nougat (API Level 24) introduced the* `Html.fromHtml` *method shown in the snippet above, which allows you to specify a flag to determine how block-level elements are separated. For applications supporting earlier versions of Android, you can continue to use the deprecated* `Html.fromHtml` *method that behaves identically to the new method using the* `FROM_HTML_MODE_LEGACY` *flag.*

You can also define alternative plural forms for your strings. This enables you to define different strings based on the number of items you refer to. For example, in English you would refer to "one Android" but "seven Androids."

By creating a plurals resource, you can specify an alternative string for any of zero, one, multiple, few, many, or other quantities. In English the singular is a special case, whereas some languages require finer detail and in others the singular is never used:

```
<plurals name="unicorn_count">
  <item quantity="one">One unicorn</item>
  <item quantity="other">%d unicorns</item>
</plurals>
```

To access the correct plural in code, use the getQuantityString method on your application's Resources object, passing in the resource ID of the plural resource, and specifying the number of objects you want to describe:

```
Resources resources = getResources();
String unicornStr = resources.getQuantityString(
  R.plurals.unicorn_count, unicornCount, unicornCount);
```

Note that in this example the object count is passed in twice—once to return the correct plural string, and again as an input parameter to complete the sentence.

Colors

Use the color tag to define a new color resource. Specify the color value using a # symbol followed by the (optional) alpha channel, and then the red, green, and blue values using one or two hexadecimal numbers with any of the following notations:

➤ #RGB

➤ #RRGGBB

➤ #ARGB

➤ #AARRGGBB

The following example shows how to specify Android green and a partially transparent blue:

```
<color name="android_green">#A4C639</color>
<color name="transparent_blue">#770000FF</color>
```

Dimensions

Dimensions are most commonly referenced within style and layout resources. They're useful for defining layout values, such as borders and font heights.

To specify a dimension resource, use the dimen tag, specifying the dimension value, followed by an identifier describing the scale of your dimension:

➤ dp (density-independent pixels)

➤ sp (scalable pixels)

➤ px (screen pixels)

➤ in (physical inches)

➤ pt (physical points)

➤ mm (physical millimeters)

Although you can use any of these measurements to define a dimension, it's best practice to use either density independent or scalable pixels. These alternatives let you define a dimension using relative scales that account for different screen resolutions and densities to simplify scaling on different hardware.

Scalable pixels are particularly well suited when defining font sizes because they automatically scale if the user changes the system font size.

The following XML snippet shows how to specify dimension values for a large font size and a standard border:

```xml
<dimen name="large_font_size">16sp</dimen>
<dimen name="activity_horizontal_margin">16dp</dimen>
```

Styles and Themes

Style resources let your applications maintain a consistent look and feel by enabling you to specify the attribute values used by Views—most commonly colors, borders, and font sizes for an application.

To create a style, use a `style` tag that includes a `name` attribute and contains one or more `item` tags. Each `item` tag should include a `name` attribute used to specify the attribute (such as font size or color) being defined. The tag itself should then contain the value, as shown in the following skeleton code:

```xml
<style name="base_text">
  <item name="android:textSize">14sp</item>
  <item name="android:textColor">#111</item>
</style>
```

Styles support inheritance using the `parent` attribute on the `style` tag, making it easy to create simple variations:

```xml
<style name="AppTheme" parent="Theme.AppCompat.Light.DarkActionBar">
  <item name="colorPrimary">@color/colorPrimary</item>
  <item name="colorPrimaryDark">@color/colorPrimaryDark</item>
  <item name="colorAccent">@color/colorAccent</item>
</style>
```

In Chapter 13 you learn more about using the themes and styles provided by the Android Support Library to create applications that are consistent with the Android platform and the material design philosophy.

Drawables

Drawable resources include bitmaps, NinePatches (stretchable PNG images), and scalable Vector Drawables. They also include complex composite Drawables, such as `LevelListDrawables` and `StateListDrawables`, which are defined in XML.

> **NOTE** *NinePatch Drawables, Vector Drawables, and complex composite resources are covered in more detail in the next chapter.*

All Drawables are stored as individual files in the `res/drawable` folder. Note that it's good practice to store bitmap image assets in the appropriate `drawable-ldpi`, `-mdpi`, `-hdpi`, and `-xhdpi` folders, as described later in this chapter. The resource identifier for a Drawable resource is the lowercase filename without its extension.

> **NOTE** *The preferred format for a Drawable bitmap resource is PNG, although JPG and GIF files are also supported.*

MipMaps

It's considered good practice to store your application's launcher icon image within the MipMap folder group—one for each resolution size up to `xxxhdpi` (as seen in your Hello World application).

Different home screen launcher apps on different devices show application launcher icons at various resolutions—some devices scale-up the launcher icons by as much as 25%. Application resource optimization techniques can remove Drawable resources for unused screen densities; however, all MipMap resources are preserved—ensuring that launcher apps can pick icons with the best resolution for display.

Note that the `mipmap-xxxhdpi` qualifier is typically supplied only to ensure a suitably high-resolution launcher icon is available in the case of up-scaling on an `xxhdpi` device; you typically won't need to supply `xxxhdpi` assets for the rest of your Drawable resources.

Layouts

Layout resources enable you to decouple your presentation layer from your business logic by designing UI layouts in XML, rather than constructing them in code.

You can use layouts to define the UI for any visual component, including Activities, Fragments, and Widgets. Once defined in XML, the layout must be "inflated" into the user interface. Within an Activity you do this using `setContentView` (usually within the `onCreate` method), whereas Fragments are inflated using the `inflate` method from the `Inflator` object passed in to the Fragment's `onCreateView` handler.

For more detailed information on using and creating layouts in Activities and Fragments, see Chapter 5, "Building User Interfaces."

Using layouts to construct your screens in XML is best practice in Android. The decoupling of the layout from the code enables you to create optimized layouts for different hardware configurations, such as varying screen sizes, orientation, or the presence of keyboards and touch screens as described later in this chapter.

Each layout definition is stored in its own XML file, within the `res/layout` folder, with the file-name becoming the resource identifier.

A thorough explanation of layout containers and View elements is included in the next chapter, but Listing 4-2 shows the layout created by the New Project Wizard. It uses a Constraint Layout container for a Text View that displays the "Hello World" greeting.

LISTING 4-2: Hello World layout

```xml
<?xml version="1.0" encoding="utf-8"?>
<android.support.constraint.ConstraintLayout
  xmlns:android="http://schemas.android.com/apk/res/android"
  xmlns:app="http://schemas.android.com/apk/res-auto"
  android:layout_width="match_parent"
  android:layout_height="match_parent">
  <TextView
    android:layout_width="wrap_content"
    android:layout_height="wrap_content"
    android:text="Hello World!"
    app:layout_constraintBottom_toBottomOf="parent"
    app:layout_constraintLeft_toLeftOf="parent"
    app:layout_constraintRight_toRightOf="parent"
    app:layout_constraintTop_toTopOf="parent"/>
</android.support.constraint.ConstraintLayout>
```

Animations

Android supports three types of animation that can be applied within a View or Activity, and is defined in XML:

➤ **Property animations**—A tweened animation that can be used to potentially animate any property on the target object by applying incremental changes between two values. This can be used for anything from changing the color or opacity of a View to gradually fade it in or out, to changing a font size, or increasing a character's hit points.

➤ **View animations**—Tweened animations that can be applied to rotate, move, fade, and stretch a View.

➤ **Frame animations**—Frame-by-frame "cell" animations used to display a sequence of Drawable images.

Android also includes the scene transition framework, which you can use to animate from one layout to another at run time by interpolating and modifying each of their property values of the views in each layout hierarchy.

> **NOTE** *You can find a comprehensive overview of creating, using, and applying animations and scene transitions in Chapter 14, "Advanced Customization of Your User Interface."*

Defining property, view, and frame animations as external resources enables you to reuse the same sequence in multiple places and provides you with the opportunity to present different animations based on device hardware or orientation.

Defining Property Animations

Property animators are a powerful framework that can be used to create interpolated animation paths for almost any value or property.

Each property animation is stored in a separate XML file in the project's res/animator folder. As with layouts and Drawable resources, the animation's filename is used as its resource identifier.

You can use a property animator to animate most numeric properties on a target object. You can define animators that are tied to a specific property, or a generic value animator that can be allocated to any property and object.

The following simple XML snippet shows a property animator that changes the opacity of the target object by calling its setAlpha method (or modifying the alpha property) incrementally between 0 and 1 over the course of a second:

```xml
<?xml version="1.0" encoding="utf-8"?>
<objectAnimator xmlns:android="http://schemas.android.com/apk/res/android"
    android:propertyName="alpha"
    android:duration="1000"
    android:valueFrom="0f"
    android:valueTo="1f"
/>
```

You can create more complex animations that modify multiple property values using the nestable set tag. Within each property animator set, you can choose to execute the grouped animations concurrently (the default option) or sequentially using the ordering tag as shown here:

```xml
<?xml version="1.0" encoding="utf-8"?>
<set xmlns:android="http://schemas.android.com/apk/res/android"
     android:ordering="sequentially">
  <set>
    <objectAnimator
      android:propertyName="x"
      android:duration="200"
      android:valueTo="0"
      android:valueType="intType"/>
    <objectAnimator
      android:propertyName="y"
      android:duration="200"
      android:valueTo="0"
      android:valueType="intType"/>
  </set>
```

```
<objectAnimator
  android:propertyName="alpha"
  android:duration="1000"
  android:valueTo="1f"/>
</set>
```

Note that property animations actually change the properties of the target object, and those modifications are persisted.

Defining View Animations

Each view animation is stored in a separate XML file in the project's `res/anim` folder. As with layouts and Drawable resources, the animation's filename is used as its resource identifier.

An animation can be defined for changes in `alpha` (fading), `scale` (scaling), `translate` (movement), or `rotate` (rotation).

> **NOTE** *While still sometimes useful, View animations have some significant restrictions compared to the new property animator described previously. As a result, it's typically good practice to use property animators whenever possible.*

Table 4-1 shows the valid attributes, and attribute values, supported by each animation type.

TABLE 4-1: Animation Type Attributes

ANIMATION TYPE	ATTRIBUTES	VALID VALUES
Alpha	fromAlpha/toAlpha	Float from 0 to 1
Scale	fromXScale/toXScale	Float from 0 to 1
	fromYScale/toYScale	Float from 0 to 1
	pivotX/pivotY	String of the percentage of graphic width/height from 0% to 100%
Translate	fromXDelta/toXDelta	One of either a float representing number of pixels relative to the normal position, a percentage relative to the element width (using "%" suffix), or a percentage relative to the parent width (using "%p" suffix).
	fromYDelta/toYDelta	One of either a float representing number of pixels relative to the normal position, a percentage relative to the element width (using "%" suffix), or a percentage relative to the parent width (using "%p" suffix).
Rotate	fromDegrees / toDegrees	Float from 0 to 360

ANIMATION TYPE	ATTRIBUTES	VALID VALUES
	pivotX/pivotY	String of the percentage of graphic width/height from 0% to 100%
		String indicating the X and Ycoordinate (respectively) in pixels relative to the object's left edge, or percentage relative to the object's left edge (using "%"), or in percentage relative to the parent container's left edge (using "%p").

You can create a combination of animations using the set tag. An animation set contains one or more animation transformations and supports various additional tags and attributes to customize when and how each animation within the set is run.

The following list shows some of the set tags available:

➤   duration—Duration of the full animation in milliseconds.

➤   startOffset—Millisecond delay before the animation starts.

➤   fillBefore—Applies the animation transformation before it begins.

➤   fillAfter—Applies the animation transformation after it ends.

➤   interpolator—Sets how the speed of this effect varies over time. Chapter 14 explores the interpolators available. To specify one, reference the system animation resources at android:anim/interpolatorName.

The following example shows an animation set that spins the target 360 degrees while it shrinks and fades out:

> **NOTE** *If you do not use the* startOffset *tag, all the animation effects within a set will execute simultaneously.*

```xml
<?xml version="1.0" encoding="utf-8"?>
<set xmlns:android="http://schemas.android.com/apk/res/android"
     android:interpolator="@android:anim/accelerate_interpolator">
  <rotate
    android:fromDegrees="0"
    android:toDegrees="360"
    android:pivotX="50%"
    android:pivotY="50%"
    android:startOffset="500"
    android:duration="1000" />
  <scale
    android:fromXScale="1.0"
    android:toXScale="0.0"
```

```
        android:fromYScale="1.0"
        android:toYScale="0.0"
        android:pivotX="50%"
        android:pivotY="50%"
        android:startOffset="500"
        android:duration="500" />
    <alpha
        android:fromAlpha="1.0"
        android:toAlpha="0.0"
        android:startOffset="500"
        android:duration="500" />
</set>
```

Defining Frame-by-Frame Animations

Frame-by-frame (cell) animations represent a sequence of Drawables, each of which is displayed for a specified duration.

Because frame-by-frame animations represent animated Drawables, they are stored in the res/ drawable folder and use their filenames (without the .xml extension) as their resource IDs.

The following XML snippet shows a simple animation that cycles through a series of bitmap resources, displaying each one for half a second. To use this snippet, you will also need to create new image resources android1 through android3:

```
<animation-list
  xmlns:android="http://schemas.android.com/apk/res/android"
  android:oneshot="false">
  <item android:drawable="@drawable/android1" android:duration="500" />
  <item android:drawable="@drawable/android2" android:duration="500" />
  <item android:drawable="@drawable/android3" android:duration="500" />
</animation-list>
```

Note that in many cases you should include multiple resolutions of each of the Drawables used within the animation list.

To play the animation, start by assigning the resource to a host View before getting a reference to the Animation Drawable object and starting it:

```
ImageView androidIV = findViewById(R.id.iv_android);
androidIV.setBackgroundResource(R.drawable.android_anim);

AnimationDrawable androidAnimation =
  (AnimationDrawable)androidIV.getBackground();

androidAnimation.start();
```

Typically, you do this in two steps; you assign the resource to the background within the onCreate handler.

Within this handler the animation is not fully attached to the window, so the animations can't be started; instead, this is usually done as a result to user action (such as a button press) or within the onWindowFocusChanged handler.

Using Resources

In addition to the resources you supply, the Android platform includes several system resources that you can use in your applications. All resources can be used within your application code, and can also be referenced from within other resources. For example, a dimension or string resource might be referenced in a layout definition.

Later in this chapter you learn how to define alternative resource values for different languages, locations, and hardware. It's important to note that when using resources, you don't choose a particular alternative; Android automatically selects the correct value for a given resource identifier based on the current hardware, device, and language configurations.

Using Resources in Code

Within your application, you access resources in code using the static R class. R is a generated class, created when your project is built, that lets you reference any resource you've included to offer design-time syntax checking.

The R class contains static subclasses for each of the resources available, such as R.string and R.drawable subclasses.

> **NOTE** *If you use Android Studio, the* R *class is created automatically when you build your application after making changes to an external resource file or folder. Remember that* R *is a build-generated class, so don't make any manual modifications to it because they will be lost when the file is regenerated.*

Each of the subclasses within R exposes its associated resources as variables, with the variable names matching the resource identifiers—for example, R.string.app_name or R.mipmap.ic_launcher.

The value of these variables is an integer that represents each resource's location in the resource table, *not* an instance of the resource itself.

Where a constructor or method, such as setContentView, accepts a resource identifier, you can pass in the resource variable, as shown in the following code snippet:

```
// Inflate a layout resource.
setContentView(R.layout.main);
// Display a transient dialog box that displays the
// app name string resource.
Toast.makeText(this, R.string.app_name, Toast.LENGTH_LONG).show();
```

When you need an instance of the resource itself, you need to use helper methods to extract them from the resource table. The resource table is represented within your application as an instance of the Resources class.

These methods perform lookups on the application's current resource table, so these helper methods can't be static. Use the getResources method on your application context, as shown in the following snippet, to access your application's Resources instance:

```
Resources myRes = getResources();
```

The `Resources` class includes getters for each of the available resource types and generally works by passing in the resource ID you'd like an instance of.

The Android Support Library also includes a `ResourcesCompat` class that offers backward-compatible getter functions where a Framework class has been deprecated (such as `getDrawable`).

The following code snippet shows an example of using the helper methods to return a selection of resource values:

```
CharSequence styledText = myRes.getText(R.string.stop_message);

float borderWidth = myRes.getDimension(R.dimen.standard_border);

Animation tranOut;
tranOut = AnimationUtils.loadAnimation(this, R.anim.spin_shrink_fade);

ObjectAnimator animator =
  (ObjectAnimator)AnimatorInflater.loadAnimator(this,
  R.animator.my_animator);

String[] stringArray;
stringArray = myRes.getStringArray(R.array.string_array);

int[] intArray = myRes.getIntArray(R.array.integer_array);
```

Android 5.0 Lollipop (API Level 21) added support for Drawable theming, so you should use the `ResourcesCompat` library to obtain both Drawable and Color resources as shown in the following snippet. Note that both methods accept `null` values for themes:

```
Drawable img = ResourcesCompat.getDrawable(myRes,
  R.drawable.an_image, myTheme);
int opaqueBlue = ResourcesCompat.getColor(myRes,
                              R.color.opaque_blue, myTheme);
```

Frame-by-frame animated resources are inflated into `AnimationResources`. You can return the value using `getDrawable` and casting the return value, as shown here:

```
AnimationDrawable androidAnimation;
androidAnimation =
  (AnimationDrawable)ResourcesCompat.getDrawable(R.myRes,
                              drawable.frame_by_frame,
                              myTheme);
```

Referencing Resources Within Resources

You can also use resource references as attribute values in other XML resources.

This is particularly useful for layouts and styles, letting you create specialized variations on themes and localized strings and image assets. It's also a useful way to support different images and spacing for a layout to ensure that it's optimized for different screen sizes and resolutions.

To reference one resource from another, use the @ notation, as shown in the following snippet:

```
attribute="@[packagename:]resourcetype/resourceidentifier"
```

> **NOTE** *Android assumes you use a resource from the same package, so you only need to fully qualify the package name if you use a resource from a different package.*

Listing 4-3 shows a layout that uses dimension, color, and string resources.

LISTING 4-3: Using resources in a layout

```xml
<?xml version="1.0" encoding="utf-8"?>
<RelativeLayout xmlns:android="http://schemas.android.com/apk/res/android"
  xmlns:tools="http://schemas.android.com/tools"
  android:id="@+id/activity_main"
  android:layout_width="match_parent"
  android:layout_height="match_parent"
  android:paddingBottom="@dimen/activity_vertical_margin"
  android:paddingLeft="@dimen/activity_horizontal_margin"
  android:paddingRight="@dimen/activity_horizontal_margin"
  android:paddingTop="@dimen/activity_vertical_margin"
  tools:context="com.professionalandroid.apps.helloworld.MainActivity">
  <TextView
    android:id="@+id/myTextView"
    android:layout_width="wrap_content"
    android:layout_height="wrap_content"
    android:textColor="@color/colorAccent"
    android:text="@string/hello"
  />
</RelativeLayout>
```

Using System Resources

The Android framework makes many native resources available, providing you with various strings, images, animations, styles, and layouts to use in your applications.

Accessing the system resources in code is similar to using your own resources. The difference is that you use the native Android resource classes available from `android.R`, rather than the application-specific `R` class. The following code snippet uses the `getString` method available in the application Context to retrieve an error message available from the system resources:

```java
CharSequence httpError = getString(android.R.string.httpErrorBadUrl);
```

To access system resources in XML, specify `android` as the package name, as shown in this XML snippet:

```xml
<EditText
  android:id="@+id/myEditText"
  android:layout_width="match_parent"
  android:layout_height="wrap_content"
  android:text="@android:string/httpErrorBadUrl"
  android:textColor="@android:color/darker_gray"
/>
```

You can find the full list of available Android resources at `developer.android.com/reference/android/R.html`.

Referring to Styles in the Current Theme

Using themes is an excellent way to ensure consistency for your application's UI. Rather than fully define each style, Android provides a shortcut to enable you to use styles from the currently applied theme.

To do this, use `?android:` rather than `@` as a prefix to the resource you want to use. The following example shows a snippet of the preceding code but uses the current theme's text color rather than a system resource:

```
<EditText
    android:id="@+id/myEditText"
    android:layout_width="match_parent"
    android:layout_height="wrap_content"
    android:text="@android:string/httpErrorBadUrl"
    android:textColor="?android:textColor"
/>
```

This technique enables you to create styles that change if the current theme changes, without you modifying each individual style resource. Note that the `textColor` resource value must be defined in the current theme. You learn more about using Themes and Styles in Chapter 13.

Creating Resources for Different Languages and Hardware

You can create different resource values for specific languages, locations, and hardware configurations using a parallel directory structure within the `res` folder.

A hyphen (-) is used to separate qualifiers that specify the conditions for which you are providing alternatives. Android chooses from among these values dynamically at run time using its dynamic resource-selection mechanism.

The following example hierarchy shows a folder structure that features default string values, with French language and French Canadian location variations:

```
Project/
  res/
    values/
      strings.xml
    values-fr/
      strings.xml
    values-fr-rCA/
      strings.xml
```

If you're using Android Studio, these parallel folders are represented as shown in Figure 4-4—a folder with the name of the file, that contains each version, followed by the qualifier in parentheses.

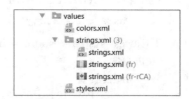

FIGURE 4-4

You can construct these qualified folders manually or, using Android Studio, you can create new folders as required when creating the alternative files they'll contain.

To do so, either right-click the parent folder (for example, `res/values`) and select "New [Values] resource file," or select the parent folder and select File ⇨ New ⇨ [Values] resource file. This displays the New Resource File dialog box as shown in Figure 4-5, which provides all the optional qualifier categories, and available options, before creating the folder and placing your new file within it. Note that not every available qualifier is available in the Android Studio dialog; in this case you'll have to create the folder manually.

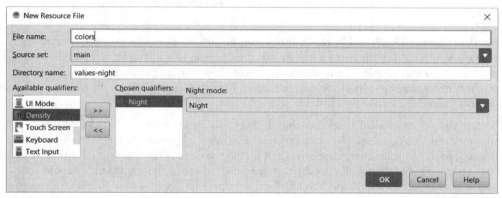

FIGURE 4-5

The following list gives the qualifiers you can use to customize your resource values:

➤ **Mobile Country Code and Mobile Network Code (MCC/MNC)**—The country, and optionally the network, associated with the SIM currently used in the device. The MCC is specified by `mcc` followed by the three-digit country code. You can optionally add the MNC using `mnc` and the two- or three-digit network code (for example, `mcc234-mnc20` or `mcc310`). You can find a list of MCC/MNC codes on Wikipedia at `en.wikipedia.org/wiki/Mobile_country_code`.

➤ **Language and Region**—Language specified by the lowercase two-letter ISO 639-1 language code, followed optionally by a region specified by a lowercase `r` followed by the uppercase two-letter ISO 3166-1-alpha-2 language code (for example, `en`, `en-rUS`, or `en-rGB`). Available under "locale" within the Android Studio "New Resource File" dialog.

➤ **Layout Direction**—The layout direction of your user interface where `ldrtl` represents right-to-left, and `ldltr` left-to-right (the default value). Use this modifier to provide a different layout (or any other resource) to better support right-to-left languages.

➤ **Smallest Screen Width**—The lowest of the device's screen dimensions (height and width) specified in the form `sw<Dimension value>dp` (for example, `sw600dp`, `sw320dp`, or `sw720dp`). This is generally used when providing multiple layouts, where the value specified should be the smallest screen width that your layout requires in order to render correctly. Where you supply multiple directories with different smallest screen width qualifiers, Android selects the largest value that doesn't exceed the smallest dimension available on the device.

➤ **Available Screen Width**—The minimum screen width required to use the contained resources, specified in the form `w<Dimension value>dp` (for example, `w600dp`, `w320dp`, or `w720dp`). Also used to supply multiple layouts alternatives, but unlike smallest screen width, the available screen width changes to reflect the current screen width when the device orientation changes. Android selects the largest value that doesn't exceed the currently available screen width.

➤ **Available Screen Height**—The minimum screen height required to use the contained resources, specified in the form `h<Dimension value>dp` (for example, `h720dp`, `h480dp`, or `h1280dp`). Like available screen width, the available screen height changes when the device orientation changes to reflect the current screen height. Android selects the largest value that doesn't exceed the currently available screen height.

➤ **Screen Size**—One of `small` (smaller than HVGA), `normal` (at least HVGA and typically smaller than VGA), `large` (VGA or larger), or `xlarge` (significantly larger than HVGA). Because each of these screen categories can include devices with significantly different screen sizes (particularly tablets), it's good practice to use the more specific smallest screen size, and available screen width and height whenever possible. Because they precede this screen size qualifier, where both are specified, the more specific qualifiers will be used in preference where supported.

➤ **Screen Aspect Ratio**—Specify `long` or `notlong` for resources designed specifically for wide screen. (For example, WVGA is `long`; QVGA is `notlong`.)

➤ **Screen Shape**—Specify `round` or `notround` for resources designed specifically for round screens (such as watches) or rectangular screens (such as phones or tablets), respectively.

➤ **Screen Color Gamut**—Specify `widecg` for resources designed for displays capable of displaying a wide color gamut such as Display P3 or AdobeRGB, or `nowidecg` for displays with a narrow color gamut such as sRGB.

➤ **Screen Dynamic Range**—Either `highdr` for displays that support a high-dynamic range (HDR) or `lowdr` for displays with a normal dynamic range.

➤ **Screen Orientation:** One of `port` (portrait) or `land` (landscape).

➤ **UI Mode**—Indicate resources (typically layouts) designed specifically for one of `car` (car dock), `desk` (desk dock), `television` (10 foot lean-back experience), `appliance` (no visible UI), `watch` (wrist mounted display), or `vrheadset` (virtual reality headset.

➤ **Night Mode**—One of `night` (night mode) or `notnight` (day mode). Used in combination with the UI mode qualifier, this provides a simple way to change the theme and/or color scheme of an application to make it more suitable for use at night.

➤ **Screen Pixel Density**—Pixel density in dots per inch (dpi). Best practice is to supply `ldpi`, `mdpi`, `hdpi`, `xhdpi`, and `xxhdpi` Drawable resources to include low (120 dpi), medium (160 dpi), high (240 dpi), extra high (320 dpi), and extra extra high (480 dpi) pixel density assets, to ensure crisp assets on all devices. For launcher icons, it's good practice to also supply an xxxhdpi resource for launchers that may choose to display a larger icon. You can specify nodpi for bitmap resources you don't want scaled to support an exact screen density, and anydpi for scalable vector graphics. To better support applications targeting televisions running Android, you can also use the tvdpi qualifier for assets of approximately 213dpi. This is generally unnecessary for most applications, where including medium- and high-resolution assets is sufficient for a good user experience. Unlike with other resource types, Android does not require an exact match to select a resource. When selecting the appropriate folder, it chooses the nearest match to the device's pixel density and scales the resulting Drawables accordingly.

➤ **Touchscreen Type**—Either notouch or finger, allowing you to provide layouts or dimensions optimized for the availability of touch screen input.

➤ **Keyboard Availability**—One of keysexposed, keyshidden, or keyssoft, representing a device that currently has a hardware keyboard available, a hardware keyboard that's not currently available, or uses a software keyboard (visible or not), respectively.

➤ **Keyboard Input Type**—One of nokeys, qwerty, or 12key representing no physical keyboard, a full qwerty keyboard, or 12-key physical keyboard, respectively—whether the keyboard is currently available or not.

➤ **Navigation Key Availability**—One of navexposed or navhidden.

➤ **UI Navigation Type**—One of nonav, dpad, trackball, or wheel.

➤ **Platform Version**—The target API level, specified in the form v<API Level> (for example, v7). Used for resources restricted to devices running at the specified API level or higher.

You can specify multiple qualifiers for any resource type, separating each qualifier with a hyphen. Any combination is supported; however, they must be used in the order given in the preceding list, and no more than one value can be used per qualifier.

The following example shows valid and invalid directory names for alternative layout resources:

Valid

```
layout-large-land
layout-xlarge-port-keyshidden
layout-long-land-notouch-nokeys
```

Invalid

```
values-rUS-en (out of order)
values-rUS-rUK (multiple values for a single qualifier)
```

When Android retrieves a resource at run time, it finds the best match from the available alternatives. Starting with a list of all the folders in which the required value exists, it selects the one with the greatest number of matching qualifiers. If two folders are an equal match, the tiebreaker is based on the order of the matched qualifiers in the preceding list.

> **WARNING** *If no resource matches are found on a given device, your application throws an exception when attempting to access that resource. To avoid this, you should always include default values for each resource type in a folder that includes no qualifiers.*

Runtime Configuration Changes

Android handles runtime changes to the language, location, and hardware by terminating and restarting the active Activity. This forces the resource resolution for the Activity to be reevaluated and the most appropriate resource values for the new configuration to be selected.

In some special cases this default behavior may be inconvenient, particularly for applications that don't want to alter UI based on screen orientation changes. You can customize your application's response to such changes by detecting and reacting to them yourself.

To have an Activity listen for runtime configuration changes, add an `android:configChanges` attribute to its manifest node, specifying the configuration changes you want to handle.

The following list describes some of the configuration changes you can specify:

➤ `mcc` and `mnc`—A SIM has been detected and the mobile country or network code (respectively) has changed.

➤ `locale`—The user has changed the device's language settings.

➤ `keyboardHidden`—The keyboard, d-pad, or other input mechanism has been exposed or hidden.

➤ `keyboard`—The type of keyboard has changed; for example, the phone may have a 12-key keypad that flips out to reveal a full keyboard, or an external keyboard might have been plugged in.

➤ `fontScale`—The user has changed the preferred font size.

➤ `uiMode`—The global UI mode has changed. This typically occurs if you switch between car mode, day or night mode, and so on.

➤ `orientation`—The screen has been rotated between portrait and landscape.

➤ `screenLayout`—The screen layout has changed; typically occurs if a different screen has been activated.

➤ `screenSize`—Occurs when the available screen size has changed; for example, a change in orientation between landscape and portrait or with multi-window mode.

➤ `smallestScreenSize`—Occurs when the physical screen size has changed, such as when a device has been connected to an external display.

➤ `layoutDirection`—The screen/text layout direction has changed; for example, switching between left-to-right and right-to-left (RTL).

In certain circumstances multiple events will be triggered simultaneously. For example, when the user slides out a keyboard, most devices fire both the keyboardHidden and orientation events, and connecting an external display is likely to trigger orientation, screenLayout, screenSize, and smallestScreenSize events.

You can select multiple events you want to handle yourself by separating the values with a pipe (|), as shown in Listing 4-4, which shows an Activity node declaring that it will handle changes in screen size and orientation, and access to a physical keyboard.

LISTING 4-4: Activity definition for handling dynamic resource changes

```
<activity
  android:name=".MyActivity"
  android:label="@string/app_name"
  android:configChanges="screenSize|orientation|keyboardHidden">
  <intent-filter >
    <action android:name="android.intent.action.MAIN" />
    <category android:name="android.intent.category.LAUNCHER" />
  </intent-filter>
</activity>
```

Adding an android:configChanges attribute suppresses the restart for the specified configuration changes, instead triggering the onConfigurationChanged handler in the associated Activity. Override this method to handle the configuration changes yourself, using the passed-in Configuration object to determine the new configuration values, as shown in Listing 4-5. Be sure to call back to the superclass and reload any resource values that the Activity uses, in case they've changed.

LISTING 4-5: Handling configuration changes in code

```
@Override
public void onConfigurationChanged(Configuration newConfig) {
  super.onConfigurationChanged(newConfig);

  // [ ... Update any UI based on resource values ... ]

  if (newConfig.orientation == Configuration.ORIENTATION_LANDSCAPE) {
    // [ ... React to different orientation ... ]
  }

  if (newConfig.keyboardHidden == Configuration.KEYBOARDHIDDEN_NO) {
    // [ ... React to changed keyboard visibility ... ]
  }
}
```

When onConfigurationChanged is called, the Activity's Resource variables have already been updated with the new values, so they'll be safe to use.

Any configuration change that you don't explicitly flag as being handled by your application will cause your Activity to restart, without a call to onConfigurationChanged.

5

Building User Interfaces

WROX.COM CODE DOWNLOADS FOR THIS CHAPTER

The code downloads for this chapter are found at www.wrox.com. The code for this chapter is divided into the following major examples:

➤ Snippets_ch5.zip

➤ Earthquake_ch5_1.zip

➤ Earthquake_ch5_2.zip

➤ Compass_ch5.zip

FUNDAMENTAL ANDROID DESIGN

At the beginning of the smart-phone era, Stephen Fry described the interplay of style and substance in the design of digital devices as follows:

> *As if a device can function if it has no style. As if a device can be called stylish that does not function superbly.... Yes, beauty matters. Boy, does it matter. It is not surface, it is not an extra, it is the thing itself.*
>
> —STEPHEN FRY, THE GUARDIAN (OCTOBER 27, 2007)

Although Fry was describing the style of the devices themselves, the same can be said of the applications that run on them.

That sentiment has only gained relevance since then—with design and user experience becoming increasingly important in the success of smart devices, and a significant focus for Android application developers.

Bigger, brighter, and higher resolution displays have made applications increasingly visual. As phones evolved beyond purely functional devices, and Android devices expanding past phone form factors, the user experience your application provides has become critically important.

For Android apps, this focus on design and user experience has most been apparent in the launch and adoption of the material design philosophy, which we'll describe in more detail in later chapters.

In this chapter, we'll focus on the Android components used to create UIs; you'll learn how to use Views to create functional and intuitive UIs within your Activities and Fragments.

The individual elements of an Android UI are arranged on screen by means of a variety of Layout Managers derived from the `ViewGroup` class. This chapter introduces several native layout classes, demonstrates how to use them, and introduces techniques to ensure your use of layouts is as efficient as possible.

You'll examine Android's data binding framework, and how it can be used to dynamically bind data to your UI based on your layouts. With many user interfaces based on lists of content, you'll learn how to use the `RecyclerView` to efficiently display lists connected to your underlying data sources.

Android also allows you to extend and customize the available Views and View Groups. Using View Groups, you'll combine Views to create atomic, reusable UI elements made up of interacting sub-controls. You'll also create your own Views to display data, and to interact with users in creative new ways.

DENSITY-INDEPENDENT DESIGN

User interface (UI) design, user experience (UX), human computer interaction (HCI), and usability are huge topics that can't be covered in the depth they deserve within the confines of this book. Nonetheless, the importance of creating a UI that your users will understand and enjoy using can't be overstated.

There is a huge variety of different Android devices, including a number of different sizes and form factors. From a UI perspective that means understanding that the number of pixels available to your application, and the underlying density of the display hardware, will vary significantly across devices.

You can abstract away the impact of different device densities by always thinking in terms of density-independent pixels (dp). Density-independent pixels represent *physical* sizes—two UI elements of the same size measured in dp, will *appear* to users as the same size on screen whether they are on a low-density device or newest super high-density screen. Knowing that users will physically interact with your UI (touching visual elements with their fingers) makes the importance and usefulness of this abstraction clear. Very few things are more frustrating than a button that is too small to tap!

For font sizes, we use the scalable pixel (sp). The sp shares the same base density independence as dp, but is also scaled independently based on the user's preferred text size: an important consideration for accessibility, allowing users to increase the font size for all apps on their device.

Android 5.0 Lollipop (API Level 21) introduced support for device-independent Vector Drawables. Vector Drawables are defined in XML, and can be scaled to support any display density. Alternatively, where you have assets that can't be described as vector graphics, the Android resource system will automatically down-scale graphics, or you can provide multiple resources in different resource folders, as described in Chapter 4.

As a result of making your designs density independent, you can focus on optimizing and adapting your designs for different screen sizes. You'll note that the UI elements throughout the book are written in terms of density-independent pixels (dp) and text sizes are written in terms of scalable pixels (sp).

ANDROID USER INTERFACE FUNDAMENTALS

All visual components in Android descend from the `View` class and are referred to generically as *Views*. You'll often see Views referred to as *controls* or *widgets* (not to be confused with home-screen App Widgets described in Chapter 19, "Invading the Home Screen")—terms you're probably familiar with if you've previously done GUI development on other platforms.

The `ViewGroup` class is an extension of `View` that supports adding child Views (commonly referred to as children). View Groups are responsible for deciding how large each child View is, and determining their positions. View Groups that focus primarily on laying out child Views are referred to as *layouts*.

View Groups are Views, so—like any other View—they can also draw their own customized UI, and handle user interactions.

The Views and View Groups included in the Android SDK provide the components you need to build an effective and accessible UI. You can create and lay out your Views within your UI programmatically, but it's strongly recommended to use XML layout resources to build and construct your UI. This approach makes it possible to specify different layouts optimized for different hardware configurations—particularly screen size variations—potentially even modifying them at run time based on hardware changes (such as orientation changes).

Each View contains a set of XML attributes that allow you to set its initial state from your layout resource. For example, to set the text on a `TextView`, you'd set the `android:text` attribute.

In the following sections you'll learn how to put together increasingly complex UIs, before being introduced to Fragments, the Views available in the SDK, how to extend these Views, build your own compound controls, and create your own custom Views from scratch.

Assigning User Interfaces to Activities

A new Activity starts with an invitingly empty screen, onto which you can place your UI. To do so, call `setContentView`, passing in the View instance, or layout resource, to display.

An empty screen lacks the visceral appeal required by today's savvy users, so you'll almost always use `setContentView` to assign an Activity's UI when overriding its `onCreate` handler. Because the `setContentView` method accepts either a layout's resource ID or a single View instance at the root of your view hierarchy, you can define your UI either in code or using the best-practice technique of external layout resources:

```
@Override
public void onCreate(Bundle savedInstanceState) {
    super.onCreate(savedInstanceState);
    setContentView(R.layout.main);
}
```

Using layout resources allows you to decouple the presentation layer from the application logic, providing the flexibility to change the presentation without changing code. This makes it possible to specify different layouts optimized for different hardware configurations, even changing them at run time based on hardware changes (such as screen orientation changes).

Once the layout has been set, you can obtain a reference to each of the Views within it using the `findViewById` method:

```
TextView myTextView = findViewById(R.id.myTextView);
```

If you're using Fragments to encapsulate portions of your Activity's UI, the View set within your Activity's `onCreate` handler will be a layout that describes the relative position of each of your Fragments (or their containers). The UI used for each Fragment is defined in its own layout and inflated within the Fragment itself and should, in almost all cases, be handled solely by that Fragment.

INTRODUCING LAYOUTS

In most cases, building your UI will include many Views contained within one or more nested *layouts*—extensions of the `ViewGroup` class. By combining different layouts and Views, you can create arbitrarily complex UIs.

The Android SDK includes a number of layout classes. You will use these, modify them, or create your own to construct UI layouts for your Views, Fragments, and Activities. Your challenge, should you choose to accept it, is to find the right combination of layouts to make your UI aesthetically pleasing, easy to use, and efficient to display.

The following list includes some of the most commonly used layout classes available in the Android SDK, as illustrated in Figure 5-1.

➤ `FrameLayout`—The simplest of the Layout Managers, the Frame Layout pins each child View within its frame. The default position is the top-left corner, though you can use the `layout_gravity` attribute on a child View to alter its location. Adding multiple children stacks each new child on top of the one before, with each new View potentially obscuring the previous ones.

➤ `LinearLayout`—The Linear Layout aligns its child Views in either a vertical or a horizontal line. A vertical layout has a column of Views, whereas a horizontal layout has a row of Views. The Linear Layout supports a `layout_weight` attribute for each child View that can control the relative size of each child View within the available space.

➤ `RelativeLayout`—One of the most flexible of the native layouts, though potentially expensive to render, the Relative Layout lets you define the positions of each child View relative to the others, and to the layout's boundaries.

➤ `ConstraintLayout`—The newest (and recommended) layout, it's designed to support large and complex layouts without the need to nest layouts. It's similar to the Relative Layout but provides greater flexibility and is more efficient to lay out. The Constraint Layout positions its child Views through a series of constraints—requiring child Views be positioned according to a boundary, other child Views, or to custom guidelines. The Constraint Layout has its own Visual Layout Editor, used to position each control and define the constraints rather than relying on manually editing the XML. The Constraint Layout is available through the Constraint Layout package of the Android Support Library, making it backward compatible.

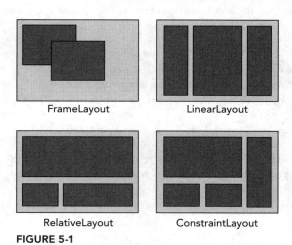

FrameLayout   LinearLayout

RelativeLayout   ConstraintLayout

FIGURE 5-1

Each of these layouts can scale to fill the host device's screen size by avoiding the use of absolute positions or predetermined pixel values. This makes them particularly useful when designing applications that work well on a diverse set of Android hardware.

Layouts use a variety of attributes assigned to the root node to modify the way in which all child nodes will be positioned (such as Linear Layout's `android:orientation` attribute):

```
<LinearLayout xmlns:android="http://schemas.android.com/apk/res/android"
  android:layout_width="match_parent"
  android:layout_height="match_parent"
  android:orientation="vertical">
  [... Child Views ...]
</LinearLayout>
```

To change the measurement and positioning of specific child Views, you will use `layout_` attributes within the child nodes directly. These attributes are used to instruct the parent `ViewGroup` on how the child should be laid out:

```
<LinearLayout xmlns:android="http://schemas.android.com/apk/res/android"
  android:layout_width="match_parent"
  android:layout_height="match_parent"
  android:orientation="vertical">
  <TextView
    android:layout_width="match_parent"
    android:layout_height="wrap_content"/>
</LinearLayout>
```

The most common `layout_` attributes are `layout_width` and `layout_height`—required attributes on all Views—but most layouts feature custom child View attributes to provide the majority of the layout-specific functionality they provide.

The Android documentation describes the features and properties of each layout class in detail; so, rather than repeat that information here, I'll refer you to `developer.android.com/guide/topics/ui/declaring-layout.html#CommonLayouts`.

> **NOTE** *When reviewing documentation on layout attributes, make sure to look at the* `LayoutParams` *class for the layout. For example, if the parent layout is a* `FrameLayout`, *documentation on its* `layout_gravity` *attribute will be found on the* `FrameLayout.LayoutParams` *class.*

You'll see practical example of how these layouts should be used as they're introduced in the examples throughout this book. Later in this chapter you'll also learn how to create compound controls by using and/or extending these layout classes.

Defining Layouts

The preferred way to define a layout is by using XML external resources, either by manually writing the XML or using the Constraint Layout's visual layout editor to create it for you.

Each layout XML must contain a single root element, which can contain as many nested layouts and Views as necessary to construct an arbitrarily complex UI.

The following snippet shows a simple layout that places a TextView above an EditText control using a vertical LinearLayout that covers the full screen height and width:

```xml
<?xml version="1.0" encoding="utf-8"?>
<LinearLayout xmlns:android="http://schemas.android.com/apk/res/android"
  android:layout_width="match_parent"
  android:layout_height="match_parent"
  android:orientation="vertical">
  <TextView
    android:layout_width="match_parent"
    android:layout_height="wrap_content"
    android:text="Enter Text Below" />
  <EditText
    android:layout_width="match_parent"
    android:layout_height="wrap_content"
    android:text="Text Goes Here!" />
</LinearLayout>
```

For each of the layout elements, the constants wrap_content and match_parent are used rather than specifying an exact height or width in pixels (or dp). These constants, combined with layouts that scale (such as the Linear Layout, Relative Layout, and Constraint Layout) offer the simplest, and most powerful, technique for ensuring your layouts are screen-size and resolution independent.

The wrap_content constant sets the size of a View to the minimum required to contain the contents it displays (such as the height required to display a wrapped text string). The match_parent constant expands the View to match the available space within the parent View, Fragment, or Activity.

Later in this chapter you'll learn how these constants are used when creating your own controls, as well as further best practices for resolution independence.

Implementing layouts in XML decouples the presentation layer from the View, Fragment, and Activity controller code and business logic. It also lets you create hardware configuration–specific variations that are dynamically loaded without requiring code changes.

When preferred, or required, you can implement layouts in code. When assigning Views to layouts in code, it's important to apply LayoutParameters using the setLayoutParams method, or by passing them into the addView call:

```java
LinearLayout ll = new LinearLayout(this);
ll.setOrientation(LinearLayout.VERTICAL);

TextView myTextView = new TextView(this);
EditText myEditText = new EditText(this);

myTextView.setText("Enter Text Below");
myEditText.setText("Text Goes Here!");

int lHeight = LinearLayout.LayoutParams.MATCH_PARENT;
int lWidth = LinearLayout.LayoutParams.WRAP_CONTENT;

ll.addView(myTextView, new LinearLayout.LayoutParams(lWidth, lHeight));
ll.addView(myEditText, new LinearLayout.LayoutParams(lWidth, lHeight));

setContentView(ll);
```

Using Layouts to Create Device-Independent User Interfaces

A defining feature of the layout classes is their ability to scale and adapt to a range of screen sizes, resolutions, and orientations.

The variety of Android devices is a critical part of the platform's success, but for us as application developers, it introduces a challenge in designing UIs that offer the best possible experience for users, regardless of which Android device they own.

Using a Linear Layout

The Linear Layout is one of the simplest layout classes. It allows you to create simple UIs (or UI elements) that align a sequence of child Views either vertically or horizontally.

The simplicity of the Linear Layout makes it easy to use, but limits its flexibility. In most cases you will use Linear Layouts to construct UI elements that will be nested within other layouts, such as the Relative or Constraint Layouts.

Listing 5-1 shows two nested Linear Layouts—a horizontal layout of two equally sized buttons within a vertical layout that places the buttons above a Recycler View.

LISTING 5-1: Using a Linear Layout

```xml
<?xml version="1.0" encoding="utf-8"?>
<LinearLayout
  xmlns:android="http://schemas.android.com/apk/res/android"
  android:layout_width="match_parent"
  android:layout_height="match_parent"
  android:orientation="vertical">
  <LinearLayout
    android:layout_width="match_parent"
    android:layout_height="wrap_content"
    android:layout_marginLeft="5dp"
    android:layout_marginRight="5dp"
    android:layout_marginTop="5dp"
    android:orientation="horizontal">
    <Button
      android:id="@+id/cancel_button"
      android:layout_width="match_parent"
      android:layout_height="wrap_content"
      android:layout_weight="1"
      android:text="@string/cancel_button_text" />
    <Button
      android:id="@+id/ok_button"
      android:layout_width="match_parent"
      android:layout_height="wrap_content"
      android:layout_weight="1"
      android:text="@string/ok_button_text" />
  </LinearLayout>
  <android.support.v7.widget.RecyclerView
    android:layout_width="match_parent"
    android:layout_height="match_parent"
```

```
          android:paddingBottom="5dp"
          android:clipToPadding="false" />
    </LinearLayout>
```

If you find yourself creating increasingly complex nesting patterns of Linear Layouts, you will likely be better served using a more flexible Layout Manager such as the Constraint Layout.

Using a Relative Layout

The Relative Layout provides a great deal of flexibility for your layouts, allowing you to define the position of each element within the layout in terms of its parent and the other Views.

Listing 5-2 modifies the layout described in Listing 5-1 to move the buttons below the Recycler View.

LISTING 5-2: Using a Relative Layout

```xml
<?xml version="1.0" encoding="utf-8"?>
<RelativeLayout
  xmlns:android="http://schemas.android.com/apk/res/android"
  android:layout_width="match_parent"
  android:layout_height="match_parent">
  <LinearLayout
    android:id="@+id/button_bar"
    android:layout_alignParentBottom="true"
    android:layout_width="match_parent"
    android:layout_height="wrap_content"
    android:layout_marginLeft="5dp"
    android:layout_marginRight="5dp"
    android:layout_marginBottom="5dp"
    android:orientation="horizontal">
    <Button
      android:id="@+id/cancel_button"
      android:layout_width="match_parent"
      android:layout_height="wrap_content"
      android:layout_weight="1"
      android:text="@string/cancel_button_text" />
    <Button
      android:id="@+id/ok_button"
      android:layout_width="match_parent"
      android:layout_height="wrap_content"
      android:layout_weight="1"
      android:text="@string/ok_button_text" />
  </LinearLayout>
  <android.support.v7.widget.RecyclerView
    android:layout_above="@id/button_bar"
    android:layout_alignParentLeft="true"
    android:layout_width="match_parent"
    android:layout_height="match_parent"
    android:paddingTop="5dp"
    android:clipToPadding="false" />
</RelativeLayout>
```

Using a Constraint Layout

The Constraint Layout provides the most flexibility of any of the Layout Managers, offering the advantage of both a visual layout editor, and a flat view hierarchy without the nesting shown in the previous examples.

It's available as part of the Android Support Library, and must be included as a dependency to your project's module-level `build.gradle` file:

```
dependencies {
  [... Existing dependencies ...]
  implementation 'com.android.support.constraint:constraint-layout:1.1.2'
}
```

As the name suggests, the Constraint Layout positions its child Views through the specification of constraints that define the relationship between a View and elements such as boundaries, other views, and custom guidelines.

While it's possible to define a Constraint Layout in XML manually, it's much simpler (and less error prone) to use the visual layout editor. Figure 5-2 shows the Layout Editor used to create the same UI as the previous example using a Constraint Layout.

FIGURE 5-2

Listing 5-3 shows the XML produced by the visual editor in Figure 5-2.

LISTING 5-3: USING A CONSTRAINT LAYOUT

```xml
<?xml version="1.0" encoding="utf-8"?>
<android.support.constraint.ConstraintLayout
  xmlns:android="http://schemas.android.com/apk/res/android"
  xmlns:app="http://schemas.android.com/apk/res-auto"
  android:layout_width="match_parent"
  android:layout_height="match_parent">
  <Button
    android:id="@+id/cancel_button"
    android:layout_width="0dp"
    android:layout_height="wrap_content"
    android:layout_marginStart="5dp"
    android:layout_marginBottom="5dp"
    app:layout_constraintStart_toStartOf="parent"
    app:layout_constraintEnd_toStartOf="@+id/ok_button"
    app:layout_constraintTop_toBottomOf="@+id/recyclerView"
    app:layout_constraintBottom_toBottomOf="parent"
    android:text="@string/cancel_button_text" />
  <Button
    android:id="@+id/ok_button"
    android:layout_width="0dp"
    android:layout_height="wrap_content"
    android:layout_marginEnd="5dp"
    android:layout_marginBottom="5dp"
    app:layout_constraintStart_toEndOf="@id/cancel_button"
    app:layout_constraintEnd_toEndOf="parent"
    app:layout_constraintTop_toBottomOf="@id/recyclerView"
    app:layout_constraintBottom_toBottomOf="parent"
    android:text="@string/ok_button_text" />
  <android.support.v7.widget.RecyclerView
    android:id="@+id/recyclerView"
    android:layout_width="0dp"
    android:layout_height="0dp"
    app:layout_constraintStart_toStartOf="parent"
    app:layout_constraintEnd_toEndOf="parent"
    app:layout_constraintTop_toTopOf="parent"
    app:layout_constraintBottom_toTopOf="@id/ok_button"
    android:paddingTop="5dp"
    android:clipToPadding="false" />
</android.support.constraint.ConstraintLayout>
```

Notice in particular that this layout removes the need to nest a second layout within the parent Constraint Layout. Flattening our hierarchy reduces the number of measure and layout passes required to render it on screen, making it more efficient as described in more detail in the following section.

Optimizing Layouts

Inflating layouts is an expensive process; each additional nested layout and included View directly impacts on the performance and responsiveness of your application. This is one of the reasons why Constraint Layout, with its ability to flatten the View hierarchy, is strongly recommended.

To keep your applications smooth and responsive, it's important to keep your layouts as simple as possible, and to avoid inflating entirely new layouts for relatively small UI changes.

Redundant Layout Containers Are Redundant

A Linear Layout within a Frame Layout, both of which are set to MATCH_PARENT, does nothing but add extra time to inflate. Look for redundant layouts, particularly if you've been making significant changes to an existing layout or are adding child layouts to an existing layout.

Layouts can be arbitrarily nested, so it's easy to create complex, deeply nested hierarchies. Although there is no hard limit, it's good practice to restrict nesting to fewer than 10 levels.

One common example of unnecessary nesting is a Frame Layout used to create the single root node required for a layout, as shown in the following snippet:

```xml
<?xml version="1.0" encoding="utf-8"?>
<FrameLayout
  xmlns:android="http://schemas.android.com/apk/res/android"
  android:layout_width="match_parent"
  android:layout_height="match_parent">
  <ImageView
    android:id="@+id/myImageView"
    android:layout_width="match_parent"
    android:layout_height="match_parent"
    android:src="@drawable/myimage"
  />
  <TextView
    android:id="@+id/myTextView"
    android:layout_width="match_parent"
    android:layout_height="wrap_content"
    android:text="@string/hello"
    android:gravity="center_horizontal"
    android:layout_gravity="bottom"
  />
</FrameLayout>
```

In this example, when the Frame Layout is added to a parent, it will become redundant. A better alternative is to use the merge tag:

```xml
<?xml version="1.0" encoding="utf-8"?>
<merge
  xmlns:android="http://schemas.android.com/apk/res/android">
  <ImageView
    android:id="@+id/myImageView"
    android:layout_width="match_parent"
    android:layout_height="match_parent"
    android:src="@drawable/myimage"
  />
  <TextView
    android:id="@+id/myTextView"
    android:layout_width="match_parent"
    android:layout_height="wrap_content"
    android:text="@string/hello"
    android:gravity="center_horizontal"
    android:layout_gravity="bottom"
  />
</merge>
```

When a layout containing a merge tag is added to another layout, the merge node is removed and its child Views are added directly to the new parent.

The merge tag is particularly useful in conjunction with the include tag, which is used to insert the contents of one layout into another:

```xml
<?xml version="1.0" encoding="utf-8"?>
<LinearLayout
  xmlns:android="http://schemas.android.com/apk/res/android"
  android:orientation="vertical"
  android:layout_width="match_parent"
  android:layout_height="match_parent">
  <include android:id="@+id/my_action_bar"
            layout="@layout/actionbar"/>
  <include android:id="@+id/my_image_text_layout"
            layout="@layout/image_text_layout"/>
</LinearLayout>
```

Combining the merge and include tags enables you to create flexible, reusable layout definitions that don't create deeply nested layout hierarchies. You'll learn more about creating and using simple and reusable layouts later in this chapter.

Avoid Using Excessive Views

Each additional View takes time and resources to inflate. To maximize the speed and responsiveness of your application, none of its layouts should include more than 80 Views. When you exceed this limit, the time taken to inflate the layout can become significant.

To minimize the number of Views inflated within a complex layout, you can use a ViewStub.

A View Stub works like a lazy include—a stub that represents the specified child Views within the parent layout—but the stub is only inflated explicitly via the inflate method or when it's made visible:

```java
// Find the stub
View stub = findViewById(R.id.download_progress_panel_stub);
// Make it visible, causing it to inflate the child layout
stub.setVisibility(View.VISIBLE);

// Find the root node of the inflated stub layout
View downloadProgressPanel = findViewById(R.id.download_progress_panel);
```

As a result, the Views contained within the child layout aren't created until they are required—minimizing the time and resource cost of inflating complex UIs.

When adding a View Stub to your layout, you can override the id and layout parameters of the root View of the layout it represents:

```xml
<?xml version="1.0" encoding="utf-8"?>
<FrameLayout "xmlns:android=http://schemas.android.com/apk/res/android"
  android:layout_width="match_parent"
  android:layout_height="match_parent">
  <ListView
```

```
    android:id="@+id/myListView"
    android:layout_width="match_parent"
    android:layout_height="match_parent"
  />
  <ViewStub
    android:id="@+id/download_progress_panel_stub"

    android:layout="@layout/progress_overlay_panel"
    android:inflatedId="@+id/download_progress_panel"

    android:layout_width="match_parent"
    android:layout_height="wrap_content"
    android:layout_gravity="bottom"
  />
</FrameLayout>
```

This snippet modifies the width, height, and gravity of the imported layout to suit the requirements of the parent layout. This flexibility makes it possible to create and reuse the same generic child layouts in a variety of parent layouts.

An ID has been specified for both the stub and the View Group it will become when inflated using the `id` and `inflatedId` attribute, respectively.

> **NOTE** *When the View Stub is inflated, it is removed from the hierarchy and replaced by the root node of the View it imported. If you need to modify the visibility of the imported Views, you must either use the reference to their root node (returned by the* `inflate` *call) or find the View by using* `findViewById`*, using the layout ID assigned to it within the corresponding View Stub node.*

Using Lint to Analyze Your Layouts

To assist you in optimizing your layout hierarchies, the Android SDK includes `lint`—a powerful tool that you can use to detect problems within your application, including layout performance issues.

The Lint tool is available within Android Studio through the Inspect Code option in the Analyze menu as shown in Figure 5-3, or as a command-line tool.

In addition to using Lint to detect each optimization issue described previously in this section, you can also use Lint to detect missing translations, unused resources, inconsistent array sizes, accessibility and internationalization problems, missing or duplicated image assets, usability problems, and manifest errors.

Lint is a constantly evolving tool, with new rules added regularly. You can find a full list of the tests performed by the Lint tool at `http://tools.android.com/tips/lint-checks`.

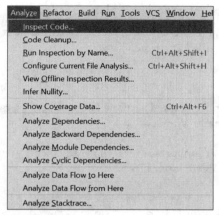

FIGURE 5-3

THE ANDROID WIDGET TOOLBOX

Android supplies a toolbox of standard Views to help you create your UIs. By using these controls (and modifying or extending them, as necessary), you can simplify your development and provide consistency across applications and with the Android system UI.

The following list highlights some of the more familiar controls:

➤ TextView—A standard read-only text label that supports multiline display, string formatting, and automatic word-wrapping.

➤ EditText—An editable text entry box that accepts multiline entry, word-wrapping, and hint text.

➤ ImageView—A View that shows a single image.

➤ Toolbar—A View that shows a title and common actions, often used as the main app bar at the top of an Activity.

➤ ProgressBar—A View that shows either an indeterminate progress indicator (a spinning circle) or a horizontal progress bar.

➤ RecyclerView—A View Group that manages displaying a large number of Views in a scrolling container. Supports a number of layout managers that allow you to lay out Views as a vertical and horizontal list or a grid.

➤ Button—A standard interactive push button.

➤ ImageButton—A push button for which you can specify a customized background image.

➤ CheckBox—A two-state button represented by a checked or unchecked box.

➤ RadioButton—A two-state grouped button. A group of these presents the user with a number of possible options, of which only one can be enabled at a time.

➤ VideoView—Handles all state management and display Surface configuration for playing videos more simply from within your Activity.

➤ ViewPager—Implements a horizontally scrolling set of Views. The View Pager allows users to swipe or drag left or right to switch between different Views.

This is only a selection of the widgets available. Android also supports several more advanced View implementations, including date-time pickers, and auto-complete input boxes.

> **NOTE** *Chapter 12, "Implementing the Android Design Philosophy," and Chapter 13, "Implementing a Modern Android User Experience," introduce the Design Library and several new material design components that are included within it, including tabs, Floating Action Buttons , and the bottom navigation bar. These material design components are expected to go through a much faster evolution, including deprecation of whole components, than these basic building block UI elements.*

WORKING WITH LISTS AND GRIDS

When you need to display a large dataset within your UI, it may be tempting to add hundreds of Views to your UI. This is almost always the wrong approach. Instead, the RecyclerView (available from the Android Support Library) offers a scrollable View Group specifically designed to efficiently display, and scroll through, a large number of items.

The Recycler View can be used in both vertical and horizontal orientations, configured using the android:orientation attribute:

```
<android.support.v7.widget.RecyclerView
  xmlns:android="http://schemas.android.com/apk/res/android"
  xmlns:app="http://schemas.android.com/apk/res-auto"
  android:id="@+id/recycler_view"
  android:layout_width="match_parent"
  android:layout_height="match_parent"
  android:orientation="vertical"
  [... Layout Manager Attributes ...]
/>
```

In a vertical orientation, items are laid out from top to bottom and the Recycler View scrolls vertically, while a horizontal orientation will lay out items from left to right and the Recycler View will scroll horizontally.

Recycler View and Layout Managers

The `RecyclerView` itself doesn't control how each item is displayed; that responsibility belongs to the associated `RecyclerView.LayoutManager`. This separation of duties allows you to substitute Layout Manager classes, without affecting other parts of your application.

A number of Layout Managers are available, as shown in Figure 5-4, and described here:

➤ `LinearLayoutManager`—Lays out items in a single vertical or horizontal list.

➤ `GridLayoutManager`—Similar to the Linear Layout Manager, but displays a grid. When laid out vertically, each row can include multiple items, where each is the same height. For horizontal orientation each item in a given column must be the same width.

➤ `StaggeredGridLayoutManager`—Similar to the Grid Layout Manager but creates a "staggered" grid, where each grid cell can have a different height or width, with cells staggered to eliminate gaps.

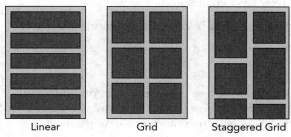

Linear   Grid   Staggered Grid

FIGURE 5-4

The Layout Manager operates in the same way as a standard layout—responsible for laying out the Views representing each item in your dataset.

The Recycler View gets its name from the way it supports scrolling. Rather than creating a view for each item upfront, or continually creating them when they're scrolled into view, the Recycler View is able to "recycle" existing Views that are no longer visible—changing their content and position to represent newly visible items.

To support this behavior, the Layout Manager is also responsible for determining when a View can safely be recycled. In most cases, this allows the Recycler View to support a nearly infinite (2^{26}) list of items, while creating just enough Views to fill a single screen.

The Layout Manager for a Recycler View can be set either in XML or programmatically.

For example, the following snippet lays out a vertically aligned Recycler View with a Grid Layout Manager that features two columns:

```
<android.support.v7.widget.RecyclerView
  xmlns:android:"http://schemas.android.com/apk/res/android"
  xmlns:app="http://schemas.android.com/apk/res-auto"
```

```
    android:id="@+id/recycler_view"
    android:layout_width="match_parent"
    android:layout_height="match_parent"
    android:orientation="vertical"
    app:layoutManager="GridLayoutManager"
    app:spanCount="2"
/>
```

To assign the same Layout Manager in code, for an existing Recycler View, you would use the following snippet:

```
RecyclerView recyclerView = findViewById(R.id.recycler_view);
GridLayoutManager gridLayoutManager = new GridLayoutManager(2);
recyclerView.setLayoutManager(gridLayoutManager);
```

Introducing Adapters

Layout Managers aren't particularly useful until you have data for them to display; that data is provided by the `RecyclerView.Adapter`. The Adapter has two important roles:

➤ The initial creation of the Views to display, including inflating the appropriate layout

➤ The creation of the View Holders you'll use to "bind" the View elements to the underlying data source

A View Holder stores the View to be displayed, and also allows the Adapter to store additional metadata and View references to simplify data binding, as shown later. This typically includes finding references to any child Views within an item layout (ensuring that work is only done once).

The Adapter's `onCreateViewHolder` method is called to get a new `RecyclerView.ViewHolder` instance whenever the Layout Manager doesn't have an unused View to reuse—typically only enough views to fill the screen.

Listing 5-4 shows a simple Adapter implementation that uses a single Text View to display a data stored in an array of strings.

LISTING 5-4: Creating a Recycler View Adapter

```
public class SimpleAdapter
    extends RecyclerView.Adapter<SimpleAdapter.ViewHolder> {

  // Underlying data to be displayed.
  private String[] mData;

  // Set the initial data in the constructor
  public SimpleAdapter(String[] data) {
    mData = data;
  }
```

```java
// Tell the Layout Manager how many items exist in the data
@Override
public int getItemCount() {
  return mData == null ? 0 : mData.length;
}

public static class ViewHolder extends RecyclerView.ViewHolder {
  public TextView textView;

  public ViewHolder(View v) {
    super(v);
    // Only do findViewById once
    textView = v.findViewById(R.id.text);
  }
}

@Override
public SimpleAdapter.ViewHolder onCreateViewHolder(
    ViewGroup parent, int viewType) {
  // Create the new View
  View v = LayoutInflater.from(parent.getContext())
            .inflate(R.layout.simple_text, parent, false);

  return new ViewHolder(v);
}
```

Notice that the View Holder itself doesn't assign values from the underlying data to the Views it contains—its role is to make the elements within the View's layout available for the adapter to bind data to them.

Every time an item needs to be displayed, the Layout Manager will call the Adapter's `onBindView-Holder` method, providing you a previously created `ViewHolder` and the position in the dataset requested. This binding phase runs very frequently when scrolling through a list (once for every element that scrolls into view) so it should be as lightweight as possible.

```java
@Override
public void onBindViewHolder(ViewHolder holder, int position) {
  holder.textView.setText(mData[position]);
}
```

> **NOTE** *When binding a new data element, it's important to reset any View element that may have been set previously. Because the View Holder (and its View elements) are constantly reused, they will retain any state set from previous* `onBindViewHolder` *calls.*

To assign your Adapter to a Recycler View, use the `setAdapter` method:

```java
RecyclerView recyclerView = findViewById(R.id.recycler_view);
SimpleAdapter adapter =
  new SimpleAdapter(new String[] {"Sample", "Sample 2"});

recyclerView.setAdapter(adapter);
```

Static datasets like this example are fun, but in reality we're rarely that lucky. In most cases the underlying data will change when new data is loaded from the server, if the user adds or deletes an item, or even if the sort order is changed.

When you update an Adapter with new or changed data, you must call one of the Adapter's `notify` methods to inform the Layout Manager that something has changed. The `RecyclerView` will then animate a transition between the previous and updated states (cross fading changed items, collapsing and removing removed items, and animating in new items).

You can customize the animations used for each state change by assigning a `RecyclerView` `.ItemAnimator` using the `setItemAnimator` method.

There are different methods for notifying the change, insertion, move, or removal of a single item, and for a range of items. You can use the `DiffUtil` class to understand which changes should be applied to transition from one dataset to another, as shown in Listing 5-5.

LISTING 5-5: Calculating the transitions between datasets

```java
public class SimpleAdapter
    extends RecyclerView.Adapter<SimpleAdapter.ViewHolder> {

  [... Existing SimpleAdapter Implementation ...]

  public void setData(final String[] newData) {
    // Store a copy of the previous data
    final String[] previousData = mData;

    // apply the new data
    mData = newData;

    // Calculate the differences between the old and new data
    DiffUtil.calculateDiff(new DiffUtil.Callback() {
      @Override
      public int getOldListSize() {
        return previousData != null ? previousData.length : 0;
      }

      @Override
      public int getNewListSize() {
        return newData != null ? previousData.length : 0;
      }

      @Override
      public boolean areItemsTheSame(int oldItemPosition,
                                     int newItemPosition) {
        // This method should compare the item's unique identifiers
        // if available. Returning true means the two items should be
        // crossfaded. In this example, we don't have an identifier,
        // so we'll compare the string values.
        return TextUtils.equals(previousData[oldItemPosition],
                                newData[newItemPosition]);
      }
```

```
      @Override
      public boolean areContentsTheSame(int oldItemPosition,
                                        int newItemPosition) {
        // This method should do a deep inspection of the items to determine
        // if their visible contents are the same.
        // If they are the same, no animation is required.
        // In this example, if the items are the same,
        // the contents are the same
        return true;
      }
  }).dispatchUpdatesTo(this);
  }
}
```

Returning to the Earthquake Viewer Application

With the newfound knowledge of layouts and Views, we can improve the Earthquake Viewer built in Chapter 3, replacing the simple `TextView` with a more complicated layout that better displays the data in the `Earthquake` class:

1. Replace the `list_item_earthquake.xml` layout resource with a new layout that uses a Constraint Layout to display the magnitude, date, and details in separate Text Views:

```xml
<?xml version="1.0" encoding="utf-8"?>
<android.support.constraint.ConstraintLayout
  xmlns:android="http://schemas.android.com/apk/res/android"
  xmlns:app="http://schemas.android.com/apk/res-auto"
  android:layout_width="match_parent"
  android:layout_height="wrap_content"
  android:paddingLeft="@dimen/activity_vertical_margin"
  android:paddingRight="@dimen/activity_vertical_margin">
  <TextView
    android:id="@+id/magnitude"
    android:layout_width="wrap_content"
    android:layout_height="0dp"
    android:gravity="center_vertical"
    app:layout_constraintRight_toRightOf="parent"
    app:layout_constraintTop_toTopOf="parent"
    app:layout_constraintBottom_toBottomOf="parent"
    android:textAppearance="?attr/textAppearanceListItem"/>
  <TextView
    android:id="@+id/date"
    android:layout_width="0dp"
    android:layout_height="wrap_content"
    android:layout_marginTop="@dimen/text_margin"
    app:layout_constraintLeft_toLeftOf="parent"
    app:layout_constraintTop_toTopOf="parent"
    app:layout_constraintRight_toLeftOf="@id/magnitude"/>
  <TextView
    android:id="@+id/details"
    android:layout_width="0dp"
    android:layout_height="wrap_content"
    android:layout_marginBottom="@dimen/text_margin"
    app:layout_constraintLeft_toLeftOf="parent"
    app:layout_constraintBottom_toBottomOf="parent"
```

```
            app:layout_constraintRight_toLeftOf="@id/magnitude"
            app:layout_constraintTop_toBottomOf="@id/date"/>
    </android.support.constraint.ConstraintLayout>
```

2. Update the `EarthquakeRecyclerViewAdapter` to cache the new Views elements added in Step 1 within the View Holder constructor, and then bind those Views to each `Earthquake` item within the `onBindViewHolder` by using `java.text.SimpleDateFormat`:

```
private static final SimpleDateFormat TIME_FORMAT =
    new SimpleDateFormat("HH:mm", Locale.US);
private static final NumberFormat MAGNITUDE_FORMAT =
    new DecimalFormat("0.0");

public static class ViewHolder extends RecyclerView.ViewHolder {
  public final TextView date;
  public final TextView details;
  public final TextView magnitude;

  public ViewHolder(View view) {
    super(view);
    date = (TextView) view.findViewById(R.id.date);
    details = (TextView) view.findViewById(R.id.details);
    magnitude = (TextView) view.findViewById(R.id.magnitude);
  }
}

@Override
public void onBindViewHolder(ViewHolder holder, int position) {
  Earthquake earthquake = mEarthquakes.get(position);

  holder.date.setText(TIME_FORMAT.format(earthquake.getDate()));
  holder.details.setText(earthquake.getDetails());
  holder.magnitude.setText(
      MAGNITUDE_FORMAT.format(earthquake.getMagnitude()));
}
```

INTRODUCING DATA BINDING

The Data Binding library makes it possible to write declarative layouts that minimize the glue code needed to bind View elements to underlying data sources by generating that code for you at compile time.

> **NOTE** *Data Binding is a complex topic that is beyond the scope of this book. We'll introduce you to the fundamentals, but recommend you refer to the Android Developer documentation to dive into the details at* `developer.android` `.com/topic/libraries/data-binding`.

Enabling Data Binding

Data Binding is an optional library, so before you can take advantage of it you must enable it in your application module's `build.gradle` file:

```
android {
  [... Existing Android Node ...]
  dataBinding.enabled = true
}

dependencies {
  [... Existing dependencies element ...]
  implementation 'com.android.support:support-v4:27.1.1'
}
```

Once enabled, you can apply Data Binding to any layout by wrapping the elements of a layout file in a new `<layout>` element, as seen in Listing 5-6:

LISTING 5-6: Enabling Data Binding in a layout

```xml
<?xml version="1.0" encoding="utf-8"?>
<layout
  xmlns:android="http://schemas.android.com/apk/res/android">
  <LinearLayout
    android:layout_width="match_parent"
    android:layout_height="wrap_content"
    android:orientation="vertical">
    <TextView
      android:id="@+id/user_name"
      android:layout_width="match_parent"
      android:layout_height="wrap_content" />
    <TextView
      android:id="@+id/email"
      android:layout_width="match_parent"
      android:layout_height="wrap_content" />
  </LinearLayout>
</layout>
```

This triggers Data Binding to generate a Binding class based on the name of the modified layout file. For example, for a layout defined in `profile_activity.xml`, the generated Binding class would be named `ProfileActivityBinding`.

You create an instance of a Binding class using `DataBindingUtil`, and use its `setContentView` method in place of the Activity's `setContentView`:

```
ProfileActivityBinding binding =
    DataBindingUtil.setContentView(this, R.layout.profile_activity);
```

For inflating the View associated with a Fragment or Recycler View item, you would use the Binding class's `inflate` method:

```
ProfileActivityBinding binding =
    ProfileActivityBinding.inflate(layoutInflater, viewGroup, false);
```

Alternatively, you can create a Data Binding class from an existing View:

```
ProfileActivityBinding binding =
    (ProfileActivityBinding) DataBindingUtil.bind(view);
```

The Binding class automatically calls `findViewById` on each View with an ID within the associated layout, so instead of keeping a reference to every View in your layout or having to call `findViewById` yourself, you can reference the View through the Binding class:

```
binding.userName.setText("professionalandroid");
binding.email.setText("example@example.com");
```

Variables in Data Binding

The power of this fully operational Data Binding is its ability to simplify the process of dynamically binding your underlying data to the layout. You do this by adding a `<data>` element and declaring variables that can be used within the layout using the `@{name.classvariable}` syntax as shown in Listing 5-7.

LISTING 5-7: Applying Data Binding variables in a layout

```xml
<?xml version="1.0" encoding="utf-8"?>
<layout
  xmlns:android="http://schemas.android.com/apk/res/android">
  <data>
    <variable name="user" type="com.professionalandroid.databinding.User" />
  </data>
  <LinearLayout
    android:layout_width="match_parent"
    android:layout_height="wrap_content"
    android:orientation="vertical">
    <TextView
      android:layout_width="match_parent"
      android:layout_height="wrap_content"
      android:text="@{user.userName}" />
    <TextView
      android:layout_width="match_parent"
      android:layout_height="wrap_content"
      android:text="@{user.email}" />
  </LinearLayout>
</layout>
```

By declaring a variable named `user`, of the class `User`, our Binding class will generate a `setUser` method.

Calling this method will set all of the properties referencing that class using the `@{}` syntax. Data Binding will look for public variables, getter methods of the style `get<Variable>` or `is<Variable>` (for example, `getEmail` or `isValid`), or the exact method name when resolving expressions:

```
User user = new User("professionalandroid", "example@example.com");
binding.setUser(user);
```

This allows you to keep all of the View-specific logic in the layout file itself while your code can focus on only providing the appropriate data to the Binding class.

You'll note that the `android:id` attributes were removed in the preceding example because Data Binding does not require IDs to evaluate variable expressions.

In addition to specifying variables, you can use almost all Java language syntax within these expressions. For example, you can use the null-coalescing operator `??` to shorten simple ternary expressions:

```
android:text='@{user.email ?? "No email"}'
```

By default, any variables binding you apply is done after the next frame redraw. This can cause a visible flicker when used in scrollable views such as Recycler View. To avoid this, call `executePendingBindings` after setting your variables, causing the binding to be done immediately:

```
User user = userList.get(position);
binding.setUser(user);
binding.executePendingBindings();
```

Data Binding for the Earthquake Viewer Application

Data Binding enables us to simplify the Earthquake Viewer's `RecyclerView.Adapter` by binding each `Earthquake` to the layout for each row:

1. Update the `build.gradle` file to enable data binding:

```
android {
  [... Existing android element ...]
  dataBinding.enabled = true
}

dependencies {
  [... Existing dependencies element ...]
  implementation 'com.android.support:support-v4:27.1.1'
}
```

2. Update the `list_item_earthquake.xml` layout resource to take advantage of Data Binding:

```
<?xml version="1.0" encoding="utf-8"?>
<layout
  xmlns:android="http://schemas.android.com/apk/res/android"
  xmlns:app="http://schemas.android.com/apk/res-auto">
  <data>
    <variable name="timeformat" type="java.text.DateFormat" />
    <variable name="magnitudeformat" type="java.text.NumberFormat" />
    <variable name="earthquake"
      type="com.professionalandroid.apps.earthquake.Earthquake" />
  </data>
  <android.support.constraint.ConstraintLayout
    android:layout_width="match_parent"
    android:layout_height="wrap_content"
    android:paddingLeft="@dimen/activity_vertical_margin"
    android:paddingRight="@dimen/activity_vertical_margin">
    <TextView
      android:id="@+id/magnitude"
      android:layout_width="wrap_content"
      android:layout_height="0dp"
      android:gravity="center_vertical"
```

```
        app:layout_constraintRight_toRightOf="parent"
        app:layout_constraintTop_toTopOf="parent"
        app:layout_constraintBottom_toBottomOf="parent"
        android:textAppearance="?attr/textAppearanceListItem"
        android:text="@{magnitudeformat.format(earthquake.magnitude)}"/>
      <TextView
        android:id="@+id/date"
        android:layout_width="0dp"
        android:layout_height="wrap_content"
        android:layout_marginTop="@dimen/text_margin"
        app:layout_constraintLeft_toLeftOf="parent"
        app:layout_constraintTop_toTopOf="parent"
        app:layout_constraintRight_toLeftOf="@id/magnitude"
        android:text="@{timeformat.format(earthquake.date)}"/>
      <TextView
        android:layout_width="0dp"
        android:layout_height="wrap_content"
        android:layout_marginBottom="@dimen/text_margin"
        app:layout_constraintLeft_toLeftOf="parent"
        app:layout_constraintBottom_toBottomOf="parent"
        app:layout_constraintRight_toLeftOf="@id/magnitude"
        app:layout_constraintTop_toBottomOf="@id/date"
        android:text="@{earthquake.details}"/>
    </android.support.constraint.ConstraintLayout>
  </layout>
```

3. Generate the Binding class by rebuilding the project. You can trigger this manually via the Build ⇨ Make Project menu item.

4. Update the `EarthquakeRecyclerViewAdapter.ViewHolder` to receive the Binding class as the input and do the one-time initialization of setting the time and magnitude format variables:

```
public static class ViewHolder extends RecyclerView.ViewHolder {
  public final ListItemEarthquakeBinding binding;

  public ViewHolder(ListItemEarthquakeBinding binding) {
    super(binding.getRoot());
    this.binding = binding;
    binding.setTimeformat(TIME_FORMAT);
    binding.setMagnitudeformat(MAGNITUDE_FORMAT);
  }
}
```

5. Update the `EarthquakeRecyclerViewAdapter` to create the Binding class in `onCreateView-Holder` and simplify `onBindViewHolder`:

```
@Override
public ViewHolder onCreateViewHolder(ViewGroup parent, int viewType) {
  ListItemEarthquakeBinding binding = ListItemEarthquakeBinding.inflate(
    LayoutInflater.from(parent.getContext()), parent, false);
  return new ViewHolder(binding);
}
```

```
@Override
public void onBindViewHolder(ViewHolder holder, int position) {
    Earthquake earthquake = mEarthquakes.get(position);
    holder.binding.setEarthquake(earthquake);
    holder.binding.executePendingBindings();
}
```

CREATING NEW VIEWS

It's only a matter of time before you, as an innovative developer, encounter a situation in which none of the built-in controls meets your needs.

The ability to extend existing Views, assemble composite controls, and create unique new Views makes it possible to implement beautiful UIs optimized for your application's specific workflow. Android lets you subclass the existing View toolbox or implement your own View controls, giving you total freedom to tailor your UI to optimize the user experience.

> **NOTE** *When designing a UI, it's important to balance raw aesthetics and usability. With the power to create your own custom controls comes the temptation to rebuild all your controls from scratch. Resist that urge. The standard Views will be familiar to users from other Android applications and will update in line with new platform releases. On small screens, with users often paying limited attention, familiarity can often provide better usability than a slightly shinier control.*

The best approach to use when creating a new View depends on what you want to achieve:

➤ **Modify or extend the appearance and/or behavior of an existing View** when it supplies the basic functionality you want. By overriding the event handlers and/or onDraw, but still calling back to the superclass's methods, you can customize a View without having to re-implement its functionality. For example, you could customize a TextView to display numbers using a set number of decimal points.

➤ **Combine Views** to create atomic, reusable controls that leverage the functionality of several interconnected Views. For example, you could create a stopwatch timer by combining a TextView and a Button that resets the counter when clicked.

➤ **Create an entirely new control** when you need a completely different interface that you can't get by changing or combining existing controls.

Modifying Existing Views

The Android widget toolbox includes Views that provide many common UI requirements, but the controls are necessarily generic. By customizing these basic Views, you avoid re-implementing existing behavior while still tailoring the UI, and functionality, to your application's needs.

To create a new View based on an existing control, create a new class that extends it, as shown with the TextView derived class shown in Listing 5-8. In this example you extend the Text View to customize its appearance and behavior.

LISTING 5-8: Extending Text View

```java
import android.content.Context;
import android.graphics.Canvas;
import android.util.AttributeSet;
import android.view.KeyEvent;
import android.widget.TextView;

public class MyTextView extends TextView {

  // Constructor used when creating the View in code
  public MyTextView (Context context) {
    this(context, null);
  }

  // Constructor used when inflating the View from XML
  public MyTextView (Context context, AttributeSet attrs) {
    this(context, attrs, 0);
  }

  // Constructor used when inflating the View from XML when it has a
  // style attribute
  public MyTextView(Context context, AttributeSet attrs, int defStyleAttr) {
    super(context, attrs, defStyleAttr);

    // Do any custom initialization here
  }
}
```

If you are building a reusable View, it is strongly recommended to override all three of these constructors to ensure that your View can be created in code and inflated in XML files just like all of the Views included in the Android SDK.

To override the appearance or behavior of your new View, override and extend the event handlers associated with the behavior you want to change.

In the following extension of the Listing 5-8 code, the onDraw method is overridden to modify the View's appearance, and the onKeyDown handler is overridden to allow custom key-press handling:

```java
public class MyTextView extends TextView {

  public MyTextView(Context context) {
    this(context, null);
  }

  public MyTextView(Context context, AttributeSet attrs) {
    this(context, attrs, 0);
  }

  public MyTextView(Context context, AttributeSet attrs, int defStyleAttr) {
    super(context, attrs, defStyleAttr);
  }
```

```
@Override
public void onDraw(Canvas canvas) {
  [ ... Draw things on the canvas under the text ... ]

  // Render the text as usual using the TextView base class.
  super.onDraw(canvas);

  [ ... Draw things on the canvas over the text ... ]
}

@Override
public boolean onKeyDown(int keyCode, KeyEvent keyEvent) {
  [ ... Perform some special processing ... ]
  [ ... based on a particular key press ... ]

  // Use the existing functionality implemented by
  // the base class to respond to a key press event.
  return super.onKeyDown(keyCode, keyEvent);
}
}
```

The event handlers available within Views are covered in more detail later in this chapter.

Defining Custom Attributes

As mentioned in the previous section, you have three primary constructors for Views, used to support creating a View in code as well as part of an XML file. This same duality applies to functionality you might add to your View—you'll want to support changing added functionality via both code and via XML.

Adding functionality in code is no different for a View or any other class, and generally involves adding a set and get method:

```
public class PriceTextView extends TextView {
  private static NumberFormat CURRENCY_FORMAT =
    NumberFormat.getCurrencyInstance();

  private float mPrice;

  // These three constructors are required for all Views
  public PriceTextView(Context context) {
    this(context, null);
  }

  public PriceTextView(Context context, AttributeSet attrs) {
    this(context, attrs, 0);
  }

  // Constructor used when inflating the View from XML when it has a
  // style attribute
  public MyTextView(Context context, AttributeSet attrs, int defStyleAttr) {
    super(context, attrs, defStyleAttr);
  }
```

```
    public void setPrice(float price) {
      mPrice = price;
      setText(CURRENCY_FORMAT.format(price));
    }

    public float getPrice() {
      return mPrice;
    }
  }
```

However, this only allows changing the price in code. To set the displayed price as part of your XML files, you can create a custom attribute, generally in a `res/values/attrs.xml` file that contains one or more `<declare-styleable>` elements:

```
<resources>
  <declare-styleable name="PriceTextView">
    <attr name="price" format="reference|float" />
  </declare-styleable>
</resources>
```

It is convention that the `<declare-styleable>` name matches the name of the class using the attribute, although it is not strictly required.

It is important to note that the names used are global—your application will not compile if the same attribute is declared more than once (such as in your application and in a library you use); consider adding a prefix to your attributes if they are likely to be common names.

The basic formats available for attributes include `color`, `boolean`, `dimension`, `float`, `integer`, `string`, `fraction`, `enum`, and `flag`. The `reference` format is particularly important and allows you to reference another resource when using your custom attribute (such as using `@string/app_name`). If you want to allow multiple formats, combine the formats with the | character.

Your View XML can then reference the custom attribute by adding a namespace declaration associated with all of the attributes declared by your application, usually using `xmlns:app` (although `app` can be any identifier you choose):

```
<PriceTextView
    xmlns:android:"http://schemas.android.com/apk/res/android"
    xmlns:app="http://schemas.android.com/apk/res-auto"
    android:layout_width="wrap_content"
    android:layout_height="wrap_content"
    app:price="1999.99" />
```

You can then read the custom attributes in your class by using the `obtainStyledAttributes` method:

```
// Constructor used when inflating the View from XML when it has a
// style attribute
public MyTextView(Context context, AttributeSet attrs, int defStyleAttr) {
  super(context, attrs, defStyleAttr);

  final TypedArray a = context.obtainStyledAttributes(attrs,
    R.styleable.PriceTextView, // The <declare-styleable> name
    defStyleAttr,
    0); // An optional R.style to use for default values
```

```
if (a.hasValue(R.styleable.PriceTextView_price)) {
  setPrice(a.getFloat(R.styleable.PriceTextView_price,
  0)); // default value
}
a.recycle();
}
```

> **NOTE** *You must always call* `recycle` *when you are done reading values from the* `TypedArray`.

Creating Compound Controls

Compound controls are atomic, self-contained View Groups that contain multiple child Views laid out and connected together.

When you create a compound control, you define the layout, appearance, and interaction of the Views it contains. You create compound controls by extending a `ViewGroup` (usually a layout). To create a new compound control, choose the layout class that's most suitable for positioning the child controls and extend it:

```
public class MyCompoundView extends LinearLayout {
  public MyCompoundView(Context context) {
    this(context, null);
  }

  public MyCompoundView(Context context, AttributeSet attrs) {
    this(context, attrs, 0);
  }

  public MyCompoundView(Context context, AttributeSet attrs,
                        int defStyleAttr) {
    super(context, attrs, defStyleAttr);
  }
}
```

As with Activities, the preferred way to design compound View UI layouts is by using an external resource.

Listing 5-9 shows the XML layout definition for a simple compound control consisting of an Edit Text for text entry, with a "Clear" Button beneath it.

LISTING 5-9: A compound View layout resource

```
<?xml version="1.0" encoding="utf-8"?>
<LinearLayout xmlns:android="http://schemas.android.com/apk/res/android"
  android:orientation="vertical"
  android:layout_width="match_parent"
```

```
      android:layout_height="wrap_content">
      <EditText
        android:id="@+id/editText"
        android:layout_width="match_parent"
        android:layout_height="wrap_content"
      />
      <Button
        android:id="@+id/clearButton"
        android:layout_width="match_parent"
        android:layout_height="wrap_content"
        android:text="Clear"
      />
    </LinearLayout>
```

To use this layout in your new compound View, override its constructor to inflate the layout resource using the `inflate` method from the `LayoutInflate` system service. The `inflate` method takes the layout resource and returns the inflated View.

For circumstances such as this, in which the returned View should be the class you're creating, you can pass in the parent View and attach the result to it automatically.

Listing 5-10 demonstrates this using the `ClearableEditText` class. Within the constructor it inflates the layout resource from Listing 5-9 and then finds a reference to the Edit Text and Button Views it contains. It also makes a call to `hookupButton` that will later be used to hook up the plumbing that will implement the *clear text* functionality.

LISTING 5-10: Constructing a compound View

```
public class ClearableEditText extends LinearLayout {

  EditText editText;
  Button clearButton;

  public ClearableEditText(Context context) {
    this(context, null);
  }

  public ClearableEditText(Context context, AttributeSet attrs) {
    this(context, attrs, 0);
  }

  public ClearableEditText(Context context, AttributeSet attrs,
                           int defStyleAttr) {
    super(context, attrs, defStyleAttr);

    // Inflate the view from the layout resource.
    String infService = Context.LAYOUT_INFLATER_SERVICE;
    LayoutInflater li;
    li = (LayoutInflater)getContext().getSystemService(infService);
    li.inflate(R.layout.clearable_edit_text, this, true);
```

```
    // Get references to the child controls.
    editText = (EditText)findViewById(R.id.editText);
    clearButton = (Button)findViewById(R.id.clearButton);

    // Hook up the functionality
    hookupButton();
  }
}
```

If you prefer to construct your layout in code, you can do so just as you would for an Activity:

```
public ClearableEditText(Context context, AttributeSet attrs,
                         int defStyleAttr) {
  super(context, attrs, defStyleAttr);

  // Set orientation of layout to vertical
  setOrientation(LinearLayout.VERTICAL);

  // Create the child controls.
  editText = new EditText(getContext());
  clearButton = new Button(getContext());
  clearButton.setText("Clear");

  // Lay them out in the compound control.
  int lHeight = LinearLayout.LayoutParams.WRAP_CONTENT;
  int lWidth = LinearLayout.LayoutParams.MATCH_PARENT;

  addView(editText, new LinearLayout.LayoutParams(lWidth, lHeight));
  addView(clearButton, new LinearLayout.LayoutParams(lWidth, lHeight));

  // Hook up the functionality
  hookupButton();
}
```

After constructing the View layout, you can hook up the event handlers for each child control to provide the functionality you need. In Listing 5-11, the `hookupButton` method is filled in to clear the Edit Text when the button is pressed.

LISTING 5-11: Implementing the "Clear" Button

```
private void hookupButton() {
  clearButton.setOnClickListener(new Button.OnClickListener() {
    public void onClick(View v) {
      editText.setText("");
    }
  });
}
```

Creating Simple Compound Controls as a Layout

It's often sufficient, and more flexible, to define the layout and appearance of a set of Views without hard-wiring their interactions.

You can create a reusable layout by creating an XML resource that encapsulates the UI pattern you want to reuse. You can then import these layout patterns when creating the UI for Activities or Fragments by using the `include` tag within their layout resource definitions:

```
<include layout="@layout/clearable_edit_text"/>
```

The `include` tag also enables you to override the `id` and `layout` parameters of the root node of the included layout:

```
<include
  layout="@layout/clearable_edit_text"
  android:id="@+id/add_new_entry_input"
  android:layout_width="match_parent"
  android:layout_height="wrap_content"
  android:layout_gravity="top"
/>
```

Creating Custom Views

Creating new Views gives you the power to fundamentally shape the way your applications look and feel. By creating your own controls, you can create UIs that are uniquely suited to your needs.

To create new controls from a blank canvas, you extend either the `View` or `SurfaceView` class. The `View` class provides a `Canvas` object with a series of `draw` methods and `Paint` classes. Use them to create a visual interface with bitmaps and raster graphics. You can then override user events, including screen touches or key presses to provide interactivity.

In situations in which extremely rapid repaints and 3D graphics aren't required, the `View` base class offers a powerful lightweight solution.

The `SurfaceView` class provides a `Surface` object that supports drawing from a background thread and optionally using `OpenGL` to implement your graphics. This is an excellent option for graphics-heavy controls that are frequently updated (such as live video) or that display complex graphical information (particularly, games and 3D visualizations).

> **REFERENCE** *This section focuses on building controls based on the* `View` *class. To learn more about the* `SurfaceView` *class and some of the more advanced Canvas paint features available in Android, see Chapter 14, "Advanced Customization of Your User Interface."*

Creating a New Visual Interface

The base `View` class presents a distinctly empty 100-pixel-by-100-pixel square. To change the size of the control and display a more compelling visual interface, you need to override the `onMeasure` and `onDraw` methods.

Within `onMeasure` your View will determine the height and width it will occupy given a set of boundary conditions. The `onDraw` method is where you draw onto the Canvas.

Listing 5-12 shows the skeleton code for a new `View` class, which will be examined and developed further in the following sections.

```java
public class MyView extends View {

  public MyView(Context context) {
    this(context, null);
  }

  public MyView (Context context, AttributeSet attrs) {
    this(context, attrs, 0);
  }

  public MyView(Context context, AttributeSet attrs, int defStyleAttr) {
    super(context, attrs, defStyleAttr);
  }

  @Override
  protected void onMeasure(int wMeasureSpec, int hMeasureSpec) {
    int measuredHeight = measureHeight(hMeasureSpec);
    int measuredWidth = measureWidth(wMeasureSpec);

    // MUST make this call to setMeasuredDimension
    // or you will cause a runtime exception when
    // the control is laid out.
    setMeasuredDimension(measuredHeight, measuredWidth);
  }

  private int measureHeight(int measureSpec) {
    int specMode = MeasureSpec.getMode(measureSpec);
    int specSize = MeasureSpec.getSize(measureSpec);

    [ ... Calculate the view height ... ]

    return specSize;
  }

  private int measureWidth(int measureSpec) {
    int specMode = MeasureSpec.getMode(measureSpec);
    int specSize = MeasureSpec.getSize(measureSpec);

    [ ... Calculate the view width ... ]

    return specSize;
  }

  @Override
  protected void onDraw(Canvas canvas) {
    [ ... Draw your visual interface ... ]
  }
}
```

> **NOTE** *The* onMeasure *method calls* setMeasuredDimension. *You must always call this method within your overridden* onMeasure *method; otherwise, your View will throw an exception when the parent container attempts to lay it out.*

Drawing Your Control

The onDraw method is where the magic happens. If you're creating a new widget from scratch, it's because you want to create a completely new visual interface. The Canvas parameter in the onDraw method is the surface you'll use to bring your imagination to life.

The Android Canvas uses the *painter's algorithm*, meaning that each time you draw on to the Canvas, it will cover anything previously drawn on the same area.

The drawing APIs provide a variety of tools to help draw your design on the Canvas using various Paint objects. The Canvas class includes helper methods for drawing primitive 2D objects, including circles, lines, rectangles, text, and Drawables (images). It also supports transformations that let you rotate, translate (move), and scale (resize) the Canvas while you draw on it.

When these tools are used in combination with Drawables and the Paint class (which offer a variety of customizable fills and pens), the complexity and detail that your control can render are limited only by the size of the screen and the power of the processor rendering it.

> **WARNING** *One of the most important techniques for writing efficient code in Android is to avoid the repetitive creation and destruction of objects. Any object created in your* onDraw *method will be created and destroyed every time the screen refreshes. Improve efficiency by making as many of these objects (particularly instances of* Paint *and* Drawable) *class-scoped and by moving their creation into the constructor.*

Listing 5-13 shows how to override the onDraw method to display a simple text string in the center of the View.

LISTING 5-13: Drawing a custom View

```
@Override
protected void onDraw(Canvas canvas) {
    // Get the size of the control based on the last call to onMeasure.
    int height = getMeasuredHeight();
    int width = getMeasuredWidth();

    // Find the center
    int px = width/2;
    int py = height/2;
```

```
    // Create the new paint brushes.
    // NOTE: For efficiency this should be done in
    // the views's constructor
    Paint mTextPaint = new Paint(Paint.ANTI_ALIAS_FLAG);
    mTextPaint.setColor(Color.WHITE);

    // Define the string.
    String displayText = "Hello View!";

    // Measure the width of the text string.
    float textWidth = mTextPaint.measureText(displayText);

    // Draw the text string in the center of the control.
    canvas.drawText(displayText, px-textWidth/2, py, mTextPaint);
}
```

So that we don't diverge too far from the current topic, a more detailed look at the Canvas and Paint classes, and the techniques available for drawing more complex visuals is included in Chapter 14, "Advanced Customization of Your User Interface."

> **NOTE** *Changes to any element of your Canvas require that the entire Canvas be repainted; modifying the color of a brush will not change your View's display until the control is invalidated and redrawn. Alternatively, you can use OpenGL to render graphics. For more details, see the discussion on* SurfaceView *in Chapter 17, "Audio, Video, and Using the Camera."*

Sizing Your Control

Unless you conveniently require a control that always occupies a space 100 pixels square, you will also need to override onMeasure.

The onMeasure method is called when the control's parent is laying out its child controls. It asks the question, "How much space will you use?" and passes in two parameters: widthMeasureSpec and heightMeasureSpec. These parameters specify the space available for the control and some metadata to describe that space.

Rather than return a result, you pass the View's height and width into the setMeasuredDimension method.

The following snippet shows how to override onMeasure. The calls to the local method stubs measureHeight and measureWidth are used to decode the widthHeightSpec and heightMeasureSpec values and calculate the preferred height and width values, respectively:

```
@Override
protected void onMeasure(int widthMeasureSpec, int heightMeasureSpec) {

    int measuredHeight = measureHeight(heightMeasureSpec);
    int measuredWidth = measureWidth(widthMeasureSpec);

    setMeasuredDimension(measuredHeight, measuredWidth);
}
```

```
private int measureHeight(int measureSpec) {
  // Return measured widget height.
}

private int measureWidth(int measureSpec) {
  // Return measured widget width.
}
```

The boundary parameters, `widthMeasureSpec` and `heightMeasureSpec`, are passed in as integers for efficiency reasons. Before they can be used, they first need to be decoded using the static `getMode` and `getSize` methods from the `MeasureSpec` class:

```
int specMode = MeasureSpec.getMode(measureSpec);
int specSize = MeasureSpec.getSize(measureSpec);
```

Depending on the *mode* value, the *size* represents either the maximum space available for the control (in the case of `AT_MOST`), or the exact size that your control will occupy (for `EXACTLY`). In the case of `UNSPECIFIED`, your control does not have any reference for what the size represents.

By marking a measurement size as `EXACT`, the parent is insisting that the View will be placed into an area of the exact size specified. The `AT_MOST` mode says the parent is asking what size the View would like to occupy, given an upper boundary. In many cases the value you return will either be the same, or the size required to appropriately wrap the UI you want to display.

In either case, you should treat these limits as absolute. In some circumstances it may still be appropriate to return a measurement outside these limits, in which case you can let the parent choose how to deal with the oversized View, using techniques such as clipping and scrolling.

Listing 5-14 shows a typical implementation for handling View measurements.

LISTING 5-14: A typical View measurement implementation

```
@Override
protected void onMeasure(int widthMeasureSpec, int heightMeasureSpec) {
  int measuredHeight = measureHeight(heightMeasureSpec);
  int measuredWidth = measureWidth(widthMeasureSpec);

  setMeasuredDimension(measuredHeight, measuredWidth);
}

private int measureHeight(int measureSpec) {
  int specMode = MeasureSpec.getMode(measureSpec);
  int specSize = MeasureSpec.getSize(measureSpec);

  //  Default size in pixels if no limits are specified.
  int result = 500;

  if (specMode == MeasureSpec.AT_MOST) {
    // Calculate the ideal size of your
    // control within this maximum size.
    // If your control fills the available
    // space return the outer bound.
    result = specSize;
```

```
    } else if (specMode == MeasureSpec.EXACTLY) {
      // If your control can fit within these bounds return that value.
      result = specSize;
    }
    return result;
  }

  private int measureWidth(int measureSpec) {
    int specMode = MeasureSpec.getMode(measureSpec);
    int specSize = MeasureSpec.getSize(measureSpec);

    //  Default size in pixels if no limits are specified.
    int result = 500;

    if (specMode == MeasureSpec.AT_MOST) {
      // Calculate the ideal size of your control
      // within this maximum size.
      // If your control fills the available space
      // return the outer bound.
      result = specSize;
    } else if (specMode == MeasureSpec.EXACTLY) {
      // If your control can fit within these bounds return that value.
      result = specSize;
    }
    return result;
  }
```

Handling User Interaction Events

For your new View to be interactive, it will need to respond to user-initiated events such as key presses, screen touches, and button clicks. Android exposes several virtual event handlers that you can use to react to user input:

➤ onKeyDown—Called when any device key is pressed; includes the D-pad, keyboard, hang-up, call, back, and camera buttons

➤ onKeyUp—Called when a user releases a pressed key

➤ onTouchEvent—Called when the touch screen is pressed or released, or when it detects movement

Listing 5-15 shows a skeleton class that overrides each of the user interaction handlers in a View.

LISTING 5-15: Input event handling for Views

```
@Override
public boolean onKeyDown(int keyCode, KeyEvent keyEvent) {
  // Return true if the event was handled.
  return true;
}
```

```
@Override
public boolean onKeyUp(int keyCode, KeyEvent keyEvent) {
  // Return true if the event was handled.
  return true;
}

@Override
public boolean onTouchEvent(MotionEvent event) {
  // Get the type of action this event represents
  int actionPerformed = event.getAction();
  // Return true if the event was handled.
  return true;
}
```

Further details on using each of these event handlers, including greater detail on the parameters received by each method and support for multitouch events, are available in Chapter 14.

Supporting Accessibility in Custom Views

Creating a custom View with a beautiful interface is only half the story. It's just as important to create accessible controls that can be used by users with disabilities that require them to interact with their devices in different ways.

The Accessibility APIs provide alternative interaction methods for users with visual, physical, or age-related disabilities that make it difficult to interact fully with a touch screen.

The first step is to ensure that your custom View is accessible and navigable using D-pad events, as described in the previous section. It's also important to use the content description attribute within your layout definition to describe the input widgets. (This is described in more detail in Chapter 14.)

To be accessible, custom Views must implement the AccessibilityEventSource interface and broadcast AccessibilityEvents using the sendAccessibilityEvent method.

The View class already implements the Accessibility Event Source interface, so you only need to customize the behavior to suit the functionality introduced by your custom View. Do this by passing the type of event that has occurred—usually one of clicks, long clicks, selection changes, focus changes, and text/content changes—to the sendAccessibilityEvent method. For custom Views that implement a completely new UI, this will typically include a broadcast whenever the displayed content changes, as shown in Listing 5-16.

LISTING 5-16: Broadcasting Accessibility Events

```
public void setSeason(Season season) {
  mSeason = season;
  sendAccessibilityEvent(AccessibilityEvent.TYPE_VIEW_TEXT_CHANGED);
}
```

Clicks, long clicks, and focus and selection changes typically will be broadcast by the underlying View implementation, although you should take care to broadcast any additional events not captured by the base View class.

The broadcast Accessibility Event includes a number of properties used by the accessibility service to augment the user experience. Several of these properties, including the View's class name and event timestamp, won't need to be altered; however, by overriding the `dispatchPopulateAccessibilityEvent` handler, you can customize details such as the textual representation of the View's contents, checked state, and selection state of your View, as shown in Listing 5-17.

LISTING 5-17: Customizing Accessibility Event properties

```
@Override
public boolean dispatchPopulateAccessibilityEvent(
                final AccessibilityEvent event) {

  super.dispatchPopulateAccessibilityEvent(event);
  if (isShown()) {
    String seasonStr = Season.valueOf(season);
    if (seasonStr.length() > AccessibilityEvent.MAX_TEXT_LENGTH)
      seasonStr =
        seasonStr.substring(0, AccessibilityEvent.MAX_TEXT_LENGTH-1);

    event.getText().add(seasonStr);
    return true;
  }
  else
    return false;
}
```

Creating a Compass View Example

In the following example you'll create a new Compass View by extending the `View` class. This View will display a traditional compass rose to indicate a heading/orientation. When complete, it should appear as in Figure 5-5.

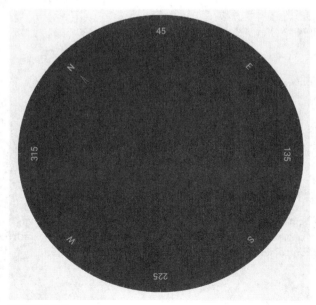

FIGURE 5-5

A compass is an example of a UI control that requires a radically different visual display from the Text Views and Buttons available in the SDK toolbox, making it an excellent candidate for building from scratch.

> **NOTE** *In Chapter 14 you will learn some advanced techniques for Canvas drawing that will let you dramatically improve its appearance. Then in Chapter 16, "Hardware Sensors," you'll use this Compass View and the device's built-in accelerometer to display the user's current orientation.*

Start by creating a new Compass project that will contain your new CompassView, and create an initially empty CompassActivity within which to display it:

1. Create a new CompassView class that extends View and add constructors that will allow the View to be instantiated, either in code or through inflation from a resource layout. Add setFocusable(true) to the final constructor to allow a user using a D-pad to select and focus the compass (this will allow them to receive accessibility events from the View):

```
package com.professionalandroid.apps.compass;

import android.content.Context;
import android.content.res.Resources;
import android.content.res.TypedArray;
import android.graphics.Canvas;
import android.graphics.Paint;
import android.support.v4.content.ContextCompat;
import android.util.AttributeSet;
import android.view.View;
import android.view.accessibility.AccessibilityEvent;

public class CompassView extends View {
  public CompassView(Context context) {
    this(context, null);
  }

  public CompassView(Context context, AttributeSet attrs) {
    this(context, attrs, 0);
  }

  public CompassView(Context context, AttributeSet attrs, int defStyleAttr) {
    super(context, attrs, defStyleAttr);

    setFocusable(true);
  }
}
```

2. The Compass View should always be a perfect circle that takes up as much of the canvas as this restriction allows. Override the onMeasure method to calculate the length of the shortest side, and use setMeasuredDimension to set the height and width using this value:

```java
@Override
protected void onMeasure(int widthMeasureSpec, int heightMeasureSpec) {
  // The compass is a circle that fills as much space as possible.
  // Set the measured dimensions by figuring out the shortest boundary,
  // height or width.
  int measuredWidth = measure(widthMeasureSpec);
  int measuredHeight = measure(heightMeasureSpec);

  int d = Math.min(measuredWidth, measuredHeight);

  setMeasuredDimension(d, d);
}

private int measure(int measureSpec) {
  int result = 0;

  // Decode the measurement specifications.
  int specMode = MeasureSpec.getMode(measureSpec);
  int specSize = MeasureSpec.getSize(measureSpec);

  if (specMode == MeasureSpec.UNSPECIFIED) {
    // Return a default size of 200 if no bounds are specified.
    result = 200;
  } else {
    // As you want to fill the available space
    // always return the full available bounds.
    result = specSize;
  }
  return result;
}
```

3. Modify the `activity_compass.xml` layout resource and replace it with a Frame Layout containing your new `CompassView`:

```xml
<?xml version="1.0" encoding="utf-8"?>
<FrameLayout xmlns:android="http://schemas.android.com/apk/res/android"
  android:orientation="vertical"
  android:layout_width="match_parent"
  android:layout_height="match_parent">
  <com.professionalandroid.apps.compass.CompassView
    android:id="@+id/compassView"
    android:layout_width="match_parent"
    android:layout_height="match_parent"
  />
</FrameLayout>
```

4. Use resource files to store the colors and text strings you'll use to draw the compass.

   4.1. Create the text string resources by replacing the `res/values/strings.xml` file with the following:

```xml
<?xml version="1.0" encoding="utf-8"?>
<resources>
  <string name="app_name">Compass</string>
  <string name="cardinal_north">N</string>
  <string name="cardinal_east">E</string>
```

```xml
    <string name="cardinal_south">S</string>
    <string name="cardinal_west">W</string>
</resources>
```

4.2. Add the following color resources to `res/values/colors.xml`:

```xml
<?xml version="1.0" encoding="utf-8"?>
<resources>

    <color name="colorPrimary">#3F51B5</color>
    <color name="colorPrimaryDark">#303F9F</color>
    <color name="colorAccent">#FF4081</color>
    <color name="background_color">#F555</color>
    <color name="marker_color">#AFFF</color>
    <color name="text_color">#AFFF</color>
</resources>
```

5. Return to the `CompassView` class. Add a new property to store the displayed bearing, and create `get` and `set` methods for it. Call `invalidate` in the set method to ensure that the View is repainted when the bearing changes:

```java
private float mBearing;

public void setBearing(float bearing) {
  mBearing = bearing;
  invalidate();
}

public float getBearing() {
  return mBearing;
}
```

6. Create a custom attribute for setting the bearing in XML.

6.1. Create the custom attribute in the res/values/attrs.xml file:

```xml
<?xml version="1.0" encoding="utf-8"?>
<resources>
  <declare-styleable name="CompassView">
    <attr name="bearing" format="reference|float" />
  </declare-styleable>
</resources>
```

6.2. Update the constructor to read the bearing from the XML attribute:

```java
public CompassView(Context context, AttributeSet attrs,
                   int defStyleAttr) {
  super(context, attrs, defStyleAttr);
  setFocusable(true);
  final TypedArray a = context.obtainStyledAttributes(attrs,
    R.styleable.CompassView, defStyleAttr, 0);
  if (a.hasValue(R.styleable.CompassView_bearing)) {
    setBearing(a.getFloat(R.styleable.CompassView_bearing, 0));
  }
  a.recycle();
}
```

7. In the constructor, get references to each resource created in Step 4. Store the string values as instance variables, and use the color values to create new class-scoped `Paint` objects. You'll use these objects in the next step to draw the compass face.

```java
private Paint markerPaint;
private Paint textPaint;
private Paint circlePaint;
private String northString;
private String eastString;
private String southString;
private String westString;
private int textHeight;

public CompassView(Context context, AttributeSet attrs, int defStyleAttr) {
  super(context, attrs, defStyleAttr);

  setFocusable(true);
  final TypedArray a = context.obtainStyledAttributes(attrs,
    R.styleable.CompassView, defStyleAttr, 0);
  if (a.hasValue(R.styleable.CompassView_bearing)) {
    setBearing(a.getFloat(R.styleable.CompassView_bearing, 0));
  }
  a.recycle();

  Context c = this.getContext();
  Resources r = this.getResources();

  circlePaint = new Paint(Paint.ANTI_ALIAS_FLAG);
  circlePaint.setColor(ContextCompat.getColor(c, R.color.background_color));
  circlePaint.setStrokeWidth(1);
  circlePaint.setStyle(Paint.Style.FILL_AND_STROKE);

  northString = r.getString(R.string.cardinal_north);
  eastString = r.getString(R.string.cardinal_east);
  southString = r.getString(R.string.cardinal_south);
  westString = r.getString(R.string.cardinal_west);

  textPaint = new Paint(Paint.ANTI_ALIAS_FLAG);
  textPaint.setColor(ContextCompat.getColor(c, R.color.text_color));

  textHeight = (int)textPaint.measureText("yY");

  markerPaint = new Paint(Paint.ANTI_ALIAS_FLAG);
  markerPaint.setColor(ContextCompat.getColor(c, R.color.marker_color));
}
```

8. The next step is to draw the compass face using the `String` and `Paint` objects you created in Step 7. The following code snippet is presented with only limited commentary. You can find more detail about drawing on the Canvas and using advanced Paint effects in Chapter 14.

8.1. Start by overriding the `onDraw` method in the `CompassView` class:

```java
@Override
protected void onDraw(Canvas canvas) {
```

8.2. Find the center of the control, and store the length of the smallest side as the Compass's radius:

```
int mMeasuredWidth = getMeasuredWidth();
int mMeasuredHeight = getMeasuredHeight();

int px = mMeasuredWidth / 2;
int py = mMeasuredHeight / 2 ;

int radius = Math.min(px, py);
```

8.3. Draw the outer boundary, and color the background of the Compass face using the `drawCircle` method. Use the `circlePaint` object you created in Step 7:

```
// Draw the background
canvas.drawCircle(px, py, radius, circlePaint);
```

8.4. This Compass displays the current heading by rotating the face so that the current direction is always at the top of the device. To achieve this, rotate the canvas in the opposite direction to the current heading:

```
// Rotate our perspective so that the 'top' is
// facing the current bearing.
canvas.save();
canvas.rotate(-mBearing, px, py);
```

8.5. All that's left is to draw the markings. Rotate the canvas through a full rotation, drawing markings every 15 degrees and the abbreviated direction string every 45 degrees:

```
int textWidth = (int)textPaint.measureText("W");
int cardinalX = px-textWidth/2;
int cardinalY = py-radius+textHeight;

// Draw the marker every 15 degrees and text every 45.
for (int i = 0; i < 24; i++) {
  // Draw a marker.
  canvas.drawLine(px, py-radius, px, py-radius+10, markerPaint);

  canvas.save();
  canvas.translate(0, textHeight);

  // Draw the cardinal points
  if (i % 6 == 0) {
    String dirString = "";
    switch (i) {
      case(0)   : {
                  dirString = northString;
                  int arrowY = 2*textHeight;
                  canvas.drawLine(px, arrowY, px-5, 3*textHeight,
                                  markerPaint);
                  canvas.drawLine(px, arrowY, px+5, 3*textHeight,
                                  markerPaint);
                  break;
                }
```

```
        case(6)  : dirString = eastString; break;
        case(12) : dirString = southString; break;
        case(18) : dirString = westString; break;
      }
      canvas.drawText(dirString, cardinalX, cardinalY, textPaint);
    }

    else if (i % 3 == 0) {
      // Draw the text every alternate 45deg
      String angle = String.valueOf(i*15);
      float angleTextWidth = textPaint.measureText(angle);

      int angleTextX = (int)(px-angleTextWidth/2);
      int angleTextY = py-radius+textHeight;
      canvas.drawText(angle, angleTextX, angleTextY, textPaint);
    }
    canvas.restore();

    canvas.rotate(15, px, py);
  }
  canvas.restore();
}
```

9. The next step is to add accessibility support. The Compass View presents a heading visually, so to make it accessible you need to broadcast an Accessibility Event signifying that the "text" (in this case, content) has changed when the bearing changes. Do this by modifying the setBearing method:

```
public void setBearing(float bearing) {
  mBearing = bearing;
  invalidate();
  sendAccessibilityEvent(AccessibilityEvent.TYPE_VIEW_TEXT_CHANGED);
}
```

10. Override the dispatchPopulateAccessibilityEvent to use the current heading as the content value to be used for accessibility events:

```
@Override
public boolean dispatchPopulateAccessibilityEvent(
              final AccessibilityEvent event) {
  super.dispatchPopulateAccessibilityEvent(event);
  if (isShown()) {
    String bearingStr = String.valueOf(mBearing);
    event.getText().add(bearingStr);
    return true;
  }
  else
    return false;
}
```

Run the Activity, and you should see the CompassView displayed. See Chapter 16, "Hardware Sensors," to learn how to bind the CompassView to the device's compass sensor.

Using Custom Controls

Having created your own custom Views, you can use them within code and layouts as you would any other View. Note that you must specify the fully qualified class name when you add a node for your new View in the layout definition:

```
<com.professionalandroid.apps.compass.CompassView
  android:id="@+id/compassView"
  android:layout_width="match_parent"
  android:layout_height="match_parent"
  app:bearing="45" />
```

You can inflate the layout and get a reference to the CompassView, as usual, using the following code:

```
@Override
public void onCreate(Bundle savedInstanceState) {
  super.onCreate(savedInstanceState);
  setContentView(R.layout.main);
  CompassView cv = findViewById(R.id.compassView);
  // Update the bearing by calling setBearing as needed
}
```

You can also add your new View to a layout in code:

```
@Override
public void onCreate(Bundle savedInstanceState) {
  super.onCreate(savedInstanceState);
  CompassView cv = new CompassView(this);
  setContentView(cv);
  cv.setBearing(45);
}
```

Custom Views are a powerful way to provide distinct functionality to your application. Once created, they can be used in the same way as any Android framework View.

Intents and Broadcast Receivers

WHAT'S IN THIS CHAPTER?

➤ Introducing Intents and Pending Intents

➤ Starting Activities and Services using implicit and explicit Intents

➤ Returning results from sub-Activities

➤ Understanding how Intents are resolved

➤ Extending application functionality using Intent Filters

➤ Adding links to text fields with Linkify

➤ Monitoring device state changes with broadcast Intents

➤ Sending broadcast Intents within your application with the Local Broadcast Manager

WROX.COM CODE DOWNLOADS FOR THIS CHAPTER

The code downloads for this chapter are found at www.wrox.com. The code for this chapter is divided into the following major examples:

➤ Snippets_ch6.zip

➤ StarSignPicker_ch6.zip

USING INTENTS AND BROADCAST RECEIVERS

Intents are a message-passing mechanism you can use within your application, between applications, and between the system and your application. Intents are used to do the following:

➤ Explicitly start a particular Service, Broadcast Receiver, Activity, or sub-Activity using its class name

➤ Start an Activity, sub-Activity, or Service to perform an action with (or on) a particular piece of data

➤ Return information from a sub-Activity

➤ Broadcast that an event has occurred

Intents are a fundamental part of the Android OS, they're also quite unique to Android, and as such can be a confusing concept to master.

Intents can be used to send information among any application components installed on an Android device, no matter which application they're a part of. This turns your device from a platform containing a collection of independent components into a single, interconnected system. Alternatively, for improved security and efficiency, you can use the Local Broadcast Manager to send Intents only to components within your application.

One of the most common uses for Intents is to launch (or "start") Activities, either *explicitly* (by specifying the class to load) or *implicitly* (by creating an action Intent that requests a specific action be performed on a piece of data). In the latter case the action does not necessarily have to be performed by an Activity within the calling application.

Using Intents, rather than explicitly loading classes, to launch application components—even within the same application—is a fundamental Android design principle.

You can also use Intents to broadcast messages across the system; these are known as broadcast Intents. Applications can register Broadcast Receivers to listen for, and react to, these broadcast Intents. This enables you to create event-driven applications based on internal or system events.

The Android system uses broadcast Intents to announce system events, such as changes in Internet connectivity or battery charge levels. The native Android applications, such as the Phone Dialer and SMS Manager, register components that listen for specific broadcast Intents and react accordingly. As a result, you can replace many of the native applications by registering Broadcast Receivers that listen for the same Intents.

USING INTENTS TO LAUNCH ACTIVITIES

The most common use of Intents is to connect your application components, and to communicate between them. For example, Intents are used within Activities to start new Activities, allowing you to create a workflow made up of multiple screens.

> **NOTE** *The instructions in this section refer to starting new Activities, but the same approach also applies to Services. Details on starting (and creating) Services are available in Chapter 11, "Working in the Background."*

To create and display an Activity, call `startActivity`, passing in an `Intent`, as follows:

```
startActivity(myIntent);
```

The `startActivity` method finds and starts the single Activity that best matches your Intent.

You can construct an Intent that explicitly specifies a particular Activity class to start, or it can include an action that the target Activity must be able to perform. In the latter case, the run time will dynamically choose an Activity to through *intent resolution.*

When you use `startActivity`, your application won't receive any notification when the newly launched Activity finishes. To track feedback from a sub-Activity, use `startActivityForResult`, as described later in this chapter.

Explicitly Starting New Activities

You learned in Chapter 3, "Applications and Activities and Fragments, Oh My!" that applications consist of a number of interrelated screens—Activities—that must be included in the application manifest.

To transition between them, you can explicitly indicate an Activity to start by creating a new Intent, specifying the current Activity's Context and the class of the Activity to launch. Once defined, pass this Intent into `startActivity` as shown in Listing 6-1 to launch the new Activity.

LISTING 6-1: Explicitly starting a specific Activity

```
Intent intent = new Intent(MyActivity.this, MyOtherActivity.class);
startActivity(intent);
```

After `startActivity` is called, the new Activity (in this example, `MyOtherActivity`) will be created, started, and resumed—replacing `MyActivity` at the top of the Activity stack.

Calling `finish` on the new Activity, or pressing the hardware back button, closes it and removes it from the stack. Alternatively, you can continue to navigate to other Activities using `startActivity`.

Note that each time you call `startActivity`, a new Activity will be added to the stack. Pressing back (or calling `finish`) will remove each of these Activities, in turn; if an Activity is not closed in this way it will remain on the stack while the application is running. As a result, it's possible to have multiple instances of the same Activity on your Activity stack.

Implicit Intents and Late Runtime Binding

An implicit Intent is used to ask the system to find and start an Activity that can perform a particular *action*, without you knowing exactly which application, or Activity, will be started.

For example, to let users make calls from your application, you *could* implement a new dialer, or (if you don't hate yourself), you could use an implicit Intent that requests the action (dialing) be performed on a phone number (represented as a URI):

```
if (somethingWeird && itDontLookGood) {
  Intent intent =
    new Intent(Intent.ACTION_DIAL, Uri.parse("tel:555-2368"));

  startActivity(intent);
}
```

Android resolves this Intent by finding, and then starting, an Activity that can perform the dial action on a telephone number URI—in this case, typically the bundled phone dialer application.

When constructing a new implicit Intent, you specify an action to perform and the URI of the data on which to perform that action. You can send additional data to the target Activity by adding extras to the Intent.

Extras are a mechanism used to attach primitive values to an Intent. You can use the overloaded putExtra method on any Intent to attach a new name/value pair (NVP):

```
intent.putExtra("STRING_EXTRA", "Beverly Hills");
intent.putExtra("INT_EXTRA", 90210);
```

The extras are stored within the Intent as a Bundle object, available from within the started Activity using the getExtras method. You can extract each extra value directly from the Intent using the corresponding get[type]Extra method:

```
Intent intent = getIntent();
String myStringExtra = intent.getStringExtra("STRING_EXTRA");
int myIntExtra = intent.getIntExtra("INT_EXTRA", DEFAULT_INT_VALUE);
```

When you use an implicit Intent to start an Activity, Android will—at run time—resolve it into the Activity class best suited to performing the required action on the type of data specified. This means you can create projects that use functionality from other applications without knowing exactly which application you're borrowing functionality from ahead of time.

In circumstances where multiple Activities can potentially perform a given action, the user is presented with a choice. The process of Intent resolution is determined through an analysis of the Activities' Intent Filters, which are described in detail later in this chapter.

Various native applications provide Activities capable of performing actions against specific data. Third-party applications, including your own, can be registered to support new actions or to provide an alternative provider of native actions. You are introduced to some of the native actions, as well as how to register your own Activities to support them, later in this chapter.

Determining If an Intent Will Resolve

Incorporating the Activities and Services of a third-party application into your own is incredibly powerful; however, there is no guarantee that any particular application will be installed on a device, or even that *any* installed application is capable of handling your request.

As a result, it's good practice to check if your implicit Intent will resolve to an Activity before passing it to `startActivity`.

You can use the Package Manager to query which, if any, Activity will be launched in response to a specific Intent by calling `resolveActivity` on your Intent object, passing in the Package Manager, as shown in Listing 6-2.

LISTING 6-2: Implicitly starting an Activity

```
if (somethingWeird && itDontLookGood) {
  // Create the implicit Intent to use to start a new Activity.
  Intent intent =
    new Intent(Intent.ACTION_DIAL, Uri.parse("tel:555-2368"));

  // Check if an Activity exists to perform this action.
  PackageManager pm = getPackageManager();
  ComponentName cn = intent.resolveActivity(pm);
  if (cn == null) {
    // There is no Activity available to perform the action
    // Log an error and modify app behavior accordingly,
    // typically by disabling the UI element that would allow
    // users to attempt this action.
    Log.e(TAG, "Intent could not resolve to an Activity.");
  }
  else
    startActivity(intent);
}
```

If no Activity is found, you can choose to either disable the related functionality (and associated user interface controls) or direct users to an appropriate application in the Google Play Store. Note that Google Play is not available on all devices, so it's good practice to check for that as well.

Returning Results from Activities

An Activity started via `startActivity` is independent of the calling Activity, and will not provide any feedback when it closes.

Where feedback is required, you can start an Activity as a sub-Activity that can pass results back to its parent. Sub-Activities are really just Activities opened in a different way; as such, you must still register them in the application manifest in the same way as any other Activity.

Any manifest-registered Activity can be opened as a sub-Activity, including those provided by the system or third-party applications.

When a sub-Activity is finished, it triggers the `onActivityResult` event handler within the calling parent Activity. Sub-Activities are particularly useful in situations where one Activity is providing data input for another, such as a user filling in a form or selecting an item from a list.

Launching Sub-Activities

The `startActivityForResult` method works much like `startActivity`, but with one important difference. In addition to passing in the explicit or implicit Intent used to determine which Activity to launch, you also pass in a *request code*. This value will later be used to uniquely identify the sub-Activity that has returned a result.

Listing 6-3 shows the skeleton code for launching a sub-Activity explicitly.

LISTING 6-3: Explicitly starting a sub-Activity for a result

```
private static final int SHOW_SUBACTIVITY = 1;

private void startSubActivity() {
  Intent intent = new Intent(this, MyOtherActivity.class);
  startActivityForResult(intent, SHOW_SUBACTIVITY);
}
```

Like regular Activities, you can start sub-Activities implicitly or explicitly. Listing 6-4 uses an implicit Intent to launch a new sub-Activity to pick a contact.

LISTING 6-4: Implicitly starting a sub-Activity for a result

```
private static final int PICK_CONTACT_SUBACTIVITY = 2;

private void startSubActivityImplicitly() {
  // Create an Intent that requests an Activity capable
  // of allowing users to pick a contact.
  Uri uri = Uri.parse("content://contacts/people");
  Intent intent = new Intent(Intent.ACTION_PICK, uri);
  startActivityForResult(intent, PICK_CONTACT_SUBACTIVITY);
}
```

Returning Results from a Sub-Activity

When your sub-Activity is ready to return, call `setResult` before `finish` to return a result to the calling Activity.

The `setResult` method takes two parameters: the result code and the result data itself, represented as an Intent.

The result code indicates the success of running the sub-Activity—generally, either `Activity.RESULT_OK` or `Activity.RESULT_CANCELED`. In some circumstances, where neither OK nor canceled sufficiently or accurately describes the result, you'll want to use your own response codes to handle application-specific choices; `setResult` supports any integer value.

The result Intent often includes a data URI that points to a piece of content (such as the selected contact, phone number, or media file) and a collection of extras used to return additional information.

Listing 6-5, taken from a sub-Activity's `onCreate` method, shows how OK and Cancel buttons might return different results to the calling Activity.

LISTING 6-5: Returning a result from a sub-Activity

```
Button okButton = findViewById(R.id.ok_button);
okButton.setOnClickListener(new View.OnClickListener() {
  public void onClick(View view) {
    // Create a URI that points to the currently selected item
    Uri selectedHorse = Uri.parse("content://horses/" +
                                  selected_horse_id);
    Intent result = new Intent(Intent.ACTION_PICK, selectedHorse);

    setResult(RESULT_OK, result);
    finish();
  }
});

Button cancelButton = findViewById(R.id.cancel_button);
cancelButton.setOnClickListener(new View.OnClickListener() {
  public void onClick(View view) {
    setResult(RESULT_CANCELED);
    finish();
  }
});
```

If the Activity is closed by the user pressing the hardware back key, or `finish` is called without a prior call to `setResult`, the result code will be set to `RESULT_CANCELED` and the result Intent set to null.

Handling Sub-Activity Results

When a sub-Activity closes, the `onActivityResult` event handler is fired within the calling Activity. Override this method to handle the results returned by sub-Activities.

The `onActivityResult` handler receives a number of parameters:

➤ **Request code**—The request code that was used to launch the returning sub-Activity.

➤ **Result code**—The result code set by the sub-Activity to indicate its result. It can be any integer value, but typically will be either `Activity.RESULT_OK` or `Activity.RESULT_CANCELED`.

➤ **Data**—An Intent used to package returned data. Depending on the purpose of the sub-Activity, it may include a URI that represents a selected piece of content. The sub-Activity can also return information as extras within the returned data Intent.

> **NOTE** *If the sub-Activity closes abnormally or doesn't specify a result code before it closes, the result code is* `Activity.RESULT_CANCELED`.

Listing 6-6 shows the skeleton code for implementing the `onActivityResult` event handler within an Activity.

LISTING 6-6: Implementing an On Activity Result handler

```
private static final int SELECT_HORSE = 1;
private static final int SELECT_GUN = 2;

Uri selectedHorse = null;
Uri selectedGun = null;

@Override
public void onActivityResult(int requestCode,
                             int resultCode,
                             Intent data) {

  super.onActivityResult(requestCode, resultCode, data);

  switch(requestCode) {
    case (SELECT_HORSE):
      if (resultCode == Activity.RESULT_OK)
        selectedHorse = data.getData();
      break;

    case (SELECT_GUN):
      if (resultCode == Activity.RESULT_OK)
        selectedGun = data.getData();
      break;

    default: break;
  }
}
```

Using Platform-Native Actions to Launch Activities

Applications distributed as part of the Android platform also use Intents to launch Activities and sub-Activities.

The following (non-comprehensive) list shows some of the native actions available as static string constants in the `Intent` class. When creating implicit Intents, you can use these actions, known as *Activity Intents*, to start Activities and sub-Activities within your own applications.

> **NOTE** *Later you are introduced to Intent Filters and how to register your own Activities as handlers for these actions.*

➤ `ACTION_DELETE`—Starts an Activity that lets you delete the data specified at the Intent's data URI.

➤ ACTION_DIAL—Brings up a dialer application with the number to dial pre-populated from the Intent's data URI. By default, this is handled by the native Android phone dialer. The dialer can normalize most number schemas—for example, `tel:555-1234` and `tel:(212) 555 1212` are both valid numbers.

➤ ACTION_EDIT—Requests an Activity that can edit the data at the Intent's data URI.

➤ ACTION_INSERT—Opens an Activity capable of inserting new items into the Cursor specified in the Intent's data URI. When called as a sub-Activity, it should return a URI to the newly inserted item.

➤ ACTION_PICK—Launches a sub-Activity that lets you pick an item from the Content Provider specified by the Intent's data URI. When closed, it should return a URI to the item that was picked. The Activity launched depends on the data being picked—for example, passing `content://contacts/people` will invoke the native contacts list.

➤ ACTION_SEARCH—Typically used to launch a specific search Activity. When it's fired without a specific Activity, the user will be prompted to select from all applications that support search. Supply the search term as a string in the Intent's extras using `SearchManager.QUERY` as the key.

➤ ACTION_SENDTO—Launches an Activity to send data to the contact specified by the Intent's data URI.

➤ ACTION_SEND—Launches an Activity that sends the data specified in the Intent. The recipient contact needs to be selected by the resolved Activity. Use `setType` to set the MIME type of the transmitted data. The data itself should be stored as an extra by means of the key `EXTRA_TEXT` or `EXTRA_STREAM`, depending on the type. In the case of email, the native Android applications will also accept extras via the `EXTRA_EMAIL`, `EXTRA_CC`, `EXTRA_BCC`, and `EXTRA_SUBJECT` keys. Use the `ACTION_SEND` action only to send data to a remote recipient (not to another application on the device).

➤ ACTION_VIEW—This is the most common generic action. View asks that the data supplied in the Intent's data URI be viewed in the most reasonable manner. Different applications will handle view requests depending on the URI schema of the data supplied. Natively `http:` addresses will open in the browser; `tel:` addresses will open the dialer to call the number; `geo:` addresses will be displayed in the Google Maps application; and contact content will be displayed in the Contact Manager.

➤ ACTION_WEB_SEARCH—Opens the Browser to perform a web search based on the query supplied using the `SearchManager.QUERY` key.

> **NOTE** *In addition to these Activity actions, Android includes a large number of broadcast actions that are used to create Intents that are broadcast to announce system events. These broadcast actions are described later in this chapter.*

CREATING INTENT FILTERS TO RECEIVE IMPLICIT INTENTS

Where an Activity Intent is a request for an action to be performed on a set of data, an Intent Filter is the corresponding declaration that an Activity is capable of performing an action on a type of data.

As you see later in this chapter, Intent Filters are also used by Broadcast Receivers to indicate the broadcast actions they wish to receive.

Defining an Intent Filter

Using Intent Filters, Activities can declare the actions and data they are able to support.

To register an Activity as a potential Intent handler, add an `intent-filter` tag to its manifest node using the following tags (and associated attributes):

➤ `action`—Uses the `android:name` attribute to specify the name of the action that can be performed. Each Intent Filter must have at least one action tag, and actions should be unique strings that are self-describing. You can define your own actions (best practice is to use a naming system based on the Java package naming conventions) or use one of the system actions provided by Android.

➤ `category`—Uses the `android:name` attribute to specify under which circumstances the action can be performed. Each Intent Filter tag can include multiple category tags. You can specify your own categories or use one of the standard values provided by Android.

➤ `data`—The data tag enables you to specify which data types your component can act on; you can include several data tags as appropriate. You can use any combination of the following attributes to specify the data your component supports:

  ➤ `android:host`—Specifies a valid hostname (for example, `google.com`).

  ➤ `android:mimetype`—Specifies the type of data your component is capable of handling. For example, `vnd.android.cursor.dir/*` would match any Android cursor.

  ➤ `android:path`—Specifies valid path values for the URI (for example, `/transport/boats/`).

  ➤ `android:port`—Specifies valid ports for the specified host.

  ➤ `android:scheme`—Requires a particular scheme (for example, `content` or `http`).

The following snippet shows an Intent Filter for an Activity that can perform the SHOW_DAMAGE action as either a primary or an alternative action based on its Earthquake cursor mime type:

```
<intent-filter>
  <action
    android:name="com.paad.earthquake.intent.action.SHOW_DAMAGE"/>
  <category
    android:name="android.intent.category.DEFAULT"/>
```

```
    <category
        android:name="android.intent.category.SELECTED_ALTERNATIVE"/>
    <data android:mimeType=
        "vnd.android.cursor.item/vnd.com.professionalandroid.provider.earthquake"
    />
</intent-filter>
```

You may have noticed that clicking a link to a YouTube video or Google Maps location on an Android device prompts you to use YouTube or Google Maps, respectively, rather than a web browser. This is achieved by specifying the scheme, host, and path attributes within the data tag of an Intent Filter, as shown in Listing 6-7. In this example, any link of the form that begins `http://blog.radioactiveyak.com` can be serviced by this Activity.

LISTING 6-7: Registering an Activity as an Intent Receiver for viewing content from a specific website using an Intent Filter

```
<activity android:name=".MyBlogViewerActivity">
  <intent-filter>
    <action android:name="android.intent.action.VIEW" />
    <category android:name="android.intent.category.DEFAULT" />
    <category android:name="android.intent.category.BROWSABLE" />
    <data android:scheme="http"
          android:host="blog.radioactiveyak.com"/>
  </intent-filter>
</activity>
```

Note that you must include the *browsable* category in order for links clicked within the browser to trigger this behavior.

How Android Resolves Intents Using Intent Filters

The process of deciding which Activity to start when an implicit Intent is passed in to `startActivity` is called *Intent resolution*. The aim of intent resolution is to find the best Intent Filter match possible by means of the following process:

1. Android puts together a list of all the Intent Filters available from the installed packages.

2. Intent Filters that do not match the action *or* category associated with the Intent being resolved are removed from the list.

➤ Action matches are made only if the Intent Filter includes the specified action. An Intent Filter will fail the action match check if *none* of its actions matches the one specified by the Intent.

➤ For category matching, Intent Filters must include *all* the categories defined in the resolving Intent, but can include additional categories not included in the Intent. An Intent Filter with no categories specified matches only Intents with no categories.

3. Each part of the Intent's data URI is compared to the Intent Filter's data tag. If the Intent Filter specifies a scheme, host/authority, path, or MIME type, these values are compared to the Intent's URI. Any mismatch will remove the Intent Filter from the list. Specifying no data values in an Intent Filter will result in a match with all Intent data values.

➤ The MIME type is the data type of the data being matched. When matching data types, you can use wildcards to match subtypes. If the Intent Filter specifies a data type, it must match the Intent; specifying no data types results in a match with all of them.

➤ The scheme is the "protocol" part of the URI (for example, `http:`, `mailto:`, or `tel:`).

➤ The hostname or *data authority* is the section of the URI between the scheme and the path (for example, `developer.android.com`). For a hostname to match, the Intent Filter's scheme must also match. If no scheme is specified the hostname is ignored.

➤ The data path is what comes after the authority (for example, `/training`). A path can match only if the scheme and hostname parts of the data tag also match.

4. When you implicitly start an Activity, if more than one component is resolved from this process, all the matching possibilities are offered to the user.

Native Android application components are part of the Intent-resolution process in exactly the same way as third-party applications. They do not have a higher priority and can be completely replaced with new Activities that declare Intent Filters that service the same actions.

As a result, when defining an Intent Filter indicating your application can view URL links, the browser will still be offered (in addition to your application.)

Finding and Using Intents Within an Activity

When an Activity is started through an implicit Intent, it needs to find the action it's been asked to perform, and the data it needs to perform it on.

To find the Intent used to start the Activity, call `getIntent`, as shown in Listing 6-8.

LISTING 6-8: Finding the launch Intent for an Activity

```
@Override
public void onCreate(Bundle savedInstanceState) {
  super.onCreate(savedInstanceState);
  setContentView(R.layout.main);

  Intent intent = getIntent();
  String action = intent.getAction();
  Uri data = intent.getData();
}
```

Use the `getData` and `getAction` methods to find the data and action, respectively, associated with the Intent. Use the type-safe `get<type>Extra` methods to extract additional information stored in its extras Bundle.

The `getIntent` method will always return the initial Intent used to create the Activity; in some circumstances your Activity may continue to receive Intents after it has been launched.

For example, if your application moves to the background, the user may click a Notification to return the running application to the foreground, resulting in a new Intent being delivered to the relevant Activity. If your Activity is configured such that when re-launched, instead of a new instance being created, the existing instance is moved to the top of the Activity stack a new Intent is delivered via the `onNewIntent` handler.

You can call `setIntent` to update the Intent returned when you call `getIntent`:

```
@Override
public void onNewIntent(Intent newIntent) {
  // TODO React to the new Intent
  setIntent(newIntent);
  super.onNewIntent(newIntent);
}
```

Selecting a Star Sign Example

In this example, you create a new Activity that services `ACTION_PICK` for a list of star signs. The picker application displays a list of star signs, and lets the user select one before closing and returning the selected sign to the calling Activity.

> **NOTE** *As with previous examples, to simplify readability, not all of the required import statements are included in these steps. You can enable "automatically add unambiguous imports on the fly" within the Android Studio settings or press Alt+Enter on each unresolved class name, as required.*

1. Create a new *StarSignPicker* project that includes a `StarSignPicker` Activity based on the Empty Activity template and using the App Compatibility library. Add an `EXTRA_SIGN_NAME` string constant that will be used to store an extra in our return Intent to indicate the star sign selected by user:

   ```
   public class StarSignPicker extends AppCompatActivity {

     public static final String EXTRA_SIGN_NAME = "SIGN_NAME";

     @Override
     protected void onCreate(Bundle savedInstanceState) {
       super.onCreate(savedInstanceState);
       setContentView(R.layout.activity_star_sign_picker);
     }
   }
   ```

2. Modify the `activity_star_sign_picker.xml` layout resource to include a single `RecyclerView` control. This control will be used to display the contacts:

```xml
<?xml version="1.0" encoding="utf-8"?>
<android.support.v7.widget.RecyclerView
  xmlns:android="http://schemas.android.com/apk/res/android"
  xmlns:app="http://schemas.android.com/apk/res-auto"
  android:id="@+id/recycler_view"
  android:layout_width="match_parent"
  android:layout_height="match_parent"
  android:orientation="vertical"
  app:layoutManager="LinearLayoutManager"
/>
```

3. Create a new `list_item_layout.xml` layout resource based on a `FrameLayout` that includes a single `TextView` control. This control will be used to display each star sign in the Recycler View:

```xml
<?xml version="1.0" encoding="utf-8"?>
<FrameLayout xmlns:android="http://schemas.android.com/apk/res/android"
  android:layout_width="match_parent"
  android:layout_height="wrap_content">
  <TextView
    android:id="@+id/itemTextView"
    android:layout_width="match_parent"
    android:layout_height="wrap_content"
    android:layout_margin="8dp"
    android:textAppearance="?attr/textAppearanceListItem"/>
</FrameLayout>
```

4. Add the Recycler View library to your app module Gradle build file:

```
dependencies {
  [... Existing dependencies ...]
  implementation 'com.android.support:recyclerview-v7:27.1.1'
}
```

5. Create a new `StarSignPickerAdapter` class that extends `RecyclerView.Adapter`, and which contains a string array of star signs:

```java
public class StarSignPickerAdapter
  extends RecyclerView.Adapter<StarSignPickerAdapter.ViewHolder> {

  private String[] mStarSigns = {"Aries", "Taurus", "Gemini", "Cancer",
                                 "Leo", "Virgo", "Libra", "Scorpio",
                                 "Sagittarius", "Capricorn", "Aquarius",
                                 "Pisces" };

  public StarSignPickerAdapter() {
  }

  @Override
  public int getItemCount() {
    return mStarSigns == null ? 0 : mStarSigns.length;
  }
}
```

5.1 Within the Adapter created in Step 5, create a new `ViewHolder` class that extends `RecyclerView.ViewHolder` and implements an `OnClickListener`. It should expose a `TextView` and an `OnClickListener`:

```
public static class ViewHolder extends RecyclerView.ViewHolder
                               implements View.OnClickListener {
  public TextView textView;
  public View.OnClickListener mListener;

  public ViewHolder(View v, View.OnClickListener listener) {
    super(v);
    mListener = listener;
    textView = v.findViewById(R.id.itemTextView);
    v.setOnClickListener(this);
  }

  @Override
  public void onClick(View v) {
    if (mListener != null)
      mListener.onClick(v);
  }
}
```

5.2 Still within the Adapter, override onCreateViewHolder using the ViewHolder created in Step 5.1, inflating the list_item_layout created in Step 3:

```
@Override
public StarSignPickerAdapter.ViewHolder
  onCreateViewHolder(ViewGroup parent, int viewType) {
  // Create the new View
  View v = LayoutInflater.from(parent.getContext())
          .inflate(R.layout.list_item_layout, parent, false);

  return new ViewHolder(v, null);
}
```

5.3 Create a new Interface that contains an onItemClicked method that takes a String argument; add a setOnAdapterItemClick method to the Adapter to store a reference to this event handler. We will use this handler notify the parent Activity which list item has been selected:

```
public interface IAdapterItemClick {
  void onItemClicked(String selectedItem);
}

IAdapterItemClick mAdapterItemClickListener;

public void setOnAdapterItemClick(
  IAdapterItemClick adapterItemClickHandler) {
  mAdapterItemClickListener = adapterItemClickHandler;
}
```

5.4 Finally, override the Adapter's onBindViewHolder method, assigning a star sign to the Text View defined in our View Holder. Take this opportunity to implement the onClickListener for each View Holder, which will call the IAdapterItemClick handler from Step 5.3 if an item in our list is clicked:

```
@Override
public void onBindViewHolder(ViewHolder holder, final int position) {
  holder.textView.setText(mStarSigns[position]);
  holder.mListener = new View.OnClickListener() {
```

```
        @Override
        public void onClick(View v) {
          if (mAdapterItemClickListener != null)
            mAdapterItemClickListener.onItemClicked(mStarSigns[position]);
        }
      };
    }
```

6. Return to the StarSignPicker Activity and modify the onCreate method. It currently begins like this:

```
@Override
protected void onCreate(Bundle savedInstanceState) {
  super.onCreate(savedInstanceState);
  setContentView(R.layout.activity_starsign_picker);
```

6.1 Now, still within onCreate, instantiate the StarSignPickerAdapter you created in Step 5:

```
StarSignPickerAdapter adapter = new StarSignPickerAdapter();
```

6.2 Create a new IAdapterItemClick handler and assign it to the Adapter using the setOnAdapterItemClick method. When an item is clicked, create a new result Intent and use the EXTRA_SIGN_NAME string to assign an extra that contains the selected star sign. Assign the new Intent as this Activity's result using setResult and call finish to close the Activity and return to the caller:

```
adapter.setOnAdapterItemClick(
  new StarSignPickerAdapter.IAdapterItemClick() {
  @Override
  public void onItemClicked(String selectedItem) {
    // Construct the result URI.
    Intent outData = new Intent();
    outData.putExtra(EXTRA_SIGN_NAME, selectedItem);
    setResult(Activity.RESULT_OK, outData);
    finish();
  }
});
```

6.3 Assign the adapter to the Recycler View using setAdapter:

```
RecyclerView rv = findViewById(R.id.recycler_view);
rv.setAdapter(adapter);
```

6.4 Close off the onCreate method:

```
}
```

7. Modify the application manifest and replace the intent-filter tag of the Activity to add support for the ACTION_PICK action on star signs:

```
<activity android:name=".StarSignPicker">
  <intent-filter>
    <action android:name="android.intent.action.PICK" />
    <category android:name="android.intent.category.DEFAULT"/>
    <data android:scheme="starsigns" />
  </intent-filter>
</activity>
```

8. This completes the sub-Activity. To test it, create a new test harness `StarSignPickerTester` launcher Activity with an `activity_star_sign_picker_tester.xml` layout file. Update the layout to include a `TextView` to display the selected star sign, and a `Button` to start the sub-Activity:

```xml
<?xml version="1.0" encoding="utf-8"?>
<LinearLayout xmlns:android="http://schemas.android.com/apk/res/android"
  android:orientation="vertical"
  android:layout_width="match_parent"
  android:layout_height="match_parent">
  <TextView
    android:id="@+id/selected_starsign_textview"
    android:layout_width="match_parent"
    android:layout_height="wrap_content"
    android:textAppearance="?attr/textAppearanceListItem"
    android:layout_margin="8dp"
  />
  <Button
    android:id="@+id/pick_starsign_button"
    android:layout_width="match_parent"
    android:layout_height="wrap_content"
    android:text="Pick Star Sign"
  />
</LinearLayout>
```

9. Override the `onCreate` method of the `StarSignPickerTester` to add a click listener to the Button so that it implicitly starts a new sub-Activity by specifying the `ACTION_PICK` and `starsign` as the data scheme:

```java
public class StarSignPickerTester extends AppCompatActivity {

  public static final int PICK_STARSIGN = 1;

  @Override
  public void onCreate(Bundle savedInstanceState) {
    super.onCreate(savedInstanceState);
    setContentView(R.layout.activity_star_sign_picker_tester);

    Button button = findViewById(R.id.pick_starsign_button);

    button.setOnClickListener(new View.OnClickListener() {
      @Override
      public void onClick(View _view) {
        Intent intent = new Intent(Intent.ACTION_PICK,
                                   Uri.parse("starsigns://"));
        startActivityForResult(intent, PICK_STARSIGN);
      }
    });
  }
}
```

10. When the sub-Activity returns, use the result to populate the Text View with the selected star sign:

```java
@Override
public void onActivityResult(int reqCode, int resCode, Intent data) {
  super.onActivityResult(reqCode, resCode, data);
```

```
        switch(reqCode) {
          case (PICK_STARSIGN) : {
            if (resCode == Activity.RESULT_OK) {
              String selectedSign =
                data.getStringExtra(StarSignPicker.EXTRA_SIGN_NAME);
              TextView tv = findViewById(R.id.selected_starsign_textview);
              tv.setText(selectedSign);
            }
            break;
          }
          default: break;
        }
      }
```

When your test Activity is running, press the "pick star sign" button. The star sign picker Activity should appear, as shown in Figure 6-1.

After you select a star sign, the parent Activity should return to the foreground with the selection displayed (see Figure 6-2).

FIGURE 6-1

FIGURE 6-2

Using Intent Filters for Plug-Ins and Extensibility

Having used Intent Filters to declare the actions your Activities can perform on different types of data, it stands to reason that applications can also query to find which actions are available to be performed on a particular piece of data.

Android provides a plug-in model that lets your applications take advantage of functionality, provided anonymously from your own or third-party application components you haven't yet conceived of, without your having to modify or recompile your projects.

Supplying Anonymous Actions to Applications

To use this mechanism to make your Activity's actions available anonymously for existing applications, publish them using intent-filter tags within their manifest nodes, as described earlier.

The Intent Filter describes the action it performs and the data upon which it can be performed. The latter will be used during the Intent-resolution process to determine when this action should be available. The category tag must be either ALTERNATIVE or SELECTED_ALTERNATIVE, or both. The android:label attribute should be a human-readable label that describes the action.

> **NOTE** *The* ALTERNATIVE *category is used to indicate that the action described is an alternative to what the user may currently be viewing. It is used to indicate an action to be displayed in a set of alternative things the user can do, usually as part of an options menu. The* SELECTED_ALTERNATIVE *category is similar but indicates an action that is typically performed on a selected item displayed within a list.*

Listing 6-9 shows an example of an Intent Filter used to advertise an Activity's capability to nuke Moon bases from orbit.

LISTING 6-9: Advertising supported Activity actions

```
<activity android:name=".NostromoController">
  <intent-filter
    android:label="Nuke From Orbit">
    <action
       android:name="com.professionalandroid.nostromo.NUKE_FROM_ORBIT"/>
    <data android:mimeType=
      "vnd.android.cursor.item/vnd.com.professionalandroid.provider.moonbase"
    />
    <category android:name="android.intent.category.ALTERNATIVE"/>
    <category
      android:name="android.intent.category.SELECTED_ALTERNATIVE"
    />
  </intent-filter>
</activity>
```

Discovering New Actions from Third-Party Intent Receivers

Using the Package Manager, you can create an Intent that specifies a type of data and a category of action, and have the system return a list of Activities capable of performing an action on that data.

The elegance of this concept is best explained by an example. If the data your Activity displays is a list of places, you might include functionality to View them on a map or "Show directions to" each. Jump a few months ahead and you've created an application that interfaces with your car, allowing your phone to set the destination for self-driving. Thanks to the runtime menu generation, when a new Intent Filter—with a DRIVE_CAR action—is included within the new Activity's node, Android will resolve this new action and make it available to your earlier application.

This provides you with the ability to retrofit functionality to your application when you create new components capable of performing actions on a given type of data.

The Intent you create will be used to resolve components with Intent Filters that supply actions for the data you specify. The Intent is being used to find actions, so don't assign it one; it should specify only the data to perform actions on. You should also specify the category of the action, either CATEGORY_ALTERNATIVE or CATEGORY_SELECTED_ALTERNATIVE.

The skeleton code for creating an Intent for menu-action resolution is shown here:

```
Intent intent = new Intent();
intent.setData(MyProvider.CONTENT_URI);
intent.addCategory(Intent.CATEGORY_ALTERNATIVE);
```

Pass this Intent into the Package Manager method queryIntentActivityOptions, specifying any options flags.

Listing 6-10 shows how to generate a list of actions to make available within your application.

LISTING 6-10: Generating a list of possible actions to be performed on specific data

```
PackageManager packageManager = getPackageManager();

// Create the intent used to resolve which actions
// should appear in the menu.
Intent intent = new Intent();
intent.setType(
  "vnd.android.cursor.item/vnd.com.professionalandroid.provider.moonbase");
intent.addCategory(Intent.CATEGORY_SELECTED_ALTERNATIVE);

// Specify flags. In this case, return all matches
int flags = PackageManager.MATCH_ALL;

// Generate the list
List<ResolveInfo> actions;
actions = packageManager.queryIntentActivities(intent, flags);

// Extract the list of action names
ArrayList<CharSequence> labels = new ArrayList<CharSequence>();
Resources r = getResources();
for (ResolveInfo action : actions)
  labels.add(action.nonLocalizedLabel);
```

Incorporating Anonymous Actions as Menu Items

The most common way to incorporate actions from third-party applications is to include them within your Menu Items of your App Bar. Menus and the App Bar are described in more detail in Chapter 13, "Implementing a Modern Android User Experience."

The `addIntentOptions` method, available from the `Menu` class, lets you specify an Intent that describes the data acted upon within your Activity, as described previously; however, rather than simply returning a list of possible actions, a new Menu Item will be created for each, with the text populated from the matching Intent Filters' labels.

To add Menu Items to your Menus dynamically at run time, use the `addIntentOptions` method on the `Menu` object in question: Pass in an Intent that specifies the data for which you want to provide actions. Generally, this will be handled within your Activities' or Fragments' `onCreateOptionsMenu` handlers.

As in the previous section, the Intent you create will be used to resolve Activities with Intent Filters that can supply actions for the data you specify. The Intent is being used to find actions, so don't assign it one; it should specify only the data to perform actions on. You should also specify the category of the action, either `CATEGORY_ALTERNATIVE` or `CATEGORY_SELECTED_ALTERNATIVE`.

The skeleton code for creating an Intent for menu-action resolution is shown here:

```
Intent intent = new Intent();
intent.setData(MyProvider.CONTENT_URI);
intent.addCategory(Intent.CATEGORY_ALTERNATIVE);
```

Pass this Intent in to `addIntentOptions` on the Menu you want to populate, as well as any options flags, the name of the calling class, the Menu group to use, and the Menu ID values. You can also specify an array of Intents you'd like to use to create additional Menu Items.

Listing 6-11 gives an idea of how to dynamically populate an Activity Menu.

LISTING 6-11: Dynamic Menu population from advertised actions

```java
@Override
public boolean onCreateOptionsMenu(Menu menu) {
  super.onCreateOptionsMenu(menu);

  // Create the intent used to resolve which actions
  // should appear in the menu.
  Intent intent = new Intent();
  intent.setType(
    "vnd.android.cursor.item/vnd.com.professionalandroid.provider.moonbase");
  intent.addCategory(Intent.CATEGORY_SELECTED_ALTERNATIVE);

  // Normal menu options to let you set a group and ID
  // values for the menu items you're adding.
  int menuGroup = 0;
  int menuItemId = 0;
  int menuItemOrder = Menu.NONE;
```

```
      // Provide the name of the component that's calling
      // the action -- generally the current Activity.
      ComponentName caller = getComponentName();

      // Define intents that should be added first.
      Intent[] specificIntents = null;
      // The menu items created from the previous Intents
      // will populate this array.
      MenuItem[] outSpecificItems = null;

      // Set any optional flags.
      int flags = Menu.FLAG_APPEND_TO_GROUP;

      // Populate the menu
      menu.addIntentOptions(menuGroup,
                            menuItemId,
                            menuItemOrder,
                            caller,
                            specificIntents,
                            intent,
                            flags,
                            outSpecificItems);

      return true;
  }
```

INTRODUCING LINKIFY

`Linkify` is a helper class that creates hyperlinks within Text View (and Text View-derived) classes through RegEx pattern matching. The hyperlinks work by creating new Intents that are used to start a new Activity when the link is clicked.

Text that matches a specified RegEx pattern will be converted into a clickable hyperlink that implicitly fires `startActivity(new Intent(Intent.ACTION_VIEW, uri))`, using the matched text as the target URI.

You can specify any string pattern to be treated as a clickable link; for convenience, the `Linkify` class provides presets for common content types.

Native Linkify Link Types

The `Linkify` class has presets that can detect and linkify web URLs, email addresses, map addresses, and phone numbers. To apply a preset, use the static `Linkify.addLinks` method, passing in a View to Linkify and a bitmask of one or more of the following self-describing `Linkify` class constants: `WEB_URLS`, `EMAIL_ADDRESSES`, `PHONE_NUMBERS`, `MAP_ADDRESSES`, and `ALL`.

```
TextView textView = findViewById(R.id.myTextView);
Linkify.addLinks(textView, Linkify.WEB_URLS|Linkify.EMAIL_ADDRESSES);
```

You can also linkify Views directly within a layout using the `android:autoLink` attribute. It supports one or more of the following values: `none`, `web`, `email`, `phone`, `map`, and `all`.

```
<TextView
  android:layout_width="match_parent"
  android:layout_height="match_parent"
  android:text="@string/linkify_me"
  android:autoLink="phone|email"
/>
```

Creating Custom Link Strings

To linkify your own data, you need to define your own linkify strings. Do this by creating a new RegEx pattern that matches the text you want to display as hyperlinks.

As with the native types, you can linkify the target Text View by calling `Linkify.addLinks`; however, rather than passing in one of the preset constants, pass in your RegEx pattern. You can also pass in a prefix that will be prepended to the target URI when a link is clicked.

Listing 6-12 shows a View being linkified to support earthquake data provided by an Android Content Provider. Note that rather than include the entire schema, the specified RegEx matches any text that starts with "quake" and is followed by a number, with optional whitespace. The full schema is then prepended to the URI before the Intent is fired.

LISTING 6-12: Creating custom link strings in Linkify

```
// Define the base URI.
String baseUri = "content://com.paad.earthquake/earthquakes/";

// Construct an Intent to test if there is an Activity capable of
// viewing the content you are Linkifying. Use the Package Manager
// to perform the test.
PackageManager pm = getPackageManager();
Intent testIntent = new Intent(Intent.ACTION_VIEW, Uri.parse(baseUri));
boolean activityExists = testIntent.resolveActivity(pm) != null;

// If there is an Activity capable of viewing the content
// Linkify the text.
if (activityExists) {
  int flags = Pattern.CASE_INSENSITIVE;
  Pattern p = Pattern.compile("\\bquake[\\s]?[0-9]+\\b", flags);
  Linkify.addLinks(myTextView, p, baseUri);
}
```

Note that in this example, including whitespace between "quake" and a number will return a match, but the resulting URI won't be valid. You can implement and specify one or both of a `TransformFilter` and `MatchFilter` interface to resolve this problem. These interfaces, defined in detail in the following section, offer additional control over the target URI structure and the definition of matching strings, and are used as in the following skeleton code:

```
Linkify.addLinks(myTextView, p, baseUri,
                 new MyMatchFilter(), new MyTransformFilter());
```

Using the Match Filter

To add additional conditions to RegEx pattern matches, implement the `acceptMatch` method in a Match Filter. When a potential match is found, `acceptMatch` is triggered, with the match start and end index (along with the full text being searched) passed in as parameters.

Listing 6-13 shows a `MatchFilter` implementation that cancels any match immediately preceded by an exclamation mark.

LISTING 6-13: Using a Linkify Match Filter

```
class MyMatchFilter implements MatchFilter {
  public boolean acceptMatch(CharSequence s, int start, int end) {
    return (start == 0 || s.charAt(start-1) != '!');
  }
}
```

Using the Transform Filter

The Transform Filter lets you modify the implicit URI generated by matching link text. Decoupling the link text from the target URI gives you more freedom in how you display data strings to your users.

To use the Transform Filter, implement the `transformUrl` method in your Transform Filter. When Linkify finds a successful match, it calls `transformUrl`, passing in the RegEx pattern used and the matched text string (before the base URI is prepended). You can modify the matched string and return it such that it can be appended to the base string as the data for a View Intent.

As shown in Listing 6-14, the `TransformFilter` implementation transforms the matched text into a lowercase URI, having also removed any whitespace characters.

LISTING 6-14: Using a Linkify Transform Filter

```
class MyTransformFilter implements TransformFilter {
  public String transformUrl(Matcher match, String url) {
    return url.toLowerCase().replace(" ", "");
  }
}
```

USING INTENTS TO BROADCAST EVENTS

So far, we've used Intents to start new application components, but you can also use Intents to broadcast messages *between* components using the `sendBroadcast` method.

As a system-level message-passing mechanism, Intents are capable of sending structured messages across process boundaries. As a result, you can implement Broadcast Receivers to listen for, and respond to, Broadcast Intents within your application for your own broadcasts as well as those from other apps or the system itself.

Android broadcasts Intents extensively, to announce system events, such as changes in network connectivity, docking state, and incoming calls.

Broadcasting Events with Intents

Within your application, construct the Intent you want to broadcast and use the `sendBroadcast` method to send it.

As with Intents used to start Activities, you can broadcast either an explicit or implicit Intent. Explicit Intents indicate the class of the Broadcast Receiver you want to trigger, whereas implicit Intents specify the action, data, and category of your Intent in a way that lets potential Broadcast Receivers accurately determine their interest.

Implicit Intent broadcasts are particularly useful where you have multiple Receivers that are potential targets for a broadcast.

For implicit Intents, the *action* string is used to identify the type of event being broadcast, so it should be a unique string that identifies the event type. By convention, action strings are constructed using the same form as Java package names:

```
public static final String NEW_LIFEFORM_ACTION =
    "com.professionalandroid.alien.action.NEW_LIFEFORM_ACTION";
```

If you want to include data within the Intent, you can specify a URI using the Intent's `data` property. You can also include extras to add additional primitive values. Considered in terms of an event-driven paradigm, the extras equate to optional parameters passed into an event handler.

Listing 6-15 shows the basic creation of explicit and implicit broadcast Intents, the latter using the action defined previously with additional event information stored as extras.

LISTING 6-15: Broadcasting an Intent

```
Intent explicitIntent = new Intent(this, MyBroadcastReceiver.class);
intent.putExtra(LifeformDetectedReceiver.EXTRA_LIFEFORM_NAME,
                detectedLifeform);
intent.putExtra(LifeformDetectedReceiver.EXTRA_LATITUDE,
                mLatitude);
intent.putExtra(LifeformDetectedReceiver.EXTRA_LONGITUDE,
                mLongitude);

sendBroadcast(explicitIntent);

Intent intent = new Intent(LifeformDetectedReceiver.NEW_LIFEFORM_ACTION);
intent.putExtra(LifeformDetectedReceiver.EXTRA_LIFEFORM_NAME,
                detectedLifeform);
intent.putExtra(LifeformDetectedReceiver.EXTRA_LATITUDE,
                mLatitude);
intent.putExtra(LifeformDetectedReceiver.EXTRA_LONGITUDE,
                mLongitude);

sendBroadcast(intent);
```

The explicit Intent will be received only by the `MyBroadcastReceiver` class indicated, whereas the implicit Intent could potentially be received by multiple Receivers.

Listening for Intent Broadcasts with Broadcast Receivers

Broadcast Receivers (commonly referred to as *Receivers*) are used to listen for broadcast Intents. For a Receiver to receive broadcasts, it must be registered, either in code or within the application manifest—the latter case is referred to as a *manifest Receiver*.

To create a new Broadcast Receiver, extend the `BroadcastReceiver` class and override the `onReceive` event handler:

```
import android.content.BroadcastReceiver;
import android.content.Context;
import android.content.Intent;

public class MyBroadcastReceiver extends BroadcastReceiver {
  @Override
  public void onReceive(Context context, Intent intent) {
    //TODO: React to the Intent received.
  }
}
```

When a broadcast Intent is started, the `onReceive` method will be executed on the main application Thread. Any non-trivial work should be performed asynchronously after calling `goAsync`—as described in Chapter 11, "Working in the Background."

In any case, all processing within the Broadcast Receiver must complete within 10 seconds or the system will consider it unresponsive, and attempt to terminate it.

To avoid this, Broadcast Receivers will typically schedule a background job or launch a bound Service to initiate potentially long-running tasks, or it can update the containing parent Activity UI or trigger a Notification to notify the user of received changes.

Listing 6-16 shows how to implement a Broadcast Receiver that extracts the data and several extras from the broadcast Intent and uses them to trigger a Notification. In the following sections you learn how to register it in code or in your application manifest.

LISTING 6-16: Implementing a Broadcast Receiver

```
public class LifeformDetectedReceiver
  extends BroadcastReceiver {

  public static final String NEW_LIFEFORM_ACTION
    = "com.professionalandroid.alien.action.NEW_LIFEFORM_ACTION";
  public static final String EXTRA_LIFEFORM_NAME
    = "EXTRA_LIFEFORM_NAME";
  public static final String EXTRA_LATITUDE = "EXTRA_LATITUDE";
  public static final String EXTRA_LONGITUDE = "EXTRA_LONGITUDE";
  public static final String FACE_HUGGER = "facehugger";

  private static final int NOTIFICATION_ID = 1;

  @Override
  public void onReceive(Context context, Intent intent) {
    // Get the lifeform details from the intent.
```

```
String type = intent.getStringExtra(EXTRA_LIFEFORM_NAME);
double lat = intent.getDoubleExtra(EXTRA_LATITUDE, Double.NaN);
double lng = intent.getDoubleExtra(EXTRA_LONGITUDE, Double.NaN);

if (type.equals(FACE_HUGGER)) {
  NotificationManagerCompat notificationManager =
    NotificationManagerCompat.from(context);

  NotificationCompat.Builder builder =
    new NotificationCompat.Builder(context);

  builder.setSmallIcon(R.drawable.ic_alien)
          .setContentTitle("Face Hugger Detected")
          .setContentText(Double.isNaN(lat) || Double.isNaN(lng) ?
                          "Location Unknown" :
                          "Located at " + lat + "," + lng);

  notificationManager.notify(NOTIFICATION_ID, builder.build());
  }
 }
}
```

Registering Broadcast Receivers in Code

Broadcast Receivers that respond to broadcasts sent from your own application, and those that alter the UI of an Activity, are typically registered dynamically in code. A Receiver registered programmatically can respond to broadcast Intents only when the application component it is registered within is running.

This is useful when the Receiver behavior is tightly bound to a particular component—for example, one that updates the UI elements of an Activity. In this case, it's good practice to register the Receiver within the onStart handler and unregister it during onStop.

Listing 6-17 shows how to register and unregister a Broadcast Receiver in code using the IntentFilter class that defines an action associated with an implicit broadcast Intent the Receiver should respond to.

LISTING 6-17: Registering and unregistering a Broadcast Receiver in code

```
private IntentFilter filter =
  new IntentFilter(LifeformDetectedReceiver.NEW_LIFEFORM_ACTION);

private LifeformDetectedReceiver receiver =
  new LifeformDetectedReceiver();

@Override
public void onStart() {
  super.onStart();

  // Register the broadcast receiver.
  registerReceiver(receiver, filter);
}
```

```
@Override
public void onStop() {
  // Unregister the receiver
  unregisterReceiver(receiver);

  super.onStop();
}
```

Registering Broadcast Receivers in Your Application Manifest

Broadcast Receivers registered statically in your application manifest are always active, and will receive Broadcast Intents even when your application has been killed or hasn't been started; your application will be started automatically when a matching Intent is broadcast.

To include a Broadcast Receiver in the application manifest, add a `receiver` tag within the `application` node, specifying the class name of the Broadcast Receiver to register:

```
<receiver android:name=".LifeformDetectedReceiver"/>
```

Prior to Android 8.0 Oreo (API Level 26), it was possible for manifest Receivers to include an intent-filter tag that specified an action to support listening for implicit broadcasts:

```
<receiver android:name=".LifeformDetectedReceiver">
  <intent-filter>
    <action android:name=
      "com.professionalandroid.alien.action.NEW_LIFEFORM_ACTION"
    />
  </intent-filter>
</receiver>
```

Manifest Receivers let you create event-driven applications that will respond to broadcast events even after your application has been closed or killed—however, it also introduces associated resource use risks. If an Intent is broadcast frequently it could cause your application to wake repeatedly, potentially resulting in significant battery drain.

To minimize this risk, Android 8.0 no longer supports manifest Receivers for arbitrary implicit Intents.

Apps can continue to register for explicit broadcasts in their manifests, and you can register Receivers at runtime for any broadcast, both implicit or explicit—but only a limited number of broadcast system actions can be used to register an implicit Intent within your manifest. The supported actions are described later in this chapter in the section, "Monitoring Device State Changes through Broadcast Intents."

Managing Manifest Receivers at Run Time

Using the Package Manager, you can enable and disable any of your application's manifest Receivers at run time using the `setComponentEnabledSetting` method. You can use this technique to enable or disable any application component (including Activities and Services), but it is particularly useful for manifest Receivers.

To minimize the potential battery drain caused by your application, it's good practice to disable manifest Receivers that listen for system events when your application doesn't need to respond to those events.

Listing 6-18 shows how to enable and disable a manifest Receiver at run time.

LISTING 6-18: Dynamically toggling manifest Receivers

```
ComponentName myReceiverName =
  new ComponentName(this,LifeformDetectedReceiver.class);
PackageManager pm = getPackageManager();

// Enable a manifest receiver
pm.setComponentEnabledSetting(myReceiverName,
  PackageManager.COMPONENT_ENABLED_STATE_ENABLED,
  PackageManager.DONT_KILL_APP);

// Disable a manifest receiver
pm.setComponentEnabledSetting(myReceiverName,
  PackageManager.COMPONENT_ENABLED_STATE_DISABLED,
  PackageManager.DONT_KILL_APP);
```

Monitoring Device State Changes Through Broadcast Intents

Many of the system Services broadcast Intents to signal changes in device state. You can monitor these broadcasts to add functionality to your own projects based on events such as the completion of device booting, time-zone changes, changes in dock state, and battery status.

A comprehensive list of the broadcast actions used and transmitted natively by Android is available at `developer.android.com/reference/android/content/Intent.html`. Due to the restrictions on registering implicit manifest Broadcast Receivers introduced in Android 8.0, only a subset of the system broadcast Intents can be registered in the manifest. You can find the list of implicit broadcast exceptions at `developer.android.com/guide/components/broadcast-exceptions.html`.

The following sections examine how to create Intent Filters to register Broadcast Receivers that can react to some of these system events, and how to extract the device state information accordingly.

Listening for Docking Changes

Some Android devices can be docked in a car dock or desk dock, where the desk dock can be analog (low-end) or digital (high-end).

By registering a Receiver to listen for the `Intent.ACTION_DOCK_EVENT` (`android.intent.action.ACTION_DOCK_EVENT`), you can determine the docking status and type of dock on devices that support docks:

```
<action android:name="android.intent.action.ACTION_DOCK_EVENT"/>
```

The dock event Broadcast Intent is sticky, meaning you will receive the current dock status when calling `registerReciver`, even if no receiver is specified. Listing 6-19 shows how to extract the current docking status from the Intent returned by calling `registerReceiver`, using the `Intent .ACTION_DOCK_EVENT` Intent. Note that if the device doesn't include support for docking, the call to `registerReceiver` will return null.

LISTING 6-19: Determining docking state

```
boolean isDocked = false;
boolean isCar = false;
boolean isDesk = false;

IntentFilter dockIntentFilter =
  new IntentFilter(Intent.ACTION_DOCK_EVENT);
Intent dock = registerReceiver(null, dockIntentFilter);

if (dock != null) {
  int dockState = dock.getIntExtra(Intent.EXTRA_DOCK_STATE,
                  Intent.EXTRA_DOCK_STATE_UNDOCKED);

  isDocked = dockState != Intent.EXTRA_DOCK_STATE_UNDOCKED;
  isCar    = dockState == Intent.EXTRA_DOCK_STATE_CAR;
  isDesk   = dockState == Intent.EXTRA_DOCK_STATE_DESK ||
             dockState == Intent.EXTRA_DOCK_STATE_LE_DESK ||
             dockState == Intent.EXTRA_DOCK_STATE_HE_DESK;
}
```

Listening for Battery State and Data Connectivity Changes

Prior to the introduction of the Job Scheduler, the most common reason for listening for battery status and data connectivity changes was to delay large downloads or similarly time-consuming, battery draining processes until the device was connected to an appropriate data network and/or charging.

Chapter 11, "Working in the Background," describes how to use the Job Scheduler and Firebase Job Dispatcher to schedule jobs using criteria including network connectivity and battery charging state, as a more efficient and comprehensive solution than manually monitoring these state changes.

To monitor changes in the battery level and charging status within an Activity, you can register a Receiver using an Intent Filter that listens for the `Intent.ACTION_BATTERY_CHANGED` broadcast by the Battery Manager.

Listing 6-20 shows how to extract the current battery charge and charging status from the sticky battery status change Intent.

LISTING 6-20: Determining battery and charge state information

```
IntentFilter batIntentFilter = new IntentFilter(Intent.ACTION_BATTERY_CHANGED);
Intent battery = context.registerReceiver(null, batIntentFilter);
```

```
int status = battery.getIntExtra(BatteryManager.EXTRA_STATUS, -1);
boolean isCharging =
  status == BatteryManager.BATTERY_STATUS_CHARGING ||
  status == BatteryManager.BATTERY_STATUS_FULL;
```

Note that you can't register the battery changed action within a manifest Receiver; however, you can monitor connection and disconnection from a power source and a low battery level using the following action strings, each prefixed with `android.intent.action`:

➤   `ACTION_BATTERY_LOW`

➤   `ACTION_BATTERY_OKAY`

➤   `ACTION_POWER_CONNECTED`

➤   `ACTION_POWER_DISCONNECTED`

Changes to the battery level and status occur regularly, so it's generally considered good practice not to register receivers to listen for these broadcasts unless your application provides functionality specifically related to these changes.

To monitor changes in network connectivity, register a Broadcast Receiver within your application to listen for the `ConnectivityManager.CONNECTIVITY_ACTION` action (apps targeting Android 7.0 Nougat (API Level 24) and higher will not receive this broadcast if they declare the Receiver in their manifest).

The connectivity change broadcast isn't sticky and doesn't contain any additional information regarding the change. To extract details on the current connectivity status, you need to use the Connectivity Manager, as shown in Listing 6-21.

LISTING 6-21: Determining connectivity state information

```
String svcName = Context.CONNECTIVITY_SERVICE;
ConnectivityManager cm =
  (ConnectivityManager)context.getSystemService(svcName);

NetworkInfo activeNetwork = cm.getActiveNetworkInfo();
boolean isConnected = activeNetwork.isConnectedOrConnecting();
boolean isMobile = activeNetwork.getType() ==
                   ConnectivityManager.TYPE_MOBILE;
```

INTRODUCING THE LOCAL BROADCAST MANAGER

The Local Broadcast Manager was introduced to the Android Support Library to simplify the process of registering for, sending, and receiving Intents broadcast only between components within your application.

Because of the reduced broadcast scope, using the Local Broadcast Manager is more efficient than sending a global broadcast. It also ensures that the Intent you broadcast cannot be received by any other applications, ensuring that there is no risk of leaking private or sensitive data.

Similarly, other applications can't transmit broadcasts to your Receivers, negating the risk of these Receivers becoming vectors for security exploits. Note that the Broadcast Receiver specified can also be used to handle global Intent broadcasts.

To use the Local Broadcast Manager, you must first include the Android Support Library in your application, as described in Chapter 2.

Use the `LocalBroadcastManager.getInstance` method to return an instance of the Local Broadcast Manager:

```
LocalBroadcastManager lbm = LocalBroadcastManager.getInstance(this);
```

To register a local Broadcast Receiver, use the Local Broadcast Manager's `registerReceiver` method, much as you would register a global receiver, passing in a Broadcast Receiver and an Intent Filter as shown in Listing 6-22.

LISTING 6-22: Registering and unregistering a local Broadcast Receiver

```java
@Override
public void onResume() {
  super.onResume();

  // Register the broadcast receiver.
  LocalBroadcastManager lbm = LocalBroadcastManager.getInstance(this);
  lbm.registerReceiver(receiver, filter);
}

@Override
public void onPause() {
  // Unregister the receiver
  LocalBroadcastManager lbm = LocalBroadcastManager.getInstance(this);
  lbm.unregisterReceiver(receiver);

  super.onPause();
}
```

To transmit a local Broadcast Intent, use the Local Broadcast Manager's `sendBroadcast` method, passing in the Intent to broadcast:

```
lbm.sendBroadcast(new Intent(LOCAL_ACTION));
```

The Local Broadcast Manager also includes a `sendBroadcastSync` method that operates synchronously, blocking until each registered Receiver has processed the broadcast Intent.

INTRODUCING PENDING INTENTS

The `PendingIntent` class provides a mechanism for creating Intents that can be fired on your application's behalf by the system, or another application, at a later time.

A Pending Intent is commonly used to package Intents that will be fired in response to a future event, such as when a user touches a Notification.

> **NOTE** *When used, Pending Intents execute the packaged Intent with the same permissions and identity as if you had executed them yourself, within your own application.*

The `PendingIntent` class offers static methods to construct Pending Intents used to start an Activity, to start background or foreground Services, or to broadcast implicit or explicit Intents:

```
int requestCode = 0;
int flags = 0;

// Start an Activity
Intent startActivityIntent = new Intent(this, MyActivity.class);
PendingIntent.getActivity(this, requestCode,
                          startActivityIntent, flags);

// Start a Service
Intent startServiceIntent = new Intent(this, MyService.class);
PendingIntent.getService(this, requestCode,
                         startServiceIntent, flags);

// Start a foreground Service (API Level 26 or higher)
Intent startForegroundServiceIntent = new Intent(this, MyFGService.class);
PendingIntent.getForegroundService(this, requestCode,
                                   startForegroundServiceIntent flags);

// Broadcast an Intent to an explicit Broadcast Receiver
Intent broadcastExplicitIntent = new Intent(this, MyReceiver.class);
PendingIntent.getBroadcast(this, requestCode,
                           broadcastExplicitIntent, flags);

// Broadcast an implicit Intent (API Level 25 or lower)
Intent broadcastImplicitIntent = new Intent(NEW_LIFEFORM_ACTION);
PendingIntent.getBroadcast(this, requestCode,
                           broadcastImplicitIntent, flags);
```

The `PendingIntent` class includes static constants that can be used to specify flags to update or cancel any existing Pending Intent that matches your specified action, as well as to specify if this Intent is to be fired only once. The various options are examined in more detail when Notifications are introduced in Chapter 11.

Because Pending Intents are triggered outside the scope of your application, it's important to consider the user's context when these Intents are likely to be executed; an Intent that starts a new Activity should be used only in response to direct user action, such as selecting a notification.

To improve battery life, Android 8.0 Oreo (API Level 26) introduced strict limits on application background execution that affect Pending Intents.

Since Android 8.0, apps can't start new background Services if the app itself is idle in the background. As a result, a Pending Intent created using the `startService` method can't start a new Service if the app is in the background when it's triggered. For this reason, the startForegroundService method was introduced in Android 8.0. Pending Intents created using this method are allowed to start a new Service, which—once started—has five seconds to become a foreground Service through a call to startForeground, or it will be stopped and the application shown as not responding.

As mentioned previously, Android 8.0 also eliminated support for using your manifest to register for implicit Intent broadcasts. As Pending Intents are commonly fired when your application isn't running, so it's necessary to use an explicit Intent to ensure the target Receiver is triggered.

7

Using Internet Resources

WROX.COM CODE DOWNLOADS FOR THIS CHAPTER

The code downloads for this chapter are found at www.wrox.com. The code for this chapter is divided into the following major examples:

➤ `Snippets_ch7.zip`

➤ `Earthquake_ch7.zip`

CONNECTING TO THE INTERNET

One of the most powerful aspects of modern smart devices is their ability to connect to Internet services, and to expose the information—or those services—to users within native applications.

This chapter introduces Android's Internet connectivity model and techniques for downloading and parsing data efficiently. You learn how to connect to an Internet resource and how to use the SAX Parser, XML Pull Parser, and JSON Reader to parse data feeds. Android requires that you perform all network tasks on a background thread, so you learn how to do this efficiently using a combination of View Models, Live Data, and Asynchronous Tasks.

Expanding the earthquake-monitoring example demonstrates how to tie together all these features.

This chapter also introduces the Download Manager, and you learn how to use it to schedule and manage long-running shared downloads. You are also introduced to the Job Scheduler, and learn the best practices for ensuring your downloads are fast, efficient, and don't drain the battery.

Finally, this chapter introduces some popular Internet cloud services you can leverage to add additional cloud-based functionality to your Android apps.

CONNECTING, DOWNLOADING, AND PARSING INTERNET RESOURCES

Using Android's network APIs, you can connect to remote server endpoints, make HTTP requests, and process server results and data feeds—including the ability to extract and process data using a parser, such as SAX, the XML Pull Parser, or the JSON Reader.

Modern mobile devices offer a number of alternatives for accessing the Internet. Broadly speaking, Android provides two connection techniques for Internet connectivity, each is offered to the application layer automatically—you don't have to indicate which technology to use when making an Internet connection:

➤ **Mobile Internet**—GPRS, EDGE, 3G, 4G, and LTE Internet access is available through carriers that offer mobile data.

➤ **Wi-Fi**—Private and public Wi-Fi access points.

If you use Internet resources in your application, remember that your users' data connections are dependent on the communications technology available to them. EDGE and GSM connections are notoriously low-bandwidth, whereas a Wi-Fi connection may be unreliable in a mobile setting.

Optimize the user experience by always minimizing the quantity of data transmitted and ensure that your application is robust enough to handle network outages and bandwidth/latency limitations.

Why Build a Native Internet App?

Given that a web browser is available on most smart devices, you might ask if there's any reason to create native Internet-based applications when you could make a web-based version instead.

While mobile web browsers are becoming increasingly powerful, there are still a number of benefits to creating thick- and thin-client native applications rather than relying on entirely web-based solutions:

➤ **Bandwidth**—Static resources such as images, layouts, and sounds can be expensive on devices with bandwidth restraints. By creating a native application, you can limit the bandwidth requirements to changed data only.

➤ **Offline availability**—With a browser-based solution, a patchy Internet connection can result in intermittent application availability. A native application can cache data and user actions to provide as much functionality as possible without a live connection, and synchronize with the cloud when a connection is reestablished.

➤ **Latency and UX**—By building a native application, you can take advantage of lower user-interaction latency as well as ensure the user experience is consistent with the OS and other first- and third-party apps.

➤ **Reducing battery drain**—Each time your application opens a connection to a server, the wireless radio will be turned on (or kept on). A native application can bundle its connections, minimizing the number of connections initiated. The longer the period between network requests, the longer the wireless radio can be left off and the lower the impact on battery life.

➤ **Native features**—Android devices are more than simple platforms for running a browser. They include location-based services, Notifications, widgets, cameras, Bluetooth radios, background Services, and hardware sensors. By creating a native application, you can combine the data available online with the hardware features available on the device to provide a richer user experience.

Connecting to an Internet Resource

Before you can access Internet resources, you need to add an `INTERNET` uses-permission node to your application manifest, as shown in the following XML snippet:

```
<uses-permission android:name="android.permission.INTERNET"/>
```

Listing 7-1 shows the basic pattern for opening an Internet data connection and receiving a stream of data from a data feed.

LISTING 7-1: Opening an Internet data stream

```
try {
  URL url = new URL(myFeed);

  // Create a new HTTP URL connection
  URLConnection connection = url.openConnection();
  HttpURLConnection httpConnection = (HttpURLConnection) connection;

  int responseCode = httpConnection.getResponseCode();
  if (responseCode == HttpURLConnection.HTTP_OK) {
    InputStream in = httpConnection.getInputStream();
    processStream(in);
  }
  httpConnection.disconnect();
```

LISTING 7-1 *(continued)*

```
} catch (MalformedURLException e) {
  Log.e(TAG, "Malformed URL Exception.", e);
} catch (IOException e) {
  Log.e(TAG, "IO Exception.", e);
}
```

> **WARNING** *On Android, attempting to perform network operations on the main UI thread will cause a* `NetworkOnMainThreadException`. *In order to connect to an Internet resource, you must do so from a background thread. The next section describes a best-practice technique for moving network operations to background threads using a combination of the View Model, Live Data, and Asynchronous Task classes.*

Android includes several classes to help you handle network communications. They are available in the `java.net.*` and `android.net.*` packages.

Performing Network Operations on Background Threads Using View Models, Live Data, and Asynchronous Tasks

It's always good practice to perform potentially time-consuming tasks such as network operations on a background thread. Doing so ensures you're not blocking the UI thread, which would make your application janky or unresponsive. On Android, this best practice is enforced for network operations through the `NetworkOnMainThreadException`, which is triggered whenever a network operation is attempted on the main UI thread.

> **NOTE** *In Chapter 11, "Working in the Background," you learn a broad range of options for moving operations to background threads. You are also introduced to APIs designed for scheduling background network operations efficiently, including the Job Scheduler.*

Within your Activity you can create and run a new `Thread` as shown in the following code. When you're ready to post to the UI thread, call `runOnUIThread` and apply your UI changes within another Runnable:

```
Thread t = new Thread(new Runnable() {
  public void run() {
    // Perform Network operations and processing.
    final MyDataClass result = loadInBackground();
    // Synchronize with the UI thread to post changes.
    runOnUiThread(new Runnable() {
```

```
      @Override
      public void run() {
        deliverResult(result);
      }
    });
  }
});
t.start();
```

Alternatively, you can take advantage of the `AsyncTask` class, which encapsulates this process for you. An Async Task lets you define an operation to be performed in the background and provides event handlers that enable you to monitor progress and post the results on the GUI Thread.

Async Task handles all the Thread creation, management, and synchronization, enabling you to create an asynchronous task consisting of processing to be done in the background, and UI updates to be performed both during the processing and once it's complete.

To create a new asynchronous task, extend the `AsyncTask` class, specifying the parameter types to use, as shown in this skeleton code:

```
private class MyAsyncTask extends AsyncTask<String, Integer, String> {
  @Override
  protected String doInBackground(String... parameter) {
    // Moved to a background thread.
    String result = "";
    int myProgress = 0;
    int inputLength = parameter[0].length();
    // Perform background processing task, update myProgress
    for (int i = 1; i <= inputLength; i++) {
      myProgress = i;
      result = result + parameter[0].charAt(inputLength-i);
      try {
        Thread.sleep(100);
      } catch (InterruptedException e) { }
      // Send progress to onProgressUpdate handler
      publishProgress(myProgress);
    }
    // Return the value to be passed to onPostExecute
    return result;
  }

  @Override
  protected void onProgressUpdate(Integer... progress) {
    // Synchronized to UI thread.
    // Update progress bar, Notification, or other UI elements
  }

  @Override
  protected void onPostExecute(String result) {
    // Synchronized to UI thread.
    // Report results via UI update, Dialog, or notifications
  }
}
```

After you've implemented an Asynchronous Task, execute it by creating a new instance and calling `execute`, passing in any parameters as required:

```
String input = "redrum ... redrum";
new MyAsyncTask().execute(input);
```

Each Async Task instance can be executed only once. If you attempt to call execute a second time, an exception will be thrown.

These approaches have several significant limitations stemming from the Activity life cycle described in Chapter 3. As you know, an Activity (and its Fragments) may be destroyed and re-created whenever the device configuration changes. As a result a user rotating the screen may interrupt your running network Thread or Async Task, which will be destroyed along with its parent Activity.

For Threads that are started through user action, this will effectively cancel the operation. For Threads initiated within the Activity's lifecycle handlers—such as `onCreate` or `onStart`—they will be re-created and rerun when the Activity is re-created—potentially executing the same network operation multiple times. This can result in duplicative data transfers and a shorter battery life.

A better approach is to use the `ViewModel` and `LiveData` classes provided as part of the Android Architecture Components. Any View Models associated with an Activity or Fragment are designed specifically to persist across configuration changes, effectively providing caching for the data they store. The data within a View Model is typically returned as Live Data.

Live Data is a lifecycle-aware class used to store, and provide observable updates for, application data. Lifecycle-awareness means that Live Data only sends updates to Observers within app components that are in an active lifecycle state.

To use View Models and Live Data, you must first add Android Architecture Components to your app module's Gradle Build file:

```
dependencies {
  [... Existing dependencies nodes ...]
  implementation "android.arch.lifecycle:extensions:1.1.1"
}
```

Listing 7-2 shows a simple View Model implementation that takes advantage of the standard `MutableLiveData` class. It uses an `AsyncTask` to download and parse an Internet resource in the background, and returns the result as a Live Data representing a List of Strings.

LISTING 7-2: Using a View Model to download on a background thread using an Async Task

```
public class MyViewModel extends AndroidViewModel {
  private static final String TAG = "MyViewModel";

  private final MutableLiveData<List<String>> data;

  public MyViewModel(Application application) {
    super(application);
  }
```

```java
public LiveData<List<String>> getData() {
  if (data == null)
    data = new MutableLiveData<List<String>>();
    loadData();
  }
  return data;
}

private void loadData() {
  new AsyncTask<Void, Void, List<String>>() {
    @Override
    protected List<String> doInBackground(Void... voids) {
      ArrayList<String> result = new ArrayList<>(0);

      String myFeed = getApplication().getString(R.string.my_feed);
      try {
        URL url = new URL(myFeed);

        // Create a new HTTP URL connection
        URLConnection connection = url.openConnection();
        HttpURLConnection httpConnection = (HttpURLConnection) connection;

        int responseCode = httpConnection.getResponseCode();
        if (responseCode == HttpURLConnection.HTTP_OK) {
          InputStream in = httpConnection.getInputStream();
          // Process the input stream to generate our result list
          result = processStream(in);
        }
        httpConnection.disconnect();
      } catch (MalformedURLException e) {
        Log.e(TAG, "Malformed URL Exception.", e);
      } catch (IOException e) {
        Log.e(TAG, "IO Exception.", e);
      }
      return result;
    }

    @Override
    protected void onPostExecute(List<String> data) {
      // Update the Live Data data value.
      data.setValue(data);
    }
  }.execute();
}
}
```

To use a View Model within your application, you must first create a new (or return the existing) instance of your View Model within the Activity or Fragment that will be observing the Live Data.

Use the `ViewModelProviders` class's static `of` method—passing in the current application component —to retrieve the View Models available, and use the `get` method to specify the View Model you wish to use:

```java
MyViewModel myViewModel = ViewModelProviders.of(this)
                                  .get(MyViewModel.class);
```

Once you have a reference to your View Model, you must add an `Observer` in order to receive the Live Data it contains. Call `getData` on the View Model, then use the `observe` method to add an `Observer` implementation whose `onChanged` handler will be triggered whenever the underlying data changes:

```
myViewModel.getData()
          .observe(this, new Observer<List<String>>() {
  @Override
  public void onChanged(@Nullable List<String> data) {
    // TODO When new View Model data is received, update the UI.
  }
});
```

The full process of obtaining a View Model for your Activity, requesting the Live Data, and observing it for changes is shown in Listing 7-3.

LISTING 7-3: Using Live Data and a View Model from an Activity

```
@Override
protected void onCreate(Bundle savedInstanceState) {
  super.onCreate(savedInstanceState);
  setContentView(R.layout.activity_main);

  // Obtain (or create) an instance of the View Model
  MyViewModel myViewModel = ViewModelProviders.of(this)
                                      .get(MyViewModel.class);

  // Get the current data and observe it for changes.
  myViewModel.getData()
            .observe(this, new Observer<List<String>>() {
    @Override
    public void onChanged(@Nullable List<String> data) {
      // Update your UI with the loaded data.
      // Returns cached data automatically after a configuration change,
      // and will be fired again if underlying Live Data object is modified.
    }
  });
}
```

Because your View Model lifecycle is based on your application—rather than the parent Activity or Fragment—the View Model's Live Data's loading function won't be interrupted by a device configuration change.

Similarly, your results are implicitly cached across device configuration changes. After a rotation, when `observe` is called on the View Model's data, it will immediately return the last result set via the `onChanged` handler—without the View Model's `loadData` method being called. This saves significant time and battery power by eliminating duplicative network downloads and the associated processing.

In Chapter 11 you are introduced to more powerful APIs for scheduling background network operations, which take into account timing and device state to improve the efficiency of your network transfers.

Parsing XML Using the XML Pull Parser

Although detailed instructions for parsing XML and interacting with specific web services are outside the scope of this book, it's important to understand the available technologies.

This section provides a brief overview of the XML Pull Parser, and the following sections demonstrate the use of the DOM parser and JSON Reader to retrieve earthquake details from the United States Geological Survey (USGS).

The XML Pull Parser API is available from the following libraries:

```
org.xmlpull.v1.XmlPullParser;
org.xmlpull.v1.XmlPullParserException;
org.xmlpull.v1.XmlPullParserFactory;
```

It enables you to parse an XML document in a single pass. Unlike the DOM parser, the Pull Parser presents the elements of your document in a sequential series of events and tags.

Your location within the document is represented by the current event. You can determine the current event by calling getEventType. Each document begins at the START_DOCUMENT event and ends at END_DOCUMENT.

To proceed through the tags, simply call next, which causes you to progress through a series of matched (and often nested) START_TAG and END_TAG events. You can extract the name of each tag by calling getName and extract the text between each set of tags using getNextText.

Listing 7-4 demonstrates how to use the XML Pull Parser to extract details from the points of interest list returned by the Google Places API.

LISTING 7-4: Parsing XML using the XML Pull Parser

```java
private void processStream(InputStream inputStream) {
  // Create a new XML Pull Parser.
  XmlPullParserFactory factory;
  try {
    factory = XmlPullParserFactory.newInstance();
    factory.setNamespaceAware(true);
    XmlPullParser xpp = factory.newPullParser();

    // Assign a new input stream.
    xpp.setInput(inputStream, null);
    int eventType = xpp.getEventType();

    // Allocate a variable for extracted name tags.
    String name;

    // Continue until the end of the document is reached.
    while (eventType != XmlPullParser.END_DOCUMENT) {
      // Check for a start tag of the results tag.
      if (eventType == XmlPullParser.START_TAG &&
          xpp.getName().equals("result")) {
        eventType = xpp.next();
        // Process each result within the result tag.
```

LISTING 7-4 *(continued)*

```
            while (!(eventType == XmlPullParser.END_TAG &&
                 xpp.getName().equals("result"))) {
              // Check for the name tag within the results tag.
              if (eventType == XmlPullParser.START_TAG &&
                  xpp.getName().equals("name")) {
                // Extract the POI name.
                name = xpp.nextText();
                doSomethingWithName(name);
              }
              // Move on to the next tag.
              eventType = xpp.next();
            }
            // Do something with each POI name.
          }
          // Move on to the next result tag.
          eventType = xpp.next();
        }
    } catch (XmlPullParserException e) {
      Log.e("PULLPARSER", "XML Pull Parser Exception", e);
    } catch (IOException e) {
      Log.e("PULLPARSER", "IO Exception", e);
    }
  }
```

Connecting the Earthquake Viewer to the Internet

In this example you extend the Earthquake Viewer you began in Chapter 3 and improved in Chapter 5. You'll replace the dummy Array List of Earthquakes with a real list, by connecting to an earthquake feed, downloading, and parsing it so it can be displayed in your List Fragment.

The earthquake feed XML is parsed here by the DOM parser. Several alternatives exist, including the XML Pull Parser described in the previous section. Alternatively, you could parse the JSON feed using the JsonReader class, as shown in the following section

1. For this example, the feed used is the one-day USGS Atom feed for earthquakes with a magnitude greater than 2.5 on the Richter scale. Add the location of your feed as an external string resource within the Strings.xml resource file in the res/values folder. This lets you potentially specify a different feed based on a user's locale:

```
<resources>
  <string name="app_name">Earthquake</string>
  <string name="earthquake_feed">
  https://earthquake.usgs.gov/earthquakes/feed/v1.0/summary/2.5_day.atom
  </string>
</resources>
```

2. Before you can access this feed, your application needs to request permission for Internet access. Add the Internet uses-permission to the top of your manifest file:

```
<?xml version="1.0" encoding="utf-8"?>
<manifest xmlns:android="http://schemas.android.com/apk/res/android"
          package="com.professionalandroid.apps.earthquake">
```

```
<uses-permission android:name="android.permission.INTERNET"/>

[... Application Node ...]

</manifest>
```

3. Our Internet access must happen on a background thread, and the results should persist on device configuration changes. Use a View Model and Live Data for this. Start by adding a dependency to the Android Architecture Components lifecycle extensions to your app module Gradle build file:

```
dependencies {
  [... Existing dependencies nodes ...]
  implementation "android.arch.lifecycle:extensions:1.1.1"
}
```

4. Create a new `EarthquakeViewModel` that extends `AndroidViewModel` and includes a `MutableLiveData` variable that represents a List of Earthquakes. This View Model will be cached and maintained across configuration changes. Create a `getEarthquakes` method that will check if our Earthquake List Live Data has been populated already, and if not, will load the Earthquakes from the feed:

```
public class EarthquakeViewModel extends AndroidViewModel {
  private static final String TAG = "EarthquakeUpdate";

  private MutableLiveData<List<Earthquake>> earthquakes;

  public EarthquakeViewModel(Application application) {
    super(application);
  }

  public LiveData<List<Earthquake>> getEarthquakes() {
    if (earthquakes == null) {
      earthquakes = new MutableLiveData<List<Earthquake>>();
      loadEarthquakes();
    }
    return earthquakes;
  }

  // Asynchronously load the Earthquakes from the feed.
  public void loadEarthquakes() {
  }
}
```

5. Update the `loadEarthquakes` method to download and parse the earthquake feed. This must be done on a background thread, so implement an `AyncTask` to simplify this process. In the background, extract each earthquake and parse the details to obtain the ID, date, magnitude, link, and location. Once the feed has been parsed, update the `onPostExecute` handler to set the value of the Mutable Live Data that represents our List of Earthquakes. This will alert any registered Observers, passing them the updated list:

```
public void loadEarthquakes() {
  new AsyncTask<Void, Void, List<Earthquake>>() {
    @Override
```

```java
protected List<Earthquake> doInBackground(Void... voids) {
  // Result ArrayList of parsed earthquakes.
  ArrayList<Earthquake> earthquakes = new ArrayList<>(0);

  // Get the XML
  URL url;
  try {
    String quakeFeed =
      getApplication().getString(R.string.earthquake_feed);
    url = new URL(quakeFeed);

    URLConnection connection;
    connection = url.openConnection();

    HttpURLConnection httpConnection = (HttpURLConnection)connection;
    int responseCode = httpConnection.getResponseCode();

    if (responseCode == HttpURLConnection.HTTP_OK) {
      InputStream in = httpConnection.getInputStream();

      DocumentBuilderFactory dbf =
        DocumentBuilderFactory.newInstance();
      DocumentBuilder db = dbf.newDocumentBuilder();

      // Parse the earthquake feed.
      Document dom = db.parse(in);
      Element docEle = dom.getDocumentElement();

      // Get a list of each earthquake entry.
      NodeList nl = docEle.getElementsByTagName("entry");
      if (nl != null && nl.getLength() > 0) {
        for (int i = 0 ; i < nl.getLength(); i++) {
          // Check to see if our loading has been cancelled, in which
          // case return what we have so far.
          if (isCancelled()) {
            Log.d(TAG, "Loading Cancelled");
            return earthquakes;
          }
          Element entry =
            (Element)nl.item(i);
          Element id =
            (Element)entry.getElementsByTagName("id").item(0);
          Element title =
            (Element)entry.getElementsByTagName("title").item(0);
          Element g =
            (Element)entry.getElementsByTagName("georss:point")
                      .item(0);
          Element when =
            (Element)entry.getElementsByTagName("updated").item(0);
          Element link =
            (Element)entry.getElementsByTagName("link").item(0);

          String idString = id.getFirstChild().getNodeValue();
          String details = title.getFirstChild().getNodeValue();
          String hostname = "http://earthquake.usgs.gov";
          String linkString = hostname + link.getAttribute("href");
```

```
                        String point = g.getFirstChild().getNodeValue();
                        String dt = when.getFirstChild().getNodeValue();
                        SimpleDateFormat sdf =
                          new SimpleDateFormat("yyyy-MM-dd'T'hh:mm:ss.SSS'Z'");
                        Date qdate = new GregorianCalendar(0,0,0).getTime();
                        try {
                          qdate = sdf.parse(dt);
                        } catch (ParseException e) {
                          Log.e(TAG, "Date parsing exception.", e);
                        }

                        String[] location = point.split(" ");
                        Location l = new Location("dummyGPS");
                        l.setLatitude(Double.parseDouble(location[0]));
                        l.setLongitude(Double.parseDouble(location[1]));

                        String magnitudeString = details.split(" ")[1];
                        int end =  magnitudeString.length()-1;
                        double magnitude =
                          Double.parseDouble(magnitudeString.substring(0, end));

                        if (details.contains("-"))
                          details = details.split("-")[1].trim();
                        else
                          details = "";

                        final Earthquake earthquake = new Earthquake(idString,
                                                          qdate,
                                                          details, l,
                                                          magnitude,
                                                          linkString);

                        // Add the new earthquake to our result array.
                        earthquakes.add(earthquake);
                      }
                  }
              }
          httpConnection.disconnect();
      } catch (MalformedURLException e) {
        Log.e(TAG, "MalformedURLException", e);
      } catch (IOException e) {
        Log.e(TAG, "IOException", e);
      } catch (ParserConfigurationException e) {
        Log.e(TAG, "Parser Configuration Exception", e);
      } catch (SAXException e) {
        Log.e(TAG, "SAX Exception", e);
      }
      // Return our result array.
      return earthquakes;
  }
```

```
      @Override
      protected void onPostExecute(List<Earthquake> data) {
        // Update the Live Data with the new list.
        earthquakes.setValue(data);
      }
    }.execute();
}
```

6. Update your Earthquake Main Activity to remove the dummy data and update the Earthquake List Fragment to use your new `EarthquakeViewModel`.

6.1. Start by updating the Activity's `onCreate` handler, removing the dummy data

```
EarthquakeViewModel earthquakeViewModel;

@Override
protected void onCreate(Bundle savedInstanceState) {
  super.onCreate(savedInstanceState);
  setContentView(R.layout.activity_earthquake_main);

  FragmentManager fm = getSupportFragmentManager();

  // Android will automatically re-add any Fragments that
  // have previously been added after a configuration change,
  // so only add it if this is an automatic restart.
  if (savedInstanceState == null) {
    FragmentTransaction ft = fm.beginTransaction();
    mEarthquakeListFragment = new EarthquakeListFragment();
    ft.add(R.id.main_activity_frame, mEarthquakeListFragment,
          TAG_LIST_FRAGMENT);
    ft.commitNow();
  } else {
    mEarthquakeListFragment =
      (EarthquakeListFragment)fm.findFragmentByTag(TAG_LIST_FRAGMENT);
  }

  // Retrieve the Earthquake View Model for this Activity.
  earthquakeViewModel = ViewModelProviders.of(this)
                        .get(EarthquakeViewModel.class);
}
```

6.2. Within the Earthquake List Fragment, update the `onActivityCreated` handler. Using the View Model Provider's static `of` method to retrieve the current instance of your Earthquake View Model. Add an Observer to the Live Data returned from your View Model—it will set the Earthquake List Fragment Earthquake List when your Activity is created, and again whenever the list of parsed Earthquakes is updated:

```
protected EarthquakeViewModel earthquakeViewModel;

@Override
public void onActivityCreated(@Nullable Bundle savedInstanceState) {
  super.onActivityCreated(savedInstanceState);

  // Retrieve the Earthquake View Model for the parent Activity.
  earthquakeViewModel = ViewModelProviders.of(getActivity())
                        .get(EarthquakeViewModel.class);
```

```
        // Get the data from the View Model, and observe any changes.
        earthquakeViewModel.getEarthquakes()
          .observe(this, new Observer<List<Earthquake>>() {
            @Override
            public void onChanged(@Nullable List<Earthquake> earthquakes) {
              // When the View Model changes, update the List
              if (earthquakes != null)
                setEarthquakes(earthquakes);
            }
          });
        }
```

7. When you run your project, you should see a Recycler View that features the earthquakes from the last 24 hours with a magnitude greater than 2.5 (Figure 7-1).

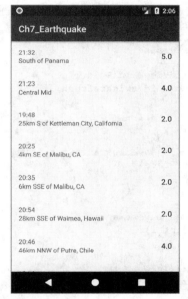

FIGURE 7-1

8. The earthquake data is cached by the View Model, so it will persist across device configuration changes, and only refresh when the app is restarted. Let's update the app to let users refresh the earthquake list using the swipe-to-refresh pattern. Update the fragment_earthquake_list .xml layout resource to include a SwipeRefreshLayout as the parent of the RecyclerView:

```xml
<?xml version="1.0" encoding="utf-8"?>
<android.support.v4.widget.SwipeRefreshLayout
  xmlns:android="http://schemas.android.com/apk/res/android"
  android:id="@+id/swiperefresh"
  android:layout_width="match_parent"
  android:layout_height="match_parent">
  <android.support.v7.widget.RecyclerView
    xmlns:android="http://schemas.android.com/apk/res/android"
    xmlns:app="http://schemas.android.com/apk/res-auto"
    android:id="@+id/list"
    android:layout_width="match_parent"
```

```
            android:layout_height="match_parent"
            android:layout_marginLeft="16dp"
            android:layout_marginRight="16dp"
            app:layoutManager="LinearLayoutManager"
        />
    </android.support.v4.widget.SwipeRefreshLayout>
```

9. Update onCreateView within the Earthquake List Fragment to get a reference to the Swipe
    Refresh Layout added in Step 8, and update onViewCreated to assign a refresh listener to
    the Swipe Refresh Layout that calls a new updateEarthquakes method when the swipe to
    refresh action is made:

```
    private SwipeRefreshLayout mSwipeToRefreshView;

    @Override
    public View onCreateView(LayoutInflater inflater, ViewGroup container,
                             Bundle savedInstanceState) {
      View view = inflater.inflate(R.layout.fragment_earthquake_list,
                                   container, false);

      mRecyclerView = (RecyclerView) view.findViewById(R.id.list);
      mSwipeToRefreshView = view.findViewById(R.id.swiperefresh);
      return view;
    }

    @Override
    public void onViewCreated(View view, Bundle savedInstanceState) {
      super.onViewCreated(view, savedInstanceState);

      // Set the Recycler View adapter
      Context context = view.getContext();
      mRecyclerView.setLayoutManager(new LinearLayoutManager(context));
      mRecyclerView.setAdapter(mEarthquakeAdapter);

      // Setup the Swipe to Refresh view
      mSwipeToRefreshView.setOnRefreshListener(new
        SwipeRefreshLayout.OnRefreshListener() {
        @Override
        public void onRefresh() {
          updateEarthquakes();
        }
      });
    }

    protected void updateEarthquakes() {
    }
```

10. Update the setEarthquakes method to disable the "refreshing" visual indicator when an
    update has been received:

```
    public void setEarthquakes(List<Earthquake> earthquakes) {
      mEarthquakes.clear();
      mEarthquakeAdapter.notifyDataSetChanged();
      for (Earthquake earthquake: earthquakes) {
        if (!mEarthquakes.contains(earthquake)) {
          mEarthquakes.add(earthquake);
          mEarthquakeAdapter.notifyItemInserted(
```

```
                mEarthquakes.indexOf(earthquake));
      }
    }
    mSwipeToRefreshView.setRefreshing(false);
  }
```

11. The update itself will be performed by the Earthquake View Model, which we communicate with through the parent Activity. Define a new OnListFragmentInteractionListener within the Earthquake List Fragment; it should include an onListFragmentRefreshRequested method that's called when we request a refresh via the updateEarthquakes method added in Step 9:

```
public interface OnListFragmentInteractionListener {
  void onListFragmentRefreshRequested();
}

private OnListFragmentInteractionListener mListener;

@Override
public void onAttach(Context context) {
  super.onAttach(context);
  mListener = (OnListFragmentInteractionListener) context;
}

@Override
public void onDetach() {
  super.onDetach();
  mListener = null;
}

protected void updateEarthquakes() {
  if (mListener != null)
    mListener.onListFragmentRefreshRequested();
}
```

12. Return to the Earthquake Main Activity and have it implement the Interface defined in Step 11, and use the Earthquake View Model to force a refresh when requested:

```
public class EarthquakeMainActivity extends AppCompatActivity implements
  EarthquakeListFragment.OnListFragmentInteractionListener {

  @Override
  public void onListFragmentRefreshRequested() {
    updateEarthquakes();
  }

  private void updateEarthquakes() {
    // Request the View Model update the earthquakes from the USGS feed.
    earthquakeViewModel.loadEarthquakes();
  }

  [... Existing Class Definition ...]
}
```

13. You should also add a refresh action as a menu item or on your app's action bar to support users who may not be able to perform a swipe gesture (for example, users with accessibility issues can trigger action bar actions using external devices, such as keyboards and D-pads). We show how to do this in Chapter 13, "Implementing a Modern Android User Experience."

Parsing JSON Using the JSON Parser

This section provides a brief overview of the `JsonParser`, demonstrating how it can be used to parse earthquake details from the JSON feed from the United States Geological Survey (USGS) found at `earthquake.usgs.gov/earthquakes/feed/v1.0/summary/2.5_day.geojson`.

As with XML parsing in the earlier sections, detailed instructions for parsing JSON are outside the scope of this book; however, with many APIs now providing JSON feeds it's important to introduce the concepts.

Like the pull parser, the JSON Parser enables you to parse a document in a single pass, presenting the elements of your document in a sequential series of objects, arrays, and values.

To create a recursive parser, you must first create an entry point method that takes an Input Stream and creates a new JSON Reader:

```
private List<Earthquake> parseJson(InputStream in) throws IOException {

  // Create a new Json Reader to parse the input.
  JsonReader reader =
    new JsonReader(new InputStreamReader(in, "UTF-8"));
    // TODO: Parse the InputStream
}
```

Data within each JSON feed are stored as names and values, structured using objects and arrays. JSON objects are used similarly to code objects—grouping together values that are semantically related. JSON also supports arrays to group multiple values or objects together.

For example, the USGS feed contains a type value, and metadata and bounding box objects at the root level, as well as an array of multiple feature objects representing each earthquake. Each feature object then contains values for type and ID, and objects to group earthquake properties and geometry details. The geometry object in turn includes a value for the geometry type, and an array of values representing the latitude, longitude, and depth of each earthquake. This structure is illustrated in part in Figure 7-2.

To parse these structures, create handler methods that will parse each object, and array, within the JSON text.

For the object structure handler methods, begin by calling your JSON Reader object's `beginObject` method to consume the opening brace. Then use the `hasNext` method to control a while loop within which you can extract values, or further objects (or arrays). Use the `endObject` method to read the object's closing brace when the object has been fully read:

```
private MyObject readMyObject(JsonReader reader) throws IOException {
  // Create variables for the return values.
  String myValue = null;

  // Consume the opening brace.
  reader.beginObject();

  // Traverse the values, objects, and arrays within this object.
  while (reader.hasNext()) {
    // Find the next name.
    String name = reader.nextName();
```

```
        // Extract each of the values based on name matches.
        if (name.equals("my_value")) {
          myValue = reader.nextString();

        // Skip any unexpected (or purposefully ignored) values.
        } else {
          reader.skipValue();
        }
      }

      // Consume closing brace.
      reader.endObject();

      // Return parsed object.
      return new MyObject(myValue);
    }
```

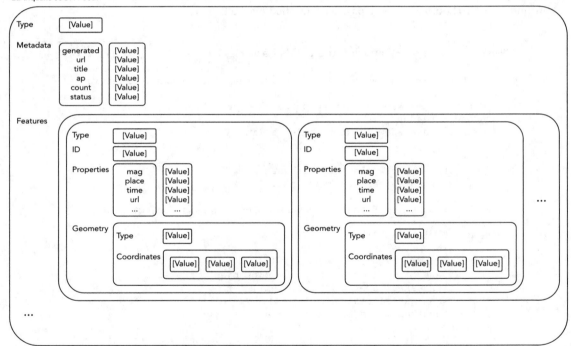

FIGURE 7-2

Arrays are handled similarly, using the beginArray and endArray methods to consume the opening and closing brackets respectively. The values within an array are homogenous, allowing you to simply add each value to a list:

```
public List<Double> readDoublesArray(JsonReader reader)
  throws IOException {
```

```
    List<Double> doubles = new ArrayList<Double>();

    reader.beginArray();

    while (reader.hasNext()) {
      doubles.add(reader.nextDouble());
    }

    reader.endArray();
    return doubles;
}
```

As you traverse each object or array, if a nested object or array is found, simply pass the JSON Reader object to the corresponding parsing method.

If an unknown name is encountered, you can choose to call skipValue to recursively skip the value's nested tokens

Listing 7-5 demonstrates how to use the JSON Parser to extract details from the JSON feed of magnitude 2.5+ earthquake over the past day supplied by the USGS.

LISTING 7-5: Parsing JSON using the JSON Parser

```
private List<Earthquake> parseJson(InputStream in) throws IOException {

  // Create a new Json Reader to parse the input.
  JsonReader reader =
    new JsonReader(new InputStreamReader(in, "UTF-8"));

  try {
    // Create an empty list of earthquakes.
    List<Earthquake> earthquakes = null;

    // The root node of the Earthquake JSON feed is an object that
    // we must parse.
    reader.beginObject();
    while (reader.hasNext()) {
      String name = reader.nextName();
      // We are only interested in one sub-object: the array of
      // earthquakes labeled as features.
      if (name.equals("features")) {
        earthquakes = readEarthquakeArray(reader);
      } else {
        // We will ignore all other root level values and objects.
        reader.skipValue();
      }
    }
    reader.endObject();

    return earthquakes;

  } finally {
```

```java
      reader.close();
  }
}

// Traverse the array of earthquakes.
private List<Earthquake> readEarthquakeArray(JsonReader reader)
  throws IOException {

  List<Earthquake> earthquakes = new ArrayList<Earthquake>();

  // The earthquake details are stored in an array.
  reader.beginArray();
  while (reader.hasNext()) {
    // Traverse the array, parsing each earthquake.
    earthquakes.add(readEarthquake(reader));
  }
  reader.endArray();

  return earthquakes;
}

// Parse each earthquake object within the earthquake array.
public Earthquake readEarthquake(JsonReader reader) throws IOException {
  String id = null;
  Location location = null;
  Earthquake earthquakeProperties = null;

  reader.beginObject();
  while (reader.hasNext()) {
    String name = reader.nextName();
    if (name.equals("id")) {
      // The ID is stored as a value.
      id = reader.nextString();
    } else if (name.equals("geometry")) {
      // The location is stored as a geometry object
      // that must be parsed.
      location = readLocation(reader);
    } else if (name.equals("properties")) {
      // Most of the earthquake details are stored as a
      // properties object that must be parsed.
      earthquakeProperties = readEarthquakeProperties(reader);
    } else {
      reader.skipValue();
    }
  }
  reader.endObject();

  // Construct a new Earthquake based on the parsed details.
  return new Earthquake(id,
                        earthquakeProperties.getDate(),
                        earthquakeProperties.getDetails(),
                        location,
                        earthquakeProperties.getMagnitude(),
                        earthquakeProperties.getLink());
}
```

LISTING 7-5 *(continued)*

```java
// Parse the properties object for each earthquake object
// within the earthquake array.
public Earthquake readEarthquakeProperties(JsonReader reader) throws IOException {
  Date date = null;
  String details = null;
  double magnitude = -1;
  String link = null;

  reader.beginObject();
  while (reader.hasNext()) {
    String name = reader.nextName();
    if (name.equals("time")) {
      long time = reader.nextLong();
      date = new Date(time);
    } else if (name.equals("place")) {
      details = reader.nextString();
    } else if (name.equals("url")) {
      link = reader.nextString();
    } else if (name.equals("mag")) {
      magnitude = reader.nextDouble();
    } else {
      reader.skipValue();
    }
  }
  reader.endObject();
  return new Earthquake(null, date, details, null, magnitude, link);
}

// Parse the coordinates object to obtain a location.
private Location readLocation(JsonReader reader) throws IOException {
  Location location = null;

  reader.beginObject();
  while (reader.hasNext()) {
    String name = reader.nextName();
    if (name.equals("coordinates")) {
      // The location coordinates are stored within an
      // array of doubles.
      List<Double> coords = readDoublesArray(reader);
      location = new Location("dummy");
      location.setLatitude(coords.get(0));
      location.setLongitude(coords.get(1));
    } else {
      reader.skipValue();
    }
  }
  reader.endObject();
  return location;
}

// Parse an array of doubles.
public List<Double> readDoublesArray(JsonReader reader) throws IOException {
  List<Double> doubles = new ArrayList<Double>();
```

```
    reader.beginArray();
    while (reader.hasNext()) {
      doubles.add(reader.nextDouble());
    }
    reader.endArray();
    return doubles;
  }
```

USING THE DOWNLOAD MANAGER

The Download Manager is a Service designed to optimize the handling of long-running downloads, by managing the HTTP connection and monitoring connectivity changes and system reboots to ensure each download completes successfully.

Downloads managed by the Download Manager are stored in a globally accessible location, so it's unsuitable for privacy-sensitive downloads.

It's good practice to use the Download Manager when a download is large—and therefore likely to continue in the background between user sessions, when successful completion is important, and when the file being downloaded will be shared with other applications (such as an image or PDF).

> **NOTE** *By default, files downloaded by the Download Manager are stored in the shared download cache directory (*Environment.getDownloadCacheDirectory*), meaning that they will be available to other apps, and deleted by the system if it requires space. Similarly, they will be managed through the Download app, meaning your downloads could be deleted manually by users. You can change these defaults as described later in this section.*

To access the Download Manager, request the DOWNLOAD_SERVICE using the getSystemService method:

```
DownloadManager downloadManager =
  (DownloadManager)getSystemService(Context.DOWNLOAD_SERVICE);
```

As the Download Manager uses the Internet, your app will need to request the INTERNET permission within its manifest in order to use the Download Manager:

```
<uses-permission android:name="android.permission.INTERNET"/>
```

Downloading Files

To request a download, create a new DownloadManager.Request, specifying the URI of the file to download and passing it in to the Download Manager's enqueue method, as shown in Listing 7-6.

LISTING 7-6: Downloading files using the Download Manager

```
DownloadManager downloadManager =
  (DownloadManager)getSystemService(Context.DOWNLOAD_SERVICE);
```

LISTING 7-6 *(continued)*

```
Uri uri = Uri.parse(
  "http://developer.android.com/shareables/icon_templates-v4.0.zip");

DownloadManager.Request request = new DownloadManager.Request(uri);
long reference = downloadManager.enqueue(request);
```

You can use the returned reference value to perform future actions or query the download, including checking its status or canceling it.

You can add an HTTP header to your request, or override the mime type returned by the server, by calling `addRequestHeader` and `setMimeType`, respectively, on your `Request` object.

You can also specify the connectivity conditions under which to execute the download. The `setAllowedNetworkTypes` method enables you to restrict downloads to either Wi-Fi or mobile networks. The `setAllowedOverRoaming` and `setAllowedOverMetered` methods allow you to prevent downloads while the phone is roaming or over a metered (paid) connection.

The following snippet shows how to ensure a large file is downloaded only when connected to Wi-Fi:

```
request.setAllowedNetworkTypes(Request.NETWORK_WIFI);
```

After calling `enqueue`, the download begins as soon as suitable connectivity is available, and the Download Manager is free.

> **NOTE** *Android Virtual Devices don't include virtualized Wi-Fi hardware, so downloads restricted to Wi-Fi only will be enqueued but never commence downloading.*

By default, ongoing and completed downloads are indicated as Notifications. You should create a Broadcast Receiver that listens for the `ACTION_NOTIFICATION_CLICKED` action, which will be broadcast whenever a user selects a download from the Notification tray or the Downloads app. It will include an `EXTRA_NOTIFICATION_CLICK_DOWNLOAD_IDS` extra that contains the reference ID of the download that was selected.

When the download is complete, the Download Manager will broadcast the `ACTION_DOWNLOAD_COMPLETE` action, with an `EXTRA_DOWNLOAD_ID` extra indicating the reference ID of the completed file download, as shown in Listing 7-7.

LISTING 7-7: Implementing a Broadcast Receiver for handling Download Manager broadcasts

```
public class DownloadsReceiver extends BroadcastReceiver {
  @Override
  public void onReceive(Context context, Intent intent) {
    String extraNotificationFileIds =
      DownloadManager.EXTRA_NOTIFICATION_CLICK_DOWNLOAD_IDS;
```

```
String extraFileId = DownloadManager.EXTRA_DOWNLOAD_ID;
String action = intent.getAction();

if (DownloadManager.ACTION_DOWNLOAD_COMPLETE.equals(action)) {
  long reference = intent.getLongExtra(extraFileId,-1);
  if (myDownloadReference == reference) {
    // Do something with downloaded file.
  }
}
else if (DownloadManager.ACTION_NOTIFICATION_CLICKED.equals(action)) {
  long[] references = intent.getLongArrayExtra(extraNotificationFileIds);
  for (long reference : references)
    if (myDownloadReference == reference) {
      // Respond to user selecting your file download notification.
    }
}
}
}
```

The Download Manager will continue downloading your files between user sessions of your app, as well as phone reboots. As a result, it's important for you to store the download reference numbers to ensure your app remembers them.

For the same reason you should register your Broadcast Receivers for Notification clicks and download completions within the manifest, as shown in Listing 7-8, because there is no guarantee your app will be running when a user selects a download notification, or the download is completed.

LISTING 7-8: Registering a Broadcast Receiver for Download Manager broadcasts

```
<receiver
  android:name="com.professionalandroid.apps.MyApp.DownloadsReceiver">
  <intent-filter>
    <action
      android:name="android.intent.action.DOWNLOAD_NOTIFICATION_CLICKED" />
    <action
      android:name="android.intent.action.DOWNLOAD_COMPLETE" />
  </intent-filter>
</receiver>
```

Once the download has completed, you can use Download Manager's `openDownloadedFile` method to receive a Parcel File Descriptor to your file, or use the ID to query the Download Manager and obtain metadata details.

You learn more about file handling in Chapter 8, "Saving State, User Preferences, and Using and Sharing Files."

Customizing Download Manager Notifications

By default, ongoing Notifications will be displayed for each file while it's being downloaded by the Download Manager. Each Notification will show the current download progress and the filename (Figure 7-3).

The Download Manager enables you to customize the Notification displayed for each download request, including hiding it completely. The following snippet shows how to use the `setTitle` and `setDescription` methods to customize the text displayed in the file download Notification. Figure 7-4 shows the result.

```
request.setTitle("Hive Husks");
request.setDescription("Downloading Splines for Reticulation");
```

FIGURE 7-3

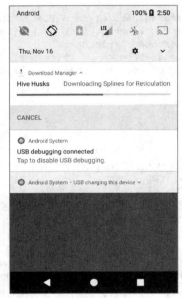

FIGURE 7-4

The `setNotificationVisibility` method lets you control when, and if, a Notification should be displayed for your download using one of the following flags:

➤ `Request.VISIBILITY_VISIBLE`—An ongoing Notification will be visible for the duration that the download is in progress. It will be removed when the download is complete. This is the default option.

➤ `Request.VISIBILITY_VISIBLE_NOTIFY_COMPLETED`—An ongoing Notification will be displayed during the download and will continue to be displayed once the download has completed, until it is selected or dismissed.

➤ `Request.VISIBILITY_VISIBLE_NOTIFY_ONLY_COMPLETION`—Useable only when using `addCompletedDownload` to add an already downloaded file to the downloads database system. When selected, a notification will be displayed after the file has been added.

➤ `Request.VISIBILITY_HIDDEN`—No Notification will be displayed for this download. In order to set this flag, your application must have the `DOWNLOAD_WITHOUT_NOTIFICATION` permission specified in its manifest:

```
<uses-permission
  android:name="android.permission.DOWNLOAD_WITHOUT_NOTIFICATION"/>
```

> **NOTE** *You learn more about creating your own custom Notifications in Chapter 11.*

Specifying a Download Location

By default, all Download Manager downloads are saved to the shared download cache using system-generated filenames, where they may be deleted automatically by the system, or manually by users.

Alternatively, a download Request can indicate a URI to a specific download location. In that case, the location must be on external storage, and accordingly your app must have the WRITE_EXTERNAL_STORAGE permission defined in its manifest:

```
<uses-permission android:name="android.permission.WRITE_EXTERNAL_STORAGE"/>
```

The following code snippet shows how to specify an arbitrary path on external storage:

```
request.setDestinationUri(Uri.fromFile(f));
```

If the downloaded file is specific to your application, you may want to place it in your application's external storage folder. Note that access control is not applied to this folder, and other applications will be able to access it. If your application is uninstalled, files stored in these folders will also be removed.

The following snippet specifies storing a file in your application's external downloads folder:

```
request.setDestinationInExternalFilesDir(this,
  Environment.DIRECTORY_DOWNLOADS, "bugdroid.png");
```

For files that can or should be shared with other applications—particularly those you want to scan with the Media Scanner—you can specify a location within the public folder on the external storage. The following snippet requests a file be stored in the public music folder:

```
request.setDestinationInExternalPublicDir(Environment.DIRECTORY_MUSIC,
  "android_anthem.mp3");
```

> **NOTE** *See Chapter 8 for more details about external storage and the static* Environment *variables you can use to indicate folders within it.*

It's important to note that by default, files downloaded by the Download Manager are not scanned by Media Scanner, so they might not appear in apps such as photo galleries and music players.

To make downloaded files scannable, call allowScanningByMediaScanner on the Request object *before* it is enqueued by the Download Manager:

```
request.allowScanningByMediaScanner();
```

By default, your files will be visible and manageable by the system's Downloads app. If you'd prefer they not be, you can call setVisibleInDownloadsUi, passing in false:

```
request.setVisibleInDownloadsUi(false);
```

Canceling and Removing Downloads

The Download Manager's `remove` method lets you cancel a pending download, abort a download in progress, or delete a completed download.

As shown in the following code snippet, the `remove` method accepts download IDs as optional arguments, enabling you to specify one or many downloads to cancel:

```
downloadManager.remove(fileRef1, fileRef2, fileRef3);
```

It returns the number of downloads successfully canceled. If a download is canceled, all associated files—both partial and complete—are removed.

Querying the Download Manager

You can query the Download Manager to find the status, progress, and details of your download requests by using the `query` method, which returns a Cursor to the list of downloads.

> **NOTE** *The* `Cursor` *class represents a data construct used by Android to return data, typically stored in a Content Provider or SQLite database. You learn more about Content Providers, Cursors, and how to find data stored in them in Chapter 10, "Content Providers and Search."*

The `query` method takes a `DownloadManager.Query` object as a parameter. Use the `setFilterById` method on a Query object to specify a sequence of download reference IDs, or use the `setFilterByStatus` method to filter on a download status using one of the `DownloadManager.STATUS_*` constants to specify running, paused, failed, or successful downloads.

The Download Manager includes a number of `COLUMN_` static String constants that you can use to query the result Cursor. You can find details for each download, including the status, files size, bytes downloaded so far, title, description, URI, media type, and Media Provider download URI.

In addition, the Download Manager includes the `getUriForDownloadedFile` and `openDownloadedFile` methods. Listing 7-9 expands on Listing 7-7 to demonstrate how to find the Uri, or Parcel File Descriptor of completed downloads from within a Broadcast Receiver registered to listen for download completions.

LISTING 7-9: Finding details of completed downloads

```
@Override
public void onReceive(Context context, Intent intent) {

  DownloadManager downloadManager =
      (DownloadManager)getSystemService(Context.DOWNLOAD_SERVICE);

  String extraNotificationFileIds =
    DownloadManager.EXTRA_NOTIFICATION_CLICK_DOWNLOAD_IDS;
  String extraFileId = DownloadManager.EXTRA_DOWNLOAD_ID;
  String action = intent.getAction();
```

```
if (DownloadManager.ACTION_DOWNLOAD_COMPLETE.equals(action)) {
  long reference = intent.getLongExtra(extraFileId,-1);
  if (myDownloadReference == reference) {
    DownloadManager.Query myDownloadQuery = new DownloadManager.Query();
    myDownloadQuery.setFilterById(reference);

    Cursor myDownload = downloadManager.query(myDownloadQuery);
    if (myDownload.moveToFirst()) {
      int fileIdIdx =
        myDownload.getColumnIndex(DownloadManager.COLUMN_ID);

      long fileId = myDownload.getLong(fileIdIdx);

      Uri fileUri = downloadManager.getUriForDownloadedFile(fileId);
      // Do something with downloaded file.
    }
    myDownload.close();
  }
}
else if (DownloadManager.ACTION_NOTIFICATION_CLICKED.equals(action)) {
  long[] references = intent.getLongArrayExtra(extraNotificationFileIds);
  for (long reference : references)
    if (myDownloadReference == reference) {
      // Respond to user selecting your file download notification.
      try {
        ParcelFileDescriptor fileDescriptor =
          downloadManager.openDownloadedFile(reference);
      } catch (FileNotFoundException e) {
        Log.e(TAG, "Downloaded file open error.", e);
      }
    }
}
}
```

For downloads that are either paused or have failed, you can query the COLUMN_REASON column to find the cause represented as an integer.

In the case of STATUS_PAUSED downloads, you can interpret the reason code by using one of the DownloadManager.PAUSED_ static constants to determine if the download has been paused while waiting for network connectivity, a Wi-Fi connection, or pending a retry.

For STATUS_FAILED downloads, you can determine the cause of failure using the DownloadManager.ERROR_ codes. Possible error codes include lack of a storage device, insufficient free space, duplicate filenames, or HTTP errors.

Listing 7-10 shows how to find a list of the currently paused downloads, extracting the reason the download was paused, the filename, its title, and the current progress.

LISTING 7-10: Finding details of paused downloads

```
// Obtain the Download Manager Service.
String serviceString = Context.DOWNLOAD_SERVICE;
DownloadManager downloadManager;
```

LISTING 7-10 *(continued)*

```
downloadManager = (DownloadManager)getSystemService(serviceString);

// Create a query for paused downloads.
DownloadManager.Query pausedDownloadQuery = new DownloadManager.Query();
pausedDownloadQuery.setFilterByStatus(DownloadManager.STATUS_PAUSED);

// Query the Download Manager for paused downloads.
Cursor pausedDownloads = downloadManager.query(pausedDownloadQuery);

// Find the column indexes for the data we require.
int reasonIdx = pausedDownloads.getColumnIndex(DownloadManager.COLUMN_REASON);
int titleIdx = pausedDownloads.getColumnIndex(DownloadManager.COLUMN_TITLE);
int fileSizeIdx = pausedDownloads.getColumnIndex(
                    DownloadManager.COLUMN_TOTAL_SIZE_BYTES);
int bytesDLIdx = pausedDownloads.getColumnIndex(
                    DownloadManager.COLUMN_BYTES_DOWNLOADED_SO_FAR);

// Iterate over the result Cursor.
while (pausedDownloads.moveToNext()) {
  // Extract the data we require from the Cursor.
  String title = pausedDownloads.getString(titleIdx);
  int fileSize = pausedDownloads.getInt(fileSizeIdx);
  int bytesDL = pausedDownloads.getInt(bytesDLIdx);

  // Translate the pause reason to friendly text.
  int reason = pausedDownloads.getInt(reasonIdx);
  String reasonString = "Unknown";
  switch (reason) {
    case DownloadManager.PAUSED_QUEUED_FOR_WIFI :
      reasonString = "Waiting for WiFi."; break;
    case DownloadManager.PAUSED_WAITING_FOR_NETWORK :
      reasonString = "Waiting for connectivity."; break;
    case DownloadManager.PAUSED_WAITING_TO_RETRY :
      reasonString = "Waiting to retry."; break;
    default : break;
  }

  // Construct a status summary
  StringBuilder sb = new StringBuilder();
  sb.append(title).append("\n");
  sb.append(reasonString).append("\n");
  sb.append("Downloaded ").append(bytesDL).append(" / " ).append(fileSize);

  // Display the status
  Log.d("DOWNLOAD", sb.toString());
}

// Close the result Cursor.
pausedDownloads.close();
```

BEST PRACTICES FOR DOWNLOADING DATA WITHOUT DRAINING THE BATTERY

Using the wireless radios to transfer data is a significant cause of battery drain. The mobile and Wi-Fi radios use a lot of power, not only transferring data, but powering up and maintaining network data connections.

The timing and approach you use to download data can have a significant effect on battery life, so to minimize the battery drain associated with network activity it's critical that you understand how your connectivity model will affect the underlying radio hardware.

> **NOTE** *For a much more detailed look at how to reduce the impact of network connections and data transfers, refer to "Reducing Network Battery Drain" at* `developer.android.com/training/performance/battery/network`.

A cellular wireless radio transmitting or receiving data consumes significant power, while at the same time, powering up to provide connectivity introduces latency. As a result, the radio transitions between different power modes in order to conserve power and minimize latency.

For a typical 3G network radio that typically involves three energy states:

➤ **Full power**—Used when a connection is actively transferring data.

➤ **Low power**—Activated a short time (~5s) after a transfer has concluded. It uses around 50% of the power of a full connection, but has improved startup latency compared to standby mode.

➤ **Standby**—The minimal power draw state, activated after a reasonable period (~15s) during which no network traffic has occurred.

Every time you create a new connection or download additional data, you risk waking the wireless radio from standby mode, and/or prolonging the amount of time it spends in full- and low-power modes.

To use a converse example, creating frequent, short-lived connections that download small amounts of data can have a dramatically negative impact on the battery. Transferring data every 15 seconds can effectively keep the network radio at full power constantly.

The solution is to reduce the frequency and size of your data transfers. You can use the following techniques to minimize your application's battery impact:

➤ **Cache and compress data**—Avoid downloading data more often than necessary by storing or caching it locally. Minimize the duration of transfers by compressing data efficiently at the server source, before transmitting it to your device.

➤ **Consider Wi-Fi versus mobile network connections**—The Wi-Fi radio can be significantly less power-hungry than the mobile network cell radio. For large files, and also where timeliness isn't as important, consider delaying transfers until the device is connected over Wi-Fi.

➤ **Aggressively prefetch**—The more data you download in a single connection, the less frequently the radio will need to be powered up to download more data. This will need to be balanced with downloading too much data that won't be used.

➤ **Bundle your connections and downloads**—Rather than sending time-insensitive data such as analytics as they're received, bundle them together and schedule them to transmit concurrently with other connections, such as when refreshing content or prefetching data. Remember, each new connection has the potential of powering up the radio.

➤ **Reuse existing connections rather than creating new ones**—Using existing connections rather than initiating new ones for each transfer can dramatically improve network performance, reduce latency, and allow the network to intelligently react to congestion and related issues.

➤ **Use server-initiated updates in preference to periodic downloads**—Every time you initiate a connection you potentially power up the radio, even if you don't end up downloading any new data. Instead of regular polling, have your server notify each client when there's new data to download using Firebase Cloud Messaging (discussed in Chapter 11).

➤ **Schedule periodic downloads as infrequently as possible**—When periodic updates are necessary, it's good practice to set the default refresh frequency to as low as usability will allow, rather than as frequent as possible. For users who require their updates to be more frequent, provide preferences that allow them to sacrifice battery life in exchange for freshness.

Android offers a number of APIs to assist you in performing data transfers efficiently, specifically the Android frameworks Job Scheduler.

This API provides facilities for you to intelligently schedule background data transfers within your application process. As a global Service, it can batch and defer transfers from multiple apps, in order to minimize the overall battery impact.

It provides:

➤ Scheduling for one-off or periodic downloads

➤ Automatic back-off and failure retry

➤ Persistence of scheduled transfers between device reboots

➤ Scheduling based on network connection type and device charging status.

We explore this API in detail in Chapter 11.

AN INTRODUCTION TO INTERNET SERVICES AND CLOUD COMPUTING

Software as a service (SaaS) and cloud computing are becoming increasingly popular as companies reduce the cost overheads associated with installing, upgrading, and maintaining their own hardware. The result is a range of rich Internet services and cloud resources with which you can build and enhance mobile applications.

The idea of using a middle tier to reduce client-side load is not a novel one, and happily there are many Internet-based options to supply your applications with the level of service you need.

The sheer volume of Internet services available makes it impossible to list them all here (let alone look at them in any detail), but the following list shows some of the more mature and common Internet services currently available. With Android being primarily developed by Google, Google's Cloud Platform offerings are particularly well supported, as summarized in the following section:

➤ **Google Cloud Platform Compute services**—A variety of services for running cloud-based servers, including Compute Engine for running large-scale workloads on virtual machines, the App Engine platform for building scalable mobile back ends, and Kubernetes Engine for running containers.

➤ **Google Cloud Platform Storage and BigQuery**—A range of products for storing data in the cloud, including Cloud Storage for object storage with global edge-caching, Cloud Spanner and Cloud SQL for relational databases supporting SQL queries, Cloud Bigtable for massively scalable NoSQL databases, and Cloud Datastore for NoSQL, schemaless databases (designed for storing non-relational data). They also offer BigQuery, a fully managed, petabyte scale, low-cost enterprise data warehouse for data analysis.

➤ **Google Machine Learning APIs**—Google offers a range of Machine Intelligence APIs built on its machine learning capabilities. That includes a Vision API that can understand the content of images, a Speech API for advanced speech recognition, a Natural Language API that derives insights from unstructured text, and a Translate API for programmatically translating text in real time.

➤ **Amazon Web Services**—Amazon offers a range of cloud-based services including a similar range of services for cloud compute and storage, including distributed storage solution (S3) and Elastic Compute Cloud (EC2).

A more detailed exploration of these products is out of scope for this book. However, Chapter 11 provides some additional details on how to use Firebase Cloud Messaging to replace client-side polling with server-driven updates.

8

Files, Saving State, and User Preferences

WROX.COM CODE DOWNLOADS FOR THIS CHAPTER

The code downloads for this chapter are found at www.wrox.com. The code for this chapter is divided into the following major examples:

➤ `Snippets_ch8.zip`

➤ `Earthquake_ch8.zip`

SAVING FILES, STATES, AND PREFERENCES

This chapter introduces some of the simplest and most versatile data-persistence and file sharing techniques in Android: Shared Preferences, instance-state Bundles, local files, and the Storage Access Framework.

At a minimum, an Activity should save its user interface (UI) state before becoming inactive, to ensure the same UI is presented when the Activity restarts. It's also likely that you'll need to save user preferences and UI selections.

Android's nondeterministic Activity and application lifetimes make persisting UI state and application data between sessions particularly important, because your application process may have been killed and restarted before it returns to the foreground.

We will explore mechanisms to store complex, structured data in Chapter 9, "Creating and Using Databases" and Chapter 10, "Content Providers and Search"—but for saving simple values or files within your application Android offers several alternatives, each optimized to fulfill a particular need:

➤ **Saved application UI state**—Activities and Fragments include specialized event handlers to record the current UI state when your application is moved to the background.

➤ **Shared Preferences**—When storing UI state, user preferences, or application settings, you want a lightweight mechanism to store a known set of values. Shared Preferences let you save groups of name/value pairs of primitive data as named preferences.

➤ **Files**—Sometimes writing to and reading from files is the only way to go, particularly when saving binary data such as images, audio, and video. Android lets you create, load, and share files on the device's internal or external media, as well as providing support for temporary caches. The File Provider and Storage Access Framework also provide the ability to share files with, and access files from, other applications.

SAVING AND RESTORING ACTIVITY AND FRAGMENT INSTANCE STATE USING THE LIFECYCLE HANDLERS

To save the state of instance variables within Activities and Fragments, Android provides the `onSaveInstanceState` handler to persist data associated with UI state across sessions.

While View state for any View with an `android:id` is automatically saved and restored by the framework, you are responsible for saving and restoring any other instance variables that are needed to re-create and restore the UI.

The `onSaveInstanceState` is designed specifically to allow you to persist UI state, in case the Activity is terminated by the run time within a single user session—either in an effort to free resources for foreground applications or to accommodate restarts caused by hardware configuration changes.

When overriding an Activity's `onSaveInstanceState` event handler, use its `Bundle` parameter to save instance variables related to your UI using the `put` methods associated with each primitive type. Remember to always call the super type method to save the default state:

```
private static final String SEEN_WARNING_KEY = "SEEN_WARNING_KEY";

// Has the user has seen an important warning during this session
private boolean mSeenWarning = false;

@Override
public void onSaveInstanceState(Bundle saveInstanceState) {
  super.onSaveInstanceState(saveInstanceState);
  // Save state associated with the UI
  saveInstanceState.putBoolean(SEEN_WARNING_KEY,
                               mSeenWarning);
}
```

This handler will be triggered whenever an Activity completes its active lifecycle, but only when it's not being explicitly finished (with a call to `finish`). As a result, it's used to ensure a consistent Activity state between active lifecycles of a single user session.

The saved Bundle is passed in to the `onRestoreInstanceState` and `onCreate` methods if the Activity is restarted:

```
@Override
public void onCreate(Bundle savedInstanceState) {
  super.onCreate(savedInstanceState);
  setContentView(R.layout.main);

  if (savedInstanceState != null &&
      savedInstanceState.containsKey(SEEN_WARNING_KEY)) {
    mSeenWarning = savedInstanceState.getBoolean(SEEN_WARNING_KEY);
  }
}
```

If an Activity is explicitly closed by the user (by pressing the Back button), or programmatically with a call to `finish`, the saved instance state Bundle will not be passed in to `onCreate` or `onRestore-InstanceState` when the Activity is next created. Data that should be persisted across user sessions should be stored using Shared Preferences, as described in the next sections.

The UI for many applications will be encapsulated within Fragments. Accordingly, Fragments also include an `onSaveInstanceState` handler that works in much the same way as its Activity counterpart.

The instance state persisted in that Bundle is passed as a parameter to the Fragment's `onCreate`, `onCreateView`, and `onActivityCreated` handlers.

For Fragments with a UI component, the same techniques used for saving Activity state apply to Fragments: they should restore their exact UI state if an Activity is destroyed and restarted to handle a hardware configuration change, such as the screen orientation changing. Because Android will automatically re-create Fragments, any Fragments programmatically added within an Activity's onCreate should only be added if the savedInstanceState parameter is null, in order to prevent duplicate Fragments, as shown in Listing 8-1.

LISTING 8-1: Programmatically adding a Fragment in onCreate

```
@Override
public void onCreate(Bundle savedInstanceState) {
  super.onCreate(savedInstanceState);
  setContentView(R.layout.main);

  if (savedInstanceState == null) {
    FragmentTransaction ft = getSupportFragmentManager().beginTransaction();
    ft.add(R.id.fragment_container, new MainFragment());
    ft.commit();
  }
}
```

RETAINING INSTANCE STATE WITH HEADLESS FRAGMENTS AND VIEW MODELS

Activities and Fragments are designed to display UI data and react to user interactions; they are destroyed and re-created each time the device configuration changes—most commonly when the display is rotated.

As a result, if you store data—or perform time consuming asynchronous operations—within these UI components, a user rotating the screen will destroy this data and interrupt any ongoing processes.

This can result in duplicative work, increased latency, and redundant processing. Instead, it is strongly recommended that you move application data and processing out of Activities and into a class that is persisted when device configuration changes cause Activity restarts.

View Models and headless Fragments provide two such mechanisms that ensure data is persisted across configuration changes, while also ensuring that your Activity or Fragment UI can be updated without risk of memory leaks.

View Models and Live Data

View Models and Live Data were introduced in Chapter 7 as part of a way to perform network operations on background Threads. They are the recommended best practice technique for persisting state across device configurations.

View Models are designed specifically to store and manage UI-related data such that it's persisted across configuration changes. View Models provide a simple way to separate the data being displayed from the UI controller logic that belongs in the Fragment or Activity. As a result, it's good practice to move all your data, business logic, and any code not directly related to UI elements out of your Activity or Fragment, and into a View Model.

Because View Models are retained during configuration changes, data they hold is immediately available to a newly re-created Activity or Fragment instance.

The data stored within a View Model is typically returned as `LiveData`, a class specifically designed to hold individual data fields for View Models.

Live Data is a lifecycle-aware class used to provide observable updates for application data. Lifecycle-awareness means that Live Data only sends updates to Observers within app components that are in an active lifecycle state. It's sometimes useful to create your own Live Data class; however, in most instances the `MutableLiveData` class is sufficient.

Each Mutable Live Data instance can be declared to represent a particular data type:

```
private final MutableLiveData<List<String>> data;
```

Within your View Model, you can modify the value stored by your Live Data using the `setValue` method while on the main UI Thread:

```
data.setValue(data);
```

Alternatively, you can use `postValue` to update the UI from a background Thread, which will post a Task to a main Thread to perform the update.

Whenever the value of a Live Data object is changed, the new value will be dispatched to any active Observers as described later in this section.

An Observer added by an Activity or Fragment will automatically be removed when the corresponding Activity or Fragment is destroyed, ensuring they can safely observe Live Data without worrying about memory leaks.

The `ViewModel` and related `LiveData` classes are available as part of the Android Architecture Components library, so to use them you first need to add a dependency to your app module's Gradle Build file:

```
dependencies {
  [... Existing dependencies nodes ...]
  implementation "android.arch.lifecycle:extensions:1.1.1"
}
```

The following snippet shows the skeleton code for a simple View Model implementation using a standard Mutable Live Data object to store UI-related data. It also uses an `AsyncTask` to encapsulate the background Threading needed to load the associated data:

```
public class MyViewModel extends AndroidViewModel {
  private static final String TAG = "MyViewModel";

  private MutableLiveData<List<String>> data = null;

  public MyViewModel(Application application) {
    super(application);
  }

  public LiveData<List<String>> getData() {
    if (data == null) {
      data = new MutableLiveData<List<String>>();
```

```
      loadData();
    }
    return data;
}

// Asynchronously load / update the data represented
// by the Live Data object.
public void loadData() {
  new AsyncTask<Void, Void, List<String>>() {
    @Override
    protected List<String> doInBackground(Void... voids) {
      ArrayList<String> result = new ArrayList<>(0);
      // TODO Load the data from this background thread.
      return result;
    }

    @Override
    protected void onPostExecute(List<String> resultData) {
      // Update the Live Data data value.
      data.setValue(resultData);
    }
  }.execute();
  }
}
```

Once defined, to use a View Model within your application you must first create a new (or return the existing) instance of your View Model from within an Activity or Fragment.

The `ViewModelProviders` class includes a static `of` method that can be used to retrieve all the View Models associated with a given Context:

```
ViewModelProvider providers = ViewModelProviders.of(this);
```

Then use the `get` method to specify the View Model you wish to use:

```
MyViewModel myViewModel = providers.get(MyViewModel.class);
```

Once you have a reference to your View Model, access any of the Live Data fields it contains and use the `observe` method to add an `Observer` that will receive updates (via the `onChanged` handler) when the Observer is added, and again whenever the underlying data changes. This is typically done within the `onCreate` handler of your Activity or Fragment:

```
myViewModel.getData().observe(this,
  new Observer<List<String>>() {
    @Override
    public void onChanged(@Nullable List<String> data) {
      // TODO When new View Model data is received, update the UI.
    }
  }
);
```

Because your View Model lifecycle is based on your application—rather than the corresponding Activity or Fragment—the View Model's loading function won't be interrupted by a device configuration change.

Similarly, your results are implicitly cached across device configuration changes. After a rotation, when `observe` is called on the View Model's data, it will immediately return the last result set via the `onChanged` handler—without the View Model's `loadData` method being called.

Headless Fragments

Prior to the availability of View Models through the Android Architecture Components, headless Fragments were useful mechanisms for retaining instance state across device configuration changes.

Fragments are not required to contain a UI—a "headless" Fragment can be created by returning `null` within its `onCreateView` method (this is the default implementation). Headless Fragments that are retained across Activity restarts can be used to encapsulate self-contained operations that need access to lifecycle methods, or that should not be terminated and restarted along with the Activity after a configuration change.

> **NOTE** *The introduction of View Models and Live Data has largely deprecated the use of headless Fragments for retaining state information across device configuration changes. Details are included here for your reference as you are likely to encounter this approach in apps that were designed prior to the introduction of Android Architecture Components.*

You can request that your Fragment instance be retained across configuration changes by calling `setRetainInstance` within a Fragment's `onCreate` handler. This will disconnect the Fragment instance's re-creation lifecycle from its parent Activity, meaning it will not be killed and restarted along with its parent Activity:

```
@Override
public void onCreate(Bundle savedInstanceState) {
  super.onCreate(savedInstanceState);

  // Retain this fragment across configuration changes.
  setRetainInstance(true);
}

@Override
public View onCreateView (LayoutInflater inflater,
                          ViewGroup container,
                          Bundle savedInstanceState){
  return null;
}
```

As a result, the `onDestroy` and `onCreate` handlers for a retained Fragment will not be called when the device configuration changes and the attached Activity is destroyed and re-created. This can provide a significant efficiency improvement if you move the majority of your object creation into this Fragment's `onCreate` handler.

Note that the rest of the Fragment's lifecycle handlers, including `onAttach`, `onCreateView`, `on ActivityCreated`, `onStart`, `onResume`, and their corresponding tear-down handlers, will still be called based on the parent Activity's lifecycle.

As headless Fragments have no View associated with them, they can't be created by adding a `<fragment>` tag to your layout; they must be created programmatically.

Fragment instances are only retained when they are active, meaning that this can only be used with Fragments not on the back stack.

> **NOTE** *When using headless Fragments that retain their instance, remember that it must not store any references to the host Activity—or any objects that contain a reference to that Activity (such as a View within its layout), because this may cause a memory leak when the Activity is destroyed but cannot be garbage collected due to the retained Fragment maintaining a reference to it.*

CREATING AND SAVING SHARED PREFERENCES

Using the `SharedPreferences` class, you can create named maps of name/value pairs that can be persisted across sessions and shared among application components running within the same application sandbox, but that aren't accessible to other apps.

To create or modify a Shared Preference, call `getSharedPreferences` on the current Context, passing in the name of the Shared Preference to change:

```
SharedPreferences prefs = getSharedPreferences(MY_PREFS,
                                               Context.MODE_PRIVATE);
```

In most cases, you can use the default Shared Preferences file by calling the static `getDefault-SharedPreferences` method from the Preference Manager:

```
Context context = getApplicationContext();
SharedPreferences prefs =
  PreferenceManager.getDefaultSharedPreferences(context);
```

To modify a Shared Preference, use the `SharedPreferences.Editor` class. Get the `Editor` object by calling `edit` on the Shared Preferences object you want to change:

```
SharedPreferences.Editor editor = prefs.edit();
```

Use the `put<type>` methods to insert or update the values associated with the specified name:

```
// Store new primitive types in the shared preferences object.
editor.putBoolean("isTrue", true);
editor.putFloat("lastFloat", 1f);
editor.putInt("wholeNumber", 2);
editor.putLong("aNumber", 31);
editor.putString("textEntryValue", "Not Empty");
```

To save edits, call `apply` or `commit` on the `Editor` object to save the changes asynchronously or synchronously, respectively:

```
// Commit the changes.
editor.apply();
```

> **NOTE** *Saving edits to Shared Preferences involves disk I/O and should be avoided on the main thread. Because the* `apply` *method causes a safe asynchronous write of the Shared Preference Editor on a separate thread, it is the preferred technique for saving Shared Preferences.*
>
> *If you require confirmation of success, you can call the* `commit` *method, which blocks the calling thread and returns true once a successful write has completed, or false otherwise.*

Android 6.0 Marshmallow (API Level 23) introduced a new Cloud Backup feature that by default (but with user permission), backs up almost all data created by an app to the cloud, including Shared Preferences files. Whenever a user installs your app on a new device, the system will automatically restore this backup data.

If you have device-specific Shared Preference values that should not be backed up with Android's Auto Backup, they must be stored in a separate file that can be excluded using a backup scheme definition XML file stored in the `res/xml` resources folder. Note that you must include the full filename of the Shared Preference, which includes the `.xml` extension:

```
<?xml version="1.0" encoding="utf-8"?>
<full-backup-content>
  <exclude domain="sharedpref" path="supersecretlaunchcodes.xml"/>
</full-backup-content>
```

You assign this scheme to your app by specifying it using the `android:fullBackupContent` attribute in the application node of your application manifest:

```
<application ...
  android:fullBackupContent="@xml/appbackupscheme">
</application>
```

More details on Auto Backup, including which files it backs up, and how to disable Auto Backup are covered later in this chapter.

RETRIEVING SHARED PREFERENCES

To access Shared Preferences, like editing and saving them, you use the `getSharedPreferences` method.

Use the type-safe `get<type>` methods to extract saved values. Each getter takes a key and a default value (returned when no value has been saved for that key):

```
// Retrieve the saved values.
boolean isTrue = prefs.getBoolean("isTrue", false);
```

```
float lastFloat = prefs.getFloat("lastFloat", 0f);
int wholeNumber = prefs.getInt("wholeNumber", 1);
long aNumber = prefs.getLong("aNumber", 0);
String stringPreference = prefs.getString("textEntryValue", "");
```

You can return a map of all the available Shared Preferences keys values by calling `getAll`, or check for the existence of a particular key by calling the `contains` method:

```
Map<String, ?> allPreferences = prefs.getAll();
boolean containsLastFloat = prefs.contains("lastFloat");
```

INTRODUCING ON SHARED PREFERENCE CHANGE LISTENERS

You can implement the `onSharedPreferenceChangeListener` to invoke a callback whenever a particular Shared Preference value is added, removed, or modified.

This is particularly useful for Activities and Services that use the Shared Preference framework to set application preferences. Using this handler, your application components can listen for changes to user preferences and update their UIs, or behavior, as required.

Register your On Shared Preference Change Listeners using the Shared Preference you want to monitor:

```
public class MyActivity extends Activity implements
  OnSharedPreferenceChangeListener {

  @Override
  public void onCreate(Bundle savedInstanceState) {
    super.onCreate(savedInstanceState);

    // Register this OnSharedPreferenceChangeListener
    // with any SharedPreferences instance
    SharedPreferences prefs =
      PreferenceManager.getDefaultSharedPreferences(this);
    prefs.registerOnSharedPreferenceChangeListener(this);
  }

  public void onSharedPreferenceChanged(SharedPreferences prefs,
                                        String key) {
    // TODO Check the shared preference and key parameters
    // and change UI or behavior as appropriate.
  }
}
```

CONFIGURING AUTO BACKUP OF APPLICATION FILES AND SHARED PREFERENCES

Introduced as part of Android 6.0 Marshmallow (API Level 23), Auto Backup automatically backs up at most 25MB of files, databases, and Shared Preferences created by your app, by encrypting and uploading it to the user's Google Drive account, such that it can automatically be restored when the app is installed on a new device, or after a device wipe.

Automatic backups occur at most once every 24 hours when the device is connected to Wi-Fi, charging, and idle.

> **NOTE** *In order for Auto Backup to be enabled on a given device, Google Services must be available, and the user must have opted in. There is no charge to you or the user for data storage, and the saved data does not count toward the user's personal Google Drive quota.*

When your app is installed by the same user on a new device, or if they reinstall your app on the same device, the system will use the last backup snapshot to restore your application data.

By default, almost all your application data files will be backed up, with the exception of all files stored in:

➤   The temporary cache directories returned by `getCacheDir` and `getCodeCacheDir`

➤   External storage, except those stored in the directory returned by `getExternalFilesDir`

➤   The directory returned by `getNoBackupFilesDir`

You can also define a backup scheme XML file using the `full-backup-content` tag, defining specific files to include or exclude from the Auto Backup. Note that if you specify an explicit include, it will prevent any file *not* specified in an include node from being backed up:

```
<?xml version="1.0" encoding="utf-8"?><full-backup-content>
  <include domain=["file" | "database" | "sharedpref" | "external" | "root"]
          path="[relative file path string]" />
  <exclude domain=["file" | "database" | "sharedpref" | "external" | "root"]
          path="[relative file path string]" />
</full-backup-content>
```

As shown here, each `include` or `exclude` tag must include a `domain` attribute, which indicates the root directory for a file of that domain, and the path to the file (including file extension) relative to that domain root directory, where:

➤   `root` is the app's root directory.

➤   `file` is the directory returned by the `getFilesDir` method.

➤   `database` is the default location for SQL databases, as returned by `getDatabasePath`.

➤   `sharedpref` indicates a Shared Preferences XML file returned by `getSharedPreferences`.

➤   `external` corresponds to a file in the directory returned by `getExternalFilesDir`.

For example, this following snippet excludes a database file from Auto Backup:

```
<?xml version="1.0" encoding="utf-8"?>
<full-backup-content>
  <exclude domain="database" path="top_secret_launch_codes.db"/>
</full-backup-content>
```

Once your backup scheme is defined, store it in your `res/xml` folder and associate it with your application using the `android:fullBackupContent` attribute in the application node of your manifest:

```
<application ...
    android:fullBackupContent="@xml/mybackupscheme">
</application>
```

Alternatively, if you wish to simply disable automatic app data backups completely, you can set the `android:allowBackup` attribute to false within the application node of your manifest:

```
<application ...
    android:allowBackup="false">
</application>
```

While it's possible to disable Auto Backup, this isn't recommended, as it offers a worse user experience for users moving between devices. Most users will expect your app to back up their settings and remember them when installing the app onto a new device. For this reason, `allowBackup` defaults to `true`. Make sure you have set up an alternate backup mechanism (for example, tied to your own custom login system) if you disable Android's built in data backup.

BUILDING A PREFERENCE UI

Android offers an XML-driven framework to create system-style Preference Screens for your applications. By using this framework you can create a user-preferences UI that is consistent with those used in both native and other third-party applications.

This has two distinct advantages:

➤ Users will be familiar with the layout and use of your settings screens.

➤ You can integrate settings from other applications (including system settings, such as location settings) into your application's preferences.

The preference framework consists of two primary components:

➤ **Preference Screen layout**—An XML file that defines the hierarchy of items displayed in your Preference Screens. It specifies the text and associated controls to display, the allowed values, and the Shared Preference keys to use for each control.

➤ **Preference Fragment**—Preference Screens are hosted within a `PreferenceFragment` or `PreferenceFragmentCompat`. It inflates the Preference Screen XML files, manages Preference dialog boxes, and handles transitions to other Preference Screens.

Using the Preference Support Library

The framework `PreferenceFragment` class must be added to a `PreferenceActivity`, meaning you can't use Activity classes such as `AppCompatActivity`. As a result, it's best practice use the `PreferenceFragmentCompat` class from the Preference Support Library, which allows you to add a support Preference Fragment to any Activity—which is what we'll be doing in the remainder of this chapter.

If you've already downloaded the Android Support Library as described in Chapter 2, you only need to add a Gradle dependency for the Preference Support Library, in order to take advantage of these features.

Open your `build.gradle` file and add the Fragment Support Library to the dependencies section:

```
dependencies {
  [... Existing dependencies ...]
  implementation "com.android.support:preference-v14:27.1.1"
}
```

Defining a Preference Screen Layout in XML

Unlike standard UI layouts, preference definitions are stored in the `res/xml` resources folder.

Although conceptually they are similar to the UI layout resources described in Chapter 5, "Building User Interfaces," Preference Screen layouts use a specialized set of UI controls designed specifically for Preference Screens. These native preference controls are described in the next section.

Each preference layout is defined as a hierarchy, beginning with a single `PreferenceScreen` element:

```
<?xml version="1.0" encoding="utf-8"?>
<PreferenceScreen
  xmlns:android="http://schemas.android.com/apk/res/android">
</PreferenceScreen>
```

You can nest Preference Screen elements, where each nested screen is represented as a selectable element that displays a new screen when tapped.

Each Preference Screen can include any combination of `PreferenceCategory` and `Preference` elements.

Preference Category elements, as shown in the following snippet, are used to break each Preference Screen into subcategories using a title bar separator:

```
<PreferenceCategory
  android:title="My Preference Category"/>
```

For example, Figure 8-1 shows the My Account and Services Preference Categories used on the Google Settings Preference Screen.

Preference elements are used to set and display the preferences themselves. The specific attributes used for each Preference element vary, but each includes at least the following:

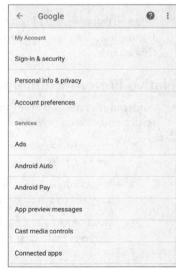

FIGURE 8-1

➤ `android:key`—The Shared Preference key against which the selected value will be recorded.

➤ `android:title`—The text displayed to represent the preference.

➤   `android:summary`—The longer text description displayed in a smaller font below the title text.

➤   `android:defaultValue`—The default value that will be displayed (and selected) if no preference value has been assigned to the associated preference key.

Listing 8-2 shows a sample Preference Screen that includes a Preference Category and Switch Preference.

LISTING 8-2: A simple Preference Screen layout

```xml
<?xml version="1.0" encoding="utf-8"?>
<PreferenceScreen
  xmlns:android="http://schemas.android.com/apk/res/android">
  <PreferenceCategory
    android:title="My Preference Category">
    <SwitchPreference
      android:key="PREF_BOOLEAN"
      android:title="Switch Preference"
      android:summary="Switch Preference Description"
      android:defaultValue="true"
    />
  </PreferenceCategory>
</PreferenceScreen>
```

When displayed, this Preference Screen will appear as shown in Figure 8-2. You learn how to display a Preference Screen later in this chapter.

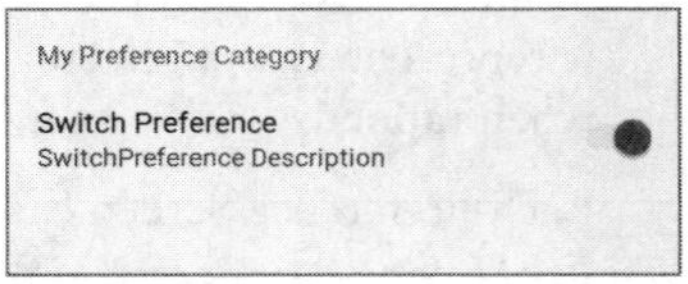

FIGURE 8-2

Native Preference Element Types

Android includes several Preference elements you can use to construct your Preference Screens:

➤   `CheckBoxPreference`—A standard preference check box control used to set preferences to true or false.

➤   `SwitchPreference`—A two-state Boolean toggle displayed as an on-or-off switch to set preferences to true or false. Generally used in preference to the Check Box preference.

➤   `EditTextPreference`—Allows users to enter a string value as a preference. Selecting the preference text at run time displays a text-entry dialog box.

➤   `ListPreference`—The preference equivalent of a spinner. Selecting this preference displays a dialog box containing a list of values from which to select. You can specify separate arrays to contain different display text and corresponding selection values.

➤   `MultiSelectListPreference`—This is the preference equivalent of a check box list, allowing users to select multiple entries from a single list of options.

➤ RingtonePreference—A specialized List Preference that presents the list of available ringtones for user selection. This is particularly useful when you're constructing a screen to configure Notification settings.

You can use a combination of each Preference element to construct your Preference Screen hierarchy. Alternatively, you can create your own specialized Preference elements by extending the `Preference` class (or any of the `Preference` subclasses from the list above.)

> **NOTE** *You can find further details about Preference elements at* `developer` `.android.com/reference/android/support/v7/preference/Preference` `.html.`

Using Intents to Add System Settings to Your Preference Screens

In addition to including your own Preference Screens, your hierarchies can include Preference Screens from other applications or—more usefully—the system Preferences.

You can invoke any Activity within your Preference Screen using an Intent; if you add an Intent element within a Preference Screen definition, the system will interpret this as a request to call `startActivity` using the specified action. The following XML snippet adds a link to the system's display settings:

```xml
<?xml version="1.0" encoding="utf-8"?>
<PreferenceScreen
  xmlns:android="http://schemas.android.com/apk/res/android">
  <PreferenceCategory
    android:title="My Preference Category">
    <Preference
      android:title="Intent preference"
      android:summary="System preference imported using an intent">
      <intent android:action="android.settings.DISPLAY_SETTINGS"/>
    </Preference>
  </PreferenceCategory>
</PreferenceScreen>
```

The `android.provider.Settings` class includes a number of `android.settings.*` constants that can be used to invoke the system settings screens including Bluetooth, location, and connectivity. You can see all of the available Intent actions at `d.android.com/reference/android/provider/` `Settings.html`.

Making Your Preference Screens Available to the System

To make your own Preference Screens available for invocation using this technique, simply add an Intent Filter to the manifest entry for the host Preference Activity (described in detail in the following section):

```xml
<activity android:name=".UserPreferences" android:label="My User Preferences">
  <intent-filter>
    <action android:name="com.paad.myapp.ACTION_USER_PREFERENCE" />
```

```
      <category android:name="android.intent.category.DEFAULT" />
    </intent-filter>
  </activity>
```

The most common use for this technique is to manage network usage. Since Android 4.0 Ice Cream Sandwich (API Level 14), the system preferences have allowed users to disable background data on a per-app basis. You can specify a Preference Activity that will be displayed when this setting is selected by adding an Intent Filter for `ACTION_MANAGE_NETWORK_USAGE`:

```
<activity android:name=".DataPreferences" android:label="Data Preferences">
  <intent-filter>
    <action android:name="android.intent.action.MANAGE_NETWORK_USAGE" />
    <category android:name="android.intent.category.DEFAULT" />
  </intent-filter>
</activity>
```

The associated Preference Activity should provide settings for your app that provide fine-grained control over your app's use of data, particularly in the background, such that users are more likely to modify data usage than disable background data completely.

Typical settings in this Preference Activity include update frequency, requirements for unmetered (Wi-Fi) connections, and charging status. In Chapter 11, "Working in the Background" you'll learn how to use the Job Scheduler to apply these settings to your background updates.

Introducing the Preference Fragment

The `PreferenceFragment` class hosts the Preference Screens defined earlier. To create a new Preference Fragment, extend the `PreferenceFragment` class. It's best practice to use the support library Fragments, in which case you'll extend the `PreferenceFragmentCompat` class:

```
public class MyPreferenceFragment extends PreferenceFragmentCompat
```

To inflate the Preference Screens, override `onCreatePreferences` and call `addPreferencesFrom-Resource`, as shown in Listing 8-3.

LISTING 8-3: Creating a Preference Fragment

```
import android.os.Bundle;
import android.support.v7.preference.PreferenceFragmentCompat;

public class MyPreferenceFragment extends PreferenceFragmentCompat {

  @Override
  public void onCreatePreferences(Bundle savedInstanceState, String rootKey) {
    setPreferencesFromResource(R.xml.preferences, rootkey);
  }
}
```

Your application can include multiple Preference Fragments, which, just like any other Fragment, can be included in any Activity and added, removed, and replaced at run time. By convention the Preference Fragment will be the only Fragment displayed within its parent Activity.

Before you can add a Preference Fragment to an Activity, you must also include a `preferenceTheme` element in your Activity's style. The following example uses the `PreferenceThemeOverlay.v14` `.Material` style available from the Preferences Support Library:

```
<style name="AppTheme" parent="@style/Theme.AppCompat">
  <item name="colorPrimary">@color/primary</item>
  <item name="colorPrimaryDark">@color/primaryDark</item>
  <item name="colorAccent">@color/colorAccent</item>

  <item
    name="preferenceTheme">@style/PreferenceThemeOverlay.v14.Material
  </item>
</style>
```

> **NOTE** *The Preference Theme shown in the previous code snippet requires a device running at least Android 4.0 Ice Cream Sandwich (API Level 14). If your application needs to support devices running an earlier Android platform, you should create a separate style definition that uses the* `@style/` `PreferenceThemeOverlay` *value for the* `preferenceTheme` *attribute.*

CREATING A SETTINGS ACTIVITY FOR THE EARTHQUAKE MONITOR

In the following example you build a settings Activity to set user preferences for the earthquake viewer last seen in the previous chapter. This Activity lets users configure settings for a more personalized experience. You'll provide the option to toggle automatic updates, control the frequency of updates, and filter the minimum earthquake magnitude displayed.

1. Open the Earthquake project you last modified in Chapter 7, "Using Internet Resources," and add the Preferences Support Library API to the app module `build.gradle` file. Our minimum SDK is 16, so we can use the v14 version of the preference support library:

    ```
    implementation 'com.android.support:preference-v14:27.1.1'
    ```

2. Add new string resources to the `res/values/strings.xml` file for the labels to be displayed in the Preference Screen. Also, add a string for the new Menu Item that will let users open the Preference Screen:

    ```
    <resources>
      <string name="app_name">Earthquake</string>
      <string name="earthquake_feed">
    https://earthquake.usgs.gov/earthquakes/feed/v1.0/summary/2.5_day.atom
      </string>
      <string name="menu_update">Refresh Earthquakes</string>
      <string name="auto_update_prompt">Auto refresh?</string>
      <string name="update_freq_prompt">Refresh Frequency</string>
      <string name="min_quake_mag_prompt">Minimum Quake Magnitude</string>
      <string name="menu_settings">Settings</string>
    </resources>
    ```

3. Create four array resources in a new `res/values/arrays.xml` file. They will provide the values to use for the update frequency and minimum magnitude spinners:

```xml
<?xml version="1.0" encoding="utf-8"?>
<resources>
  <string-array name="update_freq_options">
    <item>Every Minute</item>
    <item>5 minutes</item>
    <item>10 minutes</item>
    <item>15 minutes</item>
    <item>Every Hour</item>
  </string-array>
  <string-array name="update_freq_values">
    <item>1</item>
    <item>5</item>
    <item>10</item>
    <item>15</item>
    <item>60</item>
  </string-array>
<string-array name="magnitude_options">
    <item>All Magnitudes</item>
    <item>Magnitude 3</item>
    <item>Magnitude 5</item>
    <item>Magnitude 6</item>
    <item>Magnitude 7</item>
    <item>Magnitude 8</item>
  </string-array>
  <string-array name="magnitude_values">
    <item>0</item>
    <item>3</item>
    <item>5</item>
    <item>6</item>
    <item>7</item>
    <item>8</item>
  </string-array>
</resources>
```

4. Create a new XML resource folder at `res/xml`. Within it create a new `userpreferences` `.xml` file. This file will define the settings UI for your earthquake application settings. Include a switch for indicating the "auto refresh" toggle, and List Preferences to select the update rate and magnitude filter. Note the key values for each preference:

```xml
<?xml version="1.0" encoding="utf-8"?>
<PreferenceScreen
  xmlns:android="http://schemas.android.com/apk/res/android">
  <SwitchPreference
    android:key="PREF_AUTO_UPDATE"
    android:title="@string/auto_update_prompt"
    android:summary="Select to turn on automatic updating"
    android:defaultValue="true"
  />
<ListPreference
    android:key="PREF_UPDATE_FREQ"
    android:title="@string/update_freq_prompt"
    android:summary="Frequency at which to refresh earthquake list"
```

```
      android:entries="@array/update_freq_options"
      android:entryValues="@array/update_freq_values"
      android:dialogTitle="Refresh frequency"
      android:defaultValue="60"
    />
    <ListPreference
      android:key="PREF_MIN_MAG"
      android:title="@string/min_quake_mag_prompt"
      android:summary="Select the minimum magnitude earthquake to display"
      android:entries="@array/magnitude_options"
      android:entryValues="@array/magnitude_values"
      android:dialogTitle="Magnitude"
      android:defaultValue="3"
    />
  </PreferenceScreen>
```

5. Create a new `preferences.xml` layout resource in the `res/layout` folder for the Preferences Activity. Note that it includes a `PrefFragment` inner class defined within the `PreferencesActivty`. You'll create those in the next step.

```
<?xml version="1.0" encoding="utf-8"?>
<FrameLayout
  xmlns:android="http://schemas.android.com/apk/res/android"
  android:layout_width="match_parent"
  android:layout_height="match_parent">
  <fragment
    android:id="@+id/preferences_fragment"
    android:layout_width="match_parent"
    android:layout_height="match_parent"
    android:name=
"com.professionalandroid.apps.earthquake.PreferencesActivity$PrefFragment"/>
</FrameLayout>
```

6. Create the `PreferencesActivity` Activity by extending `AppCompatActivity`. Override `onCreate` to inflate the layout you created in Step 5, and create a static `PrefFragment` class that extends `PreferenceFragmentCompat`. Your Pref Fragment will contain your Preference Screen within the Preference Activity.

```java
import android.os.Bundle;
import android.support.v7.app.AppCompatActivity;
import android.support.v7.preference.PreferenceFragmentCompat;

public class PreferencesActivity extends AppCompatActivity {
  @Override
  public void onCreate(Bundle savedInstanceState) {
    super.onCreate(savedInstanceState);
    setContentView(R.layout.preferences);
  }

  public static class PrefFragment extends PreferenceFragmentCompat {
  }
}
```

7. Within your `PrefFragment` class, override the `onCreatePreferences` method to inflate the `userpreferences.xml` file you created in Step 4:

```java
public static class PrefFragment extends PreferenceFragmentCompat {
  @Override
```

```
public void onCreatePreferences(Bundle savedInstanceState,
                                String rootKey) {
    setPreferencesFromResource(R.xml.userpreferences, null);
}
}
```

8. Within your `PreferencesActivity`, add public static string values that correspond to the preference keys used in Step 4. You'll use these strings to access the Shared Preferences used to store each preference value.

```
public class PreferencesActivity extends AppCompatActivity {

    public static final String PREF_AUTO_UPDATE = "PREF_AUTO_UPDATE";
    public static final String USER_PREFERENCE = "USER_PREFERENCE";
    public static final String PREF_MIN_MAG = "PREF_MIN_MAG";
    public static final String PREF_UPDATE_FREQ = "PREF_UPDATE_FREQ";

    @Override
    public void onCreate(Bundle savedInstanceState) {
        super.onCreate(savedInstanceState);
        setContentView(R.layout.preferences);
    }
}
```

9. Open your `res/values/styles.xml` file and add a new item that defines your `preferenceTheme` to use the v14 Material design Preference Theme Overlay:

```
<style name="AppTheme" parent="@style/Theme.AppCompat">
  <item name="colorPrimary">@color/primary</item>
  <item name="colorPrimaryDark">@color/primaryDark</item>
  <item name="colorAccent">@color/colorAccent</item>

  <item
    name="preferenceTheme">@style/PreferenceThemeOverlay.v14.Material
  </item>
</style>
```

10. That completes your Preferences Activity. Open the application manifest and add an entry for this Activity, including an Intent Filter that it will be triggered if the user chooses to modify the app's background data settings from the system preferences.

```
<activity android:name=".PreferencesActivity">
  <intent-filter>
    <action android:name="android.intent.action.MANAGE_NETWORK_USAGE" />
    <category android:name="android.intent.category.DEFAULT" />
  </intent-filter>
</activity>
```

11. Return to the `EarthquakeMainActivity`, and add support for using the preferences selected from your Preference Activity. Start by adding a Menu Item to display the Preferences Activity. Override the `onCreateOptionsMenu` method to include a new item that will open the Preferences Activity:

```
private static final int MENU_PREFERENCES = Menu.FIRST+1;

@Override
```

```
public boolean onCreateOptionsMenu(Menu menu) {
    super.onCreateOptionsMenu(menu);

    menu.add(0, MENU_PREFERENCES, Menu.NONE, R.string.menu_settings);

    return true;
}
```

12. Override the onOptionsItemSelected method to display the PreferencesActivity when the new Menu Item from Step 11 is selected. To launch the Preferences Activity, create an explicit Intent, and pass it in to the startActivityForResult method. This will launch the Activity and alert the EarthquakeMainActivity class when the Preferences Activity is finished via the onActivityResult handler.

```
private static final int SHOW_PREFERENCES = 1;

public boolean onOptionsItemSelected(MenuItem item){
    super.onOptionsItemSelected(item);
    switch (item.getItemId()) {
        case MENU_PREFERENCES:
            Intent intent = new Intent(this, PreferencesActivity.class);
            startActivityForResult(intent, SHOW_PREFERENCES);
            return true;
    }
    return false;
}
```

13. Launch your application and select Preferences from the Activity menu. The Preferences Activity should be displayed, as shown in Figure 8-3.

FIGURE 8-3

14. All that's left is to apply the preferences to the earthquake app functionality. Implementing the automatic updates will be left until Chapter 11, "Working in the Background," where you learn to use the Job Scheduler for this. For now you can apply the magnitude filter. Start by creating a new `updateFromPreferences` method in the `EarthquakeListFragment` that reads the Shared Preference minimum magnitude value:

```
private int mMinimumMagnitude = 0;

private void updateFromPreferences() {
  SharedPreferences prefs =
    PreferenceManager.getDefaultSharedPreferences(getContext());


  mMinimumMagnitude = Integer.parseInt(
    prefs.getString(PreferencesActivity.PREF_MIN_MAG, "3"));
}
```

15. Apply the magnitude filter by updating the `setEarthquakes` method from the `EarthquakeListFragment` to update the minimum magnitude preference, and check each earthquake's magnitude before adding it to the list:

```
public void setEarthquakes(List<Earthquake> earthquakes) {
  updateFromPreferences();

  for (Earthquake earthquake: earthquakes) {
    if (earthquake.getMagnitude() >= mMinimumMagnitude) {
      if (!mEarthquakes.contains(earthquake)) {
        mEarthquakes.add(earthquake);
        mEarthquakeAdapter.notifyItemInserted(
          mEarthquakes.indexOf(earthquake));
      }
    }
  }

  if (mEarthquakes != null && mEarthquakes.size() > 0)
    for (int i = mEarthquakes.size() - 1; i >= 0; i--) {
      if (mEarthquakes.get(i).getMagnitude() < mMinimumMagnitude) {
        mEarthquakes.remove(i);
        mEarthquakeAdapter.notifyItemRemoved(i);
      }
    }

  mSwipeToRefreshView.setRefreshing(false);
}
```

16. The final step is to create a new `OnSharedPreferenceChangeListener` within the Earthquake List Fragment that will repopulate the Earthquake list, applying the magnitude filter based on the new setting. :

```
@Override
protected void onActivityCreated(Bundle savedInstanceState) {

  [... Existing onActivityCreated method ...]

  // Register an OnSharedPreferenceChangeListener
```

```
        SharedPreferences prefs =
          PreferenceManager.getDefaultSharedPreferences(getContext());
        prefs.registerOnSharedPreferenceChangeListener(mPrefListener);
    }

    private SharedPreferences.OnSharedPreferenceChangeListener mPrefListener
      = new SharedPreferences.OnSharedPreferenceChangeListener() {
      @Override
      public void onSharedPreferenceChanged(SharedPreferences
                                            sharedPreferences,
                                            String key) {
        if (PreferencesActivity.PREF_MIN_MAG.equals(key)) {
          List<Earthquake> earthquakes
            = earthquakeViewModel.getEarthquakes().getValue();
          if (earthquakes != null)
            setEarthquakes(earthquakes);
        }
      }
    };
```

INCLUDING STATIC FILES AS RESOURCES

If your application requires external file resources, you can include them in your distribution package by placing them in the `res/raw` folder of your project resources hierarchy.

To access these read-only file resources, call the `openRawResource` method from your application's `Resource` object to receive an `InputStream` based on the specified file. Pass in the filename (without the extension) as the variable name from the `R.raw` class, as shown in the following skeleton code:

```
Resources myResources = getResources();
InputStream myFile = myResources.openRawResource(R.raw.myfilename);
```

Adding raw files to your resources hierarchy is an excellent alternative for large, preexisting data sources (such as dictionaries) for which it's not desirable (or even possible) to convert them into Android databases.

Android's resource mechanism lets you specify alternative resource files for different languages, locations, and hardware configurations. For example, you could create an application that loads a different dictionary resource based on the user's language settings.

WORKING WITH THE FILESYSTEM

It's good practice to use Shared Preferences or a database (described in more detail in Chapter 9, "Creating and Using Databases") to store your application data, but there may still be times when you'll want to use files directly rather than rely on Android's managed mechanisms—particularly when working with binary files.

File-Management Tools

Android supplies some basic file-management tools to help you deal with the filesystem. Many of these utilities are located within the `java.io.File` package.

Although complete coverage of Java file-management utilities is beyond the scope of this book, Android does supply some specialized utilities for file management that are available from the application Context.

➤ `deleteFile`—Enables you to remove files created by the current application

➤ `fileList`—Returns a string array that includes all the files created by the current application

These methods are particularly useful for cleaning up temporary files left behind if your application crashes or is killed unexpectedly.

Creating Files on Application-Specific Internal Storage

Each application is provided with a data directory on internal storage where it can create files that are private to the application, and not accessible to other apps. This data directory and all files within it are automatically deleted when the app is uninstalled.

The two primary subdirectories within this data directory are the files directory and cache directory, available via the `getFilesDir` and `getCacheDir` methods of your Context respectively.

> **WARNING** *The returned path for these directories may change over time so you should only store relative paths to files in these directories.*

The location returned by `getFilesDir` is the appropriate place to store persistent, private files that your app expects to be available until/unless it removes them.

In contrast, files storied in the location returned by `getCacheDir` will potentially be erased by the system when it is running low on available storage, and should therefore be considered temporary storage. As such, these cache files won't be backed up by Auto Backup, their absence or deletion should not cause the user to lose any data, and your app should be prepared for these files to be removed at any time. In addition to the system, users can manually choose to remove these temporary cache files by selecting "Clear Cache" from the system settings for your app.

Creating Files on Application-Specific External Storage

In addition to the data directory on internal storage, your application also has access to application-specific directories on external storage. Similarly to the previously discussed internal storage directories, files created in these application-specific external storage directories are also deleted when the app is uninstalled.

When referring to *external* storage, we refer to the shared/media storage that is accessible by all applications and can typically be mounted to a computer filesystem when the device is connected via USB. Depending on the device, this can be a separate partition on the internal storage or on the SD card. `Environment.isExternalStorageEmulated` returns true if the internal storage and external storage are backed by the same underlying storage device.

The most important thing to remember when storing files on external storage is that no security is enforced on files stored here. Any application can access, overwrite, or delete files stored on the external storage.

> **NOTE** *It's important to remember that files stored on external storage may not always be available. If an SD card is ejected, or the device is mounted for access via a computer, your application will be unable to read (or create) files on the external storage.*

The Context method `getExternalFilesDir` is the external storage equivalent to `getFilesDir`. It accepts a string parameter that can be used to specify the subdirectory into which you want to place your files. The `Environment` class includes a number of `DIRECTORY_[Category]` string constants that represent standard directories, such as for images, movies, and music files.

Similar to the case for internal storage, `getExternalCacheDir` allows you to store temporary files in external storage. Note that Android does not always monitor available storage space on external storage, so you must monitor and manage the size and age of your cache, deleting files when a reasonable maximum cache size is exceeded.

For devices that have multiple external directories available such as those with an emulated external storage and a separate SD card, Android 4.4 Kit Kat (API Level 19) added the `getExternalFilesDirs` and `getExternalCacheDirs` directories, which will return an array of directories, allowing your app read and write access to application-specific directories on each external storage device. The first directories in the array correspond with the directory returned by `getExternalFilesDir` or `getExternalCacheDir`.

> **NOTE** *Prior to Android 4.4 Kit Kat (API Level 19), your app must have the* `READ_EXTERNAL_STORAGE` *and* `WRITE_EXTERNAL_STORAGE` *permissions to read and write to any folder on external storage, respectively. By adding* `android:maxSdkVersion="18"` *to the corresponding* `<uses-permission>` *elements, you can ensure that you will only request these "dangerous" permissions on the earlier platform releases that require them.*

Files stored in the application folders should be specific to the parent application and are typically not detected by the Media Scanner, and therefore won't be added to the Media Library automatically.

If your application downloads or creates files that should be added to the Media Library such as images, audio, or video files, you should store them in the location returned by the `getExternal MediaDirs` method added in Android 6.0 Marshmallow (API Level 21) so that they are automatically scanned by the Media Scanner.

> **NOTE** *As the* `getExternalMediaDirs` *method was introduced in Android 6.0 Marshmallow (API Level 21), to support earlier platform releases you should use* `MediaScannerConnection.scanFile` *to explicitly add any file stored on external storage to the media database.*

Accessing Public Directories Using Scoped Directory Access

Files stored in the application-specific directories on internal and external storage as described previously are deleted when the app is uninstalled. However, applications can also store files in shared public directories; these files will be persisted even if after your app is uninstalled.

Due to the shared nature of these public directories, users must explicitly give your app access before it can read or write files in these directories. Scoped Directory Access, introduced in Android 7.0 Nougat (API Level 24), is the process through which you can request access to these shared public directories on a given Storage Volume.

The primary Storage Volume is the same storage device as the application-specific external storage directories described previously. Secondary Storage Volumes may include SD cards and temporarily attached storage devices such as USB attached devices.

A particular `StorageVolume` object is retrieved using the `StorageManager`, as shown in the following snippet that retrieves the primary storage volume using the `getPrimaryStorageVolume` method:

```
StorageManager sm =
   (StorageManager)getSystemService(Context.STORAGE_SERVICE);
StorageVolume volume = sm.getPrimaryStorageVolume();
```

To access a particular public directory, call `createAccessIntent`, passing in a parameter that specifies the directory you require using one of the `Environment.DIRECTORY_` static constants:

```
Intent intent =
   volume.createAccessIntent(Environment.DIRECTORY_PICTURES);
```

The `Environment` class includes a number of static string constants that let you specify the public directory you wish to access, including:

➤ `DIRECTORY_ALARMS`—Audio files that should be available as user-selectable alarm sounds

➤ `DIRECTORY_DCIM`—Pictures and videos taken by the device

➤ `DIRECTORY_DOCUMENTS`—Documents created by the user

➤ `DIRECTORY_DOWNLOADS`—Files downloaded by the user

➤ `DIRECTORY_MOVIES`—Video files that represent movies

➤ `DIRECTORY_MUSIC`—Audio files that represent music

➤ `DIRECTORY_NOTIFICATIONS`—Audio files that should be available as user-selectable notification sounds

➤ `DIRECTORY_PICTURES`—Image files that represent pictures

➤ DIRECTORY_PODCASTS—Audio files that represent podcasts

➤ DIRECTORY_RINGTONES—Audio files that should be available as user-selectable ringtones

> **NOTE** *When using secondary storage volumes, passing in* null *for the directory value provides access to the entire storage volume. This option is not available for the primary storage volume. Access to the root of the primary storage is strongly discouraged due to the wide reaching consequences and security of the user's personal files.*
>
> *However, you can request the* READ_EXTERNAL_STORAGE *and* WRITE_EXTERNAL_STORAGE *permissions to read and write any directory on the primary storage volume returned by* Environment.getExternalStorageDirectory.

Once you have an Intent returned from createAccessIntent, pass it to startActivityForResult as seen in Listing 8-4:

LISTING 8-4: Requesting access with Scoped Directory Access

```
StorageManager sm =
  (StorageManager)getSystemService(Context.STORAGE_SERVICE);
StorageVolume volume = sm.getPrimaryStorageVolume();

Intent intent =
  volume.createAccessIntent(Environment.DIRECTORY_PICTURES);

startActivityForResult(intent, PICTURE_REQUEST_CODE);
```

The user will be shown a dialog box, as shown in Figure 8-4, where they can grant your app access to the specified directory (and any subdirectories) on the given storage volume. If users have previously denied your request, they will be offered a "Don't ask again" check box, which, if selected, will lead to an automatic denial on any further requests for the same location.

FIGURE 8-4

If the user accepts your request, the callback to onActivityResult will have a result code of RESULT_OK and getData will return a document tree URI to the newly accessible directory, as seen in Listing 8-5.

LISTING 8-5: Receiving access with Scoped Directory Access

```
@Override
public void onActivityResult(int requestCode, int resultCode, Intent data) {
  if (requestCode == PICTURE_REQUEST_CODE && resultCode == RESULT_OK) {
    Uri documentTreeUri = data.getData();
```

```
      // Use the returned URI to access the files within the directory
      handleDocumentTreeUri(documentTreeUri);
   }
}
```

Unlike a traditional `java.io.File`, a document URI provides access to files through methods within the `DocumentContract` class, and by using a `ContentResolver` to query metadata about the file. Similarly, you must use `openInputStream` to access the contents of each document, as seen in Listing 8-6.

LISTING 8-6: Using Document Contract to parse a document tree

```java
private void handleDocumentTreeUri(Uri documentTreeUri) {
   Uri childrenUri = DocumentsContract.buildChildDocumentsUriUsingTree(
      documentTreeUri, DocumentsContract.getDocumentId(documentTreeUri));
   try (Cursor children = getContentResolver().query(childrenUri,
      new String[] { DocumentsContract.Document.COLUMN_DOCUMENT_ID,
      DocumentsContract.Document.COLUMN_MIME_TYPE },
      null /* selection */,
      null /* selectionArgs */,
      null /* sortOrder */)) {
      if (children == null) {
         return;
      }

      while (children.moveToNext()) {
         String documentId = children.getString(0);
         String mimeType = children.getString(1);
         Uri childUri = DocumentsContract.buildDocumentUriUsingTree(
            documentTreeUri, documentId);
         if (DocumentsContract.Document.MIME_TYPE_DIR.equals(mimeType)) {
            handleDocumentTreeUri(childUri);
         } else {
            try (InputStream in =
               getContentResolver().openInputStream(childUri)) {
               // TODO Read the file
            } catch (FileNotFoundException e) {
               Log.e(TAG, e.getMessage(), e);
            } catch (IOException e) {
               Log.e(TAG, e.getMessage(), e);
            }
         }
      }
   }
}
```

Alternatively, the Support Library includes a helper `DocumentFile` class, which emulates the `File` API at the expense of additional overhead, as shown in Listing 8-7.

LISTING 8-7: Using Document File to parse directory document tree

```java
private void handleDocumentTreeUri(Uri documentTreeUri) {
  DocumentFile directory = DocumentFile.fromTreeUri(
    this, // Context
    documentTreeUri);

  DocumentFile[] files = directory.listFiles();

  for (DocumentFile file : files) {
    if (file.isDirectory()) {
      handleDocumentTreeUri(file.getUri());
    } else {
      try (InputStream in =
          getContentResolver().openInputStream(file.getUri())) {
        // TODO Read the file
      } catch (FileNotFoundException e) {
        Log.e(TAG, e.getMessage(), e);
      } catch (IOException e) {
        Log.e(TAG, e.getMessage(), e);
      }
    }
  }
}
```

You can find more details on using document URIs and using `DocumentContract` later in this chapter within the "Accessing Files from Other Applications Using the Storage Access Framework" section.

By default, each request for Scoped Directory Access will persist only for the current session. If your app needs persistent access to the requested directory, you must call `ContentResolver.take PersistableUriPermission` passing in the received document tree URI, and either (or both) `FLAG_ GRANT_READ_URI_PERMISSION` and/or `FLAG_GRANT_WRITE_URI_PERMISSION` to request persistent read and/or write permission, respectively.

If the user grants permission, subsequent access requests will automatically return successfully with no user interaction or dialog box. This will allow your app to continue to have access to the directory across multiple sessions—even after the device reboots:

```java
@Override
public void onActivityResult(int requestCode, int resultCode, Intent data) {
  if (requestCode == PICTURE_REQUEST_CODE && resultCode == RESULT_OK) {
    Uri documentTreeUri = data.getData();

    // Persist access to the directory so it can be accessed multiple times
    getContentResolver().takePersistableUriPermission(documentTreeUri,
      Intent.FLAG_GRANT_READ_URI_PERMISSION);

    // Use the returned URI to access the files within the directory
    handleDocumentTreeUri(documentTreeUri);
  }
}
```

> **NOTE** *Scoped Directory Access was introduced in Android 7.0 Nougat (API Level 24). You can access the public directories of the primary storage volume on earlier platform releases, using the* `Environment.getExternalStorage PublicDirectory` *method, which requires the* `READ_EXTERNAL_STORAGE` *and* `WRITE_EXTERNAL_STORAGE` *permissions to read and write, respectively.*

SHARING FILES USING FILE PROVIDER

The Android Support Library contains the `FileProvider` class, specifically designed for transforming files in application-specific directories into content URIs, making it possible to share them with other apps.

Creating a File Provider

Unlike Services or Activities, which you must extend and implement, File Providers are added directly to your manifest using a `provider` node:

```
<provider
  android:name="android.support.v4.content.FileProvider"
  android:authorities="${applicationId}.files"
  android:grantUriPermissions="true"
  android:exported="false">
  <meta-data
    android:name="android.support.FILE_PROVIDER_PATHS"
    android:resource="@xml/filepaths"
  />
</provider>
```

The `android:authorities` attribute must be a unique string, typically prefixed with the app's `applicationId` or package name. Gradle offers a placeholder—`${applicationId}`—that you can use to insert the application ID.

Each File Provider allows sharing from the directories you specify in the XML paths file you specify in the `android:resource` attribute of the `android.support.FILE_PROVIDER_PATHS` metadata node. This XML file lets you specify paths relative to your application's internal and external files and caches, for example:

```
<paths>
  <!-- Any number of paths can be declared here -->
  <files-path name="my_images" path="images/" />
  <cache-path name="internal_image_cache" path="imagecache/" />
  <external-files-path name="external_audio" path="audio/" />
  <external-cache-path name="external_image_cache" path="imagecache/" />
</paths>
```

Each path node requires a unique name for that directory, and its relative path.

Sharing a File Using a File Provider

Sharing a file with `FileProvider` requires that you first create a content URI for it. You can do this using `FileProvider.getUriForFile` and passing in a Context, the authority you added to your manifest, and the file itself:

```
File photosDirectory = new File(context.getFilesDir(), "images");
File imageToShare = new File(photosDirectory, "shared_image.png");

Uri contentUri = FileProvider.getUriForFile(context,
  BuildConfig.APPLICATION_ID + ".files", imageToShare);
```

The content URI can then be attached to an `ACTION_SEND` Intent to share with another app. The Android Support Library includes the `ShareCompat` class, which makes this simple:

```
ShareCompat.IntentBuilder.from(activity)
  .setType("image/png")
  .setStream(contentUri)
  .startChooser();
```

> **NOTE** *Prior to Android 4.1 Jellybean (API Level 16), you must also call* `setData(contentUri)` *and* `addFlags(Intent.FLAG_GRANT_READ_URI_PERMISSION)` *on the Intent, as described later in this chapter in the section "Using URI-Based Permissions," to ensure that the receiving app has permission to read the content URI. This is done for you on in the case of* `ACTION_SEND` *from API 16.*

Receiving a File from a File Provider

When you receive a shared file, you can get access to its contents using `ContentResolver.open InputStream`. For example, to extract a Bitmap from a received content URI:

```
Uri uri = ShareCompat.IntentReader.from(activity).getStream();
Bitmap bitmap;
try (InputStream in = getContentResolver().openInputStream(uri)) {
  bitmap = BitmapFactory.decodeStream(in);
} catch (IOException e) {
  Log.e(TAG, e.getMessage(), e);
}
```

ACCESSING FILES FROM OTHER APPLICATIONS USING THE STORAGE ACCESS FRAMEWORK

The Storage Access Framework provides a standard system-wide UI that can be used to enable users to pick files from the external public storage directories, or from apps that choose to provide files by exposing Document Providers.

This feature is useful for applications that may wish to include files, particularly images, created and stored by those applications—such as when composing an e-mail, sending a text message, or posting to social media.

Android provides a number of built in Document Providers that provide access to images, videos, and audio files on the device—as well as access to the contents of all external public directories, including those on SD cards or other external storage devices.

> **NOTE** *Document Providers can be used to provide access to files stored remotely—for example Google Drive and Google Photos. If you wish to provide other applications access to files stored remotely by your application, you can create your own* DocumentsProvider. *Coverage of how to build your own Documents Provider is out of scope for this book; however, you can learn more about it at* d.android.com/guide/topics/providers/create-document-provider.html#custom.

Document Providers accessed through the Storage Access Framework provide access to *documents*, not traditional *files*.

Documents differ from files in that they are addressed by a URI, rather than by path and file name. They also provide a level of abstraction over the usual file APIs to allow transparent access to cloud based files.

Therefore when working with documents, you can't use the java.io APIs. Instead, the DocumentsContract class contains the equivalent methods that take a document Uri.

> **NOTE** *The Storage Access Framework was added in Android 4.4 Kit Kat (API Level 19). However, the* ACTION_GET_CONTENT *described next can be used on all versions of Android in conjunction with apps that provide an Activity that has an Intent Filter for* android.intent.action.GET_CONTENT.

Requesting Temporary Access to Files

When performing a one-time operation, such as posting a file to social media, you will only need temporary access to the relevant file. You can enable users to select one or more files by using the ACTION_GET_CONTENT action within an Intent:

```
Intent intent = new Intent(Intent.ACTION_GET_CONTENT);
intent.setType("image/*");
intent.addCategory(Intent.CATEGORY_OPENABLE);
intent.putExtra(Intent.EXTRA_ALLOW_MULTIPLE, true);
startActivityForResult(intent, REQUEST_IMAGES_CODE);
```

Using `startActivityForResult`, passing in this Intent, launches the Storage Access Framework UI, which filters the available files based on the mime type specified in the Intent using `setType`.

Android supports both openable files (those with direct byte representations that you can access with `openInputStream`) and virtual files (that do not have a byte representation). By specifying `CATEGORY_OPENABLE` using `addCategory`, only openable files will be available to select.

The `EXTRA_ALLOW_MULTIPLE` extra is optional and indicates that the user can select multiple files to return to your app. You can then use `getClipData` to retrieve the list of URIs selected when the result Intent is returned. In all cases, the first URI selected is available by calling `getData`.

> **NOTE** *Because* `ACTION_GET_CONTENT` *preceded the Storage Access Framework, legacy apps will still appear in the Storage Access Framework UI. Since API Level 19, files returned using this technique will be Document URIs; however, legacy apps will return simple files. As a result, you can't assume that all returned URIs will be Document URIs. To determine if you've received a document URI and can use the* `DocumentsContract` *APIs, use* `DocumentsContract` `.isDocumentUri`*.*

Requesting Persistent Access to Files

If you require persistent access to selected files, you should use `ACTION_OPEN_DOCUMENT` instead of `ACTION_GET_CONTENT`. This allows your app to receive updates if the file is changed within the original provider.

All URIs returned when using `ACTION_OPEN_DOCUMENT` will be document URIs, allowing advanced functionality including retrieving metadata about the file (including the name and a summary of the file), as well as optional functionality (such as getting a thumbnail).

It also enables you to manage the file using operations such as copying, deleting, moving, removing, or renaming. Once you receive the document URI, you must call `ContentResolver.take` `PersistableUriPermission` for each URI to get persistent permission to access the URI across sessions and device reboots.

Requesting Access to Directories

Persistent access to files allows a client app to stay in sync with the Document Provider app, but ignores any structural changes such as the addition of new files or new subdirectories. `ACTION_OPEN_DOCUMENT_TREE` solves this problem by allowing the user to select a directory, and giving your app persistent access to the entire directory tree, as seen in Listing 8-8.

LISTING 8-8: Requesting access to a directory with the Storage Access Framework

```
Intent intent = new Intent(Intent.ACTION_OPEN_DOCUMENT_TREE);
startActivityForResult(intent, REQUEST_DIRECTORY_CODE);
```

When a directory is selected, you'll receive a document tree URI, allowing you to recursively enumerate all of the files in that directory. The same code used for Scoped Directory Access in Listings 8-6 and 8-7 can be used to parse the results of ACTION_OPEN_DOCUMENT_TREE.

Creating New Files

By creating an Intent that uses the ACTION_CREATE_DOCUMENT action, you can enable users to select a location to save content—be it locally or to a cloud-based Document Provider offered through the Storage Access Framework. The only required field is a mime type, set using setType; however, you can provide a suggested initial name by including an EXTRA_TITLE extra. To ensure that you can write the byte representation of the new file, CATEGORY_OPENABLE is also specified:

```
Intent intent = new Intent(Intent.ACTION_CREATE_DOCUMENT);
intent.setType("image/png");
intent.addCategory(Intent.CATEGORY_OPENABLE);
intent.putExtra(Intent.EXTRA_TITLE, "YourImage.png");
startActivityForResult(intent, REQUEST_CREATE_IMAGE_CODE);
```

When the user has selected a location for the new file (either by selecting an existing file of the same mime type to override, or choosing a new filename), a document URI will be returned, and the content of the file can be written using ContentResolver.openOutputStream. You can maintain persistent permission to access the newly created file by passing the returned content URI to ContentResolver.takePersistableUriPermission as described earlier in this chapter.

USING URI-BASED PERMISSIONS

Android apps can only store files in application-specific directories, effectively segmenting them from all other apps. This useful security property would normally prevent apps from sharing files to other apps; however, Android provides a number of techniques using URI-based permissions, which allow your app to grant temporary or persistent access of its files to other applications.

URI-based permissions are applied to single URIs, where each URI represents a specific file or directory. This allows a much more fine-grained security model than file permissions.

URI-based permissions are used behind the scenes to enable Scoped Directory Access, File Providers, and the Storage Access Framework described earlier in this chapter, so understanding how they operate can be useful.

Using URI-based permissions, an application can grant access to a particular file or directory within its sandbox to another app—be it on the same user profile or on a work profile. You do this by including FLAG_GRANT_READ_URI_PERMISSION or FLAG_GRANT_WRITE_URI_PERMISSION, as appropriate, within an Intent passed to the app seeking to access its files:

```
Intent sendIntent = new Intent();
sendIntent.setAction(Intent.ACTION_VIEW);
sendIntent.setType("image/png");
sendIntent.setData(contentUri);
sendIntent.addFlags(Intent.FLAG_GRANT_READ_URI_PERMISSION);
startActivity(sendIntent);
```

> **NOTE** *On Android 4.2 Jellybean (API Level 17) and higher devices,* FLAG_GRANT_READ_URI_PERMISSION *is automatically added for all URIs included in an* ACTION_SEND *Intent's* EXTRA_STREAM. *Similarly,* FLAG_GRANT_READ_URI_PERMISSION *and* FLAG_GRANT_WRITE_URI_PERMISSION *are automatically added to an* ACTION_IMAGE_CAPTURE *and* ACTION_VIDEO_CAPTURE *Intent's* EXTRA_OUTPUT.

Using FLAG_GRANT_PREFIX_URI_PERMISSION can be combined with the read or write URI permission to grant access to all URIs with a particular prefix.

URI-based permissions are short lived—as soon as the component that received the Intent with the URI permission flags is destroyed, access to that URI is revoked. However, if the receiving component forwards the Intent, including the flags to a Service for processing, the permission will remain valid until both components are destroyed.

Further, if the sending app includes FLAG_GRANT_PERSISTABLE_URI_PERMISSION with the Intent, the permission can be persisted with ContentResolver.takePersistableUriPermission and will be kept until the app calls releasePersistableUriPermission, or the sending app calls Context.revokeUriPermission.

This level of fine-grained control and ability for a sending app to grant permissions to resources to other apps make URI-based permissions ideal for sharing files between apps.

Creating and Using Databases

WROX.COM CODE DOWNLOADS FOR THIS CHAPTER

The code downloads for this chapter are found at www.wrox.com. The code for this chapter is divided into the following major examples:

➤ `Snippets_ch9.zip`

➤ `Earthquake_ch9.zip`

INTRODUCING STRUCTURED DATA STORAGE IN ANDROID

This chapter introduces structured data storage in Android, starting with the Room persistence library, before investigating the underlying SQLite relational database, and exploring the Firebase Realtime NoSQL Database.

Room provides an abstraction layer over SQLite that allows you to persist your applications data using the powerful SQLite database, while abstracting away the complexity of managing the database itself.

You learn how to define the Room database and how to query it and perform transactions using Data Access Objects (DAO). You also learn how to use Live Data to track changes in query results within your application's data layer, when the underlying data changes.

This chapter also explores the SQLite database APIs underlying Room. Using SQLite, you can create fully encapsulated relational databases for your applications, and use them to store and manage complex, structured application data.

Every application can create its own SQLite databases, over which it has complete control; all databases are private, accessible only by the application that created them.

In addition to the SQLite relational database library, you can use the Firebase Realtime Database to create and use a cloud-hosted NoSQL database.

By the end of this chapter, you'll learn how to incorporate and use a cloud-based Firebase Database, which stores its contents as a JSON tree on each device and automatically synchronizes it in real time to the cloud-host and every connected client.

STORING DATA USING THE ROOM PERSISTENCE LIBRARY

Room is a persistence library that simplifies the process of adding a structured SQL database to your app. Room provides an abstraction layer over an SQLite backend, making it easier to define and access a database for your app's structured data, while still offering the full power of SQLite.

One of the challenges of adding a database to your app is creating and maintaining an object-relational mapping (ORM). An ORM is necessary, because while your application's data is stored as variables within objects defined by your classes, relational databases store data in rows using columns within tables.

As a result, whenever you wish to store data in an SQLite table, you must first extract the data stored as variables within each object, and convert them into a row of values according to the columns of your table (using Content Values). Similarly, when extracting data from the table, you receive one or more rows of values (as a Cursor), which must be translated into one or more objects. Figure 9-1 shows the typical mapping of objects to rows within tables.

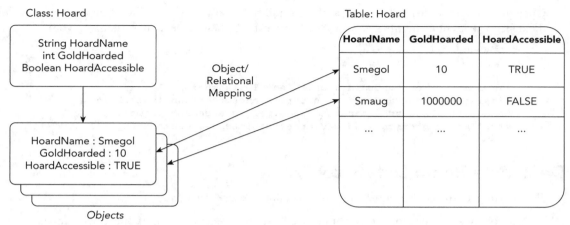

FIGURE 9-1

Creating and maintaining the ORM code required to translate between your application's class-based data model, and the relational databases tables and columns, is one of the most error prone and time-consuming aspects of using relational databases such as SQLite.

Room simplifies this by allowing you to use annotations within your class definitions, which map class variables to table columns, and methods to SQL statements. This abstracts away the underlying database, meaning you don't need to maintain a separate list of table and column names, or separately maintain SQL statements for inserting, deleting, updating, or querying SQL statements.

Query annotations use SQL, providing the full power of SQLite, while also allowing the compiler to verify each query at compile time. As a result, if a query has invalid field/column names, a compilation error occurs instead of a runtime failure.

Adding the Room Persistence Library

The Room persistence library is available as part of the Android Architecture Components suite of libraries, available from Google's Maven repository.

To add Room to your application, first ensure your project `build.gradle` file includes the Google Maven repository within the all projects repositories node:

```
allprojects {
  repositories {
    jcenter()
    maven { url 'https://maven.google.com' }
  }
}
```

Open your app module `build.gradle` file and add the following Room library dependencies within the dependencies node (as always, you should indicate the newest version available to you):

```
dependencies {
  [... Existing dependencies ...]

  implementation "android.arch.lifecycle:extensions:1.1.1"
  implementation "android.arch.persistence.room:runtime:1.1.1"
  annotationProcessor "android.arch.persistence.room:compiler:1.1.1"
  testImplementation "android.arch.persistence.room:testing:1.1.1"
}
```

Defining a Room Database

The Room persistence model requires you to define three components:

➤ **Entity**—One or more classes, annotated with the `@Entity` annotation, which define the structure of a database table that will be used to store instances of the annotated class.

➤ **Data Access Object**—A class annotated with the `@Dao` annotation that will define the methods used to modify or query the database.

➤ **Room Database**—An abstract class annotated with the `@Database` annotation that extends `RoomDatabase`. This class is the main access point for the underlying SQLite connection, and must also include an abstract method that returns the Data Access Object class and the list of entities the database will `contain`.

Figure 9-2 illustrates the relationship between the Room persistence model, the underlying database, and your application.

Classes annotated as entities are used to define the tables within your database. Each entity must include one non-nullable field annotated as the primary key using the `@PrimaryKey` annotation. The following snippet will create a table that includes three columns containing the hoard name, amount of gold hoarded, and the hoard's accessibility, where the hoard name is the primary key:

```
@Entity
public class Hoard {
  @NonNull
  @PrimaryKey
  public String HoardName;
  public int GoldHoarded;
  public boolean HoardAccessible;
}
```

By default, all public fields will be included in the table definition. You can use the `@Ignore` annotation to indicate fields that should not be persisted.

To persist fields that are accessed using getters and setters, rather than public variables, you can annotate the private variables, provided that the getters and setters use JavaBeans notation, where the methods for variable `foo` would be `getFoo` and `setFoo` respectively, as shown in Listing 9-1. Note that for Boolean values, an *is* method—`isFoo`—can be used instead of a *get* method.

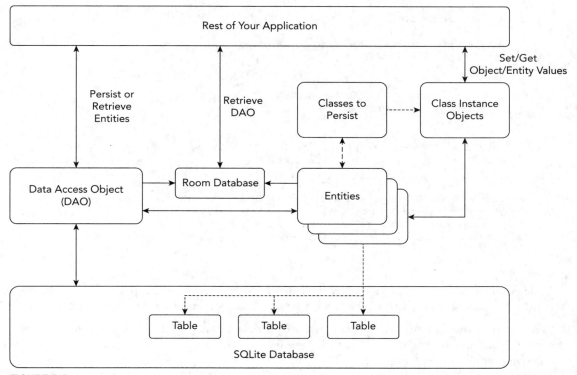

FIGURE 9-2

LISTING 9-1: Defining a Room entity

```
@Entity
public class Hoard {
  @NonNull
  @PrimaryKey
  private String hoardName;
  private int goldHoarded;
  private boolean hoardAccessible;

  public String getHoardName() {
    return hoardName;
  }
  public void setHoardName(String hoardName) {
    this.hoardName = hoardName;
  }

  public int getGoldHoarded() {
    return goldHoarded;
  }
```

continues

LISTING 9-1 *(continued)*

```
    public void setGoldHoarded(int goldHoarded) {
      this.goldHoarded = goldHoarded;
    }

    public boolean getHoardAccessible() {
      return hoardAccessible;
    }

    public void setHoardAccessible(boolean hoardAccessible) {
      this.hoardAccessible = hoardAccessible;
    }

    public Hoard(String hoardName, int goldHoarded, boolean hoardAccessible) {
      this.hoardName = hoardName;
      this.goldHoarded = goldHoarded;
      this.hoardAccessible = hoardAccessible;
    }
  }
```

The parameters for your class's constructors should contain names and types that correspond to the entity fields, as shown in Listing 9-1. Empty or partial constructors are also supported.

Once your entities are defined, create a new abstract class that extends `RoomDatabase`, annotating it with a `@Database` annotation that includes a list of each of your entity classes and the current version number—as shown in Listing 9-2.

LISTING 9-2: Defining a Room database

```
@Database(entities = {Hoard.class}, version = 1)
public abstract class HoardDatabase extends RoomDatabase{
}
```

Before you can use your database you must create a data access object class, which will be returned from your Room Database, as shown in the section, "Defining Room Database Interactions Using Data Access Objects."

Persisting Complex Objects Using Type Convertors

Room will attempt to allocate a column for each field; however, only the primitive types supported by SQLite—Booleans, Strings, integers, longs, and doubles—will work by default.

For public fields that hold class objects, you can choose to use the `@Ignore` annotation, as shown in the following snippet, to indicate a field that should not be stored in the database:

```
@Entity
public class Album {
  @NonNull
```

```
@PrimaryKey
public String albumName;
public String artistName;
@Ignore
public Bitmap albumArt;
}
```

Alternatively, if you wish to record the contents of an object within your Room database you must define a pair of Type Convertor methods—annotated using the `@TypeConverter` annotation—that can translate back-and-forth between the object stored in the field and a single primitive value.

The following snippet shows a simple pair of Type Converters that translate between a Date object and a long value representing the timestamp:

```
public class MyTypeConverters {
  @TypeConverter
  public static Date dateFromTimestamp(Long value) {
    return value == null ? null : new Date(value);
  }

  @TypeConverter
  public static Long dateToTimestamp(Date date) {
    return date == null ? null : date.getTime();
  }
}
```

Once defined, you can use the `@TypeConverters` annotation to apply the Type Converters within one or more classes, defined as an array value as shown in the following snippet:

```
@TypeConverters({MyTypeConverters.class})
```

Typically, you will apply the `@TypeConverters` annotation to the Room Database definition as shown in this snippet:

```
@Database(entities = {Album.class}, version = 1)
@TypeConverters({MyTypeConverters.class})
public abstract class AlbumDatabase extends RoomDatabase{
}
```

This will apply the Type Converters within the specified class to every Entity and DAO within your database.

Alternatively, you can restrict the scope of the Type Converters within a given class to one or more specific Entities, DAOs, specific Entity fields, DAO methods, or even individual DAO method parameters.

As a result, you can create multiple alternative Type Converters—between the same object/primitive-type pairs—that are applied to different elements within your Room Database.

For more information on why Room doesn't automatically support storage or object references, see the Room documentation at `d.android.com/training/data-storage/room/referencing-data.html`.

Defining Room Database Interactions Using Data Access Objects

Data Access Objects (DAO) are classes used to define your Room database interactions, including methods used to insert, delete, update, and query your database. If your database includes multiple tables, it's best practice to have multiple DAO classes, one for each table.

DAO's are defined either as interfaces or abstract classes, annotated using the `@Dao` annotation as shown in Listing 9-3.

LISTING 9-3: Defining a Room Data Access Object

```
@Dao
public interface HoardDAO {
}
```

Once defined, make it available to your app by adding a new abstract public method to the Room Database class that returns the new DAO, as shown in Listing 9-4 that extends Listing 9-2.

LISTING 9-4: Returning a DAO from a Room database

```
@Database(entities = {Hoard.class}, version = 1)
public abstract class HoardDatabase extends RoomDatabase{
  public abstract HoardDAO hoardDAO();
}
```

Within your DAO, create new methods to support each of your database interactions using the `@Insert`, `@Update`, `@Delete`, and `@Query` annotations.

Inserting Entities

Use the `@Insert` annotation to annotate methods that will be used to insert a new object/entity instance into your database. Each insert method can accept one or more parameters (including collections), of the type/entity represented by this DAO.

As shown in Listing 9-5, you can include multiple insert methods, and optionally use the `onConflict` annotation parameter to indicate a strategy for handling conflicts where the inserted object has the same primary key value as an existing stored object.

LISTING 9-5: Defining a Room database insert method within a DOA

```
@Dao
public interface HoardDAO {
  // Insert a list of hoards, replacing stored
  // hoards using the same name.
  @Insert(onConflict = OnConflictStrategy.REPLACE)
  public void insertHoards(List<Hoard> hoards);
```

```
// Insert one new hoard.
@Insert
public void insertHoard(Hoard hoard);
}
```

In addition to the replace strategy for conflict resolution shown in Listing 9-5, the following alternatives are available:

➤ ABORT—Cancel the ongoing transaction.

➤ FAIL—Cause the current transaction to fail.

➤ IGNORE—Ignore the conflicting new data and continue the transaction.

➤ REPLACE—Override the existing value with the newly supplied value and continue the transaction.

➤ ROLLBACK—Roll back the current transaction, reversing any previously made changes.

Updating Entities

You can create methods that update objects stored within your database using the @Update annotation, as shown in Listing 9-6.

Like insert methods, each update method can accept one or more entity parameters (including collections). Each object parameter passed in will be matched against the primary key of existing database entities and updated accordingly.

LISTING 9-6: Defining a Room database update method within a DOA

```
@Update
public void updateHoards(Hoard... hoard);

@Update
public void updateHoard(Hoard hoard);
```

Deleting Entities

To define a method that deletes or removes an object from the database, use the @Delete annotation, as shown in Listing 9-7. Room will use the primary key of each received parameter to find entities within the database and remove them.

LISTING 9-7: Defining a Room database delete method within a DOA

```
@Delete
public void deleteHoard(Hoard hoard);

@Delete
public void deleteTwoHoards(Hoard hoard1, Hoard hoard2);
```

If you wish to remove all the entities stored within a given table, you must use a @Query annotation that deletes all the entries from a given table:

```
@Query("DELETE FROM hoard")
public void deleteAllHoards();
```

Query annotations can be used to perform arbitrary SQL operations against your Room database, as shown in the following section.

Querying a Room Database

The most powerful annotation you can use within your DAO class is @Query. The @Query annotation allows you to perform read/write operations on the database using SELECT, UPDATE, and DELETE SQL statements, defined in the annotation value as shown in the snippet below, which will be executed when the associated method is called:

```
@Query("SELECT * FROM hoard")
public List<Hoard> loadAllHoards();
```

Each @Query SQL statement is verified at compile time, so if there is a problem with the query, a compilation error occurs instead of a runtime failure.

To use method parameters within the SQL query statement, you can reference them by prepending a colon (:) to the parameter name, as shown in Listing 9-8, which shows two common SELECT statements—one that returns all the database table entries, and another that returns a given row based on a primary key value.

LISTING 9-8: Querying a Room database

```
// Return all hoards
@Query("SELECT * FROM hoard")
public List<Hoard> loadAllHoards();

// Return a named hoard
@Query("SELECT * FROM hoard WHERE hoardName = :hoardName")
public Hoard loadHoardByName(String hoardName);
```

For SELECT queries that return one or more entities from a table, Room auto-generates the code that converts the query result into the return type indicated by your method.

It's also possible to pass through method parameters that contain a List or array of values as shown in Listing 9-9.

LISTING 9-9: Using a List parameter when querying a Room database

```
@Query("SELECT * FROM Hoard WHERE hoardName IN (:hoardNames)")
public List<Hoard> findByNames(String[] hoardNames);
```

Room will construct a query that binds each element in the array or list, for example if the `hoard-Names` parameter in Listing 9-9 is an array of 3 elements, Room will run the query as follows:

```
SELECT * FROM Hoard WHERE hoardName IN(?, ?, ?)
```

For efficiency reasons, it's often desirable to return only a subset of fields/columns from the underlying Room database—or to return a single calculated value such as in this snippet:

```
@Query("SELECT SUM(goldHoarded) FROM hoard")
public int totalGoldHoarded();
```

To return a subset of columns/fields, create a new class that contains public fields that match the returned columns, as shown in this snippet:

```
public class AnonymousHoard {
    public int goldHoarded;
    public boolean hoardAccessible;
}
```

Then define a SELECT statement that indicates the columns to return, and set the return type of the method to any class that contains public fields that match the returned column names, as shown in Listing 9-10.

LISTING 9-10: Returning a subset of columns from a Room database query

```
@Query("SELECT goldHoarded, hoardAccessible FROM hoard")
public List<AnonymousHoard> getAnonymousAmounts();

@Query("SELECT AVG(goldHoarded) FROM hoard")
public int averageGoldHoarded();
```

When a single row is returned, the return type can be any compatible type. For queries that return multiple values, you can use a List or array of a compatible type. It's also possible to return a raw Cursor, or have the results wrapped in a `LiveData` object as described in a later section.

Room verifies the return results of SELECT queries, such that if the fields in the method's return type don't match the columns names in the query response, you'll receive a warning (if only some field names match), or an error (if no field names match.)

Performing Room Database Interactions

Once you've defined the entities, DAO, and Room Database classes for your Room database, you can interact with it using the Room `databaseBuilder` method, passing in the application context, your Room Database, and filename to use for your database.

Creating and maintaining a Room Database instance is resource intensive, so it's best practice to use a singleton pattern to control access, as shown in Listing 9-11.

LISTING 9-11: Creating a Room Database access singleton

```java
public class HoardDatabaseAccessor {

  private static HoardDatabase HoardDatabaseInstance;
  private static final String HOARD_DB_NAME = "hoard_db";

  private HoardDatabaseAccessor() {}

  public static HoardDatabase getInstance(Context context) {
    if (HoardDatabaseInstance == null) {
      // Create or open a new SQLite database, and return it as
      // a Room Database instance.
      HoardDatabaseInstance = Room.databaseBuilder(context,
        HoardDatabase.class, HOARD_DB_NAME).build();
    }

    return HoardDatabaseInstance;
  }
}
```

You can then access your Room Database anywhere in your code, using the DAO classes to perform insert, delete, update, and query operations on your database as shown in Listing 9-12.

LISTING 9-12: Performing database interactions with Room

```java
// Access the Hoard Database instance.
HoardDatabase hoardDb =
  HoardDatabaseAccessor.getInstance(getApplicationContext());

// Add new hoards to the database.
hoardDb.hoardDAO().insertHoard(new Hoard("Smegol", 1, true));
hoardDb.hoardDAO().insertHoard(new Hoard("Smaug", 200000, false));

// Query the database.
int totalGold = hoardDb.hoardDAO().totalGoldHoarded();
List<Hoard> allHoards = hoardDb.hoardDAO().loadAllHoards();
```

> **WARNING** *As with accessing Internet resources, Room doesn't allow database interactions to occur on the main UI thread. Chapter 11, "Working in the Background" presents a number of options for moving your database interactions safely onto a background thread.*

Monitoring Query Result Changes with Live Data

The LiveData API allows you to receive updates when modifications to a database result in changes to the results of a query.

Live Data is an observable data holder that respects the lifecycle of Activities and Fragments, such that an observed Live Data only updates observers that are in an active lifecycle state.

To use Live Data, first add the Android Architecture Components Lifecycle extensions library to your project, by modifying your app module `build.gradle` file to include the following dependency:

```
implementation "android.arch.lifecycle:extensions:1.1.1"
```

To enable observing a Room query result for changes, set its return type to `LiveData`, and indicate the type being observed—as shown in Listing 9-13.

LISTING 9-13: Creating an observable query using Live Data

```
@Query("SELECT * FROM hoard")
public LiveData<List<Hoard>> monitorAllHoards()
```

To monitor a Live Data query, implement a new `Observer` of the appropriate type—overriding the `onChanged` handler. Use your Database's DAO to return an instance of the Live Data query result, and call its `observe` method, passing in the lifecycle owner (typically the Activity or Fragment whose UI is affected by the changed query result) and your Observer implementation, as shown in Listing 9-14.

Note that it's generally considered best practice to begin observing a Live Data query from within a component's `onCreate` handler.

LISTING 9-14: Observing a Room query Live Data result

```
@Override
protected void onCreate(Bundle savedInstanceState) {
  super.onCreate(savedInstanceState);
  setContentView(R.layout.activity_main);

  // The observer, which will be triggered when the Live Data changes
  final Observer<List<Hoard>> hoardObserver = new Observer<List<Hoard>>() {
    @Override
    public void onChanged(@Nullable final List<Hoard> updatedHoard) {
      // Update the UI with the updated database results.
    }
  };

  // Observe the LiveData
  LiveData hoardLiveData =
    HoardDatabaseAccessor.getInstance(getApplicationContext())
                         .hoardDAO().monitorAllHoards();
  hoardLiveData.observe(this, hoardObserver);
}
```

Calling `observe` will immediately result in the Observer's `onChanged` handler being triggered, after which it will be triggered again any time data in the underlying tables changes.

Live Data only notifies *active* observers about updates, automatically handling Activity and Fragment lifecycle changes, preventing crashes due to stopped Activities, and safely handling configuration changes.

You can learn more about the Lifecycle Library and other Android Architecture Components on the Android Developers site at: `developer.android.com/topic/libraries/architecture`

PERSISTING EARTHQUAKES TO A DATABASE WITH ROOM

In this example you modify the ongoing earthquake monitoring example application by creating a Room database to persist the earthquake data between user sessions.

1. Begin by ensuring the project's `build.gradle` file includes the Google Maven repository within the all projects repositories node:

    ```
    allprojects {
      repositories {
        jcenter()
        maven { url 'https://maven.google.com' }
      }
    }
    ```

2. Then open your app module `build.gradle` file and add dependencies for the Android Architecture Components Room and Live Data libraries within the dependencies node:

    ```
    dependencies {
      [... Existing dependencies nodes ...]

      implementation "android.arch.persistence.room:runtime:1.1.1"
      annotationProcessor "android.arch.persistence.room:compiler:1.1.1"
      testImplementation "android.arch.persistence.room:testing:1.1.1"
      implementation "android.arch.lifecycle.extensions:1.1.1"
    }
    ```

3. You will be persisting instances of the Earthquake class, so open it now, and annotate the class using the `@Entity` annotation. Take this opportunity to annotate the `mId` field to be the non-null primary key.

    ```
    @Entity
    public class Earthquake {
      @NonNull
      @PrimaryKey
      private String mId;
      private Date mDate;
      private String mDetails;
      private Location mLocation;
    ```

```
        private double mMagnitude;
        private String mLink;

        [... Existing Class definition ...]
    }
```

4. Notice that our Earthquake fields include complex Date and Location objects. Create a new
    EarthquakeTypeConverters class with static methods to convert back-and-forth between
    Date objects and Long values, and Location objects and String values. Each method must be
    annotated with the @TypeConverter annotation:

```java
public class EarthquakeTypeConverters {
    @TypeConverter
    public static Date dateFromTimestamp(Long value) {
        return value == null ? null : new Date(value);
    }

    @TypeConverter
    public static Long dateToTimestamp(Date date) {
        return date == null ? null : date.getTime();
    }

    @TypeConverter
    public static String locationToString(Location location) {
        return location == null ?
                null : location.getLatitude() + "," +
                        location.getLongitude();
    }

    @TypeConverter
    public static Location locationFromString(String location) {
        if (location != null && (location.contains(","))) {
            Location result = new Location("Generated");
            String[] locationStrings = location.split(",");
            if (locationStrings.length == 2) {
                result.setLatitude(Double.parseDouble(locationStrings[0]));
                result.setLongitude(Double.parseDouble(locationStrings[1]));
                return result;
            }
            else return null;
        }
        else
            return null;
    }
}
```

5. Create a new EarthquakeDAO interface definition. It should be annotated using the @Dao
    annotation, and will act as our Earthquake table Data Access Object. Include methods anno-
    tated with @Insert that insert one Earthquake or a List of Earthquakes, and which resolves
    conflicts by replacing existing database entries. Also define a query method that returns a

Live Data containing a List of all the Earthquakes, using the @Query annotation with an SQL statement that selects all rows from the earthquake table:

```
@Dao
public interface EarthquakeDAO {
  @Insert(onConflict = OnConflictStrategy.REPLACE)
  public void insertEarthquakes(List<Earthquake> earthquakes);

  @Insert(onConflict = OnConflictStrategy.REPLACE)
  public void insertEarthquake(Earthquake earthquake);

  @Delete
  public void deleteEarthquake(Earthquake earthquake);

  @Query("SELECT * FROM earthquake ORDER BY mDate DESC")
  public LiveData<List<Earthquake>> loadAllEarthquakes();
}
```

6. Complete the database setup by creating a new abstract EarthquakeDatabase class that extends RoomDatabase. It should be annotated using the @Database annotation, with values specifying the Earthquake class as an entity, and a database schema version number. Use the @TypeConverters annotation to specify that our Earthquake Type Converters from Step 4 should be used, and include an abstract method that returns our EarthquakeDAO data access object from Step 5:

```
@Database(entities = {Earthquake.class}, version = 1)
@TypeConverters({EarthquakeTypeConverters.class})
public abstract class EarthquakeDatabase extends RoomDatabase {
  public abstract EarthquakeDAO earthquakeDAO();
}
```

7. To interact with your new database, create a new EarthquakeDatabaseAccessor class, which uses the Singleton pattern to return an instance of the EarthquakeDatabase defined in Step 6:

```
public class EarthquakeDatabaseAccessor {

  private static EarthquakeDatabase EarthquakeDatabaseInstance;
  private static final String EARTHQUAKE_DB_NAME = "earthquake_db";

  private EarthquakeDatabaseAccessor() {}

  public static EarthquakeDatabase getInstance(Context context) {
    if (EarthquakeDatabaseInstance == null) {
      // Create or open a new SQLite database, and return it as
      // a Room Database instance.
      EarthquakeDatabaseInstance = Room.databaseBuilder(context,
        EarthquakeDatabase.class, EARTHQUAKE_DB_NAME).build();
    }

    return EarthquakeDatabaseInstance;
  }
}
```

8. Now update the `doInBackground` method within the Async Task of your `EarthquakeView-Model` to store the newly parsed List of Earthquakes into the database using the Earthquake Database Accessor from Step 7. Note that our DAO insert method has been configured to handle collisions by replacing existing rows to avoid duplicate entries:

```java
@Override
protected List<Earthquake> doInBackground(Void... voids) {
  // Result ArrayList of parsed earthquakes.
  ArrayList<Earthquake> earthquakes = new ArrayList<>(0);

  [... Existing earthquake feed downloading and parsing code ...]

  // Insert the newly parsed array of Earthquakes
  EarthquakeDatabaseAccessor
    .getInstance(getApplication())
    .earthquakeDAO()
    .insertEarthquakes(earthquakes);

  // Return our result array.
  return earthquakes;
}
```

9. Still within the Earthquake View Model, update the `onPostExecute` handler within your Async Task. The `loadEarthquakes` method will no longer directly apply the list of parsed Earthquakes to our Live Data field, instead we'll replace our Mutable Live Data with a query of the database:

```java
@Override
protected void onPostExecute(List<Earthquake> data) {
}
```

10. Update the View Model's `earthquakes` class variable to be of type `LiveData`, and update the `getEarthquakes` method to query the Room database. The Earthquake List Fragment is already expecting Live Data, so no further changes are necessary—the `onChanged` handler will be triggered whenever the Room database is modified:

```java
private LiveData<List<Earthquake>> earthquakes;

public LiveData<List<Earthquake>> getEarthquakes() {
  if (earthquakes == null) {
    // Load the Earthquakes from the database.
    earthquakes =
      EarthquakeDatabaseAccessor
        .getInstance(getApplication())
        .earthquakeDAO()
        .loadAllEarthquakes();

    // Load the earthquakes from the USGS feed.
    loadEarthquakes();
  }

  return earthquakes;
}
```

WORKING WITH SQLITE DATABASES

The SQLite APIs provide direct, low-level access to the SQLite database library. While powerful, using SQLite directly can require significant amounts of boilerplate code. It also offers no compile-time verification of SQL queries, increasing the risk of runtime errors.

To help simplify the process of storing application data within SQLite databases, Android has introduced the Room persistence library, described in the previous section. Room provides an abstraction layer over SQLite and is now considered best practice for storing and querying information for your application.

That said, there may be circumstances where you want to create or access your own SQLite database directly. This section assumes you have basic familiarity with SQL databases, and aims to help you apply that knowledge to SQLite databases on Android specifically.

SQLite is a well-regarded SQL-based relational database management system (RDBMS). It is:

➤   Open source

➤   Standards-compliant, implementing most of the SQL standard

➤   Lightweight

➤   Single-tier

➤   ACID compliant

It has been implemented as a compact C library that's included as part of the Android software stack.

By being implemented as a library, rather than running as a separate ongoing process, each SQLite database is an integrated part of the application that created it. This reduces external dependencies, minimizes latency, and simplifies transaction locking and synchronization.

Lightweight and powerful, SQLite differs from many conventional SQL database engines by loosely typing each column, meaning that column values are not required to conform to a single type; instead, each value is typed individually in each row. As a result, type checking isn't necessary when assigning or extracting values from each column within a row.

Android databases are stored in the `/data/data/<package_name>/databases` folder on your device (or emulator).

> **NOTE** *For more comprehensive coverage of SQLite, including its particular strengths and limitations, check out the official site at* `www.sqlite.org`.

Relational database design is a big topic that deserves more thorough coverage than is possible within this book. It is worth highlighting that standard database best practices still apply in Android. In particular, when you're creating databases for resource-constrained devices (such as mobile phones), it's important to normalize your data to minimize redundancy.

The SQLite databases described in detail in this chapter are only one of countless database options available for storing structured data within your application—a comprehensive investigation of available database technologies is beyond the scope of this book.

Input Validation and SQL Injection

Insufficiently validating user input is one of the most common security risks for applications, irrespective of the underlying platform or database implementation. To minimize these risks, Android has multiple platform-level features that reduce the potential impact of input validation issues.

Dynamic, string-based languages such as SQL are particularly at risk from input validation problems due to their support for escape characters and the possibility of script injection.

If user data is used within the query or transaction strings submitted to an SQLite database (or Content Provider), SQL injection may be an issue. The most important best practice is to always pass in user strings using the parameterized query methods `query`, `insert`, `update`, and `delete`, as described in the following sections. This will minimize the potential for SQL injection from untrusted sources.

Using parameterized methods is not sufficient if the `selection` parameter is built by concatenating user data prior to submitting it to the method. Instead, you should use `?` to indicate user-supplied variables that are then passed in as an array of strings using the `selectionargs` parameter. These selection arguments are bound as strings, negating the risk of escape character or SQL injection.

You can learn more about SQL injection and how to mitigate the risks associated with it here: `www.owasp.org/index.php/SQL_Injection`

Cursors and Content Values

SQLite Database and Content Provider query results are returned using `Cursor` objects. Rather than extracting and returning a copy of the result values, Cursors are pointers to the result set within the underlying data. Cursors provide a managed way of controlling your position (row) in the result set of a query.

The `Cursor` class includes a number of navigation and interaction functions, including, but not limited to, the following:

➤   `moveToFirst`—Moves the cursor to the first row in the query result

➤   `moveToNext`—Moves the cursor to the next row

➤   `moveToPrevious`—Moves the cursor to the previous row

➤   `getCount`—Returns the number of rows in the result set

➤   `getColumnIndexOrThrow`—Returns the zero-based index for the column with the specified name (throwing an exception if no column exists with that name)

➤   `getColumnName`—Returns the column name with the specified index

➤   `getColumnNames`—Returns a string array of all the column names in the current Cursor

➤   `moveToPosition`—Moves the cursor to the specified row

➤   `getPosition`—Returns the current cursor row position

Where Cursors return results, Content Values are used to insert or update rows. Each `ContentValues` object represents a single table row as a map of column names to values.

Defining a Database Contract

It's good form to encapsulate the underlying database and expose only the public methods and constants required to interact with the underlying data, generally using what's often referred to as a *contract* or *helper* class. This class should expose database constants, particularly column names, which will be required for populating and querying the database as shown in Listing 9-15.

LISTING 9-15: Skeleton code for contract class constants

```
public static class HoardContract {
  // The index (key) column name for use in where clauses.
  public static final String KEY_ID = "_id";

  // The name and column index of each column in your database.
  // These should be descriptive.
  public static final String KEY_GOLD_HOARD_NAME_COLUMN =
    "GOLD_HOARD_NAME_COLUMN";
  public static final String KEY_GOLD_HOARD_ACCESSIBLE_COLUMN =
    "OLD_HOARD_ACCESSIBLE_COLUMN";
  public static final String KEY_GOLD_HOARDED_COLUMN =
    "GOLD_HOARDED_COLUMN";
}
```

Introducing the SQLiteOpenHelper

`SQLiteOpenHelper` is an abstract class used to help implement the best practice pattern for creating, opening, and upgrading databases.

By implementing an SQLite Open Helper, you can encapsulate and hide the logic used to decide if a database needs to be created or upgraded before it's opened, as well as ensure that each operation is completed efficiently.

It's good practice to defer creating and opening databases until they're needed, and the SQLite Open Helper facilitates this pattern by caching database instances after they've been successfully opened, so you can make requests to open the database immediately prior to performing any query or transaction. For the same reason, there is no need to close the database manually until the Activity is finished.

Listing 9-16 shows how to extend the `SQLiteOpenHelper` class by overriding the constructor, `onCreate`, and `onUpgrade` methods to handle the creation of a new database, and upgrading to a new version, respectively.

LISTING 9-16: Implementing an SQLite Open Helper

```java
public static class HoardDBOpenHelper extends SQLiteOpenHelper {

  public static final String DATABASE_NAME = "myDatabase.db";
  public static final String DATABASE_TABLE = "GoldHoards";
  public static final int DATABASE_VERSION = 1;

  // SQL Statement to create a new database.
  private static final String DATABASE_CREATE =
    "create table " + DATABASE_TABLE + " (" + HoardContract.KEY_ID +
    " integer primary key autoincrement, " +
    HoardContract.KEY_GOLD_HOARD_NAME_COLUMN + " text not null, " +
    HoardContract.KEY_GOLD_HOARDED_COLUMN + " float, " +
    HoardContract.KEY_GOLD_HOARD_ACCESSIBLE_COLUMN + " integer);";

  public HoardDBOpenHelper(Context context, String name,
                          SQLiteDatabase.CursorFactory factory, int version)
  {
    super(context, name, factory, version);
  }

  // Called when no database exists in disk and the helper class needs
  // to create a new one.
  @Override
  public void onCreate(SQLiteDatabase db) {
    db.execSQL(DATABASE_CREATE);
  }

  // Called when there is a database version mismatch meaning that
  // the version of the database on disk needs to be upgraded to
  // the current version.
  @Override
  public void onUpgrade(SQLiteDatabase db, int oldVersion,
                       int newVersion) {
    // Log the version upgrade.
    Log.w("TaskDBAdapter", "Upgrading from version " +
                          oldVersion + " to " +
                          newVersion +
                          ", which will destroy all old data");

    // Upgrade the existing database to conform to the new
    // version. Multiple previous versions can be handled by
    // comparing oldVersion and newVersion values.

    // The simplest case is to drop the old table and create a new one.
    db.execSQL("DROP TABLE IF EXISTS " + DATABASE_TABLE);
    // Create a new one.
    onCreate(db);
  }
}
```

> **NOTE** *In this example* onUpgrade *simply drops the existing table and replaces it with the new definition. This is often the simplest and most practical solution; however, for important data that is not synchronized with an online service or is hard to recapture, a better approach may be to migrate existing data into the new table.*

The database creation SQL string defined in the DATABASE_CREATE variable in Listing 9-16 creates a new table that includes an auto-incrementing key. Although not strictly a requirement, it's strongly recommended that all tables include an auto-increment key field to guarantee a unique identifier for each row.

If you plan to share your table using a Content Provider (described in Chapter 10), a unique ID field is required.

Opening Databases with the SQLite Open Helper

To access a database using the SQLite Open Helper, call getWritableDatabase or getReadableDatabase to open and obtain an instance of the underlying database.

Behind the scenes, if the database doesn't exist, the helper executes its onCreate handler. If the database version has changed, the onUpgrade handler will fire. In either case, the get<read/writ>ableDatabase call will return the cached, newly opened, newly created, or upgraded database, as appropriate.

Note that in situations where the database exists and has previously been opened, both get<read/writ>ableDatabase methods will return the same, cached writeable database instance.

To create or upgrade the database, it must be opened in a writeable form; therefore, it's generally good practice to always attempt to open a writeable database. However, a call to getWritableDatabase can fail due to disk space or permission issues so it's good practice to fall back to the getReadableDatabase method for queries if possible as shown in Listing 9-17.

LISTING 9-17: Opening a database using the SQLite Open Helper

```
HoardDBOpenHelper hoardDBOpenHelper = new HoardDBOpenHelper(context,
                                HoardDBOpenHelper.DATABASE_NAME, null,
                                HoardDBOpenHelper.DATABASE_VERSION);

SQLiteDatabase db;
try {
  db = hoardDBOpenHelper.getWritableDatabase();
} catch (SQLiteException ex) {
  db = hoardDBOpenHelper.getReadableDatabase();
}
```

When a database has been successfully opened, the SQLite Open Helper will cache it, so you can (and should) use these methods each time you query or perform a transaction on the database, rather than caching the open database within your application.

Opening and Creating Databases Without the SQLite Open Helper

If you would prefer to manage the creation, opening, and version control of your databases directly, without the SQLite Open Helper, you can use the application Context's `openOrCreateDatabase` method to create the database itself:

```
SQLiteDatabase db = context.openOrCreateDatabase(DATABASE_NAME,
                                                 Context.MODE_PRIVATE,
                                                 null);
```

This approach does not check for the existence of the database, or what version it is, so you must handle the creation and upgrade logic yourself—typically using the database's `execSQL` method to create and drop tables, as required.

Adding, Updating, and Deleting Rows

The `SQLiteDatabase` class exposes `insert`, `delete`, and `update` methods that encapsulate the SQL statements required to perform these actions. Additionally, the `execSQL` method lets you execute any valid SQL statement on your database tables, should you want to execute these (or any other) operations manually.

Any time you modify the underlying database values, you should update any query result Cursors by re-running any queries.

> **NOTE** *Database operations should always be performed on a background Thread to ensure they don't interrupt the UI, as described in detail in Chapter 11. It's also best practice not to handle database interactions directly within Activities or Fragments; View Models are designed specifically as a mechanism to store database results and handle interactions so that database operations aren't interrupted on device configuration changes.*

Inserting Rows

To create a new row, construct a `ContentValues` object and use its `put` methods to add name/value pairs representing each column name and its associated value.

Insert the new row by passing the Content Values into the `insert` method called on the target database—along with the table name—as shown in Listing 9-18.

LISTING 9-18: Inserting a new row into an SQLite database

```
// Create a new row of values to insert.
ContentValues newValues = new ContentValues();

// Assign values for each row.
newValues.put(HoardContract.KEY_GOLD_HOARD_NAME_COLUMN, newHoardName);
newValues.put(HoardContract.KEY_GOLD_HOARDED_COLUMN, newHoardValue);
newValues.put(HoardContract.KEY_GOLD_HOARD_ACCESSIBLE_COLUMN,
                          newHoardAccessible);
// [ ... Repeat for each column / value pair ... ]

// Insert the row into your table
SQLiteDatabase db = hoardDBOpenHelper.getWritableDatabase();
db.insert(HoardDBOpenHelper.DATABASE_TABLE, null, newValues);
```

> **NOTE** *The second parameter used in the insert method shown in Listing 9-18 is known as the* null column hack.
>
> *If you want to add a new row to an SQLite database by passing in an empty Content Values object, you must also pass in the name of a column whose value can be explicitly set to null.*
>
> *When inserting a new row into an SQLite database, you must always explicitly specify at least one column and a corresponding value, the latter of which can be null. If you set the null column hack parameter to null, as shown in Listing 9-18, when inserting an empty Content Values object SQLite will throw an exception.*

Updating Rows

You also update rows using Content Values. Create a new `ContentValues` object, using the `put` methods to assign new values to each column you want to update. Call the `update` method on the database, passing in the table name, the updated Content Values object, and a `where` clause that specifies the row(s) to update, as shown in Listing 9-19.

LISTING 9-19: Updating a database row

```
// Create the updated row Content Values.
ContentValues updatedValues = new ContentValues();

// Assign values for each row.
updatedValues.put(HoardContract.KEY_GOLD_HOARDED_COLUMN, newHoardValue);
// [ ... Repeat for each column to update ... ]

// Specify a where clause that defines which rows should be
// updated. Specify where arguments as necessary.
```

```
String where = HoardContract.KEY_ID + "=?";
String whereArgs[] = {hoardId};

// Update the row with the specified index with the new values.
SQLiteDatabase db = hoardDBOpenHelper.getWritableDatabase();
db.update(HoardDBOpenHelper.DATABASE_TABLE, updatedValues,
          where, whereArgs);
```

Deleting Rows

To delete a row, simply call the `delete` method on a database, specifying the table name and a `where` clause that describes the rows you want to delete, as shown in Listing 9-20.

LISTING 9-20: Deleting a database row

```
// Specify a where clause that determines which row(s) to delete.
// Specify where arguments as necessary.
String where = HoardContract.KEY_ID + "=?";
String whereArgs[] = {hoardId};

// Delete the rows that match the where clause.
SQLiteDatabase db = hoardDBOpenHelper.getWritableDatabase();
db.delete(HoardDBOpenHelper.DATABASE_TABLE, where, whereArgs);
```

Querying a Database

To execute a query on an SQLite `Database` object, use its `query` method, passing in the following:

➤ An optional Boolean that specifies if the result set should contain only unique values.

➤ The name of the table to query.

➤ A projection, as an array of strings that lists the columns to include in the result set.

➤ A `where` clause that defines the criteria that will be used to limit the rows returned. You can include `?` wildcards that will be replaced by the values passed in through the selection argument parameter.

➤ An array of selection argument strings that will replace the `?` wildcards in the `where` clause, bound as String values.

➤ A `group by` clause that defines how the resulting rows will be grouped.

➤ A `having` clause that defines which row groups to include if you specified a `group by` clause.

➤ A string that describes the order of the returned rows.

➤ A string that limits the maximum number of rows in the result set.

Each database query is returned as a `Cursor`, which lets Android manage resources more efficiently by retrieving and releasing row and column values on demand.

> **NOTE** *As mentioned earlier, database operations should always be performed on a background, as described in Chapter 11, and database results and interactions should be encapsulated by a View Model, as described in Chapter 8.*

Listing 9-21 shows how to return a selection of rows from within an SQLite database.

LISTING 9-21: Querying a database

```
HoardDBOpenHelper hoardDBOpenHelper =
  new HoardDBOpenHelper(context,
                        HoardDBOpenHelper.DATABASE_NAME, null,
                        HoardDBOpenHelper.DATABASE_VERSION);

// Specify the result column projection. Return the minimum set
// of columns required to satisfy your requirements.
String[] result_columns = new String[] {
  HoardContract.KEY_ID,
  HoardContract.KEY_GOLD_HOARD_ACCESSIBLE_COLUMN,
  HoardContract.KEY_GOLD_HOARDED_COLUMN };

// Specify the where clause that will limit our results.
String where = HoardContract.KEY_GOLD_HOARD_ACCESSIBLE_COLUMN + "=?";
String whereArgs[] = {"1"};

// Replace these with valid SQL statements as necessary.
String groupBy = null;
String having = null;

// Return in ascending order of gold hoarded.
String order = HoardContract.KEY_GOLD_HOARDED_COLUMN + " ASC";

SQLiteDatabase db = hoardDBOpenHelper.getWritableDatabase();

Cursor cursor = db.query(HoardDBOpenHelper.DATABASE_TABLE,
  result_columns, where, whereArgs, groupBy, having, order);
```

> **NOTE** *It's good practice to request a database instance each time you perform a query or transaction on the database. For efficiency reasons, you should close your database instance only when you believe you will no longer require it— typically, when the Activity using it is stopped.*

Extracting Values from a Cursor

To extract values from a Cursor, first use the `moveTo<location>` methods to move to the desired row. Then use the type-safe `get<type>` methods (passing in a column index) to return the value stored at the current row for the specified column.

The use of projections means that result Cursors may contain only a subset of the full set of columns available in the queried table, so the index of each column may be different for different result Cursors. To find the current index of a particular column within each result Cursor, use the `getColumnIndexOrThrow` and `getColumnIndex` methods.

It's good practice to use `getColumnIndexOrThrow` when you expect a column to exist:

```
try {
  int columnIndex =
    cursor.getColumnIndexOrThrow(HoardContract.KEY_GOLD_HOARDED_COLUMN);
  String columnValue = cursor.getString(columnIndex);
  // Do something with the column value.
}
catch (IllegalArgumentException ex) {
  Log.e(TAG, ex.getLocalizedMessage());
}
```

Using `getColumnIndex` and checking for a –1 result, as shown in the following snippet, is a more efficient technique than catching exceptions when you expect the column might not always exist:

```
int columnIndex =
    cursor.getColumnIndex(HoardContract.KEY_GOLD_HOARDED_COLUMN);
if (columnIndex > -1) {
  String columnValue = cursor.getString(columnIndex);
    // Do something with the column value.
}
else {
  // Do something else if the column doesn't exist.
}
```

Note that the column indexes will not change within a given result cursor, so for efficiency reasons you should determine these prior to iterating over the Cursor to extract results, as shown in Listing 9-22.

> **NOTE** *Database implementations should publish static constants that provide the column names to simplify the process of extracting results from Cursors. These static constants are typically exposed from within the database contract class.*

Listing 9-22 shows how to iterate over a result Cursor, extracting and averaging a column of float values.

LISTING 9-22: Extracting values from a Cursor

```
float totalHoard = 0f;
float averageHoard = 0f;

// Find the index to the column(s) being used.
int GOLD_HOARDED_COLUMN_INDEX =
  cursor.getColumnIndexOrThrow(HoardContract.KEY_GOLD_HOARDED_COLUMN);

// Find the total number of rows.
int cursorCount = cursor.getCount();

// Iterate over the cursors rows.
// The Cursor is initialized at before first, so we can
// check only if there is a "next" row available. If the
// result Cursor is empty this will return false.
while (cursor.moveToNext())
  totalHoard += cursor.getFloat(GOLD_HOARDED_COLUMN_INDEX);

// Calculate an average -- checking for divide by zero errors.
averageHoard = cursor.getCount() > 0 ?
                 (totalHoard / cursorCount) : Float.NaN;

// Close the Cursor when you've finished with it.
cursor.close();
```

Because SQLite database columns are loosely typed, you can cast individual values into valid types, as required. For example, values stored as floats can be read back as strings.

When you have finished using your result Cursor, it's important to close it to avoid memory leaks and reduce your application's resource load:

```
cursor.close();
```

INTRODUCING THE FIREBASE REALTIME DATABASE

The Firebase Realtime Database is a cloud-hosted NoSQL database, whose data is synced across all clients in real time, and which remains available for queries and transactions on your device even when you lose Internet connectivity.

This approach to databases is significantly different from the SQLite databases described earlier in this chapter. SQLite databases are created and stored locally, and would need to be synchronized with a cloud-based data source to maintain a cloud copy of the data, or to share data across multiple devices.

Where SQLite databases are relational, and use SQL statements to execute queries and transactions that can include features such as joins across multiple tables, the Firebase Realtime Database works differently. As a NoSQL database, it is not relational and you do not use SQL statements to interact with it. The database is stored locally on each device as JSON files, which are synchronized in real time to the cloud-host and in turn with every connected client.

The Firebase Realtime Database is optimized for responsiveness and real-time updates, making it ideal for data that is frequently stored or modified by users, and which needs to be continuously synchronized across devices including mobile and web clients.

While a thorough investigation into the options available using the Firebase Realtime Database is beyond the scope of this book, within this section we will describe the simple case of adding it to your Android project, and interacting with it.

Adding Firebase to Your App

To add the Firebase Realtime Database to your app, you must install the Firebase SDK, which requires Android 4.0 Ice Cream Sandwich (API Level 14) and Google Play services version 10.2.6 or higher.

Android Studio includes a Firebase Assistant to simplify adding Firebase components to your app. To use it, select Tools ⇨ Firebase to display the assistant window shown in Figure 9-3.

Expand the Realtime Database list item and select the hyperlinked Save and retrieve data text, to display the Firebase Realtime Database assistant, as shown in Figure 9-4.

Select Connect to Firebase, and a browser window will open, where you'll be prompted to select a Google account to connect to. When you're logged in, you'll be prompted to accept a series of permissions as shown in Figure 9-5.

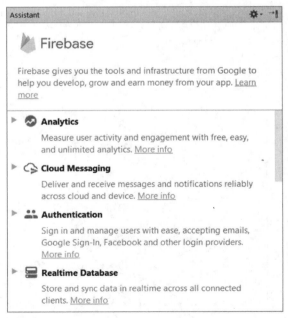

FIGURE 9-3

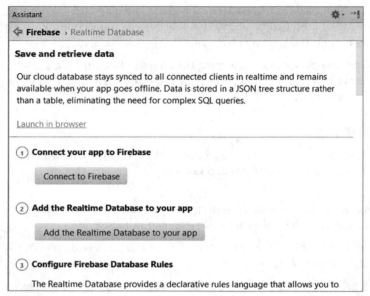

FIGURE 9-4

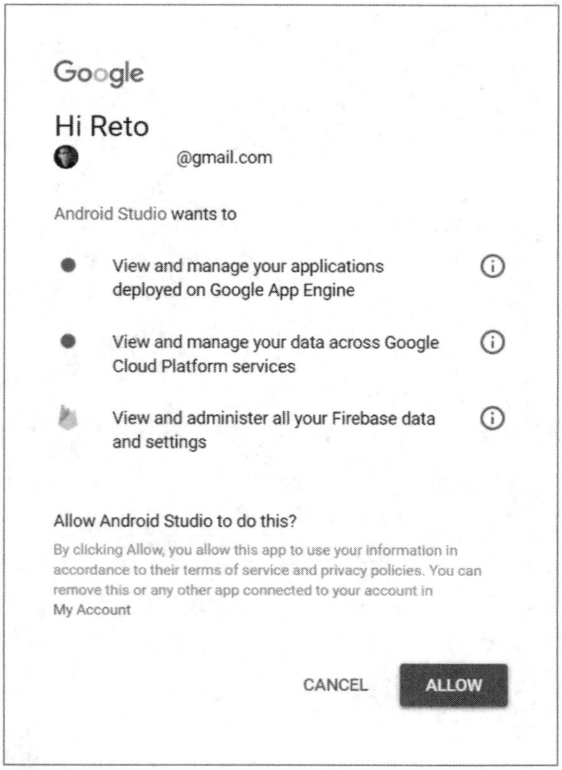

FIGURE 9-5

You are now signed into Firebase within Android Studio. Return to Android Studio and you'll see a dialog, shown in Figure 9-6, which allows you to create a new Firebase project, or select an existing one to use with your app.

With your app connected, you can choose to "Add the Realtime Database to Your App," which will add the Firebase Gradle build script dependency to your project-level `build.gradle` file, add the Firebase plug-in for Gradle, and add a dependency for the Firebase Database library to your `build .gradle` file.

Defining a Firebase Database and Defining Access Rules

Unlike SQLite databases, the Firebase Database is cloud-hosted, so we will use the Firebase Console to define our data structure and access rules.

In your browser, navigate to `console.firebase.google.com`, and select the project associated with your Android app.

Using the left-bar navigation, select the Develop item and then the Database option to display the configuration console for the Realtime Database, as shown in Figure 9-7.

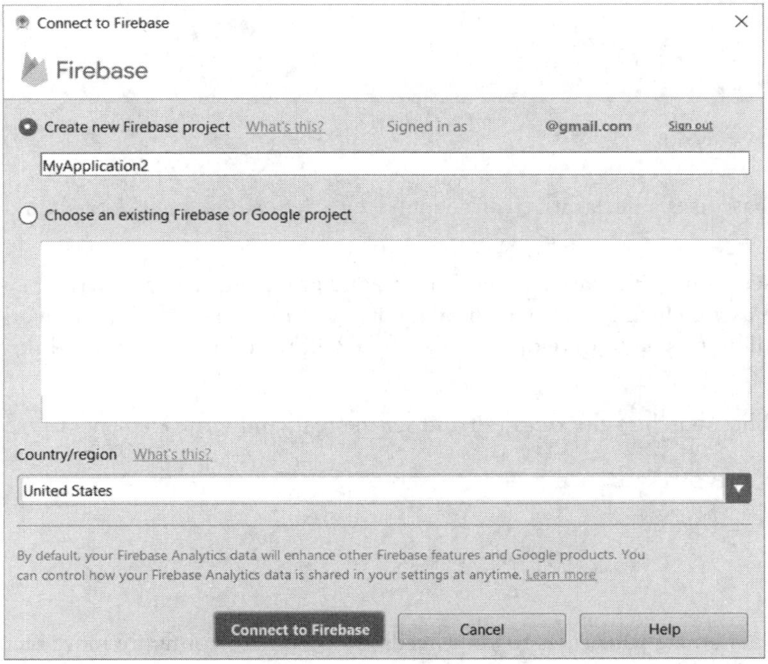

FIGURE 9-6

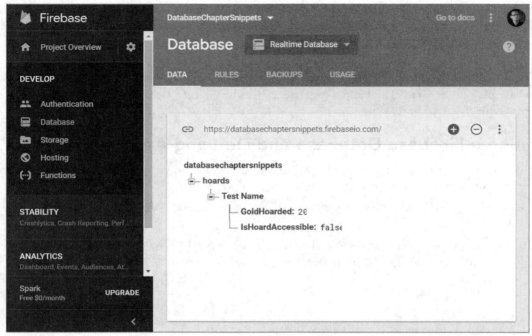

FIGURE 9-7

The Firebase Realtime Database uses a declarative rules language to define how your data should be accessed.

By default, Firebase Databases require Firebase Authentication, and grant full read and write permissions to all authenticated users. During development it can be useful to permit full unauthenticated access to get started, allowing you to develop your database before you have completed the authentication piece.

To set the access rules to public, switch to the *rules* tab and set the read and write elements to true:

```
{
  "rules": {
    ".read": true,
    ".write": true
  }
}
```

Once you're set up, you can customize your rules to your needs, so be sure to configure more secure and appropriate rules before launching your app.

Adding, Modifying, Deleting, and Querying Data from a Firebase Realtime Database

Firebase Realtime Database data is stored as JSON objects, effectively creating a cloud-hosted JSON tree. The *data* tab of the Firebase database console shows you the current state of the JSON tree representing the data you are recording in your database.

Unlike the SQLite databases described previously in this chapter, there are no tables or records. When you add new data, it becomes an element in the JSON tree, accessible using the associated key. You can define your own keys, such as unique user IDs, or you can let Firebase provide them for you automatically.

To write to a Firebase Database from within your Android app, you must first retrieve an instance of your database using the static `getInstance` method:

```
FirebaseDatabase database = FirebaseDatabase.getInstance();
```

Use the `getReference` method to find root-level nodes, and the `child` method to descend down the tree. To set a value for a given node, use the `setValue` method. Setting the value for a node or leaf element will automatically create all the parent nodes.

The following snippet shows how to add a new item to a Firebase table, using a simple data structure that stores similar information to the previous SQLite examples:

```
// Write a message to the database
FirebaseDatabase database = FirebaseDatabase.getInstance();

// Get a node corresponding to the root of our list of hoards.
DatabaseReference listRootRef = database.getReference("hoards");

// Get a node for our current hoard.
DatabaseReference itemRootRef = listRootRef.child(hoard.getHoardName());

// Set values for the properties of our hoard.
itemRootRef.child("hoardName").setValue(hoard.getHoardName());
itemRootRef.child("goldHoarded").setValue(hoard.getGoldHoarded());
itemRootRef.child("hoardAccessible").setValue(hoard.getHoardAccessible());
```

Figure 9-8 shows how that data is represented in a JSON tree in the Firebase Console.

The `setValue` method allows you to pass in objects as well as primitives. When you pass in an object, the result of all its getters are saved as children of the node you're saving to. The following snippet is the equivalent of the previous, using an object rather than passing in individual values:

FIGURE 9-8

```
// Write a message to the database
FirebaseDatabase database = FirebaseDatabase.getInstance();
```

```
// Get a node corresponding to the root of our list of hoards.
DatabaseReference listRootRef = database.getReference("hoards");

// Get a node for our current hoard and set its values.
listRootRef.child(hoard.getHoardName()).setValue(hoard);
```

When constructing your data structure it's important to keep in mind some best practices, including avoiding nested data, flattening data structures, and creating data that scales. To learn more about how to structure data in a NoSQL database like Firebase, refer to the Firebase "Structure Your Database" guide at `firebase.google.com/docs/database/android/structure-data`.

To modify an entry, simply use `setValue` as you would to create a new entry, and the previous value(s) will be overridden with the new values.

To delete an entry, call `removeValue` on the node or element you wish to remove:

```
DatabaseReference listRootRef = database.getReference("hoards");
listRootRef.child(hoard.getHoardName()).removeValue();
```

You query a Firebase Database by adding a `ValueEventListener` to the Database Reference, and overriding its `onDataChange` handler:

```
FirebaseDatabase database = FirebaseDatabase.getInstance();
DatabaseReference listRootRef = database.getReference("hoards");

// Read from the database
listRootRef.addValueEventListener(new ValueEventListener() {
  @Override
  public void onDataChange(DataSnapshot dataSnapshot) {
    // This method is called once with the initial value and again
    // whenever data at this location is updated.
    String key = dataSnapshot.getKey();
    String value = dataSnapshot.getValue().toString();
    Log.d(TAG, "Key is: " + key);
    Log.d(TAG, "Value is: " + value);
  }

  @Override
  public void onCancelled(DatabaseError error) {
    // Failed to read value
    Log.w(TAG, "Failed to read value.", error.toException());
  }
});
```

This handler is called immediately after the listener is attached, and again every time the data for it—and any of its children—is changed. As a result, you receive real-time updates whenever the database is changed, either within your app or from an external source—such as the server or another client.

To bind a Firebase Database to Android UI elements, you must store a local copy of the database tree, and use the `ValueEventListener` to observe and apply changes.

To simplify this process, the Firebase team has created the FirebaseUI open source library for Android, which allows you to quickly connect common UI elements, such as the Recycler View, to Firebase APIs like the Realtime Database or Firebase Authentication. The FirebaseUI library is available at `github.com/firebase/firebaseui-android`.

You can learn more about the Firebase Realtime Database here:

`firebase.google.com/docs/database/`

Google has also released a new databse system, Cloud Firestore, into public Beta. Firestore is a highly-scalable NoSQL cloud database that, like Firebase Realtime Database, can be used to sync application data across servers and client apps in real time.

Firestore is designed specifically to be highly scalable and supports more expressive and efficient querying, including shallow queries that don't require retrieving the entire collection, and support for sorting, filtering, and limiting query returns. It also offers seamless integration with other Firebase and Google Cloud Platform products, including Cloud Functions.

In addition to Android, web, and iOS SDKs, Firestore APIs are available in Node.js, Java, Python, and Go.

As Firestore is in beta at the time of writing this book, a more detailed exploration is beyond our scope. You can find more detail on Firestore at `firebase.google.com/docs/firestore/`.

10

Content Providers and Search

WROX.COM CODE DOWNLOADS FOR THIS CHAPTER

The code downloads for this chapter are found at www.wrox.com. The code for this chapter is divided into the following major examples:

➤ `Snippets_ch10.zip`

➤ `Earthquake_ch10.zip`

INTRODUCING CONTENT PROVIDERS

In this chapter you learn how to create and use Content Providers as a consistent way to share, and consume structured data within and between applications by providing an abstraction from the underlying data storage technique.

You see how to query Content Providers asynchronously using Cursor Loaders, to ensure your application remains responsive while you retrieve data.

In Android, access to a database is restricted to the application that created it, so Content Providers offer a standard interface your applications can use to share data with, and consume data from, other applications—including many of the native databases.

Content Providers are used extensively by the Android framework, giving you the opportunity to enhance your own applications with native Content Providers, including contacts, calendar, and the Media Store. You learn how to store and retrieve data from these core Android Content Providers to provide your users with a richer, more consistent, and fully integrated user experience.

Finally, you learn how to use Content Providers to offer rich search options, including how to provide real-time search suggestions using the Search View.

WHY SHOULD I USE CONTENT PROVIDERS?

The main reason to use a Content Provider is to facilitate data sharing across applications. Content Providers allow you to define granular data access restrictions so that other applications can securely access and modify your app's data.

Any application—with the appropriate permissions—can potentially query, add, remove, or update data provided by another application through a Content Provider, including the native Android Content Providers.

By publishing your own Content Providers, you make it possible for you (and potentially other developers) to incorporate and extend your data in other applications. Content Providers are also the mechanism used to provide search results for the Search View, and to generate real-time search suggestions.

Content Providers are also useful as a way to decouple your application layers from the underlying data layers, by encapsulating and abstracting your underlying database. This approach is useful in making your applications data-source agnostic, such that your data storage mechanism can be modified or replaced without affecting your application layer.

If you aren't planning to share your application data, you don't need to use Content Providers; however, many developers still choose to create Content Providers on top of their databases so they can take advantage of a consistent abstraction layer. Content Providers also allow you to take advantage of several convenience classes for data access, particularly the Cursor Loader, as described later in this chapter.

Several native Content Providers have been made accessible for access by third-party applications, including the contact manager, Media Store, and calendar, as described later in this chapter.

CREATING CONTENT PROVIDERS

Content Providers are an abstraction layer over an underlying data source, which provide an interface for publishing data that will be consumed using a Content Resolver, potentially across process boundaries. Content Providers use an interface for publishing and consuming data based around a simple URI addressing model using the content:// schema.

Content Providers allow you to decouple the application components that consume data from their underlying data sources, providing a generic mechanism through which applications can share their data or consume data provided by others.

They allow you to share data access across application process boundaries, and support the use of granular data access restrictions so that other applications can securely access and modify your app data.

To create a new Content Provider, extend the abstract ContentProvider class as shown in Listing 10-1.

LISTING 10-1: Creating a new Content Provider

```
public class MyHoardContentProvider extends ContentProvider {

  @Override
  public boolean onCreate() {
    return false;
  }

  @Nullable
  @Override
  public Cursor query(@NonNull Uri uri,
                      @Nullable String[] projection,
                      @Nullable String selection,
                      @Nullable String[] selectionArgs,
                      @Nullable String sortOrder) {
    // TODO: Perform a query and return Cursor.
    return null;
  }

  @Nullable
  @Override
  public String getType(@NonNull Uri uri) {
    // TODO: Return the mime-type of a query.
    return null;
  }

  @Nullable
  @Override
  public Uri insert(@NonNull Uri uri, @Nullable ContentValues values) {
    // TODO: Insert the Content Values and return a URI to the record.
    return null;
  }
```

continues

LISTING 10-1 *(continued)*

```
@Override
public int delete(@NonNull Uri uri,
                  @Nullable String selection,
                  @Nullable String[] selectionArgs) {
  // TODO: Delete the matching records and return the number
  //       of records deleted.
  return 0;
}

@Override
public int update(@NonNull Uri uri,
                  @Nullable ContentValues values,
                  @Nullable String selection,
                  @Nullable String[] selectionArgs) {
  // TODO: Update the matching records with the provided
  //       Content Values, returning the number of records updated.
  return 0;
}
}
```

In the following sections you learn how to implement the onCreate handler to initialize the underlying data source, and update the query, getType, insert, update, and delete methods to implement the interface used by the Content Resolver to interact with the data.

Creating the Content Provider's Database

To initialize the data source you plan to access through the Content Provider, override the onCreate method, as shown in Listing 10-2. If you are using an SQLite database, this can be handled using an SQLite Open Helper implementation, as described in the previous chapter.

LISTING 10-2: Creating the Content Provider's database

```
private HoardDB.HoardDBOpenHelper mHoardDBOpenHelper;

@Override
public boolean onCreate() {
  // Construct the underlying database.
  // Defer opening the database until you need to perform
  // a query or transaction.
  mHoardDBOpenHelper =
    new HoardDB.HoardDBOpenHelper(getContext(),
                                  HoardDB.HoardDBOpenHelper.DATABASE_NAME,
                                  null,
                                  HoardDB.HoardDBOpenHelper.DATABASE_VERSION);
  return true;
}
```

We'll continue to use an SQLite database for all our examples of underlying databases within this chapter, but remember that the database implementation you choose is arbitrary—you may use a cloud-based database, an entirely in-memory database, or an alternative SQL or no-SQL database library. Later in this chapter, we'll create a Content Provider over a Room database to provide search results for the ongoing Earthquake example. You can learn more about using SQLite in Chapter 9, "Creating and Using Databases."

Registering Content Providers

Like Activities and Services, Content Providers are application components that must be registered in your application manifest before the Content Resolver can discover and use them. You do this using a `provider` tag that includes a `name` attribute, describing the Provider's class name, and an `authorities` tag.

Use the `authorities` tag to define the base URI of the Provider; a Content Provider's authority is used by the Content Resolver as an address to find the database to interact with.

Each Content Provider authority must be unique, so it's good practice to base the URI path on your package name. The general form for defining a Content Provider's authority is as follows:

```
com.<CompanyName>.provider.<ApplicationName>
```

The completed `provider` tag should follow the format shown in Listing 10-3.

LISTING 10-3: Registering a new Content Provider in the application manifest

```
<provider android:name=".MyHoardContentProvider"
          android:authorities="com.professionalandroid.provider.hoarder"/>
```

Publishing Your Content Provider's URI Address

By convention, each Content Provider should expose its authority using a public static `CONTENT_URI` property that includes a data path to the primary content, as shown in Listing 10-4.

LISTING 10-4: Publishing your Content Provider authority

```
public static final Uri CONTENT_URI =
    Uri.parse("content://com.professionalandroid.provider.hoarder/lairs");
```

These content URIs will be used when accessing your Content Provider using a Content Resolver, as shown in the following sections. A query made using this form represents a request for all rows, whereas an appended trailing /<rownumber>, as shown in the following snippet, represents a request for a specific single record:

```
content://com.professionalandroid.provider.hoarder/lairs/5
```

It's good practice to support access to your provider for both of these forms. The simplest way to do this is to add a `UriMatcher` to your Content Provider implementation to parse URIs, determine their forms, and extract the provided details.

Listing 10-5 shows the implementation pattern for defining a Uri Matcher that analyzes the form of a URI—specifically determining if a URI is a request for all data or for a single row.

LISTING 10-5: Defining a Uri Matcher

```
// Create the constants used to differentiate between the different URI
// requests.
private static final int ALLROWS = 1;
private static final int SINGLE_ROW = 2;

private static final UriMatcher uriMatcher;

// Populate the UriMatcher object, where a URI ending in
// 'elements' will correspond to a request for all items,
// and 'elements/[rowID]' represents a single row.
static {
  uriMatcher = new UriMatcher(UriMatcher.NO_MATCH);
  uriMatcher.addURI("com.professionalandroid.provider.hoarder",
    "lairs", ALLROWS);
  uriMatcher.addURI("com.professionalandroid.provider.hoarder",
    "lairs/#", SINGLE_ROW);
}
```

You can use the same technique to expose alternative URIs within the same Content Provider that represent different subsets of data, or different tables within your database.

Implementing Content Provider Queries

To support queries with your Content Provider, you must override the `query` and `getType` methods. The Content Resolver uses these methods to access the underlying data, without knowing its structure or implementation. These methods enable applications to share data across application boundaries without having to publish a specific interface for each data source.

In this chapter we show how to use a Content Provider to provide access to an SQLite database, but within these methods you can access any source of data (including Room, files, application instance variables, or cloud-based databases).

Having used the Uri Matcher to distinguish between full table and single row queries, you can refine the query requests, and use the `SQLiteQueryBuilder` class to easily apply additional selection conditions to a query.

Android 4.1 Jelly Bean (API Level 16) extended the `query` method to support a `CancellationSignal` parameter:

```
CancellationSignal mCancellationSignal = new CancellationSignal();
```

By using a Cancellation Signal, you can notify the Content Provider that you wish to abort the currently running query by calling the Cancellation Signal's `cancel` method:

```
mCancellationSignal.cancel();
```

For backward compatibility reasons, Android requires that you also implement the `query` method that doesn't include the Cancellation Signal parameter, as shown in Listing 10-6.

Listing 10-6 shows the skeleton code for implementing queries within a Content Provider using an underlying SQLite database, using an SQLite Query Builder to pass each of the query parameters, including the Cancellation Signal, into a query made to the underlying SQLite database.

LISTING 10-6: Implementing queries within a Content Provider

```java
@Nullable
@Override
public Cursor query(@NonNull Uri uri,
                    @Nullable String[] projection,
                    @Nullable String selection,
                    @Nullable String[] selectionArgs,
                    @Nullable String sortOrder) {
  return query(uri, projection, selection, selectionArgs, sortOrder, null);
}


@Nullable
@Override
public Cursor query(@NonNull Uri uri,
                    @Nullable String[] projection,
                    @Nullable String selection,
                    @Nullable String[] selectionArgs,
                    @Nullable String sortOrder,
                    @Nullable CancellationSignal cancellationSignal) {
  // Open the database.
  SQLiteDatabase db;
  try {
    db = mHoardDBOpenHelper.getWritableDatabase();
  } catch (SQLiteException ex) {
    db = mHoardDBOpenHelper.getReadableDatabase();
  }

  // Replace these with valid SQL statements if necessary.
  String groupBy = null;
  String having = null;

  // Use an SQLite Query Builder to simplify constructing the
  // database query.
  SQLiteQueryBuilder queryBuilder = new SQLiteQueryBuilder();

  // If this is a row query, limit the result set to the passed in row.
  switch (uriMatcher.match(uri)) {
    case SINGLE_ROW :
      String rowID = uri.getLastPathSegment();
```

continues

LISTING 10-6 *(continued)*

```
        queryBuilder.appendWhere(HoardDB.HoardContract.KEY_ID + "=" + rowID);
      default: break;
    }

    // Specify the table on which to perform the query. This can
    // be a specific table or a join as required.
    queryBuilder.setTables(HoardDB.HoardDBOpenHelper.DATABASE_TABLE);

    // Specify a limit to the number of returned results, if any.
    String limit = null;

    // Execute the query.
    Cursor cursor = queryBuilder.query(db, projection, selection,
      selectionArgs, groupBy, having, sortOrder, limit, cancellationSignal);

    // Return the result Cursor.
    return cursor;
}
```

If a running query is canceled, SQLite will throw an `OperationCanceledException`. If your Content Provider doesn't use an SQLite database, you will need to listen for cancellation signals using an `onCancelListener` handler, and handle them yourself:

```
cancellationSignal.setOnCancelListener(
  new CancellationSignal.OnCancelListener() {
    @Override
    public void onCancel() {
      // TODO React when my query is cancelled.
    }
  }
);
```

Having implemented queries, you must also specify a MIME type to indicate the *type* of data returned. Override the `getType` method to return a string that uniquely describes your data type.

The type returned should include two forms, one for a single entry and another for all the entries, following these forms:

➤ Single item:

    `vnd.android.cursor.`**`item`**`/vnd.<companyname>.<contenttype>`

➤ All items:

    `vnd.android.cursor.`**`dir`**`/vnd.<companyname>.<contenttype>`

Listing 10-7 shows how to override the `getType` method to return the correct MIME type based on the URI passed in.

LISTING 10-7: Returning a Content Provider MIME type

```
@Nullable
@Override
```

```
public String getType(@NonNull Uri uri) {
  // Return a string that identifies the MIME type
  // for a Content Provider URI
  switch (uriMatcher.match(uri)) {
    case ALLROWS:
      return "vnd.android.cursor.dir/vnd.professionalandroid.lairs";
    case SINGLE_ROW:
      return "vnd.android.cursor.item/vnd.professionalandroid.lairs";
    default:
      throw new IllegalArgumentException("Unsupported URI: " + uri);
  }
}
```

Content Provider Transactions

To support delete, insert, and update transactions on your Content Provider, override the corresponding `delete`, `insert`, and `update` methods.

Like `query`, these methods are used by Content Resolvers to perform transactions on the underlying data without knowing its implementation.

When performing transactions that modify the dataset, it's good practice to call the Content Resolver's `notifyChange` method. This will notify any Content Observers, registered for a given Cursor using the `Cursor.registerContentObserver` method, that the underlying table (or a particular row) has been removed, added, or updated.

Listing 10-8 shows the skeleton code for implementing transactions within a Content Provider on an underlying SQLite database.

LISTING 10-8: Content Provider insert, update, and delete implementations

```
@Override
public int delete(@NonNull Uri uri,
                  @Nullable String selection,
                  @Nullable String[] selectionArgs) {

  // Open a read / write database to support the transaction.
  SQLiteDatabase db = mHoardDBOpenHelper.getWritableDatabase();

  // If this is a row URI, limit the deletion to the specified row.
  switch (uriMatcher.match(uri)) {
    case SINGLE_ROW :
      String rowID = uri.getLastPathSegment();
      selection = KEY_ID + "=" + rowID
                    + (!TextUtils.isEmpty(selection) ?
                          " AND (" + selection + ')' : "");
    default: break;
  }

  // To return the number of deleted items you must specify a where
  // clause. To delete all rows and return a value pass in "1".
  if (selection == null)
```

continues

LISTING 10-8 *(continued)*

```
      selection = "1";

  // Perform the deletion.
  int deleteCount = db.delete(HoardDB.HoardDBOpenHelper.DATABASE_TABLE,
                              selection, selectionArgs);

  // Notify any observers of the change in the data set.
  getContext().getContentResolver().notifyChange(uri, null);

  // Return the number of deleted items.
  return deleteCount;
}

@Nullable
@Override
public Uri insert(@NonNull Uri uri, @Nullable ContentValues values) {

  // Open a read / write database to support the transaction.
  SQLiteDatabase db = mHoardDBOpenHelper.getWritableDatabase();

  // To add empty rows to your database by passing in an empty
  // Content Values object you must use the null column hack
  // parameter to specify the name of a column that can be
  // explicitly set to null.
  String nullColumnHack = null;

  // Insert the values into the table
  long id = db.insert(HoardDB.HoardDBOpenHelper.DATABASE_TABLE,
                      nullColumnHack, values);

  // Construct and return the URI of the newly inserted row.
  if (id > -1) {
    // Construct and return the URI of the newly inserted row.
    Uri insertedId = ContentUris.withAppendedId(CONTENT_URI, id);

    // Notify any observers of the change in the data set.
    getContext().getContentResolver().notifyChange(insertedId, null);

    return insertedId;
  }
  else
    return null;
}

@Override
public int update(@NonNull Uri uri,
                  @Nullable ContentValues values,
                  @Nullable String selection,
                  @Nullable String[] selectionArgs) {

  // Open a read / write database to support the transaction.
  SQLiteDatabase db = mHoardDBOpenHelper.getWritableDatabase();
```

```
    // If this is a row URI, limit the deletion to the specified row.
    switch (uriMatcher.match(uri)) {
      case SINGLE_ROW :
        String rowID = uri.getLastPathSegment();
        selection = KEY_ID + "=" + rowID
                    + (!TextUtils.isEmpty(selection) ?
                        " AND (" + selection + ')' : "");
      default: break;
    }

    // Perform the update.
    int updateCount = db.update(HoardDB.HoardDBOpenHelper.DATABASE_TABLE,
                            values, selection, selectionArgs);

    // Notify any observers of the change in the data set.
    getContext().getContentResolver().notifyChange(uri, null);

    return updateCount;
}
```

> **NOTE** *When working with content URIs, the* ContentUris *class includes the* withAppendedId *convenience method to easily append a specific row ID to the* CONTENT_URI *of a Content Provider. This is used in Listing 10-8 to construct the URI of newly inserted rows.*

Sharing Files Using a Content Provider

Rather than store large files within your Content Provider, you should represent them within a table as fully qualified URIs to files stored somewhere else on the file-system.

To include files within your table, include a column labeled _data that will contain the path to the file represented by that record—this column should not be used by client applications directly. Instead, override the openFile handler within your Content Provider to provide a ParcelFileDescriptor when the Content Resolver requests a file associated with that record by providing its URI path.

To simplify this process, Android includes the openFileHelper method, which queries the Content Provider for the file path stored in the _data column and creates and returns a Parcel File Descriptor, as shown in Listing 10-9.

LISTING 10-9: Returning files from a Content Provider

```
@Nullable
@Override
public ParcelFileDescriptor openFile(@NonNull Uri uri, @NonNull String mode)
  throws FileNotFoundException {

  return openFileHelper(uri, mode);
}
```

> **NOTE** *Because the files associated with rows in the database are stored on the file-system, not within the database table, it's important to consider what the effect of deleting a row should have on the underlying file.*

A better approach for sharing files between applications is the Storage Access Framework, introduced in Android 4.4 KitKat (API Level 19). The Storage Access Framework is described in detail in Chapter 8, "Files, Saving State, and Preferences."

Adding Permission Requirements to Content Providers

The primary purpose of Content Providers is to share data with other applications; by default, any application that knows the right URIs can use the Content Resolver to access your Content Provider and query its data or perform transactions.

If you have no intention of making your Content Provider accessible to other applications, set the `android:exported` attribute to `false`, to restrict access to only your application:

```
<provider
    android:name=".MyHoardContentProvider"
    android:authorities="com.professionalandroid.provider.hoarder"
    android:exported="false">
</provider>
```

Alternatively, you can restrict read and/or write access to your Providers using permissions.

For example, native Android Content Providers that include sensitive information—such as contact details and call logs—require read and write permissions respectively to access and modify their content (native Content Providers are described in more detail in the section "Using Native Android Content Providers").

Using permissions prevents malicious applications from corrupting data, gaining access to sensitive information, or making excessive (or unauthorized) use of hardware resources or external communication channels.

The most common use of permissions with Content Providers is to restrict access only to applications signed with the same signature—meaning other apps you have created and released—in order that they can work together.

To do this, you must first define a new permission within the application manifest of *both* the consumer and Content Provider apps, indicating a protection level of *signature*:

```
<permission
    android:name="com.professionalandroid.provider.hoarder.ACCESS_PERMISSION"
    android:protectionLevel="signature">
</permission>
```

Also add the corresponding uses-permission entry in each Manifest:

```
<uses-permission
    android:name="com.professionalandroid.provider.hoarder.ACCESS_PERMISSION"
/>
```

In addition to the signature protection level, which restricts access to apps signed with the same signature, permissions can be defined as requiring *normal* or *dangerous* protection levels. Normal permissions are displayed to the user at installation time, while dangerous permissions require runtime user acceptance.

More details on creating and using your own permissions is available in Chapter 20, "Advanced Android Development."

Once you have defined a permission, you can apply it by modifying the Content Provider manifest entry, indicating the permission required to read or write to the Provider. You can specify different permissions for read or write access, or require permissions for only one or the other:

```
<provider
  android:name=".MyHoardContentProvider"
  android:authorities="com.professionalandroid.provider.hoarder"
  android:writePermission=
    "com.professionalandroid.provider.hoarder.ACCESS_PERMISSION"
/>
```

It's also possible to provide apps with temporary permission, to access or modify a particular record, using Intents. This works by having the requesting app send an Intent to the Content Provider host application, which then returns an Intent that contains the appropriate permissions for a specific URI, which lasts until the calling Activity is finished.

To support temporary permissions, start by setting the `android:grantUriPermissions` attribute to `true` in your Provider's manifest entry:

```
<provider
  android:name=".MyHoardContentProvider"
  android:authorities="com.professionalandroid.provider.hoarder"
  android:writePermission=
    "com.professionalandroid.provider.hoarder.ACCESS_PERMISSION"
  android:grantUriPermissions="true"
/>
```

This will allow you to grant temporary permissions to any URI used to access your Provider. Alternatively, you can use a `grant-uri-permission` child node within your `provider` node to define a specific path pattern or prefix.

Within your application, provide functionality that listens for an Intent from another app (as described in Chapter 6, "Intents and Broadcast Receivers"). When such an Intent is received, display a UI to support the requested action, and return an Intent with a URI to the affected/ selected record, setting either the `FLAG_GRANT_READ_URI_PERMISSION` or `FLAG_GRANT_WRITE_URI_ PERMISSION` flag as applicable:

```
protected void returnSelectedRecord(int rowId) {
  Uri selectedUri =
    ContentUris.withAppendedId(MyHoardContentProvider.CONTENT_URI,
                               rowId);

  Intent result = new Intent(Intent.ACTION_PICK, selectedUri);
  result.addFlags(FLAG_GRANT_READ_URI_PERMISSION);

  setResult(RESULT_OK, result);
  finish();
}
```

Using this approach, your app provides the intermediation between the user the third-party application and your Content Provider—for example, by providing the UI that allows the user to select a record or modify data.

This limits the risks of data leakage or corruption by restricting the amount of data accessed, and ensuring your app—and by extension the user—is able to cancel any inappropriate access or changes. As a result, the requesting app does not need to request any special permissions when using an Intent to query or modify data.

The approach of using Intents to grant temporary permissions is used extensively to provide access to native Content Providers, as described in the section "Using Native Content Providers."

ACCESSING CONTENT PROVIDERS WITH CONTENT RESOLVERS

Each application includes a `ContentResolver` instance, accessible using the `getContentResolver` method, as follows:

```
ContentResolver cr = getContentResolver();
```

Content Resolvers are used to query and perform transactions on Content Providers. The Content Resolver supplies methods to query and perform transactions on Content Providers, taking a URI that indicates which Content Provider to interact with.

A Content Provider's URI is its *authority* as defined by its manifest entry, and typically published as a static constant on the Content Provider implementation.

As described in the previous section, Content Providers usually accept two forms of URI—one for requests against all data and another that specifies only a single row. The form for the latter appends the row identifier (in the form `/<rowID>`) to the base URI.

Querying Content Providers

Content Provider queries take a form very similar to that of SQLite database queries. Query results are returned as Cursors over a result set, and the values extracted, in the same way as described in the previous chapter describing SQLite databases.

Using the `query` method on the `ContentResolver` object, pass in the following:

➤   A URI to the Content Provider content you want to query.

➤   A projection that lists the columns you want to include in the result set.

➤   A `where` clause that defines the rows to be returned. You should include ? wildcards that will be replaced by the values passed into the selection argument parameter.

➤   An array of selection argument strings that will replace the ? wildcards in the `where` clause.

➤   A String that describes the order of the returned rows.

Listing 10-10 shows how to use a Content Resolver to apply a query to a Content Provider.

LISTING 10-10: Querying a Content Provider with the Content Resolver

```
// Get the Content Resolver.
ContentResolver cr = getContentResolver();

// Specify the result column projection. Return the minimum set
// of columns required to satisfy your requirements.
String[] result_columns = new String[] {
  HoardDB.HoardContract.KEY_ID,
  HoardDB.HoardContract.KEY_GOLD_HOARD_ACCESSIBLE_COLUMN,
  HoardDB.HoardContract.KEY_GOLD_HOARDED_COLUMN };

// Specify the where clause that will limit your results.
String where = HoardDB.HoardContract.KEY_GOLD_HOARD_ACCESSIBLE_COLUMN
                  + "=?";
String[] whereArgs = {"1"};

// Replace with valid SQL ordering statement as necessary.
String order = null;

// Return the specified rows.
Cursor resultCursor = cr.query(MyHoardContentProvider.CONTENT_URI,
                        result_columns, where, whereArgs, order);
```

In this example the query is made using the column names provided as static constants from the `HoardContract` class and the `CONTENT_URI` available from the `MyHoardContentProvider` class; however, it's worth noting that a third-party application can perform the same query, provided it knows the content URI and column names, and has the appropriate permissions.

Most Content Providers also include a shortcut URI pattern that allows you to address a particular row by appending a row ID to the content URI. You can use the static `withAppendedId` method from the `ContentUris` class to simplify this, as shown in Listing 10-11.

LISTING 10-11: Querying a Content Provider for a particular row

```
private Cursor queryRow(int rowId) {
  // Get the Content Resolver.
  ContentResolver cr = getContentResolver();

  // Specify the result column projection. Return the minimum set
  // of columns required to satisfy your requirements.
  String[] result_columns = new String[] {
    HoardDB.HoardContract.KEY_ID,
    HoardDB.HoardContract.KEY_GOLD_HOARD_NAME_COLUMN,
    HoardDB.HoardContract.KEY_GOLD_HOARDED_COLUMN };

  // Append a row ID to the URI to address a specific row.
  Uri rowAddress =
    ContentUris.withAppendedId(MyHoardContentProvider.CONTENT_URI,
                        rowId);
```

continues

LISTING 10-11 *(continued)*

```
    // These are null as we are requesting a single row.
    String where = null;
    String[] whereArgs = null;
    String order = null;

    // Return the specified row.
    return cr.query(rowAddress, result_columns, where, whereArgs, order);
}
```

To extract values from a result Cursor, use the same techniques described in the previous chapter, using the moveTo<location> methods in combination with the get<type> methods to extract values from the specified row and column.

Listing 10-12 extends the code from Listing 10-11, by iterating over a result Cursor and displaying the name of the largest hoard.

LISTING 10-12: Extracting values from a Content Provider result Cursor

```
    float largestHoard = 0f;
    String largestHoardName = "No Hoards";

    // Find the index to the column(s) being used.
    int GOLD_HOARDED_COLUMN_INDEX = resultCursor.getColumnIndexOrThrow(
      HoardDB.HoardContract.KEY_GOLD_HOARDED_COLUMN);
    int HOARD_NAME_COLUMN_INDEX = resultCursor.getColumnIndexOrThrow(
      HoardDB.HoardContract.KEY_GOLD_HOARD_NAME_COLUMN);

    // Iterate over the cursors rows.
    // The Cursor is initialized at before first, so we can
    // check only if there is a "next" row available. If the
    // result Cursor is empty, this will return false.
    while (resultCursor.moveToNext()) {
      float hoard = resultCursor.getFloat(GOLD_HOARDED_COLUMN_INDEX);
      if (hoard > largestHoard) {
        largestHoard = hoard;
        largestHoardName = resultCursor.getString(HOARD_NAME_COLUMN_INDEX);
      }
    }

    // Close the Cursor when you've finished with it.
    resultCursor.close();
```

When you have finished using your result Cursor it's important to close it to avoid memory leaks and reduce your application's resource load:

```
    resultCursor.close();
```

You see more examples of querying for content later in this chapter when the native Android Content Providers are introduced in the section "Using Native Android Content Providers."

> **WARNING** *Database queries can take significant time to execute. By default, the Content Resolver will execute queries—as well as all other transactions—on the main application thread.*
>
> *To ensure your application remains smooth and responsive, you must execute all queries asynchronously, as described later in this chapter.*

Cancelling Queries

Android 4.1 Jelly Bean (API Level 16) extended the Content Resolver `query` method to support a `CancellationSignal` parameter:

```
CancellationSignal mCancellationSignal = new CancellationSignal();
```

The Android Support Library includes a `ContentResolverCompat` class that allows you to support query cancellation in a backward-compatible fashion:

```
Cursor resultCursor = ContentResolverCompat.query(cr,
                 MyHoardContentProvider.CONTENT_URI,
                 result_columns, where, whereArgs, order,
                 mCancellationSignal);
```

Through its `cancel` method, a Cancellation Signal enables you to notify a Content Provider that you wish to abort a query:

```
mCancellationSignal.cancel();
```

If the query is canceled while running, a `OperationCanceledException` will be thrown.

Querying for Content Asynchronously with a Cursor Loader

Database operations can be time-consuming, so it's particularly important that no database or Content Provider queries or transactions are performed on the main application thread.

To help simplify the process of managing Cursors, synchronizing correctly with the UI thread, and ensuring all queries occur on a background Thread, Android provides the `Loader` class.

Loaders and the Loader Manager are used to simplify asynchronous background data loading. Loaders create a background thread within which your database queries and transactions are performed, before syncing with the UI thread, and returning your processed data via callback handlers.

The Loader Manager includes simple caching, ensuring Loaders aren't interrupted by Activity restarts due to device configuration changes, and Loaders are aware of Activity and Fragment life-cycle events. This ensures Loaders are removed when the parent Activity or Fragment is permanently destroyed.

The `AsyncTaskLoader` class can be extended to load any kind of data from any data source; of particular interest is the `CursorLoader` class. The Cursor Loader is designed specifically to support asynchronous queries on Content Providers, returning a result Cursor and notifications of any updates to the underlying provider.

> **NOTE** *To maintain concise and encapsulated code, not all the examples in this chapter explicitly show a Cursor Loader being used when making a Content Provider query—which is bad and we feel bad about it. For your applications it's important to always use a Cursor Loader—or other background Threading technique—when performing queries or transactions on Content Providers or databases.*

The Cursor Loader handles all the management tasks required to use a Cursor, including managing the Cursor life cycle to ensure Cursors are closed when the Activity is terminated.

Cursor Loaders also observe changes in the underlying query, so you don't need to implement your own Content Observers.

Implementing Cursor Loader Callbacks

To use a Cursor Loader, create a new `LoaderManager.LoaderCallbacks` implementation. Loader Callbacks are implemented using generics, so you should specify the explicit type being loaded, in this case Cursors, when implementing your own:

```
LoaderManager.LoaderCallbacks<Cursor> loaderCallback
  = new LoaderManager.LoaderCallbacks<Cursor>() {

  @Override
  public Loader<Cursor> onCreateLoader(int id, Bundle args) {
    return null;
  }

  @Override
  public void onLoadFinished(Loader<Cursor> loader, Cursor data) {}

  @Override
  public void onLoaderReset(Loader<Cursor> loader) {}
};
```

If you require only a single Loader implementation within your Fragment or Activity, you typically do this by having that component implement the interface:

```
public class MyActivity extends AppCompatActivity
                    implements LoaderManager.LoaderCallbacks<Cursor>
```

The Loader Callbacks consist of three handlers:

➤ `onCreateLoader`—Called when the Loader is initialized, this handler should create and return new Cursor Loader object. The Cursor Loader constructor arguments mirror those required for executing a query using the Content Resolver. Accordingly, when this handler is executed, the query parameters you specify will be used to perform a query using the Content Resolver. Note that a Cancellation Signal is not required (or supported). Instead, the Cursor Loader creates its own Cancellation Signal object, which can be triggered by calling `cancelLoad`.

➤ onLoadFinished—When the Loader Manager has completed the asynchronous query, the onLoadFinished handler is called, with the result Cursor passed in as a parameter. Use this Cursor to update adapters and other UI elements.

➤ onLoaderReset—When the Loader Manager resets your Cursor Loader, onLoaderReset is called. Within this handler you should release any references to data returned by the query and reset the UI accordingly. The Cursor will be closed by the Loader Manager, so you shouldn't attempt to close it.

Listing 10-13 shows a skeleton implementation of the Cursor Loader Callbacks.

LISTING 10-13: Implementing Loader Callbacks

```
public Loader<Cursor> onCreateLoader(int id, Bundle args) {
  // Construct the new query in the form of a Cursor Loader. Use the id
  // parameter to construct and return different loaders.
  String[] projection = null;
  String where = null;
  String[] whereArgs = null;
  String sortOrder = null;

  // Query URI
  Uri queryUri = MyHoardContentProvider.CONTENT_URI;

  // Create the new Cursor loader.
  return new CursorLoader(this, queryUri, projection,
                          where, whereArgs, sortOrder);
}

public void onLoadFinished(Loader<Cursor> loader, Cursor cursor) {
  // You are now on the UI thread, update your UI with the loaded data.
  // Returns cached data automatically if initLoader is called after
  // a configuration change.
}

public void onLoaderReset(Loader<Cursor> loader) {
  // Handle any cleanup necessary when Loader (or its parent)
  // is completely destroyed, for example the application being
  // terminated. Note that the Cursor Loader will close the
  // underlying result Cursor so you don't have to.
}
```

Initializing, Restarting, and Cancelling a Cursor Loader

To initialize a new Loader, call the Loader Manager's initLoader method, passing in a reference to your Loader Callback implementation, an optional arguments Bundle, and a Loader identifier. Here, as in the remainder of the book, we will use the Support Library version of the Loader Manager to ensure backward compatibility. Note also that in this snippet the enclosing Activity implements the Loader Callbacks:

```
Bundle args = null;
// Initialize Loader. "this" is the enclosing Activity that implements callbacks
getSupportLoaderManager().initLoader(LOADER_ID, args, this);
```

This is generally done within the `onCreate` method of the host Activity (or the `onActivityCreated` handler in the case of Fragments).

If a Loader corresponding to the identifier used doesn't already exist, it is created within the associated Loader Callback's `onCreateLoader` handler as described in the previous section.

In most circumstances this is all that's required. The Loader Manager will handle the life cycle of any Loaders you initialize and the underlying queries and resulting Cursors, including any changes in the query results.

If your Loader completes during a device configuration change, the result Cursor will be queued, and you'll receive it via `onLoadFinished` once the parent Activity or Fragment has been re-created.

After a Loader has been created, your results are cached across device configuration changes. Repeated calls to `initLoader` will immediately return the last result set via the `onLoadFinished` handler—without the Loader's `onStartLoading` method being called. This saves significant time and battery power by eliminating duplicative database reads and the associated processing.

Should you want to discard the previous Loader and re-create it, use the `restartLoader` method:

```
getSupportLoaderManager().restartLoader(LOADER_ID, args, this);
```

This is typically necessary only when your query parameters change—such as search queries, sort order, or filter parameters.

If you want to cancel a Cursor Loader while it's running, you can call its `cancelLoad` method:

```
getSupportLoaderManager().getLoader(LOADER_ID).cancelLoad();
```

The will trigger an internal Cancellation Signal within the Cursor Loader, which will in turn be passed to the associated Content Provider.

Adding, Deleting, and Updating Content

To perform transactions on Content Providers, use the `insert`, `delete`, and `update` methods on the Content Resolver. Like queries, Content Provider transactions must be explicitly moved to a background worker Thread to avoid blocking the UI thread with potentially time-consuming operations.

Inserting Content

The Content Resolver offers two methods for inserting new records into a Content Provider: `insert` and `bulkInsert`. Both methods accept the URI of the Content Provider into which you're inserting; the `insert` method takes a single new `ContentValues` object, and the `bulkInsert` method takes an array of them.

The `insert` method returns a URI to the newly added record, whereas the `bulkInsert` method returns the number of successfully added rows.

Listing 10-14 shows how to use the `insert` method to add new rows to a Content Provider.

LISTING 10-14: Inserting new rows into a Content Provider

LISTING 10-14: Inserting new rows into a Content Provider

```
// Create a new row of values to insert.
ContentValues newValues = new ContentValues();

// Assign values for each row.
newValues.put(HoardDB.HoardContract.KEY_GOLD_HOARD_NAME_COLUMN,
  newHoardName);
newValues.put(HoardDB.HoardContract.KEY_GOLD_HOARDED_COLUMN,
  newHoardValue);
newValues.put(HoardDB.HoardContract.KEY_GOLD_HOARD_ACCESSIBLE_COLUMN,
  newHoardAccessible);

// Get the Content Resolver
ContentResolver cr = getContentResolver();

// Insert the row into your table
Uri newRowUri = cr.insert(MyHoardContentProvider.CONTENT_URI,
                          newValues);
```

Deleting Content

To delete a single record, call `delete` on the Content Resolver, passing in the URI of the row you want to remove. Alternatively, you can specify a `where` clause to remove multiple rows. Calls to `delete` will return the number of rows removed. Listing 10-15 demonstrates how to delete a number of rows matching a given condition.

LISTING 10-15: Deleting rows from a Content Provider

```
// Specify a where clause that determines which row(s) to delete.
// Specify where arguments as necessary.
String where = HoardDB.HoardContract.KEY_GOLD_HOARDED_COLUMN +
               "=?";
String[] whereArgs = {"0"};

// Get the Content Resolver.
ContentResolver cr = getContentResolver();

// Delete the matching rows
int deletedRowCount =
  cr.delete(MyHoardContentProvider.CONTENT_URI, where, whereArgs);
```

Updating Content

You can update rows by using the Content Resolver's `update` method. The `update` method takes the URI of the target Content Provider, a `ContentValues` object that maps column names to updated values, and a `where` clause that indicates which rows to update.

When the update is executed, every row matched by the where clause is updated using the specified Content Values, and the number of successful updates is returned.

Alternatively, you can choose to update a specific row by specifying its unique URI, as shown in Listing 10-16.

LISTING 10-16: Updating a record in a Content Provider

```
// Create a URI addressing a specific row.
Uri rowURI =
  ContentUris.withAppendedId(MyHoardContentProvider.CONTENT_URI,
                             hoardId);

// Create the updated row content, assigning values for each row.
ContentValues updatedValues = new ContentValues();
updatedValues.put(HoardDB.HoardContract.KEY_GOLD_HOARDED_COLUMN,
                  newHoardValue);
// [ ... Repeat for each column to update ... ]

// If we specify a specific row, no selection clause is required.
String where = null;
String[] whereArgs = null;

// Get the Content Resolver.
ContentResolver cr = getContentResolver();
// Update the specified row.
int updatedRowCount =
  cr.update(rowURI, updatedValues, where, whereArgs);
```

Accessing Files Stored in Content Providers

In the earlier section, "Storing Files in a Content Provider," we described how to store files within Content Providers. To access a file stored in, or to insert a new file into, a Content Provider, use the Content Resolver's openOutputStream or openInputStream methods.

Pass in the URI to the Content Provider row that includes the file you require, and the Content Provider will use its openFile implementation to interpret your request and return an input or output stream to the requested file, as shown in Listing 10-17.

LISTING 10-17: Reading and writing files from and to a Content Provider

```
public void addNewHoardWithImage(int rowId, Bitmap hoardImage) {
  // Create a URI addressing a specific row.
  Uri rowURI =
    ContentUris.withAppendedId(MyHoardContentProvider.CONTENT_URI, rowId);

  // Get the Content Resolver
  ContentResolver cr = getContentResolver();
```

```
    try {
      // Open an output stream using the  row's URI.
      OutputStream outStream = cr.openOutputStream(rowURI);
      // Compress your bitmap and save it into your provider.
      hoardImage.compress(Bitmap.CompressFormat.JPEG, 80, outStream);
    }
    catch (FileNotFoundException e) {
      Log.d(TAG, "No file found for this record.");
    }
  }

  public Bitmap getHoardImage(long rowId) {
    Uri myRowUri =
      ContentUris.withAppendedId(MyHoardContentProvider.CONTENT_URI, rowId);

    try {
      // Open an input stream using the new row's URI.
      InputStream inStream =
        getContentResolver().openInputStream(myRowUri);

      // Make a copy of the Bitmap.
      Bitmap bitmap = BitmapFactory.decodeStream(inStream);
      return bitmap;
    }
    catch (FileNotFoundException e) {
      Log.d(TAG, "No file found for this record.");
    }

    return null;
  }
```

Accessing Permission-Restricted Content Providers

Many Content Providers require specific permissions before you can read and write to them. For example, native Content Providers that include sensitive information such as contact details and call logs have both their read and write access protected by permissions. Native Content Providers are described in more detail in the section "Using Native Android Content Providers."

To query or modify a Content Provider that has a permission requirement, you need to declare the corresponding uses-permissions in your manifest to read and/or write to them, respectively:

```
<uses-permission android:name="android.permission.READ_CONTACTS"/>
<uses-permission android:name="android.permission.WRITE_CALL_LOG"/>
```

Manifest permissions are granted by the user as part of the regular installation flow; however, Android 6.0 Marshmallow (API Level 23) introduced an additional requirement for *dangerous* permissions—including those which guard access to potentially sensitive information.

Dangerous permissions require explicit approval from the user when they are first accessed within the app, by way of runtime permission requests.

Each time you attempt to access a Content Provider protected by a dangerous permission you must use the `ActivityCompat.checkSelfPermission` method, passing in the appropriate permission constant to determine if you have access to the Provider. It will return `PERMISSION_GRANTED` if user permission is granted, or `PERMISSION_DENIED` if the user has declined, or not yet granted, access:

```
int permission = ActivityCompat.checkSelfPermission(this,
                    Manifest.permission.READ_CONTACTS);

if (permission==PERMISSION_GRANTED) {
  // Access the Content Provider
} else {
  // Request the permission or
  // display a dialog showing why the function is unavailable.
}
```

If you have not been granted permission, you can use the `ActivityCompat` class's `shouldShow-RequestPermissionRationale` method to determine if this is the first time this app has presented the user with a request for this permission—indicated with a `false` result—or if the user has already declined a request. In the latter case you may consider providing additional context describing why you need the requested permission, before presenting them with the permission-request dialog again:

```
if (ActivityCompat.shouldShowRequestPermissionRationale(
    this, Manifest.permission.READ_CALL_LOG)) {
  // TODO: Display additional rationale for the requested permission.
}
```

To display the system's runtime permission-request dialog, call the `ActivityCompat.request-Permission` method, specifying the required permissions:

```
ActivityCompat.requestPermissions(this,
  new String[]{Manifest.permission.READ_CONTACTS},
  CONTACTS_PERMISSION_REQUEST);
```

This function runs asynchronously, displaying a standard Android dialog that can't be customized. You can receive a callback when the user has either accepted or denied your runtime request, by overriding the `onRequestPermissionsResult` handler:

```
@Override
public void onRequestPermissionsResult(int requestCode,
                                       @NonNull String[] permissions,
                                       @NonNull int[] grantResults) {
  super.onRequestPermissionsResult(requestCode, permissions, grantResults);
  // TODO React to granted / denied permissions.
}
```

It's common practice to listen for this callback, and if permission is granted to execute the functionality that was previously protected by your permission check. The result, for the user, will be an interstitial permission dialog displayed before the requested action is completed. This is generally preferable to them having to reinitiate the action; however, be careful not to create an endless loop of request-denial-request.

USING NATIVE ANDROID CONTENT PROVIDERS

Android exposes several native Content Providers that you can access directly using the techniques described earlier in this chapter. The `android.provider` package includes many useful Content Providers, including the following:

➤ **Browser**—Reads or modifies browser and browser search history.

➤ **Calendar**—Creates new events, and deletes, updates, and reads existing calendar entries. That includes modifying the attendee lists and setting reminders.

➤ **Call Log and Blocked Numbers**—The Call Log Provider stores the call history, including incoming and outgoing calls, missed calls, and call details, including caller IDs and call durations. Blocked Numbers exposes a table containing blocked numbers and e-mail addresses.

➤ **Contacts**—Retrieves, modifies, or stores contact details.

➤ **Media Store**—Provides centralized, managed access to the multimedia on your device, including audio, video, and images. You can store your own multimedia within the Media Store and make it globally available, as shown in Chapter 17, "Audio, Video, and Using the Camera."

Where possible, you should use native Content Providers rather than duplicating them whenever you are building an app that augments or replaces the native apps that use these Providers.

Accessing the Call Log

The Android Call Log contains information about placed and received calls. Access to the Call Log is protected by the `READ_CALL_LOG` manifest uses-permission:

```
<uses-permission android:name="android.permission.READ_CALL_LOG"/>
```

For Android devices running Android 6.0 Marshmallow (API Level 23) and above, you also require the corresponding runtime permission:

```
int permission = ActivityCompat.checkSelfPermission(this,
                    Manifest.permission.READ_CALL_LOG);
```

Use the Content Resolver to query the Call Log Calls table using its `CONTENT_URI` static constant: `CallLog.Calls.CONTENT_URI`.

The Call Log is used to store all the incoming and outgoing call details, such as date/time of calls, phone numbers, and call durations, as well as cached values for caller details such as name, URI, and photos. Listing 10-18 shows how to query the Call Log for all outgoing calls, showing the name, number, and duration of each call.

LISTING 10-18: Accessing the Call Log Content Provider

```
// Create a projection that limits the result Cursor
// to the required columns.
String[] projection = {
```

continues

LISTING 10-18 *(continued)*

```
    CallLog.Calls.DURATION,
    CallLog.Calls.NUMBER,
    CallLog.Calls.CACHED_NAME,
    CallLog.Calls.TYPE
};

// Return only outgoing calls.
String where = CallLog.Calls.TYPE + "=?";
String[] whereArgs = {String.valueOf(CallLog.Calls.OUTGOING_TYPE)};

// Get a Cursor over the Call Log Calls Provider.
Cursor cursor =
  getContentResolver().query(CallLog.Calls.CONTENT_URI,
    projection, where, whereArgs, null);

// Get the index of the columns.
int durIdx = cursor.getColumnIndexOrThrow(CallLog.Calls.DURATION);
int numberIdx = cursor.getColumnIndexOrThrow(CallLog.Calls.NUMBER);
int nameIdx = cursor.getColumnIndexOrThrow(CallLog.Calls.CACHED_NAME);

// Initialize the result set.
String[] result = new String[cursor.getCount()];

// Iterate over the result Cursor.
while (cursor.moveToNext()) {
  String durStr = cursor.getString(durIdx);
  String numberStr = cursor.getString(numberIdx);
  String nameStr = cursor.getString(nameIdx);

  result[cursor.getPosition()] = numberStr + " for " + durStr + "sec" +
                                   ((null == nameStr) ?
                                    "" : " (" + nameStr + ")");
  Log.d(TAG, result[cursor.getPosition()]);
}

// Close the Cursor.
cursor.close();
```

Using the Media Store Content Provider

The Android Media Store is a managed repository of audio, video, and image files.

Whenever you add a new multimedia file to the filesystem, it should also be added to the Media Store, as described in Chapter 17; this will expose it to other applications, including media players. In most circumstances it's not necessary (or recommended) to modify the contents of the Media Store Content Provider directly.

To access the media available within the Media Store, the `MediaStore` class includes `Audio`, `Video`, and `Images` subclasses, which in turn contain subclasses that are used to provide the column names and content URIs for the corresponding media providers.

The Media Store segregates media kept on the internal and external volumes of the host device. Each Media Store subclass provides a URI for either the internally or externally stored media using the forms:

➤ `MediaStore.<mediatype>.Media.EXTERNAL_CONTENT_URI`

➤ `MediaStore.<mediatype>.Media.INTERNAL_CONTENT_URI`

Listing 10-19 shows a simple code snippet used to find the song title and album name for each piece of audio stored on the internal volume.

LISTING 10-19: Accessing the Media Store Content Provider

```
// Get a Cursor over every piece of audio on the external volume,
// extracting the song title and album name.
String[] projection = new String[] {
  MediaStore.Audio.AudioColumns.ALBUM,
  MediaStore.Audio.AudioColumns.TITLE
};

Uri contentUri = MediaStore.Audio.Media.INTERNAL_CONTENT_URI;

Cursor cursor =
  getContentResolver().query(contentUri, projection,
                             null, null, null);

// Get the index of the columns we need.
int albumIdx =
  cursor.getColumnIndexOrThrow(MediaStore.Audio.AudioColumns.ALBUM);
int titleIdx =
  cursor.getColumnIndexOrThrow(MediaStore.Audio.AudioColumns.TITLE);

// Create an array to store the result set.
String[] result = new String[cursor.getCount()];

// Iterate over the Cursor, extracting each album name and song title.
while (cursor.moveToNext()) {
  // Extract the song title.
  String title = cursor.getString(titleIdx);
  // Extract the album name.
  String album = cursor.getString(albumIdx);

  result[cursor.getPosition()] = title + " (" + album + ")";
}

// Close the Cursor.
cursor.close();
```

> **NOTE** *In Chapter 17 you learn how to play audio and video resources stored in the Media Store by specifying the URI of a particular multimedia item, as well as how to properly add media to the Media Store.*

Using the Contacts Content Provider

Android makes the full database of contact information available to any application that has been granted the READ_CONTACTS permission.

The ContactsContract Provider provides an extensible database of contact-related information. This allows users to use and combine multiple sources for their contact information. More importantly, it allows developers to arbitrarily extend the data stored against each contact, or even become an alternative provider for contacts and contact details.

Rather than providing a single, fully defined table of contact detail columns, the Contacts Contract provider uses a three-tier data model to store data, associate it with a contact, and aggregate it to a single person using the following subclasses:

➤ Data—Each row in the underlying table defines a set of personal data (phone numbers, e-mail addresses, and so on), separated by MIME type. Although there is a predefined set of common column names for each personal data type available (along with the appropriate MIME types from subclasses within ContactsContract.CommonDataKinds), this table can be used to store *any* value.

The kind of data stored in a particular row is determined by the MIME type specified for that row. A series of generic columns is then used to store up to 15 different pieces of data varying by MIME type.

When adding new data to the Data table, you specify a Raw Contact to which a set of data will be associated.

➤ RawContacts—Users can add multiple contact account providers to their device—for example, if they've added multiple Gmail accounts. Each row in the Raw Contacts table defines an account to which a set of Data values is associated.

➤ Contacts—The Android Contacts app aggregates and exposes all contacts, from every account on the device, in a single list. It's possible for the same person to be included as a contact in multiple accounts—for example, your significant other may appear as an entry in both your personal and work Gmail accounts. The Contacts table represents the aggregation of multiple rows from Raw Contacts that describe the same person, so they appear as one entry in the Android Contacts app.

The contents of each of these tables are aggregated as shown in Figure 10-1.

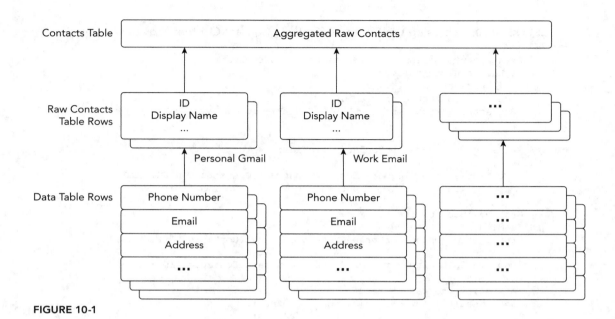

FIGURE 10-1

Typically, you will use the Data table to add, delete, or modify data stored against an existing contact account, the Raw Contacts table to create and manage accounts, and both the Contact and Data tables to query the database to extract contact details.

Reading Contact Details

To access any of the Contact Contract Providers, you must include the READ_CONTACTS uses-permission in your application manifest:

```
<uses-permission android:name="android.permission.READ_CONTACTS"/>
```

Android devices running Android 6.0 Marshmallow (API Level 23) also require the corresponding runtime permission:

```
int permission = ActivityCompat.checkSelfPermission(this,
                Manifest.permission.READ_CONTACTS);
```

Use the Content Resolver to query any of the three Contact Contracts Providers previously described using their respective CONTENT_URI static constants. Each class includes their column names as static properties.

Listing 10-20 queries the Contacts table for a Cursor to every person in the address book, creating an array of strings that holds each contact's name and unique ID.

LISTING 10-20: Accessing the Contacts Contract Contact Content Provider

```
// Create a projection that limits the result Cursor
// to the required columns.
String[] projection = {
    ContactsContract.Contacts._ID,
    ContactsContract.Contacts.DISPLAY_NAME
};

// Get a Cursor over the Contacts Provider.
Cursor cursor =
  getContentResolver().query(ContactsContract.Contacts.CONTENT_URI,
                        projection, null, null, null);

// Get the index of the columns.
int nameIdx =
  cursor.getColumnIndexOrThrow(ContactsContract.Contacts.DISPLAY_NAME);
int idIdx =
  cursor.getColumnIndexOrThrow(ContactsContract.Contacts._ID);

// Initialize the result set.
String[] result = new String[cursor.getCount()];

// Iterate over the result Cursor.
while(cursor.moveToNext()) {
    // Extract the name.
    String name = cursor.getString(nameIdx);
    // Extract the unique ID.
    String id = cursor.getString(idIdx);

    result[cursor.getPosition()] = name + " (" + id + ")";
  }

// Close the Cursor.
cursor.close();
```

The `ContactsContract.Data` Content Provider is used to store all the contact details, such as addresses, phone numbers, and e-mail addresses. In most cases, you will likely be querying for contact details based on a full or partial contact name.

To simplify this lookup, Android provides the `ContactsContract.Contacts.CONTENT_FILTER_URI` query URI. Append the full or partial name to this lookup as an additional path segment to the URI. To extract the associated contact details, find the `_ID` value from the returned Cursor, and use it to create a query on the Data table.

The content of each column with a row in the Data table depends on the MIME type specified for that row. As a result, any query on the Data table must filter the rows by MIME type to meaningfully extract data.

Listing 10-21 shows how to use the contact-detail column names available in the `CommonDataKinds` subclasses to extract the display name and mobile phone number from the Data table for a particular contact.

LISTING 10-21: Finding contact details for a contact name

```
ContentResolver cr = getContentResolver();
String[] result = null;

// Find a contact using a partial name match
String searchName = "john";
Uri lookupUri =
  Uri.withAppendedPath(ContactsContract.Contacts.CONTENT_FILTER_URI,
                       searchName);

// Create a projection of the required column names.
String[] projection = new String[] {
  ContactsContract.Contacts._ID
};

// Get a Cursor that will return the ID(s) of the matched name.
Cursor idCursor = cr.query(lookupUri,
  projection, null, null, null);

// Extract the first matching ID if it exists.
String id = null;
if (idCursor.moveToFirst()) {
  int idIdx =
    idCursor.getColumnIndexOrThrow(ContactsContract.Contacts._ID);
  id = idCursor.getString(idIdx);
}

// Close that Cursor.
idCursor.close();

// Create a new Cursor searching for the data associated
// with the returned Contact ID.
if (id != null) {
  // Return all the PHONE data for the contact.
  String where = ContactsContract.Data.CONTACT_ID +
    " = " + id + " AND " +
    ContactsContract.Data.MIMETYPE + " = '" +
    ContactsContract.CommonDataKinds.Phone.CONTENT_ITEM_TYPE +
    "'";

  projection = new String[] {
    ContactsContract.Data.DISPLAY_NAME,
    ContactsContract.CommonDataKinds.Phone.NUMBER
  };

  Cursor dataCursor =
    getContentResolver().query(ContactsContract.Data.CONTENT_URI,
      projection, where, null, null);

  // Get the indexes of the required columns.
  int nameIdx =
    dataCursor.getColumnIndexOrThrow(ContactsContract.Data.DISPLAY_NAME);
  int phoneIdx =
```

continues

LISTING 10-21 *(continued)*

```
    dataCursor.getColumnIndexOrThrow(
      ContactsContract.CommonDataKinds.Phone.NUMBER);

  result = new String[dataCursor.getCount()];

  while(dataCursor.moveToNext()) {
    // Extract the name.
    String name = dataCursor.getString(nameIdx);
    // Extract the phone number.
    String number = dataCursor.getString(phoneIdx);

    result[dataCursor.getPosition()] = name + " (" + number + ")";
  }

  dataCursor.close();
}
```

The `Contacts` subclass also offers a phone number lookup URI to help find a contact associated with a particular phone number. This query is highly optimized to return fast results for caller-ID notification.

Use `ContactsContract.PhoneLookup.CONTENT_FILTER_URI`, appending the number to look up as an additional path segment, as shown in Listing 10-22.

LISTING 10-22: Performing a caller-ID lookup

```
String incomingNumber = "(555) 123-4567";
String result = "Not Found";

Uri lookupUri =
  Uri.withAppendedPath(ContactsContract.PhoneLookup.CONTENT_FILTER_URI,
                       incomingNumber);

String[] projection = new String[] {
  ContactsContract.Contacts.DISPLAY_NAME
};

Cursor cursor = getContentResolver().query(lookupUri,
  projection, null, null, null);

if (cursor.moveToFirst()) {
  int nameIdx =
    cursor.getColumnIndexOrThrow(ContactsContract.Contacts.DISPLAY_NAME);

  result = cursor.getString(nameIdx);
}

cursor.close();
```

Using the Intents API for the Contacts Content Provider

The Contacts Contract Content Provider includes an Intent-based mechanism that can be used to view, insert, or select a contact using an existing contact application (typically, the native contact app).

This is the best practice approach and has the advantage of presenting the user with a consistent interface for performing the same task, avoiding ambiguity and improving the overall user experience. Because the user has the power to abort the action without affecting the Content Provider, you don't require any special permissions to utilize this technique for selecting or creating new contacts.

Accessing Contacts Using Intents

To display a list of contacts for your users to select from, you can use the `Intent.ACTION_PICK` action, and use the `setType` method to indicate the MIME type of the contact data you wish to use. Listing 10-23 requests that we pick a Contact with a phone number.

LISTING 10-23: Picking a contact

```
private static int PICK_CONTACT = 0;

private void pickContact() {
   Intent intent = new Intent(Intent.ACTION_PICK);
   intent.setType(ContactsContract.CommonDataKinds.Phone.CONTENT_TYPE);
   startActivityForResult(intent, PICK_CONTACT);
}
```

This will display a List View of the contacts available (as shown in Figure 10-2).

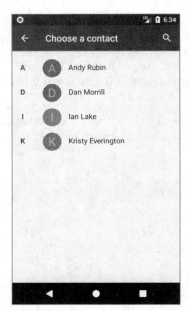

FIGURE 10-2

When the user selects a contact, it will be returned as a lookup URI within the data property of the returned Intent. To retrieve specific contact details, use the Content Resolver to perform a query using the lookup URI, and extract the required details as shown in this extension to Listing 10-23:

```
@Override
protected void onActivityResult(int requestCode, int resultCode, Intent data) {
  super.onActivityResult(requestCode, resultCode, data);
  if ((requestCode == PICK_CONTACT) && (resultCode == RESULT_OK)) {
    Uri selectedContact = data.getData();
      Cursor cursor = getContentResolver().query(selectedContact,
        null, null, null, null);
      // If the cursor returned is valid, get the phone number
      if (cursor != null && cursor.moveToFirst()) {
        int numberIndex = cursor.getColumnIndex(
          ContactsContract.CommonDataKinds.Phone.NUMBER);
        String number = cursor.getString(numberIndex);

        int nameIndex = cursor.getColumnIndex(
          ContactsContract.CommonDataKinds.Identity.DISPLAY_NAME);
        String name = cursor.getString(nameIndex);

        // TODO: Do something with the selected name and phone number.
      }
    }
  }
```

The contacts app delegates read and write permissions to this content URI for the life of your Activity, meaning you can use it to access the associated data without requesting special permission.

Inserting or Modifying Contacts with Intents

To insert a new contact, you will use an Intent specifying a phone number or e-mail address, along with extras that will pre-populate the new contact form.

The ContactsContract.Intents.SHOW_OR_CREATE_CONTACT action will search the Contacts Provider for a particular e-mail address or telephone number URI, offering to insert a new entry only if a contact with the specified contact address doesn't exist. If the contact does exist, it will be displayed.

Use the constants in the ContactsContract.Intents.Insert class to include Intent extras that can be used to pre-populate contact details, including the name, company, e-mail, phone number, notes, and postal address of the new contact, as shown in Listing 10-24.

LISTING 10-24: Inserting a new contact using an Intent

```
Intent intent =
  new Intent(ContactsContract.Intents.SHOW_OR_CREATE_CONTACT,
            ContactsContract.Contacts.CONTENT_URI);
intent.setData(Uri.parse("tel:(650)253-0000"));

intent.putExtra(ContactsContract.Intents.Insert.COMPANY, "Google");
```

```
intent.putExtra(ContactsContract.Intents.Insert.POSTAL,
  "1600 Amphitheatre Parkway, Mountain View, California");

startActivity(intent);
```

Using the Calendar Content Provider

Android 4.0 (API Level 14) introduced a supported API for accessing the Calendar Content Provider. The Calendar API allows you to insert, view, and edit the complete Calendar database, providing access to calendars, events, attendees, and event.

Like the Contacts Contract Content Provider, the Calendar Content Provider is designed to support multiple synchronized accounts. As a result, you can choose to read from, and contribute to, existing calendar applications and accounts; develop an alternative Calendar Provider by creating a calendar Sync Adapter; or create an alternative calendar application.

Querying the Calendar

The Calendar Provider requires that you include the READ_CALENDAR uses-permission in your application manifest:

```
<uses-permission android:name="android.permission.READ_CALENDAR"/>
```

Android devices running Android 6.0 Marshmallow (API Level 23) also require the granting of the corresponding runtime permission:

```
int permission = ActivityCompat.checkSelfPermission(this,
                    Manifest.permission.READ_CALENDAR);
```

Use the Content Resolver to query any of the Calendar Provider tables using their CONTENT_URI static constant. Each table is exposed from within the CalendarContract class, including:

➤ Calendars—The Calendar application can display multiple calendars associated with multiple accounts. This table holds each calendar that can be displayed, as well as details such as the calendar's display name, time zone, and color.

➤ Events—The Events table includes an entry for each scheduled calendar event, including the name, description, location, and start/end times.

➤ Instances—Each event has one or (in the case of recurring events) multiple instances. The Instances table is populated with entries generated by the contents of the Events table and includes a reference to the event that generated it.

➤ Attendees—Each entry in the Attendees table represents a single attendee of a given event. Each attendee can include a name, e-mail address, and attendance status, and if they are optional or required guests.

➤ Reminders—Event reminders are represented within the Reminders table, with each row representing one reminder for a particular event.

Each class includes its column names as static properties.

Listing 10-25 queries the Events table for every event, creating an array of strings that holds each event's name and unique ID.

LISTING 10-25: Querying the Events table

```
// Create a projection that limits the result Cursor
// to the required columns.
String[] projection = {
    CalendarContract.Events._ID,
    CalendarContract.Events.TITLE
};

// Get a Cursor over the Events Provider.
Cursor cursor =
  getContentResolver().query(CalendarContract.Events.CONTENT_URI,
                            projection, null, null, null);

// Get the index of the columns.
int nameIdx =
 cursor.getColumnIndexOrThrow(CalendarContract.Events.TITLE);
int idIdx = cursor. getColumnIndexOrThrow(CalendarContract.Events._ID);

// Initialize the result set.
String[] result = new String[cursor.getCount()];

// Iterate over the result Cursor.
while(cursor.moveToNext()) {
    // Extract the name.
    String name = cursor.getString(nameIdx);
    // Extract the unique ID.
    String id = cursor.getString(idIdx);

    result[cursor.getPosition()] = name + " (" + id + ")";
}

// Close the Cursor.
cursor.close();
```

Creating Calendar Entries Using Intents

The Calendar Content Provider includes an Intent-based mechanism that allows you to perform common actions without the need for special permissions by utilizing the Calendar application UI. Using Intents, you can open the Calendar application to a specific time, view event details, and insert a new event.

> **NOTE** *At the time of writing, the Android documentation also describes support for editing calendar entries using Intents. Unfortunately, at this time this mechanism doesn't work as described. To edit calendar entries, you can either interact with the Content Provider directly or display the entry and encourage the user to make the changes to the event themselves.*

Like the Contacts API, using Intents is the best practice approach for manipulating calendar entries and should be used in preference to direct manipulation of the underlying tables whenever possible.

Using the `Intent.ACTION_INSERT` action, specifying the `CalendarContract.Events.CONTENT_URI`, you can add new events to an existing calendar without requiring any special permissions.

Your Intent can include extras that define each of the event attributes, including the title, start and end time, location, and description, as shown in Listing 10-26. When triggered, the Intent will be received by the Calendar application, which will create a new entry pre-populated with the data provided.

LISTING 10-26: Inserting a new calendar event using an Intent

```
// Create a new insertion Intent.
Intent intent = new Intent(Intent.ACTION_INSERT,
                           CalendarContract.Events.CONTENT_URI);

// Add the calendar event details
intent.putExtra(CalendarContract.Events.TITLE, "Book Launch!");
intent.putExtra(CalendarContract.Events.DESCRIPTION,
                "Professional Android Release!");
intent.putExtra(CalendarContract.Events.EVENT_LOCATION, "Wrox.com");

Calendar startTime = Calendar.getInstance();
startTime.set(2018, 6, 19, 0, 30);
intent.putExtra(CalendarContract.EXTRA_EVENT_BEGIN_TIME,
                startTime.getTimeInMillis());

intent.putExtra(CalendarContract.EXTRA_EVENT_ALL_DAY, true);

// Use the Calendar app to add the new event.
startActivity(intent);
```

To view a calendar event, you must first know its row ID. To find this, you need to query the Events Content Provider, as described earlier in this section.

When you have the ID of the event you want to display, create a new Intent using the `Intent.ACTION_VIEW` action and a URI that appends the event's row ID to the end of the Events table's `CONTENT_URI`, as shown in Listing 10-27.

LISTING 10-27: Viewing a calendar event using an Intent

```
// Create a URI addressing a specific event by its row ID.
// Use it to  create a new edit Intent.
long rowID = 760;
Uri uri = ContentUris.withAppendedId(
  CalendarContract.Events.CONTENT_URI, rowID);

Intent intent = new Intent(Intent.ACTION_VIEW, uri);

// Use the Calendar app to view the calendar entry.
startActivity(intent);
```

To view a specific date and time, the URI should be of the form `content://com.android.calendar/time/[milliseconds since epoch]`, as shown in Listing 10-28.

LISTING 10-28: Displaying a time on the calendar using an Intent

```
// Create a URI that specifies a particular time to view.
Calendar startTime = Calendar.getInstance();
startTime.set(2012, 2, 13, 0, 30);

Uri uri = Uri.parse("content://com.android.calendar/time/" +
  String.valueOf(startTime.getTimeInMillis()));
Intent intent = new Intent(Intent.ACTION_VIEW, uri);

// Use the Calendar app to view the time.
startActivity(intent);
```

ADDING SEARCH TO YOUR APPLICATION

Surfacing your application's content through search is a simple and powerful way to make your content more discoverable and increase user engagement. On mobile devices speed is everything, and search helps users quickly find the content they need within your app.

Android includes a framework that helps you to implement a search experience within your app that's consistent with the system and other applications.

You can provide search capabilities for your application in a number of ways, but the best practice solution is to use the Search View, included as an action in the app bar, as shown in its expanded form in Figure 10-3.

FIGURE 10-3

It's possible to add the Search View anywhere within your Activity layout, though the app bar is by far the most common location.

A Search View can be configured to display search suggestions as you type, providing a powerful mechanism for improving the responsiveness of your application.

Before you can enable a Search View within your application, you need to define what is being searched and how to display the results.

Defining Your Search Metadata

The first step in utilizing the system search facilities is to create a Searchable XML file that defines the settings that will be used by the Search View.

Create a new Searchable XML resource in your project's `res/xml` folder. As shown in Listing 10-29, you must specify the `android:label` attribute (typically your application name), and an `android:hint` attribute to help users understand what they can search for. The hint is typically in the form of "Search for [content type or product name]." Note that the hint must be a reference to a string resource. If you use a String constant, it will not be displayed.

LISTING 10-29: Defining application search metadata

```xml
<?xml version="1.0" encoding="utf-8"?>
<searchable
  xmlns:android="http://schemas.android.com/apk/res/android"
  android:label="@string/app_name"
  android:hint="@string/search_hint">
</searchable>
```

In the section "Providing Search Suggestions Using a Content Provider" later in this chapter, you learn how to modify your Searchable configuration to provide as-you-type search suggestions within your application's search framework.

Creating a Search Results Activity

When a search is executed using the Search View, it launches an associated search results Activity, which receives the search query as an Intent. Your search results Activity must then extract the search query from the Intent, perform the search, and present the results.

Your search results Activity can use any UI, but is most commonly a simple list of results, typically implemented using a Recycler View. It's good practice to set your search results Activity as "single top," ensuring that the same instance will be used repeatedly, rather than creating a new instance for each search and risk stacking search results on your back stack.

To indicate that an Activity will be used to provide search results, include an Intent Filter registered for the SEARCH action:

```xml
<intent-filter>
  <action android:name="android.intent.action.SEARCH" />
</intent-filter>
```

You must also include a `meta-data` tag that includes a `name` attribute that specifies `android.app` `.searchable`, and a corresponding `resource` attribute that specifies the `searchable` XML resource described in the previous section.

Listing 10-30 shows a simple application manifest entry for a search Activity.

LISTING 10-30: Registering a search results Activity

```xml
<activity
  android:name=".MySearchActivity"
  android:label="Hoard Search"
  android:launchMode="singleTop">
  <intent-filter>
    <action android:name="android.intent.action.SEARCH" />
  </intent-filter>
```

continues

LISTING 10-30 *(continued)*

```
    <meta-data
      android:name="android.app.searchable"
      android:resource="@xml/hoard_search"
    />
</activity>
```

When a search is initiated, your search results Activity will be started and the search query will be available from within the launch Intent, accessible through the `SearchManager.QUERY` extra, as shown in Listing 10-31.

LISTING 10-31: Extracting the search query

```
@Override
public void onCreate(Bundle savedInstanceState) {
  super.onCreate(savedInstanceState);
  setContentView(R.layout.activity_my_search);

  // Parse the launch Intent to perform the search
  // and display the results.
  parseIntent();
}

@Override
protected void onNewIntent(Intent intent) {
  super.onNewIntent(intent);

  // If the search Activity exists, and another search
  // is performed, set the launch Intent to the newly
  // received search Intent and perform a new search.
  setIntent(intent);
  parseIntent();
}

private void parseIntent() {
  Intent searchIntent = getIntent();
  // If the Activity was started to service a Search request,
  // extract the search query.
  if (Intent.ACTION_SEARCH.equals(searchIntent.getAction())) {
    String searchQuery = searchIntent.getStringExtra(SearchManager.QUERY);
    // Perform the search
    performSearch(searchQuery);
  }
}

private void performSearch(String searchQuery) {
  // TODO: Perform the search and update the UI to display the results.
}
```

When your search Activity receives a new search query, execute the search and display the results within the Activity. How you choose to implement your search query and display its results depends on your application, what you're searching, and where the searchable content is stored.

Searching a Content Provider

Using a Content Provider to expose the data you plan to make searchable has a number of advantages; one of the most powerful is the ability to provide real-time search suggestions, as described later in this chapter.

If you're providing results from a Content Provider, it's good practice to use a Cursor Loader to execute a query and bind the result to the UI. In most circumstances you'll want to provide functionality for users to select a search result and navigate to an appropriate part of your app to interact with it.

Listing 10-32 shows how to create a search results Activity that searches a Content Provider, displays the results Cursor in a Recycler View, and adds a Click Listener you can use to support a user selecting a search result. For brevity, the layout resources for the Activity and the search result items are not included in this listing.

LISTING 10-32: Performing a search and displaying the results

```
public class MySearchActivity extends AppCompatActivity
                              implements LoaderManager.LoaderCallbacks<Cursor>
{

  private static final String QUERY_EXTRA_KEY = "QUERY_EXTRA_KEY";

  private MySearchResultRecyclerViewAdapter mAdapter;

  @Override
  public void onCreate(Bundle savedInstanceState) {
    super.onCreate(savedInstanceState);
    setContentView(R.layout.searchresult_list);

    // Set the adapter
    mAdapter = new MySearchResultRecyclerViewAdapter(null, mListener);

    // Update the Recycler View
    RecyclerView resultsRecyclerView = findViewById(R.id.list);
    resultsRecyclerView.setLayoutManager(new LinearLayoutManager(this));
    resultsRecyclerView.setAdapter(mAdapter);

    // Initiate the Cursor Loader
    getSupportLoaderManager().initLoader(0, null, this);
  }

  @Override
  protected void onNewIntent(Intent intent) {
    super.onNewIntent(intent);
```

continues

LISTING 10-32 *(continued)*

```java
    // If the search Activity exists, and another search
    // is performed, set the launch Intent to the newly
    // received search Intent and perform a new search.
    setIntent(intent);

    getSupportLoaderManager().restartLoader(0, null, this);
}

public Loader<Cursor> onCreateLoader(int id, Bundle args) {
  // Extract the search query from the Intent.
  String query = getIntent().getStringExtra(SearchManager.QUERY);

  // Construct the new query in the form of a Cursor Loader.
  String[] projection = {
    HoardDB.HoardContract.KEY_ID,
    HoardDB.HoardContract.KEY_GOLD_HOARD_NAME_COLUMN,
    HoardDB.HoardContract.KEY_GOLD_HOARDED_COLUMN
  };

  String where = HoardDB.HoardContract.KEY_GOLD_HOARD_NAME_COLUMN
                      + " LIKE ?";
  String[] whereArgs = {"%" + query + "%"};

  String sortOrder = HoardDB.HoardContract.KEY_GOLD_HOARD_NAME_COLUMN +
                      " COLLATE LOCALIZED ASC";

  // Create the new Cursor loader.
  return new CursorLoader(this, MyHoardContentProvider.CONTENT_URI,
                      projection, where, whereArgs, sortOrder);
}

public void onLoadFinished(Loader<Cursor> loader, Cursor cursor) {
  // Replace the result Cursor displayed by the Cursor Adapter with
  // the new result set.
  mAdapter.setCursor(cursor);
}

public void onLoaderReset(Loader<Cursor> loader) {
  // Remove the existing result Cursor from the List Adapter.
  mAdapter.setCursor(null);
}

private OnListItemInteractionListener mListener =
  new OnListItemInteractionListener() {
  @Override
  public void onListItemClick(Uri selectedContent) {
    // TODO If an item is clicked, open an Activity
    //      to display further details.
  }
};
```

```java
public class MySearchResultRecyclerViewAdapter
  extends RecyclerView.Adapter<MySearchResultRecyclerViewAdapter.ViewHolder>
{
  private Cursor mValues;
  private OnListItemInteractionListener mClickListener;

  private int mHoardIdIndex = -1;
  private int mHoardNameIndex = -1;
  private int mHoardAmountIndex = -1;

  public MySearchResultRecyclerViewAdapter(Cursor items,
    OnListItemInteractionListener clickListener) {

    mValues = items;
    mClickListener = clickListener;
  }

  public void setCursor(Cursor items) {
    mValues = items;

    if (items != null) {
      mHoardIdIndex =
        items.getColumnIndex(HoardDB.HoardContract.KEY_ID);
      mHoardNameIndex =
        items.getColumnIndex(
          HoardDB.HoardContract.KEY_GOLD_HOARD_NAME_COLUMN);
      mHoardAmountIndex =
        items.getColumnIndex(
          HoardDB.HoardContract.KEY_GOLD_HOARDED_COLUMN);
    }

    notifyDataSetChanged();
  }

  @Override
  public ViewHolder onCreateViewHolder(ViewGroup parent, int viewType) {
    View view = LayoutInflater.from(parent.getContext())
                  .inflate(R.layout.searchresult_item, parent, false);

    return new ViewHolder(view);
  }

  @Override
  public void onBindViewHolder(final ViewHolder holder, int position) {
    if (mValues != null) {
      // Move the Cursor to the correct position, extract the
      // search result values, and assign them to the UI for
      // each search result.
      mValues.moveToPosition(position);
      holder.mNameView.setText(mValues.getString(mHoardNameIndex));
      holder.mAmountView.setText(mValues.getString(mHoardAmountIndex));

      // Create a Uri that points to this search result item.
      int rowId = mValues.getInt(mHoardIdIndex);
```

```
        final Uri rowAddress =
          ContentUris.withAppendedId(MyHoardContentProvider.CONTENT_URI,
            rowId);

        // Return the Uri to this search result item if clicked.
        holder.mView.setOnClickListener(new View.OnClickListener() {
          @Override
          public void onClick(View v) {
            mClickListener.onListItemClick(rowAddress);
          }
        });
      }
    }

    @Override
    public int getItemCount() {
      if (mValues != null)
        return mValues.getCount();
      else
        return 0;
    }

    // View Holder is used as a template to encapsulate the UI
    // for each search result item.
    public class ViewHolder extends RecyclerView.ViewHolder {
      public final View mView;
      public final TextView mNameView;
      public final TextView mAmountView;

      public ViewHolder(View view) {
        super(view);
        mView = view;
        mNameView = view.findViewById(R.id.id);
        mAmountView = view.findViewById(R.id.content);
      }
    }
  }

  // Interface used to encapsulate the behavior when a user
  // clicks on a search result item.
  public interface OnListItemInteractionListener {
    void onListItemClick(Uri selectedContent);
  }
}
```

Using the Search View Widget

The Search View widget appears and behaves much the same as an Edit Text View, but is designed to offer search suggestions and to initiate search queries within your application.

You can add the Search View anywhere in your View hierarchy and configure it in the same way; however, it's best practice to add it as an action View within the app bar, as shown in Listing 10-33.

LISTING 10-33: Adding a Search View to the app bar

```xml
<menu xmlns:android="http://schemas.android.com/apk/res/android"
      xmlns:app="http://schemas.android.com/apk/res-auto"
      xmlns:tools="http://schemas.android.com/tools"
      tools:context=
        "com.professionalandroid.apps.databasechaptersnippets.MainActivity">
  <item android:id="@+id/search_view"
      android:title="@string/search_label"
      app:showAsAction="collapseActionView|ifRoom"
      app:actionViewClass="android.support.v7.widget.SearchView" />
</menu>
```

Figure 10-4 shows a collapsed Search View displaying a mag-
nifying glass icon within an app bar. You learn more about
the app bar in Chapter 12, "Implementing the Android Design
Philosophy."

FIGURE 10-4

To configure a Search View to display your search results
Activity, you must first add a new meta-data tag to the manifest entry of the Activity that hosts the
Search View, setting the `android.app.default_searchable` value to our search Activity, as shown
in Listing 10-34.

LISTING 10-34: Binding a Search View to your searchable Activity

```xml
<activity
  android:name=".MainActivity"
  android:label="@string/app_name">
  <intent-filter>
    <action android:name="android.intent.action.MAIN"/>
    <category android:name="android.intent.category.LAUNCHER"/>
  </intent-filter>
  <meta-data
    android:name="android.app.default_searchable"
    android:value=".MySearchActivity" />
</activity>
```

Extract a reference to your `SearchableInfo` using the Search Manager's `getSearchableInfo`
method. Use the Search View's `setSearchableInfo` method to bind this object to your Search
View, as shown in Listing 10-35.

LISTING 10-35: Binding a Search View to your searchable Activity

```java
@Override
public boolean onCreateOptionsMenu(Menu menu) {
  // Inflate the options menu from XML
  MenuInflater inflater = getMenuInflater();
  inflater.inflate(R.menu.menu_main, menu);
```

continues

LISTING 10-35 *(continued)*

```
    // Use the Search Manager to find the SearchableInfo related
    // to this Activity.
    SearchManager searchManager =
      (SearchManager) getSystemService(Context.SEARCH_SERVICE);
    SearchableInfo searchableInfo =
      searchManager.getSearchableInfo(getComponentName());

    SearchView searchView =
      menu.findItem(R.id.search_view).getActionView();
    searchView.setSearchableInfo(searchableInfo);
    searchView.setIconifiedByDefault(false);

    return true;
  }
```

When connected, your Search View will send the entered search query to the Search Activity for execution and results display.

By default, the Search View will be displayed as an icon that, when touched, expands to display the search edit box. You can use the setIconifiedByDefault method to disable this and have it always display as an edit box:

```
    searchView.setIconifiedByDefault(false);
```

Also by default, a Search View query is initiated when the user presses Enter. You can choose to also display a button to submit a search using the setSubmitButtonEnabled method:

```
    searchView.setSubmitButtonEnabled(true);
```

Providing Search Suggestions Using a Content Provider

One of the most engaging innovations in search is the provision of real-time search suggestions as users type their queries.

Search suggestions display a list of possible search results beneath the Search View as users enter their queries, as shown in Figure 10-5.

FIGURE 10-5

Users can then select a suggestion from this list, which allows us to handle this case directly, rather than displaying the list of potential search results as shown in the previous section. Search suggestion selections must still be handled by the search results Activity, but it can potentially start a new Activity without the search Activity being displayed.

If you want to provide search suggestions, you need to create (or modify) a Content Provider to receive search queries and return suggestions using the expected projection. Speed is critical for real-time search results; in many cases it's good practice to create a separate table specifically to store and provide suggestions.

To support search suggestions, configure your Content Provider to recognize specific URI paths as search queries. Listing 10-36 shows a Uri Matcher used within a Content Provider to compare a requested URI to the known search-query path values.

LISTING 10-36: Detecting search suggestion requests in Content Providers

```
private static final UriMatcher uriMatcher;

// Create the constants used to differentiate between the different URI
// requests.
private static final int ALLROWS = 1;
private static final int SINGLE_ROW = 2;
private static final int SEARCH = 3;

static {
  uriMatcher = new UriMatcher(UriMatcher.NO_MATCH);
  uriMatcher.addURI("com.professionalandroid.provider.hoarder",
    "lairs", ALLROWS);
  uriMatcher.addURI("com.professionalandroid.provider.hoarder",
    "lairs/#", SINGLE_ROW);

  uriMatcher.addURI("com.professionalandroid.provider.hoarder",
    SearchManager.SUGGEST_URI_PATH_QUERY, SEARCH);
  uriMatcher.addURI("com.professionalandroid.provider.hoarder",
    SearchManager.SUGGEST_URI_PATH_QUERY + "/*", SEARCH);
  uriMatcher.addURI("com.professionalandroid.provider.hoarder",
    SearchManager.SUGGEST_URI_PATH_SHORTCUT, SEARCH);
  uriMatcher.addURI("com.professionalandroid.provider.hoarder",
    SearchManager.SUGGEST_URI_PATH_SHORTCUT + "/*", SEARCH);
}
```

Use the Uri Matcher to return the search suggestion MIME type for search queries using the getType handler, as shown in Listing 10-37.

LISTING 10-37: Returning the correct MIME type for search results

```
@Nullable
@Override
public String getType(@NonNull Uri uri) {
  // Return a string that identifies the MIME type
  // for a Content Provider URI
  switch (uriMatcher.match(uri)) {
    case ALLROWS:
      return "vnd.android.cursor.dir/vnd.professionalandroid.lairs";
    case SINGLE_ROW:
      return "vnd.android.cursor.item/vnd.professionalandroid.lairs";
    case SEARCH :
      return SearchManager.SUGGEST_MIME_TYPE;
    default:
      throw new IllegalArgumentException("Unsupported URI: " + uri);
  }
}
```

The Search Manager will request search suggestions by initiating a query on your Content Provider and passing in the current search term as the last element in the URI path, making new queries as the user continues to type. To return suggestions, your Content Provider must return a Cursor with a set of predefined columns.

Two columns are required: SUGGEST_COLUMN_TEXT_1, which displays the search result text, and _id, which indicates the unique row ID. You can also supply another column containing text, and an icon to be displayed on either the left or right of the text results.

Listing 10-38 shows how to create a projection that returns a Cursor suitable for search suggestions.

LISTING 10-38: Creating a projection for returning search suggestions

```
private static final HashMap<String, String> SEARCH_SUGGEST_PROJECTION_MAP;
static {
  SEARCH_SUGGEST_PROJECTION_MAP = new HashMap<String, String>();

  // Map our ID column to "_id"
  SEARCH_SUGGEST_PROJECTION_MAP.put("_id",
    HoardDB.HoardContract.KEY_ID + " AS " + "_id");

  // Map our search field to the suggestions's first text field
  SEARCH_SUGGEST_PROJECTION_MAP.put(
    SearchManager.SUGGEST_COLUMN_TEXT_1,
    HoardDB.HoardContract.KEY_GOLD_HOARD_NAME_COLUMN +
      " AS " + SearchManager.SUGGEST_COLUMN_TEXT_1);
}
```

To perform the query that will supply the search suggestions, use the Uri Matcher within your query implementation, applying the projection map of the form defined in the previous listing, as shown in Listing 10-39.

LISTING 10-39: Returning search suggestions for a query

```
@Nullable
@Override
public Cursor query(Uri uri, String[] projection, String selection,
                    String[] selectionArgs, String sortOrder) {

  // Open the database.
  SQLiteDatabase db = null;
  try {
    db = mHoardDBOpenHelper.getWritableDatabase();
  } catch (SQLiteException ex) {
    db = mHoardDBOpenHelper.getReadableDatabase();
  }

  // Replace these with valid SQL statements if necessary.
  String groupBy = null;
  String having = null;
```

```
    // Use an SQLite Query Builder to simplify constructing the
    // database query.
    SQLiteQueryBuilder queryBuilder = new SQLiteQueryBuilder();

    // If this is a row query, limit the result set to the passed in row.
    switch (uriMatcher.match(uri)) {
      case SINGLE_ROW :
        String rowID = uri.getLastPathSegment();
        queryBuilder.appendWhere(HoardDB.HoardContract.KEY_ID + "=" + rowID);
      case SEARCH :
        String query = uri.getLastPathSegment();
        queryBuilder.appendWhere(
          HoardDB.HoardContract.KEY_GOLD_HOARD_NAME_COLUMN +
          " LIKE \"%" + query + "%\"");
        queryBuilder.setProjectionMap(SEARCH_SUGGEST_PROJECTION_MAP);
        break;
      default: break;
    }

    // Specify the table on which to perform the query. This can
    // be a specific table or a join as required.
    queryBuilder.setTables(HoardDB.HoardDBOpenHelper.DATABASE_TABLE);

    // Execute the query.
    Cursor cursor = queryBuilder.query(db, projection, selection,
      selectionArgs, groupBy, having, sortOrder);

    // Return the result Cursor.
    return cursor;
  }
```

The final step is to update your Searchable XML resource as shown in Listing 10-40. You need to specify the authority of the Content Provider that will be used to supply search suggestions for the Search View. This can be the same Content Provider used to execute regular searches (if you've mapped the columns as required), or an entirely different Provider.

It's also useful to specify both a searchSuggestIntentAction and searchSuggestIntentData attribute. These attributes are used to create an Intent that is fired when a search suggestion is selected by the user, indicating the Intent action, and the base URI that will be used in the Intent's data value.

LISTING 10-40: Configuring a searchable resource for search suggestions

```xml
<?xml version="1.0" encoding="utf-8"?>
<searchable
  xmlns:android="http://schemas.android.com/apk/res/android"
  android:label="@string/app_name"
  android:hint="@string/search_hint"

  android:searchSuggestAuthority=
    "com.professionalandroid.provider.hoarder"
```

continues

LISTING 10-41 *(continued)*

```
    android:searchSuggestIntentAction="android.intent.action.VIEW"
    android:searchSuggestIntentData=
      "content://com.professionalandroid.provider.hoarder/lairs">
</searchable>
```

If you specify an Intent action and base URI within the Searchable resource, you should update your Projection to include a column named SearchManager.SUGGEST_COLUMN_INTENT_DATA_ID that includes the row ID that will be appended to the base URI, as shown in Listing 10-41.

LISTING 10-41: Updating a search suggestion projection to include Intent data

```java
private static final HashMap<String, String> SEARCH_SUGGEST_PROJECTION_MAP;
static {
  SEARCH_SUGGEST_PROJECTION_MAP = new HashMap<String, String>();

  // Map our ID column to "_id"
  SEARCH_SUGGEST_PROJECTION_MAP.put("_id",
    HoardDB.HoardContract.KEY_ID + " AS " + "_id");

  // Map our search field to the suggestions's first text field
  SEARCH_SUGGEST_PROJECTION_MAP.put(
    SearchManager.SUGGEST_COLUMN_TEXT_1,
    HoardDB.HoardContract.KEY_GOLD_HOARD_NAME_COLUMN +
      " AS " + SearchManager.SUGGEST_COLUMN_TEXT_1);

  // Map the ID column to the suggestion's data ID. This will be
  // combined with the base URI specified in our Searchable definition
  // to supply the data value for the selection Intent.
  SEARCH_SUGGEST_PROJECTION_MAP.put(
    SearchManager.SUGGEST_COLUMN_INTENT_DATA_ID,
    KEY_ID + " AS " + SearchManager.SUGGEST_COLUMN_INTENT_DATA_ID);
}
```

It's also possible to specify unique actions and data URIs for each search suggestion, using the Search Manager's SUGGEST_COLUMN_INTENT_ACTION and SUGGEST_COLUMN_INTENT_DATA constants, respectively.

Searching the Earthquake Monitor Database

In the following example, you add search functionality to the Earthquake project, by adding a Search View that supports search suggestions to the action bar:

1. To begin, open the Earthquake project and create a new EarthquakeSearchProvider class that extends ContentProvider. It will be used exclusively to generate search suggestions for your Search View. Include the required stubs overriding the abstract onCreate, getType, query, insert, delete, and update methods:

```java
public class EarthquakeSearchProvider extends ContentProvider {
  @Override
```

```java
public boolean onCreate() {
  return false;
}

@Nullable
@Override
public Cursor query(@NonNull Uri uri, @Nullable String[] projection,
                    @Nullable String selection,
                    @Nullable String[] selectionArgs,
                    @Nullable String sortOrder) {
  return null;
}

@Nullable
@Override
public String getType(@NonNull Uri uri) {
  return null;
}

@Nullable
@Override
public Uri insert(@NonNull Uri uri, @Nullable ContentValues values) {
  return null;
}

@Override
public int delete(@NonNull Uri uri, @Nullable String selection,
                  @Nullable String[] selectionArgs) {
  return 0;
}

@Override
public int update(@NonNull Uri uri, @Nullable ContentValues values,
                  @Nullable String selection,
                  @Nullable String[] selectionArgs) {
  return 0;
}
}
```

2. Add a `UriMatcher`, which can be used to handle requests made using different URI patterns. As you will use this Content Provider exclusively for search suggestions, you only need to include matches for those query types:

```java
private static final int SEARCH_SUGGESTIONS = 1;

// Allocate the UriMatcher object, recognize search requests.
private static final UriMatcher uriMatcher;
static {
  uriMatcher = new UriMatcher(UriMatcher.NO_MATCH);
  uriMatcher.addURI("com.professionalandroid.provider.earthquake",
    SearchManager.SUGGEST_URI_PATH_QUERY, SEARCH_SUGGESTIONS);
  uriMatcher.addURI("com.professionalandroid.provider.earthquake",
    SearchManager.SUGGEST_URI_PATH_QUERY + "/*", SEARCH_SUGGESTIONS);
  uriMatcher.addURI("com.professionalandroid.provider.earthquake",
    SearchManager.SUGGEST_URI_PATH_SHORTCUT, SEARCH_SUGGESTIONS);
```

```
uriMatcher.addURI("com.professionalandroid.provider.earthquake",
  SearchManager.SUGGEST_URI_PATH_SHORTCUT + "/*", SEARCH_SUGGESTIONS);
}
```

3. Also override the Content Provider's `getType` method to return the MIME type for search suggestions:

```
@Nullable
@Override
public String getType(@NonNull Uri uri) {
  switch (uriMatcher.match(uri)) {
    case SEARCH_SUGGESTIONS :
      return SearchManager.SUGGEST_MIME_TYPE;
    default:
      throw new IllegalArgumentException("Unsupported URI: " + uri);
  }
}
```

4. Rather than accessing a SQLite database directly, you will use the Room Database created in Chapter 9 to perform searches. Confirm you can access it within the `onCreate` handler, and return true:

```
@Override
public boolean onCreate() {
  EarthquakeDatabaseAccessor
    .getInstance(getContext().getApplicationContext());
  return true;
}
```

5. Open the `EarthquakeDAO` and add a new query method that returns a Cursor of search suggestions based on a partial query passed in as a parameter. Search suggestion columns require specific names and unfortunately, it's not currently possible to use static constants, or passed parameters, when defining column aliases. Instead, while not ideal, hard-code the required String constants. You may want to shower afterwards:

```
@Query("SELECT mId as _id, " +
          "mDetails as suggest_text_1, " +
          "mId as suggest_intent_data_id " +
      "FROM earthquake " +
      "WHERE mDetails LIKE :query " +
      "ORDER BY mdate DESC")
public Cursor generateSearchSuggestions(String query);
```

6. Still within the Earthquake Data Access Object, add another query method that includes a query String parameter. This method returns full search results as a Live Data object containing a List of Earthquakes that match the query:

```
@Query("SELECT * " +
      "FROM earthquake " +
      "WHERE mDetails LIKE :query " +
      "ORDER BY mdate DESC")
public LiveData<List<Earthquake>> searchEarthquakes(String query);
```

7. Return to the Content Provider, and implement the query method stub. Check if the received URI is of the form of a request for search suggestions, and if so query the Room database using the current partial query:

```
@Nullable
@Override
public Cursor query(@NonNull Uri uri, @Nullable String[] projection,
                    @Nullable String selection,
                    @Nullable String[] selectionArgs,
                    @Nullable String sortOrder) {

  if (uriMatcher.match(uri) == SEARCH_SUGGESTIONS) {
    String searchQuery = "%" + uri.getLastPathSegment() + "%";

    EarthquakeDAO earthquakeDAO
      = EarthquakeDatabaseAccessor
          .getInstance(getContext().getApplicationContext())
          .earthquakeDAO();

    Cursor c = earthquakeDAO.generateSearchSuggestions(searchQuery);

    // Return a cursor of search suggestions.
    return c;
  }
  return null;
}
```

8. Now that it's complete, add the Content Provider to the manifest. Note that this Content Provider is very limited; it does not include the ability to insert, delete, or update records—nor does it support queries beyond supplying search suggestions:

```
<provider android:name=".EarthquakeSearchProvider"
          android:authorities=
            "com.professionalandroid.provider.earthquake"/>
```

9. Open the `strings.xml` resource file (in the `res/values` folder) and add new string resources that describe the Earthquake search label and text entry hint:

```
<resources>
  [... Existing String resource values ...]
  <string name="search_label">Search</string>
  <string name="search_hint">Search for earthquakes...</string>
</resources>
```

10. Create a new `searchable.xml` file in the `res/xml` folder that defines the metadata for your Earthquake Search Provider. Use the `search_hint` String from Step 9 as the hint value, and use the `app_name` String resource as the label value. Note that the label value *must* be the same as the application label specified in the manifest. Also set the authority to use for generating search suggestions to the Earthquake Search Provider's authority, and configure the `searchSuggestIntentAction` and `searchSuggestIntentData` attributes:

```
<?xml version="1.0" encoding="utf-8"?>
<searchable
```

```
      xmlns:android="http://schemas.android.com/apk/res/android"
      android:label="@string/app_name"
      android:hint="@string/search_hint"

      android:searchSuggestAuthority=
        "com.professionalandroid.provider.earthquake"
      android:searchSuggestIntentAction="android.intent.action.VIEW"
      android:searchSuggestIntentData=
        "content://com.professionalandroid.provider.earthquake/earthquakes">
    </searchable>
```

11.   Now create a new empty `EarthquakeSearchResultActivity` that extends `AppCompatActivity`:

```
    public class EarthquakeSearchResultActivity
               extends AppCompatActivity {

      @Override
      protected void onCreate(Bundle savedInstanceState) {
        super.onCreate(savedInstanceState);
        setContentView(R.layout.activity_earthquake_search_result);
      }
    }
```

12.   The list of Earthquake search results will be displayed using a Recycler View that uses your existing Earthquake list item layout and Recycler View Adapter. Modify the layout for the Earthquake Search Result Activity created in Step 11 to include a Recycler View:

```
    <?xml version="1.0" encoding="utf-8"?>
    <android.support.v7.widget.RecyclerView
      xmlns:android="http://schemas.android.com/apk/res/android"
      xmlns:app="http://schemas.android.com/apk/res-auto"
      android:id="@+id/search_result_list"
      android:layout_width="match_parent"
      android:layout_height="match_parent"
      android:layout_marginLeft="16dp"
      android:layout_marginRight="16dp"
      app:layoutManager="LinearLayoutManager"
    />
```

13.   Within the Earthquake Search Result Activity, update the `onCreate` handler to apply the Earthquake Recycler View Adapter to the Recycler View that will display the search results:

```
    private ArrayList<Earthquake> mEarthquakes = new ArrayList< >();

    private EarthquakeRecyclerViewAdapter mEarthquakeAdapter
      = new EarthquakeRecyclerViewAdapter(mEarthquakes);

    @Override
    protected void onCreate(Bundle savedInstanceState) {
      super.onCreate(savedInstanceState);
      setContentView(R.layout.activity_earthquake_search_result);
```

```
RecyclerView recyclerView = findViewById(R.id.search_result_list);
recyclerView.setLayoutManager(new LinearLayoutManager(this));
recyclerView.setAdapter(mEarthquakeAdapter);
}
```

14. Some of the next steps require Lambda functions, so make sure your project is targeting Java 1.8. Open your App module `build.gradle` file and confirm the target and source compatibility compile options within the Android node are set to 1.8:

```
android {
[... Existing Android node values ...]

compileOptions {
    targetCompatibility 1.8
    sourceCompatibility 1.8
}
}
```

15. Return to the Search Results Activity, and add a new Live Data `Observer` that will update the Array List of Earthquakes displayed by the Recycler View. Also create a new Mutable Live Data that will store the current search query, and a `setSearchQuery` method that will modify that query:

```
MutableLiveData<String> searchQuery;

private void setSearchQuery(String query) {
  searchQuery.setValue(query);
}

private final Observer<List<Earthquake>> searchQueryResultObserver
  = updatedEarthquakes -> {
    // Update the UI with the updated search query results.
    mEarthquakes.clear();
    if (updatedEarthquakes != null)
      mEarthquakes.addAll(updatedEarthquakes);
    mEarthquakeAdapter.notifyDataSetChanged();
  };
```

16. To simplify the process of applying updated search terms, we can use `Transformations` `.switchMap`. This method automatically modifies the underlying data of one Live Data based on changes in another. Apply a Switch Map that monitors the `searchQuery` Live Data, and when it changes—update a `searchResults` Live Data variable, by querying the database using the updated search term. Then use the Observer from Step 15 to observe changes in the `searchResults` Live Data. Finally, extract the search query from the Intent that launched the Activity, and pass it into the `setSearchQuery` method.

```
LiveData<List<Earthquake>> searchResults;

@Override
protected void onCreate(Bundle savedInstanceState) {
  super.onCreate(savedInstanceState);
  setContentView(R.layout.activity_earthquake_search_result);
```

```
RecyclerView recyclerView = findViewById(R.id.search_result_list);
recyclerView.setLayoutManager(new LinearLayoutManager(this));
recyclerView.setAdapter(mEarthquakeAdapter);

// Initialize the search query Live Data.
searchQuery = new MutableLiveData<>();
searchQuery.setValue(null);

// Link the search query Live Data to the search results Live Data.
// Configure Switch Map such that a change in the search query
// updates the search results by querying the database.
searchResults = Transformations.switchMap(searchQuery,
  query -> EarthquakeDatabaseAccessor
              .getInstance(getApplicationContext())
              .earthquakeDAO()
              .searchEarthquakes("%" + query + "%"));

// Observe changes to the search results Live Data.
searchResults.observe(EarthquakeSearchResultActivity.this,
                      searchQueryResultObserver);

// Extract the search query term and update the search query
// Live Data.
String query = getIntent().getStringExtra(SearchManager.QUERY);
setSearchQuery(query);
}
```

17. Also override the onNewIntent handler to update the search query if a new search request Intent is received:

```
@Override
protected void onNewIntent(Intent intent) {
  super.onNewIntent(intent);

  // If the search Activity exists, and another search
  // is performed, set the launch Intent to the newly
  // received search Intent.
  setIntent(intent);

  // Extract the search query and update the searchQuery Live Data.
  String query = getIntent().getStringExtra(SearchManager.QUERY);
  setSearchQuery(query);
}
```

18. Open the application Manifest, and modify the EarthquakeSearchResultActivity element, making its launch mode singleTop and adding an Intent Filter for the SEARCH Action. You will also need to add a meta-data tag that specifies the searchable XML resource you created in Step 10:

```
<activity
  android:name=".EarthquakeSearchResultActivity"
  android:launchMode="singleTop">
  <intent-filter>
    <action android:name="android.intent.action.SEARCH" />
  </intent-filter>
```

```
    <meta-data
      android:name="android.app.searchable"
      android:resource="@xml/searchable"
    />
  </activity>
```

19. Still in the manifest, add a new `meta-data` tag to the Earthquake Main Activity to specify the Earthquake Search Results Activity as its default search provider:

```
<activity android:name=".EarthquakeMainActivity">
  <intent-filter>
    <action android:name="android.intent.action.MAIN"/>
    <category android:name="android.intent.category.LAUNCHER"/>
  </intent-filter>
  <meta-data
    android:name="android.app.default_searchable"
    android:value=".EarthquakeSearchResultActivity"
  />
</activity>
```

20. Now add a Search View to the Earthquake Main Activity's app bar as an action button. Create a new `options_menu.xml` resource in the `res/menu` folder that includes a menu item for displaying settings, as well as a new Search View:

```
<?xml version="1.0" encoding="utf-8"?>
<menu xmlns:app="http://schemas.android.com/apk/res-auto"
      xmlns:android="http://schemas.android.com/apk/res/android">
  <item android:id="@+id/settings_menu_item"
        android:title="Settings" />
  <item android:id="@+id/search_view"
        android:title="@string/search_label"
        app:showAsAction="collapseActionView|ifRoom"
        app:actionViewClass="android.support.v7.widget.SearchView" />
</menu>
```

21. Return to the Earthquake Main Activity and modify the `onCreateOptionsMenu` handler to inflate the new XML menu definition, before connecting the Search View to your searchable definition:

```
@Override
public boolean onCreateOptionsMenu(Menu menu) {
  super.onCreateOptionsMenu(menu);

  // Inflate the options menu from XML
  MenuInflater inflater = getMenuInflater();
  inflater.inflate(R.menu.options_menu, menu);

  // Use the Search Manager to find the SearchableInfo related
  // to the Search Result Activity.
  SearchManager searchManager =
    (SearchManager) getSystemService(Context.SEARCH_SERVICE);

  SearchableInfo searchableInfo = searchManager.getSearchableInfo(
    new ComponentName(getApplicationContext(),
                      EarthquakeSearchResultActivity.class));
```

```
SearchView searchView =
  (SearchView)menu.findItem(R.id.search_view).getActionView();
searchView.setSearchableInfo(searchableInfo);
searchView.setIconifiedByDefault(false);

return true;
}
```

22. Modify the `onOptionsItemSelected` handler to use the Menu Item identifier from the XML definition created in Step 20:

```
public boolean onOptionsItemSelected(MenuItem item) {
  super.onOptionsItemSelected(item);
  switch (item.getItemId()) {
    case R.id.settings_menu_item:
      Intent intent = new Intent(this, PreferencesActivity.class);
      startActivityForResult(intent, SHOW_PREFERENCES);
      return true;
  }
  return false;
}
```

23. If you start the application, you can now initiate a search by touching the "Search" action bar button and entering a query. As a final step, modify the search results query to handle the case of users selecting a search suggestion. For now, you will display the search result as though the user had completed the full search String. First, return to the Earthquake DAO and add a new `getEarthquake` query method that takes an Earthquake unique ID, and returns a Live Data containing the matching Earthquake:

```
@Query("SELECT * " +
       "FROM earthquake " +
       "WHERE mId = :id " +
       "LIMIT 1")
public LiveData<Earthquake> getEarthquake(String id);
```

24. Then, within the Earthquake Search Result Activity, add a new `selectedSearchSuggestionId` Mutable Live Data variable that will store the ID of the selected search suggestion. Create a `setSelectedSearchSuggestion` method that will modify the `selectedSearchSuggestionId` Live Data based on the Earthquake ID extracted from a Content Provider Uri, and create an Observer that will set the search query term using the details extracted from the selected search suggestion:

```
MutableLiveData<String> selectedSearchSuggestionId;

private void setSelectedSearchSuggestion(Uri dataString) {
  String id = dataString.getPathSegments().get(1);
  selectedSearchSuggestionId.setValue(id);
}

final Observer<Earthquake> selectedSearchSuggestionObserver
  = selectedSearchSuggestion -> {
    // Update the search query to match the selected search suggestion.
    if (selectedSearchSuggestion != null) {
      setSearchQuery(selectedSearchSuggestion.getDetails());
    }
  };
```

25. Modify the `onCreate` handler to initialize the selected search suggestion Id Live Data and repeat the process from Step 16 to apply a Switch Map. This one should monitor the `selectedSearchSuggestionId` Live Data, and update the `selectedSearchSuggestion` Live Data variable, by querying the database using the selected suggestion's Id. Also check for the View action, which is sent when a suggested search result is selected. In that case, apply the Observer from Step 24 to the `selectedSearchSuggestion` Live Data, and use the `setSelectedSearchSuggestion` to extract and set the selected search suggestion Id.

```java
LiveData<Earthquake> selectedSearchSuggestion;

@Override
protected void onCreate(Bundle savedInstanceState) {
  super.onCreate(savedInstanceState);
  setContentView(R.layout.activity_earthquake_search_result);

  RecyclerView recyclerView = findViewById(R.id.search_result_list);
  recyclerView.setLayoutManager(new LinearLayoutManager(this));
  recyclerView.setAdapter(mEarthquakeAdapter);

  // Initialize the search query Live Data.
  searchQuery = new MutableLiveData<>();
  searchQuery.setValue(null);

  // Link the search query Live Data to the search results Live Data.
  // Configure Switch Map such that a change in the search query
  // updates the search results by querying the database.
  searchResults = Transformations.switchMap(searchQuery,
    query -> EarthquakeDatabaseAccessor
              .getInstance(getApplicationContext())
              .earthquakeDAO()
              .searchEarthquakes("%" + query + "%"));

  // Observe changes to the search results Live Data.
  searchResults.observe(EarthquakeSearchResultActivity.this,
                    searchQueryResultObserver);

  // Initialize the selected search suggestion Id Live Data.
  selectedSearchSuggestionId = new MutableLiveData<>();
  selectedSearchSuggestionId.setValue(null);

  // Link the selected search suggestion ID Live Data to the
  // selected search suggestion Live Data.
  // Configure Switch Map such that a change in the ID of the
  // selected search suggestion, updates the Live Data that
  // returns the corresponding Earthquake by querying the database.
  selectedSearchSuggestion =
    Transformations.switchMap(selectedSearchSuggestionId,
      id -> EarthquakeDatabaseAccessor
              .getInstance(getApplicationContext())
              .earthquakeDAO()
              .getEarthquake(id));

  // If the Activity was launched by a search suggestion
```

```
if (Intent.ACTION_VIEW.equals(getIntent().getAction())) {
  selectedSearchSuggestion.observe(this,
                             selectedSearchSuggestionObserver);
  setSelectedSearchSuggestion(getIntent().getData());
}
else {
  // If the Activity was launched from a search query.
  String query = getIntent().getStringExtra(SearchManager.QUERY);
  setSearchQuery(query);
}
}
```

26. Finally, update the onNewIntent handler to also check for the View action to update either the selected search suggestion or the search query as appropriate:

```
@Override
protected void onNewIntent(Intent intent) {
  super.onNewIntent(intent);

  // If the search Activity exists, and another search
  // is performed, set the launch Intent to the newly
  // received search Intent and perform a new search.
  setIntent(intent);

  if (Intent.ACTION_VIEW.equals(getIntent().getAction())) {
    // Update the selected search suggestion Id.
    setSelectedSearchSuggestion(getIntent().getData());
  }
  else {
    // Extract the search query and update the searchQuery Live Data.
    String query = getIntent().getStringExtra(SearchManager.QUERY);
    setSearchQuery(query);
  }
}
```

We'll return to the Earthquake app in later chapters.

11

Working in the Background

WHAT'S IN THIS CHAPTER?

➤ Using Asynchronous Tasks to execute background tasks

➤ Creating background Threads and using Handlers to synchronize with the GUI Thread

➤ Scheduling background jobs with the Job Scheduler and Firebase Job Dispatcher

➤ Scheduling background work with the Work Manager

➤ Displaying Notifications and setting Notification priority

➤ Creating Notification actions and responding to user interactions

➤ Receiving server-initiated messages with Firebase Cloud Messaging

➤ Using Firebase Notifications

➤ Using Alarms to schedule application events

➤ Creating bound and foreground Services

WROX.COM CODE DOWNLOADS FOR THIS CHAPTER

The code downloads for this chapter are found at www.wrox.com. The code for this chapter is divided into the following major examples:

➤ Snippets_ch11.zip

➤ Earthquake_ch11_Part1.zip

➤ Earthquake_ch11_Part2.zip

WORKING IN THE BACKGROUND

To help balance the trade-offs between timely, low-latency app data updates and longer battery life, Android provides a number of APIs and best-practice patterns designed to support running background tasks, while minimizing their impact on battery life.

By default, all Activities, Services, and Broadcast Receivers are executed on the main application UI Thread. To keep your applications responsive while they execute long-running tasks, in this chapter you learn to move any non-trivial tasks that aren't directly related to updating the UI onto background Threads, using the `HandlerThread` and `AsyncTask` classes.

It makes sense that when the screen turns off no apps should be running, and no data transferred; however, in practice such an extreme approach would result in a significantly worse user experience by delaying a variety of time-sensitive updates and behaviors. Finding the right balance between longer battery life and lower update latency is one of the biggest challenges in developing for mobile devices.

We expect alerts for everything from phone calls to SMS messages and incoming instant messages to be received immediately (and to be notified accordingly). We expect alarms to wake us each morning, for e-mail to arrive in a timely fashion, and for music to keep playing—even when the screen is off and the phone is in our pockets.

To minimize battery drain associated with running background tasks, Android 5.0 Lollipop (API Level 21) introduced the `JobScheduler`. You'll learn to use the Job Scheduler to batch background tasks (or "jobs"), scheduled by multiple apps across the entire system. The Job Scheduler executes jobs at times, and in a sequence, designed to minimize the associated battery drain by taking into consideration constraints such as network availability and charging state.

To provide a backward compatible API for devices running Android 4.0 Ice Cream Sandwich (API Level 14) or above, you'll learn to use the Firebase `JobDispatcher`, which is available on devices that include Google Play services. You'll also be introduced to the `WorkManager`, available as part of the Android Architecture Components, which dynamically selects the best way to execute background tasks—Threads, Job Scheduler, Firebase Job Dispatcher, or the Alarm Manager—based on factors including app state and platform API level.

When applications perform background tasks, they often have no visible UI to provide user feedback. In this chapter you learn to use Notifications to display information to users when your app is in the background, as well as optionally providing user actions related to that information.

The most efficient way to perform background tasks related to updating your app from a remote server is to rely on the server itself to push information or messages directly to each device; you learn to implement this using Firebase Cloud Messaging and Firebase Notifications as an alternative to client-side polling.

This chapter also introduces the Alarm Manager, a mechanism for firing Intents at set times, outside the scope of your application's life cycle. An Alarm will fire even after its owner application has been closed and can wake a device from sleep, so you learn to use Alarms to trigger actions based on a specific time or time interval.

Finally, for ongoing processing that interacts directly with the user, such as music playback or file uploads, a foreground `Service` may be necessary. You learn to use foreground Services that include the required Notification that gives users the ability to stop, control, and observe the progress of long-running background operations.

USING BACKGROUND THREADS

All Android application components—including Activities, Services, and Broadcast Receivers—run on the main application Thread. As a result, time-consuming processing in any component can block all other components, including any running Services and the visible Activity.

Activities that don't respond to an input event (such as a screen touch) within 5 seconds, and Broadcast Receivers that don't complete their `onReceive` handlers within 10 seconds, are considered unresponsive.

Not only do you want to avoid this scenario, you don't even want to come close. In practice, users will notice input delays and UI pauses of more than a couple of hundred milliseconds.

Responsiveness is one of the most critical attributes of a good user experience for Android applications. To ensure that your app responds quickly to any user interaction or system event, your app should use background Threads for all nontrivial processing that doesn't directly interact with user interface components. It's particularly important that long-running operations such as file I/O, network lookups, database transactions, and complex calculations are executed on background Threads.

The `AsyncTask` class is a wrapper around standard Java Threading; it encapsulates the most common pattern of executing background work on a child Thread, before syncing with the UI Thread to deliver progress and the final result. An Async Task allows you to execute background tasks sequentially, in parallel, or through your own Thread Pool.

Alternatively, if you need more control over your Threads, or don't need to synchronize with the UI Thread when the work has been completed, the `HandlerThread` class can be used to create a Thread to which components can send work using the `Handler` class.

Using Asynchronous Tasks to Run Tasks Asynchronously

The `AsyncTask` class implements the best-practice pattern for moving time-consuming operations onto a background Thread, and then synchronizing with the UI Thread to report updates, and again when the processing is complete.

It's important to note that Async Tasks have no built-in understanding of the life cycle of the components they're running within. This means that if you are creating an Async Task in an Activity, to avoid memory leaks you should define it as static (and ensure that it doesn't hold a strong reference to an Activity or its Views).

Creating New Asynchronous Tasks

Each Async Task implementation can specify parameter types to be used for input parameters, progress-reporting values, and the returned result value. If you don't need, or want, your implementation to take input parameters, update progress, or report a final result, specify Void for any or all the required types.

To create a new asynchronous task, extend the AsyncTask class and specify the parameter types to use, as shown in the skeleton code of Listing 11-1.

LISTING 11-1: An Asynchronous Task definition

```java
// The Views in your UI that you want to update from the AsyncTask
private ProgressBar asyncProgress;
private TextView asyncTextView;

private class MyAsyncTask extends AsyncTask<String, Integer, String> {
  @Override
  protected String doInBackground(String... parameter) {
    // Moved to a background Thread.
    String result = "";
    int myProgress = 0;

    int inputLength = parameter[0].length();

    // Perform background processing task, update myProgress]
    for (int i = 1; i <= inputLength; i++) {
      myProgress = i;
      result = result + parameter[0].charAt(inputLength-i);
      try {
        Thread.sleep(100);
      } catch (InterruptedException e) { }
      publishProgress(myProgress);
    }

    // Return the value to be passed to onPostExecute
    return result;
  }

  @Override
  protected void onPreExecute() {
    // Synchronized to UI Thread.
    // Update the UI to indicate that background loading is occurring
    asyncProgress.setVisibility(View.VISIBLE);
  }

  @Override
  protected void onProgressUpdate(Integer... progress) {
    // Synchronized to UI Thread.
    // Update progress bar, Notification, or other UI elements
    asyncProgress.setProgress(progress[0]);
  }
```

```
      @Override
      protected void onPostExecute(String result) {
        // Synchronized to UI Thread.
        // Report results via UI update, Dialog, or Notifications
        asyncProgress.setVisibility(View.GONE);
        asyncTextView.setText(result);
      }
    }
```

Your subclass should override the following event handlers:

➤ doInBackground—This method will be executed on a background Thread, so place your long-running code here, and don't attempt to interact with UI objects from within this handler. It takes a set of parameters of the type defined in your class implementation.

Immediately before this method is called, the onPreExecute method will be called. You can then use the publishProgress method from within this handler to pass parameter values to the onProgressUpdate handler. When your background task is complete return the final result, which will be passed as a parameter to the onPostExecute handler—from where you can update the UI accordingly.

➤ onPreExecute—Override this handler to update the UI immediately before doInBackground runs. For example, to show a loading Progress Bar.

This handler is synchronized with the UI Thread when executed, so you can safely modify UI elements.

➤ onProgressUpdate—Override this handler to update the UI with interim progress updates. This handler receives the set of parameters passed in to publishProgress (typically from within the doInBackground handler).

This handler is synchronized with the UI Thread when executed, so you can safely modify UI elements.

➤ onPostExecute—When doInBackground has completed, its return value is passed in to this event handler.

This handler is synchronized with the UI Thread when executed, so you can safely use this handler to update any UI components when your asynchronous task has completed.

Running Asynchronous Tasks

After you've implemented an asynchronous task, execute it by creating a new instance and calling execute, as shown in Listing 11-2. You can pass in a number of parameters, each of the type specified in your implementation.

LISTING 11-2: Executing an Async Task

```
String input = "redrum ... redrum";
new MyAsyncTask().execute(input);
```

> **NOTE** *Each* `AsyncTask` *instance can be executed only once. If you attempt to call* `execute` *a second time, an exception will be thrown.*

By default, Async Tasks are executed using the `AsyncTask.SERIAL_EXECUTOR`, which results in every Async Task within your application being executed serially, on the *same* background Thread. You can modify this behavior using the `executeOnExecutor` method instead of `execute`, which allows you to specify an alternative executor.

If you specify the `AsyncTask.THREAD_POOL_EXECUTOR` as seen in Listing 11-3, a new Thread Pool will be created, sized appropriately for the number of CPUs available on the device, and your Async Tasks will be executed in parallel.

LISTING 11-3: Executing Async Tasks in parallel

```
String input = "redrum ... redrum";
new MyAsyncTask().executeOnExecutor(AsyncTask.THREAD_POOL_EXECUTOR, input);
```

You can also pass in your own `Executor` implementation, or use the static methods found in the `Executors` class, such as `newFixedThreadPool`, to create a new Executor—in that case one that reuses a fixed number of Threads.

Using Asynchronous Tasks in a Broadcast Receiver

As described in Chapter 6 "Intents and Broadcast Receivers," a Broadcast Receiver can receive callbacks from other applications, and can handle processing a small amount of work in the background.

Like all components, its `onReceive` method runs on the main application UI Thread. By calling `goAsync` within `onReceive`, you can move work onto a background Thread for up to 10 seconds, before it is terminated as non-responsive.

Listing 11-4 shows how an Async Task can be useful in this context. It provides a simple way to marshal the background work within `doInBackground`, and uses the `onPostExecute` handler to call the `finish` method on the `BroadcastReceiver.PendingResult` as required to indicate that the asynchronous background work is complete.

LISTING 11-4: Asynchronous processing within a Broadcast Receiver using AsyncTask

```
public class BackgroundBroadcastReceiver extends BroadcastReceiver {

  @Override
  public void onReceive(Context context, final Intent intent) {
    final PendingResult result = goAsync();
    new AsyncTask<Void, Void, Boolean>() {
      @Override
      protected Boolean doInBackground(Void... voids) {
        // Do your background work, processing the Intent
```

```
        return true;
      }

      @Override
      protected void onPostExecute(Boolean success) {
        result.finish();
      }
    }.executeOnExecutor(AsyncTask.THREAD_POOL_EXECUTOR);
  }
}
```

Manual Thread Creation Using Handler Threads

An Async Task is a useful shortcut for running one-off tasks, but you may also need to create and manage your own Threads to perform background processing. This is often the case when you have long-running or inter-related Threads that require more subtle or complex management than is possible using Async Task.

A `Thread`, by itself, is very similar to an Async Task in that it runs a single `Runnable` and then stops. To provide a persistent Thread that can be used as a queue for background tasks, Android provides a special subclass, the `HandlerThread`.

A `HandlerThread` is kept alive by a `Looper`, a class that manages a queue of incoming work. Work can then be added to the work queue as a `Runnable`, posted to a `Handler` as seen in Listing 11-5.

LISTING 11-5: Moving processing to a background Handler Thread

```
private HandlerThread mWorkerThread;
private Handler mHandler;

@Override
public void onCreate(Bundle savedInstanceState) {
  super.onCreate(savedInstanceState);
  mWorkerThread = new HandlerThread("WorkerThread");
  mWorkerThread.start();
  mHandler = new Handler(mWorkerThread.getLooper());
}

// This method is called on the main Thread.
private void doBackgroundExecution() {
  mHandler.post(new Runnable() {
    public void run() {
      // [ ... Time consuming operations ... ]
    }
  });
}

@Override
public void onDestroy() {
  super.onDestroy();
  mWorkerThread.quitSafely();
}
```

Multiple Runnables posted to the same Handler Thread will be run sequentially. To ensure all the Thread's resources are properly cleaned up, you must call `quit` (which stops the Thread after the current Runnable has completed, and drops all queued Runnables) or `quitSafely` (which allows all queued Runnables to complete), to clean up the Thread's resources.

Handlers can send information across Threads using the `Message` class. A Message is constructed using the Handler's `obtainMessage` methods (which use a pool of Messages to avoid unnecessary object creation), or the helper method `sendEmptyMessage`.

An empty Message contains a single integer code in its `what` field, while an obtained Message instance can also contain a Bundle of information set via its `setData` method, making it a useful mechanism for sending information between Handlers.

When you send a new Message to a Handler, the `handleMessage` method is executed on the Thread the Handler is associated with, as seen in Listing 11-6.

LISTING 11-6: Sending information between Threads with Messages

```
private static final int BACKGROUND_WORK = 1;

private HandlerThread mWorkerThread;
private Handler mHandler;

@Override
public void onCreate(Bundle savedInstanceState) {
  super.onCreate(savedInstanceState);
  mWorkerThread = new HandlerThread("WorkerThread");
  mWorkerThread.start();
  mHandler = new Handler(mWorkerThread.getLooper(),
    new Handler.Callback() {
      @Override
      public void handleMessage(Message msg) {
        if (msg.what == BACKGROUND_WORK) {
          // [ ... Time consuming operations ... ]
        }
        // else, handle a different type of message
      }
    });
}

// This method is called on the main Thread.
private void backgroundExecution() {
  mHandler.sendEmptyMessage(BACKGROUND_WORK);
}

@Override
public void onDestroy() {
  super.onDestroy();
  mWorkerThread.quitSafely();
}
```

Operations that directly interact with objects created on the UI Thread (such as Views), or that display messages (such as Toasts), must always be invoked on the main Thread. Within an Activity, you can use the `runOnUiThread` method to force a Runnable to execute on the same Thread as the Activity UI, as shown in the following code snippet:

```
runOnUiThread(new Runnable() {
  public void run() {
    // Update a View or other Activity UI element.
  }
});
```

The UI Thread, just like a Handler Thread, has an associated Looper (`Looper.getMainLooper`). You can use this to create a `Handler` and post methods directly to the UI Thread.

The `Handler` class also enables you to delay posts or execute them at a specific time, using the `postDelayed` and `postAtTime` methods, respectively:

```
// Start work after 1sec.
handler.postDelayed(aRunnable, 1000);

// Start work after the device has been in use for 5mins.
int upTime = 1000*60*5;
handler.postAtTime(aRunnable, SystemClock.uptimeMillis()+upTime);
```

SCHEDULING BACKGROUND JOBS

Applications performing tasks in the background is one of the most powerful features of Android, but also the most likely to result in significant battery drain. Having multiple applications wake, and keep the device awake, can significantly reduce the expected battery life of a device.

The `JobScheduler` API was introduced in Android 5.0 Lollipop (API Level 21) to serve as a coordinator for all background work requested by any application running on a device. It effectively batches the background jobs of multiple applications, introducing efficiencies in both battery and memory use, which serves to reduce the overall impact of each individual background job.

More recently, Android Architecture Components introduced the Work Manager, which offers the same features as the Job Scheduler with the advantage of backward-compatible support for earlier platform releases.

As described in Chapter 7, "Using Internet Resources," every network request made while connected using a cellular network will result in the cell radio moving to a higher power-use state, and staying there for some time. As a result, poorly timed data transfers, initiated without context from multiple apps, can result in the radio staying in a high power state for prolonged periods.

By batching network data transfers from multiple apps such that they occur during the same time window, the Job Scheduler avoids the power drain caused by the cell radio turning on, and staying on, multiple times. The Job Scheduler also encapsulates the best practices of background jobs. It holds Wake Locks to ensure your jobs complete, checks for (and monitors) network connectivity, and it will defer and retry jobs if they fail.

Similarly, you can specify that your scheduled jobs should only occur when the device is connected to Wi-Fi, or while the device is charging, as described later in this chapter.

The Job Scheduler also reduces overall system memory usage. As described in Chapter 3 "Applications and Activities and Fragments—Oh My!," Android manages system memory primarily by killing Application processes until there is sufficient memory to support the highest-priority processes. On devices running Android 7.0 Nougat (API Level 24), the Job Scheduler optimizes background work by serializing and ordering jobs based on the available memory, effectively minimizing the risk of background tasks being killed—a strong likelihood if multiple background tasks attempt to execute simultaneously.

Creating a Job Service for the Job Scheduler

To use the Job Scheduler, your application must include a `JobService` that overrides the `onStartJob` handler. Within this handler you include the code that implements the background job to be run, while the Job Service itself is used by the system Job Scheduler to schedule and execute jobs.

You can include multiple Job Services within your app, so it's good practice to create a separate one for each distinct job type your app requires.

Listing 11-7 shows a simple `JobService` implementation; the Job Scheduler will call `onStartJob` on the main UI Thread when it's determined your job should begin.

LISTING 11-7: A simple Job Service class

```
import android.app.job.JobParameters;
import android.app.job.JobService;

public class SimpleJobService extends JobService {
  @Override
  public boolean onStartJob(JobParameters params) {
    // Do work directly on the main Thread

    // Return false if no time consuming
    // work remains to be completed on a background thread.
    return false;

    // Otherwise start a thread and return true.
  }

  @Override
  public Boolean onStopJob(JobParameters params) {
    // Return false if the job does not need to be rescheduled
    return false;
  }
}
```

If your background work can be completed quickly and safely on the main Thread, you can return `false` from `onStartJob` to indicate that there is no further work to be done; in this case `onStopJob` will not be called.

In most cases—such as when accessing Internet data, performing database operations, or file I/O—your job will need to be executed asynchronously. You can do this by creating and starting a new Thread within onStartJob, using the techniques described earlier in this chapter. In this case, you must return true from onStartJob, to indicate that additional work is still being completed.

When the work on the background Thread is completed, you must call the Job Service's job-Finished method, passing in any JobParameters associated with the job that finished, and a boolean indicating whether or not the job completed successfully or should be rescheduled.

Listing 11-8 shows how this asynchronous approach can be implemented using an AsyncTask created and started within onStartJob. It moves our processing to a background Thread, and supplies a convenient callback to indicate success or failure—and by utilizing the AsyncTask cancel method, we can fulfill the contract of calling onStopJob.

LISTING 11-8: A Job Service using an Async Task

```
import android.app.job.JobParameters;
import android.app.job.JobService;

public class BackgroundJobService extends JobService {
  private AsyncTask<Void, Void, Boolean> mJobTask = null;

  @Override
  public boolean onStartJob(final JobParameters params) {
    // TODO Do work directly on the main Thread

    // Execute additional work within a background thread.
    mJobTask = new AsyncTask<Void, Void, Boolean>() {
      @Override
      protected Boolean doInBackground(Void... voids) {
        // TODO Do your background work.

        // Return true if the job succeeded or false if it should be
        // rescheduled due to a transient failure
        return true;
      }

      @Override
      protected void onPostExecute(Boolean success) {
        // Reschedule the job if it did not succeed
        jobFinished(params, !success);
      }
    };

    mJobTask.executeOnExecutor(AsyncTask.THREAD_POOL_EXECUTOR);

    // You must return true to signify that you're doing work
    // in the background
    return true;
  }
```

continues

LISTING 11-8 *(continued)*

```
    @Override
    Public boolean onStopJob(JobParameters params) {
      if (mJobTask != null) {
        mJobTask.cancel(true);
      }
      // If we had to interrupt the job, reschedule it
      return true;
    }
  }
```

By calling `jobFinished` you notify the Job Scheduler that your background job is complete, which releases the Wake Lock and allows the device to return to standby.

If the `JobService` is only responsible for a single job, a single Async Task is enough. If you have multiple jobs running from the same Job Service, you should instead maintain a Map of Async Tasks.

Between returning true from `onStartJob` and calling `jobFinished`, the system may call `onStopJob` to indicate that there has been a system change such that the requirements you specified when scheduling the job are no longer being met. For example, if you required a charging device and the device is unplugged, or if you requested an unmetered connection and the Wi-Fi signal is lost.

When the `onStopJob` handler is triggered, you should cancel any ongoing processes as the system will release the Wakelock being held for your app—as a result of which your Thread may be stopped. The return value you indicate within `onStopJob` allows you to indicate if your job should be rescheduled to retry when your conditions are once again met.

Job Service extends the Service application component so, like all Service implementations, you must include each of your Job Services within your application manifest as shown in Listing 11-9.

LISTING 11-9: Adding a Job Service to the application manifest

```xml
<service
  android:name=".SimpleJobService"
  android:permission="android.permission.BIND_JOB_SERVICE"
  android:exported="true"/>
<service
  android:name=".BackgroundJobService"
  android:permission="android.permission.BIND_JOB_SERVICE"
  android:exported="true"/>
```

Scheduling Jobs with the Job Scheduler

Having defined your job by implementing a `JobService`, you use the `JobScheduler` to schedule when, and under what circumstances, it should be run.

The Job Scheduler is a system Service that you can access using the `getSystemService` method, passing in `Context.JOB_SCHEDULER_SERVICE`:

```
JobScheduler jobScheduler
  = (JobScheduler) context.getSystemService(Context.JOB_SCHEDULER_SERVICE);
```

To schedule a job, use the Job Scheduler's `schedule` method, passing in a `JobInfo` object that is used to specify the timeframe and conditions under which your job should be run.

To create a `JobInfo` object, use the `JobInfo.Builder`. The Job Info Builder requires two mandatory parameters: an Integer indicating the job ID, and the `ComponentName` for your Job Service implementation. A common pattern used to encapsulate the logic of scheduling a job is to include a static method in your `JobService` implementation as shown in Listing 11-10.

LISTING 11-10: Scheduling a job that requires unmetered network and charging

```java
// Can be any integer, just needs to be unique across your app
private static final int BACKGROUND_UPLOAD_JOB_ID = 13;

public static void scheduleBackgroundUpload(Context context) {
  // Access the Job Scheduler
  JobScheduler jobScheduler = (JobScheduler)
    context.getSystemService(Context.JOB_SCHEDULER_SERVICE);

  // Get a reference to my Job Service implementation
  ComponentName jobServiceName = new ComponentName(
    context, BackgroundJobService.class);

  // Build a Job Info to run my Job Service
  jobScheduler.schedule(
    new JobInfo.Builder(BACKGROUND_UPLOAD_JOB_ID, jobServiceName)
            .setRequiredNetworkType(JobInfo.NETWORK_TYPE_UNMETERED)
            .setRequiresCharging(true)
            // Wait at most a day before relaxing our network constraints
            .setOverrideDeadline(TimeUnit.DAYS.toMillis(1))
            .build());
}
```

The specified job ID is a unique identifier for a particular job; scheduling a new job with the same job ID will override any previously scheduled jobs. Similarly, you can pass this job ID into the Job Scheduler's `cancel` method to cancel a job scheduled with that identifier.

> **NOTE** *Note that you can schedule multiple jobs using the same Job Service by creating multiple* `JobInfo` *objects with different job IDs. You can obtain the job ID used to schedule a job from within your Job Service using the* `getJobId` *method from the passed in Job Parameters.*

The builder used to construct your `JobInfo` supports a large number of optional constraints that specify the timing and system conditions that determine when, and if, your job should be run. These include:

➤ `setRequiredNetworkType`—Defines a mandatory network type for your job. Must be one of:

➤ `NETWORK_TYPE_NONE`—The default option, meaning no network connectivity is required.

➤ `NETWORK_TYPE_ANY`—Requires a network connection, but can be of any type.

➤ `NETWORK_TYPE_UNMETERED`—Requires an unmetered network connection, meaning a connection that likely doesn't charge for data traffic (typically Wi-Fi).

➤ `NETWORK_TYPE_NOT_ROAMING`—Requires a network connection (Wi-Fi or cellular) that isn't roaming (only available on Android 7.0 (API Level 24) or higher).

➤ `NETWORK_TYPE_METERED`—Requires a metered network connection (typically a cellular connection). Only available on Android 8.0 Oreo (API Level 26) or higher.

➤ `setRequiresCharging`—Restricts your job to run only when the device is plugged in and charging.

➤ `setRequiresDeviceIdle`—Restricts your job to only run when the device is not in use and has not been in use for some time.

➤ `addTriggerContentUri`—Indicates your job should be triggered when a particular `content://` URI changes (typically indicating a database has changed). Only available on devices running Android 7.0 Nougat (API Level 24) or higher.

➤ `setPeriodic`—Schedules the job to recur, at a frequency no greater than the specified period.

➤ `setMinimumLatency`—Requires that the job be executed no sooner than after the specified time has passed. This cannot be combined with a periodic job.

➤ `setOverrideDeadline`—Indicates an amount of time after which the job must run, even if the other constraints aren't met. You can check if this has occurred from within your Job Service by checking the Job Parameter's `isOverrideDeadlineExpired` value.

Listing 11-10 schedules a job that requires unmetered network connectivity and a charging device, making it suitable for a one-time upload of information that isn't time sensitive.

> **NOTE** *It is strongly recommended that you* always *use* `setOverrideDeadline` *if you set a criterion requiring a particular network type because there are users who will never connect to Wi-Fi, and those who will never connect to a cell network. Consider rescheduling your job with relaxed network connectivity requirements if your override deadline is reached.*

In addition to setting conditions for when a job is run, you can also use the Job Info Builder to indicate the correct behavior if a job fails, or if the device is rebooted before the job executes.

As shown in Listing 11-11, you can use `setBackoffCriteria` to customize the back-off/retry policy by defining the length of an initial back-off and either a linear or exponential back-off strategy. By default, the Job Scheduler will use a 30 second initial value with and linear back-off. You can also use `setPersisted` to indicate if a job should be retained across device reboots.

LISTING 11-11: Scheduling a job with customized back-off criteria

```
jobScheduler.schedule(
    new JobInfo.Builder(BACKGROUND_UPLOAD_JOB_ID, jobServiceName)
            // Require a network connection
            .setRequiredNetworkType(JobInfo.NETWORK_TYPE_ANY)
            // Require the device has been idle
            .setRequiresDeviceIdle(true)
            // Force Job to ignore constraints after 1 day
            .setOverrideDeadline(TimeUnit.DAYS.toMillis(1))
            // Retry after 30 seconds, with linear back-off
            .setBackoffCriteria(30000, JobInfo.BACKOFF_POLICY_LINEAR)
            // Reschedule after the device has been rebooted
            .setPersisted(true)
            .build());
```

The Job Info Builder also provides the `setExtras` method to support sending additional data to your `JobInfo`.

Scheduling Jobs with the Firebase Job Dispatcher

The Job Scheduler was introduced in Android 5.0 Lollipop (API Level 21); the Firebase Job Dispatcher was created to provide support for devices running Android 4.0 Ice Cream Sandwich (API Level 14) and above.

On Android 7.0 Nougat (API Level 24) and higher devices, the Firebase Job Dispatcher passes responsibility for scheduling jobs to the framework Job Scheduler, ensuring future compatibility with system-wide background optimizations while maintaining backward compatibility for earlier platform versions.

> **NOTE** *Note that the Job Dispatcher requires Google Play services to be running on the device. To learn more about the Firebase Job Dispatcher, see* `github`
> `.com/firebase/firebase-jobdispatcher-android`.

To include the Firebase Job Dispatcher within your project, add a dependency to your App Module `Build.gradle` file:

```
dependencies {
  implementation 'com.firebase:firebase-jobdispatcher:0.8.5'
}
```

The Firebase Job Dispatcher includes a `JobService` class as part of the `com.firebase.job-dispatcher` package (rather than the framework's `com.android.job` package). Like the Job Scheduler, The Job Dispatcher includes `onStartJob` and `onStopJob` methods to override.

In cases where you only need to run a single job at a time on a background thread, Job Dispatcher provides a `SimpleJobService`, which implements `onStartJob` and `onStopJob` for you. You instead only override `onRunJob`, which is called on a background Thread, as shown in Listing 11-12:

LISTING 11-12: Implementing a Simple Job Service

```
import com.firebase.jobdispatcher.JobParameters;
import com.firebase.jobdispatcher.SimpleJobService;

public class FirebaseJobService extends SimpleJobService {
  @Override
  public int onRunJob(final JobParameters job) {
    // TODO Do your background work.
    // Return RESULT_FAIL_RETRY to back off
    // or RESULT_FAIL_NORETRY to give up
    return RESULT_SUCCESS;
  }
}
```

Once you've created your Job Dispatcher Job Service, you can add it to your application manifest as shown in Listing 11-13.

LISTING 11-13: Adding a Firebase Job Dispatcher Job Service to the application manifest

```
<service
  android:name=".FirebaseJobService"
  android:exported="false">
  <intent-filter>
    <action android:name="com.firebase.jobdispatcher.ACTION_EXECUTE"/>
  </intent-filter>
</service>
```

The Job Dispatcher allows you to define many of the same constraints as the Job Scheduler using the Job Dispatcher's `newJobBuilder` method, as shown in Listing 11-14, that re-creates the same job defined earlier using the Job Scheduler in Listing 11-10.

LISTING 11-14: Scheduling a job that requires unmetered network and charging using the Firebase Job Dispatcher

```
// Can be any String
private static final String BACKGROUND_UPLOAD_JOB_TAG = "background_upload";

public static void scheduleBackgroundUpload(Context context) {
  FirebaseJobDispatcher jobDispatcher =
      new FirebaseJobDispatcher(new GooglePlayDriver(context));
```

```
jobDispatcher.mustSchedule(
    jobDispatcher.newJobBuilder()
        .setTag(BACKGROUND_UPLOAD_JOB_TAG)
        .setService(FirebaseJobService.class)
        .setConstraints(
            Constraint.ON_UNMETERED_NETWORK,
            Constraint.DEVICE_CHARGING)
        .setTrigger(Trigger.executionWindow(
            0, // can start immediately
            (int) TimeUnit.DAYS.toSeconds(1))) // wait at most a day
        .build());
}
```

With backward compatibility and parity with Job Scheduler, Firebase Job Dispatcher allows you to write one system to handle background jobs that works on all devices with Google Play services.

Scheduling Work with the Work Manager

The Work Manager is an Android Architecture Component that provides a rich, backward-compatible way to use the features provided by the platform Job Scheduler.

Like the Job Scheduler, the Work Manager is intended for work that must be completed even if your app has been closed. Background work that can be abandoned if your app is closed or terminated by the runtime should be handled using Handlers, Threads, or Thread Pools, as described earlier in this chapter.

When work is scheduled, the Work Manager will determine the best available alternative to execute scheduled work: the latest available version of the platform Job Scheduler, the firebase Job Dispatcher, or even the Alarm Manager. The scheduled work is guaranteed to run, even if your app has been terminated or the device has been rebooted.

> **WARNING** *At the time of writing this book, the Work Manager was an alpha release. As such its API and functionality is particularly likely to change.*

To use the Work Manager, add a dependency to the Android Architecture Components Work Manager library, and (optionally) the Work Manager Firebase Job Dispatcher library, to your app module's Gradle Build file:

```
dependencies {
    implementation "android.arch.work:work-runtime:1.0.0-alpha03"
    implementation "android.arch.work:work-firebase:1.0.0-alpha03"
    androidTestImplementation "android.arch.work:work-testing:1.0.0-alpha03"
}
```

The Work Manager API is similar to the Job Scheduler and Firebase Job Dispatcher. Begin by extending the Worker class, overriding its doWork handler to implement the background work to be executed. Return `Worker.Result.SUCCESS` to indicate the background work has been successfully completed, `FAILURE` to indicate it has failed and should not be retried, or `RETRY` to indicate Work Manager should retry the Worker at a later point:

```
public class MyBackgroundWorker extends Worker {

  @Override
  public Worker.Result doWork() {
    // TODO Do your background work.

    // Return SUCCESS if the background work has executed successfully.
    return Result.SUCCESS;

    // Return RETRY to reschedule this work.
    // Return FAILURE to indicate a failure that shouldn't be retried.
  }
}
```

Once you've defined a Worker, request an instance of the Work Manager to request your Worker be executed using a `OneTimeWorkRequest` or `PeriodicWorkRequest` to schedule a one-off or repeating request, respectively:

```
// Schedule a one-off execution of the background work
OneTimeWorkRequest myOneTimeWork =
  new OneTimeWorkRequest.Builder(MyBackgroundWorker.class)
    .build();

// Schedule a background worker to repeat every 12 hours.
PeriodicWorkRequest myPeriodicWork =
  new PeriodicWorkRequest.Builder(MyBackgroundWorker.class,
                                  12, TimeUnit.HOURS)
    .build();

// Enqueue the work requests.
WorkManager.getInstance().enqueue(myOneTimeWork);
WorkManager.getInstance().enqueue(myPeriodicWork);
```

Once your Work Request has been enqueued, Work Manager will schedule a time to execute the specified Worker based on available system resources, and any constraints you've specified.

If no constraints have been specified (such as in the previous code snippet), the Work Manager will typically run the Worker immediately. Alternatively, you can use the `Constraint.Builder` to construct a `Constraint`, which specifies requirements—including battery and storage level, charging and idle status, and network connection type—and assign it to your Work Request using the `setConstraints` method:

```
Constraints myConstraints = new Constraints.Builder()
  .setRequiresDeviceIdle(true)
  .setRequiresCharging(true)
  .build();
```

```
OneTimeWorkRequest myWork =
  new OneTimeWorkRequest.Builder(MyBackgroundWorker.class)
  .setConstraints(myConstraints)
  .build();

WorkManager.getInstance().enqueue(myWork);
```

The Work Manager also provides support for Worker chaining, and using Live Data to observe Work Status and associated output values.

Chaining allows you to schedule Work Requests sequentially, effectively creating a dependency graph between independent Work Requests.

To create a new chained sequence, use the Work Manager's `beginWith` method, passing in the first Work Request to execute. This will return a `WorkContinuation` object whose `then` method allows you to add the next Work Request, and so on. When the sequence definition is complete, you call `enqueue` on the final Work Continuation object:

```
WorkManager.getInstance()
  .beginWith(myWork)
  .then(mySecondWork)
  .then(myFinalWork)
  .enqueue();
```

Each `beginWith` and `then` method can accept multiple Work Request objects, all of which will then be run in parallel, and must complete, before the next Worker (or group of Workers) is run. It's possible to create even more complex sequences by joining multiple chains together using the Work Continuation's `combine` methods.

In any case, each Worker is still subject to any Constraints you assign, and a permanent failure on any Worker in the chain will terminate the entire sequence.

The current status of any enqueued Work Request is reported using a `WorkStatus` within a Live Data object, and can be observed by calling the `getStatusById` method on a Work Manager instance, passing in the unique ID of the Work Request to monitor:

```
WorkManager.getInstance().getStatusById(myWork.getId())
  .observe(lifecycleOwner, workStatus -> {
    if (workStatus != null) {
      // TODO Do something with the current status
    }
  });
```

When the Work Request has completed, you can extract any output Data assigned within your Worker implementation:

```
@Override
public Worker.Result doWork() {
  // TODO Do your background work.
```

```
        Data outputData = new Data.Builder()
                                .putInt(KEY_RESULT, result)
                                .build();
        setOutputData(outputData);

        return Result.SUCCESS;
    }
```

To extract the output Data, use the Work Status `getOutputData` method, and specify the desired keys:

```
    if (workStatus != null && workStatus.getState().isFinished()) {
      int myResult = workStatus.getOutputData()
                            .getInt(KEY_RESULT, defaultValue));
    }
```

To cancel an enqueued Work Request, pass its UUID to the Work Manager's `cancelWorkById` method:

```
    UUID myWorkId = myWork.getId();
    WorkManager.getInstance().cancelWorkById(myWorkId);
```

An Earthquake-Monitoring Job Service Example

In this example you move the earthquake updating and processing functionality into its own `SimpleJobService` component.

> **NOTE** *At the time of writing this book, the Android Architecture Components Work Manager, described in the previous section, was still in alpha. As a result, in this example we demonstrate using the Firebase Job Dispatcher. As an exercise, we recommend you upgrade this sample to use the Work Manager instead.*

1. Update your `build.gradle` file to add a dependency on Firebase Job Dispatcher:

   ```
   dependencies {
     [...existing dependencies ...]

     implementation 'com.firebase:firebase-jobdispatcher:0.8.5'
   }
   ```

2. Update the `res/values/arrays.xml` to use more realistic frequency options (loading more often than every 15 minutes should only be done in response to push messages, described later in this chapter):

   ```
   <string-array name="update_freq_options">
     <item>Every 15 minutes</item>
     <item>Every hour</item>
     <item>Every 4 hours</item>
     <item>Every 12 hours</item>
   ```

```
      <item>Every 24 hours</item>
    </string-array>
    <string-array name="update_freq_values">
      <item>15</item>
      <item>60</item>
      <item>240</item>
      <item>720</item>
      <item>1440</item>
    </string-array>
```

3. Create a new `EarthquakeUpdateJobService` that extends `SimpleJobService` and requires a network connection for the job to be run:

```java
package com.professionalandroid.apps.earthquake;

import com.firebase.jobdispatcher.Constraint;
import com.firebase.jobdispatcher.FirebaseJobDispatcher;
import com.firebase.jobdispatcher.GooglePlayDriver;
import com.firebase.jobdispatcher.JobParameters;
import com.firebase.jobdispatcher.SimpleJobService;

public class EarthquakeUpdateJobService extends SimpleJobService {
  private static final String TAG = "EarthquakeUpdateJob ";
  private static final String UPDATE_JOB_TAG = "update_job";
  private static final String PERIODIC_JOB_TAG = "periodic_job";

  public static void scheduleUpdateJob(Context context) {
    FirebaseJobDispatcher jobDispatcher =
      new FirebaseJobDispatcher(new GooglePlayDriver(context));

    jobDispatcher.schedule(jobDispatcher.newJobBuilder()
      .setTag(UPDATE_JOB_TAG)
      .setService(EarthquakeUpdateJobService.class)
      .setContraints(Constraint.ON_ANY_NETWORK)
      .build());
  }

  @Override
  public int onRunJob(final JobParameters job) {
    return RESULT_SUCCESS;
  }
}
```

4. Add this new Service to the manifest by adding a new `service` tag within the `application` node:

```xml
<service android:name=".EarthquakeUpdateJobService"
  android:exported="true">
  <intent-filter>
    <action
      android:name="com.firebase.jobdispatcher.ACTION_EXECUTE/>
    </action>
  </intent-filter>
</service>
```

5.   Move the XML parsing code from the `doInBackground` handler within the Async Task defined in the `loadEarthquakes` method of the `EarthquakeViewModel`, into the `onRunJob` method in the `EarthquakeUpdateJobService`. Take the opportunity to also create a new `scheduleNextUpdate` method that should be called after the parsed Earthquakes have been added to the database:

```java
@Override
public int onRunJob(final JobParameters job) {
  // Result ArrayList of parsed earthquakes.
  ArrayList<Earthquake> earthquakes = new ArrayList<>();

  // Get the XML
  URL url;
  try {
    String quakeFeed = getString(R.string.quake_feed);
    url = new URL(quakeFeed);

    URLConnection connection;
    connection = url.openConnection();

    HttpURLConnection httpConnection = (HttpURLConnection)connection;
    int responseCode = httpConnection.getResponseCode();

    if (responseCode == HttpURLConnection.HTTP_OK) {
      InputStream in = httpConnection.getInputStream();

      DocumentBuilderFactory dbf
        = DocumentBuilderFactory.newInstance();
      DocumentBuilder db = dbf.newDocumentBuilder();

      // Parse the earthquake feed.
      Document dom = db.parse(in);
      Element docEle = dom.getDocumentElement();

      // Get a list of each earthquake entry.
      NodeList nl = docEle.getElementsByTagName("entry");
      if (nl != null && nl.getLength() > 0) {
        for (int i = 0 ; i < nl.getLength(); i++) {
          Element entry = (Element)nl.item(i);
          Element title
            = (Element)entry.getElementsByTagName("title").item(0);
          Element g
            = (Element)entry.getElementsByTagName("georss:point")
                .item(0);
          Element when
            = (Element)entry.getElementsByTagName("updated").item(0);
          Element link
            = (Element)entry.getElementsByTagName("link").item(0);

          String details = title.getFirstChild().getNodeValue();
          String hostname = "http://earthquake.usgs.gov";
          String linkString = hostname + link.getAttribute("href");
```

```
        String point = g.getFirstChild().getNodeValue();
        String dt = when.getFirstChild().getNodeValue();
        SimpleDateFormat sdf
          = new SimpleDateFormat("yyyy-MM-dd'T'hh:mm:ss'Z'");
        Date qdate = new GregorianCalendar(0,0,0).getTime();
        try {
          qdate = sdf.parse(dt);
        } catch (ParseException e) {
          Log.e(TAG, "Date parsing exception.", e);
        }

        String[] location = point.split(" ");
        Location l = new Location("dummyGPS");
        l.setLatitude(Double.parseDouble(location[0]));
        l.setLongitude(Double.parseDouble(location[1]));

        String magnitudeString = details.split(" ")[1];
        int end =  magnitudeString.length()-1;
        double magnitude
          = Double.parseDouble(magnitudeString.substring(0, end));

        if (details.contains("-"))
          details = details.split(",")[1].trim();
        else
          details = "";

        final Earthquake earthquake = new Earthquake(
          idString, qdate, details, l,
          magnitude, linkString);

        // Add the new earthquake to our result array.
        earthquakes.add(earthquake);
      }
    }
  }
  httpConnection.disconnect();

  EarthquakeDatabaseAccessor
    .getInstance(getApplicationContext())
    .earthquakeDAO()
    .insertEarthquakes(earthquakes);

  scheduleNextUpdate();

  return RESULT_SUCCESS;
} catch (MalformedURLException e) {
  Log.e(TAG, "Malformed URL Exception", e);
  return RESULT_FAIL_NORETRY;
} catch (IOException e) {
  Log.e(TAG, "IO Exception", e);
  return RESULT_FAIL_RETRY;
} catch (ParserConfigurationException e) {
  Log.e(TAG, "Parser Configuration Exception", e);
  return RESULT_FAIL_NORETRY;
} catch (SAXException e) {
```

```
            Log.e(TAG, "SAX Exception", e);
            return RESULT_FAIL_NORETRY;
        }
    }

    private void scheduleNextUpdate() {
    }
```

6. Update the `loadEarthquakes` method within the `EarthquakeViewModel` to remove the Async Task and instead call the static `scheduleUpdateJob` method within the `EarthquakeUpdateJobService` to schedule the job to execute:

```
public void loadEarthquakes() {
    EarthquakeUpdateJobService.scheduleUpdateJob(getApplication());
}
```

7. Return to the `EarthquakeUpdateJobService`. Update the `scheduleNextUpdate` method to create a new periodic job that will be used to regularly update the earthquake list if the user has set a preference to do so:

```
private void scheduleNextUpdate() {
    if (job.getTag().equals(UPDATE_JOB_TAG)) {
        SharedPreferences prefs =
            PreferenceManager.getDefaultSharedPreferences(this);
        int updateFreq = Integer.parseInt(
            prefs.getString(PreferencesActivity.PREF_UPDATE_FREQ, "60"));
        boolean autoUpdateChecked =
            prefs.getBoolean(PreferencesActivity.PREF_AUTO_UPDATE, false);

        if (autoUpdateChecked) {
            FirebaseJobDispatcher jobDispatcher =
                new FirebaseJobDispatcher(new GooglePlayDriver(context));

            jobDispatcher.schedule(jobDispatcher.newJobBuilder()
                .setTag(PERIODIC_JOB_TAG)
                .setService(EarthquakeUpdateJobService.class)
                .setConstraints(Constraint.ON_ANY_NETWORK)
                .setReplaceCurrent(true)
                .setRecurring(true)
                .setTrigger(Trigger.executionWindow(
                    updateFreq*60 / 2,
                    updateFreq*60))
                .setLifetime(Lifetime.FOREVER)
                .build());
        }
    }
}
```

Now, when the Earthquake Main Activity is launched, it will start the Earthquake Update Job Service, which will continue to schedule jobs—updating the database in the background—even after the Activity is suspended or closed.

Because the Earthquake List Fragment is observing the database, each new Earthquake will automatically be added to the list.

USING NOTIFICATIONS TO NOTIFY USERS

Notifications, such as those shown in Figure 11-1, are a powerful mechanism that makes it possible for your application to communicate important, timely information with users, even when none of your app's Activities are visible.

FIGURE 11-1

While it's likely that your users will have their phones with them at all times, it's quite unlikely that they will be paying attention to them, or your application, at any given time. Generally, users will have several applications open in the background, and they won't be paying attention to any of them.

Depending on priority, Notifications can be displayed visually above the active Activity; trigger sounds, lights, and/or a status bar icon; or be completely passive—visible only when the Notification tray is open.

It's also possible to dramatically change the appearance and interactivity of each Notification, or group of Notifications, using Notification Styles and actions. Actions add interactive controls to the Notification UI, making it possible for users to respond to Notifications without needing to open your app.

Notifications are the preferred mechanism for invisible application components (particularly Job Services) to alert users that events have occurred that may require timely attention. They are also required to indicate a running Service with foreground priority as described later in this chapter.

Introducing the Notification Manager

The `NotificationManager` is a system Service used to manage Notifications. To provide a consistent experience across all API levels, the Support Library provides a `NotificationManagerCompat` class, which you should use rather than the framework Notification Manager when posting Notifications.

The Support Library Notification Manager can be accessed as shown in Listing 11-15.

LISTING 11-15: Using the Notification Manager

```
NotificationManagerCompat notificationManager =
    NotificationManagerCompat.from(context);
```

Using the Notification Manager, you can trigger new Notifications, modify existing ones, or cancel those that are no longer required.

Each Notification is identified by a unique integer ID, and an optional String tag that are used to determine if a new Notification should be created, or if an existing Notification should be updated. Similarly, these properties are used to determine which Notification to cancel.

Working with Notification Channels

Starting in Android 8.0 Oreo (API Level 26), all Notifications must be associated with a Notification Channel. At minimum, each Notification Channel has a unique ID and a user-visible name, but they are also used to define a default priority, sound, light, and vibration for all Notifications posted to that Notification Channel.

After you've created a Notification Channel, and posted a Notification to it, the user can modify that Channel's settings—including raising or lowering the priority of all future Notifications posted to that Channel.

As a result, it's critical to create the right granularity of Notification Channels and carefully set the defaults to be consistent with the expectations of the majority of your users. For example, Notifications for messges received from other users should be in a separate—higher—priority Notification Channel from Notifications regarding service updates.

Mixing different Notifications types within the same Notification Channel makes it is much more likely that users will disable or demote the priority of that Channel, consistent with the expectations for the lowest priority Notifications they receive.

In most cases, an app has a fixed number of Notification Channels, each with a static String ID. This type of Notification Channel is shown in Listing 11-16. Note that you must create your Notification Channels using the system Notification Manager, and only on devices running Android 8.0 or later.

LISTING 11-16: Creating a Notification Channel

```java
private static final String MESSAGES_CHANNEL = "messages";

public void createMessagesNotificationChannel(Context context) {
  if (Build.VERSION.SDK_INT >= Build.VERSION_CODES.O) {
    CharSequence name = context
      .getString(R.string.messages_channel_name);

    NotificationChannel channel = new NotificationChannel(
      MESSAGES_CHANNEL,
      name,
      NotificationManager.IMPORTANCE_HIGH);

    NotificationManager notificationManager =
      context.getSystemService(NotificationManager.class);
    notificationManager.createNotificationChannel(channel);
  }
}
```

This method should then be called before every Notification to ensure the corresponding Notification Channel is created.

As the Android system UI allows users to directly adjust the settings for each Notification Channel, your app doesn't need to provide a separate UI for setting Notification preferences on Android 8.0 or higher devices. However, you may consider providing those settings within your app for users on older versions of Android.

For Android 8.0 or higher devices, rather than providing Notification settings within your app, you should redirect users to the system Notification settings screen:

```
Intent intent = new Intent(Settings.ACTION_CHANNEL_NOTIFICATION_SETTINGS);
intent.putExtra(Settings.EXTRA_APP_PACKAGE, context.getPackageName());
startActivity(intent);
```

Creating Notifications

In addition to a Notification Channel, every Notification is required to contain three primary elements: a small icon, a title, and descriptive text.

The small icon is displayed in the status bar, and should be immediately recognizable as representing your app. A small icon should be 24x24dp in size and should be white on a transparent background.

> **NOTE** *On Android 5.0 Lollipop (API Level 21) or higher devices, you should consider using a vector Drawable for your small icon so that the system can scale it to any size. Vector Drawables are discussed in detail in Chapter 12, "Implementing the Android Design Philosophy."*

Small icons are typically simplified versions of your app's launcher icon, and should always match the iconography used within your app so that users will recognize them in the status bar.

Pro Android · now
Reto Meier
Interested in a new book recommendation? I have o..

FIGURE 11-2

The main content of a Notification is split across two lines as shown in Figure 11-2.

The first line is the title, with the text beneath.

With these fields, it is possible to build a simple Notification using a `NotificationCompat.Builder` and post a Notification using `notify`, as shown in Listing 11-17.

LISTING 11-17: Creating and posting a Notification

```
final int NEW_MESSAGE_ID = 0;

createMessagesNotificationChannel(context);
NotificationCompat.Builder builder = new NotificationCompat.Builder(
  Context, MESSAGES_CHANNEL);
```

continues

LISTING 11-7 *(continued)*

```
// These would be dynamic in a real app
String title = "Reto Meier";
String text = "Interested in a new book recommendation?" +
            " I have one you should check out!";

builder.setSmallIcon(R.drawable.ic_notification)
    .setContentTitle(title)
    .setContentText(text);

notificationManager.notify(NEW_MESSAGE_ID, builder.build());
```

The title should contain the information needed to understand each Notification's importance to the user. It's always displayed on a single line, so whenever possible it's important to keep the title length under 30 characters to ensure it's displayed in full.

For example, Notifications indicating incoming messages from another person should display the sender's name in the title. Always avoid using your app's name within the title; it's redundant—and the app name is displayed within the header on Android 7.0 Nougat (API Level 24) and higher devices.

The content text provides the context and more detailed information. In our messaging example, the content text would be the latest message received. In all cases the content text should not duplicate information already available in the title.

It's also good practice to use the setColor method to specify a color for your Notifications consistent with your app's branding:

```
builder.setColor(ContextCompat.getColor(context, R.color.colorPrimary));
```

Between Android 5.0 Lollipop (API Level 21) and Android 6.0 Marshmallow (API Level 23), this color is used as the background color surrounding the small icon on a Notification. Since Android 7.0 Nougat (API Level 24) the specified color is used for the small icon, app name, and any actions you use as shown in Figure 11-3.

FIGURE 11-3

In either case, the color you select should contrast with the light background color used on the Notification tray.

Notifications also support the use of a large icon. The large icon is displayed in an open Notification, and provides additional context alongside the content title and text strings, as shown in Figure 11-4.

FIGURE 11-4

You can set a large icon using a Bitmap passed in to the setLargeIcon method of the Builder:

```
builder.setLargeIcon(profilePicture);
```

Handling Notification Taps

In almost all cases, a Notification should respond to a user tap by opening the corresponding application, and navigating to the correct context for the user to either get more detail or provide a response.

To support taps, each Notification can include a content Intent, specified using the setContent-Intent method of the Notification Builder. This method takes a PendingIntent that should launch the appropriate Activity.

In most cases, a Notification tap will deep link into a specific Activity within your application—for example, an e-mail to read or an image to view. In this case, it's important to also construct the correct back stack to ensure navigation occurs the way users would predict when using the back button.

To accomplish this, you should use the TaskStackBuilder class as shown in Listing 11-18:

LISTING 11-18: Adding a content Intent to start an Activity

```
// This could be any Intent. Here we use the app's
// launcher activity as a simple example
Intent launchIntent = context.getPackageManager()
  .getLaunchIntentForPackage(context.getPackageName());

PendingIntent contentIntent = TaskStackBuilder.create(context,
  .addNextIntentWithParentStack(launchIntent)
  .getPendingIntent(0, PendingIntent.FLAG_UPDATE_CURRENT);
builder.setContentIntent(contentIntent);
```

By default, Activities have no parent Activity declared, which means that tapping the Notification does not create any additional back stack. While this is appropriate for your launcher Activity, a parent Activity should be set for all other Activities in your app. The process for setting the parent Activity is described in Chapter 12.

To dismiss a Notification when it is tapped, you can set the Notification to automatically cancel with setAutoCancel:

```
builder.setAutoCancel(true);
```

Handling Notification Dismissal by Users

Users can dismiss Notifications by swiping them away individually, or by choosing to clear all of them at once. You can specify a delete Intent using the setDeleteIntent method on the Builder that will be sent to your app when a Notification is dismissed, rather than clicked or canceled.

This is useful if you need to sync dismissals across multiple devices, or update your app's internal state. The Pending Intent you specify here should almost always point to a Broadcast Receiver that can do the processing in the background, or initiate a background job if necessary:

```
Intent intent = new Intent(context, DeleteReceiver.class);

// Add any extras or a data URI that uniquely defines this Notification
```

```
PendingIntent deleteIntent = PendingIntent.getBroadcast(context, 0,
  intent, PendingIntent.FLAG_UPDATE_CURRENT);

builder.setDeleteIntent(deleteIntent);
```

Using an Expanded Notification Style

Android 4.1 Jelly Bean (API Level 16) introduced the ability to create Notifications that can be expanded to show additional information, as well as include user actions. Android provides multiple expanded Notification styles:

➤   `BigTextStyle`—Displays multiple lines of text.

➤   `BigPictureStyle`—Displays a large image within the expanded Notification.

➤   `MessagingStyle`—Displays messages received as part of conversations.

➤   `MediaStyle`—Displays information on playing media and up to five actions to control media playback.

➤   `InboxStyle`—Displays a summary Notification that represents multiple Notifications.

Each Notification style provides a different UI and set of functionality, as shown in Figure 11-5 and described below.

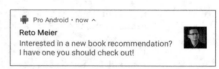

The most widely applicable is the `BigTextStyle`, which displays multiple lines of text as specified using the `bigText` method from the Big Text Style, rather than the single line of text displayed in a standard (non-styled) Notification.

FIGURE 11-5

Listing 11-19 shows how to apply the Big Text Style using the `setStyle` method of the Notification Builder.

LISTING 11-19: Applying a Big Text Style to a Notification

```
builder.setSmallIcon(R.drawable.ic_notification)
  .setContentTitle(title)
  .setContentText(text)
  .setLargeIcon(profilePicture)
  .setStyle(new NotificationCompat.BigTextStyle().bigText(text));
```

For purely visual content, the `BigPictureStyle` allows you to specify a large image using the `big-Picture` method, returned when adding the Big Picture Style, when the Notification is expanded—as shown in Listing 11-20.

LISTING 11-20: Applying a Big Picture Style to a Notification

```
builder.setSmallIcon(R.drawable.ic_notification)
  .setContentTitle(title)
  .setContentText(text)
```

```
           .setLargeIcon(profilePicture)
           .setStyle(new NotificationCompat.BigPictureStyle()
                                  .bigPicture(aBigBitmap));
```

For Notifications published by messaging apps—particularly those featuring conversations with multiple people—you can use the `MessagingStyle`.

When using this style, provide a `userDisplayName` string to represent the current user, and a set of messages using the `addMessage` method as shown in Listing 11-21.

```
builder
    .setShowWhen(true) // Show the time the Notification was posted
    .setStyle(new NotificationCompat.MessagingStyle(userDisplayName)
        .addMessage("Hi Reto!", message1TimeInMillis, "Ian Lake")
        .addMessage("How's it going?", message2TimeInMillis, "Ian Lake")
        .addMessage("Very well indeed. And you?", message3TimeInMillis, null));
```

Each added message has three main properties: the text of the incoming message, the time the message was sent (in milliseconds), and the name of the sender. A null sender indicates that the message was sent by the user of the host device. For group conversations, the conversation title can be set with `setConversationTitle`.

For media playback apps, a `MediaStyle` Notification offers users quick access to up to five actions (such as play/pause, next/previous track). This style is discussed in detail in Chapter 17, "Audio, Video, and Using the Camera."

`InboxStyle` Notifications are particularly useful for generating a summary Notification, as discussed later in this chapter within the "Grouping Multiple Notifications" section.

Setting a Notification's Priority

The priority attached to a Notification represents its relative importance to your users, and the level of user-interruption it will cause.

The lowest-priority Notifications (such as weather forecasts) are only presented when the Notification tray is expanded, while the highest-priority Notifications (such as incoming calls) trigger sounds, lights, and vibrations—as well as potentially bypassing users' Do Not Disturb settings.

Setting the importance on a Notification Channel

On Android 8.0 Oreo (API Level 26) or higher devices, the priority of a Notification is set by the importance on its Notification Channel:

```
channel.setImportance(NotificationManager.IMPORTANCE_HIGH);
```

The default importance, `IMPORTANCE_DEFAULT`, causes Notifications to show on the status bar as an icon and will alert the user. By default, this uses the default sound, but you can choose to specify a custom sound, vibration, or light pattern (as discussed below).

For time-sensitive alerts such as incoming communication messages from chat services, consider using a channel with `IMPORTANCE_HIGH`. Notifications from channels of this importance or higher will "peek" onto the user's screen (if the screen is on), as shown in Figure 11-6.

FIGURE 11-6

Alternatively, `IMPORTANCE_LOW` is appropriate for non-time-sensitive information. A status bar icon will still be displayed, but no sound, vibration, or lights will be used.

For nice-to-know information that should not intrude on the user at all, `IMPORTANCE_MIN` should be used. These Notifications are not displayed as icons in the status bar; they are shown only at the bottom of the Notification tray when it is expanded.

Understanding the Notification Priority System

Prior to Android 8.0, the priority of a Notification is set using the `setPriority` method on the Notification Builder:

```
builder.setPriority(NotificationCompat.PRIORITY_HIGH);
```

The priorities here match the importance levels of Notification Channels, with one exception: a `PRIORITY_MAX` was also available. Generally, `PRIORITY_MAX` should not be used except for the most critical, time-sensitive Notifications such as incoming phone calls, which must be handled immediately.

➤ `PRIORITY_HIGH`—Equivalent to `IMPORTANCE_HIGH`

➤ `PRIORITY_DEFAULT`—Equivalent to `IMPORTANCE_DEFAULT`

➤ `PRIORITY_LOW`—Equivalent to `IMPORTANCE_LOW`

➤ `PRIORITY_MIN`—Equivalent to `IMPORTANCE_MIN`

> **NOTE** *Unlike Notification Channels, setting the priority on a Notification does not limit the types of alerts you can add to the Notification. Stay consistent with Notification Channels by refraining from adding sound, vibration, or lights to* `PRIORITY_LOW` *or* `PRIORITY_MIN` *Notifications.*

Adding Sound, Vibration, and Lights to Notifications

Notification Channels of `IMPORTANCE_DEFAULT` or higher can alert the user via sound, vibration or lights.

By default, the default Notification ring tone is used. The default vibration or light pattern can be added by calling the appropriate methods when constructing your Notification Channel:

```
channel.enableVibration(true);
channel.enableLights(true);
```

Prior to Android 8.0, the simplest and most consistent way to add sounds, lights, and vibrations to your Notifications is to use the default settings. Using the `setDefaults` method on the Notification Builder, you can combine the following constants:

➤ `NotificationCompat.DEFAULT_SOUND`

➤ `NotificationCompat.DEFAULT_VIBRATE`

➤ `NotificationCompat.DEFAULT_LIGHTS`

For example, the following code snippet assigns the default sound and vibration settings to a Notification:

```
builder.setDefaults(NotificationCompat.DEFAULT_SOUND |
                    NotificationCompat.DEFAULT_VIBRATE);
```

If you want to use all the default values, you can use the `NotificationCompat.DEFAULT_ALL` constant.

The sound, vibration pattern, and LED color and rate can be customized from the default values using the `setSound`, `setVibrationPattern`, and `setLightColor` methods on the Notification Channel, respectively.

Generally, sounds are chosen from the `RingtoneManager` class, which respects the user's preferences. A custom vibration pattern can be specified using an array of longs, alternating between the milliseconds to remain on and milliseconds to remain off. The color of the LED can also be customized, and prior to Android 8.0, you can also set the rate at which the LED flashes using two integers—the number of milliseconds for the LED to be on and then the number of milliseconds to be off.

Listing 11-22 builds a Notification that uses the `RingtoneManager` to get an appropriate sound, vibrates the phone for a total of three times over a 5-second period, and rapidly blinks the LED red.

LISTING 11-22: Customizing a Notification's alerts

```
// For Android 8.0+ higher devices:
channel.setSound(
  RingtoneManager.getDefaultUri(RingtoneManager.TYPE_NOTIFICATION));
channel.setVibrationPattern(new long[] { 1000, 1000, 1000, 1000, 1000});
channel.setLightColor(Color.RED);

// For Android 7.1 or lower devices:
builder.setPriority(NotificationCompat.PRIORITY_HIGH)
       .setSound(
           RingtoneManager.getDefaultUri(RingtoneManager.TYPE_NOTIFICATION))
       .setVibrate(new long[] { 1000, 1000, 1000, 1000, 1000 })
       .setLights(Color.RED, 0, 1);
```

> **NOTE** *Each device may have different limitations with regard to control over the LED. If the color you specify is not available, as close an approximation as possible will be used. When using LEDs to convey information to the user, keep this limitation in mind and avoid making it the only way such information is made available.*

To only have the sound and vibrate occur the first time the Notification is posted and not every time the Notification is updated, you can use `setOnlyAlertOnce` passing in `true`:

```
builder.setOnlyAlertOnce(true);
```

Respecting Requests That You "Do Not Disturb"

Since Android 5.0 Lollipop (API Level 21), users have been able to customize which Notifications can use sound, vibration, and lights to alert them while in "Do Not Disturb" (or "Priority Only") mode.

When deciding if these alerting mechanisms are allowed while Do Not Disturb mode is active, the Notification Manager uses two pieces of metadata: the Notification category, and the person whose action triggered the Notification.

A Notification's category is set using the `setCategory` method:

```
builder.setCategory(NotificationCompat.CATEGORY_EVENT);
```

The `Notification` class includes a variety of category constants including `CATEGORY_ALARM`, `CATEGORY_REMINDER`, `CATEGORY_EVENT`, `CATEGORY_MESSAGE`, and `CATEGORY_CALL`. By setting the correct category, you ensure that the user's system settings to enable or disable certain categories while in Do Not Disturb mode are respected.

For some Notification categories, specifically message and call, users can choose to allow Notifications only from specific people—namely, their starred contacts.

You can attach people to the Notification by using `addPerson`, passing in one of three types of URIs, as shown in Listing 11-23:

➤ A `CONTENT_LOOKUP_URI` or the "permanent" link to an individual contact already in the user's Contacts Content Provider

➤ A `tel:` schema for phone numbers, which will use `ContactsContract.PhoneLookup` to find the associated user

➤ A `mailto:` schema for e-mail addresses

LISTING 11-23: Setting a Notification category and sender

```
builder.setCategory(NotificationCompat.CATEGORY_CALL)
    .addPerson("tel:5558675309");
```

Adding Notification Actions

Expanded Notifications also enable you to offer users up to three actions in addition to tapping the Notification itself. For example, an e-mail Notification might contain an action to archive or delete it.

Any action added to the Notification must offer unique functionality rather than duplicate the action taken when tapping the Notification. Actions are only available when the Notification has been expanded, so it's best practice to ensure that every action available in the expanded Notification is also available in the Activity launched when the Notification is tapped.

Each Notification action has a title, an icon (32x32dp, white on a transparent background), and a `PendingIntent`. On devices running Android 7.0 Nougat (API Level 24) or above, the icon is not displayed in the expanded Notification, but it's used on devices such as Wear OS and on earlier versions of Android.

Add new actions to a Notification using the `addAction` method on the Notification Builder as shown in Listing 11-24.

LISTING 11-24: Adding a Notification action

```
Intent deleteAction = new Intent(context, DeleteBroadcastReceiver.class);
deleteAction.setData(emailUri);

PendingIntent deleteIntent = PendingIntent.getBroadcast(context, 0,
  deleteAction, PendingIntent.FLAG_UPDATE_CURRENT);

builder.addAction(
  new NotificationCompat.Action.Builder(
    R.drawable.delete,
    context.getString(R.string.delete_action),
    deleteIntent).build());
```

> **NOTE** *After an action is triggered, it is the receiving component's responsibility to cancel the Notification if appropriate. The* `setAutoCancel` *mechanism only applies when the content Intent is fired by the user tapping the Notification itself.*

The Notification Builder offers additional support for actions on Wear OS through the `Action.WearableExtender` class. You can provide quick access to a primary action on Android Wear devices using its `setHintDisplayActionInline` method:

```
builder.addAction(
  new NotificationCompat.Action.Builder(
    R.drawable.archive,
    context.getString(R.string.archive_action),
    archiveIntent)
    .extend(new NotificationCompat.Action.WearableExtender()
      .setHintDisplayActionInline(true))
    .build());
```

The Wearable Extender can also be used to further improve the transition animation on Wear OS using the `setHintLaunchesActivity(true)` when appropriate, which will play an "Opened on the phone" animation when set to `true`.

Adding Direct Reply Actions

The actions described in the previous section are limited to firing a predefined Intent when an action is selected. Android 7.0 Nougat (API Level 24) and Wear OS expand this further with the introduction of "direct reply actions," making it possible for users to respond to a Notification by entering text directly from the Notification itself, as shown in Figure 11-7.

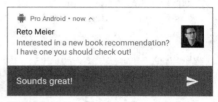

FIGURE 11-7

Direct reply actions are particularly useful for situations where the most common user response to a Notification is to provide a short reply—such as responding to an incoming message. For this reason, direct reply actions are typically paired with the `MessagingStyle`.

To add a direct reply action to your Notification, add a `RemoteInput` object to the action, as shown in Listing 11-25.

LISTING 11-25: Adding a direct reply action

```java
// The key you'll use to later retrieve the reply
final String KEY_TEXT_REPLY = "KEY_TEXT_REPLY";

Intent replyAction = new Intent(context, ReplyBroadcastReceiver.class);
replyAction.setData(chatThreadUri);
PendingIntent replyIntent = PendingIntent.getBroadcast(context, 0,
  replyAction, PendingIntent.FLAG_UPDATE_CURRENT);

// Construct the RemoteInput
RemoteInput remoteInput = new RemoteInput.Builder(KEY_TEXT_REPLY)
  .setLabel(context.getString(R.string.reply_hint_text))
  .build();

builder.addAction(
  new NotificationCompat.Action.Builder(
    R.drawable.reply,
    context.getString(R.string.reply_action),
    replyIntent)
  .addRemoteInput(remoteInput)
  .setAllowGeneratedReplies(true)
  .extend(new NotificationCompat.Action.WearableExtender()
    .setHintDisplayActionInline(true))
  .build());
```

A simple way to improve the user experience on Android Wear devices is to enable generated replies with `setAllowGeneratedReplies(true)`. Generated replies attempt to predict likely user responses, allowing the user to select a predetermined reply rather than needing to type (or say) anything at all.

When users enter their reply, it is included in your Pending Intent with the key you used to construct the `RemoteInput`. You can extract the text within your app using the static `RemoteInput.getResultsFromIntent` method to obtain a Bundle from which you can extract the user's inputted text:

```
Bundle remoteInput = RemoteInput.getResultsFromIntent(intent);
CharSequence message = remoteInput != null
  ? remoteInput.getCharSequence(KEY_TEXT_REPLY)
  : null;
```

Immediately after users have entered their reply, Android will add an indeterminate progress spinner to indicate that your app is processing the reply. Once you receive and process the user input, you must update the Notification such that it reflects their input and the progress spinner is removed.

If you're using the `MessagingStyle`, you can do this by adding a new message using `addMessage`. For any other Notification style, use `setRemoteInputHistory`.

```
// If you have multiple replies, the most recent
// should be the first in the array
builder.setRemoteInputHistory(new CharSequence[] { lastReply });
```

Grouping Multiple Notifications

Rather than sending multiple individual Notifications (such as one per e-mail), it's generally a better user experience to bundle multiple Notifications into a single group. This ensures users retain a Notification tray that can be understood at a glance, and won't be overwhelmed with multiple Notifications from any single app.

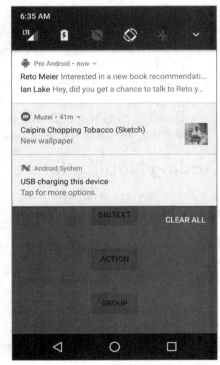

One approach is to have a single Notification that is updated to reflect multiple items that triggered it; however, the small available space limits the information you can display.

A better approach is to bundle multiple individual Notifications from your app. These grouped Notifications appear the same size as a single Notification, as shown in Figure 11-8, but can be expanded, such that a user can view and interact with multiple individual Notifications from within that group.

Notifications can be added to a group by calling `setGroup` on the Builder, passing in a String that provides a unique key for each group:

```
String accountName = "reto@example.com";
builder.setGroup(accountName);
```

FIGURE 11-8

> **NOTE** *On Android 7.0 Nougat (API Level 24) and higher devices, Notification grouping is enforced automatically for any app that posts more than four individual Notifications.*

For each group, you must also post a group summary Notification—a Notification that has the same `setGroup` call and also calls `setGroupSummary(true)`, as shown in Listing 11-26.

LISTING 11-26: Building an InboxStyle group summary Notification

```
InboxStyle inboxStyle = new NotificationCompat.InboxStyle();
for (String emailSubject : emailSubjects)
  inboxStyle.addLine(emailSubject);

builder.setSubText(accountName)
  .setGroup(accountName)
  .setGroupSummary(true)
  .setStyle(inboxStyle);
```

On devices running Android 7.0 Nougat (API Level 24) and higher, this summary Notification is used only to populate the content Intent, delete Intent, and the subtext that is seen when the bundle is collapsed.

However, on Android 6.0 Marshmallow (API Level 23) and earlier devices—where Notification bundling is not available—this summary bundle will be the only one displayed for your app. This makes Inbox Style the best style to use, as it provides a single line summary of each Notification that can be accessed when the user clicks on the summary Notification.

This means that your summary Notification should contain enough information to be useful even without the child Notifications, and every time a Notification within the group is created, updated, or deleted, the summary Notification should also be updated to reflect the current summary state.

Adding Notifications to the Earthquake Monitor

The following example enhances the `EarthquakeUpdateJobService` to trigger a Notification for the most severe new earthquake after an update. The Notification will show the magnitude and location in the Notification tray, and selecting the Notification will open the Earthquake Activity.

1. Start by adding an `earthquake_channel_name` String to the `res/values/strings.xml` file:

```
<string name="earthquake_channel_name">New earthquake!</string>
```

2. In the `EarthquakeUpdateJobService`, add new constants which we'll use for constructing each Notification:

```
private static final String NOTIFICATION_CHANNEL = "earthquake";
public static final int NOTIFICATION_ID = 1;
```

3. Still within the Earthquake Update Job Service, add a `createNotificationChannel` method to define a high importance channel with vibration and lights, suitable for something as high priority as a new earthquake:

```java
private void createNotificationChannel() {
  if (Build.VERSION.SDK_INT >= Build.VERSION_CODES.O) {
    CharSequence name = getString(R.string.earthquake_channel_name);

    NotificationChannel channel = new NotificationChannel(
      NOTIFICATION_CHANNEL,
      name,
      NotificationManager.IMPORTANCE_HIGH);
    channel.enableVibration(true);
    channel.enableLights(true);

    NotificationManager notificationManager =
      getSystemService(NotificationManager.class);
    notificationManager.createNotificationChannel(channel);
  }
}
```

4. Create a Notification icon named `notification_icon` and store it in your `res/drawable` folder by selecting the New ➪ Vector Asset menu item in Android Studio. For the icon, select the `vibration` material icon. Use the default `24 x 24 dp` (which is the correct size for Notification icons). Edit the resulting `notification_icon.xml` to change the `fillColor` to `#FFF` (white):

```xml
<vector
  xmlns:android="http://schemas.android.com/apk/res/android"
  android:width="24dp"
  android:height="24dp"
  android:viewportWidth="24.0"
  android:viewportHeight="24.0">
  <path
    android:fillColor="#FFF"
    android:pathData="M0,15h2L2,9L0,9v6z
      M3,17h2L5,7L3,7v10zM22,9v6h2L24,9h-2z
      M19,17h2L21,7h-2v10z
      M16.5,3h-9C6.67,3 6,3.67 6,4.5v15
      c0,0.83 0.67,1.5 1.5,1.5h9
      c0.83,0 1.5,-0.67 1.5,-1.5v-15
      c0,-0.83 -0.67,-1.5 -1.5,-1.5z
      M16,19L8,19L8,5h8v14z"/>
</vector>
```

5. Create a new `broadcastNotification` method that will call `createNotificationChannel`, then create the Notification Builder instance using an Earthquake object:

```java
private void broadcastNotification(Earthquake earthquake) {
  createNotificationChannel();

  Intent startActivityIntent = new Intent(this,
    EarthquakeMainActivity.class);
```

```java
PendingIntent launchIntent = PendingIntent.getActivity(this, 0,
  startActivityIntent, PendingIntent.FLAG_UPDATE_CURRENT);

final NotificationCompat.Builder earthquakeNotificationBuilder
  = new NotificationCompat.Builder(this, NOTIFICATION_CHANNEL);

earthquakeNotificationBuilder
  .setSmallIcon(R.drawable.notification_icon)
  .setColor(ContextCompat.getColor(this, R.color.colorPrimary))
  .setDefaults(NotificationCompat.DEFAULT_ALL)
  .setVisibility(NotificationCompat.VISIBILITY_PUBLIC)
  .setContentIntent(launchIntent)
  .setAutoCancel(true)
  .setShowWhen(true);

earthquakeNotificationBuilder
  .setWhen(earthquake.getDate().getTime())
  .setContentTitle("M:" + earthquake.getMagnitude())
  .setContentText(earthquake.getDetails())
  .setStyle(new NotificationCompat.BigTextStyle()
    .bigText(earthquake.getDetails()));

NotificationManagerCompat notificationManager
  = NotificationManagerCompat.from(this);

notificationManager.notify(NOTIFICATION_ID,
  earthquakeNotificationBuilder.build());
}
```

6. To avoid interrupting users with Notification for earthquakes that have already been recived, we'll need to compare any newly parsed earthquakes with those already in the database.

6.1 In the `EarthquakeDAO` class, create an `loadAllEarthquakesBlocking` method that will be used to synchronously return all Earthquakes when called from the background thread that `onRunJob` runs on:

```java
@Query("SELECT * FROM earthquake ORDER BY mDate DESC")
List<Earthquake> loadAllEarthquakesBlocking();
```

6.2 Return to the `EarthquakeUpdateJobService` class. Create a `findLargestNewEarthquake` method to compare the two lists of Earthquakes:

```java
private Earthquake findLargestNewEarthquake(
  List<Earthquake> newEarthquakes) {

  List<Earthquake> earthquakes = EarthquakeDatabaseAccessor
    .getInstance(getApplicationContext())
    .earthquakeDAO()
    .loadAllEarthquakesBlocking();

  Earthquake largestNewEarthquake = null;

  for (Earthquake earthquake : newEarthquakes) {
    if (earthquakes.contains(earthquake)) {
      continue;
    }
```

```
        if (largestNewEarthquake == null
          || earthquake.getMagnitude() >
          largestNewEarthquake.getMagnitude()) {
          largestNewEarthquake = earthquake;
        }
      }
    }
    return largestNewEarthquake;
  }
```

7. Update the onRunJob method to broadcast a new Notification when the periodic job finds a *new* earthquake that is larger than the user's specified minimum magnitude. Add a call to broadcastNotification immediately before the call to insert the new Earthquakes into the database:

```
public int onRunJob(final JobParameters job) {
  [... Existing onRunJob ...]

  if (job.getTag().equals(PERIODIC_JOB_TAG)) {
    Earthquake largestNewEarthquake
      = findLargestNewEarthquake(earthquakes);

    SharedPreferences prefs =
      PreferenceManager.getDefaultSharedPreferences(this);
    int minimumMagnitude = Integer.parseInt(
      prefs.getString(PreferencesActivity.PREF_MIN_MAG, "3"));

    if (largestNewEarthquake != null
      && largestNewEarthquake.getMagnitude() >= minimumMagnitude) {
      // Trigger a Notification
      broadcastNotification(quake);
    }
  }

  [... Existing onRunJob ...]
}
```

USING FIREBASE CLOUD MESSAGING

Firebase Cloud Messaging (FCM) can be used to "push" Notifications or data messages, directly from the cloud, or your server, to your app running on multiple devices. Using FCM you can remotely deliver simple Notifications, notify your app of updates to data on the server, or send data directly to your app.

Using FCM allows you to significantly lower the battery impact associated with synchronizing updates to your app (such as receiving new e-mail or changes to your calendar). This is an alternative to client-side polling, where your app wakes the device to check for server updates. Using a push model for updates ensures your app only wakes the device for updates when it knows they are available.

This approach also ensures more timely delivery of time-sensitive server-side messages, such as new chat messages, which users expect to be shown on their devices immediately.

Your apps can receive FCM messages even when they're not running, and while the device is asleep. FCM messages can display Notifications directly, or wake your app remotely, allowing them to respond by displaying a Notification of their own, updating their UI based on the received message data, or by starting a background job that performs a synchronization with the updated server data.

Before you can use Firebase Cloud Messaging in your app, the API must first be added as a Gradle dependency. Note that the version number in the following code snippet should be replaced with the latest version of Firebase Cloud Messaging:

```
dependencies {
  implementation 'com.google.firebase:firebase-messaging:17.0.0'
}
```

> **NOTE** *Firebase Cloud Messaging replaces the previously released "Google Cloud Messaging" (GCM) API. In this chapter we will describe features available only with FCM, and recommend that if you're using GCM, you upgrade to FCM as soon as possible.*
>
> *FCM is distributed as part of the Firebase SDK, meaning that it can be updated more frequently than the Android platform. We recommend that you always use the latest Firebase SDK; the latest version and documentation is available at* `firebase.google.com/docs/cloud-messaging/android/client`*.*

Triggering Notifications Remotely with Firebase Notifications

One of the most powerful features of Firebase Cloud Messaging is the Firebase Notifications API.

Built on top of Firebase Cloud Messaging, Firebase Notifications can be sent directly to your app from the Firebase Console at `console.firebase.google.com` (shown in Figure 11-9), without needing to write any server-side, or client-side, code.

FIGURE 11-9

Using the console, you can send Firebase Notifications to all of your users, a subset based on properties such as the app version, or an individual device—or group of devices—belonging to a particular user.

When creating a Firebase Notification, you can specify the message text that's displayed as the Notification's content title, the content text using the Notification title field, and a delivery time, as shown in Figure 11-10.

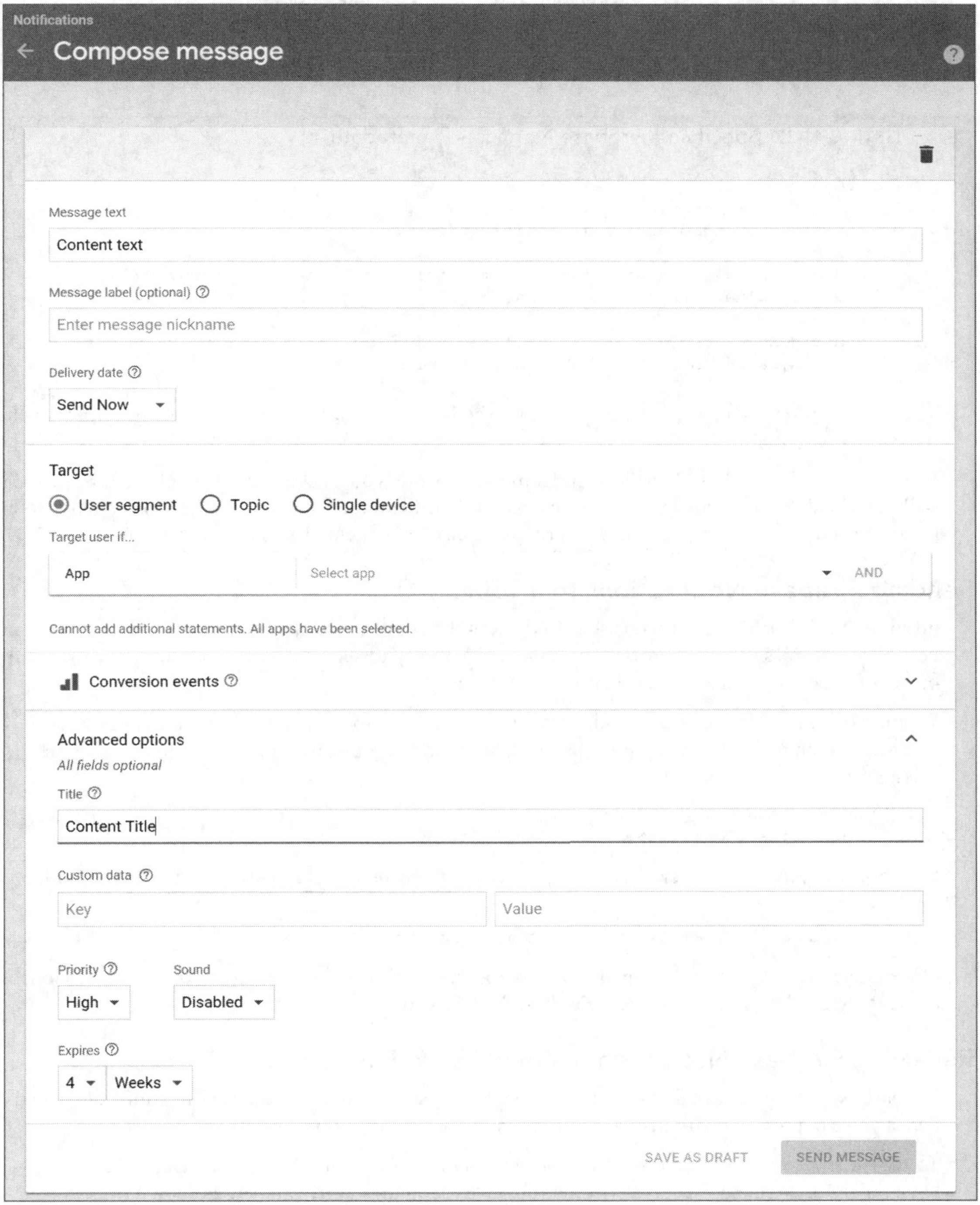
Notifications
Compose message
Message text
Content text
Message label (optional)
Enter message nickname
Delivery date
Send Now
Target
User segment
Topic
Single device
Target user if...
App
Select app
AND
Cannot add additional statements. All apps have been selected.
Conversion events
Advanced options
All fields optional
Title
Content Title
Custom data
Key
Value
Priority
Sound
High
Disabled
Expires
4
Weeks
SAVE AS DRAFT
SEND MESSAGE

FIGURE 11-10

Listing 11-27 shows the `meta-data` properties you should add to your application manifest to indicate the small icon, Notification color, and the Notification Channel that should be used for displaying received Firebase Notifications.

LISTING 11-27: Specifying Firebase Notification metadata

```
<meta-data
  android:name="com.google.firebase.messaging.default_notification_icon"
  android:value="@drawable/ic_notification" />
<meta-data
  android:name="com.google.firebase.messaging.default_notification_color"
  android:value="@color/colorPrimary" />
<meta-data
  android:name="com.google.firebase.messaging.default_notification_channel_id"
  android:value="@string/default_notification_channel" />
```

The content Intent, triggered if a user touches the Notification, is always set to your main launcher Activity.

When you send a Firebase Notification from the console, you can optionally enable sound, which will add the default Notification Ringtone to the Notification. Firebase Notifications default to high priority, so if your message is not time critical, consider reducing the priority to normal.

Sending Firebase Notifications to a Topic

Firebase Notifications can also be sent to devices that have subscribed to a specific topic. You can define these topics within your app, providing the ability to segment your users based on arbitrary business logic, app status, or explicit user selection.

Within your application, you can subscribe to a particular topic using the `subscribeToTopic` method, passing in a string representing a topic name to an instance of the `FirebaseMessaging` class:

```
FirebaseMessaging.getInstance()
  .subscribeToTopic("imminent_missile_attack");
```

Unsubscribing to a topic is similar, using the corresponding `unsubscribeFromTopic` method:

```
FirebaseMessaging.getInstance()
  .unsubscribeFromTopic("imminent_missile_attack");
```

Once an application has subscribed to a new topic, it will be available within the Firebase Console, and can be used as a target for new Firebase Notifications.

Receiving Firebase Notifications When in the Foreground

Firebase Notifications are designed to display Notifications, and like the Notifications described earlier in this chapter, they are displayed only when no Activities for your app are active.

To receive Firebase Notifications while your app is in the foreground, you must create a new `FirebaseMessagingService`, overriding the `onMessageReceived` handler, as shown in Listing 11-28.

LISTING 11-28: Handling the Firebase Notification callback

```java
public class MyFirebaseMessagingService
  extends FirebaseMessagingService {

  @Override
  public void onMessageReceived(RemoteMessage message) {
    RemoteMessage.Notification notification = message.getNotification();

    if (notification != null) {
      String title = notification.getTitle();
      String body = notification.getBody();

      // Post your own notification using NotificationCompat.Builder
      // or send the information to your UI
    }
  }
}
```

Within this callback you can extract the received Notification details and either create a Notification, or update your current Activity to display the message inline.

Once created, be sure to register the new Service in your manifest, including an Intent Filter for `com.google.firebase.MESSAGING_EVENT` as shown in Listing 11-29.

LISTING 11-29: Registering the FirebaseMessagingService

```xml
<service android:name=".MyFirebaseMessagingService>
  <intent-filter>
    <action android:name="com.google.firebase.MESSAGING_EVENT" />
  </intent-filter>
</service>
```

Receiving Data with Firebase Cloud Messaging

In addition to the Notifications described in the previous sections, Firebase Cloud Messaging (FCM) can also be used to send your app data in the form of key/value pairs.

The simplest case is by attaching custom data to a Firebase Notification, which will be received in the extras of the content Intent if the user selects your Notification, as shown in Listing 11-30.

LISTING 11-30: Receiving data from a Firebase Notification

```java
Intent intent = getIntent();
if (intent != null) {
  String value = intent.getStringExtra("your_key");
  // Change your behavior based on the value such as starting
  // the appropriate deep link activity
}
```

The same data is available from the `onMessageReceived` callback within your Firebase Messaging Service implementing using the `getData` method, as shown in Listing 11-31.

LISTING 11-31: Receiving data using the Firebase Messaging Service

```
@Override
public void onMessageReceived(RemoteMessage message) {
  Map<String,String> data = message.getData();

  if (data != null) {
    String value = data.get("your_key");

    // Post your own Notification using NotificationCompat.Builder
    // or send the information to your UI
  }
}
```

When building your own server or using the Firebase Admin API, it is possible to send a message that does not contain a Notification and only contains data. In these cases, every message results in a callback to `onMessageReceived`, whether your app is in the foreground or background, giving you complete control over your app's behavior and allowing you to use the full Notification API or trigger additional background processing.

> **NOTE** *More information on building a Firebase Cloud Messaging Server can be found at* `firebase.google.com/docs/cloud-messaging/server`, *and more information about the Firebase Admin API can be found at* `firebase.google` `.com/docs/cloud-messaging/admin`.

USING ALARMS

Alarms are a means of firing Intents at predetermined times. Unlike Handlers, alarms operate outside the scope of your application, so you can use them to trigger application events or actions even after your application has been closed.

Unlike the Job Scheduler, Firebase Job Dispatcher, and Work Manager, alarms can be set to trigger at exact times, making them particularly suitable for calendar events or alarm clocks.

> **NOTE** *For timing operations that occur only during the lifetime of your applications, using the* `Handler` *class in combination with* `postDelayed` *and Threads is a better approach than using alarms, as this allows Android better control over system resources. Alarms provide a mechanism to reduce the lifetime of your applications by moving scheduled events out of their control.*

Alarms remain active even when your app's process is killed; however, all alarms are canceled whenever the device is rebooted and must be manually re-created.

Alarm operations are handled through the `AlarmManager`, a system Service accessed via `getSystemService`, as follows:

```
AlarmManager alarmManager =
  (AlarmManager) getSystemService(Context.ALARM_SERVICE);
```

Creating, Setting, and Canceling Alarms

To create a new alarm that fires at a specific time, use the `setExactAndAllowWhileIdle` method and specify an alarm type of `RTC_WAKEUP`, a trigger time, and a Pending Intent to fire when the alarm triggers. If the trigger time you specify for the alarm occurs in the past, the alarm will be triggered immediately.

Listing 11-32 shows the Alarm-creation process.

LISTING 11-32: Creating an alarm that triggers at the top of the hour

```
// Get a reference to the Alarm Manager
AlarmManager alarmManager =
 (AlarmManager)getSystemService(Context.ALARM_SERVICE);

// Find the trigger time
Calendar calendar = Calendar.getInstance();
calendar.set(Calendar.MINUTE, 0);
calendar.set(Calendar.SECOND, 0);
calendar.set(Calendar.MILLISECOND, 0);
calendar.add(Calendar.HOUR, 1);
long time = calendar.getTimeInMillis();

// Create a Pending Intent that will broadcast and action
String ALARM_ACTION = "ALARM_ACTION";
Intent intentToFire = new Intent(ALARM_ACTION);
PendingIntent alarmIntent = PendingIntent.getBroadcast(this, 0,
  intentToFire, 0);

// Set the alarm
alarmManager.setExactAndAllowWhileIdle(AlarmManager.RTC_WAKEUP,
  time, alarmIntent);
```

When the alarm goes off, the Pending Intent you specified will be broadcast. Setting a second alarm using the same Pending Intent replaces the previous alarm.

To cancel an alarm, call `cancel` on the Alarm Manager, passing in the Pending Intent you no longer want to trigger, as shown in the Listing 11-33.

LISTING 11-33: Canceling an Alarm

```
alarmManager.cancel(alarmIntent);
```

If you have multiple exact alarms in your app (say, multiple upcoming alarm clocks), it's best practice to schedule only the *next* alarm. When your Broadcast Receiver fires, it should respond to the triggered alarm, and also set the next one. This ensures the system only needs to manage the minimal number of alarms at any given time.

Setting an Alarm Clock

Alarms, despite the name, are not user visible; only alarms set via setAlarmClock—as seen in Listing 11-34—are shown to the user, typically within the Clock app.

LISTING 11-34: Setting an Alarm Clock

```
// Create a Pending Intent that can be used to show or edit the alarm clock
// when the alarm clock icon is touched
Intent alarmClockDetails = new Intent(this, AlarmClockActivity.class);
PendingIntent showIntent = PendingIntent.getActivity(this, 0,
  alarmClockDetails, 0);

// Set the alarm clock, which will fire the alarmIntent at the set time
alarmManager.setAlarmClock(
  new AlarmManager.AlarmClockInfo(time, showIntent),
  alarmIntent);
```

You can retrieve the next scheduled alarm clock using the Alarm Manager's getNextAlarmClock method.

The system will exit the low-power doze-mode several minutes before an alarm clock fires, ensuring that apps have an opportunity to fetch fresh data before the users pick up their device.

INTRODUCING SERVICES

While short amounts of background work are best accomplished with a Broadcast Receiver, and the Job Service (or Work Manager) is preferred for batching background work, there are cases where your app will need to continue running well beyond the lifecycle of a particular Activity. These types of longer running operations that happen in the background are the focus for Services.

Most Services have their life cycle tied to other components; these are called bound Services. Many of the Services introduced in this book are extensions of bound Services, such as the JobService introduced earlier in this chapter. The Job Service is bound to the system, and unbound when your jobs have finished processing, allowing it to be terminated.

Services that have an unbounded life cycle may remain active when no Activity is visible; these are called "started Services." This type of Service should be started as a foreground Service which ensures that they are given a high priority by the system (to avoid being terminated due to low memory) and that the user is aware of the background work via a required notification.

> **WARNING** *Prior to Android 8.0 Oreo (API Level 26), started Services could be called from an idle/background app—and could continue running indefinitely. Android 8.0 introduced new restrictions to limit started Services, specifically limiting the ability to start Services to foreground apps, foreground Services, and to limited window of several minutes after an app moves to the background or after receiving a high-priority Firebase Cloud Messaging (FCM) message, receiving a broadcast, or executing a Pending Intent from a notification.*
>
> *For most use-cases, you should avoid using Services if an alternative exists—in particular the Job Scheduler is considered a best-practice alternative for scheduling operations to be performed while your app is in the background.*

Using Bound Services

Services can be bound to other components, with the latter maintaining a reference to an instance of the former, enabling you to make method calls on the running Service as you would on any other instantiated class.

Binding is useful for components that would benefit from a detailed interface with a Service, or where the Service lifetime is directly tied to its client component(s). This strong coupling is often used as the basis for a higher-level API, such as the `JobService`, that takes advantage of the direct communication available between two bound components. This same capability can be used within your own app to provide a detailed interface between two components, such as a Service and your Activity.

A bound Service has a life cycle that is intrinsically linked to one or more `ServiceConnection` objects representing application components to which it is bound; a bound Service will live until all of its clients unbind from it.

To support binding for a Service, implement the `onBind` method, returning the current instance of the Service being bound, as shown in Listing 11-35.

LISTING 11-35: Implementing a bound Service

```
public class MyBoundService extends Service {
  private final IBinder binder = new MyBinder();

  @Override
  public IBinder onBind(Intent intent) {
    return binder;
  }
```

continues

LISTING 11-35 *(continued)*

```
public class MyBinder extends Binder {
  MyBoundService getService() {
    return MyBoundService.this;
  }
}
}
```

The connection between the Service and another component is represented as a `Service-Connection`.

To bind a Service to another application component, you need to implement a new `Service-Connection`, overriding the `onServiceConnected` and `onServiceDisconnected` methods to get a reference to the Service instance after a connection has been established, as shown in Listing 11-36.

LISTING 11-36: Creating a Service Connection for Service binding

```
// Reference to the service
private MyBoundService serviceRef;

// Handles the connection between the service and activity
private ServiceConnection mConnection = new ServiceConnection() {
  public void onServiceConnected(ComponentName className,
                                 IBinder service) {
    // Called when the connection is made.
    serviceRef = ((MyBoundService.MyBinder)service).getService();
  }

  public void onServiceDisconnected(ComponentName className) {
    // Received when the service unexpectedly disconnects.
    serviceRef = null;
  }
};
```

To perform the binding, call `bindService` within your Activity, passing in an explicit Intent that selects the Service to bind to, and an instance of a `ServiceConnection` implementation.

You can also specify a number of binding flags, as shown in Listing 11-37. In this example you specify that the target Service should be created when the binding is initiated. Generally you do this in the `onCreate` of your Activity and the equivalent `unbindService` is done in `onDestroy`.

LISTING 11-37: Binding to a Service

```
// Bind to the service
Intent bindIntent = new Intent(MyActivity.this, MyBoundService.class);
bindService(bindIntent, mConnection, Context.BIND_AUTO_CREATE);
```

The last parameter to `bindService` is a flag that can be used and combined when binding a Service to an application:

➤ `BIND_ADJUST_WITH_ACTIVITY`—Causes the Service's priority to be adjusted based on the relative importance of the Activity to which it is bound. As a result, the run time will increase the priority of the Service when the Activity is in the foreground.

➤ `BIND_ABOVE_CLIENT` and `BIND_IMPORTANT`—Specify that the bound Service is so important to the binding client that it should become a foreground process when the client is in the foreground—in the case of `BIND_ABOVE_CLIENT`, you are specifying that the run time should terminate the Activity before the bound Service in cases of low memory.

➤ `BIND_NOT_FOREGROUND`—Ensures the bound Service is never brought to foreground priority. By default, the act of binding a Service increases its relative priority.

➤ `BIND_WAIVE_PRIORITY`—Indicates that binding the specified Service shouldn't alter its priority.

When the Service has been bound, all its public methods and properties are available through the `serviceBinder` object obtained from the `onServiceConnected` handler.

Android applications do not (normally) share memory, but in some cases your application may want to interact with (and bind to) Services running in different application processes.

You can communicate with a Service running in a different process by using Android Interface Definition Language (AIDL). AIDL defines the Service's interface in terms of OS-level primitives, allowing Android to transmit objects across process boundaries. AIDL definitions are described at `developer.android.com/guide/components/aidl.html`.

Creating a Started Service

A started Service can be started and stopped separate from any other application components. While the life cycle of a bound Service is explicitly tied to the components to which it's bound, the life cycle of a started Service must be explicitly managed.

Without intervention, a started Service may continue to take up system resources for several minutes, even if it is not actively doing any work, and its high priority will impact the system's efforts to terminate it (and the application that contains it.)

> **NOTE** *Before Android 8.0 Oreo (API Level 26), Services may continue running in the background indefinitely, consuming device resources and providing a worse user experience. Android 8.0 modified this behavior to stop running Services when their app has been in the background after several minutes. While this new behavior mitigates the impact of poorly managed background Services, it's critically important that you take steps to properly manage your Services regardless of the target platform.*

Started Services should be used sparingly, typically in cases where they provide user interactivity that happens without a visible user interface—such that it should continue running even after the user moves your app's Activities to the background. Wherever possible, it's best practice to use higher-level APIs that use bound Services—such as the Job Scheduler or Firebase Cloud Messaging—that take advantage of the Service architecture without requiring you to manually manage Service life cycles.

The most common use for creating your own started Service is to create foreground Services. Foreground Services run at the same priority as an active foreground Activity, ensuring that it will almost certainly not be removed due to low memory. This is useful if you're creating an application that interacts with the user without a UI always visible—such as a music player or turn-by-turn navigation.

Android also allows you to construct Services that are both bound and *started*. A common example is in audio playback, as described in Chapter 17, "Audio, Video, and Using the Camera."

Creating a Service

Every `Service` class must implement the `onBind` method, as shown in Listing 11-38. In the case of a started Service, this method can return `null`, indicating that no caller can bind to the Service.

LISTING 11-38: A skeleton Service class

```
import android.app.Service;
import android.content.Intent;
import android.os.IBinder;

public class MyService extends Service {
  @Override
  public IBinder onBind(Intent intent) {
    return null;
  }
}
```

To ensure your Service can be started and stopped only by your own application, add a `permission` attribute to its Service node in your application manifest:

```
<service android:enabled="true"
         android:name=".MyService"
         android:permission="com.paad.MY_SERVICE_PERMISSION"/>
```

This will require any third-party applications to include a uses-permission in their manifests in order to access your Service. You learn more about creating and using permissions in Chapter 20, "Advanced Android Development."

Starting and Stopping Services

To start a Service, call `startService`. Services require that you always use an explicit Intent by including the class to start. If the Service requires permissions that your application does not have, the call to `startService` will throw a `SecurityException`.

> **WARNING** *On Android 8.0 Oreo (API Level 26) and higher devices, calling* `startService` *while your app is in the background (typically from a Broadcast Receiver or a Pending Intent) will result in an* `IllegalStateException`. *You must instead use* `startForegroundService` *and call* `startForeground` *within the Service, within 5 seconds, to start a foreground Service while your app is in the background. See the "Creating Foreground Services" section for more details on foreground Services.*

Any information added to the Intent such as is demonstrated in Listing 11-39 will be available in the Service's `onStartCommand` method.

LISTING 11-39: Starting a Service

```
// Explicitly start My Service
Intent intent = new Intent(this, MyService.class);
intent.setAction("Upload");
intent.putExtra("TRACK_NAME", "Best of Chet Haase");
startService(intent);
```

To stop a Service, call `stopService`, using an Intent that defines the Service to stop (in the same way you specified which Service to start), as shown in Listing 11-40.

LISTING 11-40: Stopping a Service

```
// Stop a service explicitly.
stopService(new Intent(this, MyService.class));
```

Calls to `startService` do not nest, so a single call to `stopService` will terminate the running Service it matches, no matter how many times `startService` has been called.

Since Android 8.0, any non-foreground started Services will be automatically stopped by the system several minutes after your app goes into the background just as if you had called `stopService`. This prevents started Services from adversely affecting system performance long after the user puts the app in the background. If your Service needs to continue while your Activity is in the background, you will need to start a foreground Service as described later in this chapter.

Controlling Service Restart Behavior

The `onStartCommand` handler is called whenever a Service is started using `startService`, so it may be executed several times within a Service's lifetime. You should ensure that your Service accounts for this.

You should override the `onStartCommand` event handler to execute the task (or begin the ongoing operation) encapsulated by your Service. You can also specify your Service's restart behavior within this handler.

Like all components, Services are launched on the main Application Thread, meaning that any processing done in the onStartCommand handler will happen on the UI Thread. The standard pattern for implementing a Service is to create and run a new Thread or Async Task (as described earlier in this chapter) from onStartCommand to perform the processing in the background, and then stop the Service when it's been completed.

Listing 11-41 extends the skeleton code shown in Listing 11-38 by overriding the onStartCommand handler. Note that it returns a value that controls how the system will respond if the Service is restarted should it be killed by the run time before completing.

LISTING 11-41: Overriding Service restart behavior

```
@Override
public int onStartCommand(Intent intent, int flags, int startId) {
  // TODO Start your work on a background thread
  return START_STICKY;
}
```

This pattern lets onStartCommand complete quickly, and it enables you to control the restart behavior by returning one of the following Service constants:

➤ START_STICKY—This is the standard behavior and indicates that the system should call onStartCommand any time your Service restarts after being terminated by the run time. Note that on a restart the Intent parameter passed in to onStartCommand will be null.

This mode typically is used for Services that handle their own states and that are explicitly started and stopped as required (via startService and stopService).

➤ START_NOT_STICKY—This mode is used for Services that are started to process specific actions or commands. Typically, they will use stopSelf to terminate once that command has been completed.

Following termination by the run time, Services set to this mode restart only if there are pending start calls. If no startService calls have been made since the Service was terminated, the Service will be stopped without a call being made to onStartCommand.

➤ START_REDELIVER_INTENT—In some circumstances you will want to ensure that the commands you have requested from your Service are completed—for example, when timeliness is important.

This mode is a combination of the first two; if the Service is terminated by the run time, it will restart only if there are pending start calls *or* the process was killed prior to its calling stopSelf. In the latter case, a call to onStartCommand will be made, passing in the initial Intent whose processing did not properly complete.

Note that each mode requires you to explicitly stop your Service, through a call to stopService or stopSelf, when your processing has completed. Both methods are discussed in more detail later in this chapter.

The restart mode you specify in your onStartCommand return value will affect the parameter values passed in to it on subsequent calls. Initially, the Intent will be the parameter you passed in to startService to start your Service. After system-based restarts it will be either null, in the case of START_STICKY mode, or the original Intent if the mode is set to START_REDELIVER_INTENT.

You can use the flag parameter to discover how the Service was started. In particular, you determine if either of the following cases is true:

➤ START_FLAG_REDELIVERY—Indicates that the Intent parameter is a redelivery caused by the system run time's having terminated the Service before it was explicitly stopped by a call to stopSelf.

➤ START_FLAG_RETRY—Indicates that the Service has been restarted after an abnormal termination. It is passed in when the Service was previously set to START_STICKY.

Self-Terminating Services

By explicitly stopping the Service when your processing is complete, you allow the system to recover the resources otherwise required to keep it running.

When your Service has completed the actions or processing for which it was started, you should terminate it by making a call to stopSelf. You can call stopSelf either without a parameter to force an immediate stop, or by passing in a startId value to ensure processing has been completed for each instance of startService called so far.

Creating Foreground Services

In cases where your Service is interacting directly with the user, it may be appropriate to lift its priority to the equivalent of a foreground Activity. You can do this by setting your Service to run in the foreground by calling its startForeground method.

Because foreground Services are expected to be interacting directly with the user (for example by playing music), calls to startForeground must specify a Notification that will be displayed for as long as your Service is running in the foreground.

> **NOTE** *Moving a Service to the foreground effectively makes it impossible for the run time to kill it in order to free resources. Having multiple unkillable Services running simultaneously can make it extremely difficult for the system to recover from resource-starved situations.*
>
> *Use this technique only if it is necessary for your Service to function properly, and even then keep the Service in the foreground only as long as absolutely necessary.*

As the Notification cannot be manually dismissed by the user while your service is in the foreground, it's good practice to provide an action within the Notification that lets users cancel or stop the ongoing operation. It's also best practice to have the content Intent bring the users to an Activity where they can manage or cancel the ongoing Service.

When your Service no longer requires foreground priority, you can move it back to the background, and optionally remove the ongoing Notification, using the `stopForeground` method. The Notification will be canceled automatically if your Service stops or is terminated.

12

Implementing the Android Design Philosophy

WROX.COM CODE DOWNLOADS FOR THIS CHAPTER

The code downloads for this chapter are found at www.wrox.com. The code for this chapter is divided into the following major examples:

➤ Snippets_ch12.zip

➤ Earthquake_ch12.zip

INTRODUCING THE ANDROID DESIGN PHILOSOPHY

In Chapter 5, "Building User Interfaces," you learned the basics of creating user interfaces (UIs) in Android with an introduction to layouts and Views. These functional skills are the basis for building the UI for all apps, but creating a successful Android app requires a deeper understanding of Android's design principles, and the things to consider when building your UI.

This chapter introduces you to some best practices and techniques to create user experiences that are compelling and aesthetically pleasing on a diverse range of devices, and to an equally diverse range of users.

You are introduced to the best practices for creating resolution- and density-independent UIs, and how to use Drawables to create scalable image assets—including Vector Drawables.

Next you dive into the material design philosophy, which provides the foundation for all modern Android visual design. You learn how to apply the principles of material design to your app, including how to create screen elements that reflect physical sheets of paper, how to guide users through color and keylines, and how motion can provide continuity that will aid users' understanding.

Finally, you learn how to use three common material design UI elements: The app bar, cards—to visually group content and actions, and the Floating Action Buttons (FABs)—a high-profile circular button used to promote a single important action within your UI.

> **NOTE** *As a design philosophy material design is constantly evolving. To see the latest, complete details around material design—as well as further guidance for designing and implementing your UIs consistent with this philosophy, refer to the guidelines on the material design site at* `material.io/guidelines`.

DESIGNING FOR EVERY SCREEN

The first four Android handsets all featured identical 3.2" HVGA screens; making UI design relatively simple. Since then, tens of thousands of different Android devices have been created, resulting in thousands of different combinations of screen sizes and pixel densities—ranging from wearable devices, to phones, tablets, and even televisions. This has helped make Android incredibly popular with consumers, but creates a challenge for designers.

To provide a great experience for users no matter what Android device they own, it's important to create your UIs knowing that your applications can run on a broad variety of resolutions and physical screen sizes. It's impractical to attempt to create custom UI layouts for every possible variation, so in practice this means designing and building application interfaces with the expectation that they be capable of being used on an infinitely varied set of devices.

That means supplying image assets that can be scaled where possible, and in a variety of pixel densities where not. It means creating layouts that can scale within a known range of resolutions, and defining multiple layouts optimized for a variety of different size ranges and interaction models.

The following sections describe the range of screens you need to consider, and how to support them, before detailing some best practices for ensuring that your applications are resolution- and density-independent—and optimized for a range of different screen sizes and layouts.

> **NOTE** *The Android Developer site includes some excellent tips for supporting multiple screen types. You can find this documentation at* `d.android.com/guide/practices/screens_support.html`.

Resolution Independence

A display's pixel density is calculated as a function of the physical screen size and resolution, referring to the number of physical pixels on a display relative to the physical size of that display. It's typically measured in dots per inch (dpi).

Using Density-Independent Pixels

As a result of the variations in screen size and resolution for Android devices, the same number of pixels can correspond to different physical sizes on different devices based on the screen's DPI.

As you learned in Chapter 5, "Building User Interfaces," this makes it impossible to create consistent layouts by specifying pixels. Instead, Android uses density-independent pixels (dp) to specify screen dimensions that scale to appear the same on screens of the same physical dimensions but with different pixel densities.

In practical terms, one density-independent pixel is equivalent to one pixel on a 160dpi screen. For example, a line specified as 2dp wide appears as 3 pixels on a display with 240dpi (or 7 pixels on a Pixel XL).

When specifying your user interface, you should always use density-independent pixels, avoiding specifying any layout dimensions, View sizes, or Drawable dimensions using raw pixel values.

In addition to dp units, Android also uses a scalable pixel (sp) for the special case of font sizes. Scalable pixels use the same base unit as density-independent pixels but can be further scaled based on the user's preferred text size.

Resource Qualifiers for Pixel Density

Chapter 4, "Understanding the Android Manifest, Gradle Build Files, and Externalizing Resources" introduced you to the Android resource framework, which uses a parallel directory structure for including resources such as Drawables within your app.

The `res/drawable` directory is suitable for graphics that work on all pixel densities such as Vector Drawables and other scalable graphic assets detailed later in this chapter. It is strongly recommended that you use these types of graphics whenever possible as they will automatically scale to all pixel densities, without the requirement that you provide additional assets. This helps reduce your app's size, as well as improving forward compatibility.

There will be circumstances where scalable graphics can't be used, and you must include bitmap images in your app. Scaling bitmap images can result in either lost detail (when scaling down) or pixilation (when scaling up). To ensure that your UI is crisp, clear, and devoid of artifacts, you can create and include image assets optimized for each pixel density category, including:

➤ `res/drawable-mdpi`—Medium-density resources for screens approximately 160pi

➤ `res/drawable-hdpi`—High-density resources for screens approximately 240dpi

➤ `res/drawable-xhdpi`—Extra-high density resources for screens approximately 320dpi

➤ `res/drawable-xxhdpi`—Extra-extra-high density resources for screens approximately 480dpi

➤ `res/drawable-xxxhdpi`—Extra-extra-extra-high density resources for screens approximately 640dpi

➤ `res/drawable-nodpi`—Used for resources that must not be scaled regardless of the host screen's density

Keep in mind that including multiple sizes of bitmaps does have a cost in the form of an increased size of your application. In addition, while these pixel density buckets give you a rough set of densities to target, there are devices that exist between these generic buckets; where a specific resolution asset is unavailable, Android will automatically scale your bitmaps for these devices, preferring to scale down.

Supporting and Optimizing for Different Screen Sizes

Android devices come in countless shapes and sizes (though so far mainly quadrilaterals and circles), so when designing your UI it's important to ensure that your layouts not only *support* different screen sizes, orientations, and aspect ratios, but also that they're accordingly optimized.

It's neither practical nor desirable to create a layout specific to each possible screen configuration; instead, best practice is to take a two-phased approach:

➤ Ensure that all your layouts are capable of scaling within a reasonable set of bounds.

➤ Create a set of alternative layouts whose bounds overlap, such that all possible screen configurations are covered.

This approach is similar to that taken by most websites and desktop applications. After a fling with fixed-width pages in the '90s, most websites now scale to fit the available space on desktop browsers and offer an alternative CSS definition to provide an optimized layout based on the available window size.

The same is true for mobile devices. After those first four devices, developers were forced to use the same approach of flexible layouts. We now create optimized layouts for different screen size ranges, each capable of scaling to account for variation within that range.

Creating Scalable Layouts

The layouts provided by the framework were described in detail in Chapter 5, "Building User Interfaces." They are designed to support the implementation of UIs that scale to fit the available space. In all cases, you should avoid defining the location of your layout elements in absolute terms.

In most cases the Constraint Layout offers the most powerful and flexible alternative, supporting complex layouts that would otherwise require you to nest layouts.

For very simple UIs, the Linear Layout can be used to represent a simple column or row that fills the available width or height of the screen, respectively, whereas the Relative Layout can be used to define the position of each UI element relative to the parent Activity and other elements.

When defining the height or width of your scalable UI elements (such as Buttons and Text Views) it's good practice to avoid providing specific dimensions. Instead, you can define the height and width of Views using `wrap_content` or `match_parent` attributes, as appropriate:

```
<Button
  android:id="@+id/button"
  android:layout_width="match_parent"
  android:layout_height="wrap_content"
  android:text="@string/buttonText"
/>
```

The `wrap_content` flag enables the View to define its size based on the amount of space potentially available to it, whereas the `match_parent` flag enables the element to expand as necessary to fill the available space.

Deciding which screen element should expand (or contract) when the screen size changes is one of the most important factors in optimizing your layouts for variable screen dimensions.

Optimizing Layouts for Different Screen Types

In addition to providing layouts that scale, you should consider creating alternative layout definitions optimized for different screen sizes.

There is a significant difference in screen space available on a 3" QVGA smart phone display compared to a 4K 10" tablet. Similarly, and particularly for devices with significant aspect ratios, a layout that works well viewed in landscape mode might be unsuitable when the device is rotated into portrait.

Creating a layout that scales to accommodate the space available is a good first step; it's also good practice to consider ways that you can take advantage of the extra space (or consider the effect of reduced space) to create a better user experience.

With the introduction of multi-window support in Android 7.0 Nougat (API Level 24), the screen size available to your app might be only a fraction of the total screen size. This, combined with a spectrum of devices that include large phones and small tablets, makes it best practice to optimize your layouts based on the available space, rather than designing for a particular category of device.

The Android resource system allows you to build alternate layouts and provide alternate dimensions. Your default layouts and dimensions should be placed in the `res/layout` and `res/values` resource directories—these will be used when there is the smallest amount of screen-space available. You can then provide alternate layouts and dimensions by using additional resource qualifiers for larger screens.

For most apps, the available width is going to be the most influential factor affecting your layout design—a single column of elements might look fine on a phone in portrait, but becomes increasingly sub-optimal as the width increases, first through a rotation into landscape, and further still on a larger tablet device.

This leads to a natural system of "breaking points"—specific widths at which scaling stops being effective and you need a more fundamental change to your layout. To support this, the Android resource system provides the `w` resource qualifier to indicate a minimum supported width.

A layout in the `res/layout-w600dp` will be used instead of one in `res/layout` when the available width is over 600dp.

> **NOTE** *600dp is one of the most common breakpoints as it is the first width you would seriously consider having two levels of content hierarchy (say, a list of items and a single item's details) on screen at the same time.*

In some cases, your UI requires a minimum height—such as in cases where you have a vertically scrolling container of full-bleed images. With insufficient height, users might not be able to ever actually see a full image on screen at once! Android provides the `h` resource qualifier for this purpose; for example, `res/layout-h480dp`.

Using height and width modifiers allows you to account for different devices, and rotation from landscape to portrait on any given device. In addition to these modifiers, the `sw` resource qualifier can be used to handle the smallest width on the device.

Unlike width and height, smallest width does not change when a device is rotated—it is always the smallest value of width and height. This is incredibly useful in building a rotation-insensitive UI—a concept where all operations are available in every orientation and that the basic usage patterns are consistent across rotation.

This is even more important in multi-window mode, where "landscape" and "portrait" are not tied to the device's orientation, but whether the available width is greater than the height (landscape) or vice versa (portrait).

Figure 12-1 shows how each of the values described previously correspond to a real device in standard and multi-window mode.

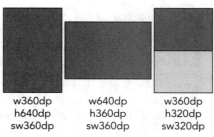

w360dp	w640dp	w360dp
h640dp	h360dp	h320dp
sw360dp	sw360dp	sw320dp

FIGURE 12-1

Building a rotation-insensitive UI, you ensure that small adjustments to the size of your app do not result in large UI changes that could be disorienting to users. A natural ordering occurs when structuring your layouts and dimensions where larger structural UI changes are tied to smallest width and smaller changes are tied to width or height breakpoints. As with any other resource qualifier, you can combine these qualifiers, allowing you to provide a layout optimized for use when a screen is a particular width now, and has the possibility of being no smaller than another value when rotated.

For example, the following resource folder is optimized for a display 800dp wide, provided that when rotated, the screen width will be no smaller than 600dp, as shown in Figure 12-2:

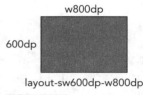
layout-sw600dp-w800dp
FIGURE 12-2

`res/layout-sw600dp-w800dp`

Layouts in this folder would share the same larger structure of the UI with layouts in the `res/layout-sw600dp` (to provide a rotation-insensitive UI) but would offer some smaller structural changes to take advantage of the extra width.

Creating Scalable Graphics Assets

Android includes a number of simple Drawable resource types that can be defined entirely in XML. These include the `ColorDrawable`, `ShapeDrawable`, and `VectorDrawable` classes. These resources are stored in the `res/drawable` folder.

When these Drawables are defined in XML, and you specify their attributes using density-independent pixels, these Drawables can be scaled dynamically at run time to display correctly, without scaling artifacts, regardless of screen size, resolution, or pixel density.

As you will see in Chapter 14, "Advanced Customization of Your User Interface," you can use these Drawables in combination with transformative Drawables and composite Drawables. Together, they can result in dynamic, scalable UI elements that require fewer resources and appear crisp on any screen.

Android also supports NinePatch PNG images, described later in this section, that enable you to mark the parts of a bitmap image that can be stretched.

Color Drawables

A `ColorDrawable`, the simplest of the XML-defined Drawables, enables you to specify an image asset based on a single solid color. Color Drawables, such as this solid red Drawable, are defined as XML files using the `color` tag in the `res/drawable` folder:

```
<color xmlns:android="http://schemas.android.com/apk/res/android"
    android:color="#FF0000"
/>
```

Shape Drawables

Shape Drawable resources let you define simple primitive shapes by defining their dimensions, background, and stroke/outline using the `shape` tag.

Each shape consists of a type (specified via the `shape` attribute), attributes that define the dimensions of that shape, and subnodes to specify padding, stroke (outline), and background color values.

Android currently supports the following shape types as values for the `shape` attribute:

➤ `line`—A horizontal line spanning the width of the parent View. The line's width and style are described by the shape's stroke.

➤ `oval`—A simple oval shape.

➤ `rectangle`—A simple rectangular shape. Also supports a `corners` subnode that uses a `radius` attribute to create a rounded rectangle.

➤ `ring`—Supports the `innerRadius` and `thickness` attributes to let you specify the inner radius of the ring shape and its thickness, respectively. Alternatively, you can use `inner RadiusRatio` and `thicknessRatio` to define the ring's inner radius and thickness, respectively, as a proportion of its width (where an inner radius of a quarter of the width would use the value 4).

Use the `stroke` subnode to specify an outline for your shapes using `width` and `color` attributes.

You can also include a `padding` node to automatically inset the contents of the View that uses this Shape Drawable, to prevent overlapping between the content and the shape's outline.

More usefully, you can include a subnode to specify the background color. The simplest case involves using the `solid` node, including the `color` attribute, to define a solid background color.

The following snippet shows a rectangular Shape Drawable with a solid fill, rounded edges, 5dp outline, and 10dp of padding. Figure 12-3 shows the result.

FIGURE 12-3

```xml
<?xml version="1.0" encoding="utf-8"?>
<shape xmlns:android="http://schemas.android.com/apk/res/android"
  android:shape="rectangle">
    <solid
      android:color="#f0600000"/>
    <stroke
      android:width="5dp"
      android:color="#00FF00"/>
    <corners
      android:radius="15dp" />
    <padding
      android:left="10dp"
      android:top="10dp"
      android:right="10dp"
      android:bottom="10dp"
    />
</shape>
```

Vector Drawables

Android 5.0 Lollipop (API Level 21) introduced the `VectorDrawable` to define more complicated, custom shapes. The Vector Support Library is also available for using Vector Drawables within apps supporting devices running at least Android 4.0 Ice Cream Sandwich (API Level 14).

> **NOTE** *For older versions of Android that don't support Vector Drawables, Vector Asset Studio can, at build time, turn your Vector Drawables into multiple bitmaps optimized for each screen density bucket.*

Vector Drawables are defined using the `vector` tag, and require four additional attributes. You must specify `height` and `width` to indicate the intrinsic size of the Drawable (its default size), and the `viewportWidth` and `viewportHeight` to define the size of the virtual canvas that the vector's `path` will be drawn on.

While you'll typically create at least one Vector Drawable with identical for height/width and their viewport equivalents, it's often useful to create duplicate Vector Drawables with different height/ width values.

This is because the Android system creates a single bitmap cache for each Vector Drawable to optimize for the re-drawing performance. If you refer to the same Vector Drawable multiple times, specifying different sizes, the bitmap will be re-created and redrawn every time a different size is required. As a result, it is more efficient to create multiple Vector Drawables, one for each required size.

Within the `vector` tag, the shape is defined using the `path` element. The color of the shape is determined by the `fillColor` attribute, while the `pathData` attribute uses the same syntax as SVG path elements to define arbitrary shapes or lines. The following snippet creates the shape shown in Figure 12-4:

FIGURE 12-4

```xml
<?xml version="1.0" encoding="utf-8"?>
<vector xmlns:android="http://schemas.android.com/apk/res/android"
  android:height="256dp"
  android:width="256dp"
  android:viewportWidth="32"
  android:viewportHeight="32">
  <path
    android:fillColor="#8f00"
    android:pathData="M20.5,9.5
                      c-1.955,0,-3.83,1.268,-4.5,3
                      c-0.67,-1.732,-2.547,-3,-4.5,-3
                      C8.957,9.5,7,11.432,7,14
                      c0,3.53,3.793,6.257,9,11.5
                      c5.207,-5.242,9,-7.97,9,-11.5
                      C25,11.432,23.043,9.5,20.5,9.5z" />
</vector>
```

The `strokeColor` and `strokeWidth` attributes indicate the color and width of the shape's outline—or if no fill color is specified, the color and width of the line being drawn.

Android Studio includes a tool called the Vector Asset Studio (shown in Figure 12-5) accessible through the New ⇨ Vector Asset menu item, which includes support for importing Scalable Vector Graphic (SVG) and Adobe Photoshop Document (PSD) files into your project as Vector Drawable resources.

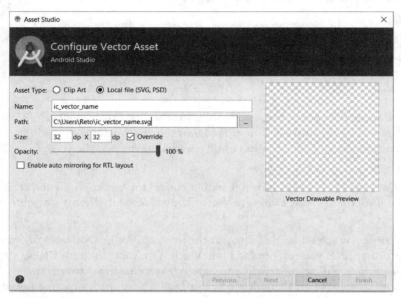

FIGURE 12-5

You can find more details on the SVG path elements at
`www.w3.org/TR/SVG/paths.html#PathData`.

Animating Vector Drawables

Vector Drawables also support animations through the aptly named `AnimatedVectorDrawable` class. When building an animation, it is important to set the `name` on each `path` that you plan to animate—this allows you to reference it when building the animation. If you have multiple paths that need to be animated together, you can put all of the paths within a named `group` element and scale, rotate, or translate all of the paths simultaneously.

When creating an Animated Vector Drawable, you can include the Vector Drawable directly within its definition:

```
<animated-vector xmlns:android="http://schemas.android.com/apk/res/android"
  xmlns:aapt="http://schemas.android.com/aapt">
  <aapt:attr name="android:drawable">
    <vector
        android:height="256dp"
        android:width="256dp"
        android:viewportWidth="32"
        android:viewportHeight="32">
      <path
        android:name="heart"
```

```
            [... Vector Drawable path definition ...]
          />
        </vector>
      </aapt:attr>
      [... Remainder of Animated Vector Drawable definition ...]
    </animated-vector>
```

Alternatively, you can reference an existing Vector Drawable by adding a `drawable` attribute to the root `animated-vector` element:

```
<animated-vector xmlns:android="http://schemas.android.com/apk/res/android"
  android:drawable="@drawable/vectordrawable">
  [... Remainder of Animated Vector Drawable definition ...]
</animated-vector>
```

You can then add a series of animations by adding `target` elements, where the `name` attribute within the target element specifies the `name` in the Vector Drawable that the animation applies to:

```
<animated-vector xmlns:android="http://schemas.android.com/apk/res/android"
  xmlns:aapt="http://schemas.android.com/aapt">
  <aapt:attr name="android:drawable">
    <vector
        android:height="256dp"
        android:width="256dp"
        android:viewportWidth="32"
        android:viewportHeight="32">
      <path
        android:name="heart"
        [... Vector Drawable path definition ...]
      />
    </vector>
  </aapt:attr>

  <target android:name="heart">
    [... Animation definition goes here ...]
  </target>

</animated-vector>
```

The `objectAnimator` node allows you to define a simple animation. The timing of each animation is determined by the `duration` in milliseconds and an optional `startOffset` (also in milliseconds). The `path` or `group` attribute that is being animated is set by the `propertyName` attribute. The initial and final values are set by the `valueFrom` and `valueTo` attributes, respectively, as shown in Listing 12-1. Figure 12-6 shows the end state of the animation.

FIGURE 12-6

LISTING 12-1: A simple Animated Vector Drawable

```
<?xml version="1.0" encoding="utf-8"?>
<animated-vector xmlns:android="http://schemas.android.com/apk/res/android"
  xmlns:aapt="http://schemas.android.com/aapt">
  <aapt:attr name="android:drawable">
    <vector
```

continues

LISTING 12-1 *(continued)*

```
        android:height="256dp"
        android:width="256dp"
        android:viewportWidth="32"
        android:viewportHeight="32">
        <path
          android:name="heart"
          android:fillColor="#8f00"
          android:pathData="M20.5,9.5
                        c-1.955,0,-3.83,1.268,-4.5,3
                        c-0.67,-1.732,-2.547,-3,-4.5,-3
                        C8.957,9.5,7,11.432,7,14
                        c0,3.53,3.793,6.257,9,11.5
                        c5.207,-5.242,9,-7.97,9,-11.5
                        C25,11.432,23.043,9.5,20.5,9.5z" />
    </vector>
  </aapt:attr>

  <target android:name="heart">
    <aapt:attr name="android:animation">
      <objectAnimator
        android:duration="1000"
        android:propertyName="fillColor"
        android:valueFrom="#8f00"
        android:valueTo="#ffc0cb"
        android:interpolator="@android:interpolator/fast_out_slow_in" />
    </aapt:attr>
  </target>
</animated-vector>
```

The `interpolator` attribute lets you control the rate of change between values within the animation. If you have multiple animations that share the same timing, you can include them all in a `set` element.

Within your application, you retrieve a reference to Animated Vector Drawables using the `ContextCompat.getDrawable` method, passing in the resource ID (the filename) of your Animated Vector Drawable:

```
AnimatedVectorDrawable avd =
  (AnimatedVectorDrawable)ContextCompat.getDrawable(context,
                                      R.drawable.avd);
```

If you are using the Android Support Library to support Animated Vector Drawables, you must instead use its associated `create` method:

```
AnimatedVectorDrawableCompat avd =
  (AnimatedVectorDrawableCompat)AnimatedVectorDrawableCompat.create(
                                      context,
                                      R.drawable.avd);
```

In either case, you can then use the Animated Vector Drawable in any operation that accepts a `Drawable`, and call `start` to trigger the animation:

```
imageView.setImageDrawable(avd);
avd.start();
```

NinePatch Drawables

NinePatch (or stretchable) images are PNG files that mark the parts of an image that can be stretched. They're stored in your `res/drawable` folders with names ending in `.9.png` extensions:

```
res/drawable/stretchable_background.9.png
```

NinePatches use a one-pixel border to define the area of the image that can be stretched if the image is enlarged. This makes them particularly useful for creating backgrounds for Views or Activities that may have a variable size.

FIGURE 12-7

To create a NinePatch, draw single-pixel black lines that represent stretchable areas along the left and top borders of your image, as shown in Figure 12-7.

The unmarked sections won't be resized, and the relative size of each of the marked sections remains the same as the image size changes, as shown in Figure 12-8.

FIGURE 12-8

To simplify the process of creating NinePatch images for your application, Android Studio includes a WYSIWIG Draw 9-Patch tool. To use it, right-click the PNG image you'd like to create a NinePatch image from, then click "Create 9-patch file."

INTRODUCING MATERIAL DESIGN

Material design is Google's design philosophy and language for mobile platforms and the web. It provides a set of guidelines and specifications that offer guidance for creating a modern look and feel for applications.

Material design became the standard design used within the Android system and core applications in Android 5.0 Lollipop (API Level 21), but many of its related APIs and design components are now available in the Android Support Library. As a result, material design is the de facto design standard for all Android devices, irrespective of API level.

As an evolving design philosophy, it's impossible to cover the full breadth of material design within the confines of this book. However, we will build an understanding of the core concepts behind material design, and introduce some of the most common iconic components that embody its philosophy.

In Chapter 13, "Implementing a Modern Android User Experience," we'll return to material design and explore the practicalities of implementing a design using its underlying philosophy.

> **NOTE** *Material design is an ever-evolving design language. Whether you are an Android designer or developer, consider reading through the latest, full material design specifications at* `material.io/guidelines`.

Thinking in Terms of Paper and Ink

The foundational principle of material design is "material is the metaphor." While acknowledging that everything visible on screen is a digital creation, our goal is to make this digital environment parallel our expectations of real-world materials.

In material design, every View displayed is imagined as being placed on a physical material—a conceptual piece of paper. Each sheet of virtual material, just like a piece of paper, is flat and 1dp thick. Just like real-world material, where you can stack paper, each piece of virtual material is imagined in a 3D environment, and has an elevation (defined using the `elevation` attribute) that is used to give your finished layout the appearance of depth.

Views with a higher elevation are shown above those at a lower elevation, and should cast shadows on the Views below them.

As a result elevation plays a meaningful role in the structural design of your UI layout, with global navigation elements being placed at a higher elevation than the Activity-specific content. Many of the built-in navigation elements discussed in Chapter 13 have their default elevations set according to this principle.

Building on the core material metaphor, material design prescribes that everything drawn in your UI should be as ink on the material surfaces.

This concept is readily apparent when handling touch feedback. Whenever a material design button is touched, it produces a ripple centered on the location the user has touched. The default touch feedback provided by the backgrounds of `selectableItemBackground` produces the same ripple, making it simple to apply to your own touchable screen elements as shown in Listing 12-2.

LISTING 12-2: A material design ripple layout

```xml
<?xml version="1.0" encoding="utf-8"?>
<LinearLayout xmlns:android="http://schemas.android.com/apk/res/android"
  android:layout_width="match_parent"
  android:layout_height="match_parent"
  android:orientation="vertical"
  android:clickable="true"
  android:background="?attr/selectableItemBackground">
  <TextView
    android:layout_width="match_parent"
    android:layout_height="wrap_content"
    android:text="Click me!" />
  <TextView
```

```
            android:layout_width="match_parent"
            android:layout_height="wrap_content"
            android:text="Clicking anywhere on the layout produces a ripple effect" />
</LinearLayout>
```

Just like ink, the ripple only flows to the material it is on. However, if your clickable layout is just a part of a larger piece of continuous material, consider using `selectableItemBackgroundBorderless` to allow the ripple of ink to spread outside of the boundaries of the single View.

Using Color and Keylines as Guides

The second principle of material design is to be bold, graphic, and intentional.

Every element of your design should be a deliberate choice not just to look good, but to enforce the hierarchy and importance of each element of your app in order to assist and guide users on their journey within your app.

Using Color in Your App

One of the most bold design choices you can make is your use of color.

A monochromatic user interface runs the risk of being more than a little bland, but will also make it difficult for users to identify the most significant Views with which they'll likely interact. A design that uses every color of the spectrum may be striking, but can also be jarring and just as difficult to understand as a black-and-white UI.

A better approach is to construct a complementary color palette that you'll to use throughout your app. This color palette should be based on a primary—signature—color, a darker variant, and an accent color.

Material design encourages you to always put the content first. Having a strong primary color can act as subtle branding, making the app feel unique and distinct—without explicit branding elements that would otherwise occupy valuable screen real estate that should be dedicated to displaying your content.

The darker variant of your primary color is commonly used to color the status bar, to visually separate it from your application's content.

The accent color should be distinct, but complementary, to your primary color; it's used to draw attention to important Views within your UI, such as Floating Action Buttons, links within body text, or as a highlight color on a text entry View.

> **NOTE** *To see examples of how to select colors, see the material design color palettes at* `material.io/guidelines/style/color.html#color-color-palette.`

You can integrate these colors into your app by building a custom theme. A theme is a collection of attributes that you can apply to an Activity using the `android:theme` attribute of your Activity node, or to all your app's Activities using the Application element within your Application manifest.

A simple theme that incorporates the color palette just described would consist of a `res/values/colors.xml` file containing a `colorPrimary`, `colorPrimaryDark`, and a `colorAccent`.

These colors are then used to construct a theme within a `res/values/styles.xml` resource:

```xml
<?xml version="1.0" encoding="utf-8"?>
<resources>
  <style name="AppTheme" parent="Theme.AppCompat">
    <item name="colorPrimary">@color/primary</item>
    <item name="colorPrimaryDark">@color/primary_dark</item>
    <item name="colorAccent">@color/accent</item>
  </style>
</resources>
```

The theme can then be applied to your entire application by adding `android:theme="@style/AppTheme"` in your application element in the manifest:

```xml
<application
  android:theme="@style/AppTheme">

  [... Remaining application node ...]
</application>
```

This will result in the app bar and status bar along the top of each activity colored according to the `colorPrimary` and `colorPrimaryDark`, respectively.

In the preceding snippet, we use a parent theme of `Theme.AppCompat`—this theme is provided by the Android Support Library and includes a consistent base for applying a material-style theme for all API levels, without you needing to define each element yourself.

We go into more details on how themes can be used in your app in Chapter 13.

Aligning to Keylines

Reducing the visual noise of your layout is vital for drawing attention to its critical elements. To help, material design incorporates techniques from traditional print design—one of the most important being aligning content to keylines.

A keyline is a vertical or horizontal guideline used to align elements, particularly text. By aligning everything to a set of keylines, users are able to easily scan your app's layout and content to find what they're looking for.

A number of keylines and dimensions are specified by the material design specifications. The most important are the horizontal margins found on the edges of the screen, and the content's left margin from the screen edge, shown in Figure 12-9.

The horizontal margins defined by material design for mobile devices is 16dp, while for tablets it expands to 24dp. The content left margin from the screen edge is 72dp on mobile and 80dp on tablets.

With more visual space on larger devices, having a larger margin allows you to make better use of the available space, and prevents content from appearing too close to the edge of the screen.

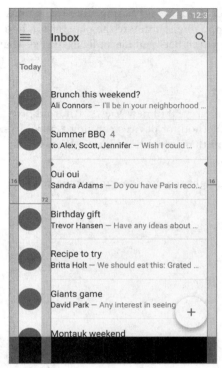

FIGURE 12-9

Note that the content left margin applies primarily to text—ensuring it's aligned with the Toolbar's title. Icons and round avatars should be aligned with the 16dp horizontal margin.

> **NOTE** *For more details on the keylines that make up material design, see* `material.io/guidelines/layout/metrics-keylines.html`.

Continuity Through Motion

The third, and final, principle of material design is that motion provides meaning.

When experimenting with motion it's tempting to move everything around, simply because you can. Don't. Unnecessary motion is distracting at best, and frustrating at worst. No one wants to chase a touch target around the screen. Material design requires a disciplined approach to using motion within your UI, with each movement intentionally designed to guide the user's eyes and attention.

The ripple animation described earlier is itself considered a form of motion, designed to provide feedback to the user. It's a common pattern in material design that a user's actions initiate motion.

The Animated Vector Drawables, discussed earlier in this chapter, are an example of how actions and feedback can be linked. For example, an audio player app might animate the play button into a pause button using an Animated Vector Drawable to transition between mutually exclusive—but tightly related—states.

Animating View Visibility Using the Reveal Effect

To provide visual continuity for user actions that result in the reveal of new Views, Android provides the `ViewAnimationUtils.createCircularReveal` method for devices running Android 5.0 Lollipop (API Level 21) or higher. This creates an animation that reveals (or hides) a View by clipping it within a circle with a growing (or shrinking) radius.

Depending on where you center the reveal animation, this might require some minor math as shown in Listing 12-3.

LISTING 12-3: Using a circular reveal to show a View

```
final View view = findViewById(R.id.hidden_view);

// Center the reveal on the middle of the View
int centerX = view.getWidth() / 2;
int centerY = view.getHeight() / 2;

// Determine what radius circle will cover the entire View
float coveringRadius = (float) Math.hypot(centerX, centerY);

// Build the circular reveal
Animator anim = ViewAnimationUtils.createCircularReveal(
  view,
  centerX,
  centerY,
  0,              // initial radius
  coveringRadius  // final covering radius
);

// Set the View to VISIBLE before starting the animation
view.setVisibility(View.VISIBLE);
anim.start();
```

The same approach can be used in reverse to hide a View as shown in Listing 12-4.

LISTING 12-4: Using a circular reveal to hide a View

```
// Build the circular hide animation
Animator anim = ViewAnimationUtils.createCircularReveal(
  view,
  centerX,
  centerY,
  coveringRadius,    // initial radius
  0                  // final radius
```

```
        );

        anim.addListener(new AnimatorListenerAdapter() {
          @Override
          public void onAnimationEnd(Animator animation) {
            // Set the view to invisible only at the end of the animation
            view.setVisibility(View.INVISIBLE);
          }
        });

        anim.start();
```

Building Shared Element Activity Transitions

Typically the largest transitions within your app will be moving between Activities. Android 5.0 Lollipop (API Level 21) introduced shared element Activity transitions that provide visual continuity for critical Views that exist in both Activities—dynamically transitioning them from their initial position in the first Activity, to their final position in the next.

To take advantage of shared element Activity transitions, add the `android:transitionName` attribute to Views within the layouts of both Activities to link the Views for animation:

```xml
<?xml version="1.0" encoding="utf-8"?>
<LinearLayout xmlns:android="http://schemas.android.com/apk/res/android"
    android:layout_width="match_parent"
    android:layout_height="wrap_content"
    android:orientation="vertical">
  <ImageView
    android:id="@+id/avatar_view"
    android:transitionName="avatar_view_transition"
    android:layout_width="match_parent"
    android:layout_height="wrap_content"/>
  <TextView
    android:id="@+id/username_view"
    android:transitionName="username_view_transition"
    android:layout_width="match_parent"
    android:layout_height="wrap_content"/>
</LinearLayout>

<?xml version="1.0" encoding="utf-8"?>
<LinearLayout xmlns:android="http://schemas.android.com/apk/res/android"
    android:layout_width="match_parent"
    android:layout_height="wrap_content"
    android:orientation="horizontal">
  <ImageView
    android:id="@+id/avatar_view"
    android:transitionName="avatar_view_transition"
    android:layout_width="wrap_content"
    android:layout_height="match_parent"/>
  <TextView
    android:id="@+id/username_view"
    android:transitionName="username_view_transition"
    android:layout_width="wrap_content"
    android:layout_height="match_parent"/>
</LinearLayout>
```

To activate an animated transition between two Activities, pass in a `Bundle` built from the `makeSceneTransitionAnimation` method of the `ActivityOptionsCompat` class, passing it `Pair` instances representing the Views in your current Activity's layout, and the `transitionName` they are transitioning to (found by passing each View to the `ViewCompat.getTransitionName` method) as shown in Listing 12-5.

LISTING 12-5: Initiating a shared element Activity transition

```
Intent intent = new Intent(context, SecondActivity.class);

Bundle bundle = ActivityOptionsCompat.makeSceneTransitionAnimation(
            this,
            Pair.create((View)avatarView,
                        ViewCompat.getTransitionName(avatarView)),
            Pair.create((View)userNameView,
                        ViewCompat.getTransitionName(userNameView))
        ).toBundle();

startActivity(intent, bundle);
```

You can apply the same animation in reverse if the second Activity is closed by calling `ActivityCompat.finishAfterTransition` instead of `finish`.

MATERIAL DESIGN UI ELEMENTS

Along with guiding principles, material design introduces a range of new UI elements. They are used frequently throughout the system UI and the core apps. By incorporating these elements within your app, you will make it more easily understood to new users, and more consistent with the system and other third-party apps using the material design philosophy.

The App Bar

The app bar, formerly known as the Action Bar, runs along the top of your app as shown in Figure 12-10.

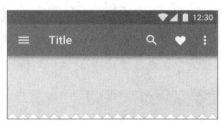

FIGURE 12-10

Its prominence at the very top of your UI means that it's often the first thing a user sees and reads. For that reason, your app bar serves as the anchor for your user interface, offering a familiar place for users to return when unsure of where they've navigated.

The app bar is automatically colored using the `colorPrimary` attribute as defined by your app's theme, offering a subtle indication of which app the user has open.

When defining a Theme, ensure that you assign a "parent" theme that will display a strong contrast between your `colorPrimary` and the text color used in the app bar. You can ensure this by selecting from one of the following:

➤ `Theme.AppCompat`—Use when you have a dark background for your UI and a dark `colorPrimary`. Text colors will be light to contrast with the dark backgrounds.

➤ `Theme.AppCompat.Light`—Use with a light background and primary color; it provides dark text.

➤ `Theme.AppCompat.Light.DarkActionBar`—Matches the light theme, but inverts the colors specifically for the app bar.

> **NOTE** *Using these themes is critical if you are using the built-in app bar. Chapter 13 explores using a `Toolbar` as your app bar, and offers alternative themes that explicitly remove the default app bar described here.*

The most prominent text displayed with the app bar is the `android:title` attribute taken from each Activity's manifest entry. It offers users a visual signpost of where they are within your app by updating as you move between Activities.

To programmatically change the title, call the `getSupportActionBar` method from your `AppCompatActivity` to retrieve the app bar and call `setTitle` to specify a new value:

```
String title = "New Title";
getSupportActionBar().setTitle(title);
```

The app bar also includes a navigation button, most often used for navigating *up* your app's navigation hierarchy.

The goal of "up" navigation differs from the Back button. Where the Back button should return the user to exactly the previous location (including restoring the state of the previous Activity), pressing "up" should serve as an escape hatch.

It should always move the user to a specific Activity in a fresh state; repeatedly pressing up should eventually take users to the main launch Activity.

Up button navigation is constructed by defining each Activity's parent. Consider a simple app that has a `MainActivity` that typically leads to `CategoryActivity`, which in turn leads to a `DetailActivity`.

As shown in Figure 12-11, MainActivity has no parent, while CategoryActivity has a parent of MainActivity and DetailActivity has a parent of CategoryActivity. As a result the up button should transition from the very specific pieces of content (a detail screen) up the content hierarchy until reaching the main Activity.

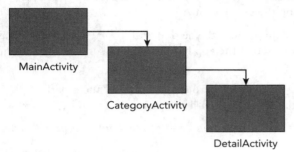

MainActivity

CategoryActivity

DetailActivity

FIGURE 12-11

You can indicate the parent of each Activity within your Application manifest using the android:parentActivityName attribute. The parentActivityName attribute was introduced in Android 4.1 Jelly Bean (API Level 16), so you must also add a <meta-data> element to support earlier platform releases:

```
<application ...>
  ...

  <activity
      android:name="com.example.MainActivity" ...>
  ...
  </activity>

  <activity
      android:name="com.example.CategoryActivity"
      android:parentActivityName="com.example.MainActivity"
      ...>
  ...
    <!-- This is only needed to support Android 4.0 or lower -->
    <meta-data
        android:name="android.support.PARENT_ACTIVITY"
        android:value="com.example.MainActivity" />
  </activity>

  <activity
      android:name="com.example.DetailActivity"
      android:parentActivityName="com.example.CategoryActivity"
      ...>
  ...
    <!-- This is only needed to support Android 4.0 or lower -->
    <meta-data
        android:name="android.support.PARENT_ACTIVITY"
        android:value="com.example.CategoryActivity" />
  </activity>

</application>
```

To enable the up button on your app bar, call `setDisplayHomeAsUpEnabled(true)` within the `onCreate` handler of each Activity.

```
getSupportActionBar().setDisplayHomeAsUpEnabled(true);
```

In cases where there may be multiple instances of a given parent Activity, you must add more detail to the `Intent` to ensure you navigate to the correct Activity.

You do this by overriding `getSupportParentActivityIntent` and adding the appropriate extras. For example, the `DetailActivity` example above may want to pass an additional extra to its parent `CategoryActivity` to ensure the correct category is shown:

```
@Override
public Intent getSupportParentActivityIntent() {
  // Get the Intent from the parentActivityName
  Intent intent = super.getSupportParentActivityIntent();
  // Add the information needed to create the CategoryActivity
  // in a fresh state
  intent.putExtra(CategoryActivity.EXTRA_CATEGORY_ID, mCategoryId);
  return intent;
}
```

Applying Material Design to the Earthquake Monitor

The default project templates in Android Studio provide the correct scaffolding to include material design in your app, but the personal branding of the app is something that must be added on top of that scaffolding. The earthquake viewer built over the previous chapters is no exception.

You'll now update the default theme to use new colors, use the Image Asset wizard to create an app icon, and ensure that each Activity has the appropriate "Up" hierarchy.

1. Open the Earthquake project and update the colors in the `res/values/colors.xml` file:

```
<?xml version="1.0" encoding="utf-8"?>
<resources>
  <color name="colorPrimary">#D32F2F</color>
  <color name="colorPrimaryDark">#9A0007</color>
  <color name="colorAccent">#448AFF</color>
</resources>
```

2. Open the Image Asset wizard by selecting File ⇨ New ⇨ Image Asset. Ensure the Icon Type is set to Launcher Icons and change the following options, and then click Finish to apply the new launcher icon:

2.1. For the foreground layer, change the Asset Type to Clip Art and select the vibration icon. Change the color to FFF and resize the icon to 80%.

2.2. For the background layer, change the Asset Type to Color and use the color D32F2F.

3. Open `AndroidManifest.xml` and add parent Activities to both `PreferencesActivity` and `EarthquakeSearchResultActivity`:

```
<activity
  android:name=".PreferencesActivity"
  android:parentActivityName=".EarthquakeMainActivity">
  <intent-filter>
```

```xml
        <action
          android:name="android.intent.action.MANAGE_NETWORK_USAGE"/>
          <category android:name="android.intent.category.DEFAULT"/>
      </intent-filter>
      <meta-data
        android:name="android.support.PARENT_ACTIVITY"
        android:value=".EarthquakeMainActivity" />
    </activity>

    <activity
      android:name=".EarthquakeSearchResultActivity"
      android:launchMode="singleTop"
      android:parentActivityName=".EarthquakeMainActivity">
      <intent-filter>
        <action android:name="android.intent.action.SEARCH" />
      </intent-filter>
      <meta-data
        android:name="android.app.searchable"
        android:resource="@xml/searchable"
        />
      <meta-data
        android:name="android.support.PARENT_ACTIVITY"
        android:value=".EarthquakeMainActivity" />
    </activity>
```

4. Update the `PreferenceActivity` to call `setDisplayHomeAsUpEnabled(true)` after the `setContentView` call:

    ```java
    @Override
    public void onCreate(Bundle savedInstanceState) {
      super.onCreate(savedInstanceState);
      setContentView(R.layout.preferences);

      getSupportActionBar().setDisplayHomeAsUpEnabled(true);
    }
    ```

5. Also update the `EarthquakeSearchResultActivity` to also call `setDisplayHomeAsUpEnabled(true)` after the `setContentView` call:

    ```java
    @Override
    public void onCreate(Bundle savedInstanceState) {
      super.onCreate(savedInstanceState);
      setContentView(R.layout.activity_earthquake_search_result);

      getSupportActionBar().setDisplayHomeAsUpEnabled(true);

      [... Existing onCreate method ...]
    }
    ```

Using Cards to Display Content

No matter your design philosophy, *content* should always be the focus of your app; providing structure for that content helps the user focus on it as well.

A card, as shown in Figure 12-12, is a raised piece of material with rounded corners that groups together information and actions about a single subject.

FIGURE 12-12

When all elements are similar, and quick scanning is important, a traditional list or grid of content works well. Cards come into their own when there are many different elements, many actions associated with each piece of content, or when it's important that users can remove individual cards.

The `CardView` class, offered as part of the Android Support Library, provides an implementation of the card concept, including the visual elements including rounded corners and elevation. In order to use Card Views in your app, you must add a dependency for the Card View library into your app module `build.gradle` file:

```
implementation 'com.android.support:cardview-v7:27.0.2'
```

`CardView` extends `FrameLayout`, so all of the layout techniques introduced in Chapter 5, "Building User Interfaces," apply to placing content within a Card View, with the exception of padding. Within Card Views you should use the `contentPadding` attribute rather than `padding` to ensure only the content within the card is padded inward (rather than the card's border).

> **NOTE** *Prior to Android 5.0 Lollipop (API Level 21),* `CardView` *padded all content rather than clipping content to the rounded corners. You can disable this using* `setPreventCornerOverlap(false)`. *If you want your Card View to look identical on all API levels, you can enable the padding on API 21+ devices by using* `setUseCompatPadding(true)`.

Cards are designed to be modular. Each card is assembled using a set of common content blocks, added in a particular order from the top to bottom as shown in Figure 12-13, including:

➤ An optional header (not pictured) with an avatar image, title, and subtitle for cards associated with a person.

➤   Rich media in a 16:9 or 1:1 aspect ratio.

➤   A primary title and subtitle (if not using a "person header"). This is used to describe the content of the card.

➤   Multiple lines of supporting text.

➤   Actions—either left aligned text or right aligned icons.

Expanded supporting text can be used by adding an expansion action that displays additional content appended to the bottom of the card.

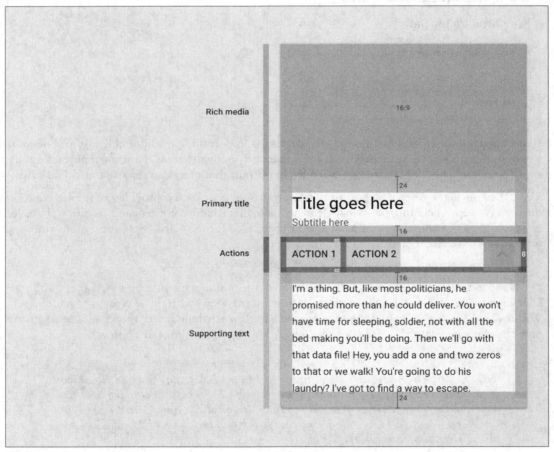

FIGURE 12-13

NOTE *For examples of cards and the content they can contain, see* `material .io/guidelines/components/cards.html#cards-content`.

Listing 12-6 shows a simple card that contains a 16:9 image, a primary title and subtitle, and two actions.

LISTING 12-6: A Card View implementation

```xml
<?xml version="1.0" encoding="utf-8"?>
<android.support.v7.widget.CardView
  xmlns:android="http://schemas.android.com/apk/res/android"
  xmlns:app="http://schemas.android.com/apk/res-auto"
  android:layout_width="match_parent"
  android:layout_height="match_parent">
  <android.support.constraint.ConstraintLayout
    android:layout_width="match_parent"
    android:layout_height="match_parent">
  <ImageView
    android:id="@+id/image"
    android:layout_width="0dp"
    app:layout_constraintDimensionRatio="16:9"
    app:layout_constraintLeft_toLeftOf="parent"
    app:layout_constraintRight_toRightOf="parent"
    app:layout_constraintTop_toTopOf="parent" />
  <TextView
    android:id="@+id/title"
    android:layout_width="0dp"
    android:layout_height="wrap_content"
    android:paddingTop="24dp"
    android:paddingLeft="16dp"
    android:paddingRight="16dp"
    app:layout_constraintLeft_toLeftOf="parent"
    app:layout_constraintRight_toRightOf="parent"
    app:layout_constraintTop_toBottomOf="@id/image"
    android:textAppearance="@style/TextAppearance.AppCompat.Headline" />
  <TextView
    android:id="@+id/subtitle"
    android:layout_width="0dp"
    android:layout_height="wrap_content"
    android:padding="16dp"
    app:layout_constraintLeft_toLeftOf="parent"
    app:layout_constraintRight_toRightOf="parent"
    app:layout_constraintTop_toBottomOf="@id/title"
    android:textAppearance="@style/TextAppearance.AppCompat.Body2" />
  <Button
    android:id="@+id/first_action"
    android:layout_width="wrap_content"
    android:layout_height="wrap_content"
    android:layout_marginTop="8dp"
    android:layout_marginLeft="8dp"
    android:layout_marginBottom="8dp"
    app:layout_constraintLeft_toLeftOf="parent"
    app:layout_constraintTop_toBottomOf="@id/subtitle"
    app:layout_constraintBottom_toBottomOf="parent"
    android:text="@string/first_action_text"
    style="?borderlessButtonStyle" />
```

continues

LISTING 12-6 *(continued)*

```
    <Button
        android:id="@+id/second_action"
        android:layout_width="wrap_content"
        android:layout_height="wrap_content"
        android:layout_margin="8dp"
        app:layout_constraintLeft_toRightOf="@id/first_action"
        app:layout_constraintTop_toBottomOf="@id/subtitle"
        app:layout_constraintBottom_toBottomOf="parent"
        android:text="@string/second_action_text"
        style="?borderlessButtonStyle" />
   </android.support.constraint.ConstraintLayout>
</android.support.v7.widget.CardView>
```

Floating Action Buttons

The Floating Action Button (FAB), shown in Figure 12-14, is an iconic pattern of material design, designed to draw attention to the single most important action the user can take within an Activity.

FIGURE 12-14

A FAB is represented as a circular icon with an increased elevation that appears above the rest of the UI, colored with your application's accent color. The floating action button should stand out considerably, making it possible for users to easily identify and find the action.

The Android Design Support Library contains the `FloatingActionButton` class, which implements the material design specifications for a FAB. It supports both the default size of 56dp and the mini size of 40dp with the `fabSize` attribute.

In almost all cases, the default size is most appropriate—the only exception is when you have other elements such as avatar images (which are also 40dp) that the FAB should align with. In either case, the icon it contains is 24dp square.

Unlike other Views, where visibility is set using `setVisibility`, it is strongly recommended to use the `show` and `hide` methods to control FAB visibility. This will animate the FAB by scaling it up from a 0 radius or back down to a 0 radius, respectively.

Where you position the FAB is ultimately a design choice, and it's important to note that not every app, nor every Activity, needs a floating action button. If there is not primary action, then you should avoid including a floating action button.

13

Implementing a Modern Android User Experience

WHAT'S IN THIS CHAPTER?

➤ Creating and applying themes to user interfaces

➤ Creating Menus and app bar actions

➤ Using Action Views and Action Providers

➤ Customizing the app bar using Toolbars

➤ Implementing advanced scrolling techniques

➤ Utilizing tabs, bottom navigation bars, and the navigation drawer for effective navigation

➤ Alerting the user with Dialogs, Toasts, and Snackbars

WROX.COM CODE DOWNLOADS FOR THIS CHAPTER

The code downloads for this chapter are found at www.wrox.com. The code for this chapter is divided into the following major examples:

➤ `Snippets_ch13.zip`

➤ `Earthquake_ch13_part1.zip`

➤ `Earthquake_ch13_part2.zip`

THE MODERN ANDROID UI

To help you create a user interface (UI) that's stylish, easy to use, and that offers a user experience consistent with the underlying platform and other applications, this chapter demonstrates techniques to expand the user experience beyond layouts and UI components.

This starts with an exploration of the AppCompat API, provided as part of the Android Support Library, which makes it possible to create a consistent, modern look for your app across all Android API levels using themes.

The app bar, introduced in Chapter 5, is an important component of your application. In this chapter you learn how to customize it further through the addition of Menus and actions. You also learn to utilize Toolbars to replace the app bar within your own layouts, and to take advantage of the functionality it supports, including specialized scrolling techniques.

When your app grows beyond a single screen, you need to incorporate a navigation pattern to facilitate user interaction. Tabs are one pattern that allows users to easily swipe between top-level Activities, while a bottom navigation bar offers persistent access to 3–5 top-level Activities, and finally a navigation drawer makes it possible for users to focus solely on content, while still making simple navigation easily accessible.

In addition to navigation, you are introduced to techniques used to alert users of exceptional circumstances. Modal dialogs force users to handle issues before continuing their work, while Toasts provide a mechanism for completely non-interactive floating messages. The Snackbar provides a non-modal alert that's interactive, and makes it simple for users to recover from potentially destructive interactions through a single action.

CREATING CONSISTENT, MODERN USER INTERFACES USING APPCOMPAT

The Android platform is constantly evolving, and the prevailing design language evolves with it; each Android release introduces new UI patterns, elements, and functionality.

The AppCompat API is available within the Android Support Library, and provides a single, backward compatible API, which developers can use to offer a consistent, modern user interface across all versions of Android.

AppCompat provides a set of themes, each prefixed with `Theme.AppCompat`. To take advantage of AppCompat's ability to make your app's appearance backward compatible, you must create a new theme that uses one of these AppCompat themes as its parent—and extend the `AppCompatActivity` within your app when creating new Activities.

AppCompat provides a number of attributes that have the same name as the framework equivalents. For example, `android:colorAccent` defines the accent color for many views on Android 5.0 Lollipop (API Level 21) and higher devices. To produce the same behavior on older versions of Android—when `android:colorAccent` wasn't available—you can instead use the `colorAccent` attribute within your theme.

In cases where an attribute exists both in AppCompat and the framework, you should always pick the AppCompat equivalent to ensure compatibility across all API levels.

> **NOTE** *In order to support theming, if you are extending standard Views such as* TextView *or* CheckBox *to implement custom behavior, or creating Views programmatically, make sure you are extending (or creating) Views from the* android.support.v7.widget *package such as* AppCompatTextView *and* AppCompatCheckBox.

Creating and Applying Themes Using AppCompat

In Chapter 12, "Implementing the Android Design Philosophy," you were introduced to the need to define a basic color palette for your app using colorPrimary, colorPrimaryDark, and color-Accent within your application's theme. We can use similar techniques to further customize the appearance of your app's Views without needing to extend or create custom Views.

For controlling the "normal" state of components such as an unselected EditText, Checkbox, and RadioButton, you can override the colorControlNormal attribute. The default value for this attribute is ?android:attr/textColorSecondary.

The activated or checked state for Checkboxes and Radio Buttons can be separately controlled by colorControlActivated if you wish to override the default color of ?attr/colorAccent.

Finally, the colorControlHighlight attribute controls the ripple coloring. In almost all cases, this should be kept to the default 20% white color (#33ffffff) for dark themes, and 12% black (#1f000000) for light themes.

Listing 13-1 shows a custom theme that specifies custom View colors.

LISTING 13-1: Defining a custom theme for Views

```xml
<resources>
  <style name="AppTheme"
    parent="Theme.AppCompat.Light.DarkActionBar">
    <item name="colorPrimary">@color/colorPrimary</item>
    <item name="colorPrimaryDark">@color/colorPrimaryDark</item>
    <item name="colorAccent">@color/colorAccent</item>
  </style>

  <!-- The implied parent here is AppTheme -->
  <style name="AppTheme.Custom">
    <item name="colorControlNormal">
      @color/colorControlNormal</item>
    <item name="colorControlActivated">
      @color/colorControlActivated</item>
  </style>
</resources>
```

Once defined, a theme can be added to the application manifest, where it can be applied to the entire application (via the `android:theme` attribute on the `application` element) or a specific Activity (using the `android:theme` attribute on the `activity` element):

```
<application ...
  android:theme="@style/AppTheme">
  <activity
    android:theme="@style/AppTheme.Custom" />
</application>
```

Creating Theme Overlays for Specific Views

It's also possible to apply a theme to a specific View (and its children) by applying the `android:theme` attribute to an individual View within a layout definition.

Unlike themes applied at the Application or Activity level, themes applied directly to Views should have a parent theme of `ThemeOverlay.AppCompat` (rather than `Theme.AppCompat`).

Theme overlays are designed to be applied over the base AppCompat theme, only affecting specific elements and ignoring attributes that are only applicable at the Activity level.

The two most common theme overlays are `ThemeOverlay.AppCompat.Light` and `ThemeOverlay.AppCompat.Dark`. The light theme alters the background colors, text colors, and highlight colors so that they are appropriate for a light background, and the dark theme does the same when using a dark background.

This approach can be particularly useful if you choose to color a portion of your screen with your primary color, and overlay it with text that must be readable:

```
<!-- Ensure text is readable on a dark
     primary color background by using
     a Dark ThemeOverlay -->
<FrameLayout
  android:layout_width="match_parent"
  android:layout_height="wrap_content"
  android:background="?attr/colorPrimary"
  android:theme="@style/ThemeOverlay.AppCompat.Dark">
  [... Remaining Layout Definition ...]
</FrameLayout>
```

A custom theme overlay is defined like any other theme. Start by declaring a parent theme using the `parent` attribute, and then specify any attributes you wish to modify:

```
<style name="ThemeOverlay.AccentSecondary"
       parent="ThemeOverlay.AppCompat">
  <item name="colorAccent">@color/accent_secondary</item>
</style>
```

ADDING A MENU AND ACTIONS TO THE APP BAR

With the app bar a standard fixture within most apps, it's a useful surface onto which we can add functionality. For common actions that are associated with the entire Activity, or a Fragment that takes up the majority of the screen, you can define a menu that will appear on the app bar in the form of icons, or within an overflow menu, as shown in Figure 13-1.

FIGURE 13-1

Defining a Menu Resource

Menus can be defined as an XML resource, stored in the res/menu folder of your project. This gives you the ability to create different Menus for alternative hardware configurations, screen sizes, languages, or Android versions.

Each Menu consists of a menu tag at the root node, and a series of item tags each specifying a Menu Item. The android:title is what is displayed to the user. Each Menu hierarchy must be created as a separate file.

Each item should also have an android:id, which you will use within your app to determine which Menu Item was tapped, as shown in Listing 13-2.

LISTING 13-2: Defining a menu in XML

```xml
<menu xmlns:android="http://schemas.android.com/apk/res/android">
  <item
    android:id="@+id/action_settings"
    android:title="@string/action_settings" />
  <item
    android:id="@+id/action_about"
    android:title="@string/action_about" />
</menu>
```

By default, Menu Items will appear in the overflow menu. To promote a Menu Item onto the app bar, you must add the app:showAsAction attribute, which controls where the Menu Item is shown:

➤ always—Forces the Menu Item to always be displayed as an action on the app bar.

➤ ifRoom—Indicates that the Menu Item should be displayed as an action provided there is enough space in the app bar to display it. It is good practice to use this option in preference to always giving the system flexibility when displaying actions.

➤ never—The default value, which ensures the Menu Item is only shown in the overflow menu.

> **NOTE** app:showAsAction *is one example of an AppCompat equivalent to the*
> *framework* android:showAsAction. *You should always use* app:showAsAction
> *when using AppCompat.*

For each Menu Item that uses always or ifRoom, you should also include an android:icon
attribute.

When shown in the overflow menu, only the text title will be displayed. When displayed as part of
the app bar, the Menu Item will be represented as an icon (a long press will briefly display the title).
By including a withText modifier (separated with a |), both the icon and title are displayed on the
App Bar. This should be used rarely, and only when there is ample space.

```
<menu xmlns:android="http://schemas.android.com/apk/res/android"
  xmlns:app="http://schemas.android.com/apk/res/res-auto">
  <item
    android:id="@+id/action_filter"
    android:icon="@drawable/action_filter"
    android:title="@string/action_filter"
    app:showAsAction="ifRoom|withText"
  />
</menu>
```

Displaying Menu Items as actions on the app bar should be reserved for those that are very frequently used, critically important for users to discover, or highly expected based on actions available
in similar applications.

Generic and seldom used Menu Items, such as settings, help, or about, should never be presented as
action items.

Adding a Menu to an Activity

To associate a Menu with an Activity, you must first inflate your Menu XML resource into a Menu
instance by overriding the Activity's onCreateOptionsMenu handler. You must return true to display your Menu (false hides the Menu entirely), as shown in Listing 13-3.

LISTING 13-3: Adding a Menu to an Activity

```
@Override
public boolean onCreateOptionsMenu(Menu menu) {
  // You should always call super.onCreateOptionsMenu()
  // to ensure this call is also dispatched to Fragments
  super.onCreateOptionsMenu(menu);

  MenuInflater inflater = getMenuInflater();
  inflater.inflate(R.menu.my_menu, menu);

  return true;
}
```

As with layouts, it's also possible to programmatically create Menu Items, and add them to the Menu object using its `add` method. The ID used when creating these dynamic Menu Items must always be greater than or equal to the `Menu.FIRST` constant, to avoid conflicting with any previously inflated Menu Items.

Adding a Menu to a Fragment

Menus can also be associated with Fragments. Fragment Menus will only be visible on the app bar when the host Fragment is visible. This allows you to dynamically change the actions available to match the content being displayed.

Fragment Menus should be inflated within the Fragment's `onCreateOptionsMenu` handler; however, unlike Activities you must also call `setHasOptionsMenu(true)` within the Fragment's `onCreate` handler, as shown in Listing 13-4.

LISTING 13-4: Adding a Menu to a Fragment

```
@Override
public void onCreate(Bundle savedInstanceState) {
  super.onCreate(savedInstanceState);
  setHasOptionsMenu(true);
}

@Override
public void onCreateOptionsMenu(Menu menu, MenuInflater inflater) {
  inflater.inflate(R.menu.my_menu, menu);
}
```

Updating Menu Items Dynamically

By overriding your Activity's or Fragment's `onPrepareOptionsMenu` method, you can modify a Menu based on an application's current state at run time, immediately before the Menu is displayed. This lets you dynamically disable/enable Menu Items, set visibility, and even modify text.

To modify Menu Items dynamically, you can either record a reference to them from within the `onCreateOptionsMenu` method when they're created, or you can use the `findItem` method on the Menu object, as shown in Listing 13-5:

LISTING 13-5: Modifying Menu Items dynamically

```
@Override
public boolean onPrepareOptionsMenu(Menu menu) {
  super.onPrepareOptionsMenu(menu);

  MenuItem menuItem = menu.findItem(R.id.action_filter);

  // Modify Menu Items
  menuItem.setVisible(false);

  return true;
}
```

Handling Menu Selections

Android handles the app bar actions and overflow Menu using a single event handler, `onOptions-ItemSelected`. The Menu Item selected is passed in to this method as the `MenuItem` parameter.

To react to the menu selection, compare the `item.getItemId` value to the resource identifiers in your Menu XML (or the Menu Item identifiers you used when populating the Menu programmatically), as shown in Listing 13-6, and perform the corresponding action.

LISTING 13-6: Handling Menu Item selections

```
public boolean onOptionsItemSelected(MenuItem item) {
  // Find which Menu Item has been selected
  switch (item.getItemId()) {

    // Check for each known Menu Item
    case (R.id.action_settings):
      [ ... Perform menu handler actions ... ]
      return true;

    // Pass on any unhandled Menu Items to super.onOptionsItemSelected
    // This is required to ensure that the up button and Fragment Menu Items
    // are dispatched properly.
    default: return super.onOptionsItemSelected(item);
  }
}
```

If you have supplied Menu Items from within a Fragment, you can choose to handle them within the `onOptionsItemSelected` handler of either the Activity or the Fragment. Note that the Activity will receive the selected Menu Item first, and that the Fragment will not receive it if the Activity handles it and returns `true`.

Adding Action Views and Action Providers

To support cases where a simple icon is not a rich enough interface, Menu Items can also display an arbitrary layout. This comes in two varieties: a `CollapsibleActionView` and an `ActionProvider`.

When an icon (and/or text) is suitable as a prompt, but a richer interface is required after it's selected, you should consider adding an `app:actionLayout` or `app:actionViewClass` attribute to your Menu Item definition.

The `app:actionLayout` attribute is suitable when you have defined a Menu Item layout as a layout resource, while `app:actionViewClass` is optimized for a single View (or View Group).

Add the `collapseActionView` value to your `app:showAsAction` attribute to ensure your Menu Item uses the Collapsible Action View specified, as shown in Listing 13-7.

LISTING 13-7: Adding an Action View to a Menu Item

```
<menu xmlns:android="http://schemas.android.com/apk/res/android"
  xmlns:app="http://schemas.android.com/apk/res-auto">
  <item
```

```
        android:id="@+id/action_search"
        android:icon="@drawable/action_search"
        android:title="@string/action_search"
        app:showAsAction="ifRoom|collapseActionView"
        app:actionViewClass="android.support.v7.widget.SearchView" />
</menu>
```

When the Menu Item is tapped, it will be expanded to fill the app bar, as shown in Figure 13-2.

FIGURE 13-2

Once added, you will need to implement handlers to react to user interaction with the collapsible Action View. This is typically done within the onCreateMenuOptions handler:

```
MenuItem searchItem = menu.findItem(R.id.action_search);
SearchView searchView = (SearchView) searchItem.getActionView();

searchView.setOnSearchClickListener(new OnClickListener() {
  public void onClick(View v) {
    // TODO React to the button press.
  }
});
```

The example in Listing 13-7 uses the SearchView, which is implemented to receive callbacks when it's collapsed or expanded. If you're using your own custom layout, you should make sure it also implements this approach. Alternatively, you can set an OnActionExpandListener via the setOn-ActionExpandListener method.

In circumstances where the custom layout should remain visible in the app bar at all times, you can use an ActionProvider. The Action Provider is attached to a Menu Item using the app:actionProviderClass attribute, and is responsible for displaying the appropriate layout—and handling any user interactions with it.

Listing 13-8 demonstrates adding a MediaRouteActionProvider—an Action Provider used to support Google Cast integration, which handles the connection status and selection of Cast devices.

LISTING 13-8: Adding an Action Provider to a Menu Item

```
<menu xmlns:android="http://schemas.android.com/apk/res/android"
  xmlns:app="http://schemas.android.com/apk/res-auto">
  <item
    android:id="@+id/action_media_route"
    android:title="@string/action_cast"
    app:showAsAction="always"
    app:actionProviderClass="android.support.v7.app.MediaRouteActionProvider"
  />
</menu>
```

GOING BEYOND THE DEFAULT APP BAR

Any Activity that applies a `Theme.AppCompat` theme will display an AppCompat-style app bar by default. You can choose to customize this, by delegating the responsibilities of the app bar to a Toolbar that you can add directly to your Activity layout.

This flexibility makes it possible to take advantage of scrolling behaviors, such as having your Toolbar scroll "off screen" as part of your content scrolling, to offer more room for content to be displayed.

Toolbars support all of the same functionality as the app bar, including the "up" navigation affordance, an Activity title, Menu Item actions, and the overflow Menu.

Replacing Your App Bar with a Toolbar

To add a Toolbar to an Activity, you must first disable the default app bar by applying a `NoActionBar` theme such as `Theme.AppCompat.NoActionBar` or `Theme.AppCompat.Light.NoActionBar` to your Activity within the manifest:

```
android:theme="@style/Theme.AppCompat.NoActionBar"
```

Within the Activity layout, add a Toolbar element aligned with the top of the screen, and sized to match the app bar:

```
<android.support.v7.widget.Toolbar
  android:id="@+id/toolbar"
  android:layout_width="match_parent"
  android:layout_height="?attr/actionBarSize"
/>
```

Within your Activity's `onCreate` handler, specify the Toolbar within your layout to be used as your app bar replacement using the `setSupportActionBar` method, as shown in Listing 13-9. Any Menu Items added within the `onCreateOptionsMenu` handler will then be added to, and displayed, on your Toolbar.

LISTING 13-9: Setting a Toolbar as your App Bar

```
@Override
public void onCreate(Bundle savedInstanceState) {
  super.onCreate(savedInstanceState);
  setContentView(R.layout.basic_toolbar_activity);
  Toolbar toolbar = findViewById(R.id.toolbar);
  setSupportActionBar(toolbar);
}
```

The Toolbar is available as part of the Android Design Support Library. Before it can be used, you must add the Android Design Support Library to your app module `build.gradle` file:

```
implementation 'com.android.support:design:27.1.1'
```

Listing 13-10 shows how to style the look and feel of the standard app bar for your Toolbar by wrapping the Toolbar in an `AppBarLayout`, part of the Android Design Support Library. The App

Bar Layout automatically sets the background color to your `colorPrimary` resource value, and adds the correct elevation; the App Bar Layout should always be used when using a Toolbar to replace the app bar. To set the correct text and icon colors, select a theme from:

➤ `ThemeOverlay.AppCompat.ActionBar`—Sets the correct styling to support a Search View, and sets the `colorControlNormal` to `android:textColorPrimary`.

➤ `ThemeOverlay.AppCompat.Dark.ActionBar`—As above, but also sets the text colors to be light for use on a dark background.

➤ `ThemeOverlay.AppCompat.Light.ActionBar`—As for the first item, but also sets the text colors to be dark for use on a light background.

LISTING 13-10: Styling a Toolbar to match the app bar

```xml
<!-- Ensure text is readable on a dark primary color background
by using a Dark ThemeOverlay -->
<android.support.design.widget.AppBarLayout
    android:layout_width="match_parent"
    android:layout_height="wrap_content"
    android:theme="@style/ThemeOverlay.AppCompat.Dark.ActionBar">

    <Toolbar
        android:id="@+id/toolbar"
        android:layout_width="match_parent"
        android:layout_height="?attr/actionBarSize"/>
</android.support.design.widget.AppBarLayout>
```

Advanced Scrolling Techniques for the Toolbar

While app bars and toolbars present users with important information and priority actions, they're also part of the app's "chrome"—and as such steal space from the *content*, which should always be prioritized. To help balance these two considerations, material design includes a number of techniques that can be used to alter the behavior of the Toolbar when users scroll app content.

> **NOTE** *Much of what's described in this section relies on understanding different gestures and motions. It will be useful to review videos of these effects on the material design page at* `material.io/guidelines/patterns/scrolling-techniques.html`.

Scrolling techniques often involve interaction between multiple Views—the View being scrolled and any View (or Views) reacting to the scrolling (typically the Toolbar replacing your app bar.)

To ensure this interaction is properly coordinated, each affected View must be the direct child of a `CoordinatorLayout`. The Coordinator Layout is used to attach Behaviors to specific Views using the `app:layout_behavior` attribute in their layout element. Each Behavior can intercept touch events, window insets, measurement and layout, and nested scrolling events for the affected View without requiring you to subclass the Views to add that additional functionality.

> **NOTE** *More information on Behaviors and examples of custom Behaviors can be found at* `medium.com/google-developers/intercepting-everything-with-coordinatorlayout-behaviors-8c6adc140c26.`

The most basic scrolling technique is to have the Toolbar scroll "off-screen," such that it disappears when the user begins scrolling the content, and then have it scroll back on-screen when the user scrolls in the opposite direction.

This is achieved by placing your Toolbar within an `AppBarLayout` and adding the `ScrollingViewBehavior` to the View being scrolled (typically a Recycler View or Nested Scroll View), as demonstrated in Listing 13-11.

LISTING 13-11: Scrolling a Toolbar off-screen

```
<android.support.design.widget.CoordinatorLayout
  xmlns:android="http://schemas.android.com/apk/res/android"
  xmlns:app="http://schemas.android.com/apk/res-auto"
  android:layout_width="match_parent"
  android:layout_height="match_parent">

  <! -- Your Scrollable View -->
  <android.support.v7.widget.RecyclerView
    android:layout_width="match_parent"
    android:layout_height="match_parent"
    app:layout_behavior="@string/appbar_scrolling_view_behavior" />

  <! - App bar style Toolbar -->
  <android.support.design.widget.AppBarLayout
    android:layout_width="match_parent"
    android:layout_height="wrap_content"
    android:theme="@style/ThemeOverlay.AppCompat.Dark.ActionBar">

    <android.support.v7.widget.Toolbar
      android:layout_width="match_parent"
      android:layout_height="wrap_content"
      app:layout_scrollFlags="scroll|snap|enterAlways" />
  </android.support.design.widget.AppBarLayout>
</android.support.design.widget.CoordinatorLayout>
```

In this layout, as the Recycler View scrolls, the `ScrollingViewBehavior` attached to it causes the App Bar Layout to respond based on the `app:layout_scrollFlags` attribute on each of the App

Bar Layout's child views. This flag controls the behavior for the View as it scrolls on, and off, the screen:

➤ scroll—Required for any View that is to scroll off the screen—Views without this flag will always remain at the top of the screen.

➤ snap—When a scroll event ends, Views with this flag will be scrolled to the closest edge, ensuring they are either fully visible, or completely scrolled off screen.

➤ enterAlways—Indicates that the View will immediately begin entering the screen on any reverse (downward) scroll event. This enables the "quick return" pattern, without which the user would need to scroll to the very top of the Recycler View before the Toolbar was scrolled back into frame.

➤ enterAlwaysCollapsed—Can be added to enterAlways to ensure the View is only scrolled back to its "collapsed" height, as described later within this section.

➤ exitUntilCollapsed—When scrolling off the screen, the view will first "collapse" before exiting and scrolling off the screen.

The App Bar Layout supports multiple children, laying them out similarly to a vertical Linear Layout. Every View that includes the scroll flag must be positioned above Views without it. This ensures that views are always scrolled off the top of the screen.

The collapsing flags are useful if you have a view that initially has a larger height (set with android:layout_height), but a smaller minimum height set with android:minHeight. This pattern is often found in combination with the CollapsingToolbarLayout, as shown in Listing 13-12. It provides fine-grained control over which elements collapse, and which should be "pinned" to the top of the Collapsing Toolbar Layout.

LISTING 13-12: Collapsing Toolbar

```
<android.support.design.widget.AppBarLayout
  android:layout_width="match_parent"
  android:layout_height="192dp"
  android:theme="@style/ThemeOverlay.AppCompat.Dark.ActionBar">

  <android.support.design.widget.CollapsingToolbarLayout
    android:layout_width="match_parent"
    android:layout_height="match_parent"
    app:layout_scrollFlags="scroll|exitUntilCollapsed">

    <android.support.v7.widget.Toolbar
      android:layout_width="match_parent"
      android:layout_height="?attr/actionBarSize"
      app:layout_collapseMode="pin" />
  </android.support.design.widget.CollapsingToolbarLayout>
</android.support.design.widget.AppBarLayout>
```

Note that the AppBarLayout has a fixed height—this is the expanded height. The Toolbar's height is set to ?attr/actionBarSize, which is the default height of the app bar. The Collapsing Toolbar Layout ensures the title text animates correctly while the View collapses, moving from the bottom of the View to the appropriate location on the Toolbar, which has its navigation button and actions pinned using the `app:layout_collapseMode="pin"`.

The Collapsing Toolbar Layout supports multiple children, laying them out similar to a Frame Layout. This is useful when adding an additional `ImageView` serving as a "hero image" behind the expanded app bar. Use the attribute `app:layout_collapseMode="parallax"` to have the image scroll at a different rate than the scrolling content to provide a parallax effect:

```
<android.support.design.widget.AppBarLayout
  android:layout_width="match_parent"
  android:layout_height="192dp"
  android:theme="@style/ThemeOverlay.AppCompat.Dark.ActionBar">

  <android.support.design.widget.CollapsingToolbarLayout
    android:layout_width="match_parent"
    android:layout_height="match_parent"
    app:layout_scrollFlagts="scroll|exitUntilCollapsed">

  <ImageView
    android:id="@+id/hero_image"
    android:layout_width="match_parent"
    android:layout_height="match_parent"
    app:layout_collapseMode="parallax" />

  <android.support.v7.widget.Toolbar
    android:id="@+id/toolbar"
    android:layout_width="match_parent"
    android:layout_height="?attr/actionBarSize"
    app:layout_collapseMode="pin" />
  </android.support.design.widget.CollapsingToolbarLayout>
</android.support.design.widget.AppBarLayout>
```

Incorporating Menus Without the App Bar

The app bar is the first place users will look for actions related to your app, but its top-level context makes it an inappropriate place for actions associated with only a portion of your layout. This can commonly be the case for large layouts, such as those optimized for tablets.

To provide actions for a specific portion of your layout, you can include a Toolbar specifically for that region. Actions can be added to that Toolbar using `inflateMenu` or programmatically by using the Toolbar's `getMenu` method. Any Menu Item selected will trigger a callback to the `OnMenuItemClickListener` you've set using with the Toolbar's `setOnMenuItemClickListener`.

If you don't need a navigation icon or a title, you can use the `ActionMenuView` as an alternative. Similar to the Toolbar, you can add Menu Items using the `getMenu` method and use `setOnMenuItemClickListener` to allocate a Menu Item Click Listener to handle selections, as shown in Listing 13-13.

LISTING 13-13: Adding a menu to an Action Menu View

```java
ActionMenuView actionMenuView = findViewById(R.id.menu_view);

MenuInflater menuInflater = getMenuInflater();
menuInflater.inflate(actionMenuView.getMenu(), R.menu.action_menu);
actionMenuView.setOnMenuItemClickListener(new OnMenuItemClickListener() {
  public boolean onMenuItemClick(MenuItem item) {
    switch (item.getItemId()) {
      case (R.id.action_menu_item) :
        // TODO Handle menu clicks.
        return true;
      default: return false;
    }
  }
});
```

IMPROVING THE EARTHQUAKE MONITOR'S APP BAR

In the following example, the earthquake-monitoring application, which you updated to material design in Chapter 12, "Implementing the Android Design Philosophy," will be enhanced to use a Toolbar and scroll techniques:

1. Update the app `build.gradle` file to include Design Support Library:

```gradle
dependencies {
  [... Existing dependencies ...]
  implementation 'com.android.support:design:27.1.1'
}
```

2. Update the `styles.xml` resource, adding a new `AppTheme.NoActionBar` theme:

```xml
<style name="AppTheme.NoActionBar"
  parent="Theme.AppCompat.Light.NoActionBar">
  <item name="colorPrimary">@color/colorPrimary</item>
  <item name="colorPrimaryDark">@color/colorPrimaryDark</item>
  <item name="colorAccent">@color/colorAccent</item>
</style>
```

3. Modify the `AndroidManifest.xml` entry for `EarthquakeMainActivity` to use the new theme added in Step 2:

```xml
<activity
  android:name=
    "com.professionalandroid.apps.earthquake.EarthquakeMainActivity"
  android:theme="@style/AppTheme.NoActionBar">
  <intent-filter>
    <action android:name="android.intent.action.MAIN"/>
    <category android:name="android.intent.category.LAUNCHER"/>
  </intent-filter>
```

```xml
    <meta-data
      android:name="android.app.default_searchable"
      android:value=".EarthquakeSearchResultActivity"
    />
  </activity>
```

4. Update the `activity_earthquake_main.xml` layout to use a `CoordinatorLayout`, `AppBarLayout`, and `Toolbar` using the `scroll|enterAlways|snap` scroll flags so that the Toolbar scrolls off the screen, returns immediately when the user scrolls up, and snaps to avoid being only partially visible:

```xml
<?xml version="1.0" encoding="utf-8"?>
<android.support.design.widget.CoordinatorLayout
  xmlns:android="http://schemas.android.com/apk/res/android"
  xmlns:app="http://schemas.android.com/apk/res-auto"
  android:layout_width="match_parent"
  android:layout_height="match_parent">

  <android.support.design.widget.AppBarLayout
    android:layout_width="match_parent"
    android:layout_height="wrap_content"
    android:theme="@style/ThemeOverlay.AppCompat.Dark.ActionBar">

    <android.support.v7.widget.Toolbar
      android:id="@+id/toolbar"
      android:layout_width="match_parent"
      android:layout_height="wrap_content"
      app:layout_scrollFlags="scroll|enterAlways|snap"/>
  </android.support.design.widget.AppBarLayout>

  <FrameLayout
    android:id="@+id/main_activity_frame"
    android:layout_width="match_parent"
    android:layout_height="match_parent"
    app:layout_behavior="@string/appbar_scrolling_view_behavior"/>
</android.support.design.widget.CoordinatorLayout>
```

5. Update the `onCreate` method in the Earthquake Main Activity to set the Toolbar as the app bar:

```java
@Override
protected void onCreate(Bundle savedInstanceState) {
  super.onCreate(savedInstanceState);
  setContentView(R.layout.activity_earthquake_main);

  Toolbar toolbar = findViewById(R.id.toolbar);
  setSupportActionBar(toolbar);

  [... Existing onCreate Method ...]
}
```

While a static image won't show any visible difference, scrolling the earthquake list will cause the app bar to scroll off-screen, ensuring users have the maximum amount of space to interact with the content. By using the `enterAlways` scroll flag, the app bar will return as soon as the user scrolls back, allowing quick access to the overflow menu and Search View.

APP NAVIGATION PATTERNS

Apps come in many different sizes and complexities, resulting in a number of different patterns to help users navigate your app easily.

Three primary navigation patterns are in common use:

➤ Tabs—allow users to swipe between equally important top-level screens

➤ Bottom navigation bar—an always visible bar containing 3 to 5 generally independent top-level screens

➤ Navigation drawer—a drawer generally only accessed by manually opening it, suitable for apps that have one primary screen and multiple independent secondary screens

Navigating with Tabs

Tabs are an effective navigation pattern when you have two equally important top-level Views. When using Tabs, users can switch between these Views either by tapping the Tab, or swiping between the Views.

FIGURE 13-3

Tabs are displayed using `TabLayout`, and are always shown along the top of the screen, as shown in Figure 13-3.

Tabs are generally included as a second child View of an App Bar Layout beneath a Toolbar, as shown in Listing 13-14.

Note that the swipe functionality is provided by the incorporation of a `ViewPager`.

LISTING 13-14: Using Tabs for app navigation

```
<android.support.design.widget.CoordinatorLayout
   xmlns:android="http://schemas.android.com/apk/res/android"
   xmlns:app="http://schemas.android.com/apk/res-auto"
   android:layout_width="match_parent"
   android:layout_height="match_parent">

   <!-- Your Main Content View -->
   <android.support.v4.view.ViewPager
```

continues

LISTING 13-14 *(continued)*

```
      android:id="@+id/view_pager"
      android:layout_width="match_parent"
      android:layout_height="match_parent"
      app:layout_behavior="@string/appbar_scrolling_view_behavior" />

  <android.support.design.widget.AppBarLayout
      android:layout_width="match_parent"
      android:layout_height="wrap_content"
      android:theme="@style/ThemeOverlay.AppCompat.Dark.ActionBar">

    <android.support.v7.widget.Toolbar
      android:layout_width="match_parent"
      android:layout_height="wrap_content"
      app:layout_scrollFlags="scroll|snap|enterAlways" />

    <android.support.design.widget.TabLayout
      android:id="@+id/tab_layout"
      android:layout_width="match_parent"
      android:layout_height="wrap_content" />
  </android.support.design.widget.AppBarLayout>
</android.support.design.widget.CoordinatorLayout>
```

The `TabLayout` in Listing 13-14 does not include any `app:layout_scrollFlags`—as a result, the tabs remain visible when the user scrolls.

The content displayed within the View Pager is populated using a `PagerAdapter`. By default, the Pager Adapter inflates a single View for each page; however, when working with Tabs, it's often more convenient to use the `FragmentPagerAdapter` and use a Fragment to represent each page.

This structure allows each Fragment to add actions using `onCreateOptionsMenu` that will only be visible when the associated Tab is selected.

To build a Fragment Pager Adapter, extend `FragmentPagerAdapter` and override `getCount` to return the number of pages, and `getItem` to return the appropriate Fragment for a given position.

To use your Fragment Pager Adapter with Tab navigation, you'll also need to override `getPage-Title` to return a title for a given position, which will be displayed within the Tab Layout.

When using a View Pager and Tab Layout for your main navigation with a fixed set of elements, `getItem` and `getPageTitle` can be simple `switch` statements mapping positions to fixed data, as shown in Listing 13-15.

LISTING 13-15: Creating a Fragment Pager Adapter for a Tab Layout

```
class FixedTabsPagerAdapter extends FragmentPagerAdapter {
  public FixedTabsPagerAdapter(FragmentManager fm) {
```

```
    super(fm);
  }

  @Override
  public int getCount() {
    return 2;
  }

  @Override
  public Fragment getItem(int position) {
    switch(position) {
      case 0:
        return new HomeFragment();
      case 1:
        return new ProfileFragment();
      default:
        return null;
    }
  }

  @Override
  public CharSequence getPageTitle(int position) {
    // To support internationalization, use string
    // resources for these titles
    switch(position) {
      case 0:
        return "Home";
      case 1:
        return "Profile";
      default:
        return null;
    }
  }
}
```

Connect your `PagerAdapter` and your `ViewPager` using the `setAdapter` method, then call `setupWithViewPager` on the `TabLayout` to create the correct Tabs. Ensure that Tab selection events change the selected page and that swiping through pages updates the selected tab, as shown in Listing 13-16.

LISTING 13-16: Connecting the View Pager to a Tab Layout

```
@Override
public void onCreate(Bundle savedInstanceState) {
  super.onCreate(savedInstanceState);
  setContentView(R.layout.app_bar_tabs);
```

```
    ViewPager viewPager = findViewById(R.id.view_pager);
    PagerAdapter pagerAdapter =
      new FixedTabsPagerAdapter(getSupportFragmentManager());
    viewPager.setAdapter(pagerAdapter);

    TabLayout tabLayout = findViewById(R.id.tab_layout);
    tabLayout.setupWithViewPager(viewPager);
  }
```

Navigating between Tabs does *not* affect the back stack, so pressing the back button won't reverse Tab navigation. As a result, individual pages should not include any internal navigation or back stack history—all navigation should be done by opening a Dialog (as discussed later in this chapter), or through a new Activity.

By following these guidelines, users will always have a consistent experience when tapping the back button.

> **NOTE** *While we've focused on* `TabLayout` *and* `ViewPager` *as a high-level navigation pattern, both components can be used in many other places within your app. For example, scrollable tabs via the* `app:tabMode="scrollable"` *attribute can be useful in splitting up a large set of elements into categories (consider extending from* `FragmentStatePagerAdapter` *to only keep a few Fragments in memory rather than all of them). For more information, see* `developer.android.com/training/implementing-navigation/lateral.html`.

Implementing a Bottom Navigation Bar

A bottom navigation bar, as shown in Figure 13-4, is presented along the bottom of the screen; users can switch between Views by tapping on the desired item.

Users will generally read from top to bottom, so this layout puts more emphasis on the content, while still ensuring that the top-level Views are available.

FIGURE 13-4

Bottom navigation bars are ideal when your app has three to five top-level navigation destinations that are of similar importance but generally independent of each other.

Unlike Tabs, a bottom navigation bar navigation pattern should *not* support swiping between Views, and transitions should cross-fade from the current item to the new, rather than using a lateral animation to "slide in."

As a result, any of the Views available from the bottom navigation can support swiping behaviors—for example, you may want to swipe to delete an e-mail from a list, or embed scrollable tabs to categorize content.

Selecting a bottom navigation item should reset that View's task state instead of restoring any previous intermediate state (such as scroll position).

The items displayed in the bottom navigation bar are defined as a Menu, as shown in Listing 13-17. Each item is defined using `item` elements, where the `android:id` attribute is later used to identify which item has been selected, and the `android:icon` and `android:title` attributes are used to populate the title and icon displayed for the bottom navigation bar items.

LISTING 13-17: Defining a Menu for a bottom navigation bar

```xml
<menu xmlns:android="http://schemas.android.com/apk/res/android"
  xmlns:app="http://schemas.android.com/apk/res-auto">
  <item
    android:id="@+id/nav_home"
    android:icon="@drawable/nav_home"
    android:title="@string/nav_home" />
  <item
    android:id="@+id/nav_profile"
    android:icon="@drawable/nav_profile"
    android:title="@string/nav_profile" />
  <item
    android:id="@+id/nav_notifications"
    android:icon="@drawable/nav_notifications"
    android:title="@string/nav_notifications" />
</menu>
```

To add a bottom navigation bar, add a `BottomNavigationView` element, part of the Android Design Support Library, to your layout. Use the `app:menu` attribute to associate a Menu resource that defines the available selections, as shown in Listing 13-18.

LISTING 13-18: Adding a Bottom Navigation View to a Layout

```xml
<android.support.design.widget.CoordinatorLayout
  xmlns:android="http://schemas.android.com/apk/res/android"
  xmlns:app="http://schemas.android.com/apk/res-auto"
  android:layout_width="match_parent"
  android:layout_height="match_parent">

  <!-- Your Main Content View -->
  <FrameLayout
    android:id="@+id/main_content"
    android:layout_width="match_parent"
    android:layout_height="match_parent"
    android:layout_marginBottom="56dp"
    app:layout_behavior="@string/appbar_scrolling_view_behavior" />

  <android.support.design.widget.AppBarLayout
    android:layout_width="match_parent"
```

```xml
      android:layout_height="wrap_content"
      android:background="?attr/colorPrimary"
      android:theme="@style/ThemeOverlay.AppCompat.Dark.ActionBar">

    <android.support.v7.widget.Toolbar
      android:id="@+id/toolbar"
      android:layout_width="match_parent"
      android:layout_height="wrap_content"
      app:layout_scrollFlags="scroll|snap|enterAlways" />
  </android.support.design.widget.AppBarLayout>

  <android.support.design.widget.BottomNavigationView
    android:id="@+id/bottom_nav"
    android:layout_width="match_parent"
    android:layout_height="56dp"
    android:layout_gravity="bottom"
    app:menu="@menu/bottom_nav_menu" />
</android.support.design.widget.CoordinatorLayout>
```

Set an `OnNavigationItemSelectedListener` to the Bottom Navigation View to listen for selection changes. Each selection should result in a `FragmentTransaction` that replaces the currently displayed content with a new Fragment based on the selection.

An `OnNavigationItemReselectedListener` is also available to receive callbacks when the currently selected item is reselected. By convention, selecting the currently selected item should scroll the content to the top. Listing 13-19 implements this by having each Fragment extend `ScrollableFragment`, which adds a single method—`scrollToTop`.

LISTING 13-19: Handling bottom navigation Item selection events

```java
private static final String CURRENT_ITEM_KEY = "current_item";
// This should be saved in onSaveInstanceState() using CURRENT_ITEM_KEY
int mCurrentItem = R.id.nav_home;

@Override
public void onCreate(Bundle savedInstanceState) {
  super.onCreate(savedInstanceState);
  setContentView(R.layout.app_bar_bottom_nav);

  // Restore the ID of the current tab
  if (savedInstanceState != null) {
    mCurrentItem = savedInstanceState.getInt(CURRENT_ITEM_KEY);
  }

  BottomNavigationView bottomNav = findViewById(R.id.bottom_nav);
  bottomNav.setOnNavigationItemSelectedListener(
    new OnNavigationItemSelectedListener() {
      @Override
      public boolean onNavigationItemSelected(MenuItem item) {
        FragmentManager fm = getSupportFragmentManager();
        // Create the newly selected item's Fragment
        Fragment newFragment;
```

```
          switch(item.getItemId()) {
            case R.id.nav_home:
              newFragment = new HomeFragment();
              getSupportActionBar().setTitle(R.string.nav_home);
              break;
            case R.id.nav_profile:
              newFragment = new ProfileFragment();
              getSupportActionBar().setTitle(R.string.nav_profile);
              break;
            case R.id.nav_notifications:
              newFragment = new NotificationsFragment();
              getSupportActionBar().setTitle(R.string.nav_notifications);
              break;
            default: break;
          }
          // Replace the current fragment with the newly selected item
          fm.beginTransaction()
            .replace(R.id.main_content, newFragment)
            .setTransition(FragmentTransaction.TRANSIT_FRAGMENT_FADE)
            .commit();
        }
        return true;
      }
    });

    bottomNav.setOnNavigationItemReselectedListener(
      new OnNavigationItemReselectedListener() {
        @Override
        public boolean onNavigationItemReselected(MenuItem item) {
          // Scroll to the top of the current tab if it supports scrolling
          // This can be done in many ways: this code assumes all Fragments
          // implement a ScrollableFragment subclass you've created
          ScrollableFragment fragment =
            (ScrollableFragment) fm.findFragmentById(R.id.main_content);
          fragment.scrollToTop();
        }
      });
  }
```

As with Tabs, bottom navigation bar navigation should not add to the back stack, and pressing the back button should not undo a selection.

Using a Navigation Drawer

The navigation drawer, shown in Figure 13-5, is typically hidden until invoked by the user tapping the navigation icon in the app bar.

FIGURE 13-5

Because the navigation options are hidden by default, this pattern is particularly appropriate when a single, main screen is significantly more important than the others. It also supports app architectures that require six or more equally important top-level screens.

The `NavigationView` class, also part of the Android Design Support Library, provides the UI for a Navigation Drawer. Like the Bottom Navigation View, the Navigation View is populated using a Menu resource, either through the `app:menu` attribute in your layout XML resource, or programmatically using the `inflateMenu` or `getMenu` methods.

When creating your navigation drawer Menu definition, use menu groups via the `android:checkableBehavior="single"` attribute, as shown in Listing 13-20.

LISTING 13-20: Defining a Menu for a Navigation View

```xml
<menu xmlns:android="http://schemas.android.com/apk/res/android"
  xmlns:app="http://schemas.android.com/apk/res-auto">
  <group android:checkableBehavior="single">
    <item
      android:id="@+id/nav_home"
      android:icon="@drawable/nav_home"
      android:title="@string/nav_home"
      android:checked="true" />
    <item
      android:id="@+id/nav_account"
      android:icon="@drawable/nav_account"
      android:title="@string/nav_account" />
    <item
      android:id="@+id/nav_settings"
      android:icon="@drawable/nav_settings"
      android:title="@string/nav_settings" />
    <item
      android:id="@+id/nav_about"
      android:icon="@drawable/nav_about"
      android:title="@string/nav_about" />
  </group>
</menu>
```

Using this approach, only one Menu Item can be selected at a time, and calling `setChecked` on a different Menu Item will automatically uncheck the previous selection.

The Navigation View also supports the `app:headerLayout` attribute (and corresponding `addHeaderView` method), to add headers to be displayed above any following Menu Items. The header can be retrieved in code using the `getHeaderView` method.

For larger screen UIs, a Navigation View can be included within the layout and made permanently visible as a side navigation affordance (see Figure 13-6).

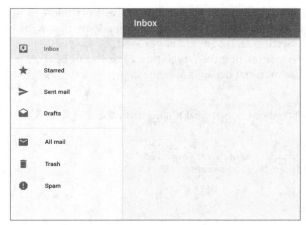

FIGURE 13-6

However, in most cases where side navigation is used, it's common to use a Navigation View within a `DrawerLayout`. Using a Drawer Layout makes it possible for users to swipe from the left screen edge to open the drawer, and swipe in the opposite direction to close the drawer.

This also allows the temporary side navigation to be toggled open and closed by selecting the navigation affordance on the left of the app bar, causing the Navigation View to appear *over* the content while the user selects a new top-level screen, as shown in Figure 13-7.

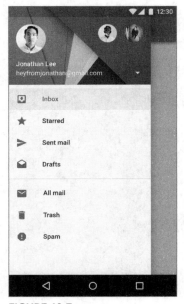

FIGURE 13-7

A Drawer Layout's first child view should always be the main layout that is always visible—in turn, this layout contains the `CoordinatorLayout`, `AppBarLayout`, and the layout or View that will contain your content, as shown in Listing 13-21. Setting `android:fitsSystemWindows="true"` on both the `DrawerLayout` and `NavigationView` ensures that the navigation drawer will be drawn underneath the status bar—as suggested by the material design guidelines.

LISTING 13-21: Building a layout using a Drawer Layout and Navigation View

```
<android.support.v4.widget.DrawerLayout
  xmlns:android="http://schemas.android.com/apk/res/android"
  xmlns:app="http://schemas.android.com/apk/res-auto"
  android:id="@+id/drawer_layout"
  android:layout_height="match_parent"
  android:layout_width="match_parent"
  android:fitsSystemWindows="true">

  <!-- Your Main Content View -->
  <android.support.design.widget.CoordinatorLayout
    android:layout_width="match_parent"
    android:layout_height="match_parent">

    <FrameLayout
      android:id="@+id/main_content"
      android:layout_width="match_parent"
      android:layout_height="match_parent"
      app:layout_behavior="@string/appbar_scrolling_view_behavior" />

    <android.support.design.widget.AppBarLayout
      android:layout_width="match_parent"
      android:layout_height="wrap_content"
      android:background="?attr/colorPrimary"
      android:theme="@style/ThemeOverlay.AppCompat.Dark.ActionBar">

      <android.support.v7.widget.Toolbar
        android:layout_width="match_parent"
        android:layout_height="wrap_content"
        app:layout_scrollFlags="scroll|snap|enterAlways" />
    </android.support.design.widget.AppBarLayout>
  </android.support.design.widget.CoordinatorLayout>

  <!-- Side navigation view -->
  <android.support.design.widget.NavigationView
    android:id="@+id/nav_view"
    android:layout_height="match_parent"
    android:layout_width="wrap_content"
    android:layout_gravity="start"
    android:fitsSystemWindows="true"
    app:headerLayout="@layout/nav_header"
    app:menu="@menu/side_nav_menu"/>
</android.support.v4.widget.DrawerLayout>
```

To connect the app bar's navigation icon to the Navigation Drawer, use the ActionBarDrawer-Toggle. To ensure that the state of the ActionBarDrawerToggle is updated correctly, you must override onPostCreate and onConfigurationChanged, including a call to the syncState method.

By calling your Action Bar Drawer Toggle's onOptionsItemSelected method from within the Activity's onOptionsMenuSelected handler, as shown in Listing 13-22, selecting the app bar navigation affordance will toggle the navigation drawer visibility.

LISTING 13-22: Connecting the App Bar and Navigation Drawer

```
private ActionBarDrawerToggle mDrawerToggle;

@Override
public void onCreate(Bundle savedInstanceState) {
  super.onCreate(savedInstanceState);
  setContentView(R.layout.app_bar_side_nav);

  // Ensure the navigation button is visible
  getSupportActionBar().setDisplayHomeAsUpEnabled(true);

  DrawerLayout drawerLayout = findViewById(R.id.drawer_layout);
  mDrawerToggle = new ActionBarDrawerToggle(this,
    drawerLayout,
    R.string.drawer_open_content_description,
    R.string.drawer_closed_content_description);
}

@Override
public void onPostCreate(Bundle savedInstanceState) {
  super.onPostCreate(savedInstanceState);
  mDrawerToggle.syncState();
}

@Override
public void onConfigurationChanged(Configuration newConfig) {
  super.onConfigurationChanged(newConfig);
  mDrawerToggle.syncState();
}

@Override
public boolean onOptionsMenuSelected(MenuItem item) {
  if (mDrawerToggle.onOptionsMenuSelected(item)) {
    return true;
  }

  // Follow with your own Menu Item selection logic
  return super.onOptionsMenuSelected(item);
}
```

When a Navigation View item is selected, the `OnNavigationItemSelectedListener` callback is called. Within that handler, the received Menu Item should be compared to the currently visible screen—and then the drawer should be closed—before the transition to the newly selected screen (if it's different from that currently displayed) should begin.

The content transition should begin only *after* the drawer has completely closed. This reduces jank by avoiding multiple concurrent animations, as well as making it easier for users to understand what is changing.

Listing 13-23 demonstrates how to configure the Action Bar Drawer Toggle by implementing a `DrawerListener`, an interface that provides callbacks for the drawer opening and closing.

Note that the main content transition, and related events such as updating the title in the app bar, are run within the `onDrawerClosed` handler.

LISTING 13-23: Connecting the App Bar and Navigation Drawer

```java
private int mSelectedItem = 0;
private ActionBarDrawerToggle mDrawerToggle;

@Override
public void onCreate(Bundle savedInstanceState) {
  super.onCreate(savedInstanceState);
  setContentView(R.layout.app_bar_side_nav);

  // Ensure the navigation button is visible
  getSupportActionBar().setDisplayHomeAsUpEnabled(true);

  final DrawerLayout drawerLayout = findViewById(R.id.drawer_layout);

  mDrawerToggle = new ActionBarDrawerToggle(this,
                        drawerLayout,
                        R.string.drawer_open_content_description,
                        R.string.drawer_closed_content_description) {

    @Override
    public void onDrawerClosed(View view) {
      // Create the newly selected item's Fragment
      Fragment newFragment;
      switch(mSelectedItem) {
        case R.id.nav_home:
          newFragment = new HomeFragment();
          getSupportActionBar().setTitle(R.string.nav_home);
          break;
        case R.id.nav_account:
          newFragment = new AccountFragment();
          getSupportActionBar().setTitle(R.string.nav_account);
          break;
```

```
    case R.id.nav_settings:
      newFragment = new SettingsFragment();
      getSupportActionBar().setTitle(R.string.nav_settings);
      break;
    case R.id.nav_about:
      newFragment = new AboutFragment();
      getSupportActionBar().setTitle(R.string.nav_about);
      break;
    default:
      return;
  }
  // Replace the current fragment with the newly selected item
  fm.beginTransaction()
    .replace(R.id.main_content, newFragment)
    .setTransition(FragmentTransaction.TRANSIT_FRAGMENT_FADE)
    .commit();
  // Reset the selected item
  mSelectedItem = 0;
  }
};

final NavigationView navigationView = findViewById(R.id.nav_view);

navigationView.setNavigationItemSelectedListener(
  new OnNavigationItemSelectedListener() {
    @Override
    public boolean onNavigationItemSelected(MenuItem item) {
      mSelectedItem = item.getItemId();
      item.setChecked(true);
      drawerLayout.closeDrawer(navigationView);
    }
  });
}
```

Combining Navigation Patterns

It can often be useful to combine multiple navigation patterns. For example, when using tabs it's common to have one or two additional secondary views accessible as app bar actions (for example, Settings and About). When you have three or more of these secondary views, you might consider adding a navigation drawer, as shown in Figure 13-8.

FIGURE 13-8

This provides users with a visual cue (in the form of the drawer indicator icon) that additional screens are available, without distracting from the tabs that should be the focus of user navigation attention.

Similarly, if you are using a bottom navigation bar, you should consider also using a navigation drawer when there are three or more secondary views, as shown in Figure 13-9.

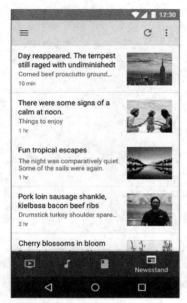

FIGURE 13-9

In both of these examples, the navigation drawer should *not* contain the items available within the primary navigation element.

ADDING TABS TO THE EARTHQUAKE MONITOR

Let's improve the earthquake-monitoring example by incorporating Tab navigation. The two tabs will be the existing list of earthquakes, and a second tab will be used to display a map of the earthquake locations.

In this example, we'll add the navigation elements—the map itself will be added in Chapter 15, "Location, Contextual Awareness, and Mapping."

1. Start by creating the layout for the Fragment that will be used to display the map by creating a new `fragment_earthquake_map.xml` layout in the `res/layout` folder. A Text View will serve as a placeholder until we add a map in Chapter 15:

```
<?xml version="1.0" encoding="utf-8"?>
<FrameLayout xmlns:android="http://schemas.android.com/apk/res/android"
  android:layout_width="match_parent"
  android:layout_height="match_parent">
  <TextView
    android:layout_width="match_parent"
    android:layout_height="match_parent"
    android:gravity="center"
    android:text="Map Goes Here!"
  />
</FrameLayout>
```

2. Create a new `EarthquakeMapFragment` class that extends `Fragment`, overriding the `onCreateView` handler to inflate the `fragment_earthquake_map` layout from Step 1:

```java
public class EarthquakeMapFragment extends Fragment  {

  @Override
  public View onCreateView(@NonNull LayoutInflater inflater,
      ViewGroup container, Bundle savedInstanceState) {
    return inflater.inflate(R.layout.fragment_earthquake_map,
      container, false);
  }
}
```

3. On larger screens (such as a tablet) we can display the list and map side-by-side. Create a variation of the `activity_earthquake_main.xml` layout within the `res/layout-sw720dp` folder that we'll optimize for displays with at least 720dp of screen width. This layout will display the Earthquake List Fragment and Earthquake Map Fragment side-by-side, limiting the width of the list Fragment to half the minimum width for this layout (360dp). With the additional screen space available, we can also use an expanded toolbar pattern, built with an `AppBarLayout` that is double the height of a normal Toolbar on tablets (64dp), a `CollapsingToolbarLayout` and a `Toolbar`:

```xml
<?xml version="1.0" encoding="utf-8"?>
<android.support.design.widget.CoordinatorLayout
  xmlns:android="http://schemas.android.com/apk/res/android"
  xmlns:app="http://schemas.android.com/apk/res-auto"
  android:layout_width="match_parent"
  android:layout_height="match_parent">

  <android.support.design.widget.AppBarLayout
    android:layout_width="match_parent"
    android:layout_height="128dp"
    android:theme="@style/ThemeOverlay.AppCompat.Dark.ActionBar">

    <android.support.design.widget.CollapsingToolbarLayout
      android:layout_width="match_parent"
      android:layout_height="match_parent">
      <android.support.v7.widget.Toolbar
        android:id="@+id/toolbar"
        android:layout_width="match_parent"
        android:layout_height="?attr/actionBarSize"/>
    </android.support.design.widget.CollapsingToolbarLayout>
  </android.support.design.widget.AppBarLayout>

  <LinearLayout
    android:layout_width="match_parent"
    android:layout_height="match_parent"
    android:baselineAligned="false"
    android:orientation="horizontal"
    app:layout_behavior="@string/appbar_scrolling_view_behavior">

    <fragment
      android:id="@+id/EarthquakeListFragment"
      android:name=
        "com.professionalandroid.apps.earthquake.EarthquakeListFragment"
```

```
      android:layout_width="360dp"
      android:layout_height="match_parent"/>
   <fragment
      android:id="@+id/EarthquakeMapFragment"
      android:name=
        "com.professionalandroid.apps.earthquake.EarthquakeMapFragment"
      android:layout_width="0dp"
      android:layout_weight="1"
      android:layout_height="match_parent"
      android:layout_weight="1"/>
 </LinearLayout>
</android.support.design.widget.CoordinatorLayout>
```

4. On smaller screens (such as a phone) we will display only the list or the map at any given time, using tabs to switch between them. Modify strings.xml to add the labels for the new tabs:

```
<string name="tab_list">List</string>
<string name="tab_map">Map</string>
```

5. Modify the activity_earthquake_main.xml layout in the res/layout folder, adding a ViewPager that will contain the list and map Fragments. Also take this opportunity to add a TabLayout to the App Bar Layout:

```
<?xml version="1.0" encoding="utf-8"?>
<android.support.design.widget.CoordinatorLayout
  xmlns:android="http://schemas.android.com/apk/res/android"
  xmlns:app="http://schemas.android.com/apk/res-auto"
  android:layout_width="match_parent"
  android:layout_height="match_parent">

  <android.support.design.widget.AppBarLayout
    android:layout_width="match_parent"
    android:layout_height="wrap_content"
    android:theme="@style/ThemeOverlay.AppCompat.Dark.ActionBar">

    <android.support.v7.widget.Toolbar
      android:id="@+id/toolbar"
      android:layout_width="match_parent"
      android:layout_height="wrap_content"
      app:layout_scrollFlags="scroll|enterAlways|snap" />

    <android.support.design.widget.TabLayout
      android:id="@+id/tab_layout"
      android:layout_width="match_parent"
      android:layout_height="wrap_content" />
  </android.support.design.widget.AppBarLayout>

  <android.support.v4.view.ViewPager
    android:id="@+id/view_pager"
    android:layout_width="match_parent"
    android:layout_height="match_parent"
    app:layout_behavior="@string/appbar_scrolling_view_behavior"/>
</android.support.design.widget.CoordinatorLayout>
```

6. Now add navigation support for switching between the list and map. In your Earthquake Main Activity, create a `FragmentPagerAdapter` that displays the list as the first tab, and the map as the second:

```
class EarthquakeTabsPagerAdapter extends FragmentPagerAdapter {

  EarthquakeTabsPagerAdapter(FragmentManager fm) {
    super(fm);
  }

  @Override
  public int getCount() {
    return 2;
  }

  @Override
  public Fragment getItem(int position) {
    switch(position) {
      case 0:
        return new EarthquakeListFragment();
      case 1:
        return new EarthquakeMapFragment();
      default:
        return null;
    }
  }

  @Override
  public CharSequence getPageTitle(int position) {
    switch(position) {
      case 0:
        return getString(R.string.tab_list);
      case 1:
        return getString(R.string.tab_map);
      default:
        return null;
    }
  }
}
```

7. Still within the Earthquake Main Activity, modify the `onCreate` handler to remove the Fragment Transaction code and instead set up tab navigation when the View Pager is detected, using the Pager Adapter from Step 6:

```
@Override
public void onCreate(Bundle savedInstanceState) {
  super.onCreate(savedInstanceState);
  setContentView(R.layout.activity_earthquake_main);
  Toolbar toolbar = findViewById(R.id.toolbar);
  setSupportActionBar(toolbar);

  ViewPager viewPager = findViewById(R.id.view_pager);
  if (viewPager != null) {
```

```
        PagerAdapter pagerAdapter =
          new EarthquakeTabsPagerAdapter(getSupportFragmentManager());
        viewPager.setAdapter(pagerAdapter);

        TabLayout tabLayout = findViewById(R.id.tab_layout);
        tabLayout.setupWithViewPager(viewPager);
    }

    [... Existing code for loading and observing data ...]
    }
```

Figure 13-10 shows the app running on a phone, where it displays the App Bar with two Tabs, and on a tablet device, where the two Fragments are shown side-by-side.

FIGURE 13-10

CHOOSING THE RIGHT LEVEL OF INTERRUPTION

In Chapter 11, "Working on the Background," you were introduced to Notifications as a method of informing users of important information while your app is in the background. Android also offers a number of mechanisms that can be used to inform—and even interrupt—the user while your app is in the foreground, including Dialogs, Toast messages, and Snackbars.

Whenever possible, your app should allow users to continue with their regular workflow unhindered. In exceptional cases, though, it may make sense to interrupt the users to inform them of a significant event or change.

Note that every interruption or significant change in your app's appearance has an inherent cost; users must process what has changed and what, if any, actions they need to perform in response.

Initiating a Dialog

Android Dialogs are partially transparent, floating windows that partially obscure the UI that launched them, as shown in Figure 13-11.

Dialog boxes are a common UI metaphor in desktop, web, and mobile applications. Modal Dialogs are the most intrusive of the options available for interrupting users—presenting information and requiring a response before allowing users to continue.

FIGURE 13-11

In terms of Android UX design, Dialogs should be used to represent global system-level events, such as displaying system errors or supporting required account selection. It's good practice to limit the use of Dialogs within your applications, and to minimize the degree to which you customize them.

Create Dialogs by extending the `AppCompatDialogFragment` class, a Fragment subclass that includes all of the AppCompat styling, and handles saving and restoring the Dialog appropriately during configuration changes.

Most Dialogs fall into a number of standard Dialog categories:

➤ A confirmation message with positive and negative response buttons

➤ A single-choice list of items for the user to make a selection

➤ A multiple-select list of items with checkboxes

These standard cases can be accommodated using an `AlertDialog`. To take advantage of the standard Alert Dialog UI, you must create a new `AlertDialog.Builder` object within the `onCreateDialog` handler of your `AppCompatDialogFragment`, before assigning values for the title, message to display, and optionally for any buttons, selection items, and text input boxes required—as shown in Listing 13-24.

Clicking either button will close the Dialog after executing the attached On Click Listeners.

LISTING 13-24: Configuring an Alert Dialog in an AppCompat Dialog Fragment

```java
public class PitchBlackDialogFragment extends AppCompatDialogFragment {
  @Override
  public Dialog onCreateDialog(Bundle savedInstanceState) {
    AlertDialog.Builder builder = new AlertDialog.Builder(getActivity());

    builder.setTitle("It is Pitch Black")
      .setMessage("You are likely to be eaten by a Grue.")
      .setPositiveButton(
        "Move Forward",
        new DialogInterface.OnClickListener() {
          @Override
          public void onClick(DialogInterface dialog, int arg1) {
            eatenByGrue();
```

```
              }
          })
        .setNegativeButton(
          "Go Back",
          new DialogInterface.OnClickListener(){
            @Override
            public void onClick(DialogInterface dialog, int arg1) {
              // do nothing
            }
        });
      // Create and return the AlertDialog
      return builder.create();
    }
  }
```

Use the setCancelable method to determine if the user should be able to close the Dialog by pressing the back button without making a selection. If you choose to make the Dialog cancelable, you can override the onCancel method in the App Compat Dialog Fragment to react to this event.

It's also possible to build an entirely custom Dialog by overriding the onCreateView and inflating your own layout.

Whether you are using a totally custom Dialog, an AlertDialog, or one of the other specialized Dialog subclasses such as DatePickerDialog or TimePickerDialog, the dialog is shown by calling the show method, as shown in Listing 13-25.

LISTING 13-25: Displaying a Dialog Fragment

```
String tag = "warning_dialog";
DialogFragment dialogFragment = new PitchBlackDialogFragment();

dialogFragment.show(getSupportFragmentManager(), tag);
```

Let's Make a Toast

On the other end of the interruption spectrum are Toast messages. Toasts are transient notifications that don't steal focus, cannot be interacted with, and are non-modal; they appear, show a brief message, and then disappear.

Given these limitations, they should only be used to confirm a user's action immediately after it occurs, or for system-level messages. They should only be displayed when your app has an active Activity visible.

The Toast class includes a static makeText method that creates a standard Toast display window. To construct a new Toast, pass the current Context, the text to display, and the length of time to display it (LENGTH_SHORT or LENGTH_LONG) into the makeText method. After creating a Toast, you can display it by calling show, as shown in Listing 13-26.

LISTING 13-26: Displaying a Toast

```
Context context = this;
String msg = "To health and happiness!";
int duration = Toast.LENGTH_SHORT;

Toast toast = Toast.makeText(context, msg, duration);

// Remember, you must *always* call show()
toast.show();
```

Figure 13-12 shows a Toast. It will remain on-screen for approximately 2 seconds before fading out. The application behind it remains fully responsive and interactive while the Toast is visible.

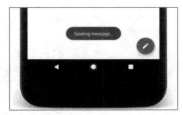

FIGURE 13-12

> **NOTE** *It should be noted that a Toast message must always be created and shown on the UI thread. Make sure that if you're building a Toast after the completion of background work, that your UI is still visible and you show it on the UI thread—for example, within an Async Task's* `onPostExecute` *handler.*

Inline Interruptions with Snackbars

A Snackbar allows you to build interruptions directly into your UI using a temporary View that is displayed by animating up from the bottom of the screen, as shown in Figure 13-13.

FIGURE 13-13

Users can choose to swipe away a Snackbar immediately, or allow it to time out and disappear automatically—similar to a Toast.

The Snackbar API, available as part of the Android Design Support Library, includes a `make` method that takes a View, the text to display, and the length of time to display it. Unlike Toasts, Snackbars also offer the ability to add a single action using the `setAction` method, as shown in Listing 13-27.

LISTING 13-27: Building and showing a Snackbar

```
Snackbar snackbar = Snackbar.make(coordinatorLayout, "Deleted",
                                  Snackbar.LENGTH_LONG);

// Define the action
snackbar.setAction("Undo", new View.OnClickListener() {
  @Override
  public void onClick(View view) {
    // Undo the deletion
  }
});

// React to the Snackbar being dismissed
snackbar.addCallback(new Snackbar.Callback() {
  @Override
  public void onDismissed(Snackbar transientBottomBar, int event) {
    // Finalize the deletion
  }
});

// Show the Snackbar
snackbar.show();
```

This is often used to offer users an "undo" facility to recover from destructive actions. For example, when a user deletes an object, it can be marked for deletion while the Snackbar is displayed, while a callback is added using the `addCallback` method. Selecting the "undo" action simply unmarks the object for deletion, while the `onDismissed` callback would apply the deletion.

The position of the Snackbar is dependent on what View you pass into `make`. If the View you pass in is a Coordinator Layout or has a Coordinator Layout as one of its parents (either directly or indirectly), the Snackbar will be positioned at the bottom of that Coordinator Layout. If no Coordinator Layout is found, the Snackbar will be positioned at the bottom of your Activity.

> **NOTE** *When a Snackbar is used with a Coordinator Layout, users are able to swipe it away and any* `FloatingActionButton` *that would potentially overlap the incoming Snackbar will be smoothly animated alongside the Snackbar.*

The Snackbar mechanism reduces risk and anxiety with your users by eliminating the potential of a mistake causing an inadvertent—and unrecoverable—destructive action, without regularly interrupting experienced users.

Strongly consider replacing blocking "are you sure?" confirmation Dialogs with Snackbars that include restorative actions, as it allows both new users and frequent users to recover when needed without constantly interrupting their workflow.

14

Advanced Customization of Your User Interface

WHAT'S IN THIS CHAPTER?

➤ Making applications accessible

➤ Using the text-to-speech and speech recognition libraries

➤ Controlling device vibration

➤ Going full screen

➤ Using property animators

➤ Advanced Canvas drawing

➤ Handling touch events

➤ Advanced Drawable resources

➤ Copy, paste, and the clipboard

WROX.COM CODE DOWNLOADS FOR THIS CHAPTER

The code downloads for this chapter are found at www.wrox.com. The code for this chapter is divided into the following major examples:

➤ Snippets_ch14.zip

➤ Compass_ch14.zip

EXPANDING THE USER EXPERIENCE

Material design serves as the basis for the structure, UI, and the interaction patterns that make for a great user experience (UX) on Android, but it's only a base to build upon.

In this chapter you learn to think beyond basic necessities and create applications that combine purpose with beauty and simplicity, even (or especially) when they're providing complex functionality.

You also discover how to ensure your app offers a great user experience to all users, including those users who take advantage of accessibility services when using their devices.

Next, you are introduced to the text-to-speech, speech recognition, and vibration APIs, in order to expand the range of interactions available to users.

To further immerse the user within your app, you then learn to control the visibility of the system UI including the status bar and navigation bar on the top and bottom of the screen, respectively.

You also discover how to use property animations to change individual views and how to enhance the custom Views you created in Chapter 5, "Building User Interfaces," using advanced canvas-drawing techniques and your own touch event handling.

SUPPORTING ACCESSIBILITY

An important part of creating a compelling UI is to ensure that it can be used by everyone, including people with disabilities that require them to interact with their devices in different ways.

The Accessibility APIs provide alternative interaction methods for users with visual, physical, or age-related disabilities that make it difficult to interact fully with a touch screen.

In Chapter 5 you learned how to make your custom Views accessible and navigable. This section summarizes some of the best practices to ensure your entire user experience is accessible.

Supporting Navigation Without a Touch Screen

While physical directional controllers, such as D-pads and arrow keys, are no longer common on smartphone devices, they are emulated when users enable the Accessibility Services, making them the primary means of navigation for many users.

To ensure that your UI is navigable without requiring a touch screen, it's important that your application supports each of these input mechanisms.

The first step is to ensure that each input View is focusable and clickable. Pressing the center or OK button should then affect the focused control in the same way as touching it using the touch screen.

It's good practice to visually indicate when a control has the input focus, allowing users to know which control they are interacting with. All the Views included in the Android SDK are focusable.

The Android run time determines the focus order for each control in your layout based on an algorithm that finds the nearest neighbor in a given direction. You can manually override that order using the `android:nextFocusDown`, `android:nextFocusLeft`, `android:nextFocusRight`, and `android:nextFocusUp` attributes for any View within your layout definition. It's good practice to ensure that consecutive navigation movements in the opposite direction should return you to the original location.

Providing a Textual Description of Each View

Context is of critical importance when designing your UI. Button images, text labels, or even the relative location of each control can be used to indicate the purpose of each input View.

To ensure your application is accessible, consider how a user without visual context can navigate and use your UI. To assist, each View can include an `android:contentDescription` attribute that can be read aloud to users who have enabled the accessibility speech tools:

```
<Button
  android:id="@+id/pick_contact_button"
  android:layout_width="match_parent"
  android:layout_height="wrap_content"
  android:text="@string/pick_contact_button"
  android:contentDescription="@string/pick_contact_button_description"
/>
```

Every View within your layout that can hold focus should have a content description that provides the entire context necessary for a user to act on it.

INTRODUCING ANDROID TEXT-TO-SPEECH

The text-to-speech (TTS) libraries, also known as *speech synthesis*, enable you to output synthesized speech from within your applications, allowing them to "talk" to your users.

Due to storage space constraints on some Android devices, the language packs are not always preinstalled on each device. Before using the TTS engine, it's good practice to confirm the language packs are installed.

To check for the TTS libraries, start a new Activity for a result using the `ACTION_CHECK_TTS_DATA` action from the `TextToSpeech.Engine` class:

```
Intent intent = new Intent(TextToSpeech.Engine.ACTION_CHECK_TTS_DATA);
startActivityForResult(intent, TTS_DATA_CHECK);
```

The `onActivityResult` handler receives `CHECK_VOICE_DATA_PASS` if the voice data has been installed successfully. If the voice data is not currently available, start a new Activity using the `ACTION_INSTALL_TTS_DATA` action from the TTS Engine class to initiate its installation:

```
Intent installVoice = new Intent(Engine.ACTION_INSTALL_TTS_DATA);
startActivity(installVoice);
```

After confirming the voice data is available, you need to create and initialize a new `TextToSpeech` instance. Note that you cannot use the new Text To Speech object until initialization is complete. Pass an `OnInitListener` into the constructor that will be fired when the TTS engine has been initialized:

```
boolean ttsIsInit = false;
TextToSpeech tts = null;
```

```
    protected void onActivityResult(int requestCode,
                          int resultCode, Intent data) {
  if (requestCode == TTS_DATA_CHECK) {
    if (resultCode == Engine.CHECK_VOICE_DATA_PASS) {
      tts = new TextToSpeech(this, new OnInitListener() {
        public void onInit(int status) {
          if (status == TextToSpeech.SUCCESS) {
            ttsIsInit = true;
            // TODO Speak!
          }
        }
      });
    }
  }
}
```

After initializing Text To Speech, you can use the `speak` method to synthesize voice data using the default device audio output:

```
Bundle parameters = null;
String utteranceId = null; // Can be used with setOnUtteranceProgressListener
tts.speak("Hello, Android", TextToSpeech.QUEUE_ADD, parameters, utteranceId);
```

The `speak` method enables you to specify either to add the new voice output to the existing queue or to flush the queue and start speaking immediately.

You can affect the way the voice output sounds using the `setPitch` and `setSpeechRate` methods. Each method accepts a float parameter that modifies the pitch and speed, respectively, of the voice output.

You can also change the pronunciation of your voice output using the `setLanguage` method. This method takes a `Locale` parameter to specify the country and language of the text to speak. This affects the way the text is spoken to ensure the correct language and pronunciation models are used.

When you have finished speaking, use `stop` to halt voice output and `shutdown` to free the TTS resources:

```
tts.stop();
tts.shutdown();
```

Listing 14-1 determines whether the TTS voice library is installed, initializes a new TTS engine, and uses it to speak in UK English.

LISTING 14-1: Using text-to-speech

```
private static int TTS_DATA_CHECK = 1;

private TextToSpeech tts = null;
private boolean ttsIsInit = false;

private void initTextToSpeech() {
  Intent intent = new Intent(Engine.ACTION_CHECK_TTS_DATA);
  startActivityForResult(intent, TTS_DATA_CHECK);
}
```

```java
protected void onActivityResult(int requestCode,
                                int resultCode, Intent data) {
  if (requestCode == TTS_DATA_CHECK) {
    if (resultCode == Engine.CHECK_VOICE_DATA_PASS) {
      tts = new TextToSpeech(this, new OnInitListener() {
        public void onInit(int status) {
          if (status == TextToSpeech.SUCCESS) {
            ttsIsInit = true;
            if (tts.isLanguageAvailable(Locale.UK) >= 0)
              tts.setLanguage(Locale.UK);
            tts.setPitch(0.8f);
            tts.setSpeechRate(1.1f);
            speak();
          }
        }
      });
    } else {
      Intent installVoice = new Intent(Engine.ACTION_INSTALL_TTS_DATA);
      startActivity(installVoice);
    }
  }
}

private void speak() {
  if (tts != null && ttsIsInit) {
    tts.speak("Hello, Android old chap!", TextToSpeech.QUEUE_ADD, null);
  }
}

@Override
public void onDestroy() {
  if (tts != null) {
    tts.stop();
    tts.shutdown();
  }
  super.onDestroy();
}
```

USING SPEECH RECOGNITION

Android supports voice input and speech recognition using the `RecognizerIntent` class. This API enables you to accept voice input into your application using the standard voice input dialog, as shown in Figure 14-1.

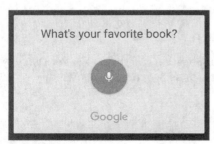

FIGURE 14-1

To add voice input to your app, your app must hold the `RECORD_AUDIO` permission:

```
<uses-permission android:name="android.permission.RECORD_AUDIO"/>
```

> **NOTE** *The* `RECORD_AUDIO` *permission is a dangerous permission that must be requested at run time on Android 6.0 Marshmallow (API Level 23) and higher devices.*

To initialize voice recognition, call `startNewActivityForResult`, passing in an Intent that specifies the `RecognizerIntent.ACTION_RECOGNIZE_SPEECH` or `RecognizerIntent.ACTION_WEB_SEARCH` actions. The former action enables you to receive the input speech within your application, whereas the latter action enables you to trigger a web search or voice action using the native providers.

The launch Intent must include the `RecognizerIntent.EXTRA_LANGUAGE_MODEL` extra to specify the language model used to parse the input audio. This can be either `LANGUAGE_MODEL_FREE_FORM` or `LANGUAGE_MODEL_WEB_SEARCH`; both are available as static constants from the `RecognizerIntent` class.

You can also specify a number of optional extras to control the language, potential result count, and display prompt using the following Recognizer Intent constants:

➤ `EXTRA_LANGUAGE`—Specifies a language constant from the `Locale` class to use an input language other than the device default. You can find the current default by calling the static `getDefault` method on the `Locale` class.

➤ `EXTRA_MAXRESULTS`—Uses an integer value to limit the number of potential recognition results returned.

➤ `EXTRA_PROMPT`—Specifies a string that displays in the voice input dialog (shown in Figure 14-1) to prompt the user to speak.

> **NOTE** *The engine that handles the speech recognition may not be capable of understanding spoken input from all the languages available from the* `Locale` *class.*
>
> *Not all devices include support for speech recognition. In such cases it is generally possible to download the voice recognition library from the Google Play Store.*

Using Speech Recognition for Voice Input

When using voice recognition to provide user input to your application, call `startNewActivityForResult` using the `RecognizerIntent.ACTION_RECOGNIZE_SPEECH` action, as shown in Listing 14-2.

LISTING 14-2: Initiating a speech recognition request

```
Intent intent = new Intent(RecognizerIntent.ACTION_RECOGNIZE_SPEECH);
// Specify free form input
intent.putExtra(RecognizerIntent.EXTRA_LANGUAGE_MODEL,
                RecognizerIntent.LANGUAGE_MODEL_FREE_FORM);
intent.putExtra(RecognizerIntent.EXTRA_PROMPT,
                "or forever hold your peace");
intent.putExtra(RecognizerIntent.EXTRA_MAX_RESULTS, 1);
intent.putExtra(RecognizerIntent.EXTRA_LANGUAGE, Locale.ENGLISH);
startActivityForResult(intent, VOICE_RECOGNITION);
```

When the user finishes speaking, the speech recognition engine analyzes and processes the resulting audio and returns the results through the onActivityResult handler as an Array List of strings in the EXTRA_RESULTS extra, as shown in Listing 14-3.

LISTING 14-3: Finding the results of a speech recognition request

```
@Override
protected void onActivityResult(int requestCode,
                                int resultCode,
                                Intent data) {
  if (requestCode == VOICE_RECOGNITION && resultCode == RESULT_OK) {
    ArrayList<String> results =
      data.getStringArrayListExtra(RecognizerIntent.EXTRA_RESULTS);

    float[] confidence =
      data.getFloatArrayExtra(
        RecognizerIntent.EXTRA_CONFIDENCE_SCORES);

    // TODO Do something with the recognized voice strings
  }}
```

Each string returned in the Array List represents a potential match for the spoken input. You can find the recognition engine's confidence in each result using the float array returned in the EXTRA_ CONFIDENCE_SCORES extra. Each value in the array is the confidence score between 0 (no confidence) and 1 (high confidence) that the speech has been correctly recognized.

Using Speech Recognition for Search

When using speech recognition to facilitate search, rather than handling the received speech yourself you can use the RecognizerIntent.ACTION_WEB_SEARCH action to display a web search result or to trigger another type of voice action based on the user's speech, as shown in Listing 14-4.

LISTING 14-4: Finding the results of a speech recognition request

```
Intent intent = new Intent(RecognizerIntent.ACTION_WEB_SEARCH);
intent.putExtra(RecognizerIntent.EXTRA_LANGUAGE_MODEL,
                RecognizerIntent.LANGUAGE_MODEL_WEB_SEARCH);
startActivityForResult(intent, 0);
```

CONTROLLING DEVICE VIBRATION

In Chapter 11, "Working in the Background," you learned how to create Notifications that can use vibration to enrich event feedback. In some circumstances, you may want to vibrate the device independently of Notifications.

For example, vibrating the device is an excellent way to provide haptic user feedback, and is particularly popular as a feedback mechanism for games.

To control device vibration, your applications needs the VIBRATE permission:

```
<uses-permission android:name="android.permission.VIBRATE"/>
```

Device vibration is controlled through the Vibrator Service, accessible via the getSystemService method:

```
String vibratorService = Context.VIBRATOR_SERVICE;
Vibrator vibrator = (Vibrator)getSystemService(vibratorService);
```

Not all devices contain a vibrator (for example, televisions), so use the hasVibrator method to determine if you should use a different mechanism to provide feedback to the user:

```
boolean hasVibrator = vibrator.hasVibrator();
```

Call vibrate to start device vibration; you can pass in either a vibration duration or a pattern of alternating vibration/pause sequences along with an optional index parameter that repeats the pattern starting at the index specified:

```
long[] pattern = {1000, 2000, 4000, 8000, 16000 };
vibrator.vibrate(pattern, 0);   // Execute vibration pattern.
Vibrator.vibrate(pattern, -1);  // Execute vibration pattern just once
vibrator.vibrate(1000);         // Vibrate for 1 second.
```

To cancel vibration, call cancel; exiting your application automatically cancels any vibration it has initiated:

```
vibrator.cancel();
```

GOING FULL SCREEN

If, and only if, you're building an application that is designed to be fully immersive it may make sense for your application to occupy the entire screen, hiding or obscuring the system UI including the status bar along the top of the screen and any on-screen navigation controls. Examples of immersive applications include games such as first-person racers or shooters, e-learning applications, and video players.

To control the visibility of the navigation bar on handsets, or the appearance of the system bar in tablets, you can use the setSystemUiVisibility method on any View visible within your Activity hierarchy. The SYSTEM_UI_FLAG_HIDE_NAVIGATION flag hides the navigation bar while the SYSTEM_UI_FLAG_FULLSCREEN flag will result in the status bar being hidden.

By default, any user interaction with the Activity will show the navigation bar, and swiping down from the top edge of the screen will show the status bar, resetting the flags. This is appropriate for apps such as video players where you expect minimal user interaction.

Android 4.4 Kit Kat (API Level 19) added the ability to provide truly immersive experiences even when the user is interacting with your Activity. This comes with the addition of two additional flags:

➤ SYSTEM_UI_FLAG_IMMERSIVE—In Immersive mode, users can interact with the Activity, requiring that they swipe down from the top edge of the screen in order to reveal the hidden system UI and exit immersive mode. This is appropriate for a book or news reader, where users will need to touch the Activity to scroll or change pages.

➤ SYSTEM_UI_FLAG_IMMERSIVE_STICKY—Similar to Immersive mode, the user can fully interact with the Activity. However, swiping down only temporarily reveals the system UI, before it automatically hides again. This is appropriate for a game or drawing app that expects infrequent use of the system UI.

When using only these flags, the position of your Views will be adjusted whenever the system UI is hidden or shown. To stabilize your UI, you can use the additional flags of SYSTEM_UI_FLAG_LAYOUT_FULLSCREEN, SYSTEM_UI_FLAG_LAYOUT_HIDE_NAVIGATION, and SYSTEM_UI_FLAG_LAYOUT_STABLE to request that the Activity always be laid out as if the system UI is always hidden:

```
private void hideSystemUI() {
  // Hide the navigation bar, status bar, and use IMMERSIVE
  // Note the usage of the _LAYOUT flags to keep a stable layout
  getWindow().getDecorView().setSystemUiVisibility(
    View.SYSTEM_UI_FLAG_LAYOUT_STABLE
    | View.SYSTEM_UI_FLAG_LAYOUT_HIDE_NAVIGATION
    | View.SYSTEM_UI_FLAG_LAYOUT_FULLSCREEN
    | View.SYSTEM_UI_FLAG_HIDE_NAVIGATION // hide nav bar
    | View.SYSTEM_UI_FLAG_FULLSCREEN      // hide status bar
    | View.SYSTEM_UI_FLAG_IMMERSIVE);
}

// Show the system UI - note how the _LAYOUT flags are kept to maintain
// a stable layout
private void showSystemUI() {
  getWindow().getDecorView().setSystemUiVisibility(
    View.SYSTEM_UI_FLAG_LAYOUT_STABLE
    | View.SYSTEM_UI_FLAG_LAYOUT_HIDE_NAVIGATION
    | View.SYSTEM_UI_FLAG_LAYOUT_FULLSCREEN);
}
```

It's good practice to synchronize other changes within your UI with changes in navigation visibility. For example, you may choose to hide and display the App Bar and other navigational controls based on entering and exiting full screen mode.

You can do this by registering an OnSystemUiVisibilityChangeListener to a View—typically, the View you're using to control the navigation visibility—as shown in Listing 14-5.

LISTING 14-5: Reacting to changes in system UI visibility

```
myView.setOnSystemUiVisibilityChangeListener(
  new OnSystemUiVisibilityChangeListener() {

  public void onSystemUiVisibilityChange(int visibility) {
    if (visibility == View.SYSTEM_UI_FLAG_VISIBLE) {
      // TODO Display Action Bar and Status Bar
    }
    else {
      // TODO Hide Action Bar and Status Bar
    }
  }
});
```

Note that the system UI flags are reset whenever the user leaves (and subsequently returns to) your app. As a result the timing of calls to set these flags is important to ensure the UI is always in the state you expect. It's recommended that you set and reset any system UI flags within the `onResume` and `onWindowFocusChanged` handlers.

WORKING WITH PROPERTY ANIMATIONS

In Chapter 12, "Implementing the Android Design Philosophy," you learned how to build "reveal" animations and shared element Activity transitions, to help construct larger transitions within your app. When it comes to animating individual Views, you can use property animators.

A property animator directly modifies any property—visual or otherwise—to transition from one value to another, over a specified period of time, using the interpolation algorithm of your choice, and repeating as required. The *value* can be any variable or object, from a regular integer to a complex Class instance.

You can use property animators to create a smooth transition for anything within your code; the target property doesn't even need to represent something visual. Property animations are effectively iterators implemented using a background timer to increment or decrement a value according to a given interpolation path over a given period of time.

This is an incredibly powerful tool that can be used for anything from a simple View effect (such as moving, scaling, or fading a View), to complex animations, including runtime layout changes and curved transitions.

Creating Property Animations

The simplest technique for creating property animations is using an `ObjectAnimator`. The Object Animator class includes the `ofFloat`, `ofInt`, and `ofObject` static methods to easily create an animation that transitions the specified property of the target object between the values provided:

```
String propertyName = "alpha";
float from = 1f;
float to = 0f;
```

```
ObjectAnimator anim = ObjectAnimator.ofFloat(targetObject, propertyName,
                                             from, to);
// Make sure to start your animation!
anim.start();
```

Alternatively, you can provide a single value to animate the property from its current value to its final value:

```
ObjectAnimator anim = ObjectAnimator.ofFloat(targetObject, propertyName, to);
anim.start();
```

> **NOTE** *To animate a given property, there must be associated getter/setter functions on the underlying object. In the preceding example, the* `targetObject` *must include* `getAlpha` *and* `setAlpha` *methods that return and accept a float value, respectively.*

To target a property of a type other than integer or float, use the `ofObject` method. This method requires that you supply an implementation of the `TypeEvaluator` class. Implement the `evaluate` method to return an object that should be returned when the animation is a given fraction of the way through animating between the start and end objects:

```
TypeEvaluator<MyClass> evaluator = new TypeEvaluator<MyClass>() {
    public MyClass evaluate(float fraction,
                            MyClass startValue,
                            MyClass endValue) {
        MyClass result = new MyClass();
        // TODO Modify the new object to represent itself the given
        // fraction between the start and end values.
        return result;
    }
};

// Animate between two instances
ValueAnimator oa
    = ObjectAnimator.ofObject(evaluator, myClassFromInstance, myClassToInstance);

oa.setTarget(myClassInstance);
oa.start();
```

By default, each animation will run once with a 300ms duration. Use the `setDuration` method to alter the amount of time the interpolator should use to complete the transition:

```
anim.setDuration(500);
```

You can use the `setRepeatMode` and `setRepeatCount` methods to cause the animation to be applied either a set number of times or infinitely:

```
anim.setRepeatCount(ValueAnimator.INFINITE);
```

You can set the repeat mode either to restart from the beginning or to apply the animation in reverse:

```
anim.setRepeatMode(ValueAnimator.REVERSE);
```

To create the same Object Animator as an XML resource, create a new XML file in the `res/animator` folder:

```
<objectAnimator xmlns:android="http://schemas.android.com/apk/res/android"
    android:valueTo="0"
    android:propertyName="alpha"
    android:duration="500"
    android:valueType="floatType"
    android:repeatCount="-1"
    android:repeatMode="reverse"
/>
```

The filename can then be used as the resource identifier. To affect a particular object with an XML animator resource, use the `AnimatorInflator.loadAnimator` method, passing in the current context and the resource ID of the animation to apply in order to obtain a copy of the Object Animator, and then use the `setTarget` method to apply it to an object:

```
Animator anim = AnimatorInflater.loadAnimator(context, resID);
anim.setTarget(targetObject);
```

By default, the interpolator used to transition between the start and end values of each animation uses a nonlinear `AccelerateDecelerateInterpolator`, which provides the effect of accelerating at the beginning of the transition and decelerating when approaching the end.

You can use the `setInterpolator` method to apply one of the following SDK interpolators:

➤ `AccelerateDecelerateInterpolator`—The rate of change starts and ends slowly but accelerates through the middle.

➤ `AccelerateInterpolator`—The rate of change starts slowly but accelerates through the middle.

➤ `AnticipateInterpolator`—The change starts backward and then flings forward.

➤ `AnticipateOvershootInterpolator`—The change starts backward, flings forward, overshoots the target value, and finally goes back to the final value.

➤ `BounceInterpolator`—The change bounces at the end.

➤ `CycleInterpolator`—The change is repeated following a sinusoidal pattern.

➤ `DecelerateInterpolator`—The rate of change starts out quickly and then decelerates.

➤ `LinearInterpolator`—The rate of change is constant.

➤ `OvershootInterpolator`—The change flings forward, overshoots the last value, and then comes back.

➤ `PathInterpolator`—The change follows a Path object that extends from Point (0, 0) to (1, 1). The x coordinate along the Path is the input value and the output is the y coordinate of the line at that point:

```
anim.setInterpolator(new OvershootInterpolator());
```

You can also extend your own `TimeInterpolator` class to specify a custom interpolation algorithm.

To execute an animation, you must call its `start` method:

```
anim.start();
```

Creating Property Animation Sets

Android includes the `AnimatorSet` class to make it easier to create complex, interrelated animations:

```
AnimatorSet bouncer = new AnimatorSet();
```

To add a new animation to an Animator Set, use the `play` method. This returns an `AnimatorSet`
`.Builder` object that lets you specify when to play the new animation in relation to the existing set:

```
AnimatorSet mySet = new AnimatorSet();
mySet.play(firstAnimation).before(concurrentAnim1);
mySet.play(concurrentAnim1).with(concurrentAnim2);
mySet.play(lastAnim).after(concurrentAnim2);
```

Use the `start` method to execute the sequence of animations:

```
mySet.start();
```

Using Animation Listeners

The `Animator.AnimationListener` class lets you create event handlers that are fired when an animation begins, ends, repeats, or is canceled:

```
Animator.AnimatorListener animListener = new AnimatorListener() {

    public void onAnimationStart(Animator animation) {
        // TODO Auto-generated method stub
    }

    public void onAnimationRepeat(Animator animation) {
        // TODO Auto-generated method stub
    }

    public void onAnimationEnd(Animator animation) {
        // TODO Auto-generated method stub
    }

    public void onAnimationCancel(Animator animation) {
        // TODO Auto-generated method stub
    }
};
```

To apply an Animation Listener to your property animation, use the `addListener` method:

```
anim.addListener(animListener);
```

ENHANCING YOUR VIEWS

Custom Views were introduced in Chapter 5 and can serve as an important differentiator among a sea of standard apps when used properly—overuse often leads to additional user confusion as they are overwhelmed with custom controls and new UI elements to understand.

It's important when building custom Views to ensure this additional risk is offset by a dramatically improved user experience. This could be through improved visual effects or through intuitive interactions by handling touch events.

ADVANCED CANVAS DRAWING

You were introduced to the `Canvas` class in Chapter 5, where you learned how to go beyond the included Views and build custom UIs. In this section you learn more about the Canvas, and take advantage of advanced UI visual effects such as Shaders and translucency.

The concept of the *canvas* is a common metaphor in graphics programming, and generally consists of three basic drawing components:

➤ `Canvas`—Supplies the draw methods that paint drawing primitives onto the underlying bitmap.

➤ `Paint`—Also referred to as a "brush," `Paint` lets you specify how a primitive is drawn on the bitmap.

➤ `Bitmap`—The surface being drawn on.

Most of the advanced techniques described in this chapter involve variations and modifications to the `Paint` object that enable you to add depth and texture to otherwise flat raster drawings.

The Android drawing API supports translucency, gradient fills, rounded rectangles, and anti-aliasing. These drawing APIs use a traditional raster-style painter's algorithm. The result of this raster approach is improved efficiency, but changing a `Paint` object does not affect primitives that have already been drawn; it affects only new elements.

What Can You Draw?

The `Canvas` class encapsulates the bitmap used as a surface for your artistic endeavors; it also exposes the `draw` methods used to implement your designs.

Without going into detail about each `draw` method, the following list provides a taste of the primitives available:

➤ `drawARGB/drawRGB/drawColor`—Fills the canvas with a single color.

➤ `drawArc`—Draws an arc between two angles within an area bounded by a rectangle.

➤ `drawBitmap`—Draws a bitmap on the Canvas. You can alter the appearance of the target bitmap by specifying a target size or using a matrix to transform it.

➤ `drawBitmapMesh`—Draws a bitmap using a mesh that lets you manipulate the appearance of the target by moving points within it.

➤ `drawCircle`—Draws a circle of a specified radius centered on a given point.

➤ `drawLine[s]`—Draws a line (or series of lines) between two points.

➤ `drawOval`—Draws an oval bounded by the rectangle specified.

➤ drawPaint—Fills the entire Canvas with the specified Paint.

➤ drawPath—Draws the specified Path. A Path object is often used to hold a collection of drawing primitives within a single object.

➤ drawPicture—Draws a Picture object within the specified rectangle.

➤ drawRect—Draws a rectangle.

➤ drawRoundRect—Draws a rectangle with rounded edges.

➤ drawText—Draws a text string on the Canvas. The text font, size, color, and rendering properties are set in the Paint object used to render the text.

➤ drawTextOnPath—Draws text that follows along a specified path (not supported when using hardware acceleration).

➤ drawVertices—Draws a series of tri-patches specified as a series of vertex points (not supported when using hardware acceleration).

Each drawing method lets you specify a Paint object to render it. In the following sections, you learn how to create and modify Paint objects to get the most out of your drawings.

Getting the Most from Your Paint

The Paint class represents a paintbrush and palette. It lets you choose how to render the primitives you draw onto the Canvas using the draw methods described in the previous section. By modifying the Paint object, you can control the color, style, font, and special effects used when drawing.

> **NOTE** *Not all the Paint options described here are available if you're using hardware acceleration to improve 2D drawing performance. As a result, it's important to check how hardware acceleration affects your 2D drawing.*

Most simply, setColor enables you to select the color of a Paint, whereas the style of a Paint object (controlled using setStyle) enables you to decide if you want to draw only the outline of a drawing object (STROKE), just the filled portion (FILL), or both (STROKE_AND_FILL).

Beyond these simple controls, the Paint class also supports transparency and can be modified with a variety of Shaders, filters, and effects to provide a rich palette of complex paints and brushes.

In the following sections, you learn what some of the features available in the Paint class are and how to use them. These sections outline what can be achieved (such as gradients and edge embossing) without exhaustively listing all possible alternatives.

Using Translucency

All colors in Android include an opacity component (alpha channel). You define an alpha value for a color when you create it using the argb or parseColor methods:

```
// Make color red and 50% transparent
int opacity = 127;
```

```
int intColor = Color.argb(opacity, 255, 0, 0);
int parsedColor = Color.parseColor("#7FFF0000");
```

Alternatively, you can set the opacity of an existing `Paint` object using the `setAlpha` method:

```
// Make color 50% transparent
int opacity = 127;
myPaint.setAlpha(opacity);
```

Creating a paint color that's not 100 percent opaque means that any primitive drawn with it will be partially transparent—making whatever is drawn beneath it partially visible.

You can use transparency effects in any class or method that uses colors including Paint colors, Shaders, and Mask Filters.

Introducing Shaders

Extensions of the `Shader` class let you create Paints that fill drawn objects with more than a single solid color.

The most common use of Shaders is to define gradient fills; gradients are an excellent way to add depth and texture to 2D drawings. Android includes three gradient Shaders as well as a Bitmap Shader and a Compose Shader.

Trying to describe painting techniques seems inherently futile, so Figure 14-2 shows how each Shader works. Represented from left to right are `LinearGradient`, `RadialGradient`, and `SweepGradient`.

> **NOTE** *Not included in the image in Figure 14-2 is the* `ComposeShader`, *which lets you create a composite of multiple Shaders, nor the* `BitmapShader`, *which lets you create a brush based on a bitmap image.*

FIGURE 14-2

Creating Gradient Shaders

Gradient Shaders let you fill drawings with an interpolated color range. You can define the gradient in two ways. The first is a simple transition between two colors:

```
int colorFrom = Color.BLACK;
int colorTo = Color.WHITE;

LinearGradient myLinearGradient =
  new LinearGradient(x1, y1, x2, y2,
                     colorFrom, colorTo, TileMode.CLAMP);
```

The second alternative is to specify a more complex series of colors distributed at set proportions:

```
int[] gradientColors = new int[3];
gradientColors[0] = Color.GREEN;
gradientColors[1] = Color.YELLOW;
gradientColors[2] = Color.RED;

float[] gradientPositions = new float[3];
gradientPositions[0] = 0.0f;
gradientPositions[1] = 0.5f;
gradientPositions[2] = 1.0f;

RadialGradient radialGradientShader
  = new RadialGradient(centerX, centerY,
                       radius,
                       gradientColors,
                       gradientPositions,
                       TileMode.CLAMP);
```

Each gradient Shader (linear, radial, and sweep) lets you define the gradient fill using either of these techniques.

Applying Shaders to Paint

To use a Shader when drawing, apply it to a Paint using the `setShader` method:

```
shaderPaint.setShader(myLinearGradient);
```

Anything you draw with this Paint will be filled with the Shader you specified rather than the paint color.

Using Shader Tile Modes

The brush sizes of the gradient Shaders are defined using explicit bounding rectangles or center points and radius lengths; the Bitmap Shader implies a brush size through its bitmap size.

If the area defined by your Shader brush is smaller than the area being filled, the `TileMode` determines how the remaining area will be covered. You can define which tile mode to use with the following static constants:

➤ `CLAMP`—Uses the edge colors of the Shader to fill the extra space

➤ `MIRROR`—Flips the Shader image horizontally and vertically so that each image seams with the last

➤ `REPEAT`—Repeats the Shader image horizontally and vertically, but doesn't flip it

Using Mask Filters

The `MaskFilter` classes let you assign edge effects to your Paint. Mask Filters are not supported when the Canvas is hardware-accelerated.

Extensions to `MaskFilter` apply transformations to the alpha-channel of a Paint along its outer edge. Android includes the following Mask Filters:

➤ `BlurMaskFilter`—Specifies a blur style and radius to feather the edges of your Paint

➤ `EmbossMaskFilter`—Specifies the direction of the light source and ambient light level to add an embossing effect

To apply a Mask Filter, use the `setMaskFilter` method, passing in a `MaskFilter` object:

```
// Set the direction of the light source
float[] direction = new float[]{ 1, 1, 1 };
// Set the ambient light level
float light = 0.4f;
// Choose a level of specularity to apply
float specular = 6f;
// Apply a level of blur to apply to the mask
float blur = 3.5f;
EmbossMaskFilter emboss = new EmbossMaskFilter(direction, light,
                                               specular, blur);

// Apply the mask
if (!canvas.isHardwareAccelerated())
  myPaint.setMaskFilter(emboss);
```

Using Color Filters

Whereas Mask Filters are transformations of a Paint's alpha-channel, a `ColorFilter` applies a transformation to each of the RGB channels. All `ColorFilter`-derived classes ignore the alpha-channel when performing their transformations.

Android includes three Color Filters:

➤ `ColorMatrixColorFilter`—Lets you specify a 4 x 5 `ColorMatrix` to apply to a Paint. Color Matrixes are commonly used to perform image processing programmatically and are useful because they support chaining transformations using matrix multiplication.

➤ `LightingColorFilter`—Multiplies the RGB channels by the first color before adding the second. The result of each transformation will be clamped between 0 and 255.

➤ `PorterDuffColorFilter`—Lets you use any one of the 18 Porter-Duff rules for digital image compositing to apply a specified color to the Paint. The Porter-Duff rules are defined at `developer.android.com/reference/android/graphics/PorterDuff.Mode.html`.

Apply `ColorFilters` using the `setColorFilter` method:

```
myPaint.setColorFilter(new LightingColorFilter(Color.BLUE, Color.RED));
```

Using Path Effects

The effects described so far affect the way the Paint *fills* a drawing; Path Effects are used to control how its outline (stroke) is drawn.

Using Path Effects, you can change the appearance of a shape's corners and control the appearance of the outline. Path Effects are particularly useful for drawing Path primitives, but they can be applied to any Paint via the setPathEffect method:

```
borderPaint.setPathEffect(new CornerPathEffect(5));
```

Android includes several Path Effects, including the following:

➤ CornerPathEffect—Lets you smooth sharp corners in the shape of a primitive by replacing them with rounded corners.

➤ DashPathEffect—Rather than drawing a solid outline, you can use the Dash Path Effect to create an outline of broken lines (dashes/dots). You can specify any repeating pattern of solid/empty line segments.

➤ DiscretePathEffect—Similar to the Dash Path Effect, but with added randomness. Specifies the length of each segment and a degree of deviation from the original path to use when drawing it.

➤ PathDashPathEffect—Enables you to define a new shape (path) to use as a stamp to outline the original path.

The following effects let you combine multiple Path Effects to a single Paint:

➤ SumPathEffect—Adds two effects to a path in sequence, such that each effect is applied to the original path and the two results are combined.

➤ ComposePathEffect—Applies first one effect and then applies the second effect to the result of the first.

Path Effects that modify the shape of the object being drawn change the area of the affected shape. This ensures that any fill effects applied to the same shape are drawn within the new bounds.

Changing the Transfer Mode

Change a Paint's Xfermode to affect the way it paints new colors on top of what's already on the Canvas. Under normal circumstances, painting on top of an existing drawing layers the new shape on top. If the new Paint is fully opaque, it totally obscures the paint underneath; if it's partially transparent, it tints the colors underneath.

The PorterDuffXfermode is a powerful transfer mode with which you can use any of the 18 Porter-Duff rules for image composition to control how the paint interacts with the existing canvas image.

To apply transfer modes, use the setXferMode method:

```
PorterDuffXfermode mode = new PorterDuffXfermode(
                         PorterDuff.Mode.DST_OVER);
borderPen.setXfermode(mode);
```

Improving Paint Quality with Anti-Aliasing

When you create a new `Paint` object, you can pass in several flags that affect the way the Paint will be rendered. One of the most interesting is the `ANTI_ALIAS_FLAG`, which ensures that diagonal lines drawn with this paint are anti-aliased to give a smooth appearance (at the cost of performance).

Anti-aliasing is particularly important when drawing text, as anti-aliased text can be significantly easier to read. To create even smoother text effects, you can apply the `SUBPIXEL_TEXT_FLAG`, which applies subpixel anti-aliasing.

```
Paint paint = new Paint(Paint.ANTI_ALIAS_FLAG|Paint.SUBPIXEL_TEXT_FLAG);
```

You can also set both of these flags manually using the `setSubpixelText` and `setAntiAlias` methods:

```
myPaint.setSubpixelText(true);
myPaint.setAntiAlias(true);
```

Canvas Drawing Best Practice

2D owner-draw operations tend to be expensive in terms of processor use; inefficient drawing routines can block the GUI thread and have a detrimental effect on application responsiveness. This is particularly true for resource-constrained mobile devices.

In Chapter 5 you learned how to create your own Views by overriding the `onDraw` method within a View-derived class. To ensure you don't end up with an attractive application that's unresponsive, laggy, or "janky," you should be conscious of the resource drain and CPU-cycle cost of your `onDraw` method.

Rather than focus on general principles, I'll describe some Android-specific considerations for ensuring that you can create Views that look good and remain interactive. (Note that list is not exhaustive.)

➤ **Consider size and orientation**—When you design your Views and Overlays, be sure to consider (and test!) how they look at different resolutions, pixel densities, and sizes.

➤ **Create static objects once**—Object creation and garbage collection are particularly expensive operations. Where possible, create drawing objects such as `Paint` objects, Paths, and Shaders once, rather than re-creating them each time the View is invalidated.

➤ **Remember that** `onDraw` **is expensive**—Performing the `onDraw` method is an expensive process that forces Android to perform several image composition and bitmap construction operations. Many of the following points suggest ways to modify the appearance of your Canvas without having to call redraw:

➤ **Use Canvas transforms**—Use Canvas transforms, such as `rotate` and `translate`, to simplify complex relational positioning of elements on your canvas. For example, rather than positioning and rotating each text element around a clock face, simply rotate the canvas 22.5 degrees, and draw the text in the same place.

➤ **Use Animations**—Consider using Animations to perform preset transformations of your View rather than manually redrawing it. Scale, rotation, and translation Animations can be performed on any View within an Activity and provide a resource-efficient way to provide zoom, rotate, or shake effects.

➤ **Consider using bitmaps, Vector Drawables, NinePatches, and Drawable resources**— It is less computationally expensive to add a pre-rendered bitmap to a Canvas than drawing it from scratch. Where possible, you should consider using a Drawable such as a bitmap, scalable NinePatch, Vector Drawable, or static XML Drawable rather than dynamically creating it at run time.

➤ **Avoid overdrawing**—A combination of raster painting and layered Views can result in many layers being drawn on top of each other. Before drawing a layer or object, check to confirm if it will be completely obscured by a layer above it. It's good practice to avoid drawing more than 2.5 times the number of pixels on screen per frame. Transparent pixels still count—and are more expensive to draw than opaque colors.

Advanced Compass Face Example

In Chapter 5, you created a simple compass UI. In the following example, you make some significant changes to the Compass View's onDraw method to change it from a simple, flat compass to a dynamic artificial horizon, as shown in Figure 14-3. Because the image in Figure 14-3 is limited to black and white, you need to create the control to see it in its full technicolor glory.

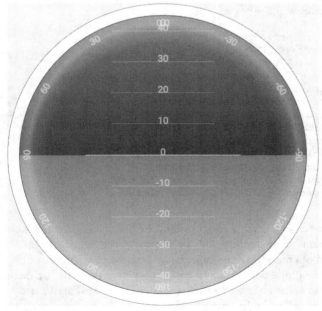

FIGURE 14-3

1. Start by adding properties to store the pitch and roll values to the CompassView class:

```
private float mPitch;

public void setPitch(float pitch) {
  mPitch = pitch;
  sendAccessibilityEvent(AccessibilityEvent.TYPE_VIEW_TEXT_CHANGED);
}

public float getPitch() {
  return mPitch;
}

private float mRoll;

public void setRoll(float roll) {
  mRoll = roll;
  sendAccessibilityEvent(AccessibilityEvent.TYPE_VIEW_TEXT_CHANGED);
}

public float getRoll() {
  return mRoll;
}
```

2. Modify the colors.xml resource file to include color values for the border gradient, the glass compass shading, the sky, and the ground. Also update the colors used for the border and the face markings:

```
<?xml version="1.0" encoding="utf-8"?>
<resources>
  <color name="background_color">#F000</color>
  <color name="marker_color">#FFFF</color>
  <color name="text_color">#FFFF</color>

  <color name="shadow_color">#7AAA</color>
  <color name="outer_border">#FF444444</color>
  <color name="inner_border_one">#FF323232</color>
  <color name="inner_border_two">#FF414141</color>
  <color name="inner_border">#FFFFFFFF</color>
  <color name="horizon_sky_from">#FFA52A2A</color>
  <color name="horizon_sky_to">#FFFFC125</color>
  <color name="horizon_ground_from">#FF5F9EA0</color>
  <color name="horizon_ground_to">#FF00008B</color>
</resources>
```

3. The Paint and Shader objects used for the sky and ground in the artificial horizon are created based on the size of the current View, so they can't be static like the Paint objects you created in Chapter 5. Instead of creating Paint objects, update the constructor of the CompassView class to construct the gradient arrays and colors they use. The existing method code can be left largely intact, with some changes to the textPaint, circlePaint, and markerPaint variables, as highlighted in the following code:

```
int[] borderGradientColors;
float[] borderGradientPositions;
```

```java
int[] glassGradientColors;
float[] glassGradientPositions;

int skyHorizonColorFrom;
int skyHorizonColorTo;
int groundHorizonColorFrom;
int groundHorizonColorTo;

public CompassView(Context context, AttributeSet attrs,
                   int defStyleAttr) {
  setFocusable(true);
  final TypedArray a = context.obtainStyledAttributes(attrs,
    R.styleable.CompassView, defStyleAttr, 0);
  if (a.hasValue(R.styleable.CompassView_bearing)) {
    setBearing(a.getFloat(R.styleable.CompassView_bearing, 0));
  }

  Context c = this.getContext();
  Resources r = this.getResources();

  circlePaint = new Paint(Paint.ANTI_ALIAS_FLAG);
  circlePaint.setColor(ContextCompat.getColor(c,
    R.color.background_color));
  circlePaint.setStrokeWidth(1);
  circlePaint.setStyle(Paint.Style.STROKE);

  northString = r.getString(R.string.cardinal_north);
  eastString = r.getString(R.string.cardinal_east);
  southString = r.getString(R.string.cardinal_south);
  westString = r.getString(R.string.cardinal_west);

  textPaint = new Paint(Paint.ANTI_ALIAS_FLAG);
  textPaint.setColor(ContextCompat.getColor(c,
    R.color.text_color));
  textPaint.setFakeBoldText(true);
  textPaint.setSubpixelText(true);
  textPaint.setTextAlign(Align.LEFT);
  textPaint.setTextSize(30);

  textHeight = (int)textPaint.measureText("yY");

  markerPaint = new Paint(Paint.ANTI_ALIAS_FLAG);
  markerPaint.setColor(r.getColor(R.color.marker_color));
  markerPaint.setAlpha(200);
  markerPaint.setStrokeWidth(1);
  markerPaint.setStyle(Paint.Style.STROKE);
  markerPaint.setShadowLayer(2, 1, 1, ContextCompat.getColor(c,
    R.color.shadow_color));
}
```

3.1 Still within the constructor, create the color and position arrays that will be used by a radial Shader to paint the outer border:

```
public CompassView(Context context, AttributeSet attrs,
                   int defStyleAttr) {

  [ ... Existing code ... ]

  borderGradientColors = new int[4];
  borderGradientPositions = new float[4];

  borderGradientColors[3] = ContextCompat.getColor(c,
    R.color.outer_border);
  borderGradientColors[2] = ContextCompat.getColor(c,
    R.color.inner_border_one);
  borderGradientColors[1] = ContextCompat.getColor(c,
    R.color.inner_border_two);
  borderGradientColors[0] = ContextCompat.getColor(c,
    R.color.inner_border);
  borderGradientPositions[3] = 0.0f;
  borderGradientPositions[2] = 1-0.03f;
  borderGradientPositions[1] = 1-0.06f;
  borderGradientPositions[0] = 1.0f;
}
```

3.2 Then create the radial gradient color and position arrays that will be used to create the semitransparent "glass dome" that sits on top of the View to give it the illusion of depth:

```
public CompassView(Context context, AttributeSet attrs,
                   int defStyleAttr) {

  [ ... Existing code ... ]

  glassGradientColors = new int[5];
  glassGradientPositions = new float[5];

  int glassColor = 245;
  glassGradientColors[4] = Color.argb(65, glassColor,
                                      glassColor, glassColor);
  glassGradientColors[3] = Color.argb(100, glassColor,
                                      glassColor, glassColor);
  glassGradientColors[2] = Color.argb(50, glassColor,
                                      glassColor, glassColor);
  glassGradientColors[1] = Color.argb(0, glassColor,
                                      glassColor, glassColor);
  glassGradientColors[0] = Color.argb(0, glassColor,
                                      glassColor, glassColor);
  glassGradientPositions[4] = 1-0.0f;
  glassGradientPositions[3] = 1-0.06f;
  glassGradientPositions[2] = 1-0.10f;
  glassGradientPositions[1] = 1-0.20f;
  glassGradientPositions[0] = 1-1.0f;
}
```

3.3 Finally, get the colors you'll use to create the linear gradients that will represent the sky and the ground in the artificial horizon:

```
public CompassView(Context context, AttributeSet attrs,
                    int defStyleAttr) {

[ ... Existing code ... ]

skyHorizonColorFrom = ContextCompat.getColor(c,
   R.color.horizon_sky_from);
skyHorizonColorTo = ContextCompat.getColor(c,
   R.color.horizon_sky_to);

groundHorizonColorFrom = ContextCompat.getColor(c,
   R.color.horizon_ground_from);
groundHorizonColorTo = ContextCompat.getColor(c,
   R.color.horizon_ground_to);
}
```

4. Before you start drawing the face, create a new enum that stores each of the cardinal directions:

```
private enum CompassDirection { N, NNE, NE, ENE,
                                E, ESE, SE, SSE,
                                S, SSW, SW, WSW,
                                W, WNW, NW, NNW }
```

5. Now you need to completely replace the existing onDraw method. You start by figuring out some size-based values, including the center of the View, the radius of the circular control, and the rectangles that will enclose the outer (heading) and inner (tilt and roll) face elements. To start, replace the existing onDraw method:

```
@Override
protected void onDraw(Canvas canvas) {
```

6. Calculate the width of the outer (heading) ring based on the size of the font used to draw the heading values:

```
float ringWidth = textHeight + 4;
```

7. Calculate the height and width of the View, and use those values to establish the radius of the inner and outer face dials, as well as to create the bounding boxes for each face:

```
int height = getMeasuredHeight();
int width = getMeasuredWidth();

int px = width/2;
int py = height/2;
Point center = new Point(px, py);

int radius = Math.min(px, py)-2;

RectF boundingBox = new RectF(center.x - radius,
                              center.y - radius,
                              center.x + radius,
                              center.y + radius);

RectF innerBoundingBox = new RectF(center.x - radius + ringWidth,
                                   center.y - radius + ringWidth,
```

```
                                        center.x + radius - ringWidth,
                                        center.y + radius - ringWidth);

        float innerRadius = innerBoundingBox.height()/2;
```

8. With the dimensions of the View established, it's time to start drawing the faces.

Start from the bottom layer at the outside, and work your way in and up, starting with the outer face (heading). Create a new `RadialGradient` Shader using the colors and positions you defined in Step 3.2, and assign that Shader to a new Paint before using it to draw a circle:

```
RadialGradient borderGradient = new RadialGradient(px, py, radius,
borderGradientColors, borderGradientPositions, TileMode.CLAMP);

Paint pgb = new Paint();
pgb.setShader(borderGradient);

Path outerRingPath = new Path();
outerRingPath.addOval(boundingBox, Direction.CW);

canvas.drawPath(outerRingPath, pgb);
```

9. Now you need to draw the artificial horizon. You do this by dividing the circular face into two sections, one representing the sky and the other the ground. The proportion of each section depends on the current pitch.

Start by creating the `Shader` and `Paint` objects that will be used to draw the sky and earth:

```
LinearGradient skyShader = new LinearGradient(center.x,
   innerBoundingBox.top, center.x, innerBoundingBox.bottom,
   skyHorizonColorFrom, skyHorizonColorTo, TileMode.CLAMP);

Paint skyPaint = new Paint();
skyPaint.setShader(skyShader);

LinearGradient groundShader = new LinearGradient(center.x,
   innerBoundingBox.top, center.x, innerBoundingBox.bottom,
   groundHorizonColorFrom, groundHorizonColorTo, TileMode.CLAMP);

Paint groundPaint = new Paint();
groundPaint.setShader(groundShader);
```

10. Normalize the pitch and roll values to clamp them within ±90 degrees and ±180 degrees, respectively:

```
float tiltDegree = mPitch;
while (tiltDegree > 90 || tiltDegree < -90) {
   if (tiltDegree > 90) tiltDegree = -90 + (tiltDegree - 90);
   if (tiltDegree < -90) tiltDegree = 90 - (tiltDegree + 90);
}

float rollDegree = mRoll;
while (rollDegree > 180 || rollDegree < -180) {
   if (rollDegree > 180) rollDegree = -180 + (rollDegree - 180);
   if (rollDegree < -180) rollDegree = 180 - (rollDegree + 180);
}
```

11. Create paths that will fill each segment of the circle (ground and sky). The proportion of each segment should be related to the clamped pitch:

```
Path skyPath = new Path();
skyPath.addArc(innerBoundingBox,
               -tiltDegree,
               (180 + (2 * tiltDegree)));
```

12. Spin the canvas around the center in the opposite direction to the current roll, and draw the sky and ground paths using the Paints you created in Step 4:

```
canvas.save();
canvas.rotate(-rollDegree, px, py);
canvas.drawOval(innerBoundingBox, groundPaint);
canvas.drawPath(skyPath, skyPaint);
canvas.drawPath(skyPath, markerPaint);
```

13. Next is the face marking. Start by calculating the start and endpoints for the horizontal horizon markings:

```
int markWidth = radius / 3;
int startX = center.x - markWidth;
int endX = center.x + markWidth;
```

14. To make the horizon values easier to read, you should ensure that the pitch scale always starts at the current value. The following code calculates the position of the UI between the ground and sky on the horizon face:

```
double h = innerRadius*Math.cos(Math.toRadians(90-tiltDegree));
double justTiltY = center.y - h;
```

15. Find the number of pixels representing each degree of tilt:

```
float pxPerDegree = (innerBoundingBox.height()/2)/45f;
```

16. Iterate over 180 degrees, centered on the current tilt value, to give a sliding scale of possible pitch:

```
for (int i = 90; i >= -90; i -= 10) {
  double ypos = justTiltY + i*pxPerDegree;

  // Only display the scale within the inner face.
  if ((ypos < (innerBoundingBox.top + textHeight)) ||
     (ypos > innerBoundingBox.bottom - textHeight))
    continue;

  // Draw a line and the tilt angle for each scale increment.
  canvas.drawLine(startX, (float)ypos,
                  endX, (float)ypos,
                  markerPaint);
  int displayPos = (int)(tiltDegree - i);
  String displayString = String.valueOf(displayPos);
  float stringSizeWidth = textPaint.measureText(displayString);
```

```
canvas.drawText(displayString,
                (int)(center.x-stringSizeWidth/2),
                (int)(ypos)+1,
                textPaint);
}
```

17. Draw a thicker line at the earth/sky interface. Change the stroke thickness of the marker-
    Paint object before drawing the line (and then set it back to the previous value):

```
markerPaint.setStrokeWidth(2);
canvas.drawLine(center.x - radius / 2,
                (float)justTiltY,
                center.x + radius / 2,
                (float)justTiltY,
                markerPaint);
markerPaint.setStrokeWidth(1);
```

18. To make it easier to read the exact roll, you should draw an arrow and display a text string
    that shows the value.

    Create a new Path, and use the moveTo/lineTo methods to construct an open arrow that
    points straight up. Draw the path and a text string that shows the current roll:

```
// Draw the arrow
Path rollArrow = new Path();
rollArrow.moveTo(center.x - 3, (int)innerBoundingBox.top + 14);
rollArrow.lineTo(center.x, (int)innerBoundingBox.top + 10);
rollArrow.moveTo(center.x + 3, innerBoundingBox.top + 14);
rollArrow.lineTo(center.x, innerBoundingBox.top + 10);
canvas.drawPath(rollArrow, markerPaint);

// Draw the string
String rollText = String.valueOf(rollDegree);
double rollTextWidth = textPaint.measureText(rollText);
canvas.drawText(rollText,
                (float)(center.x - rollTextWidth / 2),
                innerBoundingBox.top + textHeight + 2,
                textPaint);
```

19. Spin the canvas back to upright so that you can draw the rest of the face markings:

```
canvas.restore();
```

20. Draw the roll dial markings by rotating the canvas 10 degrees at a time, drawing a value
    every 30 degrees and otherwise draw a mark. When you've completed the face, restore the
    canvas to its upright position:

```
canvas.save();
canvas.rotate(180, center.x, center.y);

for (int i = -180; i < 180; i += 10) {
  // Show a numeric value every 30 degrees
  if (i % 30 == 0) {
    String rollString = String.valueOf(i*-1);
    float rollStringWidth = textPaint.measureText(rollString);
    PointF rollStringCenter =
```

```
            new PointF(center.x-rollStringWidth/2,
                        innerBoundingBox.top+1+textHeight);
        canvas.drawText(rollString,
                        rollStringCenter.x, rollStringCenter.y,
                        textPaint);
    }

    // Otherwise draw a marker line
    else {
        canvas.drawLine(center.x, (int)innerBoundingBox.top,
                        center.x, (int)innerBoundingBox.top + 5,
                        markerPaint);
    }

    canvas.rotate(10, center.x, center.y);
}
canvas.restore();
```

21. The final step in creating the face is drawing the heading markers around the outside edge:

```
canvas.save();
canvas.rotate(-1*(mBearing), px, py);

double increment = 22.5;

for (double i = 0; i < 360; i += increment) {
    CompassDirection cd = CompassDirection.values()
                        [(int)(i / 22.5)];
    String headString = cd.toString();

    float headStringWidth = textPaint.measureText(headString);
    PointF headStringCenter =
        new PointF(center.x - headStringWidth / 2,
                    boundingBox.top + 1 + textHeight);

    if (i % increment == 0)
        canvas.drawText(headString,
                        headStringCenter.x, headStringCenter.y,
                        textPaint);
    else
        canvas.drawLine(center.x, (int)boundingBox.top,
                        center.x, (int)boundingBox.top + 3,
                        markerPaint);

    canvas.rotate((int)increment, center.x, center.y);
}

canvas.restore();
```

22. With the face complete, you can add some finishing touches.

Start by adding a "glass dome" over the top to give the illusion of a watch face. Using the radial gradient array you constructed earlier, create a new Shader and Paint object. Use them to draw a circle over the inner face that makes it look like it's covered in glass:

```
RadialGradient glassShader =
    new RadialGradient(px, py, (int)innerRadius,
```

```
                            glassGradientColors,
                            glassGradientPositions,
                            TileMode.CLAMP);
            Paint glassPaint = new Paint();
            glassPaint.setShader(glassShader);

            canvas.drawOval(innerBoundingBox, glassPaint);
```

23. All that's left is to draw two more circles as clean borders for the inner and outer face boundaries. Then restore the canvas to upright, and finish the onDraw method:

```
            // Draw the outer ring
            canvas.drawOval(boundingBox, circlePaint);

            // Draw the inner ring
            circlePaint.setStrokeWidth(2);
            canvas.drawOval(innerBoundingBox, circlePaint);
    }
```

If you run the parent activity, you will see an artificial horizon, as shown at the beginning of this example in Figure 14.3.

Creating Interactive Controls

The primary interaction model for Android Devices is through the touch screen, however—as noted above in the accessibility section—you can't take this for granted. As Android continues to expand to devices including TVs and laptop form factors, your app must consider that user input may also come from D-pads, keyboards, and mice.

The challenge for you as a developer is to create intuitive UIs that make the most of whatever input hardware is available, while introducing as few hardware dependencies as possible.

The techniques described in this section show how to listen for (and react to) user input from touch-screen taps and key presses using the following event handlers in Views and Activities:

➤ onTouchEvent—The touch-screen event handler, triggered when the touch screen is touched, released, or dragged

➤ onKeyDown—Called when any hardware key is pressed

➤ onKeyUp—Called when any hardware key is released

Using the Touch Screen

The physical size and dimensions of mobile devices are inexorably tied to the size of their touch screens, so it should come as no surprise that touch screen input is all about fingers—a design principle that assumes users will use their fingers rather than a specialized stylus to touch the screen and navigate your UI.

Finger-based touch makes interaction less precise and is often based more on movement than simple contact. Android's native applications make extensive use of finger-based, touch-screen UIs—including the use of dragging motions to scroll through lists, swipe between screens, or perform actions.

Android supports two types of touch interactions: traditional touch interactions using a finger or stylus and "faketouch" where a trackpad or mouse input is interpreted as touch input events. By default, all Android apps require faketouch support, making them compatible with devices such as TVs and laptops without a touch screen.

If you'd like your app to be available *only* on devices with a real touch screen you must specify this in your manifest by adding `required="true"` to the `android.hardware.touchscreen` feature:

```
<manifest xmlns:android=http://schemas.android.com/apk/res/android
        ... >
  <uses-feature android:name="android.hardware.touchscreen"
                android:required="true" />
</manifest>
```

To create a View or Activity that uses touch-screen interaction (including faketouch), override the `onTouchEvent` handler:

```
@Override
public boolean onTouchEvent(MotionEvent event) {
  return super.onTouchEvent(event);
}
```

Return `true` if you have handled the screen press; otherwise, return `false` to pass events down through the View stack until the touch has been successfully handled.

Processing Single and Multiple Touch Events

For each gesture, the `onTouchEvent` handler is fired several times. Starting when the user touches the screen, multiple times while the system tracks the current finger position, and, finally, once more when the contact ends.

Android supports processing an arbitrary number of simultaneous touch events. Each touch event is allocated a separate pointer identifier that is referenced in the Motion Event parameter of the `onTouchEvent` handler.

Call `getAction` on the `MotionEvent` parameter to find the event type that triggered the handler. For either a single touch device, or the first touch event on a multi-touch device, you can use the `ACTION_UP[DOWN/MOVE/CANCEL/OUTSIDE]` constants to find the event type:

```
@Override
public boolean onTouchEvent(MotionEvent event) {
  int action = event.getAction();
  switch (action) {
    case (MotionEvent.ACTION_DOWN):
      // Touch screen pressed
      return true;
    case (MotionEvent.ACTION_MOVE):
      // Contact has moved across screen
      return true;
    case (MotionEvent.ACTION_UP):
      // Touch screen touch ended
      return true;
    case (MotionEvent.ACTION_CANCEL):
      // Touch event cancelled
```

```
        return true;
      case (MotionEvent.ACTION_OUTSIDE):
        // Movement has occurred outside the
        // bounds of the current screen element
        return true;
      default: return super.onTouchEvent(event);
    }
  }
}
```

To track touch events from multiple pointers, you need to apply the `MotionEvent.ACTION_MASK` and `MotionEvent.ACTION_POINTER_INDEX_MASK` constants to find the touch event (either `ACTION_POINTER_DOWN` or `ACTION_POINTER_UP`) and the pointer ID that triggered it, respectively. Call `getPointerCount` to find if this is a multiple-touch event:

```
@Override
public boolean onTouchEvent(MotionEvent event) {
  int action = event.getAction();

  if (event.getPointerCount() > 1) {
    int actionPointerId = action & MotionEvent.ACTION_POINTER_INDEX_MASK;
    int actionEvent = action & MotionEvent.ACTION_MASK;
    // Do something with the pointer ID and event.
  }
  return super.onTouchEvent(event);
}
```

The Motion Event also includes the coordinates of the current screen contact. You can access these coordinates using the `getX` and `getY` methods. These methods return the coordinate relative to the responding View or Activity.

In the case of multiple-touch events, each Motion Event includes the current position of each pointer. To find the position of a given pointer, pass its index into the `getX` or `getY` methods. Note that its index is *not* equivalent to the pointer ID. To find the index for a given pointer, use the `findPointerIndex` method, passing in the pointer ID whose index you need:

```
int xPos = -1;
int yPos = -1;

if (event.getPointerCount() > 1) {
  int actionPointerId = action & MotionEvent.ACTION_POINTER_INDEX_MASK;
  int actionEvent = action & MotionEvent.ACTION_MASK;

  int pointerIndex = event.findPointerIndex(actionPointerId);
  xPos = (int)event.getX(pointerIndex);
  yPos = (int)event.getY(pointerIndex);
}
else {
  // Single touch event.
  xPos = (int)event.getX();
  yPos = (int)event.getY();
}
```

The Motion Event parameter also includes the pressure being applied to the screen using `getPressure`, a method that returns a value usually between 0 (no pressure) and 1 (normal pressure).

You use the `getToolType` method to determine whether the touch event was from a finger, mouse, stylus, or eraser, allowing you to handle them differently.

Finally, you can also determine the normalized size of the current contact area by using the `getSize` method. This method returns a value between 0 and 1, where 0 suggests a precise measurement and 1 indicates a possible "fat touch" event in which the user may not have intended to press anything.

> **NOTE** *Depending on the calibration of the hardware, it may be possible to return values greater than 1.*

Tracking Movement

Whenever the current touch contact position, pressure, or size changes, a new `onTouchEvent` is triggered with an `ACTION_MOVE` action.

The Motion Event parameter can include historical values, in addition to the fields described previously. This history represents all the movement events that have occurred between the previously handled `onTouchEvent` and this one, allowing Android to buffer rapid movement changes to provide fine-grained capture of movement data.

You can find the size of the history by calling `getHistorySize`, which returns the number of movement positions available for the current event. You can then obtain the times, pressures, sizes, and positions of each of the historical events by using a series of `getHistorical*` methods and passing in the position index. Note that as with the `getX` and `getY` methods described earlier, you can pass in a pointer index value to track historical touch events for multiple cursors:

```
int historySize = event.getHistorySize();

if (event.getPointerCount() > 1) {
  int actionPointerId = action & MotionEvent.ACTION_POINTER_ID_MASK;
  int pointerIndex = event.findPointerIndex(actionPointerId);
  for (int i = 0; i < historySize; i++) {
    float pressure = event.getHistoricalPressure(pointerIndex, i);
    float x = event.getHistoricalX(pointerIndex, i);
    float y = event.getHistoricalY(pointerIndex, i);
    float size = event.getHistoricalSize(pointerIndex, i);
    long time = event.getHistoricalEventTime(i);
    // TODO Do something with each point
  }
}
else {
  for (int i = 0; i < historySize; i++) {
    float pressure = event.getHistoricalPressure(i);
    float x = event.getHistoricalX(i);
    float y = event.getHistoricalY(i);
    float size = event.getHistoricalSize(i);
    // TODO Do something with each point
  }
}
```

The normal pattern for handling movement events is to process each of the historical events first, followed by the current Motion Event values, as shown in Listing 14-6.

LISTING 14-6: Handling touch screen movement events

```
@Override
public boolean onTouchEvent(MotionEvent event) {

  int action = event.getAction();

  switch (action) {
    case (MotionEvent.ACTION_MOVE):
    {
      int historySize = event.getHistorySize();
      for (int i = 0; i < historySize; i++) {
        float x = event.getHistoricalX(i);
        float y = event.getHistoricalY(i);
        processMovement(x, y);
      }

      float x = event.getX();
      float y = event.getY();
      processMovement(x, y);

      return true;
    }
  }

  return super.onTouchEvent(event);
}

private void processMovement(float x, float y) {
  // TODO Do something on movement.
}
```

Using an On Touch Listener

You can listen for touch events without subclassing an existing View by attaching an OnTouchListener to any View object, using the setOnTouchListener method:

```
myView.setOnTouchListener(new OnTouchListener() {
  public boolean onTouch(View view, MotionEvent event) {
    // TODO Respond to motion events
    return false;
  }
});
```

Using the Device Keys, Buttons, and D-Pad

Button and key-press events for all hardware keys are handled by the onKeyDown and onKeyUp handlers of the active Activity or the focused View. This includes keyboard keys, the D-pad, and the back button. The only exception is the *home* key, which is reserved to ensure that users can never get locked within an application.

To have your View or Activity react to button presses, override the `onKeyUp` and `onKeyDown` event handlers:

```
@Override
public boolean onKeyDown(int keyCode, KeyEvent event) {
  // Perform on key pressed handling, return true if handled
  return false;
}

@Override
public boolean onKeyUp(int keyCode, KeyEvent event) {
  // Perform on key released handling, return true if handled
  return false;
}
```

The `keyCode` parameter contains the value of the key being pressed; compare it to the static key code values available from the `KeyEvent` class to perform key-specific processing.

> **NOTE** *You should never unconditionally return* `true` *in the* `onKeyUp` *or* `onKey-Down` *methods as this will cause system-level key events to be incorrectly consumed by your app, causing issues such as media button events being consumed rather than being sent to the appropriate music app. Only return* `true` *if you handle the* `KeyEvent`.

The `KeyEvent` parameter also includes the `isCtrlPressed`, `isAltPressed`, `isShiftPressed`, `isFunctionPressed`, and `isSymPressed` methods to determine if the Control, Alt, Shift, function, or symbols keys are also being held. The static `isModifierKey` method accepts the `keyCode` and determines whether this key event was triggered by the user pressing one of these modifier keys.

Using the On Key Listener

To respond to key presses within existing Views in your Activities, implement an `OnKeyListener`, and assign it to a View using the `setOnKeyListener` method. Rather than implementing a separate method for key-press and key-release events, the `OnKeyListener` uses a single `onKey` event:

```
myView.setOnKeyListener(new OnKeyListener() {
  public boolean onKey(View v, int keyCode, KeyEvent event) {
    // TODO Process key press event, return true if handled
    return false;
  }
});
```

Use the `keyCode` parameter to find the key pressed. The `KeyEvent` parameter is used to determine if the key has been pressed or released, where `ACTION_DOWN` represents a key press and `ACTION_UP` signals its release.

COMPOSITE DRAWABLE RESOURCES

In Chapter 12, "Implementing the Android Design Philosophy," you examined a number of scalable Drawable resources, including shapes, colors, and vectors. This section introduces a number of additional XML-defined Drawables.

Composite Drawables are used to combine and manipulate other Drawable resources. You can use any Drawable resource within the following composite resource definitions, including bitmaps, shapes, and colors. Similarly, you can use these new Drawables within each other and assign them to Views in the same way as all other Drawable assets.

Transformative Drawables

You can scale and rotate existing Drawable resources using the aptly named ScaleDrawable and RotateDrawable classes. These transformative Drawables are particularly useful for creating progress bars or animating Views:

➤ **ScaleDrawable**—Within the scale tag, use the scaleHeight and scaleWidth attributes to define the target height and width relative to the bounding box of the original Drawable, respectively. Use the scaleGravity attribute to control the anchor point for the scaled image:

```xml
<?xml version="1.0" encoding="utf-8"?>
<scale xmlns:android="http://schemas.android.com/apk/res/android"
  android:drawable="@drawable/icon"
  android:scaleHeight="100%"
  android:scaleWidth="100%"
  android:scaleGravity="center_vertical|center_horizontal"
/>
```

➤ **RotateDrawable**—Within the rotate tag, use fromDegrees and toDegrees to define the start and end rotation angle around a pivot point, respectively. Define the pivot using the pivotX and pivotY attributes, specifying a percentage of the Drawable's width and height, respectively, using nn% notation:

```xml
<?xml version="1.0" encoding="utf-8"?>
<rotate xmlns:android="http://schemas.android.com/apk/res/android"
  android:drawable="@drawable/icon"
  android:fromDegrees="0"
  android:toDegrees="90"
  android:pivotX="50%"
  android:pivotY="50%"
/>
```

To apply the scaling and rotation at run time, use the setImageLevel method on the View object hosting the Drawable to move between the start and finish values on a scale of 0 to 10,000. This allows you to define a single Drawable that can be modified to suit particular circumstances—such as an arrow that can point in multiple directions.

When moving through levels, level 0 represents the start angle (or smallest scale result). Level 10,000 represents the end of the transformation (the finish angle or highest scale). If you do not specify the image level, it will default to 0:

```
ImageView rotatingImage
  = findViewById(R.id.RotatingImageView);
ImageView scalingImage
  = findViewById(R.id.ScalingImageView);

// Rotate the image 50% of the way to its final orientation.
rotatingImage.setImageLevel(5000);

// Scale the image to 50% of its final size.
scalingImage.setImageLevel(5000);
```

Layer Drawables

A `LayerDrawable` lets you composite several Drawable resources on top of one another. If you define an array of partially transparent Drawables, you can stack them on top of one another to create complex combinations of dynamic shapes and transformations.

Similarly, you can use Layer Drawables as the source for the transformative Drawable resources described in the preceding section, or the State List and Level List Drawables that follow.

Layer Drawables are defined via the `layer-list` node tag. Within that tag, create a new `item` node using the `drawable` attribute to specify each Drawables to add. Each Drawable will be stacked in index order, with the first item in the array at the bottom of the stack:

```xml
<?xml version="1.0" encoding="utf-8"?>
<layer-list xmlns:android="http://schemas.android.com/apk/res/android">
  <item android:drawable="@drawable/bottomimage"/>
  <item android:drawable="@drawable/image2"/>
  <item android:drawable="@drawable/image3"/>
  <item android:drawable="@drawable/topimage"/>
</layer-list>
```

State List Drawables

A State List Drawable is a composite resource that enables you to specify a different Drawable to display based on the state of the View to which it has been assigned.

Most native Android Views use State List Drawables, including the image used on Buttons and the background used for standard List View items.

To define a State List Drawable, create an XML file containing a root `selector` tag. Add a series of item nodes, each of which uses an `android:state_` attribute and `android:drawable` attribute to assign a specific Drawable to a particular state:

```xml
<selector xmlns:android="http://schemas.android.com/apk/res/android">
<item android:state_pressed="true"
```

```
            android:drawable="@drawable/widget_bg_pressed"/>
  <item android:state_focused="true"
        android:drawable="@drawable/widget_bg_selected"/>
  <item android:state_window_focused="false"
        android:drawable="@drawable/widget_bg_normal"/>
  <item android:drawable="@drawable/widget_bg_normal"/>
</selector>
```

Each state attribute can be set to `true` or `false`, allowing you to specify a different Drawable for each combination of the following list View states:

➤ `android:state_pressed`—Pressed or not pressed.

➤ `android:state_focused`—Has focus or does not have focus.

➤ `android:state_hovered`—Introduced in API Level 11, the cursor is hovering over the view or is not hovering.

➤ `android:state_selected`—Selected or not selected.

➤ `android:state_checkable`—Can or can't be checked.

➤ `android:state_checked`—Is or isn't checked.

➤ `android:state_enabled`—Enabled or disabled.

➤ `android:state_activated`—Activated or not activated.

➤ `android:state_window_focused`—The parent window has focus or does not have focus.

When deciding which Drawable to display for a given View, Android will apply the first item in the state list that matches the current state of the object. As a result, your default value should be the last in the list.

Level List Drawables

Using a Level List Drawable you can create an array of Drawable resources, assigning an integer index value for each layer. Use the `level-list` node to create a new Level List Drawable, using `item` nodes to define each layer, with `android:drawable` / `android:maxLevel` attributes defining the Drawable for each layer and its corresponding index:

```
<level-list xmlns:android="http://schemas.android.com/apk/res/android">
  <item android:maxLevel="0"  android:drawable="@drawable/earthquake_0"/>
  <item android:maxLevel="1"  android:drawable="@drawable/earthquake_1"/>
  <item android:maxLevel="2"  android:drawable="@drawable/earthquake_2"/>
  <item android:maxLevel="4"  android:drawable="@drawable/earthquake_4"/>
  <item android:maxLevel="6"  android:drawable="@drawable/earthquake_6"/>
  <item android:maxLevel="8"  android:drawable="@drawable/earthquake_8"/>
  <item android:maxLevel="10" android:drawable="@drawable/earthquake_10"/>
</level-list>
```

To select which image to display in code, call `setImageLevel` on the View displaying the Level List Drawable resource, passing in the index of the Drawable you want to display:

```
imageView.setImageLevel(5);
```

The View will display the image corresponding to the index with an equal or greater value to the one specified.

COPY, PASTE, AND THE CLIPBOARD

Android includes full support for copy and paste operations within (and between) Android applications using the Clipboard Manager:

```
ClipboardManager clipboard =
    (ClipboardManager)getSystemService(CLIPBOARD_SERVICE);
```

The clipboard supports text strings, URIs (typically directed at a Content Provider item), and Intents (for copying application shortcuts). To copy an object to the clipboard, create a new `ClipData` object that contains a `ClipDescription` that describes the metadata related to the copied object, and any number of `ClipData.Item` objects, as described in the following section. Add it to the clipboard using the `setPrimaryClip` method:

```
clipboard.setPrimaryClip(newClip);
```

The clipboard can contain only one Clip Data object at any time. Copying a new object replaces the previously held clipboard item. As a result, you can assume neither that your application will be the last to have copied something to the clipboard nor that it will be the only application that pastes it.

Copying Data to the Clipboard

The `ClipData` class includes a number of static convenience methods to simplify the creation of typical Clip Data objects. Use the `newPlainText` method to create a new Clip Data that includes the specified string, sets the description to the label provided, and sets the MIME type to `MIMETYPE_TEXT_PLAIN`:

```
ClipData newClip = ClipData.newPlainText("copied text","Hello, Android!");
```

For Content Provider-based items, use the `newUri` method, specifying a Content Resolver, label, and URI from which the data is to be pasted:

```
ClipData newClip = ClipData.newUri(getContentResolver(),"URI", myUri);
```

Pasting Clipboard Data

To provide a good user experience, you should enable and disable the paste option from your UI based on whether there is data copied to the clipboard. You can do this by querying the clipboard service using the `hasPrimaryClip` method:

```
if (!(clipboard.hasPrimaryClip())) {
  // TODO Disable paste UI option.
}
```

It's also possible to query the data type of the Clip Data object currently in the clipboard. Use the `getPrimaryClipDescription` method to extract the metadata for the clipboard data, using its `has-MimeType` method to specify the MIME type you support pasting into your application:

```
if (!(clipboard.getPrimaryClipDescription().hasMimeType(MIMETYPE_TEXT_PLAIN)))
{
  // TODO Disable the paste UI option if the content in
  // the clipboard is not of a supported type.
}
else
{
  // TODO Enable the paste UI option if the clipboard contains data
  // of a supported type.
}
```

To access the data itself, use the `getItemAt` method, passing in the index of the item you want to retrieve:

```
ClipData.Item item = clipboard.getPrimaryClip().getItemAt(0);
```

You can extract the text, URI, or Intent using the `getText`, `getUri`, and `getIntent` methods, respectively:

```
CharSequence pasteData = item.getText();
Intent pastIntent = item.getIntent();
Uri pasteUri = item.getUri();
```

It's also possible to paste the content of any clipboard item, even if your application supports only text. Using the `coerceToText` method you can transform the contents of a `ClipData.Item` object into a string:

```
CharSequence pasteText = item.coerceToText(this);
```

15

Location, Contextual Awareness, and Mapping

WHAT'S IN THIS CHAPTER?

➤ Installing and using Google Play services

➤ Determining and updating the device's physical location

➤ Using the emulator to test location-based functionality

➤ Setting and monitoring Geofences

➤ Finding addresses and address locations with the Geocoder

➤ Adding interactive maps to your application

➤ Changing the map camera position

➤ Displaying user location on a map

➤ Adding markers, shapes, and image overlays to maps

➤ Adding awareness of the user's context using awareness snapshots

➤ Setting and monitoring contextual awareness fences

WROX.COM CODE DOWNLOADS FOR THIS CHAPTER

The code downloads for this chapter are found at www.wrox.com. The code for this chapter is divided into the following major examples:

➤ Snippets_ch15.zip

➤ WhereAmI_ch15_part1.zip

➤ WhereAmI_ch15_part2.zip

➤ WhereAmI_ch15_part3.zip

➤ WhereAmI_ch15_part4.zip

➤ Earthquake_ch15.zip

ADDING LOCATION, MAPS, AND CONTEXTUAL AWARENESS TO YOUR APPLICATIONS

One of the defining features of mobile devices is their portability, so it's not surprising that some of the most enticing APIs are those that enable you to find, contextualize, and map the user's physical location, environment, and context. In this chapter you learn how to install and use Google Play services to take advantage of these powerful and efficient APIs.

Location Services enable you to find the device's current location, and get updates as it changes. You'll learn how to use the Fused Location Provider to take advantage of underlying GPS-, cell-, or Wi-Fi-based location-sensing technologies. You'll also learn about the legacy platform *location-based services* (LBS) and how to use them when Google Play services aren't available.

Using the Google Maps API, also included as part of the Google Play services library, you can create map-based Activities using Google Maps as a user interface element. You have full access to the map, which enables you to control the camera position, alter the zoom level, and annotate maps using markers, shapes, and image overlays—as well as handling user interactions.

Maps and location-based services use latitude and longitude to pinpoint geographic locations, but your users are more likely to think in terms of a street address. Android includes a geocoder that you can use to convert back and forth between latitude/longitude values and real-world addresses.

Finally, you are introduced to the Awareness API that helps you understand and react to changes in your user's context. The Awareness API combines device state with the results from a dozen different sensors, and additional web-sourced environmental information such as weather. It provides access to this information through snapshots or "fences" in a way that's fast and battery efficient.

INTRODUCING GOOGLE PLAY SERVICES

The Google Play services SDK (often referred to as *Play Services* or *GMS*) is a set of libraries that you can include in your projects to access over 20 Google-proprietary features including Location Services, Google Maps, and the Awareness APIs—each of which is described within this chapter.

Like the support package introduced in Chapter 2, "Getting Started," Google Play services APIs often replace or extend framework API features, helping you provide a consistently updated user experience—as well as taking advantage of new features, bug fixes, and efficiencies.

Like the Android Support Library and SDK platform releases, new versions of the Google Play services client library are delivered through the Android SDK Manager. Note that like the support library, Google Play services are updated far more frequently than the Android platform SDK.

By downloading new versions of the SDK, and updating your dependencies to reference the newest releases, you can continue to incorporate bug fixes and improvements to your app as the Google

Play services are updated. The Google Play services libraries interact with the Google Play services application, which is automatically distributed and updated through the Google Play store. The Google Play services app runs as a background service on supported devices.

Unlike the Android Support Library, Google Play services are not guaranteed to be available on all Android devices. Because the Google Play services SDK depends on the Google Play services APK, which is delivered through the Google Play Store, both must be installed on the host device in order for your app to successfully use the SDK.

> **NOTE** *Due to the Google Play services SDK's dependency on the Google Play Store, if you plan to release via other distribution channels you may need to include alternative implementations for functionality that depends on Google Play services. If you plan to distribute your application exclusively through the Google Play Store, you can assume Google Play services will be available, but not necessarily the specific version required by your application.*
>
> *To assist you, the Google Play services can resolve issues such as a missing, disabled, or out-of-date Google Play services at run time.*

It's good practice to use the Google Play services SDK, rather than the framework API libraries, whenever the host device is capable of supporting them.

Adding Google Play Services to Your Application

To incorporate Google Play services into your project, start by downloading the Google Play services SDK.

Within Android Studio, open the SDK Manager (Figure 15-1), which is available through a shortcut on the toolbar, or from within the Android Studio settings dialog. It offers a tab for SDK Platforms and SDK Tools.

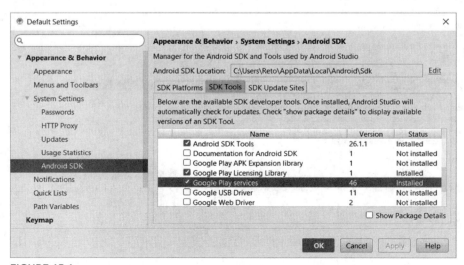

FIGURE 15-1

The SDK Tools tab shows which SDK, platform, and build tools you have downloaded, as well as the support repository, emulator, and Google Play services SDK.

Ensure the Google Play services check box is ticked, and click Apply or OK to download and install the SDK.

Once the SDK is installed, you can add it as a dependency to your application's project using your application module's `build.gradle` file within the dependencies node:

```
dependencies {
    ...
    implementation 'com.google.android.gms:play-services:15.0.1'
}
```

> **NOTE** *The specific version number specified in your dependency node must correspond to the version of the Google Play services SDK you have downloaded and installed. Similarly, when you install newer versions of the SDK, you must update the dependency node accordingly.*

Alternatively, you can use Android Studio's Project Structure UI as shown in Figure 15-2. Click File ➪ Project Structure, select "app" within the Modules section of the left navigation, and then choose the Dependencies tab. Add a new library by selecting the green "+" symbol and indicating the desired library.

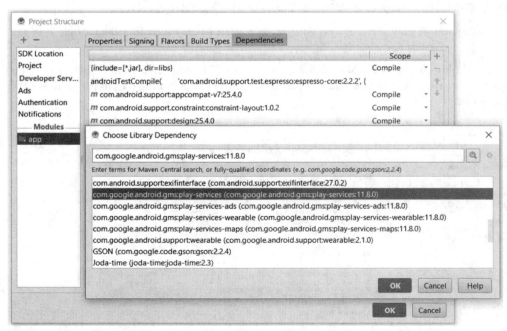

FIGURE 15-2

The Google Play services SDK contains more than 20 individual libraries, each of which offers an API related to a specific Google Service. The dependency declaration in the preceding code snippet includes all the Google Play services libraries, many of which you may not use.

Instead, it's best practice to include only the libraries you plan to use within your application, as shown in Listing 15-1, which adds only the Location, Maps, and Awareness libraries. Note again that the version number specified here should be updated to correspond to the SDK version you are developing against.

LISTING 15-1: Adding Google Play services as app dependencies

```
dependencies {
    ...
    implementation 'com.google.android.gms:play-services-awareness:15.0.1'
    implementation 'com.google.android.gms:play-services-maps:15.0.1'
    implementation 'com.google.android.gms:play-services-location:15.0.1'
}
```

You can find a full list of the available Google Play services libraries and their `build.gradle` descriptions at `developers.google.com/android/guides/setup`.

Notice that we're adding a dependency to a specific version of Google Play services. New releases of the Google Play services APK are regularly distributed, automatically, to all supported devices through the Google Play Store. It's best practice to update your app dependencies to the latest version of Google Play services so that you can take advantage of bug fixes, new features, and efficiency improvements. To update the version of Google Play services used by your app, install the updated SDK and modify your dependency node accordingly.

Determining the Availability of Google Play Services

The Google Play services APK is delivered and updated on all Android devices running Google Play. However, updates can take time to roll out to all devices so it's possible that a user's device will receive your updated application before it receives the Google Play services update upon which your app depends.

If you are using the Google Maps or Location Services, or using the Google API Client to connect to any of the other Google Services, the API will handle situations where a compatible device is running an outdated, missing, or disabled Google Play services APK.

For issues that can be resolved by the user at run time, a dialog will be displayed with instructions on how to fix the error.

Should you choose to distribute your app outside the Google Play ecosystem, it may be installed and run on a device that doesn't include, or support, Google Play services; in this case you will need to consider how to handle the missing libraries.

For some, such as location-based services, you may be able to fall back on platform functionality. In others, such as mapping, you may consider reverting to an alternative library such as Open Street Map. In the most extreme case, where critical functionality requires Google Play services, you may choose to display an error, disable functionality, or even force an exit of the application. You can detect the availability (or lack thereof) of Google Play services by looking for an unresolvable error using the `isGooglePlayServicesAvailable` method on the `GoogleApiAvailability` class as shown in Listing 15-2.

LISTING 15-2: Checking if Google Play services is available

```
GoogleApiAvailability availability = GoogleApiAvailability.getInstance();
int result = availability.isGooglePlayServicesAvailable(this);
if (result != ConnectionResult.SUCCESS) {
  if (!availability.isUserResolvableError(result))
    // TODO: Google Play services not available.
}
```

FINDING DEVICE LOCATION USING GOOGLE LOCATION SERVICES

The Location Services library, offered through Google Play services, provides a best-practice wrapper around a number of different platform technologies used to find and monitor a device's location. In addition to dramatically simplifying the process of using location services within your app, the Google Play Location Services also offer a dramatic improvement in accuracy and battery efficiency.

> **NOTE** *The Android framework includes location-based services through the Location Manager, as described in the section "Using the Legacy Platform Location-Based Services." For efficiency and accuracy reasons, the Google Play services location APIs are strongly preferred over the legacy platform APIs and should be used whenever possible.*

Using the Location Service, you can do the following:

➤ Obtain your current location

➤ Follow movement

➤ Set geofences for detecting movement into and out of a specified area

Access to the Location Services is provided by the Google Play service location library, which must be added as a dependency to your app module's `build.gradle` file after you've installed Google Play services as described earlier in this chapter:

```
dependencies {
   [... Existing dependencies ...]
   implementation 'com.google.android.gms:play-services-location:15.0.1'
}
```

> **NOTE** *The version number indicated in the previous snippet was the latest version when this book was written. You should always target the newest available version of the library within your app.*

Obtaining the current device location requires one of two `uses-permission` tags in your manifest, specifying the degree of location accuracy you require, where:

➤ *Fine* represents high accuracy, and will enable you to receive the most accurate possible location to the maximum resolution supported by the hardware.

➤ *Coarse* represents low accuracy, limiting the resolution of returned location results to approximately a city block.

The following snippet shows how to request the *fine* and *coarse* permissions in your application manifest; note that requesting/granting fine permission implicitly grants coarse permission:

```
<uses-permission android:name="android.permission.ACCESS_FINE_LOCATION"/>
<uses-permission android:name="android.permission.ACCESS_COARSE_LOCATION"/>
```

Both location permissions are marked as dangerous, meaning you need to check for—and if necessary request, and be granted—runtime user permission before you can receive location results, as shown in Listing 15-3.

LISTING 15-3: Requesting the fine location permission at runtime

```java
int permission = ActivityCompat.checkSelfPermission(this,
  Manifest.permission.ACCESS_FINE_LOCATION);

if (permission == PERMISSION_GRANTED) {
  // TODO Access the location-based services.
} else {
  // Request fine location permission.
  if (ActivityCompat.shouldShowRequestPermissionRationale(
    this, Manifest.permission.ACCESS_FINE_LOCATION)) {
    // TODO Display additional rationale for the requested permission.
  }
  ActivityCompat.requestPermissions(this,
    new String[]{Manifest.permission.ACCESS_FINE_LOCATION},
    LOCATION_PERMISSION_REQUEST);
}
```

The `requestPermissions` method runs asynchronously, displaying a standard Android dialog that can't be customized. You can receive a callback when the user has either accepted or denied your runtime request, by overriding the `onRequestPermissionsResult` handler:

```java
@Override
public void onRequestPermissionsResult(int requestCode,
                                       @NonNull String[] permissions,
                                       @NonNull int[] grantResults) {
  super.onRequestPermissionsResult(requestCode, permissions, grantResults);
  // TODO React to granted / denied permissions.
}
```

It's common practice to listen for this callback, and if permission is granted, to execute the functionality that was previously protected by the permission check.

To find or follow the device location, use the Fused Location Provider (FLP). The FLP uses a combination of software and hardware (including Wi-Fi, GPS, and other sensors available on the device) to determine the current location in a way that optimizes both accuracy and battery power.

To access the Fused Location Provider, request an instance of the `FusedLocationProviderClient` by calling the static `getFusedLocationProviderClient` method from the `LocationServices` class, as shown in Listing 15-4.

LISTING 15-4: Accessing the Fused Location Provider

```
FusedLocationProviderClient fusedLocationClient;
fusedLocationClient = LocationServices.getFusedLocationProviderClient(this);
```

Using the Emulator to Test Location-Based Functionality

All location-based functionality is dependent on the host hardware being able to determine the current location. When you develop and test with the emulator, your hardware is virtualized, and you're likely to stay in pretty much the same location.

To compensate, Android includes hooks that enable you to emulate movement for testing location-based applications.

Updating the Emulator's Virtual Location

Use the Location tab available from the emulator's Extended Controls window, as shown in Figure 15-3, to push a new location directly to the emulator.

You can specify a particular latitude/longitude pair in decimal or sexigesimal format along with an altitude value. Alternatively, click the Load GPX/KML button to import Keyhole Markup Language (KML) or GPS Exchange Format (GPX) files, respectively. After these load, you can jump to particular waypoints (locations) or play back each sequence of locations at up to 5x speed.

> **NOTE** *Most GPS systems record track-files using GPX, whereas KML is used extensively online to define geographic information. You can handwrite your own KML file or generate one by using Google Earth to create a path between locations.*

Enabling Location Services on the Emulator

The location results returned by the location APIs are not updated unless at least one application has requested location updates. Similarly, the techniques used to update the emulator's location, described in the previous section, take effect only when at least one application has requested location updates from the GPS.

FIGURE 15-3

As a result, when the Emulator is first started, the result returned from the current location may be null.

To ensure all Location Services are enabled, and location updates are being received, you should start the Google Maps app within the emulator and accept the prompts regarding location as shown in Figure 15-4.

Finding the Last Known Location

One of the most powerful uses of the Location Services is to find the physical location of the device. The accuracy of the returned location is dependent on the hardware available, the permissions requested by and granted to your application, and the user's system location settings.

Using the Fused Location Provider, you can find the last location fix received by the device using the `getLastLocation` method.

FIGURE 15-4

> **NOTE** *The underlying Android framework includes multiple Location Providers of varying power drain and accuracy, such as GPS, Wi-Fi, and cell network. Location Providers are described later in this chapter.*
>
> *In addition to improved accuracy and efficiency, another advantage of using the Fused Location Provider is that it will return the last Location value found using any underlying provider, with the best accuracy available within the constraints of your app's location permissions. If the last Location available is more accurate than your application can receive, the precision of the result will be "smudged" to preserve the user's privacy.*

The Location Service uses the Tasks API, which makes it easier to compose asynchronous operations, and handles the underlying connection process between your app and the Location Service—including the resolution for some connection failures.

As a result, to obtain the Location value, add an `OnSuccessListener` to the returned Task using the `addOnSuccessListener` method, as shown in Listing 15-5. The new `OnSuccessListener` should use a `Location` type, and implement the `onSuccess` handler.

LISTING 15-5: Obtaining the last known device Location

```
FusedLocationProviderClient fusedLocationClient;
fusedLocationClient = LocationServices.getFusedLocationProviderClient(this);
fusedLocationClient.getLastLocation()
  .addOnSuccessListener(this, new OnSuccessListener<Location>() {
    @Override
    public void onSuccess(Location location) {
      // In some rare situations this can be null.
      if (location != null) {
        // TODO Do something with the returned location.
      }
    }
  });
```

Similarly, you can use the `addOnFailureListener` method to add an `OnFailureListener` whose `onFailure` method will be triggered if the Location Service is unable to successfully return a last known Location value:

```
fusedLocationClient.getLastLocation()
  .addOnSuccessListener(this, new OnSuccessListener<Location>() {
    @Override
    public void onSuccess(Location location) {
      // In some rare situations this can be null.
      if (location != null) {
        // TODO Do something with the returned location.
      }
    }
  })
```

```
.addOnFailureListener(this, new OnFailureListener() {
  @Override
  public void onFailure(@NonNull Exception e) {
    // TODO Failed to obtain the last location.
  }
});
```

> **WARNING** *Requesting the last Location does not ask the Location Service to find the current position. If the device has not recently updated the current position, it may be out of date. In some rare cases a last Location value may not exist, in which case null will be returned.*

The Location object returned includes all the position information available from the provider that supplied it. This can include the time it was obtained, the accuracy of the coordinate found, and its latitude, longitude, bearing, altitude, and speed. All these properties are available via get methods on the Location object.

"Where Am I" Example

The following example—Where Am I—features a new Activity that finds the device's last known location using the Fused Location Provider from the Google Play services Location Services library.

> **NOTE** *For this example to work, the test device (or emulator) must have recorded at least one location update. This is most easily achieved by starting the Google Maps application and sending a location update as described earlier in this chapter.*

1. Create a new Where Am I project with an empty WhereAmIActivity. This example will use fine accuracy, so you need to include the uses-permission tag for ACCESS_FINE_LOCATION in your application manifest. We'll also add the ACCESS_COARSE_LOCATION:

```xml
<?xml version="1.0" encoding="utf-8"?>
<manifest xmlns:android="http://schemas.android.com/apk/res/android"
        package="com.professionalandroid.apps.whereami">

  <uses-permission
    android:name="android.permission.ACCESS_COARSE_LOCATION"
  />
  <uses-permission
    android:name="android.permission.ACCESS_FINE_LOCATION"
  />

  <application
    android:allowBackup="true"
    android:icon="@mipmap/ic_launcher"
    android:label="@string/app_name"
```

```
android:roundIcon="@mipmap/ic_launcher_round"
android:supportsRtl="true"
android:theme="@style/AppTheme">
<activity android:name=".WhereAmIActivity">
  <intent-filter>
    <action android:name="android.intent.action.MAIN"/>
    <category android:name="android.intent.category.LAUNCHER"/>
  </intent-filter>
</activity>
</application>

</manifest>
```

2. Add a dependency to the Location library within the app module `build.gradle` file:

```
dependencies {
    implementation fileTree(dir: 'libs', include: ['*.jar'])
    implementation 'com.android.support:appcompat-v7:27.1.1'
    implementation 'com.android.support.constraint:constraint-layout:1.1.0'
    testImplementation 'junit:junit:4.12'
    androidTestImplementation 'com.android.support.test:runner:1.0.2'
    androidTestImplementation 'com.android.support.test.espresso' +
                             ':espresso-core:3.0.2'
    implementation 'com.android.support:support-media-compat:27.1.1'
    implementation 'com.android.support:support-v4:27.1.1'

    implementation 'com.google.android.gms:play-services-location:15.0.1'
}
```

3. Modify the `activity_where_am_i.xml` layout resource to use a Linear Layout and add an `android:id` attribute for the `TextView` control so that you can access it from within the Activity:

```
<?xml version="1.0" encoding="utf-8"?>
<LinearLayout
    xmlns:android="http://schemas.android.com/apk/res/android"
    xmlns:app="http://schemas.android.com/apk/res-auto"
    xmlns:tools="http://schemas.android.com/tools"
    android:layout_width="match_parent"
    android:layout_height="match_parent"
    android:orientation="vertical"
    tools:context="com.professionalandroid.apps.whereami.WhereAmIActivity">
    <TextView
        android:id="@+id/myLocationText"
        android:layout_width="match_parent"
        android:layout_height="wrap_content"
        android:padding="16dp"
        android:text="Hello World!"/>
</LinearLayout>
```

4. Override the `onCreate` method of the Where Am I Activity to confirm that Google Play services are (or could be) available on this device, and obtain a reference to the Text View from the layout:

```
private static final String ERROR_MSG
    = "Google Play services are unavailable.";

private TextView mTextView;

@Override
```

```
  protected void onCreate(Bundle savedInstanceState) {
    super.onCreate(savedInstanceState);
    setContentView(R.layout.activity_where_am_i);
    mTextView = findViewById(R.id.myLocationText);

    GoogleApiAvailability availability
      = GoogleApiAvailability.getInstance();
    int result = availability.isGooglePlayServicesAvailable(this);
    if (result != ConnectionResult.SUCCESS) {
      if (!availability.isUserResolvableError(result)) {
        Toast.makeText(this, ERROR_MSG, Toast.LENGTH_LONG).show();
      }
    }
  }
```

5. We'll update the current location each time the app becomes visible, so override the `onStart` method to check for runtime permission to access fine location accuracy. Add the stub method `getLastLocation` to call when permission is granted or rejected:

```
private static final int LOCATION_PERMISSION_REQUEST = 1;

@Override
protected void onStart() {
  super.onStart();

  // Check if we have permission to access high accuracy fine location.
  int permission = ActivityCompat.checkSelfPermission(this,
    Manifest.permission.ACCESS_FINE_LOCATION);

  // If permission is granted, fetch the last location.
  if (permission == PERMISSION_GRANTED) {
    getLastLocation();
  } else {
    // If permission has not been granted, request permission.
    ActivityCompat.requestPermissions(this,
      new String[]{Manifest.permission.ACCESS_FINE_LOCATION},
      LOCATION_PERMISSION_REQUEST);
  }
}

@Override
public void onRequestPermissionsResult(int requestCode,
                                       @NonNull String[] permissions,
                                       @NonNull int[] grantResults) {
  super.onRequestPermissionsResult(requestCode, permissions,
                                   grantResults);

  if (requestCode == LOCATION_PERMISSION_REQUEST) {
    if (grantResults[0] != PERMISSION_GRANTED)
      Toast.makeText(this, "Location Permission Denied",
                     Toast.LENGTH_LONG).show();
    else
      getLastLocation();
  }
}

private void getLastLocation() {
}
```

6. Now update the `getLastLocation` stub. Get a reference to the Fused Location Provider and use the `getLastLocation` method to find the last known location. Create a method stub `updateTextView` that will take the returned Location and update the Text View. It's worth noting that the Location Service is capable of detecting and resolving multiple potential issues with the Google Play services APK, so we don't need to handle the connection or failure cases within our code:

```
private void getLastLocation() {
  FusedLocationProviderClient fusedLocationClient;
  fusedLocationClient =
    LocationServices.getFusedLocationProviderClient(this);

  if (
    ActivityCompat
    .checkSelfPermission(this, ACCESS_FINE_LOCATION)
     ==PERMISSION_GRANTED ||
    ActivityCompat
    .checkSelfPermission(this, ACCESS_COARSE_LOCATION)
     ==PERMISSION_GRANTED) {
       fusedLocationClient.getLastLocation()
       .addOnSuccessListener(this, new OnSuccessListener<Location>() {
         @Override
         public void onSuccess(Location location) {
           updateTextView(location);
         }
       });
    }
}

private void updateTextView(Location location) {
}
```

7. Finally, update the `updateTextView` method stub to extract the latitude and longitude from each location and display it in the Text View:

```
private void updateTextView(Location location) {
  String latLongString = "No location found";
  if (location != null) {
    double lat = location.getLatitude();
    double lng = location.getLongitude();
    latLongString = "Lat:" + lat + "\nLong:" + lng;
  }

  mTextView.setText(latLongString);
}
```

When running, your Activity should look like Figure 15-5.

FIGURE 15-5

Requesting Location Change Updates

In most circumstances, getting the last known Location is unlikely to be sufficient for your needs. Not only is the value likely to be quickly out of date, but most location-sensitive applications need to be reactive to user movement—and querying the Location Service for the last known Location does not force it to update.

The `requestLocationUpdates` method is used to request regular updates of the device's location using a `LocationCallback`. The Location Callback also notifies you of changes to device location information availability.

The `requestLocationUpdates` method accepts a `LocationRequest` object that provides information the Fused Location Provider uses to determine the most efficient way to return results at the level of accuracy and precision required.

To optimize efficiency and minimize cost and power use, you can specify a number of criteria based on your application needs:

➤ `setPriority`—Allows you to indicate the relative importance of reducing battery drain and getting accurate results, using one of the following constants:

➤ PRIORITY_HIGH_ACCURACY—Indicates that high accuracy is the priority. As a result the FLP will attempt to obtain the most precise location possible at a cost of increased battery drain. This can return results accurate to within a few feet and is typically used for mapping and navigation apps.

➤ PRIORITY_BALANCED_POWER_ACCURACY—Attempts to balance accuracy and power drain, resulting in precision to within a city block or approximately 100 meters.

➤ PRIORITY_LOW_POWER—Indicates that low battery drain is the priority. As a result, coarse location updates at city-level precision of approximately 10 kilometers are acceptable.

➤ PRIORITY_NO_POWER—Indicates that your app should not trigger location updates, but should receive location updates caused by other apps.

➤ setInterval—Your preferred rate of updates in milliseconds. This will force the Location Service to attempt to update the location at this rate. Updates may be less frequent if it is unable to determine the location, or more frequent if other applications are receiving updates more often.

➤ setFastestInterval—The fastest update rate your application can support. Specify this if more frequent updates may cause UI issues or data overflow within your app.

Listing 15-6 shows the skeleton code for defining a Location Request that requires high accuracy updates every 5 seconds. Note that you can specify a Looper parameter, this allows you to schedule the callbacks on a particular thread—setting the parameter to null will force it to return on the calling thread.

LISTING 15-6: Requesting location updates using a Location Request

```
LocationCallback mLocationCallback = new LocationCallback() {
  @Override
  public void onLocationResult(LocationResult locationResult) {
    for (Location location : locationResult.getLocations()) {
      // TODO React to newly received locations.
    }
  }
};

private void startTrackingLocation() {
  if (
    ActivityCompat
    .checkSelfPermission(this, ACCESS_FINE_LOCATION)==PERMISSION_GRANTED ||
    ActivityCompat
    .checkSelfPermission(this, ACCESS_COARSE_LOCATION)==PERMISSION_GRANTED) {

    FusedLocationProviderClient locationClient =
      LocationServices.getFusedLocationProviderClient(this);

    LocationRequest request = new LocationRequest()
```

```
        .setPriority(LocationRequest.PRIORITY_HIGH_ACCURACY)
        .setInterval(5000); // Update every 5 seconds.

    locationClient.requestLocationUpdates(request, mLocationCallback, null);
  }
}
```

When a new location update is received, the attached Location Callback executes its onLocation-Result event.

Note that it's possible to receive multiple Locations within a Location Result parameter; this occurs if you set the max wait time to more than twice the update interval:

```
LocationRequest request = new LocationRequest()
    .setPriority(LocationRequest.PRIORITY_HIGH_ACCURACY)
    .setInterval(5000)          // Check for changes every 5s
    .setMaxWaitTime(25000); // App can wait up to 25s to receive updates.
```

The max wait time indicates the maximum amount of time your application can wait before receiving location updates, at which point it will receive a batch of all the new Locations received during that interval. This can be a useful way to improve the efficiency of your app if you need to receive updates in a short interval but don't need to update the UI immediately, such as when tracking a path—for example, hiking or running.

To minimize the cost to battery life, you should disable updates whenever possible in your application, especially in cases where your application isn't visible and Location updates are used only to update an Activity's UI. You can improve performance further by making the minimum time and distance between updates as large as possible.

To remove a Location Request, call removeLocationUpdates, passing in the relevant Location Callback instance. It's generally good practice to disable location updates within the onStop handler, as shown in Listing 15-7, which is triggered when your UI is no longer visible.

LISTING 15-7: Cancelling location updates

```
@Override
protected void onStop () {
  super.onStop();

  FusedLocationProviderClient fusedLocationClient =
    LocationServices.getFusedLocationProviderClient(this);

  fusedLocationClient.removeLocationUpdates(mLocationCallback);
}
```

If you remove Location Requests when the Activity stops, you'll need to keep track of when updates have been enabled to ensure they are restarted if the Activity is restarted due to a configuration change. You can find details for maintaining application state in Chapter 8, "Files, Saving State, and User Preferences."

Receiving Location Updates with Pending Intents

In rare cases, it may be necessary for your application to continue receiving location updates when it is in the background. To support this, the Fused Location Provider allows you to use Pending Intents to receive updates rather than the Location Callback.

> **NOTE** *The most common example of an application continuing to receive updates while in the background is one with a foreground service—such as real-time driving navigation that continues to receive high accuracy updates at a short frequency. However, when using a foreground Service it's still recommended that you use the Location Callback as described in the previous section.*

When receiving location updates in the background, it's important to minimize the impact on battery life. As such, it's good practice to set the priority to low- or no-battery. To further improve battery life, on devices running Android 8.0 Oreo (API Level 26) or newer, the system strictly limits background location updates, and your app will receive updates only a few times each hour.

Rather than creating a Location Callback, you can specify a Pending Intent that will be triggered whenever the location changes or the location availability status changes. Pass the received Intent into the `hasResult` and `extractResult` methods to determine if it contains a new Location Result and to extract the Location Result, respectively.

> **WARNING** *To ensure your application doesn't leak sensitive location information, you should target a specific Broadcast Receiver, as shown in Listing 15-8.*

Listing 15-8 shows how to create a Pending Intent that triggers a Broadcast Receiver to handle new location updates.

LISTING 15-8: Requesting location updates using a Pending Intent

```
FusedLocationProviderClient fusedLocationClient
  = LocationServices.getFusedLocationProviderClient(this);

LocationRequest request = new LocationRequest()
                            .setInterval(60000*10) // Update every 10 minutes.
                            .setPriority(LocationRequest.PRIORITY_NO_POWER);

final int locationUpdateRC = 0;
int flags = PendingIntent.FLAG_UPDATE_CURRENT;
Intent intent = new Intent(this, MyLocationUpdateReceiver.class);
PendingIntent pendingIntent =
  PendingIntent.getBroadcast(this, locationUpdateRC, intent, flags);

fusedLocationClient.requestLocationUpdates(request, pendingIntent);
```

Listing 15-9 shows how to create a Broadcast Receiver that listens for changes in location broadcast using the Pending Intent as shown in Listing 15-8.

LISTING 15-9: Receiving location updates using a Broadcast Receiver

```
public class MyLocationUpdateReceiver extends BroadcastReceiver {

  @Override
  public void onReceive(Context context, Intent intent) {
    if (LocationResult.hasResult(intent)) {
      LocationResult locationResult = LocationResult.extractResult(intent);
      for (Location location : locationResult.getLocations()) {
        // TODO React to newly received location.
      }
    }
  }
}
```

Remember that you must add your Broadcast Receiver to the application manifest before it can begin receiving the Pending Intents.

To stop location updates, call removeLocationUpdates, as shown in the following code, passing in the Pending Intent that you no longer want to have broadcast:

```
fusedLocationClient.removeLocationUpdates(pendingIntent);
```

Defining Expiration Criteria for Updates

Not every app requires continuous location updates. In some cases only a single location fix is required, or updates may be required for only a short length of time to provide adequate context for the functionality they provide or information they display.

When defining your Location Request, you can indicate several additional criteria that will limit the number of location updates you receive, and will automatically remove the Location Request once the limit is reached:

➤ setExpirationDuration—Updates will expire after the specified duration in milliseconds.

➤ setExpirationTime—Updates will expire when the elapsed real time since device boot (in milliseconds) is reached.

➤ setNumUpdates—Only the specified number of updates will be received.

The following snippet shows an (unlikely) Location Request that specifies an expiration duration, time, and fixed number of updates:

```
LocationRequest request = new LocationRequest()
  .setExpirationDuration(3600000)                        // Expire in 1 hour
  .setExpirationTime(SystemClock.elapsedRealtime()+360000)) // Expire in 1 hour
  .setNumUpdates(10)    // Receive 10 updates.
```

```
.setInterval(60000)   // Update every minute.
.setPriority(LocationRequest.PRIORITY_NO_POWER);
```

If you want to start receiving more updates after an expiration condition is met, you must request location updates again.

Background Location Update Limits

In order to reduce the battery life impact of Location updates, Android 8.0 Oreo (API Level 26) introduced strict limits on the frequency at which apps can receive Location updates while they are in the background. Specifically, apps that have no active foreground Activities or Services will receive updates only a few times each hour. These new limits are applied to all apps on devices running Android 8.0 or above, irrespective of your apps' target SDK.

Foreground apps continue to receive updates at the rate you specify. This includes apps with a visible Activity or with a running foreground Service. Location Requests that specify a max wait time will receive batches of updates at the reduced interval, making this a useful approach if your app requires frequent updates but doesn't require them in real time.

Alternatively, the Geofencing API has been optimized for background operation and will receive transition events more frequently than Location updates from the Fused Location Provider. By comparison, Geofences are checked for transitions once every few minutes.

Changing Device Location Settings

The combination of the location accuracy permission you request and the priority of your Location Request indicates the level of location accuracy and precision your application requires. This typically corresponds to one or more hardware devices used to determine location—such as Wi-Fi and/or GPS.

For privacy and battery efficiency reasons, users can select their preferred Location mode, as shown in Figure 15-6.

As a result, it's possible that when your app makes a request to receive location updates, the system settings may prevent it from obtaining the accuracy of location data that it needs; for example, GPS or Wi-Fi scanning may be disabled.

FIGURE 15-6

To ensure your application receives Location results of the required accuracy, you can use the Google Play services Settings API to check the users' current system-wide location settings and prompt them to modify their selection if required.

Use the static `LocationSettingsRequest.Builder` to add each of the Location Request objects your application will use to request location updates.

Get an instance of the Location Services `SettingsClient` using the `getSettingsClient` method, and use its `checkLocationSettings` method—passing in the Location Settings Request—to start a Task that will deliver a `LocationSettingsResponse`, as shown in Listing 15-10.

LISTING 15-10: Check if the current Location Settings satisfy your requirements

```
// Get the settings client.
SettingsClient client = LocationServices.getSettingsClient(this);

// Create a new Location Settings Request, adding our Location Requests
LocationSettingsRequest.Builder builder =
  new LocationSettingsRequest.Builder().addLocationRequest(request);

// Check if the Location Settings satisfy our requirements.
Task<LocationSettingsResponse> task =
  client.checkLocationSettings(builder.build());
```

You can find the results of the Location Settings Response Task by adding onSuccess and onFailure handlers.

A successful response indicates that the location settings are sufficient for your application's Location Request so you can initiate your location updates, as shown in Listing 15-11.

LISTING 15-11: Create a handler for when Location Settings satisfy your requirements

```
task.addOnSuccessListener(this,
  new OnSuccessListener<LocationSettingsResponse>() {
    @Override
    public void onSuccess(LocationSettingsResponse locationSettingsResponse) {
      // Location settings satisfy the requirements of the Location Request
      startTrackingLocation();
    }
});
```

When the onFailure handler of the onFailureListener is triggered, it indicates that the current system location settings may not be capable of satisfying the requirements you specified in your Location Requests. You can extract the status code from the returned exception to determine your next step. A status of RESOLUTION_REQUIRED indicates that the issue could be resolved through user action, while SETTINGS_CHANGE_UNAVAILABLE indicates that the issue can't be resolved:

```
int statusCode = ((ApiException) e).getStatusCode();

switch (statusCode) {
  case CommonStatusCodes.RESOLUTION_REQUIRED:
    // Issue can be user resolved.
    break;
  case LocationSettingsStatusCodes.SETTINGS_CHANGE_UNAVAILABLE:
    // Issue can't be user resolved.
    break;
  default: break;
}
```

In the former case, you can prompt the user to change the location settings to meet your requirements by calling `startResolutionForResult` on the Resolvable API Exception received by the `onFailure` handler:

```
ResolvableApiException resolvable = (ResolvableApiException) e;
resolvable.startResolutionForResult(MainActivity.this, CHECK_SETTINGS);
```

This will display a dialog, such as the one shown in Figure 15-7, requesting the user's permission to modify location settings as required.

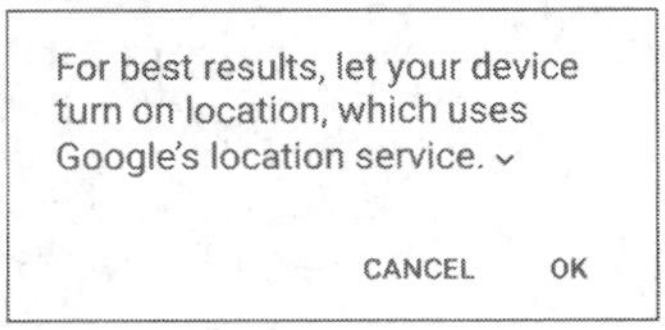

The full skeleton code for an `onFailureListener` implementation that displays a user dialog requesting a change in location settings is shown in Listing 15-12.

> For best results, let your device turn on location, which uses Google's location service. ⌄
>
> CANCEL   OK

FIGURE 15-7

LISTING 15-12: Request user changes to location settings

```
task.addOnFailureListener(this, new OnFailureListener() {
  @Override
  public void onFailure(@NonNull Exception e) {
    // Extract the status code for the failure from within the Exception.
    int statusCode = ((ApiException) e).getStatusCode();
    switch (statusCode) {
      case CommonStatusCodes.RESOLUTION_REQUIRED:
        // Location settings don't satisfy the requirements of the
        // Location Request, but they could be resolved through user
        // selection within a Dialog.
        try {
          // Display a user dialog to resolve the location settings issue.
          ResolvableApiException resolvable = (ResolvableApiException) e;
          resolvable.startResolutionForResult(MainActivity.this,
            REQUEST_CHECK_SETTINGS);
        } catch (IntentSender.SendIntentException sendEx) {
          Log.e(TAG, "Location Settings resolution failed.", sendEx);
        }
        break;
      case LocationSettingsStatusCodes.SETTINGS_CHANGE_UNAVAILABLE:
        // Location settings don't satisfy the requirements of the
        // Location Request, however it can't be resolved with a user
        // dialog.
        // TODO Start monitoring location updates anyway, or abort.
        break;
    }
  }
});
```

The result of the user's interaction with the dialog is returned within the `onActivityResult` handler as shown in Listing 15-13.

If the result is `RESULT_OK` it indicates the requested settings changes were applied, and you are free to request location updates. If `RESULT_CANCELED` is received, the user chose not to apply the requested changes.

> **LISTING 15-13:** Handling the user's response to our request to change location settings

```
@Override
protected void onActivityResult(int requestCode, int resultCode, Intent data){
  final LocationSettingsStates states =
    LocationSettingsStates.fromIntent(data);

  if (requestCode == REQUEST_CHECK_SETTINGS) {
    switch (resultCode) {
      case Activity.RESULT_OK:
        // TODO Changes were applied.
        break;
      case Activity.RESULT_CANCELED:
        // TODO Changes were not applied.
        // TODO Check states to confirm if we can attempt
        // TODO to request location updates anyway.
        break;
      default: break;
    }
  }
}
```

If the user declines the requested settings changes you must decide how to respond. You could attempt to request location results knowing the accuracy is less than desired, disable the functionality that requires the updates, or—in extreme cases—display an error and exit the application.

To help decide on the best approach, you can extract additional Location Settings States from the Intent returned to the onActivityResult handler:

```
final LocationSettingsStates states =
  LocationSettingsStates.fromIntent(data);
```

The Location Settings States includes a number of methods indicating the availability and usability of location-related support including location itself, GPS, cell network/Wi-Fi, and BLE.

Updating the Location in the "Where Am I" Example

In the following example, the Where Am I project is enhanced to update your current location by listening for location changes with a 5-second interval:

1. Open the WhereAmIActivity in the Where Am I project. Update the onCreate method to create a new LocationRequest that prioritizes high accuracy and has a 5-second update interval:

```
private LocationRequest mLocationRequest;

@Override
protected void onCreate(Bundle savedInstanceState) {
  super.onCreate(savedInstanceState);
  setContentView(R.layout.activity_where_am_i);
  mTextView = findViewById(R.id.myLocationText);

  GoogleApiAvailability availability
```

```
            = GoogleApiAvailability.getInstance();
      int result = availability.isGooglePlayServicesAvailable(this);
      if (result != ConnectionResult.SUCCESS) {
        if (!availability.isUserResolvableError(result)) {
          Toast.makeText(this, ERROR_MSG, Toast.LENGTH_LONG).show();
        }
      }

      mLocationRequest = new LocationRequest()
        .setInterval(5000)
        .setPriority(LocationRequest.PRIORITY_HIGH_ACCURACY);
    }
```

2. Create a new `LocationCallback` that calls the `updateTextView` method to update the Text
   View whenever a new Location update is received:

```
      LocationCallback mLocationCallback = new LocationCallback() {
        @Override
        public void onLocationResult(LocationResult locationResult) {
          Location location = locationResult.getLastLocation();
          if (location != null) {
            updateTextView(location);
          }
        }
      };
```

3. Create a new `requestLocationUpdates` method that will initiate a request to receive
   Location updates using the Location Request defined in Step 1 and the Location Callback
   from Step 2:

```
      private void requestLocationUpdates() {
        if (ActivityCompat
            .checkSelfPermission(this, ACCESS_FINE_LOCATION)
             ==PERMISSION_GRANTED ||
            ActivityCompat
            .checkSelfPermission(this, ACCESS_COARSE_LOCATION)
             ==PERMISSION_GRANTED) {

          FusedLocationProviderClient fusedLocationClient
            = LocationServices.getFusedLocationProviderClient(this);

          fusedLocationClient.requestLocationUpdates(mLocationRequest,
            mLocationCallback, null);
        }
      }
```

4. Update the `onStart` method to compare the system location settings with the requirements
   of our Location Request. If the settings are compatible, or if they can't be resolved, call the
   `requestLocationUpdates` method from Step 3. If they do not meet our requirements, but
   can be resolved through user action, display a dialog asking the users to change their settings
   accordingly:

```
      public static final String TAG = "WhereAmIActivity";
      private static final int REQUEST_CHECK_SETTINGS = 2;
```

```java
@Override
protected void onStart() {
  super.onStart();

  // Check if we have permission to access high accuracy fine location.
  int permission = ActivityCompat.checkSelfPermission(this,
    ACCESS_FINE_LOCATION);

  // If permission is granted, fetch the last location.
  if (permission == PERMISSION_GRANTED) {
    getLastLocation();
  } else {
    // If permission has not been granted, request permission.
    ActivityCompat.requestPermissions(this,
      new String[]{ACCESS_FINE_LOCATION},
      LOCATION_PERMISSION_REQUEST);
  }

  // Check of the location settings are compatible with our Location
  //Request.
  LocationSettingsRequest.Builder builder =
    new LocationSettingsRequest.Builder()
          .addLocationRequest(mLocationRequest);

  SettingsClient client = LocationServices.getSettingsClient(this);

  Task<LocationSettingsResponse> task =
    client.checkLocationSettings(builder.build());

  task.addOnSuccessListener(this,
    new OnSuccessListener<LocationSettingsResponse>() {
    @Override
    public void onSuccess(LocationSettingsResponse
                          locationSettingsResponse) {
      // Location settings satisfy the requirements of the Location
      // Request.
      // Request location updates.
      requestLocationUpdates();
    }
  });

  task.addOnFailureListener(this, new OnFailureListener() {
    @Override
    public void onFailure(@NonNull Exception e) {
      // Extract the status code for the failure from within the
      // Exception.
      int statusCode = ((ApiException) e).getStatusCode();
      switch (statusCode) {
        case CommonStatusCodes.RESOLUTION_REQUIRED:
          try {
            // Display a user dialog to resolve the location settings
            // issue.
            ResolvableApiException resolvable
              = (ResolvableApiException) e;
            resolvable.startResolutionForResult(WhereAmIActivity.this,
```

```
                         REQUEST_CHECK_SETTINGS);
              } catch (IntentSender.SendIntentException sendEx) {
                Log.e(TAG, "Location Settings resolution failed.", sendEx);
              }
              break;
           case LocationSettingsStatusCodes.SETTINGS_CHANGE_UNAVAILABLE:
              // Location settings issues can't be resolved by user.
              // Request location updates anyway.
              Log.d(TAG, "Location Settings can't be resolved.");
              requestLocationUpdates();
              break;
         }
       }
     });
   }
```

5. Override the `onActivityResult` handler to listen for a return from the dialog potentially displayed in Step 4. If the user accepts the requested changes, request location updates. If they are rejected, check to see if any location services are available—and request updates if so:

```
@Override
protected void onActivityResult(int requestCode,
                                int resultCode, Intent data){
  final LocationSettingsStates states =
    LocationSettingsStates.fromIntent(data);

  if (requestCode == REQUEST_CHECK_SETTINGS) {
    switch (resultCode) {
      case Activity.RESULT_OK:
        // Requested changes made, request location updates.
        requestLocationUpdates();
        break;
      case Activity.RESULT_CANCELED:
        // Requested changes were NOT made.
        Log.d(TAG, "Requested settings changes declined by user.");
        // Check if any location services are available, and if so
        // request location updates.
        if (states.isLocationUsable())
          requestLocationUpdates();
        else
          Log.d(TAG, "No location services available.");
        break;
      default: break;
    }
  }
}
```

If you run the application and start changing the device location, you see the Text View update accordingly.

Best Practices When Using Location

Incorporating user location within your application can add powerful personalization and contextualization features that improve the user experience and make unique features possible. These powerful features must be balanced against the impact on battery life and user privacy.

To take advantage of these features without draining the device battery, consider the following factors:

> **Battery life versus accuracy**—Carefully consider how accurate your location updates need to be, and consider modifying the requirements at run time to minimize the impact on battery life.

> **Minimize update rate**—Slower updates can reduce battery drain at the price of less timely updates.

> **Modify the fastest interval**—Increasing the fastest interval is useful when your application is performing a time-consuming operation that will prevent it from processing further location updates. Increase this value to allow the Location Services to buffer location updates until your app can process them. Once the long-running work is done, reset the fastest interval back to a faster value.

> **Unsubscribe when appropriate**—Your app should always unsubscribe from updates whenever they aren't needed. This is especially important if location updates are updating your UI, and your Activity is no longer visible.

Access to the user's current location introduces significant privacy considerations. As such, it's important that your application treats location data in a way that respects user privacy:

➤ Obtain the current location and request location updates only when it is strictly necessary for your application to function. When possible, allow users to decline location-dependent features while still using the rest of your app.

➤ Inform users of how and why using their location is necessary.

➤ Notify users when you are tracking their location, and if and how that location information is used, transmitted, and stored.

➤ Avoid storing or transmitting user location; when storage and transmission is necessary, take every precaution to prevent other applications from accessing this information.

➤ Be careful not to leak location information through broadcast Intents or unsecured databases.

➤ Respect user settings and system location preferences. Allow users to disable location updates within your app, and provide as much functionality as possible even when users restrict location accuracy.

SETTING AND MANAGING GEOFENCES

Geofences are defined by a given latitude and longitude, combined with an effective radius. Using Geofences, you can set Pending Intents that are fired based on the user's proximity to specified locations. Your app can specify up to 100 Geofences per device user.

> **NOTE** *Internally, Geofences use the Fused Location Provider, using different accuracy priorities depending on how close you are to the outside edge of your target area. This allows the power use and cost to be minimized when the alert is unlikely to be fired based on your distance from the target area interface.*

The Geofence API is part of the Google Play service Location Services library, which must be added as a dependency to your app module's `build.gradle` file after you've installed Google Play services as described earlier in this chapter:

```
dependencies {
  ...
  implementation 'com.google.android.gms:play-services-location:15.0.1'
}
```

The Geofence API requires the *fine* location permission to be defined in your application manifest:

```
<uses-permission android:name="android.permission.ACCESS_FINE_LOCATION" />
```

As a dangerous permission, fine location access must also be requested at run time prior to setting a Geofence:

```
// Check if we have permission to access high accuracy fine location.
int permission = ActivityCompat.checkSelfPermission(this,
  Manifest.permission.ACCESS_FINE_LOCATION);

// If permission is granted, fetch the last location.
if (permission == PERMISSION_GRANTED) {
  setGeofence();
} else {
  // If permission has not been granted, request permission.
  ActivityCompat.requestPermissions(this,
    new String[]{Manifest.permission.ACCESS_FINE_LOCATION},
    LOCATION_PERMISSION_REQUEST);
}
```

To set a Geofence, request an instance of the `GeofencingClient` by calling the static `getGeofencingClient` method from the `LocationServices` class, as shown in Listing 15-14.

LISTING 15-14: Accessing the Geofencing Client

```
GeofencingClient geofencingClient =
  LocationServices.getGeofencingClient(this);
```

As shown in Listing 15-15, you can define a Geofence around a given location using the `Geofence.Builder` class. Specify a unique ID, the center point (using longitude and latitude values), a radius around that point, an expiry time-out, and the transition types that will cause the Pending Intent to fire: entry, exit, and/or dwell.

LISTING 15-15: Defining a Geofence

```
Geofence newGeofence = new Geofence.Builder()
  .setRequestId(id) // unique name of geofence
  .setCircularRegion(location.getLatitude(),
                     location.getLongitude(),
                     30) // 30 meter radius.
  .setExpirationDuration(Geofence.NEVER_EXPIRE) // Or expiration time in ms
  .setLoiteringDelay(10*1000)                 // Dwell after 10 seconds
  .setNotificationResponsiveness(10*1000)     // Notify within 10 seconds
  .setTransitionTypes(Geofence.GEOFENCE_TRANSITION_DWELL)
  .build();
```

The loitering delay indicates the time (in milliseconds) that the device must be within the radius before the transition type moves from enter to dwell, while the notification responsiveness allows you to indicate your preferred latency between a transition and the firing of an Intent. This defaults to 0, but setting a large value here can significantly improve battery performance.

To add a Geofence you need to pass a `GeofencingRequest` and a Pending Intent to fire to the Geofencing Client.

Create the Geofencing Request using the `GeofencingRequest.Builder`, adding either a list of Geofences, or an individual one as shown in Listing 15-16. You can also specify the initial trigger, which can be useful if you're triggering on entering the Geofence and want to receive a trigger if the device is already within the proximity radius when the Geofence is created.

LISTING 15-16: Creating a Geofencing Request

```
GeofencingRequest geofencingRequest = new GeofencingRequest.Builder()
  .addGeofence(newGeofence)
  .setInitialTrigger(GeofencingRequest.INITIAL_TRIGGER_DWELL)
  .build();
```

To specify the Intent to fire, you use a `PendingIntent`, a class that wraps an Intent in a kind of method pointer, as described in Chapter 6, "Intents and Broadcast Receivers.":

```
Intent intent = new Intent(this, GeofenceBroadcastReceiver.class);
PendingIntent geofenceIntent = PendingIntent.getBroadcast(this, -1,
                                                          intent, 0);
```

Listing 15-17 shows how to initiate a Geofencing Request with the Geofencing Client, indicating the specified Pending Intent to be broadcast when the Geofence is triggered. You can use On Success and On Failure Listeners to observe if the attempt to add the Geofence(s) was successful.

LISTING 15-17: Initiating a Geofencing Request

```
geofencingClient.addGeofences(geofencingRequest, geofenceIntent)
  .addOnSuccessListener(this, new OnSuccessListener<Void>() {
    @Override
```

continues

LISTING 15-17 *(continued)*

```
    public void onSuccess(Void aVoid) {
      // TODO Geofence added.
    }
  })
  .addOnFailureListener(this, new OnFailureListener() {
    @Override
    public void onFailure(@NonNull Exception e) {
      Log.d(TAG, "Adding Geofence failed", e);
      // TODO Geofence failed to add.
    }
  });
```

When the Location Service detects that you have crossed the Geofence radius boundary, the Pending Intent fires. Depending on your Pending Intent, the Intent fired when the Geofence is triggered can trigger a Broadcast Receiver, such as the one shown in Listing 15-18.

LISTING 15-18: Creating a Geofence Broadcast Receiver

```
public class GeofenceBroadcastReceiver extends BroadcastReceiver {

  private static final String TAG = "GeofenceReceiver";

  @Override
  public void onReceive(Context context, Intent intent) {
    GeofencingEvent geofencingEvent = GeofencingEvent.fromIntent(intent);
    if (geofencingEvent.hasError()) {
      int errorCode = geofencingEvent.getErrorCode();
      String errorMessage =
        GeofenceStatusCodes.getStatusCodeString(errorCode);
      Log.e(TAG, errorMessage);
    } else {
      // Get the transition type.
      int geofenceTransition = geofencingEvent.getGeofenceTransition();

      // A single event can trigger multiple geofences.
      // Get the geofences that were triggered.
      List<Geofence> triggeringGeofences =
        geofencingEvent.getTriggeringGeofences();

      // TODO React to the Geofence(s) transition(s).
    }
  }
}
```

You can extract the GeofencingEvent by passing the received Intent into the Geofencing Event's fromIntent method. Using the Geofencing Event, you can determine what, if any, errors occurred—as well as the type of transition and List of the Geofences that triggered the Intent broadcast.

Geofences will automatically be removed once their time expires, or you can manually remove them using the Geofence Client's `removeGeofences` method, passing in either a List of identifier strings or the Pending Intent associated with the Geofences you want to remove:

```
geofencingClient.removeGeofences(geofenceIntent);
```

> **NOTE** *At the time of writing this book, it was not possible to test Geofences using the Android emulator, as they never trigger. At this time, in order to test Geofences, you must run them on a physical device. If you want to avoid having to actually move, enable "Allow mock locations" within the Developer options settings on your device, and add the* `ACCESS_MOCK_LOCATION` *permission within your manifest. This will enable you to send mock locations to your app, as described at* `d.android.com/guide/topics/location/strategies .html#MockData`.

Once added, Geofences are kept active within the Location Services process even if your app is closed or killed by the system. They will be persisted except in the cases of device reboot, uninstallation of your application, a user-initiated clear of your app data (or Google Play services app data), or if you receive a `GEOFENCE_NOT_AVAILABLE` error.

Android 8.0 Oreo (API Level 26) introduced strict limits on the frequency at which apps can receive Location updates while they are in the background. However, because the Geofencing API has been optimized for background operation, it receives transition events more frequently than Location updates from the Fused Location Provider while your app is in the background—typically once every few minutes.

Nonetheless, just as receiving location updates within your app can have a significant impact on power consumption, so too will setting multiple Geofences likely to trigger often. To minimize the associated battery impact, set the notification responsiveness to as slow a value as possible, and increase the size of your Geofence radius to at least 150 meters—reducing the need for the device to check its location.

USING THE LEGACY PLATFORM LOCATION-BASED SERVICES

In addition to the Google Play services Location Services, the Android framework includes location-based services that are available on all Android devices. The Google Play Location library utilizes these platform location APIs to implement its functionality.

The Fused Location provider implements many of the best practices described in this section, providing increased battery efficiency and location accuracy, making it the recommended API to use whenever possible.

"Location-based services" is an umbrella term that describes the different technologies used by the platform to find a device's current location. The two main LBS elements are:

➤ **Location Manager**—Provides hooks to the location-based services.

➤ **Location Providers**—Each of these represents a different location-finding technology used to determine the device's current location.

Using the Location Manager, you can do the following:

➤ Obtain your current location

➤ Follow movement

➤ Find available Location Providers

➤ Monitor the status of the GPS receiver

Access to the location-based services is provided by the Location Manager. To access the Location Manager, request a reference to it by passing in the LOCATION_SERVICE constant to the getSystem-Service method:

```
LocationManager
  = (LocationManager) getSystemService(Context.LOCATION_SERVICE);
```

As with the Google Play services Location Services library, the platform location-based services require one or more uses-permission tags in your manifest:

```
<uses-permission android:name="android.permission.ACCESS_FINE_LOCATION"/>
<uses-permission android:name="android.permission.ACCESS_COARSE_LOCATION"/>
```

As dangerous permissions, both *fine* and *coarse* location access require the user to accept runtime permissions before your app can retrieve location information using the location-based services.

Selecting a Location Provider

Depending on the device, you can use several technologies to determine the current location. Each technology, available as a Location Provider, offers different capabilities—including differences in power consumption, accuracy, and the ability to determine altitude, speed, or heading information.

> **NOTE** *The Fused Location Provider, provided by the Google Play Location library described in the previous section, incorporates all of the available Location Providers in order to provide the most accurate location results with the least battery drain.*

Finding Location Providers

The LocationManager class includes static string constants that return the provider name for three Location Providers:

➤ GPS_PROVIDER

➤ NETWORK_PROVIDER

➤ PASSIVE_PROVIDER

> **NOTE** *The GPS provider requires fine permission, as does the passive provider, whereas the network (Cell ID/Wi-Fi) provider requires only coarse.*

To get a list of the names of all the Providers available (based on hardware available on the device, and the permissions granted the application), call `getProviders`, using a Boolean to indicate if you want all, or only the enabled, Providers to be returned:

```
boolean enabledOnly = true;
List<String> providers = locationManager.getProviders(enabledOnly);
```

Finding Location Providers by Specifying Criteria

In most scenarios it's unlikely that you want to explicitly choose a Location Provider. It's better practice to specify your requirements and let Android determine the best technology to use.

Use the `Criteria` class to dictate the requirements of a Provider in terms of accuracy, power use (low, medium, high), financial cost, and the ability to return values for altitude, speed, and heading:

```
Criteria criteria = new Criteria();
criteria.setAccuracy(Criteria.ACCURACY_COARSE);
criteria.setPowerRequirement(Criteria.POWER_LOW);
criteria.setAltitudeRequired(false);
criteria.setBearingRequired(false);
criteria.setSpeedRequired(false);
criteria.setCostAllowed(true);
```

The coarse/fine values passed in to the `setAccuracy` represent a subjective level of accuracy, where fine represents GPS or better and coarse represents any technology significantly less accurate than that.

It's also possible to specify additional Criteria properties to get more control over the level of accuracy you require including horizontal (latitude/longitude), vertical (elevation), speed, and bearing accuracy:

```
criteria.setHorizontalAccuracy(Criteria.ACCURACY_HIGH);
criteria.setVerticalAccuracy(Criteria.ACCURACY_MEDIUM);

criteria.setBearingAccuracy(Criteria.ACCURACY_LOW);
criteria.setSpeedAccuracy(Criteria.ACCURACY_LOW);
```

In terms of horizontal and vertical accuracy, high accuracy represents a requirement for results correct to within 100m. Low accuracy Providers are correct to more than 500m, whereas medium accuracy Providers represent accuracy between 100 and 500 meters.

When specifying accuracy requirements for bearing and speed, only `ACCURACY_LOW` and `ACCURACY_HIGH` are valid parameters.

Having defined the required Criteria, you can use `getBestProvider` to return the best matching Location Provider or `getProviders` to return all the possible matches. The following snippet demonstrates the use of `getBestProvider` to return the best Provider for your Criteria where the Boolean enables you restrict the result to currently enabled Providers:

```
String bestProvider = locationManager.getBestProvider(criteria, true);
```

In most cases, if more than one Location Provider matches your Criteria, the one with the greatest accuracy is returned. If no Location Providers meet your requirements, the Criteria are loosened, in the following order, until a Provider is found:

➤ Power use

➤ Accuracy of returned location

➤ Accuracy of bearing, speed, and altitude

➤ Availability of bearing, speed, and altitude

The criterion for allowing a device with monetary cost is never implicitly relaxed. If no Provider is found, `null` is returned.

To get a list of names for all the Providers matching your Criteria, use `getProviders`. It accepts a Criteria object and returns a List of Strings containing all Location Providers that match it. As with the `getBestProvider` call, if no matching providers are found, this method returns `null` or an empty List:

```
List<String> matchingProviders = locationManager.getProviders(criteria,
                                                              false);
```

Determining Location Provider Capabilities

To get an instance of a specific Provider, call `getProvider`, passing in the name:

```
String providerName = LocationManager.GPS_PROVIDER;

LocationProvider gpsProvider
  = locationManager.getProvider(providerName);
```

This is useful only for obtaining the capabilities of a particular Provider—specifically the accuracy and power requirements through the `getAccuracy` and `getPowerRequirement` methods.

In the following sections, most Location Manager methods require only a Provider name or a Criteria to perform location-based functions.

Finding the Last Known Location

You can find the last location fix obtained by a particular Location Provider using the `getLast-KnownLocation` method, passing in the name of the Location Provider. The following example finds the last location fix taken by the GPS provider:

```
String provider = LocationManager.GPS_PROVIDER;
Location location = locationManager.getLastKnownLocation(provider);
```

> **WARNING** `getLastKnownLocation` *does not ask the Location Provider to update the current position. If the device has not recently updated the current position, this value may be out of date or may not exist.*

The Location object returned includes all the position information available from the provider that supplied it. This can include the time it was obtained, the accuracy of the location found, and its latitude, longitude, bearing, altitude, and speed. All these properties are available via `get` methods on the Location object.

Note that each device has multiple Location Providers, each of which may have been updated at a different time and different accuracy. To get the best last known location, you may need to query multiple Location Providers and compare their accuracies and timestamps. Alternatively, the Fused Location Provider described earlier in this chapter handles this for you with a single method call.

Requesting Location Change Updates

The Location Manager's `requestLocationUpdates` methods are used to request regular updates of location changes using a `LocationListener`. Location Listeners also contain handlers that trigger based on changes in a provider's status and availability.

The `requestLocationUpdates` method accepts either a specific Location Provider name or a set of Criteria to determine the provider to use. To optimize efficiency and minimize cost and power use, you can also specify the minimum time and the minimum distance between location change updates:

```
String provider = LocationManager.GPS_PROVIDER;

int t = 5000;    // milliseconds
int distance = 5; // meters

LocationListener myLocationListener = new LocationListener() {

  public void onLocationChanged(Location location) {
    // Update application based on new location.
  }

  public void onProviderDisabled(String provider){
    // Update application if provider disabled.
  }

  public void onProviderEnabled(String provider){
    // Update application if provider enabled.
  }

  public void onStatusChanged(String provider, int status,
                              Bundle extras){
    // Update application if provider hardware status changed.
  }
};

locationManager.requestLocationUpdates(provider, t, distance,
                                       myLocationListener);
```

When the minimum time and distance values are exceeded, the attached Location Listener executes its `onLocationChanged` event.

> **NOTE** *You can request multiple location updates pointing to the same or different Location Listeners using different minimum time and distance thresholds or Location Providers.*

It's also possible to specify a Pending Intent that will be broadcast whenever the location changes or the location provider status or availability changes, rather than using a Location Listener. The new location is stored as an extra with the key KEY_LOCATION_CHANGED:

```
String provider = LocationManager.GPS_PROVIDER;

int t = 5000;      // milliseconds
int distance = 5; // meters

final int locationUpdateRC = 0;
int flags = PendingIntent.FLAG_UPDATE_CURRENT;

Intent intent = new Intent(this, MyLocationUpdateReceiver.class);
PendingIntent pendingIntent = PendingIntent.getBroadcast(this,
  locationUpdateRC, intent, flags);

locationManager.requestLocationUpdates(provider, t,
                                       distance, pendingIntent);
```

> **WARNING** *To ensure your application doesn't leak sensitive location information, you need to either target a specific Broadcast Receiver, or require permissions for your location update Intents to be received. More details on applying permissions to Broadcast Intents are available in Chapter 20, "Advanced Android Development."*

When broadcasting Pending Intents for location changes, you will need to create a Broadcast Receiver that listens for changes in location broadcast:

```
public class MyLocationUpdateReceiver extends BroadcastReceiver {

  @Override
  public void onReceive(Context context, Intent intent) {
    String key = LocationManager.KEY_LOCATION_CHANGED;
    Location location = (Location)intent.getExtras().get(key);
    // TODO Do something with the new location
  }

}
```

To stop location updates, call removeUpdates, as shown in the following code. Pass in either the Location Listener instance or Pending Intent that you no longer want to have triggered:

```
locationManager.removeUpdates(myLocationListener);
locationManager.removeUpdates(pendingIntent);
```

To minimize the cost to battery life, you should disable updates whenever possible in your application, especially in cases where your application isn't visible and location changes are used only to update an Activity's UI. You can improve performance further by making the minimum time and distance between updates as large as possible.

Where timeliness is not a significant factor, you might consider using the Passive Location Provider, as shown in the following snippet:

```
String passiveProvider = LocationManager.PASSIVE_PROVIDER;
locationManager.requestLocationUpdates(passiveProvider, 0, 0,
                                        myLocationListener);
```

The Passive Location Provider receives location updates if, and only if, another application requests them, letting your application passively receive updates without activating a Location Provider.

Because the updates may come from any Location Provider, your application must request the ACCESS_FINE_LOCATION permission to use the Passive Location Provider. Call getProvider on the Location received by the registered Location Listener to determine which Location Provider generated each update.

Best Practice for Using the Legacy Location-Based Services

When using the platform location-based services within your application, you should consider the same factors as described earlier in "Best Practices when Using Location." In addition, the platform location-based services require you to consider the following additional factors that are handled automatically by the Fused Location Provider:

➤ **Startup time**—In a mobile environment the time taken to get an initial location can have a dramatic effect on the user experience—particularly if your app requires a location to be used. GPS, for example, can have a significant startup time, which you may need to mitigate.

➤ **Provider availability**—Users can toggle the availability of Location Providers, so your application needs to monitor changes in Location Provider status to ensure the best alternative is used at all times.

Having used Criteria to select the best Provider available for receiving location updates, you need to monitor changes in the availability of Location Providers to ensure that the one selected remains available and the best alternative.

The following snippet shows how to monitor the status of your selected Provider, dynamically switching to a new Provider should it become unavailable and switching to a better alternative should one be enabled:

```
public class DynamicProvidersActivity extends Activity {
  private LocationManager locationManager;
  private final Criteria criteria = new Criteria();
  private static final int minUpdateTime = 30*1000; // 30 Seconds
  private static final int minUpdateDistance = 100; // 100m

  private static final String TAG = "DYNAMIC_LOCATION";
  private static final int LOCATION_PERMISSION_REQUEST = 1;

  @Override
  public void onCreate(Bundle savedInstanceState) {
    super.onCreate(savedInstanceState);
    setContentView(R.layout.activity_dynamic_providers);
```

```java
    // Get a reference to the Location Manager
    locationManager
      = (LocationManager)getSystemService(Context.LOCATION_SERVICE);

    // Specify Location Provider criteria
    criteria.setAccuracy(Criteria.ACCURACY_FINE);
    criteria.setPowerRequirement(Criteria.POWER_LOW);
    criteria.setAltitudeRequired(true);
    criteria.setBearingRequired(true);
    criteria.setSpeedRequired(true);
    criteria.setCostAllowed(true);

    criteria.setHorizontalAccuracy(Criteria.ACCURACY_HIGH);
    criteria.setVerticalAccuracy(Criteria.ACCURACY_MEDIUM);
    criteria.setBearingAccuracy(Criteria.ACCURACY_LOW);
    criteria.setSpeedAccuracy(Criteria.ACCURACY_LOW);
  }

  @Override
  protected void onStop() {
    super.onStop();
    unregisterAllListeners();
  }

  @Override
  protected void onStart() {
    super.onStart();
    registerListener();
  }

  private void registerListener() {
    unregisterAllListeners();
    String bestProvider =
      locationManager.getBestProvider(criteria, false);
    String bestAvailableProvider =
      locationManager.getBestProvider(criteria, true);

    Log.d(TAG, bestProvider + " / " + bestAvailableProvider);

    // Check permissions.
    if (ActivityCompat
        .checkSelfPermission(this, ACCESS_FINE_LOCATION) !=
                                        PERMISSION_GRANTED ||
      ActivityCompat
        .checkSelfPermission(this, ACCESS_COARSE_LOCATION) !=
                                        PERMISSION_GRANTED) {
      permissionsRequest();
    }

    if (bestProvider == null)
      Log.d(TAG, "No Location Providers exist.");
    else if (bestProvider.equals(bestAvailableProvider))
      locationManager.requestLocationUpdates(bestAvailableProvider,
        minUpdateTime, minUpdateDistance,
        bestAvailableProviderListener);
```

```
    else {
      locationManager.requestLocationUpdates(bestProvider,
        minUpdateTime, minUpdateDistance, bestProviderListener);

      if (bestAvailableProvider != null)
        locationManager.requestLocationUpdates(bestAvailableProvider,
          minUpdateTime, minUpdateDistance,
          bestAvailableProviderListener);
      else {
        List<String> allProviders = locationManager.getAllProviders();
        for (String provider : allProviders)
          locationManager.requestLocationUpdates(provider, 0, 0,
            bestProviderListener);
        Log.d(TAG, "No Location Providers available.");
      }
    }
  }

  private void unregisterAllListeners() {
    locationManager.removeUpdates(bestProviderListener);
    locationManager.removeUpdates(bestAvailableProviderListener);
  }

  private void permissionsRequest() {
    if (ActivityCompat.shouldShowRequestPermissionRationale(
      this, ACCESS_FINE_LOCATION)) {
      // TODO: Display additional rationale for the requested permission.
    }
    ActivityCompat.requestPermissions(this,
      new String[]{ACCESS_FINE_LOCATION, ACCESS_COARSE_LOCATION},
      LOCATION_PERMISSION_REQUEST);
  }

  @Override
  public void onRequestPermissionsResult(int requestCode,
                                         @NonNull String[] permissions,
                                         @NonNull int[] grantResults) {
    super.onRequestPermissionsResult(requestCode, permissions, grantResults);

    if (requestCode == LOCATION_PERMISSION_REQUEST) {
      if (grantResults[0] != PERMISSION_GRANTED) {
        Log.d(TAG, "Location Permission Denied.");
        // TODO React to denied permission.
      } else {
        registerListener();
      }
    }
  }

  private void reactToLocationChange(Location location) {
    // TODO [ React to location change ]
  }

  private LocationListener bestProviderListener
    = new LocationListener() {
```

```
    public void onLocationChanged(Location location) {
      reactToLocationChange(location);
    }

    public void onProviderDisabled(String provider) {
    }

    public void onProviderEnabled(String provider) {
      registerListener();
    }

    public void onStatusChanged(String provider,
                                int status, Bundle extras) {}
  };

  private LocationListener bestAvailableProviderListener =
    new LocationListener() {
      public void onProviderEnabled(String provider) {
      }

      public void onProviderDisabled(String provider) {
        registerListener();
      }

      public void onLocationChanged(Location location) {
        reactToLocationChange(location);
      }

      public void onStatusChanged(String provider,
                                  int status, Bundle extras) {}
    };
}
```

USING THE GEOCODER

Geocoding enables you to translate in both directions between street addresses and longitude/latitude map coordinates. This can give you a recognizable context for the locations and coordinates used in location-based services and map-based Activities.

The Geocoder class provides access to two geocoding functions:

➤ **Forward geocoding**—Finds the latitude and longitude of an address

➤ **Reverse geocoding**—Finds the street address for a given latitude and longitude

The results from these calls are contextualized by means of a locale (used to define your usual location and language). The following snippet shows how you set the locale when creating your Geocoder. If you don't specify a locale, it assumes the device's default:

```
Geocoder geocoder = new Geocoder(this, Locale.getDefault());
```

Both geocoding functions return a list of Address objects. Each list can contain several possible results, up to a limit you specify when making the call.

Each Address is populated with as much detail as the Geocoder is able to resolve. This can include the latitude, longitude, phone number, and increasingly granular address details from country to street and house number.

> **NOTE** *Geocoder lookups are performed synchronously, so they block the calling thread. It's important to move these lookups into a background thread, as demonstrated in Chapter 11, "Working in the Background."*

The Geocoder uses a web service to implement its lookups that may not be included on all Android devices. Use the isPresent method to determine if a Geocoder implementation exists on a given device:

```
boolean geocoderExists = Geocoder.isPresent();
```

If no Geocoder implementation exists on the device, the forward and reverse geocoding queries described in the following sections will return an empty list.

As the geocoding lookups are done on the server, your app also requires the Internet uses-permission in your manifest:

```
<uses-permission android:name="android.permission.INTERNET"/>
```

The web service used to implement the Geocoder can vary by device, but is most commonly the Google Maps API. Note that these backend services may have limits to the number and frequency of requests. The limits of the Google Maps-based service include:

➤ A maximum of 2,500 requests per day per device

➤ No more than 50 QPS (queries per second)

The Google Maps geocoding API limitations are described in more detail at developers.google .com/maps/documentation/geocoding/geocoding-strategies?csw=1#quota-limits. In order to minimize the chance of exceeding your quota it's best practice to use techniques such as caching to reduce the number of geocoding requests made.

Reverse Geocoding

Reverse geocoding returns street addresses for physical locations specified by latitude/longitude pairs. It's a useful way to get a recognizable context for the Locations returned by location-based services.

To perform a reverse lookup, pass the target latitude and longitude to a Geocoder object's getFromLocation method and it will return a list of possible address matches. If the Geocoder could not resolve any addresses for the specified coordinate, it returns null.

Listing 15-19 shows how to reverse-geocode a given Location, limiting the number of possible addresses to the top 10.

LISTING 15-19: Reverse-geocoding a given location

```
private void reverseGeocode(Location location) {

  double latitude = location.getLatitude();
  double longitude = location.getLongitude();
  List<Address> addresses = null;

  Geocoder gc = new Geocoder(this, Locale.getDefault());
  try {
    addresses = gc.getFromLocation(latitude, longitude, 10);
  } catch (IOException e) {
    Log.e(TAG, "Geocoder I/O Exception", e);
  }
}
```

The accuracy and granularity of reverse lookups are entirely dependent on the quality of data in the geocoding database; as a result, the quality of the results may vary widely between different countries and locales.

Forward Geocoding

Forward geocoding (or just geocoding) determines map coordinates for a given location.

> **NOTE** *What constitutes a valid location varies depending on the Locale within which you search. Generally, it includes regular street addresses of varying granularity (from country to street name and number), postcodes, train stations, landmarks, and hospitals. As a general guide, valid search terms are similar to the addresses and locations you can enter into a Google Maps search.*

To geocode an address, call getFromLocationName on a Geocoder object. Pass in a string that describes the address you want the coordinates for, the maximum number of results to return, and optionally provide a geographic bounding box within which to restrict your search results:

```
List<Address> result = geocoder.getFromLocationName(streetAddress, 5);
```

The returned list of Addresses may include multiple possible matches for the named location. Each Address includes latitude and longitude and any additional address information available for those coordinates. This is useful to confirm that the correct location was resolved, and for providing location specifics in searches for landmarks.

> **NOTE** *As with reverse geocoding, if no matches are found, null is returned. The availability, accuracy, and granularity of geocoding results depend entirely on the database available for the area you search.*

When you do forward lookups, the Locale specified when instantiating the Geocoder is particularly important. The Locale provides the geographical context for interpreting your search requests because the same location names can exist in multiple areas.

Where possible, consider selecting a regional Locale to help avoid place-name ambiguity, and try to provide as many address details as possible, as shown in Listing 15-20.

LISTING 15-20: Geocoding an address

```
Geocoder geocoder = new Geocoder(this, Locale.US);
String streetAddress = "160 Riverside Drive, New York, New York";

List<Address> locations = null;
try {
  locations = geocoder.getFromLocationName(streetAddress, 5);
} catch (IOException e) {
  Log.e(TAG, "Geocoder I/O Exception", e);
}
```

For even more specific results, you can restrict your search to within a geographical area by specifying the lower-left and upper-right latitude and longitude as shown here:

```
List<Address> locations = null;
try {
  locations = geocoder.getFromLocationName(streetAddress, 10,
                                           llLat, llLong, urLat, urLong);
} catch (IOException e) {
  Log.e(TAG, "IO Exception", e);
}
```

This overload is particularly useful when working with a map, letting you restrict the search to the visible area.

Geocoding Where Am I

In this example you extend the Where Am I project to include and update the current street address whenever the device moves.

1. Start by modifying the manifest to include the Internet uses-permission:

```
<uses-permission android:name="android.permission.ACCESS_COARSE_LOCATION"/>
<uses-permission android:name="android.permission.ACCESS_FINE_LOCATION"/>
<uses-permission android:name="android.permission.INTERNET"/>
```

2. Then open the WhereAmIActivity. Create a new geocodeLocation method that takes a Location and returns a String:

```
private String geocodeLocation(Location location) {
  String returnString = "";
  return returnString;
}
```

3. Within the new method, check if the Geocoder is available, and if so instantiate a new
    `Geocoder` object and pass the Location parameter into the Geocoder's `getFromLocation`
    method to find and return the street address:

```java
private String geocodeLocation(Location location) {
  String returnString = "";

  if (location == null) {
    Log.d(TAG, "No Location to Geocode");
    return returnString;
  }

  if (!Geocoder.isPresent()) {
    Log.e(TAG, "No Geocoder Available");
    return returnString;
  } else {
    Geocoder gc = new Geocoder(this, Locale.getDefault());
    try {
      List<Address> addresses
        = gc.getFromLocation(location.getLatitude(),
                             location.getLongitude(),
                             1); // One Result
      StringBuilder sb = new StringBuilder();
      if (addresses.size() > 0) {
        Address address = addresses.get(0);

        for (int i = 0; i < address.getMaxAddressLineIndex(); i++)
          sb.append(address.getAddressLine(i)).append("\n");

        sb.append(address.getLocality()).append("\n");
        sb.append(address.getPostalCode()).append("\n");
        sb.append(address.getCountryName());
      }
      returnString = sb.toString();
    } catch (IOException e) {
      Log.e(TAG, "I/O Error Geocoding.", e);
    }
    return returnString;
  }
}
```

4. Update the `updateTextView` method to geocode each Location and append the result to our
    Text View:

```java
private void updateTextView(Location location) {
  String latLongString = "No location found";
  if (location != null) {
    double lat = location.getLatitude();
    double lng = location.getLongitude();
    latLongString = "Lat:" + lat + "\nLong:" + lng;
  }

  String address = geocodeLocation(location);

  String outputText = "Your Current Position is:\n" + latLongString;
```

```
            if (!address.isEmpty())
              outputText += "\n\n" + address;

            mTextView.setText(outputText);
        }
```

If you run the example now, it should appear as shown in Figure 15-8.

FIGURE 15-8

CREATING MAP-BASED ACTIVITIES

One of the most intuitive ways to provide context for a physical location or address is to use a map. Using a `GoogleMap` from within a `MapFragment`, you can create Activities that include an interactive map.

Google Maps support annotation using markers, shapes, and image overlays that can be pinned to geographical locations. Google Maps offer full programmatic control of the map display, letting you control camera angle, zoom, location target, and display modes—including the option to display a satellite or terrain view, and to style the appearance of the map.

Access to the Google Maps API is provided by the Google Play services Maps library, which must be added as a dependency to your app module's `build.gradle` file after you've installed Google Play services (as described earlier in this chapter):

```
dependencies {
   ...
   implementation 'com.google.android.gms:play-services-maps:15.0.1'
}
```

Getting Your Maps API Key

To use a Google Map within your application, you must first obtain an API key from the Google API Console. Navigate to `developers.google.com/maps/documentation/android-api/signup` and click Get a Key, after which you'll be asked to select an existing, or create a new, project for your Android app. Follow the guide to register your project and activate the Google Maps Android API to receive a generic, unrestricted key for your app development, as shown in Figure 15-9.

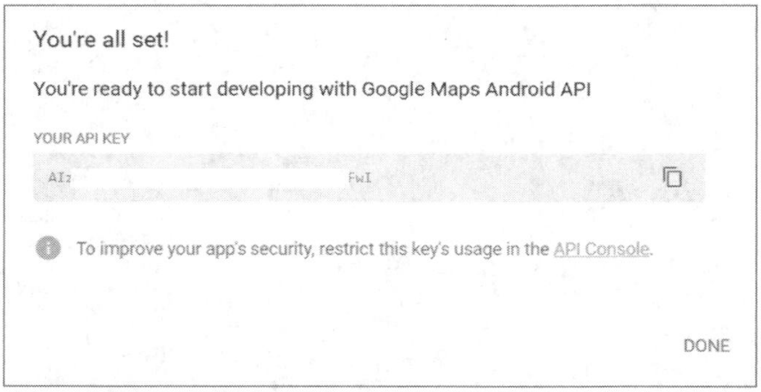

You're all set!

You're ready to start developing with Google Maps Android API

YOUR API KEY

AIz   FwI

To improve your app's security, restrict this key's usage in the API Console.

DONE

FIGURE 15-9

> **NOTE** *The unrestricted key provided here is appropriate for development and testing, but* **not** *for production deployment. When you're ready to distribute or publish your app, create a new production project with a new key that's Android-restricted, using the Google API console. Full details for creating keys and adding restrictions are available at* `developers.google.com/maps/documentation/android-api/signup#detailed-guides`*.*

Copy the key value, as you'll need to add it to your project before you can use the Google Map.

Once you've obtained your API key, add it to your application manifest by adding a new meta-data node immediately prior to the closing application tag, as shown in Listing 15-21.

LISTING 15-21: Adding your map API key to the application manifest

```
<meta-data
  android:name="com.google.android.geo.API_KEY"
  android:value="[YOUR_API_KEY]"
/>
```

Creating a Map-Based Activity

To use maps in your application, you need to create an Activity that includes a `MapFragment` or `SupportMapFragment` within its layout (the latter allows you to include a Map Fragment when using the Support Library Fragment Manager, which is best practice and the approach we'll use in all our examples).

The Map Fragment includes a `GoogleMap` with which you'll interact to modify the map UI.

The simplest way to add a new map-based Activity to your project within Android Studio is by selecting menu option File ➪ New ➪ Activity ➪ Gallery and selecting the *Google Maps Activity*, as highlighted in Figure 15-10.

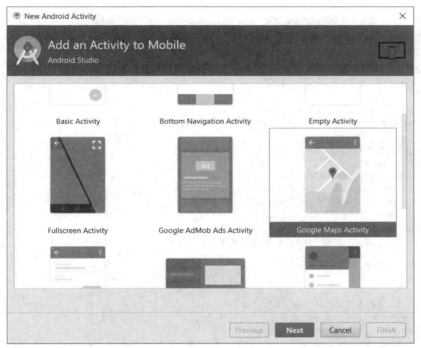

FIGURE 15-10

> **NOTE** *If you use the wizard mechanism just described to add a map Activity to your project, you can skip the step of adding your API key directly to your manifest as described in Listing 15-21. Instead, the wizard creates a* `google_maps_api.xml` *resource file into which you can paste your API key.*

The wizard will create a layout that includes a Support Map Fragment, and an Activity that includes the boilerplate code needed to inflate the Fragment and prepare the map for display and use.

Alternatively, you can create your own layout, and include a Support Map Fragment element as shown in Listing 15-22.

LISTING 15-22: Adding a Support Map Fragment to your layout

```xml
<fragment
  android:id="@+id/map"
  android:name="com.google.android.gms.maps.SupportMapFragment"
  android:layout_width="match_parent"
  android:layout_height="match_parent"
/>
```

The Activity that inflates the layout containing the Support Map Fragment must extend `FragmentActivity` and implement `OnMapReadyCallback`. Within its `onCreate` handler, get a reference to the Map Fragment and call `getMapAsync` to initiate an asynchronous request for access to the Google Map; then implement the `onMapReady` handler to be notified when the Google Map is ready to be used—as shown in Listing 15-23.

LISTING 15-23: Accessing a Google Map within your Activity

```java
import android.support.v4.app.FragmentActivity;
import android.os.Bundle;
import com.google.android.gms.maps.GoogleMap;
import com.google.android.gms.maps.OnMapReadyCallback;
import com.google.android.gms.maps.SupportMapFragment;

public class MapsActivity extends FragmentActivity
                          implements OnMapReadyCallback {

  private GoogleMap mMap;

  @Override
  protected void onCreate(Bundle savedInstanceState) {
    super.onCreate(savedInstanceState);
    setContentView(R.layout.activity_maps);
    // Obtain the SupportMapFragment and request the Google Map object.
    SupportMapFragment mapFragment =
      (SupportMapFragment)getSupportFragmentManager()
        .findFragmentById(R.id.map);
    mapFragment.getMapAsync(this);
  }


  /**
   * This callback is triggered when the map is ready to be used.
   * If Google Play services is not installed on the device, the user
   * will be prompted to install it inside the SupportMapFragment.
   * This method will only be triggered once the user has
   * installed Google Play services and returned to the app.
   */
  @Override
  public void onMapReady(GoogleMap googleMap) {
    mMap = googleMap;

    // TODO Manipulate the map.
  }
}
```

Configuring Google Maps

By default the Map View shows the standard street map as shown in Figure 15-11.

FIGURE 15-11

Alternatively, you can choose to display one of satellite, terrain, or hybrid views—as well as optionally display 3D buildings, indoor maps, and a traffic overlay as indicated by the following code snippet:

```
mMap.setMapType(GoogleMap.MAP_TYPE_NORMAL);
// mMap.setMapType(GoogleMap.MAP_TYPE_SATELLITE);
// mMap.setMapType(GoogleMap.MAP_TYPE_TERRAIN);
// mMap.setMapType(GoogleMap.MAP_TYPE_HYBRID);

mMap.setBuildingsEnabled(true);
mMap.setIndoorEnabled(true);
mMap.setTrafficEnabled(true);
```

You can also use the `getUiSettings` to obtain the current map UI settings and customize them as required:

```
mMap.getUiSettings().setCompassEnabled(false);
mMap.getUiSettings().setAllGesturesEnabled(false);
mMap.getUiSettings().setIndoorLevelPickerEnabled(false);
mMap.getUiSettings().setMapToolbarEnabled(false);
mMap.getUiSettings().setRotateGesturesEnabled(false);
mMap.getUiSettings().setScrollGesturesEnabled(false);
mMap.getUiSettings().setTiltGesturesEnabled(false);
mMap.getUiSettings().setZoomControlsEnabled(false);
mMap.getUiSettings().setZoomGesturesEnabled(false);
```

Changing the Camera Position with Camera Updates

The perspective of the map display can best be described in terms of an artificial camera pointing at a Mercator projection of the Earth's surface. Users can move, rotate, and tilt the camera using a series of gestures to modify what part of the map they're viewing, at what zoom level, orientation, and angle.

You can modify the camera perspective programmatically using the `CameraUpdateFactory` and `CameraPosition.Builder` to produce `CameraUpdates` that can be passed to the Google Map's `moveCamera` or `animateCamera` methods.

The camera's target is the latitude/longitude coordinate at the center of the displayed map. You can create a Camera Update that will modify the camera's target using the Camera Update Factory's static `newLatLng` method, passing in a `LatLng` object indicating the new latitude and longitude coordinates:

```
Double lat = 37.422006;
Double lng = -122.084095;
LatLng latLng = new LatLng(lat, lng);
CameraUpdate cameraUpdate = CameraUpdateFactory.newLatLng(latLng);
```

You can adjust how much of the world is visible on the Google Map by adjusting the camera's zoom level, indicated as a float between 1, representing the widest (or most distant) zoom, and 21, representing the tightest (nearest) view.

Each integer increase in the zoom level doubles the width of the visible world; however, the zoom level doesn't need to be an integer. The maximum zoom level available for a specific location depends on a number of factors, including the resolution of Google's maps and the available imagery for the visible area, map type, and screen size. You can find the max zoom by calling the Google Map's `getMaxZoomLevel` method.

The following list shows the approximate level of detail corresponding with a range of zoom levels:

➤   1—World

➤   5—Landmass/continent

➤   10—City

➤   15—Streets

➤   20—Buildings

To modify the camera zoom level, use the Camera Update Factory's static `zoomIn` or `zoomOut` methods to increase or decrease the zoom level by 1, or `zoomTo` to set the zoom to a specific level. Alternatively, you can use the `newLatLngZoom` method to create a Camera Update that targets a new location at a specific zoom level:

```
Double lat = 37.422006;
Double lng = -122.084095;
LatLng latLng = new LatLng(lat, lng);
CameraUpdate cameraUpdate = CameraUpdateFactory.newLatLngZoom(latLng, 16);
```

If you want to display a particular area bound by a latitude and longitude span, you can use the Camera Update Factory's `newLatLngBounds` method to specify a pair of latitude/longitude points that define the total area to be displayed. Alternatively, you can use the `LatLngBounds.Builder` to add multiple points and generate the smallest bounding box that includes all of them:

```
mMap.setOnMapLoadedCallback(new GoogleMap.OnMapLoadedCallback() {
  @Override
  public void onMapLoaded() {
    Double firstLat = 20.288193;
    Double firstLng = -155.881057;
    LatLng firstLatLng = new LatLng(firstLat, firstLng);

    Double secondLat = 18.871097;
    Double secondLng = -154.747620;
    LatLng secondLatLng = new LatLng(secondLat, secondLng);

    LatLngBounds llBounds = LatLngBounds.builder()
                            .include(firstLatLng)
                            .include(secondLatLng)
                            .build();

    int padding = 16;
    CameraUpdate bUpdate = CameraUpdateFactory.newLatLngBounds(llBounds,
                                                    padding);
  }
});
```

Because this method must know the size of the Map in order to determine the correct bounding box and zoom level, the View containing the Map must have been layed out before this method can be called. To ensure layout has completed, you can add a handler to listen for the `OnMapLoadedCallback` callback on the Map object, once the `onMapReady` handler has been triggered.

To modify the heading (rotation) or tilt (angle) of the camera, use the Camera Position Builder to generate a new Camera Position, to be passed into the Camera Update Factory's static `newCamera-Position` method:

```
CameraPosition cameraPosition = CameraPosition.builder()
  .bearing(0)
  .target(latLng)
  .tilt(10)
  .zoom(15)
  .build();

CameraUpdate posUpdate
  = CameraUpdateFactory.newCameraPosition(cameraPosition);
```

The Camera Position Builder enables you to specify every aspect of the camera's position including the target, zoom, heading, and tilt. Conversely, you can get the current Camera Position using the Google Maps's `getCameraPosition` method and extract the position elements.

Once you've created a new Camera Update, you must apply it using either the `moveCamera` or `animateCamera` methods on the Google Map object as shown in Listing 15-24.

LISTING 15-24: Moving the Google Maps camera

```
mMap.setOnMapLoadedCallback(new GoogleMap.OnMapLoadedCallback() {
  @Override
  public void onMapLoaded() {
    Double firstLat = 20.288193;
    Double firstLng = -155.881057;
    LatLng firstLatLng = new LatLng(firstLat, firstLng);

    Double secondLat = 18.871097;
    Double secondLng = -154.747620;
    LatLng secondLatLng = new LatLng(secondLat, secondLng);

    LatLngBounds llBounds = LatLngBounds.builder()
                            .include(firstLatLng)
                            .include(secondLatLng)
                            .build();

    CameraUpdate bUpdate = CameraUpdateFactory.newLatLngBounds(llBounds, 0);
    mMap.animateCamera(bUpdate);
  }
});
```

The moveCamera method will cause the camera to immediately "jump" to the new position and orientation, while animateCamera will smoothly transition from the current Camera Position to the new one; you can optionally choose to specify the duration of the animation.

Animated camera updates can be interrupted, either by a user gesture or through a call to stop-Animation. If you want to be notified of a successful completion or interruption, you can pass in an optional CancelableCallback as shown in Listing 15-25.

LISTING 15-25: Animating a Google Maps camera update

```
int duration = 2000; // 2 seconds.

mMap.animateCamera(bUpdate, duration, new GoogleMap.CancelableCallback() {
  @Override
  public void onFinish() {
    // TODO The camera update animation completed successfully.
  }

  @Override
  public void onCancel() {
    // TODO The camera update animation was cancelled.
  }
});
```

Mapping Where Am I

The following code example extends the Where Am I project again. This time you will add mapping functionality by adding a Map Fragment. As the device location changes, the map automatically re-centers on the new position.

1. Modify your app module `build.gradle` file to include a dependency on the Google Play service Maps library:

```
dependencies {
  implementation fileTree(dir: 'libs', include: ['*.jar'])
  implementation 'com.android.support:appcompat-v7:27.1.1'
  implementation 'com.android.support.constraint:constraint-layout:1.1.0'
  testImplementation 'junit:junit:4.12'
  androidTestImplementation 'com.android.support.test:runner:1.0.2'
  androidTestImplementation 'com.android.support.test.espresso' +
                            ':espresso-core:3.0.2'
  implementation 'com.android.support:support-media-compat:27.1.1'
  implementation 'com.android.support:support-v4:27.1.1'

  implementation 'com.google.android.gms:play-services-location:15.0.1'
  implementation 'com.google.android.gms:play-services-maps:15.0.1'
}
```

2. Navigate to `developers.google.com/maps/documentation/android-api/signup` to create a new project and obtain an API key. Modify the application manifest to include a new meta-data node and enter your API key accordingly:

```
<?xml version="1.0" encoding="utf-8"?>
<manifest xmlns:android="http://schemas.android.com/apk/res/android"
          package="com.professionalandroid.apps.whereami">

  <uses-permission
    android:name="android.permission.ACCESS_COARSE_LOCATION"
  />
  <uses-permission
    android:name="android.permission.ACCESS_FINE_LOCATION"
  />
  <uses-permission android:name="android.permission.INTERNET"/>

  <application
    android:allowBackup="true"
    android:icon="@mipmap/ic_launcher"
    android:label="@string/app_name"
    android:roundIcon="@mipmap/ic_launcher_round"
    android:supportsRtl="true"
    android:theme="@style/AppTheme">
    <activity android:name=".WhereAmIActivity">
      <intent-filter>
        <action android:name="android.intent.action.MAIN"/>
        <category android:name="android.intent.category.LAUNCHER"/>
      </intent-filter>
    </activity>
    <meta-data
      android:name="com.google.android.geo.API_KEY"
      android:value="[YOUR_API_KEY]"
    />
  </application>
</manifest>
```

3. Modify the `WhereAmIActivity` to implement `OnMapReadyCallback`, and add the `onMapReady` handler accordingly. It should assign the passed-in Google Map to a member variable:

```
public class WhereAmIActivity extends AppCompatActivity
                              implements OnMapReadyCallback {
```

```java
private GoogleMap mMap;

@Override
public void onMapReady(GoogleMap googleMap) {
  mMap = googleMap;
}

[ ... existing Activity code ... ]
}
```

4. Modify the `activity_where_am_i.xml` layout resource to include a `SupportMapFragment` beneath the existing Text View:

```xml
<?xml version="1.0" encoding="utf-8"?>
<LinearLayout
  xmlns:android="http://schemas.android.com/apk/res/android"
  xmlns:app="http://schemas.android.com/apk/res-auto"
  xmlns:tools="http://schemas.android.com/tools"
  android:layout_width="match_parent"
  android:layout_height="match_parent"
  android:orientation="vertical"
  tools:context="com.professionalandroid.apps.whereami.WhereAmIActivity">
  <TextView
    android:id="@+id/myLocationText"
    android:layout_width="match_parent"
    android:layout_height="wrap_content"
    android:padding="16dp"
    android:text="Hello World!"/>
  <fragment
    android:id="@+id/map"
    android:name="com.google.android.gms.maps.SupportMapFragment"
    android:layout_width="match_parent"
    android:layout_height="match_parent"/>
</LinearLayout>
```

5. Returning to the `WhereAmIActivity`, update the `onCreate` handler to find a reference to the Map Fragment and request a reference to the Google Map:

```java
@Override
protected void onCreate(Bundle savedInstanceState) {
  super.onCreate(savedInstanceState);
  setContentView(R.layout.activity_where_am_i);
  mTextView = findViewById(R.id.myLocationText);

  // Obtain the SupportMapFragment and request the Google Map object.
  SupportMapFragment mapFragment =
    (SupportMapFragment)getSupportFragmentManager()
    .findFragmentById(R.id.map);
  mapFragment.getMapAsync(this);

  GoogleApiAvailability availability
    = GoogleApiAvailability.getInstance();
  int result = availability.isGooglePlayServicesAvailable(this);
  if (result != ConnectionResult.SUCCESS) {
```

```
        if (!availability.isUserResolvableError(result)) {
          Toast.makeText(this, ERROR_MSG, Toast.LENGTH_LONG).show();
        }
      }

      mLocationRequest = new LocationRequest()
        .setInterval(5000)
        .setPriority(LocationRequest.PRIORITY_HIGH_ACCURACY);
    }
```

6. Running the application now should display the original address text with a `MapView` beneath it, as shown in Figure 15-12.

FIGURE 15-12

7. Now update the `onMapReady` handler to display the satellite view and zoom in to building level:

```
@Override
public void onMapReady(GoogleMap googleMap) {
  mMap = googleMap;

  mMap.setMapType(GoogleMap.MAP_TYPE_SATELLITE);
  mMap.animateCamera(CameraUpdateFactory.zoomTo(17));
}
```

8. The final step is to modify the Location Callback to re-center the map on the current location:

```
LocationCallback mLocationCallback = new LocationCallback() {
  @Override
```

```
public void onLocationResult(LocationResult locationResult) {
  Location location = locationResult.getLastLocation();
  if (location != null) {
    updateTextView(location);
    if (mMap != null) {
      LatLng latLng = new LatLng(location.getLatitude(),
                                 location.getLongitude());
      mMap.animateCamera(CameraUpdateFactory.newLatLng(latLng));
    }
  }
}
};
```

Displaying the Current Location with the My Location Layer

The My Location layer is designed to show the device's current location on the Google Map, represented as a flashing blue marker. Adding the My Location layer also enables the My Location button, displayed as crosshairs at the upper right of the map, as shown in Figure 15-13.

Selecting the My Location button will re-center the camera target on the device's last known location.

FIGURE 15-13

The My Location layer depends on the Fused Location Provider to provide the device location, and as such requires either *coarse* or *fine* location permissions to be requested in your application manifest, and to have been granted at runtime by the user, before the layer can be enabled:

```
if (ActivityCompat.checkSelfPermission(this,
      Manifest.permission.ACCESS_FINE_LOCATION)
      == PackageManager.PERMISSION_GRANTED ||
    ActivityCompat.checkSelfPermission(this,
      Manifest.permission.ACCESS_COARSE_LOCATION)
      == PackageManager.PERMISSION_GRANTED) {
  mMap.setMyLocationEnabled(true);
}
```

For more details on the location permissions, refer to the earlier section "Finding the Location Using Google Location Services."

Displaying Interactive Map Markers

You can add interactive, customizable markers to a Google Map (Figure 15-14) using the addMarker method, passing in a MarkerOptions object that specifies a latitude/longitude position at which to place the Marker:

```
Double lat = -32.0;
Double lng = 115.5;
```

```
LatLng position = new LatLng(lat, lng);

Marker newMarker = mMap.addMarker(new MarkerOptions().position(position));
```

When a Marker is selected, the map toolbar is displayed, providing the user with a shortcut to display, or navigate to, the Marker location in the Google Maps app. To disable the toolbar modify the Google Map UI settings:

```
mMap.getUiSettings().setMapToolbarEnabled(false);
```

By providing a title and snippet text, as shown in Listing 15-26, markers can become interactive.

LISTING 15-26: Adding a marker to a Google Map

```
Marker newMarker = mMap.addMarker(new MarkerOptions()
                    .position(latLng)
                    .title("Honeymoon Location")
                    .snippet("This is where I had my honeymoon!"));
```

When a user selects a given Marker, an information window with the associated title and snippet text is displayed, as shown in Figure 15-15.

FIGURE 15-14

FIGURE 15-15

The Google Map handles the drawing, placement, click handling, focus control, and layout optimization of each marker for you. To remove a Marker, you must maintain a reference to it when it's added and call its `remove` method:

```
newMarker.remove();
```

By default, the Marker displays the standard "Google Maps" icon, which can be customized by altering its color, or replacing the icon entirely with a custom image.

To alter the color of a Marker icon, or to use a custom Marker icon, use the `icon` method of the Marker Options. It takes a `BitmapDescriptor` that can be created using the `BitmapDescriptorFactory`.

To change the color of the default Marker icon, use the `defaultMarker` method passing in the hue, either as a value between 0 and 360, or one of the predefined hues available as constants from the Bitmap Descriptor Factory:

```
BitmapDescriptor icon
  = BitmapDescriptorFactory.defaultMarker(BitmapDescriptorFactory.HUE_GREEN);

Marker newMarker = mMap.addMarker(new MarkerOptions()
                            .position(latLng)
                            .icon(icon));
```

To change the Marker opacity, use the alpha method to indicate an opacity value between 0 (transparent) and 1 (opaque):

```
Marker newMarker = mMap.addMarker(new MarkerOptions()
                            .position(latLng)
                            .alpha(0.6f));
```

Alternatively, if you want to replace the Marker icon entirely, you can use the various `from[source]` methods from the Bitmap Descriptor Factory to select a Bitmap from a file, path, resource, asset, or Bitmap object:

```
BitmapDescriptor icon
  = BitmapDescriptorFactory.fromResource(R.mipmap.ic_launcher);

Marker newMarker = mMap.addMarker(new MarkerOptions()
                            .position(latLng)
                            .icon(icon));
```

By default, Markers will be displayed with respect to the screen, meaning that rotating, tilting, or zooming the Map won't change the appearance of the Marker.

Using the flat method, you can set the orientation of the Marker to be flat against the Map, causing it to rotate and change perspective as the map is rotated or tilted:

```
Marker newMarker = mMap.addMarker(new MarkerOptions()
                            .position(latLng)
                            .flat(true));
```

It's also possible to rotate a Marker around a specified anchor point, using a combination of the `anchor` and `rotation` methods within the Marker Options. Rotation is measured in degrees clockwise, and anchor represents the center of rotation in terms of a proportion of the size of the image in the horizontal and vertical directions:

```
Marker newMarker = mMap.addMarker(new MarkerOptions()
                            .position(latLng)
                            .anchor(0.5, 0.5)
                            .rotation(90));
```

It's also possible to customize the behavior of a Marker when selected, and the appearance of the info window that's displayed.

To alter the Marker selection behavior, add an `OnMarkerClickListener` to the Google Map. The `onMarkerClick` handler will receive an instance of the Marker selected. Return true if your handler should replace the default behavior, or false if the info window should still be displayed:

```
mMap.setOnMarkerClickListener(new GoogleMap.OnMarkerClickListener() {
  @Override
  public boolean onMarkerClick(Marker marker) {
    if (marker.equals(newMarker)) {
      // TODO React to marker selection.
    }
    // Return false to display the Info Window.
    return false;
  }
});
```

To modify the info window appearance, use the Google Map's `setInfoWindowAdapter` method, passing in an implementation of the `InfoWindowAdapter` interface to define a populated View that should be used for the Marker passed in as a parameter:

```
mMap.setInfoWindowAdapter(new GoogleMap.InfoWindowAdapter() {
  @Override
  public View getInfoWindow(Marker marker) {
    // TODO Define a view to entirely replace the default info window.
    return myView;
  }

  @Override
  public View getInfoContents(Marker marker) {
    // TODO Define a view to replace the interior of the  info window.
    return myView;
  }
});
```

Returning a View from the `getInfoWindow` handler will replace the info window in its entirety, while returning a View only from the `getInfoContents` handler will keep the same frame and background as the default info window, replacing only the contents. If `null` is returned from both handlers the default info window will be displayed.

Adding Shapes to Google Maps

In addition to Markers, Google Maps allows you to overlay lines, polygons, and circles onto the map surface. You can set the visibility, z-order, fill color, line caps, joint types, and the stroke (outline) width, style, and color for each shape.

You can draw multiple shapes on top of each map, and optionally choose to have user touches handled by one or more of them. All three shape types (Circles, Polygons, and Polylines) are mutable, meaning that they can be adjusted (or deleted) after they've been created and added to the map.

The simplest available shape is a circle, represented as a target latitude/longitude with a radius in meters. The circle is drawn as a geographically accurate projection on the Earth's surface.

Depending on the size and location of the circle, and the current zoom—the Mercator project used by the Google Map may result in the circle appearing as an ellipse.

To add a circle to your map, create a new `CircleOptions` object, specifying the center and radius of the circle and any additional settings such as fill color or stroke:

```
CircleOptions circleOptions = new CircleOptions()
                        .center(new LatLng(37.4, -122.1))
                        .radius(1000) // 1000 meters
                        .fillColor(Color.argb(50, 255, 0, 0))
                        .strokeColor(Color.RED);
```

Pass the Circle Options into the Google Map's `addCircle` method. Note that it will return a mutable `Circle` object that can be modified at run time:

```
Circle circle = mMap.addCircle(circleOptions);
```

You can create an irregular enclosed shape by defining a polygon using the `PolygonOptions` class. Use the `add` method to define a series of latitude/longitude pairs that each define a node in the shape. The default fill is transparent, so specify the fill, stroke, and joint types as needed to modify the shape's appearance:

```
PolygonOptions polygonOptions = new PolygonOptions()
                        .add(new LatLng(66.992803, -26.369462),
                            new LatLng(51.540138, -2.990557),
                            new LatLng(50.321568, -6.066729),
                            new LatLng(49.757089, -5.231768),
                            new LatLng(50.934844, 1.425947),
                            new LatLng(52.873063, 2.107099),
                            new LatLng(56.124692, -1.738115),
                            new LatLng(67.569820, -13.625322))
                        .fillColor(Color.argb(44,00,00,44));
```

Note that the polygon will automatically join the last point to the first, so there's no need to close it yourself. You can also use the Polygon Options `addAll` method to supply a List of `LatLng` objects.

Using the `addHole` method, you can create complex shapes such as filled rings or donuts by composing multiple paths. After defining the outer shape, use the `addHole` method to define a second, fully enclosed, smaller path:

```
List<LatLng> holePoints = new ArrayList<>();
holePoints.add(new LatLng(53.097936, -2.331377));
holePoints.add(new LatLng(52.015946, -2.067705));
holePoints.add(new LatLng(52.117943, 0.383657));
holePoints.add(new LatLng(53.499125, -1.088511));

mMap.addPolygon(new PolygonOptions()
            .add(new LatLng(66.992803, -26.369462),
                new LatLng(51.540138, -2.990557),
                new LatLng(50.321568, -6.066729),
                new LatLng(49.757089, -5.231768),
                new LatLng(50.934844, 1.425947),
                new LatLng(52.873063, 2.107099),
                new LatLng(56.124692, -1.738115),
                new LatLng(67.569820, -13.625322))
```

```
                       .fillColor(Color.argb(44,00,00,44))
                    .addHole(holePoints);
```

When drawn, it will appear as though a section of the surrounding polygon has been removed.

By default, the Polygon is drawn as straight lines on the Mercator projection used to display the Google Map. You can use the `geodesic` method within the Polygon Options to request each segment be drawn such that it represents the shortest path along the Earth's surface. Geodesic segments will typically appear as curved lines when observed on the Google Map:

```
PolygonOptions polygonOptions = new PolygonOptions()
                .add(new LatLng(66.992803, -26.369462),
                    new LatLng(51.540138, -2.990557),
                    new LatLng(50.321568, -6.066729),
                    new LatLng(49.757089, -5.231768),
                    new LatLng(50.934844, 1.425947),
                    new LatLng(52.873063, 2.107099),
                    new LatLng(56.124692, -1.738115),
                    new LatLng(67.569820, -13.625322))
                .fillColor(Color.argb(44,00,00,44))
                .geodesic(true);
```

Add each Polygon to your Google Map using its `addPolygon` method, passing in the Polygon Options. It will return a mutable Polygon object that can be modified at run time:

```
Polygon polygon = mMap.addPolygon(polygonOptions);
```

Finally, if you don't want to enclose an area, you can create a Polyline, which will draw a series of connected line segments based on a series of latitude/longitude pairs.

A Polyline is defined in much the same way as a Polygon; however, the ends won't be connected and the shape can't be filled. Create a new `PolyLineOptions` object, specifying the points individually, or as a List, using the `add` method as described for Polygons:

```
PolylineOptions polylineOptions = new PolylineOptions()
                .add(new LatLng(66.992803, -26.369462),
                    new LatLng(51.540138, -2.990557),
                    new LatLng(50.321568, -6.066729),
                    new LatLng(49.757089, -5.231768),
                    new LatLng(50.934844, 1.425947),
                    new LatLng(52.873063, 2.107099),
                    new LatLng(56.124692, -1.738115),
                    new LatLng(67.569820, -13.625322))
                .geodesic(true);
```

Polyline segments can be geodesic, and you can define the color and style of the stroke, the joint types, and end caps. Once defined, use the `addPolyline` method to add the Polyline Options to your Google Map:

```
Polyline polyline = mMap.addPolyline(polylineOptions);
```

By default, none of the shapes respond to user touches; however, each shape class includes a `setClickable` method that can make them clickable:

```
polyline.setClickable(true);
circle.setClickable(true);
polygon.setClickable(true);
```

To respond to shape clicks, use the Google Map's `setOnCircleClickListener`, `setOnPolygon-ClickListener`, and `setOnPolylineClickListener` to add Circle, Polygon, and Polyline Click Listeners. The click handlers for each Listener receive an instance of the shape that was clicked:

```
mMap.setOnCircleClickListener(new OnCircleClickListener() {
  @Override
  public void onCircleClick(Circle circle) {
    // TODO React to the cicle being clicked.
  }
});
```

If multiple shapes or Markers overlap at the touch point, the click event is sent first to the markers, then to each shape (in z-index order) until a marker or shape with a click handler is found—note that at most one handler will be triggered.

Adding Image Overlays to Google Maps

In addition to Markers and shapes, it's also possible to create a `GroundOverlay`, which will place an image tied to latitude/longitude coordinates over a section of the map.

To add a Ground Overlay, create a new `GroundOverlayOptions`, specifying the image to overlay as a `BitmapDescriptor` as well as the position at which to place the image. The image position can be specified as either a `LatLng` anchor at the South West point with a width (and optionally height), or as a `LatLngBounds` that contains both the South West and North East anchors:

```
LatLng rottnest = new LatLng(40.714086, -74.228697);
GroundOverlayOptions rottnestOverlay = new GroundOverlayOptions()
  .image(BitmapDescriptorFactory.fromResource(R.drawable.rottnest_wa_1902))
  .position(rottnest, 8600f, 6500f);
```

> **NOTE** *The length and width of Ground Overlays must be powers of two. If your source image doesn't conform to this requirement, it will be adjusted.*

To apply the Ground Overlay to the Google Map, call the `addGroundOverlay` method, passing in the Ground Overlay Options:

```
GroundOverlay groundOverlay = mMap.addGroundOverlay(rottnestOverlay);
```

You can remove a Ground Overlay at any time by calling its `remove` method:

```
groundOverlay.remove();
```

Adding Markers and Shapes to Where Am I

This final modification to the *Where Am I* example adds a new marker each time the location changes, and updates a Polyline connecting each marker.

We'll also take this opportunity to enable the My Location layer to show the current device position.

1. Create new member variables to store a List of Markers and the polyline:

```
private List<Marker> mMarkers = new ArrayList<>();
private Polyline mPolyline;
```

2. Update the onMapReady handler to enable the My Location layer and create a new Polyline without any points:

```
@Override
public void onMapReady(GoogleMap googleMap) {
  mMap = googleMap;

  mMap.setMapType(GoogleMap.MAP_TYPE_SATELLITE);
  mMap.animateCamera(CameraUpdateFactory.zoomTo(17));

  if (ActivityCompat.checkSelfPermission(this,
      Manifest.permission.ACCESS_FINE_LOCATION)
        == PackageManager.PERMISSION_GRANTED ||
      ActivityCompat.checkSelfPermission(this,
      Manifest.permission.ACCESS_COARSE_LOCATION)
        == PackageManager.PERMISSION_GRANTED) {
    mMap.setMyLocationEnabled(true);
  }

  PolylineOptions polylineOptions = new PolylineOptions()
                                    .color(Color.CYAN)
                                    .geodesic(true);
  mPolyline = mMap.addPolyline(polylineOptions);
}
```

3. Update the Location Callback to add a new Marker at each location, using the info window to display the date and time it was added and its place in the sequence:

```
LocationCallback mLocationCallback = new LocationCallback() {
  @Override
  public void onLocationResult(LocationResult locationResult) {
    Location location = locationResult.getLastLocation();
    if (location != null) {
      updateTextView(location);
      if (mMap != null) {
        LatLng latLng = new LatLng(location.getLatitude(),
                                   location.getLongitude());
        mMap.animateCamera(CameraUpdateFactory.newLatLng(latLng));

        Calendar c = Calendar.getInstance();
        String dateTime
          = DateFormat.format("MM/dd/yyyy HH:mm:ss",
                              c.getTime()).toString();

        int markerNumber = mMarkers.size()+1;
```

```
        mMarkers.add(mMap.addMarker(new MarkerOptions()
                              .position(latLng)
                              .title(dateTime)
                              .snippet("Marker #" + markerNumber +
                                     " @ " + dateTime)));
      }
    }
  }
};
```

4.   Make a final update to the Location Callback that modifies the Polyline to connect each Marker location:

```
LocationCallback mLocationCallback = new LocationCallback() {
  @Override
  public void onLocationResult(LocationResult locationResult) {
    Location location = locationResult.getLastLocation();
    if (location != null) {
      updateTextView(location);
      if (mMap != null) {
        LatLng latLng = new LatLng(location.getLatitude(),
                                location.getLongitude());
        mMap.animateCamera(CameraUpdateFactory.newLatLng(latLng));

        Calendar c = Calendar.getInstance();
        String dateTime
          = DateFormat.format("MM/dd/yyyy HH:mm:ss",
                              c.getTime()).toString();

        int markerNumber = mMarkers.size()+1;
        mMarkers.add(mMap.addMarker(new MarkerOptions()
                              .position(latLng)
                              .title(dateTime)
                              .snippet("Marker #" + markerNumber +
                                     " @ " + dateTime)));

        List<LatLng> points = mPolyline.getPoints();
        points.add(latLng);
        mPolyline.setPoints(points);
      }
    }
  }
};
```

When run, your application displays your current device location with a blue dot using the My Location overlay, with Markers at each location received, connected with a blue Polyline, as shown in Figure 15-16.

FIGURE 15-16

MAPPING THE EARTHQUAKE EXAMPLE

The following step-by-step guide demonstrates how to add a map to the Earthquake project you last saw in Chapter 13. The map will be used to display the recent earthquakes.

1. Start by downloading the Google Play services SDK, and adding a dependency to the Maps library within the app module `build.gradle` file:

```
dependencies {
  [... Existing Dependencies ...]
  implementation 'com.google.android.gms:play-services-maps:15.0.1'
}
```

2. Navigate to `developers.google.com/maps/documentation/android-api/signup` to create a new project and obtain an API key. Modify the application manifest to include a new meta-data node immediately before the closing `application` tag, and enter your API key accordingly:

```
<meta-data
  android:name="com.google.android.geo.API_KEY"
  android:value="[Your API Key Goes Here]"
/>
```

3. Modify the `EarthquakeMapFragment` to implement `OnMapReadyCallback`, and add the `onMapReady` handler accordingly. It should assign the passed-in Google Map to a member variable:

```
public class EarthquakeMapFragment extends Fragment
                                   implements OnMapReadyCallback {

  private GoogleMap mMap;

  @Override
  public void onMapReady(GoogleMap googleMap) {
    mMap = googleMap;
  }

  [ ... existing Fragment code ... ]
}
```

4. Modify the `fragment_earthquake_map.xml` layout resource, replacing the existing Frame Layout and Text View with a `SupportMapFragment`:

```
<fragment
  xmlns:android="http://schemas.android.com/apk/res/android"
  xmlns:map="http://schemas.android.com/apk/res-auto"
  xmlns:tools="http://schemas.android.com/tools"
  android:id="@+id/map"
  android:name="com.google.android.gms.maps.SupportMapFragment"
  android:layout_width="match_parent"
  android:layout_height="match_parent"
/>
```

5. Return to the `EarthquakeMapFragment` and override the `onViewCreated` handler to find a reference to the Map Fragment and request a reference to the Google Map:

```
@Override
public void onViewCreated(@NonNull View view,
                          Bundle savedInstanceState) {
  super.onViewCreated(view, savedInstanceState);
  // Obtain the SupportMapFragment and request the Google Map object.
  SupportMapFragment mapFragment
    = (SupportMapFragment)getChildFragmentManager()
                          .findFragmentById(R.id.map);
  mapFragment.getMapAsync(this);
}
```

At this point, starting your application should make the Map View visible either in the tablet view or when the Map tab is selected on a phone.

6. Create a new `updateFromPreferences` method, identical to the same method from the Earthquake List Fragment, which finds the current user preference for the minimum magnitude of earthquake to display:

```
private int mMinimumMagnitude = 0;

private void updateFromPreferences() {
  SharedPreferences prefs =
    PreferenceManager.getDefaultSharedPreferences(getContext());
```

```
mMinimumMagnitude = Integer.parseInt(
  prefs.getString(PreferencesActivity.PREF_MIN_MAG, "3"));
}
```

7. Create a new `setEarthquakeMarkers` method that iterates over a List of Earthquakes and creates a Marker for each, and then removes any previous Markers that should no longer be displayed:

```
Map<String, Marker> mMarkers = new HashMap<>();
List<Earthquake> mEarthquakes;

public void setEarthquakeMarkers(List<Earthquake> earthquakes) {
  updateFromPreferences();

  mEarthquakes = earthquakes;
  if (mMap == null || earthquakes == null) return;
  Map<String, Earthquake> newEarthquakes = new HashMap<>();

  // Add Markers for each earthquake above the user threshold.
  for (Earthquake earthquake : earthquakes) {
    if (earthquake.getMagnitude() >= mMinimumMagnitude) {
      newEarthquakes.put(earthquake.getId(), earthquake);

      if (!mMarkers.containsKey(earthquake.getId())) {
        Location location = earthquake.getLocation();
        Marker marker = mMap.addMarker(
          new MarkerOptions()
            .position(new LatLng(location.getLatitude(),
                                 location.getLongitude()))
            .title("M:" + earthquake.getMagnitude()));

        mMarkers.put(earthquake.getId(), marker);
      }
    }
  }

  // Remove any Markers representing earthquakes that should no longer
  // be displayed.
  for (Iterator<String> iterator = mMarkers.keySet().iterator();
       iterator.hasNext();) {
    String earthquakeID = iterator.next();
    if (!newEarthquakes.containsKey(earthquakeID)) {
      mMarkers.get(earthquakeID).remove();
      iterator.remove();
    }
  }
}
```

8. Override the `onMapReady` handler to observe the Live Data from the Earthquake View Model, which represents changes in the underlying Earthquake database; call the `setEarthquakeMarkers` method from Step 7 to update the map Markers accordingly:

```
@Override
public void onMapReady(GoogleMap googleMap) {
  mMap = googleMap;
```

```
// Retrieve the Earthquake View Model for this Fragment.
earthquakeViewModel = ViewModelProviders.of(getActivity())
                              .get(EarthquakeViewModel.class);

// Get the data from the View Model, and observe any changes.
earthquakeViewModel.getEarthquakes()
  .observe(this, new Observer<List<Earthquake>>() {
    @Override
    public void onChanged(@Nullable List<Earthquake> earthquakes) {
      // Update the UI with the updated database results.
      if (earthquakes != null)
        setEarthquakeMarkers(earthquakes);
    }
  });
}
```

9. Create a new On Shared Preference Change Listener that refreshes the Markers whenever the user alters their minimum Earthquake magnitude value, and register it within the `onActivityCreated` handler:

```
@Override
public void onActivityCreated(Bundle savedInstanceState) {
  super.onActivityCreated(savedInstanceState);

  // Register an OnSharedPreferenceChangeListener
  SharedPreferences prefs =
    PreferenceManager.getDefaultSharedPreferences(getContext());

  prefs.registerOnSharedPreferenceChangeListener(mPListener);
}

private SharedPreferences.OnSharedPreferenceChangeListener mPListener
  = new SharedPreferences.OnSharedPreferenceChangeListener() {
    @Override
    public void onSharedPreferenceChanged(SharedPreferences
                                          sharedPreferences,
                                          String key) {
      if (PreferencesActivity.PREF_MIN_MAG.equals(key)) {
        // Repopulate the Markers.
        List<Earthquake> earthquakes
          = earthquakeViewModel.getEarthquakes().getValue();

        if (earthquakes != null)
          setEarthquakeMarkers(earthquakes);
      }
    }
  };
```

If you run the application and view the Map tab, your application should appear, as shown in Figure 15-17.

FIGURE 15-17

ADDING CONTEXTUAL AWARENESS

The Awareness API combines multiple signals including location, user context, and the environment to provide a mechanism that allows you to add context-based functionality to your app, with minimal impact on system resources.

There are two variations of the Awareness API: Snapshots and Fences; both are optimized for efficiency—particularly battery life—through caching and cross-app optimizations.

The Snapshot API offers a snapshot of the user's current environment. Awareness Fences—similar to Geofences (described earlier in this chapter)—let you receive callbacks based on a combination of specific context signals whose specified conditions must be met.

The Awareness API currently supports up to seven different context signals:

> **Time**—The local time window during which a fence can trigger, defined as specific time or semantic descriptions (that is, "holidays" or "Tuesdays").
>
> **Location**—The physical user location defined as distance from a specific latitude/longitude target.
>
> **User Activity**—What activity the user is engaged in.

Nearby Beacons—The physical proximity of specific Beacons.

Places—Nearby businesses and points of interest as defined by the Google Places API.

Device state—Currently limited to headphone connection state.

Environmental conditions—Currently limited to the local weather.

Access to the Awareness API is provided by the Google Play services Awareness library, which must be added as a dependency to your app module's `build.gradle` file after you've installed Google Play services, as described earlier in this chapter:

```
dependencies {
    [... Existing Dependencies ...]
    implementation 'com.google.android.gms:play-services-awareness:15.0.1'
}
```

As a dynamic API available through Google Play services, you should expect that the range of available signals will increase over time.

Connecting to the Google Play Services API Client and Obtaining API Keys

The Awareness API, like many of the Google APIs available from the Google Play services library, requires you to create and connect an instance of the `GoogleApiClient`. The Google API Client manages the network connection between the user's device and the Google Services you want to use.

You can manage the Google API Client's connection yourself; however, it's best practice to use the automatic connection management mechanism instead.

When your auto-managed Google API Client attempts to connect to the Google APIs, it will display user dialogs as needed to attempt to fix any user resolvable connection failures.

For issues that can't be resolved, have your Activity implement the `OnConnectionFailedListener` interface, whose `onConnectionFailed` handler will be used to notify you of any user-unresolvable errors.

Create an instance of the Google API Client using the `GoogleApiClient.Builder` within your Activity's `onCreate` handler, specifying the Google APIs you want to use, along with the Activity and On Connection Failed Listener for the auto-manage functionality, as shown in the skeleton code in Listing 15-27.

LISTING 15-27: Connecting to the Google API Client

```
public class MainActivity extends AppCompatActivity
            implements GoogleApiClient.OnConnectionFailedListener {

    private static final String TAG = "CONTEXT_ACTIVITY";
```

```java
GoogleApiClient mGoogleApiClient;

@Override
protected void onCreate(Bundle savedInstanceState) {
  super.onCreate(savedInstanceState);
  setContentView(R.layout.activity_main);

  mGoogleApiClient = new GoogleApiClient.Builder(this)
                        .addApi(Awareness.API)
                        .enableAutoManage(this, // MainActivity
                                          this) // OnConnectionFailedListener
                        .build();
}

@Override
public void onConnectionFailed(@NonNull ConnectionResult connectionResult){
  Log.e(TAG, "Failed to connect to Google Services: " +
            connectionResult.getErrorMessage() +
            " (" + connectionResult.getErrorCode() + ")");
  // TODO Handled failed connection.
}
```

When auto-managed, your Google API Client will automatically connect during onStart and disconnect after onStop.

The Awareness API takes advantage of multiple Google Services. To extract Snapshots or create fences using data from these services, you must obtain API keys for each, and include them in your application manifest.

First and foremost you'll need to obtain a key for the Awareness API from developers.google.com/awareness/android-api/get-a-key.

Once obtained, add it to your application manifest immediately before the closing application tag enclosed within a meta-data node as shown in the following snippet:

```xml
<meta-data
  android:name="com.google.android.awareness.API_KEY"
  android:value="[YOUR_API_KEY]"
/>
```

The preceding URL also provides details for obtaining API keys for the Places and Nearby (beacons) APIs, which can be added in the same way as the Awareness API key:

```xml
<meta-data
  android:name="com.google.android.geo.API_KEY"
  android:value="[YOUR_API_KEY]"
/>

<meta-data
  android:name="com.google.android.nearby.messages.API_KEY"
  android:value="[YOUR_API_KEY]"
/>
```

Using Awareness Snapshots

Awareness Snapshots allow you to retrieve details about the user's current context from multiple Services. It's optimized to return results quickly while minimizing battery drain and memory impact.

The Awareness API uses cached values for the data associated with each Service; if there is no data—or the data is stale—it will use sensing and inference to return fresh values.

To obtain snapshot context signal values, use one of the `get` methods on the `Awareness` `.SnapshotApi` class, passing in your Google API Client.

Attach a `ResultCallBack`, parameterized with the result type. The returned value will be passed to the `onResult` handler. Call `getStatus` to determine if the lookup was successful, and if so extract the result using the getter, as shown in Listing 15-28.

LISTING 15-28: Retrieving Snapshot context signal results

```
Awareness.SnapshotApi.getDetectedActivity(mGoogleApiClient)
  .setResultCallback(new ResultCallback<DetectedActivityResult>() {
    @Override
    public void onResult(@NonNull DetectedActivityResult
                                  detectedActivityResult) {
      if (!detectedActivityResult.getStatus().isSuccess()) {
        Log.e(TAG, "Current activity unknown.");
      } else {
        ActivityRecognitionResult ar =
          detectedActivityResult.getActivityRecognitionResult();
        DetectedActivity probableActivity = ar.getMostProbableActivity();
        // TODO: Do something with the detected user activity.
      }
    }
  });
```

The Snapshot API includes static `get` methods corresponding to each of the context signals available. The returned values for each are consistent with the classes and values returned if you were to query the underlying Services directly. Note also that several of these methods require manifest and runtime permissions:

➤ **getBeaconState**—Provides the state of nearby beacons by returning a `BeaconStateResult`. Call `getBeaconState` to extract Beacon details. Requires the `ACCESS_FINE_LOCATION` manifest and runtime permission.

➤ **getDetectedActivity**—Returns the user's detected physical Activity (running, walking, and so on) by returning a `DetectedActivityResult`. Extract the activity recognition results by calling `getActivityRecognitionResult`. Requires the `ACTIVITY_RECOGNITION` manifest permission.

➤ **getHeadphoneState**—Indicates if the headphones are currently plugged in by returning a `HeadphoneStateResult` object, on which you must call `getState` to determine if the headphones are `PLUGGED_IN` or `UNPLUGGED`.

➤ **getLocation**—Returns the user's last known Location using a `LocationResult`. The Location value can be extracted with `getLocation`. Requires the `ACCESS_FINE_LOCATION` manifest and runtime permission.

➤ **getPlaces**—Returns a list of nearby *places*, such as businesses and points of interest, within a `PlacesResult`. Call `getPlaceLikelihoods` for a list of potential places ranked by likelihood. Requires the `ACCESS_FINE_LOCATION` manifest and runtime permission.

➤ **getWeather**—Returns the weather conditions in your current location within a `WeatherResult`. Call `getWeather` to extract a `Weather` object that includes the temperature, "feels like" temperature, humidity, dew point, and an array of descriptive weather conditions. Requires the `ACCESS_FINE_LOCATION` manifest and runtime permission.

You can find full details on each of the Snapshot methods, with examples of how to extract the data, on the Google Developer's site at `developers.google.com/awareness/android-api/snapshot-get-data`.

Setting and Monitoring Awareness Fences

Awareness Fences allow your app to adapt to the user's changing environment by defining a series of conditions that, when met, will trigger a callback, even while your app is in the background.

The concept of an Awareness "fence" is an expansion of the Geofences described earlier in this chapter in the section "Setting and Managing Geofences." Whereas a Geofence is based on the user's proximity to a specific location, Awareness Fences expand the trigger to include contextual conditions including time, nearby Beacons, headphone state, and the user's current activity.

Each of these signals can be combined using logical operators, allowing you to define custom fences based on combinations of criteria, such as:

➤ Starting to run while your headphones are plugged in on a weekend afternoon

➤ Starting to drive away from a given location on a weekday morning

➤ Moving within range of a beacon on your bicycle between 8am and 9am on Wednesdays

Awareness Fences are stored as instances of the `AwarenessFence` class. You can create new Awareness Fences for each of the available context triggers using the static methods available in the following classes:

BeaconFence—Use the `found`, `lost`, and `near` methods to specify that one or more Beacons matching the specified `TypeFilter` objects are initially detected, just lost, or nearby, respectively. Requires the `ACCESS_FINE_LOCATION` permission.

DetectedActivityFence—Use the `starting`, `stopping`, and `during` methods to indicate the user has just begun, just stopped, or is currently performing a given activity. Detectable activities include `IN_VEHICLE`, `ON_BICYCLE`, `ON_FOOT`, `RUNNING`, `WALKING`, or `STILL`. Requires the `ACTIVITY_RECOGNITION` permission.

HeadphoneFence—Use the `pluggingIn`, `unplugging`, and `during` methods to indicate the headphones have just been connected, just unplugged, or are currently plugged in.

LocationFence—Works like the Geofence. Use the `entering`, `exiting`, and `in` methods specifying a latitude, longitude, radius, and dwell time to indicate the user has entered, exited, or remained within the given area for the specified dwell time.

TimeFence—Provides a variety of static methods allowing you to indicate semantic and specific days and times:

➤ `aroundTimeInstant`—Specify a time instant, currently sunset or sunrise, and a start and stop offset around that time.

➤ `inDailyInterval`—Specify a daily start and stop time within a given time zone.

➤ `inInterval`—Specify an absolute one-off start and stop time.

➤ `inIntervalofDay`—Specify a repeating start and stop time for a given day of the week in a given time zone.

➤ `inTimeInterval`—Specify a specific semantic time interval such as day of the week, morning, afternoon, evening, night, weekday, weekend, or holiday.

For example, Listing 15-29 shows Awareness Fences based on each of the context signals.

LISTING 15-29: Creating Awareness Fences

```
// Near one of my custom beacons.
BeaconState.TypeFilter typeFilter
  = BeaconState.TypeFilter.with("com.professionalandroid.apps.beacon",
                                "my_type");
AwarenessFence beaconFence = BeaconFence.near(typeFilter);

// While walking.
AwarenessFence activityFence
  = DetectedActivityFence.during(DetectedActivityFence.WALKING);

// Having just plugged in my headphones.
AwarenessFence headphoneFence = HeadphoneFence.pluggingIn();

// Within 1km of Google for longer than a minute.
double lat = 37.4220233;
double lng = -122.084252;
double radius = 1000;  // meters
long dwell = 60000;    // milliseconds.
AwarenessFence locationFence = LocationFence.in(lat, lng, radius, dwell);

// In the morning
AwarenessFence timeFence =
  TimeFence.inTimeInterval(TimeFence.TIME_INTERVAL_MORNING);

// During holidays
AwarenessFence holidayFence =
  TimeFence.inTimeInterval(TimeFence.TIME_INTERVAL_HOLIDAY);
```

To combine multiple Awareness Fences, use the static `and`, `or`, and `not` methods within the `AwarenessFence` class as shown in Listing 15-30.

LISTING 15-30: Combining Awareness Fences

```
// Trigger when headphones are plugged in and walking in the morning
// either within a kilometer of Google or near one of my beacons --
// but not on a holiday.
AwarenessFence morningWalk = AwarenessFence
                                .and(activityFence,
                                     headphoneFence,
                                     timeFence,
                                     AwarenessFence.or(locationFence,
                                                       beaconFence),
                                     AwarenessFence.not(holidayFence));
```

Like Geofences, when triggered an Awareness Fence will broadcast a Pending Intent that can be used to trigger a Broadcast Receiver. If you have multiple Awareness Fences, you could create a unique Pending Intent for each; however, for efficiency reasons it's best practice to use a single Pending Intent each with a unique key String, specified when registering the fence:

```
int flags = PendingIntent.FLAG_UPDATE_CURRENT;
Intent intent = new Intent(this, WalkFenceReceiver.class);
PendingIntent awarenessIntent = PendingIntent.getBroadcast(this, -1,
                                                           intent, flags);
```

To add an Awareness Fence you need to create a `FenceUpdateRequest` that includes the Fences you want to add, the Pending Intent to be broadcast when the Awareness Fence is triggered, and a unique identifier.

Create the Fence Update Request using the `FenceUpdateRequest.Builder`, adding one or more Awareness Fences as shown in Listing 15-31.

LISTING 15-31: Creating an Awareness Fence Update Request

```
FenceUpdateRequest fenceUpdateRequest = new FenceUpdateRequest.Builder()
  .addFence(WALK_FENCE_KEY, morningWalk, awarenessIntent)
  .build();
```

Listing 15-32 shows how to update your app's Awareness Fences by passing in your Fence Update Request to the Fence API's `updateFences` method. You can use the `setResultCallback` to receive an `onResult` callback indicating the success or failure of the update request.

LISTING 15-32: Adding a new Awareness Fence

```
Awareness.FenceApi.updateFences(
  mGoogleApiClient,
  fenceUpdateRequest)
```

```
      .setResultCallback(new ResultCallback<Status>() {
        @Override
        public void onResult(@NonNull Status status) {
          if(!status.isSuccess()) {
            Log.d(TAG, "Fence could not be registered: " + status);
          }
        }
      });
```

When the Awareness Service detects that each of your conditions has been met, the Pending Intent fires. The Pending Intent will also be fired immediately after it has been added, regardless of the state of each condition; this allows you to extract the initial state.

When the Pending Intent has been received, you can examine the current state of the Fence using the `FenceState` class, which you can extract from the Intent using the `FenceState.extract` method:

```
FenceState fenceState = FenceState.extract(intent);
```

To receive Awareness Fence trigger notifications, create and register a Broadcast Receiver to listen for the broadcast Intent, such as the one shown in Listing 15-33.

LISTING 15-33: Listening for Awareness Fence trigger Intent broadcasts

```
public class WalkFenceReceiver extends BroadcastReceiver {

  @Override
  public void onReceive(Context context, Intent intent) {
    FenceState fenceState = FenceState.extract(intent);

    String fenceKey = fenceState.getFenceKey();
    int fenceStatus = fenceState.getCurrentState();

    if (fenceKey.equals(WALK_FENCE_KEY)) {
      if (fenceStatus == FenceState.TRUE) {
        // TODO React to fence being triggered.
      }
    }
  }
}
```

To remove an Awareness Fence use the `removeFence` method within the Fence Update Request, specifying either the unique key or the Pending Intent associated with a Fence. Pass the resulting Fence Update Request to the `updateFences` method of the Fence API as shown in Listing 15-34.

LISTING 15-34: Removing an Awareness Fence

```
FenceUpdateRequest fenceUpdateRequest = new FenceUpdateRequest.Builder()
  .removeFence(WalkFenceKey)
  .build();

Awareness.FenceApi.updateFences(
  mGoogleApiClient,
```

```
fenceUpdateRequest)
.setResultCallback(new ResultCallback<Status>() {
    @Override
    public void onResult(@NonNull Status status) {
        if(!status.isSuccess()) {
            Log.d(TAG, "Fence could not be removed: " + status);
        }
    }
});
```

Awareness Best Practices

Adding contextual awareness to your app means asking your users to trust you with that information. The more context you ask for, the more trust you're requesting—remember that it's hard to build that trust but very easy to lose it—even if what you're doing is confusing or obscure rather than malicious.

To maintain that trust, it's important to use contextual information responsibly, in a way that maximizes user control and privacy. While aiming for delight, it's important not to miss and shock or surprise users.

The following is a selection of best practices to help ensure you maintain that trust:

➤ Tell your users what you're doing, why you're doing it, and whenever possible let them say no.

➤ Always explain how you're using their context, and what you're doing with the data—both on the device, and especially if that data is being stored or transmitted.

➤ Don't transmit or store location or contact details unless that's clear to the user, and a critical part of your app's functionality.

➤ If you are storing any context data, make it simple and easy for users to erase it—both on their device and on your servers.

➤ Have a clear privacy policy that's easy for users to find and understand.

➤ Your app should be an intuitive friend, not a creepy stalker; use Awareness to improve the quality of notifications, not to spam your users.

16

Hardware Sensors

WHAT'S IN THIS CHAPTER?

➤ Using the Sensor Manager

➤ Introducing the different types of sensors

➤ Discovering available sensors and their capabilities

➤ Finding and using dynamic sensors

➤ Learning best practices for using sensors

➤ Testing sensors using the Emulator

➤ Finding a device's natural orientation

➤ Remapping a device's orientation reference frame

➤ Monitoring sensors and interpreting sensor values

➤ Using sensors to monitor a device's movement and orientation

➤ Using sensors to monitor a device's environment

➤ Using sensors to monitor a user's vital signs

➤ User activity tracking using Activity Recognition

WROX.COM CODE DOWNLOADS FOR THIS CHAPTER

The code downloads for this chapter are found at www.wrox.com. The code for this chapter is divided into the following major examples:

➤ Snippets_ch16.zip

➤ Weatherstation.zip

➤ GForceMeter.zip

➤ Compass_ch16.zip

INTRODUCING ANDROID SENSORS

Android devices are much more than simple communications and web browsing platforms; they're extra-sensory input devices using movement, the environment, and body sensors to extend your users' perceptions.

Sensors that detect physical and environmental properties offer an exciting avenue for innovations that enhance the user experience of mobile applications. The incorporation of an increasingly rich array of sensor hardware in modern devices provides new possibilities for user interaction and application development, including augmented or virtual reality, movement-based input, and environmental customizations.

This chapter introduces you to the sensors currently available in Android and how to use the Sensor Manager to monitor them.

You take a closer look at how to determine movement, and changes in the device orientation—regardless of the natural orientation of the host device.

You also explore the environmental sensors, including how to use the barometer to detect the current altitude, the light Sensor to determine the level of cloud cover, and the temperature Sensor to measure the ambient temperature.

Finally, you learn about body sensors, which are attached directly to the user and can be used to determine vital signs, such as heart rate, and to use the Activity Recognition APIs to monitor the users current physical activity.

Using the Sensor Manager

The Sensor Manager is used to manage the sensor hardware available on Android devices. Use getSystemService to return a reference to the Sensor Manager Service:

```
SensorManager sensorManager
    = (SensorManager)getSystemService(Context.SENSOR_SERVICE);
```

Rather than interact with the sensor hardware directly, you work with a series of Sensor objects that represent that hardware. These Sensor objects describe the properties of the hardware sensor they represent, including the type, name, manufacturer, and details on accuracy and range.

The Sensor class includes a set of constants that describe which type of hardware sensor is being represented by a particular Sensor object. These constants take the form of Sensor.TYPE_ followed by the name of a supported Sensor. The following section describes each supported Sensor type, after which you learn how to find and use these Sensors.

Understanding the Android Sensors

The availability of specific Sensors varies based on the platform version and the hardware available in the host device. The section, "Discovering and Identifying Sensors" describes how to identify which sensors are available to your application on a given host device.

Sensors can generally be divided into two categories: physical hardware sensors and virtual sensors.

Hardware Sensors, such as the light and barometric pressure Sensors, report results directly from a physical hardware sensor designed for that purpose. These hardware-based Sensors typically work independently of each other, each reporting the results obtained from a particular piece of hardware and generally don't apply any filtering or smoothing.

Virtual Sensors are used to present simplified, corrected, or composite sensor data in a way that makes them easier to use within some applications. Sensors such as the rotation vector and linear-acceleration Sensors are examples of virtual Sensors that may use a smoothed and filtered combination of accelerometers, magnetic-field Sensors, and gyroscopes, rather than the output of one specific hardware sensor.

In some circumstances, Android offers virtual sensors based on a particular hardware sensor. For example, there are virtual gyroscope and orientation Sensors that attempt to improve the quality and performance of their respective hardware; this involves using filters and the output of multiple Sensors to smooth, correct, or filter the raw output.

Environmental Sensors

Environmental Sensors are used to monitor the surrounding physical environment, including the current temperature, light levels, and atmospheric pressure.

➤ `Sensor.TYPE_AMBIENT_TEMPERATURE`—Introduced in Android 4.0 (API Level 14), this is a thermometer that returns the ambient room temperature in degrees Celsius.

➤ `Sensor.TYPE_GRAVITY`—A three-axis gravity sensor that returns the current direction and magnitude of gravity along three axes in m/s². The gravity sensor typically is implemented as a virtual sensor by applying a low-pass filter to the accelerometer results.

➤ `Sensor.TYPE_LIGHT`—An ambient light sensor that returns a single value describing the ambient illumination in lux. A light sensor is typically used by the system to alter the screen brightness dynamically.

➤ `Sensor.TYPE_MAGNETIC_FIELD`—A magnetometer that finds the current magnetic field in microteslas (μT) along three axes.

➤ `Sensor.TYPE_PRESSURE`—An atmospheric pressure sensor (barometer) that returns the current atmospheric pressure in millibars (mbars) as a single value. The pressure Sensor can be used to determine altitude using the `getAltitude` method on the Sensor Manager to compare the atmospheric pressure in two locations. Barometers can also be used in weather forecasting by measuring changes in atmospheric pressure in the same location over time.

➤ `Sensor.TYPE_PROXIMITY`—A proximity sensor that indicates the distance between the device and the target object in centimeters. How a target object is selected, and the distances supported, will depend on the hardware implementation of the proximity detector.

➤ `Sensor.TYPE_RELATIVE_HUMIDITY`—A relative humidity sensor that returns the relative humidity as a percentage. This Sensor was introduced in Android 4.0 (API Level 14).

Device Movement and Orientation Sensors

Device movement and orientation sensors help you to track device movement and changes in the device's physical orientation. Using these sensors, you can determine the device's relative orientation on all three axes, acceleration, and device movement (or lack thereof).

➤ `Sensor.TYPE_ACCELEROMETER`—A three-axis accelerometer that returns the current acceleration along three axes in m/s^2 (meters per second, per second.) The accelerometer is explored in greater detail later in this chapter.

➤ `Sensor.TYPE_GYROSCOPE`—A three-axis gyroscope that returns the rate of device rotation along three axes in radians/second. You can integrate the rate of rotation over time to determine the current orientation of the device; however, it generally is better practice to use this in combination with other sensors (typically the accelerometers) to provide a smoothed and corrected orientation. You learn more about the gyroscope later in this chapter.

➤ `Sensor.TYPE_LINEAR_ACCELERATION`—A three-axis linear acceleration Sensor that returns the acceleration, minus gravity, along three axes in m/s^2. Like the gravity sensor, the linear acceleration is typically implemented as a virtual sensor using the accelerometer output. In this case, to obtain the linear acceleration, a high-pass filter is applied to the accelerometer output.

➤ `Sensor.TYPE_ROTATION_VECTOR`—Returns the orientation of the device as a combination of an angle around an axis. It typically is used as an input to the `getRotationMatrixFromVector` method from the Sensor Manager to convert the returned rotation vector into a rotation matrix. The rotation vector is typically implemented as a virtual sensor that can combine and correct the results obtained from multiple sensors, such as the accelerometers and gyroscope, to provide a smoother rotation matrix.

➤ `Sensor.TYPE_GEOMAGNETIC_ROTATION_VECTOR`—An alternative to the rotation vector, implemented as a virtual Sensor using the magnetometer rather than gyroscope. As a result, it uses lower power but is noisier and best used outdoors. Introduced in Android 4.4 (API Level 19).

➤ `Sensor.TYPE_POSE_6DOF`—A pose sensor with 6 degrees of freedom; similar to the rotation vector, but with an additional delta translation from an arbitrary reference point. This is a high-power sensor that is expected to be more accurate than the rotation vector. Introduced in Android 7.0 (API Level 24).

➤ `Sensor.TYPE_MOTION_DETECT`—A virtual Sensor that returns a value of 1.0 if it determines that the device has been in motion for at least 5 seconds, with a maximum latency of another 5 seconds. Introduced in Android 7.0 (API Level 24).

➤ Sensor.TYPE_STATIONARY_DETECT—A virtual Sensor that returns a value of 1.0 if it determines that the device has been stationary for at least 5 seconds, with a maximum latency of another 5 seconds. Introduced in Android 7.0 (API Level 24).

➤ Sensor.TYPE_SIGNIFICANT_MOTION—A one-shot Sensor that is triggered when a significant device movement is detected, and then automatically disables itself to prevent further results. This is a wakeup sensor, meaning that it will continue to monitor for changes while the device is asleep, and will wake the device when motion is detected. Introduced in Android 4.3 (API Level 18).

Body and Exercise Sensors

With new hardware such as watches and fitness monitors available through devices including Android Wear, a new set of external sensors is available. Body Sensors are typically placed on—or in proximity to—the user's body, allowing you to detect body and health data such as heart beat, heart rate, and step count.

➤ Sensor.TYPE_HEART_BEAT—A Sensor that monitors heart-beats, returning a single value whenever a heart-beat-peak is detected, corresponding to the positive peak in the QRS complex of an ECG signal. Introduced in Android 7.0 (API Level 24).

➤ Sensor.TYPE_HEART_RATE—A heart-rate monitor that returns a single value describing the user's heart rate in beats-per-minute (bpm). Introduced in Android 4.4 (API Level 20).

➤ Sensor.TYPE_LOW_LATENCY_OFFBODY_DETECT—Returns a single value whenever a wearable device transitions from being in contact/not in contact with a person's body. Introduced in Android 8.0 (API Level 26.)

➤ Sensor.TYPE_STEP_COUNTER—Returns the cumulative number of steps detected while active since the last device reboot. This sensor is implemented as a low-power hardware Sensor that can be used to continuously track steps over a long period of time. Unlike most of the Sensors described, you should *not* unregister this Sensor when your Activity is stopped if you want to continue counting steps while your app is in the background. Introduced in Android 4.4 (API Level 19).

➤ Sensor.TYPE_STEP_DETECTOR—Returns a single value of 1.0 whenever a step is taken, corresponding with the foot touching the ground. If you want to track the number of steps, the step counter sensor is more appropriate. Introduced in Android 4.4 (API Level 19).

Discovering and Identifying Sensors

You can determine if a particular type of Sensor is available on the host device using the Sensor Manager's getDefaultSensor method, passing in the relevant Sensor.TYPE_ constant. If no Sensor of that type is available, null will be returned; if one or more Sensors are available, the default implementation will be returned.

Listing 16-1 shows how to determine if an atmospheric pressure Sensor is available.

LISTING 16-1: Determining if a type of sensor is available

```
SensorManager sensorManager
  = (SensorManager) getSystemService(Context.SENSOR_SERVICE);

if (sensorManager.getDefaultSensor(Sensor.TYPE_PRESSURE) != null){
  // TODO Barometer is available.
} else {
  // TODO No barometer is available.
}
```

> **NOTE** *Where a Sensor is required for your application to function, you can specify it as a required feature in the application's manifest, as described in Chapter 4, "Defining the Android Manifest and Gradle Build Files, and Externalizing Resources."*

As the name suggests, the `getDefaultSensor` method returns the *default* sensor of a given type, so it's worth noting that some Android devices may have multiple independent hardware sensors, or virtual Sensors, of a given type.

To discover every Sensor available on the host platform, you can use the `getSensorList` method on the Sensor Manager, passing in a Sensor type, or `Sensor.TYPE_ALL` to return a list of every Sensor:

```
List<Sensor> allSensors = sensorManager.getSensorList(Sensor.TYPE_ALL);
```

To find a list of all the available Sensors of a particular type, use the Sensor constants to indicate the type of Sensor you require, as shown in the following code that returns all the available gyroscopes:

```
List<Sensor> gyroscopes = sensorManager.getSensorList(Sensor.TYPE_GYROSCOPE);
```

By convention, any hardware Sensor implementations are returned at the top of the list, followed by virtual implementations, though this is not guaranteed. Since Android 5.0 (API Level 21), the default Sensor is the first Sensor in this list that isn't a wakeup Sensor (unless the Sensor is by definition a wakeup sensor). The difference between wakeup and non-wakeup Sensors is described in the "Wakeup and Non-Wakeup Sensors" section,

You can also use an overloaded implementation of `getDefaultSensor` that takes both a Sensor type, and a Boolean indicating if you specifically require a wakeup sensor:

```
Sensor wakeupProximitySensor =
  sensorManager.getDefaultSensor(Sensor.TYPE_PROXIMITY, TRUE);
```

Android 7.0 Nougat (API Level 24) introduced the concept of *dynamic* Sensors, primarily to support the Android Things platform. Dynamic Sensors behave like traditional Sensors but can be connected or disconnected at run time.

You can determine if dynamic Sensors are available on the current host platform using the Sensor Manager's `isDynamicSensorDiscoverySupported` method. To determine if a specific Sensor is dynamic, call its `isDynamicSensor` method.

To return a list of the available dynamic Sensors you can use `getDynamicSensorList` in the same way as described previously for all Sensors, specifying `Sensor.TYPE_ALL` to return all the dynamic Sensors, or the Sensor type constants for a particular Sensor type:

```
if (sensorManager.isDynamicSensorDiscoverySupported()) {
  List<Sensor> allDynamicSensors
    = sensorManager.getDynamicSensorList(Sensor.TYPE_ALL);
  // TODO Do something with the dynamic sensor list.
}
```

Because they can be added or removed at run time, the result of the `getDynamicSensor` call may change while your app is running.

To track the addition or removal of dynamic Sensors, you can implement the `DynamicSensorCallback`, and register it with the Sensor Manager, as shown in the following code:

```
SensorManager.DynamicSensorCallback dynamicSensorCallback =
  new SensorManager.DynamicSensorCallback() {
  @Override
  public void onDynamicSensorConnected(Sensor sensor) {
    super.onDynamicSensorConnected(sensor);
    // TODO React to the new Sensor being connected.
  }

  @Override
  public void onDynamicSensorDisconnected(Sensor sensor) {
    super.onDynamicSensorDisconnected(sensor);
    // TODO React to the Sensor being disconnected.
  }
};

sensorManager.registerDynamicSensorCallback(dynamicSensorCallback);
```

Determining Sensor Capabilities

If there are multiple Sensor implementations for a given sensor type, you may want to decide which of the returned Sensors to use by querying the returned Sensors and comparing their capabilities.

Each Sensor provides methods to report its name, power use while active (in mA), minimum delay latency (minimum delay between two subsequent events in microseconds), maximum range and resolution (in the units of its return values), module version, and vendor string:

```
String name = sensor.getName();
float power = sensor.getPower();
float maxRange = sensor.getMaximumRange();
float resolution = sensor.getResolution();
float minLatency = sensor.getMinDelay();
int version = sensor.getVersion();
String vendor = sensor.getVendor();

Log.d(TAG, "Sensor " + name + " (" + vendor + ":" + version +
         ") Power:" + power + ", Range: " + maxRange +
         ", Resolution: " + resolution + ", Latency: " + minLatency);
```

It can be useful to examine and experiment with the available Sensors in order to utilize the most appropriate implementation for your needs. In many cases the smoothing, filtering, and corrections applied to the virtual Sensors may provide better results for your applications than the default hardware results.

The following code snippet shows how to select a light Sensor with the highest maximum range and lowest power requirement:

```
List<Sensor> lightSensors
  = sensorManager.getSensorList(Sensor.TYPE_LIGHT);

Sensor bestLightSensor
  = sensorManager.getDefaultSensor(Sensor.TYPE_LIGHT);

if (bestLightSensor != null)
  for (Sensor lightSensor : lightSensors) {
    float range = lightSensor.getMaximumRange();
    float power = lightSensor.getPower();

    if (range >= bestLightSensor.getMaximumRange())
      if (power < bestLightSensor.getPower() ||
          range > bestLightSensor.getMaximumRange())
        bestLightSensor = lightSensor;
  }
```

Android 5.0 Lollipop (API Level 21) introduced support for finding the maximum delay latency, which returns the slowest frequency supported by a sensor—typically corresponding to when the batch FIFO (first-in-first-out) queue will be full. Ignore this value if it returns zero or a negative value:

```
float maxLatency = sensor.getMaxDelay();
```

API Level 21 also introduced the concept of a reporting mode for each sensor. By calling a Sensor's getReportingMode method, you can determine how it reports its results, represented as one of the following return constants:

➤ REPORTING_MODE_CONTINUOUS—Events are returned at least at the constant rate defined by the rate parameter used when you register a listener (as described in the following section).

➤ REPORTING_MODE_ON_CHANGE—Events are returned only when the value changes, limited to be no more often than the rate parameter used when registering a listener.

➤ REPORTING_MODE_ONE_SHOT—Events are reported only once, when the event is detected. Sensors of this type are monitored by requesting a trigger listener rather than an event listener, as described in the following section.

➤ REPORTING_MODE_SPECIAL_TRIGGER—Used by Sensors that have special triggers that aren't continuous, one-off, nor change-triggered. For example, step detectors, which return results when a step is detected.

Wakeup and Non-Wakeup Sensors

Typically, if your application is not holding a Wake Lock, a period of non–user-interaction will result in the system's application processor entering a low-power suspend mode to preserve battery (Wake Locks can be used to force the processor to remain active).

When the processor goes into low-power mode, non-wakeup Sensors will continue to consume power and generate events, but they will *not* wake the processor in order for your application to receive and process them. Instead, they will be placed into their hardware FIFO data queue, if one is available.

Older events will be lost when the maximum queue sized is reached, meaning you risk losing data that has been collected at significant battery cost. As a result, it's best practice to start and stop listening to Sensor results within the onResume and onPause methods of your Activities, respectively. This ensures your non-wakeup Sensors are drawing power only when the Activity is active.

Conversely, wakeup Sensors *will* wake the processor when their FIFO buffer is full or when it reaches the maximum latency you specify when requesting updates. Waking the processor will significantly increase battery use, so the larger the latency you specify, the lower the battery impact from your Sensor use. The process for requesting updates is described in the following section.

You can determine if a particular Sensor is a wakeup Sensor using the isWakeupSensor method:

```
boolean isWakeup = sensor.isWakeUpSensor();
```

You can find the maximum FIFO queue size for a Sensor using its maxFifoEventCount method.

Monitoring Sensor Results

How you monitor the values observed by a Sensor depends on the reporting mode used by that Sensor.

For most Sensors—those that report results continuously, on change, or caused by a special trigger—you receive Sensor Events by implementing a SensorEventListener, and registering it using the Sensor Manager's registerListener method.

Override the onSensorChanged handler to receive new Sensor values, and onAccuracyChanged to react to changes in a Sensor's accuracy, as shown in the skeleton code in Listing 16-2.

LISTING 16-2: Sensor Event Listener skeleton code

```
final SensorEventListener mySensorEventListener = new SensorEventListener() {
  public void onSensorChanged(SensorEvent sensorEvent) {
    // TODO React to new Sensor result.
  }

  public void onAccuracyChanged(Sensor sensor, int accuracy) {
    // TODO React to a change in Sensor accuracy.
  }
};
```

The `SensorEvent` parameter received by the `onSensorChanged` method includes the following four properties to describe each Sensor Event:

➤ `sensor`—The Sensor object that triggered the event.

➤ `accuracy`—The accuracy of the Sensor when the event occurred (as described in the next list).

➤ `values`—A float array that contains the new value(s) observed. The following section explains the values returned for each Sensor type.

➤ `timestamp`—The time (in nanoseconds) at which the Sensor Event occurred.

You can monitor changes in the accuracy of a Sensor separately, using the `onAccuracyChanged` method.

In both handlers the `accuracy` value represents the Sensor's accuracy, using one of the following Sensor Manager constants:

➤ `SENSOR_STATUS_ACCURACY_LOW`—Indicates that the Sensor is reporting with low accuracy and needs to be calibrated.

➤ `SENSOR_STATUS_ACCURACY_MEDIUM`—Indicates that the Sensor data is of average accuracy and that calibration might improve the accuracy of the reported results.

➤ `SENSOR_STATUS_ACCURACY_HIGH`—Indicates that the Sensor is reporting with the highest possible accuracy.

➤ `SENSOR_STATUS_UNRELIABLE`—Indicates that the Sensor data is unreliable, meaning that either calibration is required or readings are not currently possible.

➤ `SENSOR_STATUS_NO_CONTACT`—Indicates that the Sensor data is unreliable because the Sensor has lost contact with what it measures (for example, the heart rate monitor is not in contact with the user).

To listen for Sensor Events, register your Sensor Event Listener with the Sensor Manager. Specify the Sensor to observe, and the minimum frequency at which you want to receive updates, either in microseconds or using one of the `SensorManager.SENSOR_DELAY_` constants, as shown in Listing 16-3.

LISTING 16-3: Registering a Sensor Event Listener

```
Sensor sensor = sensorManager.getDefaultSensor(Sensor.TYPE_PROXIMITY);
sensorManager.registerListener(mySensorEventListener,
                               sensor,
                               SensorManager.SENSOR_DELAY_NORMAL);
```

The rate you select is not binding; the Sensor Manager may return results faster or slower than you specify, though it will tend to be faster. To minimize the associated resource cost of using the Sensor in your application, it is best practice to select the slowest acceptable rate.

You can (and must) unregister your Sensor Event Listeners when your application no longer needs to receive updates:

```
sensorManager.unregisterListener(mySensorEventListener);
```

Android 4.4 KitKat (API Level 19) introduced an overloaded `registerListener` method, as shown in Listing 16-4, that also allows you to indicate a maximum reporting latency, representing the longest time (in microseconds) that events can be delayed before being returned to the handler.

LISTING 16-4: Registering a Sensor Event Listener with a maximum Latency

```
Sensor sensor = sensorManager.getDefaultSensor(Sensor.TYPE_PROXIMITY);
sensorManager.registerListener(mySensorEventListener,
                               sensor,
                               SensorManager.SENSOR_DELAY_NORMAL,
                               10000000);
```

Specifying a large reporting latency is an effective way to reduce battery use when using *wakeup Sensors*.

For one-shot Sensors, such as the significant motion detector, you should monitor updates by implementing a `TriggerEventListener`, rather than the Sensor Event Listener, and overriding the `onTrigger` handler as shown in Listing 16-5.

LISTING 16-5: Trigger Event Listener skeleton code

```
TriggerEventListener triggerEventListener = new TriggerEventListener() {
  @Override
  public void onTrigger(TriggerEvent event) {
    // TODO React to trigger event.
  }
};
```

The `TriggerEvent` parameter received by the `onTrigger` handler includes the following properties to describe each Trigger Event:

➤   `sensor`—The Sensor object that triggered the event.

➤   `values`—A float array that contains the new value(s) observed. The following section explains the values returned for each sensor type.

➤   `timestamp`—The time (in nanoseconds) at which the Sensor Event occurred.

To listen for Sensor Events, register your Trigger Event Listener with the Sensor Manager, specifying the Sensor to observe, as shown in Listing 16-6.

LISTING 16-6: Registering a Trigger Event Listener

```
Sensor sensor = sensorManager.getDefaultSensor(Sensor.TYPE_SIGNIFICANT_MOTION);
sensorManager.requestTriggerSensor(triggerEventListener, sensor);
```

Unlike continuous or on-change Sensors, which deliver multiple events as their values change, one-shot trigger Sensors return an event only once. When the Sensor detects the trigger condition the Trigger Event Listener will be fired, and the trigger Sensor request automatically cancelled.

To receive additional Trigger Events for the same Sensor, you must call `requestTriggerSensor` again. Alternatively, if you have not received a Trigger Event, and your application no longer needs to respond to it, you should cancel your Trigger Event Listeners manually:

```
sensorManager.cancelTriggerSensor(triggerEventListener, sensor);
```

Android 7.0 Nougat (API Level 24) also introduced support for Sensors to return information beyond the accuracy status and value arrays described earlier. You can determine if a Sensor is capable of reporting this additional information using the `isAdditionalInfoSupported` method.

If a Sensor is capable of returning Sensor Additional Info, you can use the new `SensorEventCallback`, an extension of the Sensor Event Listener that includes additional callback handlers, as shown in the skeleton code of Listing 16-7.

LISTING 16-7: Registering a Sensor Event Callback to receive Sensor Additional Info

```java
SensorEventCallback sensorEventCallback = new SensorEventCallback() {
  @Override
  public void onSensorChanged(SensorEvent event) {
    super.onSensorChanged(event);
    // TODO Monitor Sensor changes.
  }

  @Override
  public void onAccuracyChanged(Sensor sensor, int accuracy) {
    super.onAccuracyChanged(sensor, accuracy);
    // TODO React to a change in Sensor accuracy.
  }

  @Override
  public void onFlushCompleted(Sensor sensor) {
    super.onFlushCompleted(sensor);
    // FIFO of this sensor has been flushed.
  }

  @Override
  public void onSensorAdditionalInfo(SensorAdditionalInfo info) {
    super.onSensorAdditionalInfo(info);
    // TODO Monitor additional sensor information.
  }
};

sensorManager.registerListener(sensorEventCallback, sensor,
                               SensorManager.SENSOR_DELAY_NORMAL);
```

The `onSensorChanged` and `onAccuracyChanged` handlers for the Sensor Event Callback behave identically to the Sensor Event Listener described previously. Additionally, you can override the `onFlushCompleted` and `onSensorAdditionalInfo` handlers.

Use the `onFlushCompleted` handler to be notified when the Sensor Manager's `flush` method has been called and completed:

```
sensorManager.flush(sensorEventCallback);
```

When called, this method will flush the FIFO of any Sensors associated with the passed-in Sensor Event Listener. As a result, if there are events currently in Sensor's FIFO queue, they will be returned to the listener as though the specified maximum report latency has expired.

The `onSensorAdditionalInfo` handler returns a `SensorAdditionalInfo` object that includes additional information regarding the current state of the sensor, including:

➤ `intValues` and `floatValues`—Integer and float arrays that may contain payload value(s) for the Sensor, as described by the information type.

➤ `type`—Sensors can return multiple types of additional sensor information. They are grouped together within a *frame* of data. Each frame is bound by the `TYPE_FRAME_BEGIN` and `TYPE_FRAME_END` types, between which data for multiple additional types can be returned, and the results made available using the integer or float value arrays. The type of the current data returned can be identified using the `type` value, corresponding to one of the following:

    ➤ `TYPE_FRAME_BEGIN` and `TYPE_FRAME_END`—Mark the beginning and end of this frame of additional information.

    ➤ `TYPE_INTERNAL_TEMPERATURE`—The internal Sensor temperature, returned in degrees Celsius as the first value in the `floatValues` array.

    ➤ `TYPE_SAMPLING`—The raw sampling period, in seconds, returned as the first value in the float array; and the estimated sample time-jitter returned as the standard deviation, available in the second value in the float array.

    ➤ `TYPE_SENSOR_PLACEMENT`—The physical location and angle of the Sensor relative to the device's geometric Sensor. The values are returned as a homogeneous matrix in the first twelve values in the float array.

    ➤ `TYPE_UNTRACKED_DELAY`—The delays to the Sensor results introduced by data processing (such as filtering or smoothing), which have not been taken into account in the Sensor Event timestamps. The first float array value is the estimated delay, the second value is the estimated standard deviation in estimated delays.

    ➤ `TYPE_VEC3_CALIBRATION`—The vector calibration parameter, representing the calibration applied to a Sensor with three-element vector output. Returns a homogeneous matrix in the first 12 values in the float array describing any linear transformation, including rotation, scaling, shear, and shift.

➤ `serial`—Each information type returned within a frame is numbered sequentially, with the serial value identifying the sequence number within the frame.

A Sensor may return multiple Sensor Additional Info values for each new Sensor value, corresponding to the multiple possible info types. The collection of values is referred to as a frame. As a result, the `onSensorAdditionalInfo` handler is likely to be triggered many times for each `onSensorChanged` trigger.

Interpreting Sensor Values

The length and composition of the `values` array within the Sensor Event parameter returned to the `onSensorChanged` handler vary depending on the type of Sensor being monitored. The details are summarized in Table 16-1. You can find further details on the use of the accelerometer, orientation, magnetic field, gyroscopic, and environmental Sensors in the following sections.

> **NOTE** *The Android documentation describes the values returned by each sensor type with some additional commentary at* `d.android.com/reference/` `android/hardware/SensorEvent.html`.

TABLE 16-1 Sensor Return Values

SENSOR TYPE	VALUE COUNT	VALUE COMPOSITION	COMMENTARY
TYPE_ACCELEROMETER	3	`value[0]`: X-axis (Lateral) `value[1]`: Y-axis (Longitudinal) `value[2]`: Z-axis (Vertical)	Acceleration along three axes in m/s². Note that when at rest, these values will include the acceleration due to gravity.
TYPE_GRAVITY	3	`value[0]`: X-axis (Lateral) `value[1]`: Y-axis (Longitudinal) `value[2]`: Z-axis (Vertical)	Force of gravity along three axes in m/s². The Sensor Manager includes a set of gravity constants of the form `SensorManager.GRAVITY_`
TYPE_RELATIVE_HUMIDITY	1	`value[0]`: Relative humidity	Relative humidity as a percentage (%).
TYPE_LINEAR_ACCELERATION	3	`value[0]`: X-axis (Lateral) `value[1]`: Y-axis (Longitudinal) `value[2]`: Z-axis (Vertical)	Linear acceleration along three axes in m/s² without the force of gravity.

SENSOR TYPE	VALUE COUNT	VALUE COMPOSITION	COMMENTARY
TYPE_GYROSCOPE	3	value[0]: X-axis value[1]: Y-axis value[2]: Z-axis	Rate of rotation around three axes in radians/second (rad/s).
TYPE_ROTATION_ VECTOR and TYPE_GEOMAGNETIC_ ROTATION_VECTOR	4	values[0]: $x*\sin(\theta/2)$ values[1]: $y*\sin(\theta/2)$ values[2]: $z*\sin(\theta/2)$ values[3]: $\cos(\theta/2)$ values[4]: Estimated heading accuracy (in radians)	Device orientation described as an angle of rotation around an axis (°). Note that the third value was optional, and the fourth unavailable, until API 18. Both will now always be returned.
TYPE_MAGNETIC_ FIELD	3	value[0]: X-axis (Lateral) value[1]: Y-axis (Longitudinal) value[2]: Z-axis (Vertical)	Ambient magnetic field measured in microteslas (µT) across three axes.
TYPE_LIGHT	1	value[0]: Illumination	Ambient light measured in lux (lx). The Sensor Manager includes a set of constants representing different standard illuminations of the form `SensorManager.LIGHT_`
TYPE_PRESSURE	1	value[0]: Atmospheric Pressure	Atmospheric pressure measured in millibars/hectopascals (hPa).
TYPE_PROXIMITY	1	value[0]: Distance	Distance from target measured in centimeters (cm). Some sensors are capable only of returning binary "far" or "near" values, which are represented as the maximum range for the former, and a lesser value for the latter.
TYPE_AMBIENT_ TEMPERATURE	1	value[0]: Temperature	Ambient temperature measured in degrees Celsius (°C).

continues

TABLE 16-1 *(continued)*

SENSOR TYPE	VALUE COUNT	VALUE COMPOSITION	COMMENTARY
TYPE_POSE_6DOF	15	value[0]: $x*\sin(\theta/2)$ value[1]: $y*\sin(\theta/2)$ value[2]: $z*\sin(\theta/2)$ value[3]: $\cos(\theta/2)$ value[4]: Translation along x-axis from an arbitrary origin. value[5]: Translation along y-axis from an arbitrary origin. value[6]: Translation along z-axis from an arbitrary origin. value[7]: Delta quaternion rotation $x*\sin(\theta/2)$ value[8]: Delta quaternion rotation $y*\sin(\theta/2)$ value[9]: Delta quaternion rotation $z*\sin(\theta/2)$ value[10]: Delta quaternion rotation $\cos(\theta/2)$ value[11]: Delta translation along x-axis. value[12]: Delta translation along y-axis. value[13]: Delta translation along z-axis. value[14]: Sequence number	A rotation expressed as a quaternion and a translation expressed in SI units. Also includes rotation and translation deltas indicating the change in pose since the previous pose.

SENSOR TYPE	VALUE COUNT	VALUE COMPOSITION	COMMENTARY
TYPE_STATIONARY_DETECT	1	value[0]: 1.0	Event indicating the device has been stationary for at least 5 seconds.
TYPE_MOTION_DETECT	1	value[0]: 1.0	Event indicating the device has been in motion for at least 5 seconds.
TYPE_HEART_BEAT	1	value[0]: Correctness confidence	Confidence (0 to 1) that the associated timestamp correctly represents the positive peak in the QRS complex of an ECG signal indicating a heart beat.
TYPE_LOW_LATENCY_OFFBODY_DETECT	1	value[0]: Off-body state	Indication if the device is in contact with a body. 1.0 indicates on-body, 0.0 indicates off-body.
TYPE_SIGNIFICANT_MOTION	1	value[0]: 1.0	Event indicating the device has registered a significant movement.
TYPE_HEART_RATE	1	value[0]: Heart rate	The user's heart rate in beats-per-minute (bpm).
TYPE_STEP_COUNTER	1	value[0]: Step count	Cumulative number of steps detected since the last device reboot.
TYPE_STEP_DETECTOR	1	value[0]: 1.0	Event corresponding with the moment a foot touches the ground.

TESTING SENSORS WITH THE ANDROID VIRTUAL DEVICE AND EMULATOR

The availability of particular Sensors is heavily dependent on the physical hardware available on particular devices. To help with testing, the Android Virtual Device and emulator include a set of virtual sensor controls that emulate physical hardware sensors, returning values through the Sensor Manager.

You can control the values returned by the emulator's sensors using the extended controls screen, as shown in Figure 16-1.

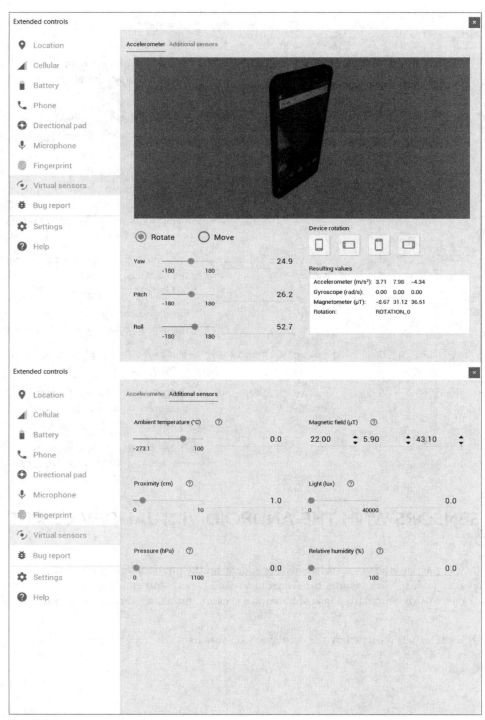

FIGURE 16-1

The emulator currently supports virtualized sensors to simulate movement and rotation through the accelerometer, magnetometer, and rotation vector Sensors, as well as environmental Sensors including ambient temperature, proximity, light level, atmospheric pressure, and relative humidity.

BEST PRACTICES FOR WORKING WITH SENSORS

Using Sensors in your applications can be incredibly powerful; like all good things, their use comes at a price—primarily the cost of increased battery drain.

You should follow several best practices to ensure you make the most of the device Sensors, without having a negative overall impact on the user experience:

Always verify Sensors exist before attempting to use them—The Android framework doesn't require Android devices to include any particular Sensor. The wide variety of devices, form-factors, and manufacturers ensures that you can't assume any particular Sensor is available.

Provide alternatives to Sensor input—If you are using Sensors to provide user-input to your app, it's good practice to offer an alternative mechanism to account for devices that don't support those Sensors.

Don't use deprecated Sensor types—For historical and legacy reasons, the framework includes several Sensor types and convenience methods that have since been deprecated and replaced with more accurate and efficient alternatives.

Be conservative when selecting Sensor reporting frequencies—Always opt for the slowest possible update rate. If your app isn't using every received Sensor result, it's wasting resources and battery.

Don't block the `onSensorChanged` handler—The high frequency at which some sensors are capable of returning new values means you should limit the work being done within the `onSensorChanged` handler to ensure you aren't blocking it from receiving new results.

Unregister your Sensor Event Listeners—The most important pattern to follow is ensuring all your Sensor Listeners are unregistered when you no longer need them to continue collecting data. If you are using Sensor data to alter the UI, you should always unregister the listener when the Activity is paused.

MONITORING A DEVICE'S MOVEMENT AND ORIENTATION

Sensors such as accelerometers, compasses, and gyroscopes make it possible to use the device's direction, orientation, and movement to offer new and innovative input mechanisms.

The availability of specific Sensors depends on the hardware and software platform on which your application is running. A 70" flat screen is difficult to lift and awkward to maneuver, so as a result Android TVs are unlikely to include orientation and movement Sensors.

Where they are available, movement and orientation sensors can be used by your application to:

➤ Determine the device orientation

➤ React to changes in orientation

> ➤ React to movement or acceleration

> ➤ Understand which direction the user is facing

> ➤ Monitor gestures based on movement, rotation, or acceleration

This opens some intriguing possibilities for your applications. By monitoring orientation, direction, and movement, you can:

> ➤ Use the device's heading or orientation with a map, camera, and location-based service to create augmented-reality apps.

> ➤ Use the rotation vector and pose Sensors to create low-latency virtual reality applications.

> ➤ Monitor for rapid acceleration to detect if a device has been dropped, thrown, or picked up.

> ➤ Measure movement or vibration.

> ➤ Create app interfaces that use physical gestures and movement as input.

> ➤ Use orientation and linear acceleration Sensors to monitor physical activity and movement to track fitness.

Determining the Natural Orientation of a Device

Before calculating the device's orientation, you must first understand its "at rest" (natural) orientation. The natural orientation of a device is the position at which the orientation is 0 on all three axes. The natural orientation can be either portrait or landscape, but it typically is identifiable by the placement of branding and hardware buttons.

For a typical smartphone, the natural orientation is with the device laying on its back on a desk, with the top of the device pointing due north.

More creatively, you can imagine yourself perched on top of a jet fuselage during level flight. An Android device has been strapped to the fuselage in front of you. In its natural orientation the screen is pointing up into space, the top of the device pointing toward the nose of the plane, and the plane is heading due north, as shown in Figure 16-2.

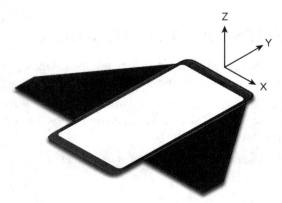

FIGURE 16-2

> **NOTE** *Before you head out to an airfield, note that this example is contrived to provide a useful metaphor for understanding the standard reference frame. The electronic compass and accelerometers included in most Android devices make them unsuitable for determining the heading, pitch, and roll of an aircraft in flight. It's also really unsafe to sit on top of a jet fuselage during flight.*

Android can rotate the display for your convenience; however, the Sensor axes described in Table 16-1 do not change as the device rotates. As a result, the display orientation and device orientation can be different.

Sensor values are always returned relative to the natural orientation of the device, whereas your application is likely to want the current orientation relative to the display orientation. As a result, if your application uses device orientation or linear acceleration as an input, it may be necessary to adjust your Sensor inputs based on the display orientation relative to the natural orientation. This is particularly important because the natural orientation of most early Android phones was portrait; however, with the range of Android devices having expanded to also include tablets and televisions, many Android devices (including smartphones) are naturally oriented when the display is in landscape.

You can find the current screen rotation using the `getRotation` method on the default Display object, as shown in Listing 16-8.

LISTING 16-8: Finding the screen orientation relative to the natural orientation

```
WindowManager wm = (WindowManager)getSystemService(Context.WINDOW_SERVICE);
Display display = wm.getDefaultDisplay();
int rotation = display.getRotation();
switch (rotation) {
  case (Surface.ROTATION_0) : break;    // Natural
  case (Surface.ROTATION_90) : break;   // On its left side
  case (Surface.ROTATION_180) : break;  // Upside down
  case (Surface.ROTATION_270) : break;  // On its right side
  default: break;
}
```

Note that in some cases Android will not rotate the screen to accommodate the device being upside down. As a result, the user may be holding the phone upside down, but the screen will still be displayed at (and report as) the same relative orientation.

Introducing Accelerometers

Acceleration is defined as the rate of change of velocity; that means accelerometers measure how quickly the speed of the device is changing in a given direction. Using an accelerometer you can detect movement and, more usefully, the rate of change of the speed of that movement in a given direction (also known as *linear acceleration*).

> **NOTE** *Accelerometers are also known as* gravity sensors *because they measure acceleration caused both by movement and by gravity. As a result, an accelerometer detecting acceleration on an axis perpendicular to the earth's surface will read* $-9.8m/s^2$ *when it's at rest. (This value is available as the* `SensorManager.STANDARD_GRAVITY` *constant.)*

Generally, you'll be interested in acceleration changes relative to a rest state, or rapid movement (signified by rapid changes in acceleration), such as gestures used for user input. In the former case you'll often need to calibrate the device to calculate the initial acceleration to take those effects into account for future results.

> **NOTE** *It's important to note that accelerometers do* not *measure velocity, so you can't measure speed directly based on a single accelerometer reading. Instead, you need to integrate the acceleration over time to find the velocity. You can then integrate the velocity over time to determine the distance traveled.*

Detecting Acceleration Changes

Acceleration is a measure of the rate of change in velocity, where velocity is the speed of movement in a particular direction. The rate of acceleration can tell you how much faster (or slower) you are moving, but by itself offers no information on the current speed or the direction of travel.

As a result, at a given moment *deceleration* in a given direction will produce the same result as acceleration in the opposite direction.

Acceleration can be measured along three directional axes:

➤ Left-right (lateral)

➤ Forward-backward (longitudinal)

➤ Up-down (vertical)

The Sensor Manager reports accelerometer sensor changes along all three axes.

The sensor values returned through the `values` property of the Sensor Event Listener's Sensor Event parameter represent lateral, longitudinal, and vertical acceleration, in that order.

Figure 16-3 illustrates the mapping of the three directional acceleration axes in relation to the device at rest in its natural orientation. Note that for the remainder of this section, I will refer to the movement of the device in relation to its natural orientation, which may be either landscape or portrait.

➤ **x-axis (lateral)**—Sideways (left or right) acceleration, for which positive values represent acceleration toward the right (or deceleration to the left), and negative values indicate acceleration toward the left (or deceleration toward the right).

➤ **y-axis (longitudinal)**—Forward or backward acceleration, for which forward acceleration, such as the device being pushed in the direction of the top of the device, is represented by a positive value and acceleration backward represented by negative values. Deceleration in either direction is reversed—deceleration while moving forward results in negative results, and while moving backwards results in positive numbers.

➤ **z-axis (vertical)**—Upward or downward acceleration, for which positive represents upward acceleration, such as the device being lifted. While at rest at the device's natural orientation, the vertical accelerometer will register -9.8m/s^2 as a result of gravity.

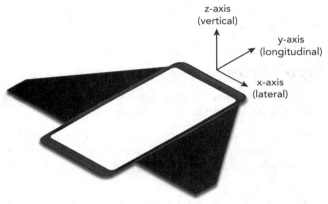

FIGURE 16-3

As described earlier, you can monitor changes in acceleration using a Sensor Event Listener. Register an implementation of `SensorEventListener` with the Sensor Manager, using a Sensor object of type `Sensor.TYPE_ACCELEROMETER` to request accelerometer updates. Listing 16-9 registers the default accelerometer using the default update rate.

LISTING 16-9: Monitoring an accelerometer sensor

```
SensorManager sm = (SensorManager)getSystemService(Context.SENSOR_SERVICE);
int sensorType = Sensor.TYPE_ACCELEROMETER;
sm.registerListener(mySensorEventListener,
                    sm.getDefaultSensor(sensorType),
                    SensorManager.SENSOR_DELAY_NORMAL);
```

Your Sensor Listener should implement the `onSensorChanged` method, which will be fired when acceleration in any direction is measured.

The `onSensorChanged` method receives a `SensorEvent` that includes a `values` float-array parameter, containing the acceleration measured along all three axes. When a device is held in its natural orientation, the first element represents lateral acceleration; the second element represents longitudinal acceleration; and the final element represents vertical acceleration, as shown in the following extension to Listing 16-9:

```
final SensorEventListener mySensorEventListener = new SensorEventListener() {
  public void onSensorChanged(SensorEvent sensorEvent) {
    if (sensorEvent.sensor.getType() == Sensor.TYPE_ACCELEROMETER) {
      float xAxis_lateralA = sensorEvent.values[0];
      float yAxis_longitudinalA = sensorEvent.values[1];
      float zAxis_verticalA = sensorEvent.values[2];
      // TODO apply the acceleration changes to your application.
    }
  }

  public void onAccuracyChanged(Sensor sensor, int accuracy) {}
};
```

Creating a Gravitational Force Meter

In the following example you create a simple device to measure gravitational force (g-force) using the accelerometers to determine the current force being exerted on the device.

The acceleration force exerted on the device at rest is 9.8 m/s^2 toward the center of the Earth. In this example you'll negate the force of gravity by accounting for it using the SensorManager.STANDARD_GRAVITY constant. If you plan to use this application on another planet, you can use an alternative gravity constant, as appropriate.

1. Start by creating a new GForceMeter project that includes a backwards compatible blank ForceMeterActivity Activity. Modify the new Activity's layout resource to display two centered lines of large, bold text that will be used to display the current g-force and maximum observed g-force:

```
<?xml version="1.0" encoding="utf-8"?>
<LinearLayout
  xmlns:android="http://schemas.android.com/apk/res/android"
  android:orientation="vertical"
  android:layout_width="match_parent"
  android:layout_height="match_parent">
  <TextView
    android:id="@+id/acceleration"
    android:gravity="center"
    android:layout_width="match_parent"
    android:layout_height="wrap_content"
    android:textStyle="bold"
    android:textSize="32sp"
    android:text="Current Acceleration"
    android:layout_margin="10dp"/>
  <TextView
    android:id="@+id/maxAcceleration"
    android:gravity="center"
    android:layout_width="match_parent"
    android:layout_height="wrap_content"
    android:textStyle="bold"
    android:textSize="40sp"
    android:text="Maximum Acceleration"
    android:layout_margin="10dp"/>
</LinearLayout>
```

2. Within the `ForceMeterActivity`, create instance variables to store references to the Text Views and the Sensor Manager. Also create variables to record the current and maximum detected acceleration values:

```
private SensorManager mSensorManager;
private TextView mAccelerationTextView;
private TextView mMaxAccelerationTextView;
private float mCurrentAcceleration = 0;
private float mMaxAcceleration = 0;
```

3. Add a calibration constant that represents the acceleration due to gravity:

```
private final double calibration = SensorManager.STANDARD_GRAVITY;
```

4. Create a new `SensorEventListener` implementation that sums the acceleration detected along each axis and negates the acceleration due to gravity. It should update the current (and possibly maximum) acceleration whenever a change in acceleration is detected:

```
private final SensorEventListener mSensorEventListener
  = new SensorEventListener() {

  public void onAccuracyChanged(Sensor sensor, int accuracy) { }

  public void onSensorChanged(SensorEvent event) {
    double x = event.values[0];
    double y = event.values[1];
    double z = event.values[2];

    double a = Math.round(Math.sqrt(Math.pow(x, 2) +
                                    Math.pow(y, 2) +
                                    Math.pow(z, 2)));
    mCurrentAcceleration = Math.abs((float)(a-calibration));

    if (mCurrentAcceleration > mMaxAcceleration)
      mMaxAcceleration = mCurrentAcceleration;
  }
};
```

5. Update the `onCreate` method to get a reference to the two Text Views and the Sensor Manager:

```
@Override
protected void onCreate(Bundle savedInstanceState) {
  super.onCreate(savedInstanceState);
  setContentView(R.layout.activity_force_meter);

  mAccelerationTextView = findViewById(R.id.acceleration);
  mMaxAccelerationTextView = findViewById(R.id.maxAcceleration);
  mSensorManager =
    (SensorManager) getSystemService(Context.SENSOR_SERVICE);
}
```

6. Override the `onResume` handler to register your new Listener for accelerometer updates using the `SensorManager`:

```
@Override
protected void onResume() {
```

```
      super.onResume();

      Sensor accelerometer
        = mSensorManager.getDefaultSensor(Sensor.TYPE_ACCELEROMETER);
      mSensorManager.registerListener(mSensorEventListener,
        accelerometer,
        SensorManager.SENSOR_DELAY_FASTEST);
    }
```

7. Also override the corresponding onPause method to unregister the Sensor Event Listener when the Activity is no longer active:

```
    @Override
    protected void onPause() {
      super.onPause();

      mSensorManager.unregisterListener(mSensorEventListener);
    }
```

8. The accelerometers can update hundreds of times a second, so updating the Text Views for every change in acceleration would quickly flood the UI event queue. Instead, create a new updateGUI method that synchronizes with the GUI thread and updates the Text Views. This will be executed regularly using a Timer introduced in the next step:

```
    private void updateGUI() {
      runOnUiThread(new Runnable() {
        public void run() {
          String currentG = mCurrentAcceleration /
                          SensorManager.STANDARD_GRAVITY
                          + "Gs";
          mAccelerationTextView.setText(currentG);
          mAccelerationTextView.invalidate();
          String maxG = mMaxAcceleration/SensorManager.STANDARD_GRAVITY
                      + "Gs";
          mMaxAccelerationTextView.setText(maxG);
          mMaxAccelerationTextView.invalidate();
        }
      });
    }
```

9. Update the onCreate method to create a timer that triggers the UI update method defined in Step 8 every 100 milliseconds:

```
    @Override
    protected void onCreate(Bundle savedInstanceState) {
      super.onCreate(savedInstanceState);
      setContentView(R.layout.activity_force_meter);

      mAccelerationTextView = findViewById(R.id.acceleration);
      mMaxAccelerationTextView = findViewById(R.id.maxAcceleration);
      mSensorManager =
        (SensorManager) getSystemService(Context.SENSOR_SERVICE);


      Timer updateTimer = new Timer("gForceUpdate");
      updateTimer.scheduleAtFixedRate(new TimerTask() {
        public void run() {
```

```
            updateGUI();
        }
    }, 0, 100);
}
```

10. Finally, because this application is functional only when the host device features an acceler-ometer sensor, modify the manifest to include a `uses-feature` node specifying the require-ment for accelerometer hardware:

```
<uses-feature android:name="android.hardware.sensor.accelerometer" />
```

When finished, you'll want to test this out. Ideally, you can do this in an F16 while Maverick performs high-g maneuvers over the Atlantic. That's been known to end badly, so, failing that, you can experiment with spinning around in circles while holding your phone at arm's length. Remember to grip your phone tightly.

The Sensor processing performed within this example is effectively the same as the preprocessing performed by the linear acceleration Sensor. As an exercise, update this sample to use the linear acceleration Sensor rather than processing the raw accelerometer results.

Determining a Device's Orientation

You typically calculate a device's orientation using the combined output of the magnetic field, accel-erometers, and gyroscope.

If you've done a bit of trigonometry, you've got the skills required to calculate the device orientation based on the results from these three Sensors. If you enjoyed trig as much as I did, you'll be happy to learn that Android can do these calculations for you.

Understanding the Standard Reference Frame

Using the standard reference frame, the device orientation is reported along three dimensions, as shown in Figure 16-4.

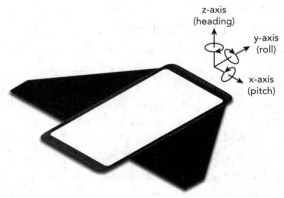

FIGURE 16-4

The standard reference frame is described relative to the device's natural orientation, as described earlier in this chapter.

Continuing the airplane analogy, imagining yourself perched on top of a jet fuselage during level flight, the z-axis comes out of the screen toward space; the y-axis comes out of the top of the device toward the nose of the plane; and the x-axis heads out toward the starboard wing. Relative to that, pitch, roll, and azimuth can be described as follows:

➤ **Pitch**—The angle of the device around the x-axis. During level flight, the pitch will be 0; as the nose angles upward, the pitch increases. It will hit 90 when the jet is pointed straight up. Conversely, as you angle the nose downward past level, the pitch will decrease until it reaches –90 as you hurtle toward imminent death. If the plane flips onto its back the pitch will report either +/–180.

➤ **Roll**—The device's sideways rotation between –90 and 90 degrees around the y-axis. During level flight the roll is zero. As you execute a roll toward the starboard (right) side, the roll will increase, reaching 90 when the wings are perpendicular to the ground. As you continue, you will reach 180 when the plane is upside down. Rolling from level toward port (left) will decrease the roll in the same way.

➤ **Azimuth**—The azimuth (also referred to as heading or yaw) is the direction the device is facing around the z-axis, where 0/360 degrees is magnetic north, 90 east, 180 south, and 270 west. Changes in the plane's heading will be reflected in changes in the azimuth value.

Determining Orientation Using the Rotation Vector Sensors

The Android framework offers a number of virtual orientation Sensors implemented to combine and correct the results obtained from multiple hardware sensors—including accelerometers, magnetometers, and gyroscopes—to provide smoother, more accurate orientation results.

The rotation vector Sensors return the orientation of the device as a vector describing an angle around an axis. This vector can be passed into the `getRotationMatrixFromVector` method from the Sensor Manager to convert a rotation vector into a rotation matrix, from which you can extract the orientation along each axis using the `getOrientation` method.

The three variations of the rotation vector sensor, each with subtle differences, are:

➤ `Sensor.TYPE_ROTATION_VECTOR`—The basic rotation vector Sensor introduced in Android 2.3 (API Level 9), which uses the accelerometer and gyroscope to calculate orientation changes.

➤ `Sensor.TYPE_GEOMAGNETIC_ROTATION_VECTOR`—An alternative to the rotation vector, implemented using the magnetometer rather than gyroscope. It uses lower power but is noisier and best used outdoors. Introduced in Android 4.4 (API Level 19).

➤ `Sensor.TYPE_GAME_ROTATION_VECTOR`—Identical to the rotation vector Sensor, except that the y-axis doesn't point north, but instead to some other reference, which is allowed to drift by the same order of magnitude as the gyroscope drift around the z-axis. Introduced in Android 4.3 (API Level 18).

Listing 16-10 shows how to use the `getRotationMatrixFromVector` and `getOrientation` methods to extract the current device orientation from the results of a rotation vector Sensor.

LISTING 16-10: Calculating the device orientation using the rotation vector

```java
public void onSensorChanged(SensorEvent sensorEvent) {
  float[] rotationMatrix = new float[9];
  float[] orientation = new float[3];

  // Convert the result Vector to a Rotation Matrix.
  SensorManager.getRotationMatrixFromVector(rotationMatrix,
                                            sensorEvent.values);

  // Extract the orientation from the Rotation Matrix.
  SensorManager.getOrientation(rotationMatrix, orientation);
  Log.d(TAG, "Yaw: " + orientation[0]);   // Yaw
  Log.d(TAG, "Pitch: " + orientation[1]); // Pitch
  Log.d(TAG, "Roll: " + orientation[2]);  // Roll
}
```

Note that `getOrientation` returns its results in radians, not degrees, with positive values representing anticlockwise rotation around the axis:

➤ `values[0]`—The azimuth, or rotation around the z-axis, is zero when the device is heading magnetic north.

➤ `values[1]`—The pitch, or rotation around the x-axis.

➤ `values[2]`—The roll, or rotation around the y-axis.

Calculating Orientation Using the Accelerometer, Magnetometer, and Gyroscope

It's also possible to determine the current device orientation using the unfiltered results provided directly by the accelerometer, magnetometer, and gyroscope.

Because you're using multiple sensors, you need to create and register a Sensor Event Listener to monitor each of them. Within the `onSensorChanged` methods for each Sensor Event Listener, record the `values` array property received in separate field variables, as shown in Listing 16-11.

LISTING 16-11: Monitoring the accelerometer and magnetometer

```java
private float[] mAccelerometerValues;
private float[] mMagneticFieldValues;

final SensorEventListener mCombinedSensorListener = new SensorEventListener() {
  public void onSensorChanged(SensorEvent sensorEvent) {
    if (sensorEvent.sensor.getType() == Sensor.TYPE_ACCELEROMETER)
      mAccelerometerValues = sensorEvent.values;
```

continues

LISTING 16-11: *(continued)*

```
    if (sensorEvent.sensor.getType() == Sensor.TYPE_MAGNETIC_FIELD)
      mMagneticFieldValues = sensorEvent.values;
  }

  public void onAccuracyChanged(Sensor sensor, int accuracy) {}
};
```

Register each Sensor with the Sensor Manager, as shown in the following code extension to Listing 16-11; this snippet uses the default hardware and UI update rate for both Sensors:

```
SensorManager sm = (SensorManager)getSystemService(Context.SENSOR_SERVICE);
Sensor aSensor = sm.getDefaultSensor(Sensor.TYPE_ACCELEROMETER);
Sensor mfSensor = sm.getDefaultSensor(Sensor.TYPE_MAGNETIC_FIELD);

sm.registerListener(mCombinedSensorListener,
                    aSensor,
                    SensorManager.SENSOR_DELAY_UI);

sm.registerListener(mCombinedSensorListener,
                    mfSensor,
                    SensorManager.SENSOR_DELAY_UI);
```

To calculate the current orientation from these Sensor values, use the `getRotationMatrix` and `getOrientation` methods from the Sensor Manager, as shown in Listing 16-12.

LISTING 16-12: Finding the current orientation using the accelerometer and magnetometer

```
float[] values = new float[3];
float[] R = new float[9];
SensorManager.getRotationMatrix(R, null,
                                mAccelerometerValues,
                                mMagneticFieldValues);
SensorManager.getOrientation(R, values);

// Convert from radians to degrees if preferred.
values[0] = (float) Math.toDegrees(values[0]); // Azimuth
values[1] = (float) Math.toDegrees(values[1]); // Pitch
values[2] = (float) Math.toDegrees(values[2]); // Roll
```

As in the previous section, the `getOrientation` method returns its results in radians, with positive values representing anticlockwise rotation around the axis in order of azimuth, pitch, and roll around the z-, x-, and y-axes, respectively.

Many Android devices also feature a gyroscope in addition to the accelerometer and magnetometer sensors. The gyroscope is used to measure angular speed around a given axis in radians per second, using the same coordinate system as described for the acceleration Sensor.

Android gyroscopes return the rate of rotation around three axes, where their sensitivity and high-frequency update rates provide extremely smooth and accurate updates. This makes them particularly good candidates for applications that use changes in orientation (as opposed to absolute orientation) as an input mechanism.

Because gyroscopes measure speed rather than direction, their results must be integrated over time in order to determine the current orientation, as shown in Listing 16-13. The calculated result will represent a change in orientation around a given axis, so you will need to either calibrate or use additional Sensors in order to determine the initial orientation.

LISTING 16-13: Calculating an orientation change using the gyroscope Sensor

```
final float nanosecondsPerSecond = 1.0f / 100000000.0f;
private long lastTime = 0;
final float[] angle = new float[3];

SensorEventListener myGyroListener = new SensorEventListener() {
  public void onSensorChanged(SensorEvent sensorEvent) {
    if (lastTime != 0) {
      final float dT = (sensorEvent.timestamp - lastTime) *
                       nanosecondsPerSecond;
      angle[0] += sensorEvent.values[0] * dT;
      angle[1] += sensorEvent.values[1] * dT;
      angle[2] += sensorEvent.values[2] * dT;
    }
    lastTime = sensorEvent.timestamp;
  }

  public void onAccuracyChanged(Sensor sensor, int accuracy) {}
};

SensorManager sm
  = (SensorManager)getSystemService(Context.SENSOR_SERVICE);
int sensorType = Sensor.TYPE_GYROSCOPE;
sm.registerListener(myGyroListener,
                    sm.getDefaultSensor(sensorType),
                    SensorManager.SENSOR_DELAY_NORMAL);
```

It's worth noting that orientation values derived solely from a gyroscope can become increasingly inaccurate due to calibration errors and noise. To account for this effect, gyroscopes are often used in combination with other sensors—particularly accelerometers—to provide smoother and more accurate orientation results.

Remapping the Orientation Reference Frame

To measure the device orientation using a reference frame other than the natural orientation, use the `remapCoordinateSystem` method from the Sensor Manager. This typically is done to simplify the calculations required to create applications that can be used on devices whose natural orientation is portrait, as well as those that are landscape.

The `remapCoordinateSystem` method accepts four parameters:

➤ The initial rotation matrix, found using `getRotationMatrix`, as described earlier

➤ A variable used to store the output (transformed) rotation matrix

➤ The remapped x-axis

➤ The remapped y-axis

The Sensor Manager provides a set of constants that let you specify the remapped x- and y-axes relative to the reference frame: AXIS_X, AXIS_Y, AXIS_Z, AXIS_MINUS_X, AXIS_MINUS_Y, and AXIS_MINUS_Z.

Listing 16-14 shows how to remap the reference frame so that the current *display* orientation (either portrait or landscape) is used as the reference frame for calculating the current *device* orientation. This is useful for games or applications that are locked to either landscape or portrait mode, as the device will report either 0 or 90 degrees based on the natural orientation of the device. By modifying the reference frame, you can ensure that the orientation values you use already take into account the orientation of the display relative to the natural orientation.

LISTING 16-14: Remapping the orientation reference frame based on the natural orientation of the device

```
// Determine the current orientation relative to the natural orientation
WindowManager wm = (WindowManager) getSystemService(Context.WINDOW_SERVICE);
Display display = wm.getDefaultDisplay();
int rotation = display.getRotation();

int x_axis = SensorManager.AXIS_X;
int y_axis = SensorManager.AXIS_Y;

switch (rotation) {
  case (Surface.ROTATION_0): break;
  case (Surface.ROTATION_90):
    x_axis = SensorManager.AXIS_Y;
    y_axis = SensorManager.AXIS_MINUS_X;
    break;
  case (Surface.ROTATION_180):
    y_axis = SensorManager.AXIS_MINUS_Y;
    break;
  case (Surface.ROTATION_270):
    x_axis = SensorManager.AXIS_MINUS_Y;
    y_axis = SensorManager.AXIS_X;
    break;
  default: break;
}

SensorManager.remapCoordinateSystem(inR, x_axis, y_axis, outR);

// Obtain the new, remapped, orientation values.
SensorManager.getOrientation(outR, values);
```

Creating a Compass and Artificial Horizon

In Chapter 14, "Advanced Customization of Your User Interface," you improved the CompassView to display pitch, roll, and heading. In this example, you finally connect your Compass View to the hardware sensors to display the device orientation.

1. Open the Compass project you last changed in Chapter 14 and open the `CompassActivity`. Use the Sensor Manager to listen for orientation changes using the rotation vector Sensor. Start by adding local variables to store the `CompassView`, `SensorManager`, screen rotation value, and latest Sensor results:

```
private CompassView mCompassView;
private SensorManager mSensorManager;
private int mScreenRotation;
private float[] mNewestValues;
```

2. Create a new `updateOrientation` method that uses new heading, pitch, and roll values to update the `CompassView`:

```
private void updateOrientation(float[] values) {
  if (mCompassView!= null) {
    mCompassView.setBearing(values[0]);
    mCompassView.setPitch(values[1]);
    mCompassView.setRoll(-values[2]);
    mCompassView.invalidate();
  }
}
```

3. Update the `onCreate` method to get references to the `CompassView` and `SensorManager`. Also determine the current screen orientation relative to the natural device orientation and initialize the heading, pitch, and roll:

```
@Override
public void onCreate(Bundle savedInstanceState) {
  super.onCreate(savedInstanceState);
  setContentView(R.layout.main);

  mCompassView = findViewById(R.id.compassView);

  mSensorManager
    = (SensorManager) getSystemService(Context.SENSOR_SERVICE);
  WindowManager wm
    = (WindowManager) getSystemService(Context.WINDOW_SERVICE);

  Display display = wm.getDefaultDisplay();
  mScreenRotation = display.getRotation();

  mNewestValues = new float[] {0, 0, 0};
}
```

4. Create a new `calculateOrientation` method to evaluate the device orientation using the last received rotation vector values. Remember to account for the natural orientation of the device by remapping the reference frame, if necessary:

```
private float[] calculateOrientation(float[] values) {
  float[] rotationMatrix = new float[9];
  float[] remappedMatrix = new float[9];
  float[] orientation = new float[3];

  // Determine the rotation matrix
  SensorManager.getRotationMatrixFromVector(rotationMatrix, values);
```

```
      // Remap the coordinates based on the natural device orientation.
      int x_axis = SensorManager.AXIS_X;
      int y_axis = SensorManager.AXIS_Y;

      switch (mScreenRotation) {
        case (Surface.ROTATION_90):
          x_axis = SensorManager.AXIS_Y;
          y_axis = SensorManager.AXIS_MINUS_X;
          break;
        case (Surface.ROTATION_180):
          y_axis = SensorManager.AXIS_MINUS_Y;
          break;
        case (Surface.ROTATION_270):
          x_axis = SensorManager.AXIS_MINUS_Y;
          y_axis = SensorManager.AXIS_X;
          break;
        default: break;
      }

      SensorManager.remapCoordinateSystem(rotationMatrix,
                                          x_axis, y_axis,
                                          remappedMatrix);


      // Obtain the current, corrected orientation.
      SensorManager.getOrientation(remappedMatrix, orientation);

      // Convert from Radians to Degrees.
      values[0] = (float) Math.toDegrees(orientation[0]);
      values[1] = (float) Math.toDegrees(orientation[1]);
      values[2] = (float) Math.toDegrees(orientation[2]);

      return values;
    }
```

5. Create a new `updateGUI` method that synchronizes with the GUI thread and calls `updateOrientation` to update the Compass View. This will be executed regularly using a Timer introduced in the next step:

```
    private void updateGUI() {
      runOnUiThread(new Runnable() {
        public void run() {
          updateOrientation(mNewestValues);
        }
      });
    }
```

6. Update the `onCreate` method to create a Timer that triggers the UI update method defined in Step 5 sixty times a second:

```
    @Override
    public void onCreate(Bundle savedInstanceState) {
      super.onCreate(savedInstanceState);
      setContentView(R.layout.main);
```

```
    mCompassView = findViewById(R.id.compassView);

    mSensorManager
      = (SensorManager) getSystemService(Context.SENSOR_SERVICE);
    WindowManager wm
      = (WindowManager) getSystemService(Context.WINDOW_SERVICE);

    Display display = wm.getDefaultDisplay();
    mScreenRotation = display.getRotation();

    mNewestValues = new float[] {0, 0, 0};

    Timer updateTimer = new Timer("compassUpdate");
    updateTimer.scheduleAtFixedRate(new TimerTask() {
      public void run() {
        updateGUI();
      }
    }, 0, 1000/60);
  }
```

7. Implement a `SensorEventListener` as a field variable. Within its `onSensorChanged` it should update the latest Sensor result array based on sending the received Sensor values to `calculateOrientation`, created in Step 4:

```
    private final SensorEventListener mSensorEventListener
      = new SensorEventListener() {

    public void onSensorChanged(SensorEvent sensorEvent) {
      mNewestValues = calculateOrientation(sensorEvent.values);
    }

    public void onAccuracyChanged(Sensor sensor, int accuracy) {}
  };
```

8. Override `onResume` and `onPause` to register and unregister the `SensorEventListener` when the Activity becomes active and inactive, respectively:

```
    @Override
    protected void onResume() {
      super.onResume();

      Sensor rotationVector
        = mSensorManager.getDefaultSensor(Sensor.TYPE_ROTATION_VECTOR);

      mSensorManager.registerListener(mSensorEventListener,
                                      rotationVector,
                                      SensorManager.SENSOR_DELAY_FASTEST);
    }

    @Override
    protected void onPause() {
      super.onPause();
      mSensorManager.unregisterListener(mSensorEventListener);
    }
```

If you run the application now, you should see the Compass View "centered" at 0, 0, 0 when the device is laying flat on a table with the top of the device pointing North. Moving the device should result in the Compass View dynamically updating as the orientation of the device changes.

You will also find that as you rotate the device through 90 degrees, the screen will rotate and the Compass View will reorient accordingly. You can extend this project by disabling automatic screen rotation.

USING THE ENVIRONMENTAL SENSORS

Like orientation Sensors, the availability of specific environmental Sensors depends on the host hardware. Where they are available, environmental Sensors can be used by your application to:

➤ Improve location detection and track movement based on altitude

➤ Alter the screen brightness or functionality based on ambient light

➤ Make environmental weather observations

➤ Determine on which planetary body the device is currently located

Using the Barometer Sensor

A barometer is used to measure atmospheric pressure. The inclusion of this Sensor in some Android devices makes it possible for users to determine their current altitude and, potentially, to forecast weather changes.

To monitor changes in atmospheric pressure, register an implementation of `SensorEventListener` with the Sensor Manager, using a Sensor object of type `Sensor.TYPE_PRESSURE`. The current atmospheric pressure is returned as the first (and only) value in the returned values array in hectopascals (hPa), which is an equivalent measurement to millibars (mbar).

To calculate the current altitude in meters, you can use the static `getAltitude` method from the Sensor Manager, as shown in Listing 16-15, supplying it with the current pressure and the local pressure at sea level.

> **NOTE** *To ensure accurate results, you should use a local value for sea-level atmospheric pressure, although the Sensor Manager provides a value for one standard atmosphere via the* `PRESSURE_STANDARD_ATMOSPHERE` *constant as a useful approximation.*

LISTING 16-15: Finding the current altitude using the barometer Sensor

```
final SensorEventListener myPressureListener = new SensorEventListener() {
  public void onSensorChanged(SensorEvent sensorEvent) {
    if (sensorEvent.sensor.getType() == Sensor.TYPE_PRESSURE) {
```

```
      float currentPressure = sensorEvent.values[0];

      // Calculate altitude
      float altitude = SensorManager.getAltitude(
        SensorManager.PRESSURE_STANDARD_ATMOSPHERE,
        currentPressure);
    }
  }

  public void onAccuracyChanged(Sensor sensor, int accuracy) {}
};

SensorManager sm
  = (SensorManager)getSystemService(Context.SENSOR_SERVICE);
int sensorType = Sensor.TYPE_PRESSURE;
sm.registerListener(myPressureListener,
                    sm.getDefaultSensor(sensorType),
                    SensorManager.SENSOR_DELAY_NORMAL);
```

It's important to note that `getAltitude` calculates altitude using the current atmospheric pressure relative to local sea-level values, not two arbitrary atmospheric pressure values. As a result, to calculate the difference in altitude represented by two observed pressure values, you need to determine the altitude for each pressure and find the difference between those results, as shown in the following snippet:

```
float altitudeChange =
  SensorManager.getAltitude(SensorManager.PRESSURE_STANDARD_ATMOSPHERE,
                            newPressure) -
  SensorManager.getAltitude(SensorManager.PRESSURE_STANDARD_ATMOSPHERE,
                            initialPressure);
```

Creating a Weather Station

To fully explore the environmental Sensors available to Android devices, the following project implements a simple weather station that monitors barometric pressure, ambient temperature, relative humidity, and ambient light levels.

1. Start by creating a new WeatherStation project that includes a blank, backwards compatible `WeatherStationActivity` Activity. Modify the resulting `activity_weather_station` layout resource to display four centered lines of large, bold text that will be used to display the current temperature, barometric pressure, humidity, and cloud level:

```xml
<?xml version="1.0" encoding="utf-8"?>
<LinearLayout
  xmlns:android="http://schemas.android.com/apk/res/android"
  android:orientation="vertical"
  android:layout_width="match_parent"
  android:layout_height="match_parent">
  <TextView
    android:id="@+id/temperature"
    android:gravity="center"
    android:layout_width="match_parent"
    android:layout_height="wrap_content"
```

```xml
      android:textStyle="bold"
      android:textSize="28sp"
      android:text="Temperature"
      android:layout_margin="10dp"/>
  <TextView
      android:id="@+id/pressure"
      android:gravity="center"
      android:layout_width="match_parent"
      android:layout_height="wrap_content"
      android:textStyle="bold"
      android:textSize="28sp"
      android:text="Pressure"
      android:layout_margin="10dp"/>
  <TextView
      android:id="@+id/humidity"
      android:gravity="center"
      android:layout_width="match_parent"
      android:layout_height="wrap_content"
      android:textStyle="bold"
      android:textSize="28sp"
      android:text="Humidity"
      android:layout_margin="10dp"/>
  <TextView
      android:id="@+id/light"
      android:gravity="center"
      android:layout_width="match_parent"
      android:layout_height="wrap_content"
      android:textStyle="bold"
      android:textSize="28sp"
      android:text="Light"
      android:layout_margin="10dp"/>
</LinearLayout>
```

2. Within the `WeatherStationActivity`, create instance variables to store references to each of the Text Views, and the Sensor Manager. Also create variables to record the last recorded value obtained from each sensor:

```java
private SensorManager mSensorManager;
private TextView mTemperatureTextView;
private TextView mPressureTextView;
private TextView mHumidityTextView;
private TextView mLightTextView;

private float mLastTemperature = Float.NaN;
private float mLastPressure = Float.NaN;
private float mLastLight = Float.NaN;
private float mLastHumidity = Float.NaN;
```

3. Update the `onCreate` method to get a reference to the Text Views and the Sensor Manager:

```java
@Override
public void onCreate(Bundle savedInstanceState) {
  super.onCreate(savedInstanceState);
  setContentView(R.layout.activity_weather_station);
```

```
mTemperatureTextView = findViewById(R.id.temperature);
mPressureTextView = findViewById(R.id.pressure);
mLightTextView = findViewById(R.id.light);
mHumidityTextView = findViewById(R.id.humidity);
mSensorManager
  = (SensorManager) getSystemService(Context.SENSOR_SERVICE);
}
```

4. Create a new `SensorEventListener` implementation that records results from each of the pressure, temperature, humidity, and light sensors. It should simply record the last observed value:

```
private final SensorEventListener mSensorEventListener
  = new SensorEventListener() {

  public void onAccuracyChanged(Sensor sensor, int accuracy) { }

  public void onSensorChanged(SensorEvent event) {
    switch (event.sensor.getType()) {
      case (Sensor.TYPE_AMBIENT_TEMPERATURE):
        mLastTemperature = event.values[0];
        break;
      case (Sensor.TYPE_RELATIVE_HUMIDITY):
        mLastHumidity = event.values[0];
        break;
      case (Sensor.TYPE_PRESSURE):
        mLastPressure = event.values[0];
        break;
      case (Sensor.TYPE_LIGHT):
        mLastLight = event.values[0];
        break;
      default: break;
    }
  }
};
```

5. Override the `onResume` handler to register your new Listener for updates using the `SensorManager`. Atmospheric and environmental conditions are likely to change slowly over time, so you can choose a relatively slow update rate. You should also check to confirm a default Sensor exists for each of the conditions being monitored, notifying the user where one or more Sensors are unavailable:

```
@Override
protected void onResume() {
  super.onResume();

  Sensor lightSensor = mSensorManager.getDefaultSensor(Sensor.TYPE_LIGHT);
  if (lightSensor != null)
    mSensorManager.registerListener(mSensorEventListener,
      lightSensor,
      SensorManager.SENSOR_DELAY_NORMAL);
  else
    mLightTextView.setText("Light Sensor Unavailable");
```

```
        Sensor pressureSensor =
          mSensorManager.getDefaultSensor(Sensor.TYPE_PRESSURE);
        if (pressureSensor != null)
          mSensorManager.registerListener(mSensorEventListener,
            pressureSensor,
            SensorManager.SENSOR_DELAY_NORMAL);
        else
          mPressureTextView.setText("Barometer Unavailable");

        Sensor temperatureSensor =
          mSensorManager.getDefaultSensor(Sensor.TYPE_AMBIENT_TEMPERATURE);
        if (temperatureSensor != null)
          mSensorManager.registerListener(mSensorEventListener,
            temperatureSensor,
            SensorManager.SENSOR_DELAY_NORMAL);
        else
          mTemperatureTextView.setText("Thermometer Unavailable");

        Sensor humiditySensor =
          mSensorManager.getDefaultSensor(Sensor.TYPE_RELATIVE_HUMIDITY);
        if (humiditySensor != null)
          mSensorManager.registerListener(mSensorEventListener,
            humiditySensor,
            SensorManager.SENSOR_DELAY_NORMAL);
        else
          mHumidityTextView.setText("Humidity Sensor Unavailable");
      }
```

6. Override the corresponding onPause method to unregister the Sensor Event Listener when the Activity is no longer active:

```
    @Override
    protected void onPause() {
      super.onPause();
      mSensorManager.unregisterListener(mSensorEventListener);
    }
```

7. Create a new updateGUI method that synchronizes with the GUI thread and updates the Text Views. This will be executed regularly using a Timer introduced in the next step:

```
    private void updateGUI() {
      runOnUiThread(new Runnable() {
        public void run() {
          if (!Float.isNaN(mLastPressure)) {
            mPressureTextView.setText(mLastPressure + "hPa");
            mPressureTextView.invalidate();
          }
          if (!Float.isNaN(mLastLight)) {
            String lightStr = "Sunny";
            if (mLastLight <= SensorManager.LIGHT_CLOUDY)
              lightStr = "Night";
            else if (mLastLight <= SensorManager.LIGHT_OVERCAST)
              lightStr = "Cloudy";
            else if (mLastLight <= SensorManager.LIGHT_SUNLIGHT)
              lightStr = "Overcast";
```

```
            mLightTextView.setText(lightStr);
            mLightTextView.invalidate();
          }
          if (!Float.isNaN(mLastTemperature)) {
            mTemperatureTextView.setText(mLastTemperature + "C");
            mTemperatureTextView.invalidate();
          }
          if (!Float.isNaN(mLastHumidity)) {
            mHumidityTextView.setText(mLastHumidity + "% Rel. Humidity");
            mHumidityTextView.invalidate();
          }
        }
      });
    }
```

8. Update the `onCreate` method to create a Timer that triggers the UI update method defined in Step 7 once every second:

```
@Override
public void onCreate(Bundle savedInstanceState) {
  super.onCreate(savedInstanceState);
  setContentView(R.layout.activity_weather_station);

  mTemperatureTextView = findViewById(R.id.temperature);
  mPressureTextView = findViewById(R.id.pressure);
  mLightTextView = findViewById(R.id.light);
  mHumidityTextView = findViewById(R.id.humidity);
  mSensorManager =
    (SensorManager) getSystemService(Context.SENSOR_SERVICE);

  Timer updateTimer = new Timer("weatherUpdate");
  updateTimer.scheduleAtFixedRate(new TimerTask() {
    public void run() {
      updateGUI();
    }
  }, 0, 1000);
}
```

USING BODY SENSORS

The launch of Android Wear introduced the concept of Android Sensors that aren't physically incorporated into the primary Android device. Instead, they are available through peripherals, such as an Android Wear device, or attached remotely using Bluetooth LE.

This made it possible to incorporate *body sensors*—such as the heart rate monitor—into the Android framework. Body sensors require physical contact with the user in order to operate. Because they monitor and report sensitive personal information from the user, they require the BODY_SENSORS permission be granted before they will be returned from getDefaultSensor or getSensorsList:

```
<uses-permission android:name="android.permission.BODY_SENSORS" />
```

As a dangerous permission, in addition to a manifest entry, it requires explicit approval from the user when first used, by way of a run-time permission requests.

Before attempting to find a body sensor, use the `ActivityCompat.checkSelfPermission` method, passing in the `Manifest.permission.BODY_SENSORS` constant to determine if you have been granted access, in which case it will return `PERMISSION_GRANTED`:

```
int permission = ActivityCompat.checkSelfPermission(this,
                 Manifest.permission.BODY_SENSORS);

if (permission==PERMISSION_GRANTED) {
  // Access the body sensor
} else {
  if (ActivityCompat.shouldShowRequestPermissionRationale(
      this, Manifest.permission.BODY_SENSORS)) {
    // TODO: Display additional rationale for the requested permission.
  }
  // Request the permission or display a dialog
  // showing why the function is unavailable.
}
```

To display the permission request dialog, call the `ActivityCompat.requestPermission` method, specifying the required permissions:

```
ActivityCompat.requestPermissions(this,
    new String[]{Manifest.permission.BODY_SENSORS},
    BODY_SENSOR_PERMISSION_REQUEST);
```

This function runs asynchronously, displaying a standard Android dialog that can't be customized. You will receive a callback when the user has either accepted or denied your runtime request, received by the `onRequestPermissionsResult` handler:

```
@Override
public void onRequestPermissionsResult(int requestCode,
                                       @NonNull String[] permissions,
                                       @NonNull int[] grantResults) {
  super.onRequestPermissionsResult(requestCode, permissions, grantResults);
  // TODO React to granted / denied permissions.
}
```

Body Sensors are only accurate and useful when in physical contact with the body whose vital signs are being monitored. As a result, it's important to always monitor the accuracy of body sensors. If the Sensor is not in contact with a body, it will return `SENSOR_STATUS_NO_CONTACT`:

```
if (sensorEvent.accuracy == SensorManager.SENSOR_STATUS_NO_CONTACT ||
    sensorEvent.accuracy == SensorManager.SENSOR_STATUS_UNRELIABLE) {
  // TODO Ignore Sensor results.
```

Listing 16-16 shows the skeleton code for connecting a Sensor Event Listener to a heart rate Sensor that returns a single value describing the user's heart rate in beats-per-minute (bpm). Remember that in addition to this code, you also need to add the body sensor permission to the application manifest.

LISTING 16-16: Connecting a Sensor Event Listener to a heart rate monitor

```java
private static final String TAG = "HEART_RATE";
private static final int BODY_SENSOR_PERMISSION_REQUEST = 1;

private void connectHeartRateSensor() {
  int permission = ActivityCompat.checkSelfPermission(this,
    Manifest.permission.BODY_SENSORS);

  if (permission == PERMISSION_GRANTED) {
    // If permission granted, connect the event listener.
    doConnectHeartRateSensor();
  } else {
    if (ActivityCompat.shouldShowRequestPermissionRationale(
      this, Manifest.permission.BODY_SENSORS)) {
      // TODO: Display additional rationale for the requested permission.
    }
    // Request the permission
    ActivityCompat.requestPermissions(this,
      new String[]{Manifest.permission.BODY_SENSORS},
      BODY_SENSOR_PERMISSION_REQUEST);
  }
}

@Override
public void onRequestPermissionsResult(int requestCode,
                                       @NonNull String[] permissions,
                                       @NonNull int[] grantResults) {
  super.onRequestPermissionsResult(requestCode, permissions, grantResults);

  if (requestCode == BODY_SENSOR_PERMISSION_REQUEST &&
      grantResults.length > 0 &&
      grantResults[0] == PERMISSION_GRANTED) {
    // If permission granted, connect the heart rate sensor.
    doConnectHeartRateSensor();
  } else {
    Log.d(TAG, "Body Sensor access permission denied.");
  }
}

private void doConnectHeartRateSensor() {
  SensorManager sm = (SensorManager)getSystemService(Context.SENSOR_SERVICE);
  Sensor heartRateSensor = sm.getDefaultSensor(Sensor.TYPE_HEART_RATE);

  if (heartRateSensor == null)
    Log.d(TAG, "No Heart Rate Sensor Detected.");
  else {
    sm.registerListener(mHeartRateListener, heartRateSensor,
                        SensorManager.SENSOR_DELAY_NORMAL);
  }
}
```

continues

LISTING 16-16 *(continued)*

```
final SensorEventListener mHeartRateListener = new SensorEventListener() {
  public void onSensorChanged(SensorEvent sensorEvent) {
    if (sensorEvent.sensor.getType() == Sensor.TYPE_HEART_RATE) {

      if (sensorEvent.accuracy == SensorManager.SENSOR_STATUS_NO_CONTACT ||
          sensorEvent.accuracy == SensorManager.SENSOR_STATUS_UNRELIABLE) {
        Log.d(TAG, "Heart Rate Monitor not in contact or unreliable");
      } else {
        float currentHeartRate = sensorEvent.values[0];
        Log.d(TAG, "Heart Rate: " + currentHeartRate);
      }
    }
  }

  public void onAccuracyChanged(Sensor sensor, int accuracy) {}
};
```

USER ACTIVITY RECOGNITION

Google's Activity Recognition API enables you to understand what activity your users are performing in the physical world. By periodically analyzing short bursts of data received from device Sensors, Activity Recognition attempts to detect what activities the user is performing, including walking, driving, cycling, and running.

Access to the Activity Recognition API is provided by the Google Play services Location library, which must be added as a dependency to your app module's build.gradle file (after you've installed Google Play services as described in Chapter 15, "Location, Contextual Awareness, and Mapping"):

```
dependencies {
  ...
  implementation 'com.google.android.gms:play-services-location:11.8.0'
}
```

You must also include the ACTIVITY_RECOGNITION permission in your manifest:

```
<uses-permission
  android:name="com.google.android.gms.permission.ACTIVITY_RECOGNITION"
/>
```

To receive updates on the user's current activity, first get an instance of the ActivityRecognitionClient using the ActivityRecognition.getClient static method, and passing in a Context:

```
ActivityRecognitionClient activityRecognitionClient
  = ActivityRecognition.getClient(this);
```

To request updates, use the `requestActivityUpdates` method, passing in a preferred detection interval in milliseconds and a Pending Intent that will be fired when a change in user activity is detected. Typically, the Pending Intent is used to start an Intent Service that will respond to the change in user activity:

```
long updateFreq = 1000*60;

Intent startServiceIntent = new Intent(this, MyARService.class);
PendingIntent pendingIntent
  = PendingIntent.getService(this, ACTIVITY_RECOGNITION_REQUEST_CODE,
                             startServiceIntent, 0);

Task task
  = activityRecognitionClient.requestActivityUpdates(updateFreq,
                                                     pendingIntent);
```

> **NOTE** *The returned Task can be used to check the success of the call, using the* `addSuccessListener` *and* `addOnFailureListener` *methods to add On Success and On Failure Listeners, respectively.*

Any subsequent request using the same Pending Intent will remove and replace earlier requests.

The specified update frequency determines the rate at which changes in the user's activity are returned; larger values result in fewer updates, which improves battery life by waking the device and turning on the Sensors less often. Like all Sensors, it's best practice to request updates as infrequently as possible.

The requested update rate is used as a guide by the Activity Recognition API; in some circumstances you may receive updates more often (for example, if other apps have requested more frequent updates). More often, you may receive less frequent updates. The API may pause updates to conserve battery when it detects that the device has remained stationary for an extended period, or when the screen is off and the device is in power saver mode.

To extract the Activity Recognition Result from the Intent fired when a new user activity has been detected, use the `extractResult` method.

```
ActivityRecognitionResult activityResult = extractResult(intent);
```

The returned Activity Recognition Result includes the `getMostProbableActivity` method that returns a `DetectedActivity` that describes the activity type for which it has the highest confidence that it's being performed:

```
DetectedActivity detectedActivity = activityResult.getMostProbableActivity();
```

Alternately, you can use the `getProbableActivities` method to return a list of all the likely activities:

```
List<DetectedActivity> allActivities = activityResult.getProbableActivities();
```

For any Detected Activity, use the getType and getConfidence methods to find the type of activity detected and the percent confidence in that result, respectively:

```
@Override
protected void onHandleIntent(@Nullable Intent intent) {
  ActivityRecognitionResult activityResult = extractResult(intent);

  DetectedActivity detectedActivity = activityResult.getMostProbableActivity();
  int activityType = detectedActivity.getType();
  int activityConfidence = detectedActivity.getConfidence(); /* Pecent */

  switch (activityType) {
    case (DetectedActivity.IN_VEHICLE): /* TODO Driving */ break;
    case (DetectedActivity.ON_BICYCLE): /* TODO Cycling */ break;
    case (DetectedActivity.ON_FOOT)   : /* TODO On Foot */ break;
    case (DetectedActivity.STILL)     : /* TODO Still   */ break;
    case (DetectedActivity.WALKING)   : /* TODO Walking */ break;
    case (DetectedActivity.RUNNING)   : /* TODO Running */ break;
    case (DetectedActivity.UNKNOWN)   : /* TODO Unknown */ break;
    case (DetectedActivity.TILTING)   : {
      // TODO Device angle changed significantly
      break;
    }
    default : break;
  }
}
```

When you no longer need to receive activity change updates, call removeActivityUpdates, passing in the Pending Intent used to request the update results:

```
activityRecognitionClient.removeActivityUpdates(pendingIntent);
```

Note that active requests for updates will keep the Google Play services connection active, so it's important to explicitly remove the request for updates when they are no longer needed—both to reduce battery drain and to maintain the advantages of automatic connection management with Google Play services.

17

Audio, Video, and Using the Camera

WHAT'S IN THIS CHAPTER?

➤ Playing audio and video with the Media Player and Exoplayer

➤ Handling audio focus

➤ Working with a Media Session

➤ Building Media Controls

➤ Background audio playback

➤ Using the Media Router and Cast Application Framwork

➤ Creating Media Style Notifications

➤ Recording audio

➤ Recording video and taking pictures using Intents

➤ Previewing recorded video and displaying live camera streams

➤ Taking pictures and controlling the camera directly

➤ Adding recorded media the Media Store

WROX.COM CODE DOWNLOADS FOR THIS CHAPTER

The following code download for this chapter is found at www.wrox.com on the Download Code tab:

➤ Snippets_ch17.zip

PLAYING AUDIO AND VIDEO, AND USING THE CAMERA

Smartphones and tablets have become so popular that for many people they have entirely replaced all other portable electronics—including cameras, music players, and audio recorders. As a result Android's media APIs, which allow us to build apps that offer a rich audio, video, and camera experiences, have become increasingly powerful and important.

This chapter introduces you to the Android APIs for controlling audio and video recording and playback, controlling the audio focus of the device, and reacting appropriately when other applications take focus or the output channel is changed (for example, when headphones are unplugged).

You also learn how to use the Media Session APIs to communicate information about your media playback to the system and to other apps as well as receive play, pause, and other media events from Notifications, headsets, and connected devices including Wear OS and Android Auto.

You learn how to build an audio playback service, and how to keep your UI synchronized with the current audio state. You also explore the importance of the life cycle and foreground status for audio playback, and how to build Media Style Notifications.

The best camera is the one that's with you, and for most people that's their smartphone camera. You learn to use the Android camera APIs to take photos and record video, as well as how to display the live camera feed.

PLAYING AUDIO AND VIDEO

Android 8.1 Oreo (API Level 27) supports the following multimedia formats for playback as part of the framework. Note that some devices may support playback of additional file formats:

➤ **Audio**

   ➤ AAC LC

   ➤ HE-AACv1 (AAC+)

   ➤ HE-AACv2 (Enhanced AAC+)

   ➤ AAC ELD (Enhanced Low Delay AAC)

   ➤ AMR-NB

   ➤ AMR-WB

   ➤ FLAC

   ➤ MP3

   ➤ MIDI

   ➤ Ogg Vorbis

   ➤ PCM/WAVE

   ➤ Opus

➤ **Image**

    ➤ JPEG

    ➤ PNG

    ➤ WEBP

    ➤ GIF

    ➤ BMP

➤ **Video**

    ➤ H.263

    ➤ H.264 AVC

    ➤ H.265 HEVC

    ➤ MPEG-4 SP

    ➤ VP8

    ➤ VP9

The following network protocols are supported for streaming media:

➤ RTSP (RTP, SDP)

➤ HTTP/HTTPS progressive streaming

➤ HTTP/HTTPS live streaming (on devices running Android 3.0 or above)

> **NOTE** *For full details on the currently supported media formats and recommendations for video encoding and audio streaming, see the Supported Media Formats page on the Android Developer documentation site:* `developer` `.android.com/guide/topics/media/media-formats.html`.

Introducing the Media Player

Using the Media Player, you can play audio and video stored in application resources, local files, Content Providers, or streamed from a network URL. The `MediaPlayer` class is available as part of the Android framework on all devices for supporting audio and video playback.

> **NOTE** *For applications supporting Android 4.1 (API Level 16) or later, the ExoPlayer library is available as an alternative to the Media Player API. Details on using ExoPlayer are described later in this chapter.*

The Media Player's management of audio/video files and streams is handled as a state machine. In the most simplistic terms, transitions through the state machine can be described as follows:

1. Initialize the Media Player with media to play.

2. Prepare the Media Player for playback.

3. Start the playback.

4. Pause or stop the playback prior to it completing.

5. The playback is complete.

> **NOTE** *A more detailed and thorough description of the Media Player state machine is provided at the Android developer site, at* `developer.android.com/reference/android/media/MediaPlayer.html#StateDiagram`*.*

To play a media resource, you need to create a new `MediaPlayer` instance, initialize it with a media source, and prepare it for playback. `MediaPlayer` contains a number of static `create` methods that combine all three of these steps.

Alternatively, you can use the `setDataSource` method on an existing Media Player instance, as shown in Listing 17-1. This method accepts a file path, Content Provider URI, streaming media URL path, or File Descriptor.

Because preparing the data source involves potentially expensive operations like fetching data over the network and decoding the data stream, you should never call the `prepare` method on the UI thread. Instead set a `MediaPlayer.OnPreparedListener` and use `prepareAsync` to keep your UI responsive while preparing for media playback.

LISTING 17-1: Playback using the Media Player

```
MediaPlayer mediaPlayer = new MediaPlayer();
mediaPlayer.setDataSource("http://site.com/audio/mydopetunes.mp3");
mediaPlayer.setOnPreparedListener(myOnPreparedListener);
mediaPlayer.prepareAsync();
```

To stream Internet media using the Media Player, your application manifest must include the `INTERNET` permission:

```
<uses-permission android:name="android.permission.INTERNET"/>
```

> **WARNING** *Android supports a limited number of simultaneous Media Player objects; not releasing them can cause runtime exceptions when the system runs out. When you finish playback, call* `release` *on your Media Player object to free the associated resources:*
>
> ```
> mediaPlayer.release();
> ```

When a Media Player has finished preparing, the associated on Prepared Listener handler will be triggered, and you can call start to begin playback of the associated media:

```
private MediaPlayer.OnPreparedListener myOnPreparedListener =
  new MediaPlayer.OnPreparedListener() {

  @Override
  public void onPrepared(MediaPlayer mp) {
    mp.start();
  }
};
```

Once playback has begun, you can use the Media Player's stop and pause methods to stop and pause playback, respectively.

The Media Player also provides the getDuration method to find the length of the media being played and the getCurrentPosition method to find the playback position. Use the seekTo method to jump to a specific position in the media.

> **WARNING** MediaPlayer *is a relatively expensive object to create and maintain, so you should avoid creating multiple instances. Consider using the* SoundPool *class if you need low-latency playback of many audio streams such as would be common in a game with background music and multiple sound effects.*

Using Media Player for Video Playback

The steps of initializing, setting a playback source, and preparing for playback apply to both audio and video playback. In addition, video playback requires that you also must have a Surface on which to display the video.

This is generally handled using a SurfaceView object. The Surface View class is a wrapper around a Surface Holder, which, in turn, is a wrapper around the Surface that is used to support visual updates from background threads.

> **NOTE** *Prior to Android 7.0 (API Level 24), each* SurfaceView *was rendered in its own window, separately from the rest of your UI. As a result, unlike View-derived classes it could not be moved, transformed, or animated. As an alternative for earlier platform versions, the* TextureView *class offers support for these operations, but is less battery-efficient.*

To include a Surface Holder in your UI layout, use the SurfaceView class:

```xml
<?xml version="1.0" encoding="utf-8"?>
<LinearLayout
  xmlns:android="http://schemas.android.com/apk/res/android"
  android:layout_width="match_parent"
  android:layout_height="match_parent"
```

```
        android:orientation="vertical" >
        <SurfaceView
          android:id="@+id/surfaceView"
          android:layout_width="match_parent"
          android:layout_height="match_parent"
          android:layout_weight="30"
        />
        <LinearLayout
          android:id="@+id/linearLayout1"
          android:layout_width="match_parent"
          android:layout_height="wrap_content"
          android:layout_weight="1">
          <Button
            android:id="@+id/buttonPlay"
            android:layout_width="wrap_content"
            android:layout_height="wrap_content"
            android:text="Play"
          />
          <Button
            android:id="@+id/buttonPause"
            android:layout_width="wrap_content"
            android:layout_height="wrap_content"
            android:text="Pause"
          />
          <Button
            android:id="@+id/buttonSkip"
            android:layout_width="wrap_content"
            android:layout_height="wrap_content"
            android:text="Skip"
          />
        </LinearLayout>
      </LinearLayout>
```

Use the Media Player's `setDisplay` method to assign a `SurfaceHolder` object that will display your video content.

Listing 17-2 shows the skeleton code used to initialize a Surface View within your Activity, and assigns it as a display target for a Media Player.

LISTING 17-2: Initializing and assigning a Surface View to a Media Player

```java
public class SurfaceViewVideoViewActivity extends Activity
  implements SurfaceHolder.Callback {

  static final String TAG = "VideoViewActivity";

  private MediaPlayer mediaPlayer;

  public void surfaceCreated(SurfaceHolder holder) {
    try {
      // When the surface is created, assign it as the
      // display surface and assign and prepare a data
      // source.
      mediaPlayer.setDisplay(holder);
```

```
      // Specify the path, URL, or Content Provider URI of
      // the video resource to play.
      File file = new File(Environment.getExternalStorageDirectory(),
                           "sickbeatsvideo.mp4");
      mediaPlayer.setDataSource(file.getPath());

      mediaPlayer.prepare();
    } catch (IllegalArgumentException e) {
      Log.e(TAG, "Illegal Argument Exception", e);
    } catch (IllegalStateException e) {
      Log.e(TAG, "Illegal State Exception", e);
    } catch (SecurityException e) {
      Log.e(TAG, "Security Exception", e);
    } catch (IOException e) {
      Log.e(TAG, "IO Exception", e);
    }
  }

  public void surfaceDestroyed(SurfaceHolder holder) {
    mediaPlayer.release();
  }

  public void surfaceChanged(SurfaceHolder holder,
                             int format, int width, int height) { }


  @Override
  public void onCreate(Bundle savedInstanceState) {
    super.onCreate(savedInstanceState);

    setContentView(R.layout.surfaceviewvideoviewer);

    // Create a new Media Player.
    mediaPlayer = new MediaPlayer();

    // Get a reference to the Surface View.
    final SurfaceView surfaceView =
      findViewById(R.id.surfaceView);

    // Configure the Surface View.
    surfaceView.setKeepScreenOn(true);

    // Configure the Surface Holder and register the callback.
    SurfaceHolder holder = surfaceView.getHolder();
    holder.addCallback(this);
    holder.setFixedSize(400, 300);

    // Connect a play button.
    Button playButton = findViewById(R.id.buttonPlay);
    playButton.setOnClickListener(new OnClickListener() {
      public void onClick(View v) {
        mediaPlayer.start();
      }
    });
```

continues

LISTING 17-2 *(continued)*

```
        // Connect a pause button.
        Button pauseButton = findViewById(R.id.buttonPause);
        pauseButton.setOnClickListener(new OnClickListener() {
          public void onClick(View v) {
            mediaPlayer.pause();
          }
        });

        // Add a skip button.
        Button skipButton = findViewById(R.id.buttonSkip);
        skipButton.setOnClickListener(new OnClickListener() {
          public void onClick(View v) {
            mediaPlayer.seekTo(mediaPlayer.getDuration()/2);
          }
        });
      }
    }
```

Note that Surface Holders are created asynchronously, so you must wait until the `surfaceCreated` handler has been fired, before assigning the returned Surface Holder object to the Media Player, by implementing the `SurfaceHolder.Callback` interface.

As shown in Listing 17-2, `setDataSource` is used to specify either a path, URL, or Content Provider URI of a video resource to play.

After you select your media source, call `prepare` to initialize the Media Player in preparation for playback.

Using ExoPlayer for Video Playback

For applications supporting Android 4.1 (API Level 16) or later, the Media Player API can be replaced with the ExoPlayer library. ExoPlayer has been built by Google to provide a consistent experience, better extensibility, and additional format support for media playback on all devices running Android 4.1 (API Level 16) or higher.

The `exoplayer-core` library is the only required dependency for integrating ExoPlayer into your app; however, ExoPlayer also provides a number of subcomponents that offer additional functionality. For example, the `exoplayer-ui` library provides pre-built UI components that greatly simplify common operations including playback controls.

To use ExoPlayer for video playback, you must add the ExoPlayer core and UI libraries as dependencies to your app module's `build.gradle` file:

```
    implementation "com.google.android.exoplayer:exoplayer-core:2.8.2"
    implementation "com.google.android.exoplayer:exoplayer-ui:2.8.2"
```

The ExoPlayer UI library provides a `PlayerView` class that encapsulates both the playback surface and playback controls including play, pause, fast forward, rewind, and a seek bar for skipping through the video, and which can be added to your Activity or Fragment layout:

```xml
<?xml version="1.0" encoding="utf-8"?>
<FrameLayout
  xmlns:android="http://schemas.android.com/apk/res/android"
  android:layout_width="match_parent"
  android:layout_height="match_parent">
  <com.google.android.exoplayer2.ui.PlayerView
    android:id="@+id/player_view"
    android:layout_width="match_parent"
    android:layout_height="match_parent"
  />
</FrameLayout>
```

Listing 17-3 shows the skeleton code used to initialize a Player View within your Activity, and start video playback.

LISTING 17-3: Playing a video using Player View

```java
public class SurfaceViewVideoViewActivity extends Activity {

  private PlayerView playerView;
  private SimpleExoPlayer player;

  @Override
  public void onCreate(Bundle savedInstanceState) {
    super.onCreate(savedInstanceState);
    setContentView(R.layout.playerview);

    playerView = findViewById(R.id.player_view);
  }

  @Override
  protected void onStart() {
    // Create a new Exo Player
    player = ExoPlayerFractory.newSimpleInstance(this,
      new DefaultTrackSelector());

    // Associate the ExoPlayer with the Player View
    playerView.setPlayer(player);

    // Build a DataSource.Factory capable of
    // loading http and local content
    DataSource.Factory dataSourceFactory = new DefaultDataSourceFactory(
      this,
      Util.getUserAgent(this, getString(R.string.app_name)));

    // Specify the URI to play
    File file = new File(Environment.getExternalStorageDirectory(),
                        "test2.mp4");
    ExtractorMediaSource mediaSource =
      new ExtractorMediaSource.Factory(dataSourceFactory)
      .createMediaSource(Uri.fromFile(file));
```

continues

LISTING 17-3 *(continued)*

```
      // Start loading the media source
      player.prepare(mediaSource);

      // Start playback automatically when ready
      player.setPlayWhenReady(true);
    }

    @Override
    protected void onStop() {
      playerView.setPlayer(null);
      player.release();
      player = null;
      super.onStop();
    }
  }
```

You can learn more about ExoPlayer at `github.com/google/ExoPlayer`.

Requesting and Managing Audio Focus

Audio focus is the implementation of the concept that only one app can be the focus of what the user is listening to at any given time. This could be an ongoing phone call, a video being played, or transient sounds such as a notification sound or navigation directions.

Sound output is an inherently shared channel—like sitting in a room and having multiple simultaneous conversions, having multiple apps simultaneously playing audio would quickly become unintelligible. A critical portion of being a good citizen when playing audio is in sharing and respecting audio focus.

For your app, that means always requesting audio focus before beginning audio playback, holding audio only until your playback is finished, and relinquishing focus when another app requests it.

Requesting Audio Focus

To request audio focus before beginning playback, use the Audio Manager's `requestAudioFocus` method. When requesting the audio focus, you can specify which stream you require (typically `STREAM_MUSIC`), and for how long you expect to require focus—either ongoing (such as when playing music) or transiently (such as when providing navigation instructions). In the latter case you can also specify if your transient interruption can be handled by the currently focused application "ducking" (lowering its volume) until your interruption is complete.

Specifying the nature of the audio focus you require allows other applications to better react to losing the audio focus, as described later in this section.

Listing 17-4 shows the skeleton code for an Activity that requests ongoing audio focus for the music stream. You must also specify an `OnAudioFocusChangeListener` object, which lets you monitor for loss of audio focus and respond accordingly (and is described in more detail later in this section).

LISTING 17-4: Requesting audio focus

```
AudioManager am = (AudioManager)getSystemService(Context.AUDIO_SERVICE);

// Request audio focus for playback
int result = am.requestAudioFocus(focusChangeListener,
                // Use the music stream.
                AudioManager.STREAM_MUSIC,
                // Request ongoing focus.
                AudioManager.AUDIOFOCUS_GAIN);

if (result == AudioManager.AUDIOFOCUS_REQUEST_GRANTED) {
  mediaPlayer.start();
}
```

There are cases—such as when the user is in a phone call—when a request for audio focus will fail. As a result, you should be careful to only start playback if you receive AUDIOFOCUS_REQUEST_ GRANTED after making the request.

> **NOTE** *The sounds generated by Notifications are a special case. Android will automatically request temporary audio focus for Notification sounds added via* setSound, *or by using the* DEFAULT_SOUND *or* DEFAULT_ALL *flag for* set- Defaults. *It's important to utilize these methods for associating audio with your Notifications to ensure that you honor the user's Do Not Disturb settings.*

Responding to Audio Focus Changes

Audio focus is assigned to each application that requests it. That means that if another application requests audio focus, your application will lose it.

You will be notified of the loss of audio focus through the onAudioFocusChange handler of the Audio Focus Change Listener you registered when requesting the audio focus, as shown in Listing 17-5.

The focusChange parameter indicates the nature of the focus loss—either transient or ongoing— and whether ducking is permitted.

It's best practice to pause your media playback whenever you lose audio focus, or, in the case of a transient loss that supports ducking, to lower the volume of your audio output.

LISTING 17-5: Responding to the loss of audio focus

```
private OnAudioFocusChangeListener focusChangeListener =
  new OnAudioFocusChangeListener() {
```

continues

LISTING 17-5 *(continued)*

```java
    public void onAudioFocusChange(int focusChange) {
      AudioManager am =
        (AudioManager)getSystemService(Context.AUDIO_SERVICE);

      switch (focusChange) {
        case (AudioManager.AUDIOFOCUS_LOSS_TRANSIENT_CAN_DUCK) :
          // Lower the volume while ducking.
          mediaPlayer.setVolume(0.2f, 0.2f);
          break;

        case (AudioManager.AUDIOFOCUS_LOSS_TRANSIENT) :
          mediaPlayer.pause();
          break;

        case (AudioManager.AUDIOFOCUS_LOSS) :
          mediaPlayer.stop();
          am.abandonAudioFocus(this);
          break;

        case (AudioManager.AUDIOFOCUS_GAIN) :
          // Return the volume to normal and resume if paused.
          mediaPlayer.setVolume(1f, 1f);
          mediaPlayer.start();
          break;

        default: break;
      }
    }
  }
};
```

In the case of a transient focus loss, you will be notified when you have regained focus by receiving an `AudioManager.AUDIOFOCUS_GAIN` event, at which point you can return to playing your audio at the previous volume.

For a permanent focus loss, you should stop playback and it should only be restarted through a user interaction (such as pressing the play button within your UI). You will not receive any further callbacks to your `OnAudioFocusChangeListener` after permanently losing audio focus.

For cases where your app is requesting transient audio focus, consider using Media Player's `OnCompletionListener` to know when your audio has finished so that you can abandon audio focus in a timely manner.

Pausing Playback When the Output Changes

If the current output stream is a headset, disconnecting it will result in the system automatically switching output to the device's speakers. It's considered good practice to pause (or reduce the volume of) your audio output in these circumstances.

To do so, create a Broadcast Receiver that listens for the `AudioManager.ACTION_AUDIO_BECOMING_NOISY` broadcast and pauses your playback:

```
private class NoisyAudioStreamReceiver extends BroadcastReceiver {
  @Override
  public void onReceive(Context context, Intent intent) {
    if (AudioManager.ACTION_AUDIO_BECOMING_NOISY.equals
      (intent.getAction())) {
      pauseAudioPlayback();
    }
  }
}
```

Because this broadcast is only needed when your app is actively playing audio/video, it is not appropriate to register this receiver in your manifest. Instead, you should create an instance of your `BroadcastReceiver` and register it programmatically when you start playback (after receiving audio focus) and unregister it when you pause playback:

```
// Create the Receiver.
NoisyAudioStreamReceiver mNoisyAudioStreamReceiver =
  new NoisyAudioStreamReceiver();

// On Play
public void registerNoisyReceiver() {
  IntentFilter filter = new
    IntentFilter(AudioManager.ACTION_AUDIO_BECOMING_NOISY);
  registerReceiver(mNoisyAudioStreamReceiver, filter);
}

// On Pause
public void unregisterNoisyReceiver() {
  unregisterReceiver(mNoisyAudioStreamReceiver);
}
```

Responding to the Volume Controls

To ensure a consistent user experience, it's important that your application correctly handles users pressing the volume keys.

By default, using the volume keys, on either the device or an attached headset, changes the volume of whichever audio stream is currently playing.

Using the Activity's `setVolumeControlStream` method—typically within its `onCreate` method—allows you to specify which audio stream should be controlled by the volume keys while the current Activity is active:

```
@Override
public void onCreate(Bundle savedInstanceState) {
  super.onCreate(savedInstanceState);
  setContentView(R.layout.audioplayer);

  setVolumeControlStream(AudioManager.STREAM_MUSIC);
}
```

You can specify any of the available audio streams, but when using the Media Player, you should specify the STREAM_MUSIC stream to make it the focus of the volume keys.

> **WARNING** *Although it's also possible to listen for volume key presses directly, this is generally considered poor practice. A user can modify the audio volume in several ways, including the hardware buttons as well as software controls. Triggering volume changes manually based only on the hardware buttons is likely to make your application respond unexpectedly and frustrate your users. Frustrated users lower your application's volume by uninstalling it.*

Working with a Media Session

The Media Session API offers a consistent interface for your app to provide metadata and playback controls for the media being played by your app through any media playback mechanism available to the system.

By creating a Media Session and responding to its user-initiated commands, your app will support playback and control from connected devices such as Bluetooth-enabled cars or headsets, WearOS, and Android Auto—all of which can retrieve metadata about your media, and allow users to control playback without needing to interact directly with their mobile device, or by opening your app.

> **NOTE** *One of the most useful and common clients for displaying media meta-data and hosting media playback controls is a Notification. We discuss how to create custom Notifications for this purpose later in this chapter in the section, "Constructing Media Style Notifications."*

Controlling Playback with Media Session

The Media Session API is provided as part of the Android Support Library. To create and initialize a Media Session, create a new instance of the MediaSessionCompat class from within the onCreate method of your Activity, passing in a Context and a String for logging error messages:

```
MediaSessionCompat mMediaSession = new MediaSessionCompat(context, LOG_TAG);
```

To receive media controls from devices such as Bluetooth headsets, Wear OS, and Android Auto, you must then call setFlags, indicating that you wish the Media Session to handle media buttons and transport controls:

```
mMediaSession.setFlags(
   MediaSessionCompat.FLAG_HANDLES_MEDIA_BUTTONS |
   MediaSessionCompat.FLAG_HANDLES_TRANSPORT_CONTROLS);
```

The final step is to create and set an instance of the `MediaSessionCompat.Callback` class. The callback methods you implement within this class will receive the media button requests and allow you to respond to them appropriately:

```
mMediaSession.setCallback(new MediaSessionCompat.Callback() {
  @Override
  public void onPlay() {
    mediaPlayer.start();
  }

  @Override
  public void onPause() {
    mediaPlayer.pause();
  }

  @Override
  public void onSeekTo(long pos) {
    mediaPlayer.seekTo((int) pos);
  }
});
```

To start receiving callbacks, you must first indicate which actions your Media Session supports. You can do this by building a `PlaybackStateCompat` and passing it in using the `setPlaybackState` method:

```
public void updatePlaybackState() {
  PlaybackStateCompat.Builder playbackStateBuilder =
    new PlaybackStateCompat.Builder();

  playbackStateBuilder
    // Available actions
    .setActions(
      PlaybackStateCompat.ACTION_PLAY_PAUSE |
      PlaybackStateCompat.ACTION_PLAY |
      PlaybackStateCompat.ACTION_PAUSE |
      PlaybackStateCompat.ACTION_STOP |
      PlaybackStateCompat.ACTION_SEEK_TO)
    // Current playback state
    .setState(
      PlaybackStateCompat.STATE_PLAYING,
      0,       // Track position in ms
      1.0f); // Playback speed
  mMediaSession.setPlaybackState(playbackStateBuilder.build());
}
```

> **NOTE** *A playback state has two components: the actions you support and the current state. These are related as generally two will be simultaneously changed (for example, disabling* ACTION_FAST_FORWARD *when* STATE_BUFFERING*).*

You must always update your Media Session playback state whenever your Media Player state changes, to ensure they remain synchronized. It's also considered best practice to maintain the `PlaybackStateCompat.Builder` object, and only perform incremental updates rather than rebuilding it from scratch each time.

Finally, you need to activate your Media Session by calling `setActive(true)`, typically after receiving audio focus:

```
mMediaSession.setActive(true);
```

Correspondingly, call `setActive(false)` after stopping playback and abandoning audio focus. When you've finished playback, call `release` on your Media Session object to free the associated resources:

```
mMediaSession.release();
```

Sharing Metadata Using Media Session

In addition to controlling playback, you can use the Media Session API to surface metadata about the media your application is playing, including album art, track names, and durations, using the `setMetadata` method.

Use the `MediaMetadataCompat.Builder` to create the `MediaMetadataCompat` object that contains the metadata for your media.

Using the builder object, use the `putBitmap` method to specify an associated bitmap using the `MediaMetadataCompat.METADATA_KEY_ART` or `MediaMetadataCompat.METADATA_KEY_ALBUM_ART` keys:

```
builder.putBitmap(MediaMetadataCompat.METADATA_KEY_ART, artworkthumbnail);
builder.putString(MediaMetadataCompat.METADATA_KEY_ART_URI,
                  fullSizeArtworkUri);
```

> **WARNING** *There is a considerable cost with passing bitmaps between processes. Strongly consider using the* `METADATA_KEY_ART_URI` *and* `METADATA_KEY_ALBUM_ART_URI` *keys to add a world-readable URI to a full-size image instead of directly including the full-size image. A good rule of thumb is to only include a single Bitmap of at most 640x640 pixels.*

```
public void updateMetadata() {
  MediaMetadataCompat.Builder builder = new MediaMetadataCompat.Builder();

  builder.putString(MediaMetadataCompat.METADATA_KEY_ART_URI,
                    fullSizeArtworkUri);

  mMediaSession.setMetadata(builder.build());
```

You can also indicate the track number, CD number, year of recording, and duration using the `putLong` method with the respective `MediaMetadataCompat.METADATA_KEY_` constants:

```
builder.putLong(MediaMetadataCompat.METADATA_KEY_DURATION, duration);
```

Similarly, using the putString method you can specify the album name, album artist, track title, author, compilation, composer, release date, genre, and writer of the current media:

```
builder.putString(MediaMetadataCompat.METADATA_KEY_ALBUM, album);
builder.putString(MediaMetadataCompat.METADATA_KEY_ARTIST, artist);
builder.putString(MediaMetadataCompat.METADATA_KEY_TITLE, title);
```

> **NOTE** *Since Android 5.0 (API Level 21), the framework contains a* MediaSession *class. However, it's best practice to use the Android Support Library's* MediaSessionCompat *to ensure a consistent experience across all platform releases, as well as to take advantage of new features and bug fixes.*

Connecting Your Application's Media Controls to the Media Session Using the Media Controller

Using the Media Session callbacks to receive the media button requests, as described earlier, helps you to centralize all your media control code—and ensures that the system can display consistent media controls across multiple possible interfaces (including Notifications, Wear OS, and Android Auto).

As a result, it's considered best practice to have the media playback controls within your own UI use the same Media Session callback mechanism as other parts of the system, such that they send commands to the Media Session rather than controlling your Media Player directly.

You can do this using the MediaControllerCompat class. Create a new Media Controller using the Media Session you've constructed:

```
// After creating your Media Session
final MediaControllerCompat mediaController =
  new MediaControllerCompat(context, mMediaSession);
```

Then connect the media control buttons in your UI, such that when they are clicked, they use the Media Controller to send commands to the Media Session, rather than directly modifying the media playback:

```
// Connect a play button.
Button playButton = findViewById(R.id.buttonPlay);
playButton.setOnClickListener(new OnClickListener() {
  public void onClick(View v) {
    mediaController.getTransportControls().play();
  }
});

// Connect a pause button.
Button pauseButton = findViewById(R.id.buttonPause);
pauseButton.setOnClickListener(new OnClickListener() {
  public void onClick(View v) {
    mediaController.getTransportControls().pause();
  }
});
```

USING THE MEDIA ROUTER AND CAST APPLICATION FRAMEWORK

The Media Router APIs provide a consistent mechanism that can be used to enable your users to redirect video display and audio playback to remote devices wirelessly. This is most commonly implemented as Google Cast, a Google Play services API that allows you to "cast" video or audio to Google Cast, Google TV, and Google Home devices.

To add support for Google Cast to your app, you must add dependencies for appcompat, Media Router, and the Google Play services Cast framework to your App Module `build.gradle` file:

```
dependencies {
   compile 'com.android.support:appcompat-v7:25.1.0'
   compile 'com.android.support:mediarouter-v7:25.1.0'
   compile 'com.google.android.gms:play-services-cast-framework:10.0.1'
}
```

To add Cast functionality to an Activity, start by creating a new `OptionsProvider` implementation that will define the Google Cast options, and return them via a `CastOptions` object from the `getCastOptions` handler:

```
public class CastOptionsProvider implements OptionsProvider {
   @Override
   public CastOptions getCastOptions(Context context) {
     CastOptions castOptions = new CastOptions.Builder()
       .setReceiverApplicationId(CastMediaControlIntent
                            .DEFAULT_MEDIA_RECEIVER_APPLICATION_ID)
       .build();
     return castOptions;
   }

   @Override
   public List<SessionProvider> getAdditionalSessionProviders(Context context) {
     return null;
   }
}
```

Only the receiver application ID is a required option, as it's used to filter the list of available destinations and to launch the receiver app on the selected target device when a Cast session is started.

The destination for your app's routed media is a Cast receiver application, an HTML5/JavaScript application running on a receiver device, which provides the UI to display your app's content and handle media control messages.

The Cast Application Framework includes a pre-built receiver application hosted by Google that can be used by providing `CastMediaControlIntent.DEFAULT_MEDIA_RECEIVER_APPLICATION_ID` as the application ID.

It is also possible to create your own custom Media Receiver, although that is beyond the scope of this book. Instructions for building a custom receiver can be found at `developers.google.com/cast/docs/android_sender_setup`.

Once your Options Provider has been defined, declare it within your Application manifest using a meta-data tag:

```
<meta-data
  android:name=
    "com.google.android.gms.cast.framework.OPTIONS_PROVIDER_CLASS_NAME"
  android:value="com.professionalandroid.CastOptionsProvider"
/>
```

All of your application's interactions with the Cast Application Framework are coordinated through the CastContext object, accessed by calling getSharedInstance on the CastContext class—typically within the onCreate handler of the Activity from which you plan to Cast media:

```
CastContext mCastContext;

@Override
public void onCreate() {
  super.onCreate(savedInstanceState);
  setContentView(R.layout.activity_layout);

  mCastContext = CastContext.getSharedInstance(this);
}
```

The Cast Application Framework provides several user interface elements that you can use to initiate, and interact with, a Cast session—including the Cast Button and Mini and Expanded Controllers.

The Cast Button is displayed when Cast discovers an available Receiver to which your app can cast. When the user clicks the Cast Button, a dialog is displayed listing either all the available remote devices to cast to or the metadata associated with the currently cast content.

The Cast Button can be added to the app bar of your Activity as Media Route Action Provider:

```
<menu xmlns:app="http://schemas.android.com/apk/res-auto"
      xmlns:android="http://schemas.android.com/apk/res/android">
  <item
    android:id="@+id/media_route_menu_item"
    android:title="@string/media_route_menu_title"
    app:actionProviderClass="android.support.v7.app.MediaRouteActionProvider"
    app:showAsAction="always" />
</menu>
```

Then within the Fragments or Activities from which you want to Cast, override the onCreateOptionsMenu handler to setup the Media Route Button:

```
@Override public boolean onCreateOptionsMenu(Menu menu) {
  super.onCreateOptionsMenu(menu);
  getMenuInflater().inflate(R.menu.main, menu);
  CastButtonFactory.setUpMediaRouteButton(getApplicationContext(),
                                          menu,
                                          R.id.media_route_menu_item);

  return true;
}
```

Alternatively, you can add a Media Route Button to your Activity Layout:

```
<android.support.v7.app.MediaRouteButton
  android:id="@+id/media_route_button"
  android:layout_width="wrap_content"
  android:layout_height="wrap_content"
  android:layout_weight="1"
  android:mediaRouteTypes="user"
  android:visibility="gone"
/>
```

Connect the Media Route Button to the Cast Application Framework within your Activity's onCreate handler:

```
CastContext mCastContext;
MediaRouteButton mMediaRouteButton;

@Override
protected void onCreate(Bundle savedInstanceState) {
  super.onCreate(savedInstanceState);
  setContentView(R.layout.activity_layout);

  mCastContext = CastContext.getSharedInstance(this);

  mMediaRouteButton = findViewById(R.id.media_route_button);
  CastButtonFactory.setUpMediaRouteButton(getApplicationContext(),
                                          mMediaRouteButton);
}
```

Once the Cast Button has been added to your app, you will use a Cast Session to specify the media (and its associated metadata) that your app will cast.

Each Cast Session starts when the user selects a remote receiver from the Cast destination selection dialog, and ends when they choose to stop casting (or another sender casts to the same device).

Sessions are managed by the SessionManager; you can access the current CastSession using the getCurrentCastSession method on the CastContext, typically within the onResume handler of your Activity.

```
CastContext mCastContext;
MediaRouteButton mMediaRouteButton;

CastSession mCastSession;
SessionManager mSessionManager;

@Override
protected void onCreate(Bundle savedInstanceState) {
  super.onCreate(savedInstanceState);
  setContentView(R.layout.activity_layout);

  mCastContext = CastContext.getSharedInstance(this);

  mMediaRouteButton = findViewById(R.id.media_route_button);
  CastButtonFactory.setUpMediaRouteButton(getApplicationContext(),
                                          mMediaRouteButton);
```

```
    mSessionManager = mCastContext.getSessionManager();
}

@Override
protected void onResume() {
  super.onResume();
  mCastSession = mSessionManager.getCurrentCastSession();
}

@Override
protected void onPause() {
  super.onPause();
  mCastSession = null;
}
```

You can also attach a `SessionManagerListener` to your Session Manager instance to listen for creation, suspension, resumption, and termination of new Cast Sessions.

Once the user has established a Cast Session, a new instance of the `RemoteMediaClient` will be created, which can be accessed by calling `getRemoteMediaClient` on the current Cast Session.

You can use the Remote Media Client to set the content to stream to the remote device, and the metadata that describes it using the `MediaMetadata` class:

```
MediaMetadata movieMetadata =
  new MediaMetadata(MediaMetadata.MEDIA_TYPE_MOVIE);

movieMetadata.putString(MediaMetadata.KEY_TITLE, mCurrentMovie.getTitle());
movieMetadata.addImage(new WebImage(Uri.parse(mCurrentMovie.getImage(0))));
```

Define the media to be played on the remote device using the `MediaInfo.Builder`, specifying a URL to the selected content, details of the format and type of stream, and the Media Metadata defined above:

```
private void castMovie() {
  MediaInfo mediaInfo = new MediaInfo.Builder(mCurrentMovie.getUrl())
                      .setStreamType(MediaInfo.STREAM_TYPE_BUFFERED)
                      .setContentType("videos/mp4")
                      .setMetadata(movieMetadata)
                      .setStreamDuration(mCurrentMovie.getDuration()
                                    * 1000)
                      .build();

  RemoteMediaClient remoteMediaClient = mCastSession.getRemoteMediaClient();
  remoteMediaClient.load(mediaInfo, autoPlay, currentPosition);
}
```

You can then control media playback on the remote device using the Remote Media Client.

The Cast design checklist requires your sender app provide a mini controller that's displayed whenever the user navigates away from the primary content page, and an expanded controller that displays a full-screen UI when the user clicks the media Notification or the mini controller.

The mini controller is available as a Fragment that can be added to the bottom of your Activities:

```
<fragment
  android:id="@+id/castMiniController"
  android:layout_width="fill_parent"
  android:layout_height="wrap_content"
  android:layout_alignParentBottom="true"
  android:visibility="gone"
  class=
    "com.google.android.gms.cast.framework.media.widget.MiniControllerFragment"
/>
```

The expanded controller is provided as the abstract `ExpandedControllerActivity`, which you must subclass to add a Cast Button, as described at `developers.google.com/cast/docs/android_sender_integrate#add_expanded_controller`.

Detailed instructions for customizing the controllers and integrating Cast control through Notifications can be found in the Google Cast SDK reference documentation at `developers.google.com/cast/docs/android_sender_setup`.

BACKGROUND AUDIO PLAYBACK

When playing video, there's a good chance users will have an Activity visible in the foreground. For audio playback, it's much more likely to happen while your app is in the background.

To support this, your Media Player and Media Session must be part of a Service that will continue to run when your Activity isn't visible (or even running).

Android provides the `MediaBrowserServiceCompat` and `MediaBrowserCompat` APIs, to simplify the separation of your audio playback Service from any connected clients—including your playback Activity.

> **NOTE** *As with the* `MediaSession` *class, Android 5.0 (API Level 21) introduced a* `MediaBrowserService` *and* `MediaBrowser` *class. However, we strongly recommend using* `MediaBrowserServiceCompat` *and* `MediaBrowserCompat` *from the Android Support Library, and will use the compatibility library classes throughout this chapter.*

Building an Audio Playback Service

Listing 17-6 provides the minimal implementation of a new Media Browser Service.

Once the Media Session is created, use `setSessionToken` to pass its session token to our Media Browser Service, and implement the two abstract methods `onGetRoot` and `onLoadChildren`.

The `onGetRoot` and `onLoadChildren` methods are used to provide support for Android Auto and Wear OS. They provide a list of media items that users can select from the Auto and Wear UIs in order to start playback of specific songs, albums, or artists. A minimal implementation, as shown in the previous listing, should return a non-null result in `onGetRoot`, because a null result will cause connections to fail.

LISTING 17-6: A skeleton Media Browser Service implementation

```
public class MediaPlaybackService extends MediaBrowserServiceCompat {
  private static final String LOG_TAG = "MediaPlaybackService";

  private MediaSessionCompat mMediaSession;

  @Override
  public void onCreate() {
    super.onCreate();
    mMediaSession = new MediaSessionCompat(this, LOG_TAG);

    // Other initialization such as setFlags, setCallback, etc.

    setSessionToken(mMediaSession.getSessionToken());
  }

  @Override
  public BrowserRoot onGetRoot(@NonNull String clientPackageName,
                               int clientUid, Bundle rootHints) {
    // Returning null == no one can connect so we'll return something
    return new BrowserRoot(
      getString(R.string.app_name), // Name visible in Android Auto
      null);                        // Bundle of optional extras
  }

  @Override
  public void onLoadChildren(String parentId,
    Result<List<MediaBrowserCompat.MediaItem>> result) {

    // If you want to allow users to browse media content your app returns on
    // Android Auto or Wear OS, return those results here.
    result.sendResult(new ArrayList<MediaBrowserServiceCompat.MediaItem>());
  }
}
```

Note that we initialize our Media Session within the Service's `onCreate` method rather than the playback Activity. The same should be done for all the media playback mechanisms described previously as we move control of media playback to this Service.

> **NOTE** *For more information on implementing the browsing APIs required for Android Auto support, see* `developer.android.com/training/auto/audio`.

Once your Media Browser Service has been constructed, in order for your Activities and other potential media playback clients to connect to it, you must add it, with a corresponding `android` `.media.browse.MediaBrowserService` Intent Filter to your manifest, as shown in Listing 17-7.

LISTING 17-7: Manifest entry for a Media Browser Service

```xml
<service android:name=".MediaPlaybackService"
         android:exported="true">
  <intent-filter>
    <action android:name="android.media.browse.MediaBrowserService" />
  </intent-filter>
</service>
```

Using a Media Browser to Connect Your Activity to a Media Browser Service

Once you've moved your Media Session to a Media Browser Service, it's important to ensure the media playback and control UI within your Activity is kept in sync.

While your Activity no longer has direct access to the underlying Media Player, your Activity can connect to your Media Browser Service, and create a new Media Controller using the `MediaBrowserCompat` API as shown in Listing 17-8.

LISTING 17-8: Connecting to your Media Browser Service from your Activity

```java
private MediaBrowserCompat mMediaBrowser;
private MediaControllerCompat mMediaController;

@Override
protected void onCreate(Bundle savedInstanceState) {
  super.onCreate(savedInstanceState);
  setContentView(R.layout.main_activity);

  // Create the MediaBrowserCompat
  mMediaBrowser = new MediaBrowserCompat(
    this,
    new ComponentName(this, MediaPlaybackService.class),
    new MediaBrowserCompat.ConnectionCallback() {
      @Override
      public void onConnected() {
        try {
          // We can construct a media controller from the session's token
          MediaSessionCompat.Token token = mMediaBrowser.getSessionToken();
          mMediaController = new MediaControllerCompat(
            MainActivity.this, token);
        } catch (RemoteException e) {
          Log.e(TAG, "Error creating controller", e);
        }
      }
    }
```

```
      @Override
      public void onConnectionSuspended() {
        // We were connected, but no longer are.
      }

      @Override
      public void onConnectionFailed() {
        // The attempt to connect failed completely.
        // Check the ComponentName!
      }
    },
    null);
  mMediaBrowser.connect();
}

@Override
protected void onDestroy() {
  super.onDestroy();
  mMediaBrowser.disconnect();
}
```

Within your Activity, you can now use the Media Controller to send media commands such as play and pause to the Media Session as described in the previous section. The Media Session will then, in turn, send your commands to the associated Media Browser Service.

The Media Controller also provides APIs for retrieving the Media Metadata and Playback State from the Media Session using the getMetadata and getPlaybackState methods, respectively.

To ensure your UI stays in sync with your Service, register a MediaControllerCompat.Callback using the registerCallback method on the Media Controller, as shown in Listing 17-9. This will ensure you receive a callback whenever the metadata or playback state changes, allowing you to keep your UI updated at all times.

LISTING 17-9: Keeping your UI in sync with playback state and metadata changes

```
@Override
public void onConnected() {
  try {
    // We can construct a media controller from the session's token
    MediaSessionCompat.Token token = mMediaBrowser.getSessionToken();
    mMediaController = new MediaControllerCompat(
      MainActivity.this, token);
    mMediaController.registerCallback(new MediaControllerCompat.Callback() {
      @Override
      public void onPlaybackStateChanged(PlaybackStateCompat state) {
        // Update the UI based on playback state change.
      }

      @Override
      public void onMetadataChanged(MediaMetadataCompat metadata) {
        // Update the UI based on Media Metadata change.
      }
```

```
        });

      } catch (RemoteException e) {
        Log.e(TAG, "Error creating controller", e);
      }
    }
```

Life Cycle of a Media Browser Service

When a Media Browser connects to your Media Browser Service, it binds to it—creating it if necessary. This allows you to prepare your media playback, and to minimize the latency between the user selecting media to play and hearing the audio. Note, however, that a bound service does not begin running until it's started.

Because we have decoupled the playback controls in our Activity from the Service that handles media playback, the Service will handle starting and stopping itself, based on the callbacks it receives from its Media Session, triggered when the Activity UI sends playback commands via the Media Controller.

In Listing 17-10, you can see how the Media Browser Service starts itself after receiving a play command, successfully gaining audio focus, and beginning media playback.

Once started, your Service will continue playback even if the playback Activity is closed. Once the Service receives the command to stop playback—from any source—it terminates itself using stopSelf.

LISTING 17-10: Starting playback on a Media Browser Service

```
mMediaSession.setCallback(new MediaSessionCompat.Callback() {
  @Override
  public void onPlay() {
    AudioManager am = (AudioManager) getSystemService(Context.AUDIO_SERVICE);

    // Request audio focus for playback
    int result = am.requestAudioFocus(focusChangeListener,
                            AudioManager.STREAM_MUSIC,
                            AudioManager.AUDIOFOCUS_GAIN);

    if (result == AudioManager.AUDIOFOCUS_REQUEST_GRANTED) {
      registerNoisyReceiver();
      mMediaSession.setActive(true);

      updateMetadata();
      updatePlaybackState();
      mediaPlayer.start();

      // Call startService to keep your Service alive during playback.
      startService(new Intent(MediaPlaybackService.this,
                          MediaPlaybackService.class));
    }
  }
```

```
      @Override
      public void onStop() {
        AudioManager am = (AudioManager) getSystemService(Context.AUDIO_SERVICE);
        am.abandonAudioFocus();

        updatePlaybackState();
        mMediaSession.setActive(false);
        mediaPlayer.stop();

        // Then call stopSelf to allow your service to be destroyed
        // now that playback has stopped
        stopSelf();
      }
    });
```

Similarly, if your playback Activity is closed by the user *before* media playback is started, your Service would be destroyed. This ensures that your app is not unnecessarily taking up resources in the background when there is no media being played.

Playing Audio as a Foreground Service

As described in Chapter 11, "Working in the Background," by default, Services run in the background and can be killed to free resources as needed. Interruptions in audio playback is very noticeable to users, so it's good practice to give your Service foreground priority when you begin media playback, to minimize the possibility of interrupted playback.

> **NOTE** *Foreground Services require an associated Notification to be visible while running. The following section, "Creating Media Style Notifications," provides details on how to build a Notification tailored for a Media Playback Service.*

Your Service should only maintain foreground priority when it is actively playing audio, as described by the following process:

1. Call `startForeground` (passing in a Media Style Notification) when you begin media playback.

2. Call `stopForeground(false)` when playback is paused to remove the foreground status, but maintain the notification.

3. Call `stopForeground(true)` when playback has stopped, to remove the foreground status and remove the notification.

This flow can be seen in Listing 17-11, which updates Listing 17-10 to set the started Service as a foreground Service.

LISTING 17-11: Using a foreground Service for media playback

```java
mMediaSession.setCallback(new MediaSessionCompat.Callback() {
  @Override
  public void onPlay() {
    AudioManager am = (AudioManager)getSystemService(Context.AUDIO_SERVICE);

    // Request audio focus for playback
    int result = am.requestAudioFocus(focusChangeListener,
              AudioManager.STREAM_MUSIC,
              AudioManager.AUDIOFOCUS_GAIN);

    if (result == AudioManager.AUDIOFOCUS_REQUEST_GRANTED) {
      registerNoisyReceiver();
      mMediaSession.setActive(true);

      updateMetadata();
      updatePlaybackState();
      mediaPlayer.start();

      // Construct a Media Style Notification and start the foreground Service
      startForeground(NOTIFICATION_ID, buildMediaNotification());
    }
  }

  @Override
  public void onPause() {
    unregisterNoisyReceiver();
    updatePlaybackState();
    mediaPlayer.pause();

    // Stop being a foreground service, but don't remove the notification
    stopForeground(false);
  }

  @Override
  public void onStop() {
    AudioManager am = (AudioManager) getSystemService(Context.AUDIO_SERVICE);
    am.abandonAudioFocus();

    updatePlaybackState();
    mMediaSession.setActive(false);
    mediaPlayer.stop();

    // Stop being a foreground service and remove the notification
    stopForeground(true);

    // Then call stopSelf to allow your service to be destroyed
    // now that playback has stopped
    stopSelf();
  }
}
```

Creating Media Style Notifications

Notifications are one of the most convenient, and therefore frequently used, mechanisms for users to control media playback.

As described in Chapter 11, Android provides a number of templates or "styles" for notifications—with the MediaStyle specifically designed for controlling media playback.

Media Style Notifications embed the media playback controls directly within the Notification, making it possible for users to control media playback in both the collapsed and expanded form of the Notification, as shown in Figure 17-1.

FIGURE 17-1

You construct your Notification using the NotificationCompat.Builder. The primary source for constructing your Notification is the media metadata available from your Media Session; this ensures a consistent display of media information across all mechanisms (including Wear OS and Android Auto).

Use the getDescription method to extract the title, subtitle, description, and icon from the Media Metadata, and pass each into the corresponding set methods on the Notification Builder.

You can specify which (if any) playback controls should appear in the collapsed mode using setShowActionsInCompactView.

It is important that you also pass the token associated with your Media Session into setMediaSession or actions taken on Wear OS devices will not be received by your app.

Listing 17-12 shows the creation of a typical Media Style Notification.

LISTING 17-12: Building a Media Style Notification

```
public Notification buildMediaNotification() {
  MediaControllerCompat controller = mMediaSession.getController();
  MediaMetadataCompat mediaMetadata = controller.getMetadata();
  MediaDescriptionCompat description = mediaMetadata.getDescription();

  NotificationCompat.Builder builder = new
                              NotificationCompat.Builder(context);

  // Add description metadata from the media session
  builder
    .setContentTitle(description.getTitle())
    .setContentText(description.getSubtitle())
    .setSubText(description.getDescription())
    .setLargeIcon(description.getIconBitmap())
    .setContentIntent(controller.getSessionActivity())
    .setDeleteIntent(MediaButtonReceiver.buildMediaButtonPendingIntent(
```

continues

LISTING 17-12 *(continued)*

```
      this, // Context
      PlaybackStateCompat.ACTION_STOP))
    .setVisibility(NotificationCompat.VISIBILITY_PUBLIC);

  // Add branding from your app
  builder
    .setSmallIcon(R.drawable.notification_icon)
    .setColor(ContextCompat.getColor(this, R.color.primary));

  // Add actions
  builder
    .addAction(new NotificationCompat.Action(
      R.drawable.pause, getString(R.string.pause),
      MediaButtonReceiver.buildMediaButtonPendingIntent(
        this, PlaybackStateCompat.ACTION_PLAY_PAUSE)))
    .addAction(new NotificationCompat.Action(
      R.drawable.skip_to_next, getString(R.string.skip_to_next),
      MediaButtonReceiver.buildMediaButtonPendingIntent(
        this, PlaybackStateCompat.ACTION_SKIP_TO_NEXT)));

  // Add the MediaStyle
  builder
    .setStyle(new NotificationCompat.MediaStyle()
    .setShowActionsInCompactView(0)
    .setMediaSession(mMediaSession.getSessionToken())

    // These two lines are only required if your minSdkVersion is <API 21
    .setShowCancelButton(true)
    .setCancelButtonIntent(MediaButtonReceiver.buildMediaButtonPendingIntent(
      this, PlaybackStateCompat.ACTION_STOP)));

  return builder.build();
}
```

> **NOTE** *For versions of Android prior to Android 7.0 (API Level 24), the color set with* `setColor` *was used as the background color for the entire notification. Make sure text is readable and the color is not too bright; your primary dark color is typically a good choice.*

When a Notification, or any of its associated controls, is selected by the user, it fires Pending Intents that must be handled by your application. This can be done using the `MediaButtonReceiver` from the Android Support Library, and its `buildMediaButtonPendingIntent` method.

Add the `MediaButtonReceiver` to your manifest:

```
<receiver android:name="android.support.v4.media.session.MediaButtonReceiver" >
  <intent-filter>
```

```
    <action android:name="android.intent.action.MEDIA_BUTTON" />
  </intent-filter>
</receiver>
```

Within your Media Browser Service implementation, call the `MediaButtonReceiver`'s `handleIntent` method in the `onStartCommand` handler:

```
@Override
public int onStartCommand(Intent intent, int flags, int startId) {
  MediaButtonReceiver.handleIntent(mMediaSession, intent);
  return super.onStartCommand(intent, flags, startId);
}
```

This technique will route Notification commands into your Media Session and Media Controller, allowing you to handle them as you would playback controls within your Activity.

USING THE MEDIA RECORDER TO RECORD AUDIO

Most Android devices have a microphone and, in many cases, multiple microphones to ensure clear audio input (important for legacy device uses such as "making phone calls"). The microphone is also available to Android apps that hold the `RECORD_AUDIO` permission:

```
<uses-permission android:name="android.permission.RECORD_AUDIO"/>
```

> **NOTE** *For privacy reasons, the* `RECORD_AUDIO` *permission is considered a* dangerous *permission. It must be requested at run time on devices running Android 6.0 (API Level 23) or higher.*

You can use the `MediaRecorder` class to record audio files that can be used in your own applications or added to the Media Store.

The Media Recorder lets you specify the audio source, the output file format, and the audio encoders to use when recording your file.

Much like the Media Player, the Media Recorder manages recording as a state machine. This means that the order in which you configure and manage the Media Recorder is important. In the simplest terms, the transitions through the state machine can be described as follows:

1. Create a new Media Recorder.

2. Specify the input sources to record from.

3. Specify the output format and audio encoder.

4. Select an output file.

5. Prepare the Media Recorder for recording.

6. Record.

7. End the recording.

> **NOTE** *A more detailed and thorough description of the Media Recorder state machine is provided at the Android developer site, at* `developer.android.com/reference/android/media/MediaRecorder.html`.

When you finish recording your media, call `release` on your Media Recorder object to free the associated resources:

```
mediaRecorder.release();
```

Configuring the Audio Recorder

As described in the preceding section, before recording you must specify the input source, choose the output format and audio encoder, and assign an output file—in that order.

The `setAudioSource` method lets you specify a `MediaRecorder.AudioSource.static` constant that defines the audio source. For audio recording, this is almost always `MediaRecorder.AudioSource.MIC`.

After selecting your input source, you need to select the output format using the `setOutputFormat` method with a `MediaRecorder.OutputFormat` constant, and use the `setAudioEncoder` methods with an audio encoder constant from the `MediaRecorder.AudioEncoder` class.

Finally, assign a file to store the recorded media using the `setOutputFile` method before calling `prepare`.

Listing 17-13 shows how to configure a Media Recorder to record audio from the microphone and save it to a file in your application's external media folder (which makes it available to other apps).

LISTING 17-13: Preparing to record audio using the Media Recorder

```
// Configure the input sources.
mediaRecorder.setAudioSource(MediaRecorder.AudioSource.MIC);

// Set the output format and encoder.
mediaRecorder.setOutputFormat(MediaRecorder.OutputFormat.THREE_GPP);
mediaRecorder.setAudioEncoder(MediaRecorder.AudioEncoder.AMR_NB);

// Specify the output file
File mediaDir = getExternalMediaDirs()[0];
File outputFile = new File(getExternalMediaDirs()[0], "myaudiorecording.3gp");
mediaRecorder.setOutputFile(outputFile.getPath());

// Prepare to record
mediaRecorder.prepare();
```

> **WARNING** *The* `setOutputFile` *method must be called before* `prepare` *and after* `setOutputFormat`*; otherwise, it will throw an* `IllegalStateException`*.*

Controlling the Recording

After configuring the Media Recorder and preparing, you can begin recording at any time by calling the `start` method:

```
mediaRecorder.start();
```

When you finish recording, call `stop` to end the playback, followed by `reset` and `release` to free the Media Recorder resources, as shown in Listing 17-14.

LISTING 17-14: Stopping an audio recording

```
mediaRecorder.stop();

// Reset and release the media recorder.
mediaRecorder.reset();
mediaRecorder.release();
```

The resulting file can then be played with a `MediaPlayer`, as described earlier in this chapter.

USING THE CAMERA FOR TAKING PICTURES

With the quality and capabilities of camera hardware available on Android devices improving dramatically, taking full advantage of that hardware can be an important differentiator for apps using the camera.

The following sections demonstrate the ways in which you can configure and control the camera, and to take photos programmatically within your applications.

Using Intents to Take Pictures

The easiest way to take a picture from within your application is to fire an Intent using the `MediaStore.ACTION_IMAGE_CAPTURE` action:

```
startActivityForResult(
    new Intent(MediaStore.ACTION_IMAGE_CAPTURE), TAKE_PICTURE);
```

This launches a camera application to take the photo, providing your users with the full suite of camera functionality without you having to rewrite the native camera application yourself.

> **NOTE** *This Intent is not intended to be used as a fallback if the user denies the* CAMERA *permission in your app. Users declining a permission is a clear signal that they don't want your app to use this feature, and you must respect that.*

Once users are satisfied with the image, the result is returned to your application within the Intent received by the onActivityResult handler.

By default, the picture taken will be returned as a thumbnail, available as a raw bitmap within the data extra within the returned Intent.

To obtain a full image, you must specify a target URI in which to store it using the MediaStore .EXTRA_OUTPUT extra in the launch Intent, as shown in Listing 17-15.

LISTING 17-15: Requesting a full-size picture using an Intent

```
// Create an output file.
File outputFile = new File(
  context.getExternalFilesDir(Environment.DIRECTORY_PICTURES),
                            "test.jpg");
Uri outputUri = FileProvider.getUriForFile(context,
  BuildConfig.APPLICATION_ID + ".files", outputFile);

// Generate the Intent.
Intent intent = new Intent(MediaStore.ACTION_IMAGE_CAPTURE);
intent.putExtra(MediaStore.EXTRA_OUTPUT, outputUri);

// Launch the camera app.
startActivityForResult(intent, TAKE_PICTURE);
```

The full-size image taken by the camera will then be saved to the specified location. No thumbnail will be returned in the Activity result callback, and the received Intent's data will be null.

Listing 17-16 shows how to use getParcelableExtra to extract a thumbnail where one is returned, or to decode the saved file when a full-size image is saved.

LISTING 17-16: Receiving pictures from an Intent

```
@Override
protected void onActivityResult(int requestCode,
                                int resultCode, Intent data) {
  if (requestCode == TAKE_PICTURE) {
    // Check if the result includes a thumbnail Bitmap
    if (data != null) {
      if (data.hasExtra("data")) {
        Bitmap thumbnail = data.getParcelableExtra("data");
        imageView.setImageBitmap(thumbnail);
      }
```

```
      } else {
        // If there is no thumbnail image data, the image
        // will have been stored in the target output URI.

        // Resize the full image to fit in our image view.
        int width = imageView.getWidth();
        int height = imageView.getHeight();

        BitmapFactory.Options factoryOptions = new
          BitmapFactory.Options();

        factoryOptions.inJustDecodeBounds = true;
        BitmapFactory.decodeFile(outputFile.getPath(),
                                 factoryOptions);

        int imageWidth = factoryOptions.outWidth;
        int imageHeight = factoryOptions.outHeight;

        // Determine how much to scale down the image
        int scaleFactor = Math.min(imageWidth/width,
                                   imageHeight/height);

        // Decode the image file into a Bitmap sized to fill the View
        factoryOptions.inJustDecodeBounds = false;
        factoryOptions.inSampleSize = scaleFactor;

        Bitmap bitmap =
          BitmapFactory.decodeFile(outputFile.getPath(),
                                   factoryOptions);

        imageView.setImageBitmap(bitmap);
      }
    }
  }
```

To make photos you save available to other applications, it's good practice to add them to the Media Store—as described in the section "Adding Media to the Media Store."

Controlling the Camera Directly

To access the camera hardware directly, you need to add the CAMERA permission to your application manifest:

```
<uses-permission android:name="android.permission.CAMERA"/>
```

> **NOTE** *For privacy reasons, the* CAMERA *permission is considered a* dangerous *permission; as such it must be requested at run time on Android 6.0 (API Level 23) and higher devices.*

The `CameraManager` allows you to enumerate all of the connected cameras, query their characteristics, and open one or more camera devices:

```
CameraManager cameraManager =
   (CameraManager) getSystemService(Context.CAMERA_SERVICE);
```

You can retrieve the list of identifiers for the currently connected camera devices using `getCameraIdList`:

```
String[] cameraIds = cameraManager.getCameraIdList();
```

Android 5.0 (API Level 21) introduced the Camera2 API, which replaced the now deprecated Camera API. For the remainder of this chapter, we will focus on the features provided within the Camera2 API, meaning the required API Level to use these features is 21.

Camera Characteristics

Each camera device has a set of immutable properties called the *characteristics* of the device. These characteristics are stored using the `CameraCharacteristics` class, accessible by calling the `getCameraCharacteristics` method of `CameraManager` and passing in the camera's identifier:

```
CameraCharacteristics characteristics =
   cameraManager.getCameraCharacteristics(cameraId);
```

The Camera Characteristics contain the capabilities of the camera device, including the direction of the lens, auto-exposure modes, auto-focus modes, focal lengths, noise reduction modes, and the ISO sensitivity range.

Use the `LENS_FACING` characteristic to determine if a given camera faces the back, front, or if the camera is external to the device, as shown in Listing 17-17.

LISTING 17-17: Determining the direction of a camera device

```
int facing = characteristics.get(CameraCharacteristics.LENS_FACING);
if (facing == CameraCharacteristics.LENS_FACING_BACK) {
  // back camera
} else if (facing == CameraCharacteristics.LENS_FACING_FRONT) {
  // front camera
} else {
  // external cameraCameraCharacteristics.LENS_FACING_EXTERNAL
}
```

This information is extremely useful in selecting the appropriate camera and rotating any taken pictures as needed (for example, the front-facing camera is mirrored).

Other Camera Characteristics include:

➤ `SCALER_STREAM_CONFIGURATION_MAP`—Returns a `StreamConfigurationMap`, which stores the output formats and sizes supported by this camera that you can use to set the appropriate preview size and image capture size.

➤ `CONTROL_AF_AVAILABLE_MODES`—Returns the auto-focus modes that are available where `CONTROL_AF_MODE_OFF` means unavailable and `CONTROL_AF_MODE_CONTINUOUS_PICTURE` and `CONTROL_AF_MODE_CONTINUOUS_VIDEO` would be appropriate for picture or video capture, respectively.

➤ SENSOR_ORIENTATION—Returns the orientation of the sensor that the output image needs to be rotated to be upright on the device screen in its native orientation. This will always be a multiple of 90.

You can find the full list of Camera Characteristics on the Android developer documentation: developer.android.com/reference/android/hardware/camera2/CameraCharacteristics .html

Opening a Connection to a Camera Device

To take a picture you must open a connection to the camera device you wish to use. Once you've identified a camera to use, open a connection with the openCamera method of CameraManager, as shown in Listing 17-18.

Opening a camera is an asynchronous operation, so openCamera also takes a CameraDevice .StateCallback in addition to the cameraId associated with the camera you want to open.

The onOpened callback is returned when the connection is open, and you have access to a CameraDevice ready for use. Make sure you override onError and onDisconnected to properly handle error cases.

LISTING 17-18: Opening a camera device

```java
CameraDevice.StateCallback cameraDeviceCallback =
  new CameraDevice.StateCallback() {

  @Override
  public void onOpened(@NonNull CameraDevice camera) {
    mCamera = camera;
  }

  @Override
  public void onDisconnected(@NonNull CameraDevice camera) {
    camera.close();
    mCamera = null;
  }

  @Override
  public void onError(@NonNull CameraDevice camera, int error) {
    // Something went wrong, tell the user
    camera.close();
    mCamera = null;
    Log.e(TAG, "Camera Error: " + error);
  }
};

try {
  cameraManager.openCamera(cameraId, cameraDeviceCallback, null);
} catch (Exception e) {
  Log.e(TAG, "Unable to open the camera", e);
}
```

Camera Capture Requests and the Camera Preview

Once you have an open connection to a `CameraDevice`, you can request image data by creating a `CameraCaptureSession`.

The Android Camera2 API offers a number of different session types and configurations, including high-speed (120fps) video recording, but the most common session type can be created using the `createCaptureSession` method.

Creating a session is an expensive operation, often taking hundreds of milliseconds as the camera hardware is powered on and configured to handle the `List` of `Surface` objects that will receive the camera output. You must make sure each Surface is set to the appropriate size (using the values from the `SCALER_STREAM_CONFIGURATION_MAP` characteristic) before creating your session.

At a minimum, you should display a preview of what's being captured by the camera to allow users to compose their photos. The camera preview is typically displayed on a `SurfaceView` within your UI hierarchy.

> **NOTE** *Prior to Android 7.0 (API Level 24), each* `SurfaceView` *was rendered in its own window, separately from the rest of your UI. As a result, unlike View-derived classes it could not be moved, transformed, or animated. As an alternative for earlier platform versions, the* `TextureView` *class offers support for these operations, but is less battery-efficient.*

To display a preview, you must implement a `SurfaceHolder.Callback` that listens for the construction of a valid Surface (and ideally set its size with `setFixedSize`):

```
SurfaceHolder.Callback surfaceHolderCallback = new SurfaceHolder.Callback() {
  @Override
  public void surfaceCreated(SurfaceHolder holder) {
    startCameraCaptureSession();
  }

  @Override
  public void surfaceDestroyed(SurfaceHolder holder) {}

  @Override
  public void surfaceChanged(SurfaceHolder holder, int format,
                             int width, int height) {}
};

mHolder.addCallback(surfaceHolderCallback);
mHolder.setFixedSize(400, 300);

try {
  cameraManager.openCamera(cameraId, cameraDeviceCallback, null);
} catch (Exception e) {
  Log.e(TAG, "Unable to open the camera", e);
}
```

Once your session is configured and you receive a callback to onConfigured, you can proceed to display data by passing in a CaptureRequest to setRepeatingRequest, which indicates that you'd like to repeatedly capture new frames.

The Camera Device's createCaptureRequest method allows you to retrieve a CaptureRequest .Builder based on a number of predefined templates. For a display preview, you'd use CameraDevice.TEMPLATE_PREVIEW and use addTarget with the same Surface you used to create your session:

```java
CameraCaptureSession mCaptureSession;
CaptureRequest mPreviewCaptureRequest;

private void startCameraCaptureSession() {
  // We require both the surface and camera to be ready
  if (mCamera == null || mHolder.isCreating()) {
    return;
  }

  Surface previewSurface = mHolder.getSurface();

  // Create our preview CaptureRequest.Builder
  mPreviewCaptureRequest = mCamera.createCaptureRequest(
    CameraDevice.TEMPLATE_PREVIEW);
  mPreviewCaptureRequest.setTarget(previewSurface);

  CameraCaptureSession.StateCallback captureSessionCallback
    = new CameraCaptureSession.StateCallback() {

    @Override
    public void onConfigured(@NonNull CameraCaptureSession session) {
      mCaptureSession = session;
      try {
        mCaptureSession.setRepeatingRequest(
          mPreviewCaptureRequest.build(),
          null,  // optional CaptureCallback
          null); // optional Handler
      } catch (CameraAccessException | IllegalStateException e) {
        Log.e(TAG, "Capture Session Exception", e);
        // Handle failures
      }
    }
  };

  try {
    mCamera.createCaptureSession(Arrays.asList(previewSurface),
      captureSessionCallback,
      null); // optional Handler
  } catch (CameraAccessException e) {
    Log.e(TAG, "Camera Access Exception", e);
  }
}
```

While the template `CaptureRequest.Builder` provides a set of common defaults, this is also where you can set the auto-focus mode (`CaptureRequest.CONTROL_AF_MODE`) or flash mode (`CaptureRequest.CONTROL_AE_MODE_ON` and `CaptureRequest.FLASH_MODE`) with `set` making sure to only use values returned by the Camera Characteristics. Note that you will need to call `setRepeatingRequest` again after changing the Capture Request values.

Taking a Picture

Displaying a camera preview is an expected feature of any camera app, but it's normally not sufficient. If you want to take the extra step and take a picture, you'll need to pass in an additional Surface when creating your capture session.

This Surface can be created with the help of `ImageReader`, which provides a `Surface` that can be used with a `CameraDevice.TEMPLATE_STILL_CAPTURE` Capture Request and the `capture` method that returns the raw bytes captured by the camera.

Listing 17-19 shows the skeleton code for taking a picture and saving the JPEG image to external storage.

LISTING 17-19: Taking a picture

```
private ImageReader mImageReader;
private ImageReader.onImageAvailableListener mOnImageAvailableListener;

@Override
public void onCreate(Bundle savedInstanceState) {
  super.onCreate(savedInstanceState);

  SurfaceHolder.Callback surfaceHolderCallback = new SurfaceHolder.Callback() {
    @Override
    public void surfaceCreated(SurfaceHolder holder) {
      startCameraCaptureSession();
    }

    @Override
    public void surfaceDestroyed(SurfaceHolder holder) {}

    @Override
    public void surfaceChanged(SurfaceHolder holder, int format,
                               int width, int height) {}
  };

  mHolder.addCallback(surfaceHolderCallback);
  mHolder.setFixedSize(400, 300);

  int largestWidth = 400;  // Read from characteristics
  int largestHeight = 300; // Read from characteristics

  mOnImageAvailableListener
      = new ImageReader.OnImageAvailableListener() {
    @Override
```

```java
    public void onImageAvailable(ImageReader reader) {
      try (Image image = reader.acquireNextImage()) {
        Image.Plane[] planes = image.getPlanes();
        if (planes.length > 0) {
          ByteBuffer buffer = planes[0].getBuffer();
          byte[] data = new byte[buffer.remaining()];
          buffer.get(data);
          saveImage(data);
        }
      }
    }
  };
  mImageReader = ImageReader.newInstance(largestWidth, largestHeight,
    ImageFormat.JPEG,
    2); // maximum number of images to return
  mImageReader.setOnImageAvailableListener(mOnImageAvailableListener,
    null); // optional Handler

  try {
    cameraManager.openCamera(cameraId, cameraDeviceCallback, null);
  } catch (Exception e) {
    Log.e(TAG, "Unable to open the camera", e);
  }
}

private void takePicture() {
  try {
    CaptureRequest.Builder takePictureBuilder = mCamera.createCaptureRequest(
      CameraDevice.TEMPLATE_STILL_CAPTURE);
    takePictureBuilder.addTarget(mImageReader.getSurface());
    mCaptureSession.capture(takePictureBuilder.build(),
      null, // CaptureCallback
      null); // optional Handler
  } catch (CameraAccessException e) {
    Log.e(TAG, "Error capturing the photo", e);
  }
}

private void saveImage(byte[] data) {
  // Save the image JPEG data to external storage
  FileOutputStream outStream = null;
  try {
    File outputFile = new File(
        getExternalFilesDir(Environment.DIRECTORY_PICTURES), "test.jpg");
    outStream = new FileOutputStream(outputFile);
    outStream.write(data);
    outStream.close();
  } catch (FileNotFoundException e) {
    Log.e(TAG, "File Not Found", e);
  } catch (IOException e) {
    Log.e(TAG, "IO Exception", e);
  }
}
```

Reading and Writing JPEG EXIF Image Details

The `ExifInterface` class provides mechanisms for you to read and modify the Exchangeable Image File Format (EXIF) metadata stored within a JPEG file. Create a new `ExifInterface` instance by passing the full filename of the target JPEG in to the constructor:

```
ExifInterface exif = new ExifInterface(jpegfilename);
```

EXIF data is used to store a wide range of metadata on photographs, including date and time, camera settings (such as make and model), and image settings (such as aperture and shutter speed), as well as image descriptions and locations.

To read an EXIF attribute, call `getAttribute` on the `ExifInterface` object, passing in the name of the attribute to read. The `Exifinterface` class includes a number of static `TAG_` constants that can be used to access common EXIF metadata. To modify an EXIF attribute, use `setAttribute`, passing in the name of the attribute to read and the value to set it to.

Listing 17-20 shows how to read the camera model from a file stored on the external storage, before modifying the camera manufacturer details.

LISTING 17-20: Reading and modifying EXIF data

```
File file = new File(getExternalFilesDir(Environment.DIRECTORY_PICTURES),
    "test.jpg");

try {
  ExifInterface exif = new ExifInterface(file.getCanonicalPath());
  // Read the camera model
  String model = exif.getAttribute(ExifInterface.TAG_MODEL);
  Log.d(TAG, "Model: " + model);
  // Set the camera make
  exif.setAttribute(ExifInterface.TAG_MAKE, "My Phone");
  // Finally, call saveAttributes to save the updated tag data
  exif.saveAttributes();
} catch (IOException e) {
  Log.e(TAG, "IO Exception", e);
}
```

RECORDING VIDEO

Android offers two options for recording video within your application.

The simplest technique is to use an Intent to launch the video camera application. This option lets you specify the output location and video recording quality, while letting another video recording application handle the user experience and error handling. This is the best practice approach and should be used in most circumstances, unless you are building your own replacement video recorder.

In cases where you want to replace the default video camera application, or simply need more fine-grained control over the video capture UI or recording settings, you can use the `MediaRecorder` class.

Using Intents to Record Video

The easiest, and best practice, way to initiate video recording is using the `MediaStore.ACTION_VIDEO_CAPTURE` action Intent.

Starting a new Activity with this Intent launches a video recorder app that's capable of allowing users to start, stop, review, and retake their video. When they're satisfied, a URI to the recorded video is provided to your Activity as the data parameter of the returned Intent:

A video capture action Intent can contain the following three optional extras:

➤ `MediaStore.EXTRA_OUTPUT`—By default, the video recorded by the video capture action will be stored in the default Media Store. If you want to record it elsewhere, you can specify an alternative URI using this extra.

➤ `MediaStore.EXTRA_VIDEO_QUALITY`—The video capture action allows you to specify an image quality using an integer value. There are currently two possible values: 0 for low (MMS) quality videos, or 1 for high (full resolution) videos. By default, the high-resolution mode is used.

➤ `MediaStore.EXTRA_DURATION_LIMIT`—The maximum length of the recorded video (in seconds).

Listing 17-21 shows how to use the video capture action to record a new video.

LISTING 17-21: Recording video using an Intent

```
private static final int RECORD_VIDEO = 0;

private void startRecording() {
  // Generate the Intent.
  Intent intent = new Intent(MediaStore.ACTION_VIDEO_CAPTURE);

  // Launch the camera app.
  startActivityForResult(intent, RECORD_VIDEO);
}

@Override
protected void onActivityResult(int requestCode,
                                int resultCode, Intent data) {
  if (requestCode == RECORD_VIDEO) {
    VideoView videoView = findViewById(R.id.videoView);
    videoView.setVideoURI(data.getData());
    videoView.start();
  }
}
```

Using the Media Recorder to Record Video

Recording a video within your app uses the same basic framework as displaying a camera preview and taking a picture. However, instead of using an `ImageReader` to read a single image, the

MediaRecorder class is used to record video files with audio that can be used in your own applications or added to the Media Store.

In addition to the CAMERA permission needed to access the camera, your application manifest needs to include the RECORD_AUDIO and/or RECORD_VIDEO permissions:

```
<uses-permission android:name="android.permission.RECORD_AUDIO"/>
<uses-permission android:name="android.permission.RECORD_VIDEO"/>
<uses-permission android:name="android.permission.CAMERA"/>
```

> **NOTE** *For privacy reasons, the* CAMERA, RECORD_AUDIO, *and* RECORD_VIDEO *permissions are both considered* dangerous *permissions, and as such must be requested at run time on Android 6.0 (API Level 23) and higher devices.*

The Media Recorder state machine described in the "Using the Media Recorder to Record Audio" also applies to video recording. To add video recording, you must set the video source with setVideoSource and set the video encoder with setVideoEncoder before setting the output file, as shown in Listing 17-22.

LISTING 17-22: Preparing to record video using the Media Recorder

```java
public void prepareMediaRecorder() {
    // Configure the input sources.
    mediaRecorder.setAudioSource(MediaRecorder.AudioSource.MIC);
    mediaRecorder.setVideoSource(MediaRecorder.VideoSource.SURFACE);

    // Set the output format and encoder.
    mediaRecorder.setOutputFormat(MediaRecorder.OutputFormat.MPEG_4);
    mediaRecorder.setAudioEncoder(MediaRecorder.AudioEncoder.AAC);
    mediaRecorder.setVideoEncoder(MediaRecorder.VideoEncoder.H264);

    // Specify the output file
    File mediaDir = getExternalMediaDirs()[0];
    File outputFile = new File(mediaDir, "myvideorecording.mp4");
    mediaRecorder.setOutputFile(outputFile.getPath());

    // Prepare to record
    mediaRecorder.prepare();
}
```

Because video recording is a continuous operation, it functions very similarly to setting up the camera preview, but instead of creating a CameraCaptureSession and CaptureRequest that only outputs to a single Surface representing the camera display, you also output to the MediaRecorder's Surface, which can be retrieved via getSurface.

It's best practice to use the `CameraDevice.TEMPLATE_RECORD` template when you create your `CaptureRequest`. Once the `CaptureRequest` is started with `setRepeatingRequest`, you can start recording video by calling `start` on your `MediaRecorder`, as shown in Listing 17-23.

LISTING 17-23: Recording video

```
MediaRecorder mMediaRecorder = new MediaRecorder();
CaptureRequest.Builder mVideoRecordCaptureRequest;

void startVideoRecording() {
  // We require both the preview surface and camera to be ready
  if (mCamera == null || mHolder.isCreating()) {
    return;
  }

  Surface previewSurface = mHolder.getSurface();

  prepareMediaRecorder();

  Surface videoRecordSurface = mediaRecorder.getSurface();

  // Create our video record CaptureRequest.Builder
  mVideoRecordCaptureRequest = mCamera.createCaptureRequest(
      CameraDevice.TEMPLATE_RECORD);
  // Add both the video record Surface and the preview Surface
  mVideoRecordCaptureRequest.addTarget(videoRecordSurface);
  mVideoRecordCaptureRequest.addTarget(previewSurface);

  CameraCaptureSession.StateCallback captureSessionCallback
    = new CameraCaptureSession.StateCallback() {
    @Override
    public void onConfigured(@NonNull CameraCaptureSession session) {
      mCaptureSession = session;
      try {
        mCaptureSession.setRepeatingRequest(
          mVideoRecordCaptureRequest.build(),
          null, // optional CaptureCallback
          null); // optional Handler

        mediaRecorder.start();
      } catch (CameraAccessException | IllegalStateException e) {
        // Handle failures
      }
    }

    @Override
    public void onConfigureFailed(@NonNull CameraCaptureSession session) {
      // Handle failures
    }
  };
```

```
      try {
        mCamera.createCaptureSession(
          Arrays.asList(previewSurface, videoRecordSurface),
          captureSessionCallback,
          null); // optional Handler
      } catch (CameraAccessException e) {
        Log.e(TAG, "Camera Access Exception", e);
      }
    }
```

When recording is stopped, you must call `stop` and `reset` on the `MediaRecorder`. You should then start a new `CameraCaptureSession` for continuing to display the preview until a new video recording is started. This ensures that the camera output is no longer sent to the Media Recorder's Surface and allows you to set a new output file for the next video.

When you finish recording, or previewing, all videos (typically in `onStop`), call `release` on your `MediaRecorder` to free the associated resources:

```
    mediaRecorder.release();
```

ADDING MEDIA TO THE MEDIA STORE

By default, media files created by your application that are stored in private application folders will be unavailable to other applications, with the exception of the files added to the `getExternalMediaDirs` directories.

To make files in other folders visible, you need to insert them into the Media Store. Android provides two options for this. The preferred approach is to use the Media Scanner to interpret your file and insert it automatically. Alternatively, you can manually insert a new record in the appropriate Content Provider.

Inserting Media Using the Media Scanner

If you have recorded new media of any kind, the `MediaScannerConnection` class provides the `scanFile` method as a simple way for you to add it to the Media Store without needing to construct the full record for the Media Store Content Provider.

Before you can use the `scanFile` method to initiate a content scan on your file, you must call `connect` and wait for the connection to the Media Scanner to complete. This call is asynchronous, so you will need to implement a `MediaScannerConnectionClient` to notify you when the connection has been made. You can use this same class to notify you when the scan is complete, at which point you can disconnect your Media Scanner Connection.

Listing 17-24 shows the skeleton code for creating a new `MediaScannerConnectionClient` that defines a `MediaScannerConnection`, which is used to add a new file to the Media Store.

```java
private void mediaScan(final String filePath) {

  MediaScannerConnectionClient mediaScannerClient = new
    MediaScannerConnectionClient() {

    private MediaScannerConnection msc = null;

    {
      msc = new MediaScannerConnection(
        VideoCameraActivity.this, this);
      msc.connect();
    }

    public void onMediaScannerConnected() {
      // Optionally specify a MIME Type, or
      // have the Media Scanner imply one based
      // on the filename.
      String mimeType = null;
      msc.scanFile(filePath, mimeType);
    }

    public void onScanCompleted(String path, Uri uri) {
      msc.disconnect();
      Log.d(TAG, "File Added at: " + uri.toString());
    }
  };
}
```

Inserting Media Manually

Rather than relying on the Media Scanner, you can add new media to the Media Store directly by creating a new ContentValues object and inserting it into the appropriate Media Store Content Provider yourself.

The metadata you specify here can include the title, timestamp, and geocoding information for your new media file:

```java
ContentValues content = new ContentValues(3);
content.put(Audio.AudioColumns.TITLE, "TheSoundandtheFury");
content.put(Audio.AudioColumns.DATE_ADDED,
            System.currentTimeMillis() / 1000);
content.put(Audio.Media.MIME_TYPE, "audio/amr");
```

You must also specify the absolute path of the media file being added:

```java
content.put(MediaStore.Audio.Media.DATA, "/sdcard/myoutputfile.mp4");
```

Get access to the application's `ContentResolver`, and use it to insert this new row into the Media Store:

```
ContentResolver resolver = getContentResolver();
Uri uri = resolver.insert(MediaStore.Video.Media.EXTERNAL_CONTENT_URI,
                          content);
```

After inserting the media file into the Media Store, you should announce its availability using a Broadcast Intent, as follows:

```
sendBroadcast(new Intent(Intent.ACTION_MEDIA_SCANNER_SCAN_FILE, uri));
```

18

Communicating with Bluetooth, NFC, and Wi-Fi Peer-to-Peer

WHAT'S IN THIS CHAPTER?

- ➤ Managing the local Bluetooth adapter
- ➤ Discovering Bluetooth client devices
- ➤ Transferring data using Bluetooth and Bluetooth LE
- ➤ Discovering Wi-Fi Direct Peer-to-Peer devices
- ➤ Transferring data using Wi-Fi Peer-to-Peer
- ➤ Scanning NFC tags
- ➤ Transferring data using Android Beam

WROX.COM CODE DOWNLOADS FOR THIS CHAPTER

The code downloads for this chapter are found at www.wrox.com. The code for this chapter is divided into the following major example:

- ➤ Snippets_ch18.zip

NETWORKING AND PEER-TO-PEER COMMUNICATION

This chapter explores Android's hardware communications features by examining the Bluetooth, Wi-Fi Peer-to-Peer, Near Field Communication (NFC), and Android Beam APIs.

The Android SDK includes a full Bluetooth stack, which enables you to manage and monitor your Bluetooth settings, control discoverability, discover nearby Bluetooth devices, and use

Bluetooth as a proximity-based peer-to-peer transport layer for your applications using Bluetooth and Bluetooth LE (Low Energy).

For situations requiring faster or higher-bandwidth data transfers, Wi-Fi Peer-To-Peer (or Wi-Fi Direct) offers a solution for peer-to-peer communication between two or more devices over Wi-Fi without the need of an intermediary access point.

Android also provides support for NFC, including reading smart tags, and using Android Beam to communicate directly between two NFC-enabled Android devices.

TRANSFERRING DATA USING BLUETOOTH

Bluetooth is a communications protocol designed for short-range, low-bandwidth peer-to-peer communications.

Using the Bluetooth APIs you can search for, and connect to, other Bluetooth devices within range. By initiating a communications link using Bluetooth Sockets, you can then transmit and receive streams of data between devices from within your applications.

> **NOTE** *At the time of writing, only encrypted communication is supported between devices, meaning that you can form connections only between devices that have been paired.*

Managing the Local Bluetooth Device Adapter

The local Bluetooth adapter is controlled via the `BluetoothAdapter` class, which represents the host Android device on which your application is running.

To access the default Bluetooth Adapter, call `getDefaultAdapter`, as shown in Listing 18-1. Some Android devices feature multiple Bluetooth adapters, though it is currently only possible to access the default device.

LISTING 18-1: Accessing the default Bluetooth Adapter

```
BluetoothAdapter bluetooth = BluetoothAdapter.getDefaultAdapter();
```

The Bluetooth Adapter offers methods for reading and setting properties of the local Bluetooth hardware.

To read any of the local Bluetooth Adapter properties, initiate discovery, or find bonded devices, you need to include the `BLUETOOTH` permission in your application manifest:

```
<uses-permission android:name="android.permission.BLUETOOTH"/>
```

Bluetooth scans can be used to gather information about the user's current location, so use of Bluetooth also requires the ACCESS_COARSE_LOCATION or ACCESS_FINE_LOCATION permissions to be declared in your manifest:

```
<uses-permission android:name="android.permission.ACCESS_COARSE_LOCATION"/>
```

You must also request at least one location permission at runtime, as described in Chapter 15.

To modify any of the local device properties, the BLUETOOTH_ADMIN permission is also required:

```
<uses-permission android:name="android.permission.BLUETOOTH_ADMIN"/>
```

The Bluetooth Adapter properties can be read and changed only if the Bluetooth Adapter is currently turned on—that is, if its device state is enabled.

Use the isEnabled method to confirm the device is enabled, after which you can access the Bluetooth Adapter's *friendly name* (an arbitrary string that users can set to identify a particular device) and hardware address, using the getName and getAddress methods, respectively:

```
if (bluetooth.isEnabled()) {
  String address = bluetooth.getAddress();
  String name = bluetooth.getName();
}
```

If the device is off, these methods will return null.

If you have the BLUETOOTH_ADMIN permission, you can change the friendly name of the Bluetooth Adapter using the setName method:

```
bluetooth.setName("Blackfang");
```

To find a more detailed description of the current Bluetooth Adapter state, use the getState method, which will return one of the following BluetoothAdapter constants:

- ➤ STATE_TURNING_ON
- ➤ STATE_ON
- ➤ STATE_TURNING_OFF
- ➤ STATE_OFF

If Bluetooth is currently disabled, you can request the user enable it by using the BluetoothAdapter.ACTION_REQUEST_ENABLE static constant as a startActivityForResult action:

```
startActivityForResult(
  new Intent(BluetoothAdapter.ACTION_REQUEST_ENABLE), ENABLE_BLUETOOTH);
```

Figure 18-1 shows the resulting system dialog.

Use the result code parameter returned in the onActivityResult handler of your Activity to determine the success of this request, as shown in Listing 18-2.

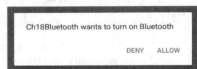

FIGURE 18-1

LISTING 18-2: Enabling Bluetooth

```
private BluetoothAdapter mBluetooth;
private static final int ENABLE_BLUETOOTH = 1;

private void initBluetooth() {
  if (!mBluetooth.isEnabled()) {
    // Bluetooth isn't enabled, prompt the user to turn it on.
    Intent intent = new Intent(BluetoothAdapter.ACTION_REQUEST_ENABLE);
    startActivityForResult(intent, ENABLE_BLUETOOTH);
  } else {
    // Bluetooth is enabled, initialize the UI.
    initBluetoothUI();
  }
}

protected void onActivityResult(int requestCode,
                                int resultCode, Intent data) {
  if (requestCode == ENABLE_BLUETOOTH)
    if (resultCode == RESULT_OK) {
      // Bluetooth has been enabled, initialize the UI.
      initBluetoothUI();
    }
}
```

Being Discoverable and Remote Device Discovery

The process of two devices finding each other to connect is called *discovery*. Before you can establish a Bluetooth Socket for communications, the local Bluetooth Adapter must bond with the remote device. Before two devices can bond and connect, they first need to discover each other.

> **NOTE** *Although the Bluetooth protocol supports ad-hoc connections for data transfer, this mechanism is not currently available in Android. Android Bluetooth communication is currently supported only between bonded devices.*

Making Your Device Discoverable

For another Android device to find your local Bluetooth Adapter during a discovery scan, you need to ensure that your Bluetooth Adapter is discoverable. Discoverability is indicated by the scan mode, found using the getScanMode method on the BluetoothAdapter object.

It will return one of the following BluetoothAdapter constants:

➤ SCAN_MODE_CONNECTABLE_DISCOVERABLE—Inquiry scan and page scan are both enabled, meaning that the device is discoverable from any Bluetooth device performing a discovery scan.

➤ SCAN_MODE_CONNECTABLE—Page scan is enabled but inquiry scan is not. This means that devices that have previously connected and bonded to the local device's Bluetooth Adapter can find it now, but new devices can't discover it.

> ➤ SCAN_MODE_NONE—Discoverability is turned off. No remote devices can find the local Bluetooth Adapter.

For privacy reasons, Android devices will default to having discoverability disabled. To turn on discovery, you need to obtain explicit permission from the user; you do this by starting a new Activity using the ACTION_REQUEST_DISCOVERABLE action, as shown in Listing 18-3.

LISTING 18-3: Enabling discoverability

```
private static final int DISCOVERY_REQUEST = 2;

private void enable_discovery() {
  startActivityForResult(
    new Intent(BluetoothAdapter.ACTION_REQUEST_DISCOVERABLE),
    DISCOVERY_REQUEST);
}
```

By default, discoverability will be enabled for 2 minutes. You can modify this setting by adding an EXTRA_DISCOVERABLE_DURATION extra to the launch Intent, specifying the number of seconds you want discoverability to last.

The user will be prompted by a system dialog, as shown in Figure 18-2, to turn on discoverability for the specified duration.

To learn if the user has allowed or rejected your discovery request, override the onActivityResult handler, as shown in Listing 18-4. The returned resultCode parameter indicates the duration of discoverability, or the RESULT_CANCELED constant if the user has rejected the request.

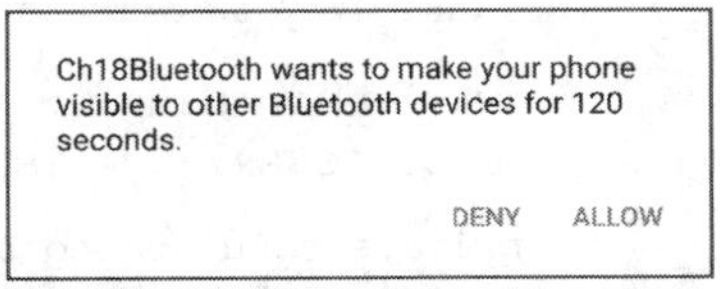

Ch18Bluetooth wants to make your phone visible to other Bluetooth devices for 120 seconds.

DENY   ALLOW

FIGURE 18-2

LISTING 18-4: Monitoring discoverability request approval

```
@Override
protected void onActivityResult(int requestCode,
                                int resultCode, Intent data) {
  if (requestCode == DISCOVERY_REQUEST) {
    if (resultCode == RESULT_CANCELED) {
      Log.d(TAG, "Discovery canceled by user.");
    }
  }
}
```

Discovering Remote Devices

Once a device has been made discoverable, it can then be discovered by another device. To discover a new device, initiate a discovery scan from your local Bluetooth Adapter.

> **NOTE** *The discovery process can take some time to complete (up to 12 seconds). During this time, performance of your Bluetooth Adapter communications will be seriously degraded. Use the techniques in this section to check and monitor the discovery status of the Bluetooth Adapter, and avoid doing high-bandwidth Bluetooth operations (including connecting to a new remote Bluetooth Device) while discovery is in progress.*

Knowledge of which Bluetooth Device's are nearby may provide information that can be used to determine the user's current location. Accordingly, you must include the ACCESS_COARSE_LOCATION permission in the application manifest and request it as a runtime permission before performing device discovery.

You can check if the local Bluetooth Adapter is already performing a discovery scan by using the isDiscovering method.

To initiate the discovery process, call startDiscovery on the Bluetooth Adapter:

```
if (mBluetooth.isEnabled() && !mBluetooth.isDiscovering())
  mBluetooth.startDiscovery();
```

The discovery process is asynchronous. Android broadcasts Intents to notify you of the start and end of discovery, as well as notifying you of remote devices discovered during the scan.

You can monitor changes in the discovery process by creating Broadcast Receivers to listen for the ACTION_DISCOVERY_STARTED and ACTION_DISCOVERY_FINISHED Broadcast Intents:

```
private void monitorDiscovery() {
  registerReceiver(discoveryMonitor,
    new IntentFilter(BluetoothAdapter.ACTION_DISCOVERY_STARTED));
  registerReceiver(discoveryMonitor,
    new IntentFilter(BluetoothAdapter.ACTION_DISCOVERY_FINISHED));
}

BroadcastReceiver discoveryMonitor = new BroadcastReceiver() {
  @Override
  public void onReceive(Context context, Intent intent) {
    if (BluetoothAdapter.ACTION_DISCOVERY_STARTED
        .equals(intent.getAction())) {
      // Discovery has started.
      Log.d(TAG, "Discovery Started...");
    }
    else if (BluetoothAdapter.ACTION_DISCOVERY_FINISHED
            .equals(intent.getAction())) {
      // Discovery has completed.
      Log.d(TAG, "Discovery Complete.");
    }
  }
};
```

Discovered Bluetooth Devices are returned via Broadcast Intents using the ACTION_FOUND broadcast action.

As shown in Listing 18-5, each Broadcast Intent includes the name of the remote device in an extra indexed as `BluetoothDevice.EXTRA_NAME`, and an immutable representation of the remote Bluetooth Device as a `BluetoothDevice` Parcelable object stored under the `BluetoothDevice.EXTRA_DEVICE` extra.

LISTING 18-5: Discovering remote Bluetooth Devices

```
private BluetoothAdapter mBluetooth;
private List<BluetoothDevice> deviceList = new ArrayList<>();

private void startDiscovery() {
  if (ContextCompat.checkSelfPermission(this,
    Manifest.permission.ACCESS_COARSE_LOCATION)
    == PackageManager.PERMISSION_GRANTED) {

    mBluetooth = BluetoothAdapter.getDefaultAdapter();

    registerReceiver(discoveryResult,
                    new IntentFilter(BluetoothDevice.ACTION_FOUND));

    if (mBluetooth.isEnabled() && !mBluetooth.isDiscovering()) {
      deviceList.clear();
      mBluetooth.startDiscovery();
    }
  }
  else
    ActivityCompat.requestPermissions(this,
      new String[]{Manifest.permission.ACCESS_COARSE_LOCATION},
      REQUEST_ACCESS_COARSE_LOCATION);
}

BroadcastReceiver discoveryResult = new BroadcastReceiver() {
  @Override
  public void onReceive(Context context, Intent intent) {
    String remoteDeviceName =
      intent.getStringExtra(BluetoothDevice.EXTRA_NAME);

    BluetoothDevice remoteDevice =
      intent.getParcelableExtra(BluetoothDevice.EXTRA_DEVICE);

    deviceList.add(remoteDevice);

    Log.d(TAG, "Discovered " + remoteDeviceName);
  }
};
```

Each `BluetoothDevice` object returned through the discovery broadcasts represents a remote Bluetooth Device that has been discovered.

The discovery process consumes significant resources, so you should be sure to cancel a discovery in progress using the `cancelDiscovery` method, prior to attempting to connect with any discovered devices.

Bluetooth Communications

The Android Bluetooth communications APIs are wrappers around RFCOMM, the Bluetooth radio frequency communications protocol. RFCOMM supports RS232 serial communication over the Logical Link Control and Adaptation Protocol (L2CAP) layer.

In practice, this alphabet soup provides a mechanism for opening communication sockets between two paired Bluetooth devices.

> **NOTE** *Before your application can communicate between devices, the devices must be paired (bonded). If you attempt to connect two unpaired devices, the users will be prompted to pair them before the connection is established.*

You can establish an RFCOMM communication channel for bidirectional communications using the following classes:

➤ `BluetoothServerSocket`—Used to establish a listening socket for initiating a link between devices. To establish a handshake, one device acts as a server to listen for, and accept, incoming connection requests.

➤ `BluetoothSocket`—Used to create a new client to connect to a listening Bluetooth Server Socket. Also returned by the Bluetooth Server Socket after a connection is established. Once a connection is established, Bluetooth Sockets are used by both the server and client to transfer data streams.

When creating an application that uses Bluetooth as a peer-to-peer transport layer across devices, you'll need to implement both a Bluetooth Server Socket to listen for connections and a Bluetooth Socket to initiate a new channel and handle communications.

When connected, the Bluetooth Server Socket returns a `BluetoothSocket` that can be used to send and receive data. This server-side Bluetooth Socket is used in exactly the same way as the client socket. The designations of *server* and *client* are relevant only to how the connection is established; they don't affect how data flows after that connection is made.

Opening a Bluetooth Server Socket Listener

A Bluetooth Server Socket is used to listen for incoming Bluetooth Socket connection requests from remote Bluetooth Devices. In order for two Bluetooth Devices to be connected, one must act as a server (listening for and accepting incoming requests) and the other as a client (initiating the request to connect to the server). After the two are connected, the communications between the server and host device are handled through a `BluetoothSocket` instance at both ends.

To have your Bluetooth Adapter act as a server, call its `listenUsingRfcommWithServiceRecord` method to listen for incoming connection requests. Pass in a name to identify this server, along with a universally unique identifier (UUID):

```
String name = "mybluetoothserver";
UUID uuid = UUID.randomUUID();
```

```
final BluetoothServerSocket btserver =
  bluetooth.listenUsingRfcommWithServiceRecord(name, uuid);
```

The method will return a `BluetoothServerSocket` object—note that the client Bluetooth Socket that is to connect to this server will need to know the server's UUID in order to connect.

Call `accept` on the Server Socket, optionally passing in a timeout duration, to have it start listening for connections. The Server Socket will now block until a remote Bluetooth Socket client with a matching UUID attempts to connect:

```
// Block until client connection established.
BluetoothSocket serverSocket = btserver.accept();
```

If a connection request is made from a remote device that is not yet paired with the local Bluetooth Adapter, the users on each devices will be prompted to accept a pairing request before the accept call returns. This prompt is made via a Notification, as shown in Figure 18-3.

FIGURE 18-3

If an incoming connection request is successful, `accept` will return a Bluetooth Socket connected to the client device. You can use this socket to transfer data, as shown later in this section.

> **WARNING** *Note that* `accept` *is a blocking operation, so it's important to listen for incoming connection requests on a background thread rather than block the UI thread until a connection has been made.*

It's also important to note that your Bluetooth Adapter must be discoverable for remote Bluetooth Devices to connect to it. Listing 18-6 shows some typical skeleton code that uses the `ACTION_REQUEST_DISCOVERABLE` broadcast to request that the device be made discoverable, before listening for incoming connection requests for the returned discoverability duration.

LISTING 18-6: Listening for Bluetooth Socket connection requests

```
private BluetoothAdapter mBluetooth;
private BluetoothSocket mBluetoothSocket;

private UUID startServerSocket() {
  UUID uuid = UUID.randomUUID();
  String name = "bluetoothserver";

  mBluetooth = BluetoothAdapter.getDefaultAdapter();
  try {
    final BluetoothServerSocket btserver =
      mBluetooth.listenUsingRfcommWithServiceRecord(name, uuid);

    Thread acceptThread = new Thread(new Runnable() {
      public void run() {
        try {
```

LISTING 18-6 *(continued)*

```
                // Block until client connection established.
                mBluetoothSocket = btserver.accept();
                // Start listening for messages.
                listenForMessages();
            } catch (IOException e) {
                Log.e(TAG, "Server connection IO Exception", e);
            }
        }
    });
    acceptThread.start();
  } catch (IOException e) {
    Log.e(TAG, "Socket listener IO Exception", e);
  }
  return uuid;
}

private void listenForMessages() {
  // TODO Listen for messages between sockets.
}
```

Selecting Remote Bluetooth Devices for Communications

To create a client-side Bluetooth Socket, you utilize a `BluetoothDevice` object that represents the target remote server.

You can obtain a reference to a remote Bluetooth Device in a number of ways, with some important caveats regarding the devices with which you can create a communications link.

For a Bluetooth Socket to establish a connection to a remote Bluetooth Device, the following conditions must be true:

➤ The remote device must be discoverable.

➤ The remote device must be accepting connections through a Bluetooth Server Socket.

➤ The local and remote devices must be paired (bonded). If the devices are not paired, the users of each device will be prompted to pair them when the connection request is initiated.

Bluetooth Device objects are proxies that represent remote devices. You can query them for the properties of the remote devices they represent, and to initiate Bluetooth Socket connections.

You have several ways to obtain `BluetoothDevices` in code. In each case you should check to ensure that the device you intend to connect to is discoverable and (optionally) determine whether you are bonded to it. If you can't discover the remote device, you should prompt the user to enable discoverability on it.

You learned one technique for finding discoverable Bluetooth Devices earlier in this section. Using the `startDiscovery` method and monitoring `ACTION_FOUND` broadcasts allows you to receive Broadcast Intents that include a `BluetoothDevice.EXTRA_DEVICE` extra containing the discovered Bluetooth Device.

You can also use the `getRemoteDevice` method on your local Bluetooth Adapter, specifying the hardware address of the remote Bluetooth Device you want to connect to:

```
BluetoothDevice device = mBluetooth.getRemoteDevice("01:23:97:35:2F:AA");
```

This is particularly useful when you know the hardware address of the target device, such as when using a technology such as Android Beam to share this information between devices.

To find the set of currently paired devices, call `getBondedDevices` on the local Bluetooth Adapter. You can query the returned set to find out if the target Bluetooth Device is already paired with the local Bluetooth Adapter:

```
Set<BluetoothDevice> bondedDevices = mBluetooth.getBondedDevices();

if (bondedDevices.contains(knownDevice)) {
  // TODO Target device is bonded / paired with the local device.
}
```

Opening a Client Bluetooth Socket Connection

To initiate a communications channel with a remote device, create a Bluetooth Socket by calling `createRfcommSocketToServiceRecord` on the Bluetooth Device object representing the target remote device, passing in the UUID of the corresponding open Bluetooth Server Socket listener.

The returned Bluetooth Socket can then be used to initiate the connection with a call to `connect`, as shown in Listing 18-7.

> **NOTE** *Note that* `connect` *is a blocking operation, so connection requests must be initiated on a background thread rather than block the UI thread until a connection has been made.*

LISTING 18-7: Creating a client Bluetooth Socket

```java
private BluetoothSocket mBluetoothSocket;

private void connectToServerSocket(BluetoothDevice device, UUID uuid) {
  try{
    BluetoothSocket clientSocket
      = device.createRfcommSocketToServiceRecord(uuid);

    // Block until server connection accepted.
    clientSocket.connect();

    // Add a reference to the socket used to send messages.
    mBluetoothSocket = clientSocket;

    // Start listening for messages.
    listenForMessages();
  } catch (IOException e) {
    Log.e(TAG, "Bluetooth client I/O Exception.", e);
  }
}
```

If you attempt to connect to a Bluetooth Device that has not yet been paired (bonded) with the host device, the users will be prompted to accept a pairing request on both the server and client devices before the `connect` (and `accept`) calls return.

Transmitting Data Using Bluetooth Sockets

After a connection has been established, you will have an open Bluetooth Socket on both the client and the server devices. From this point onward there is no significant distinction between them; you can send and receive data using the Bluetooth Socket on either device.

Data transfer across Bluetooth Sockets is handled via `InputStream` and `OutputStream` objects, which you can obtain from a Bluetooth Socket using the appropriately named `getInputStream` and `getOutputStream` methods, respectively.

Listing 18-8 shows two simple skeleton methods—the first used to send a string to a remote device using an Output Stream, and the second to listen for incoming strings using an Input Stream. The same technique can be used to transfer any streamable data.

LISTING 18-8: Sending and receiving strings using Bluetooth Sockets

```
private void sendMessage(BluetoothSocket socket, String message) {
  OutputStream outputStream;

  try {
    outputStream = socket.getOutputStream();

    // Add a stop character.
    byte[] byteArray = (message + " ").getBytes();
    byteArray[byteArray.length-1] = 0;

    outputStream.write(byteArray);
  } catch (IOException e) {
    Log.e(TAG, "Failed to send message: " + message, e);
  }
}

private boolean mListening = false;

private String listenForMessages(BluetoothSocket socket,
                                 StringBuilder incoming) {
  String result = "";
  mListening = true;

  int bufferSize = 1024;
  byte[] buffer = new byte[bufferSize];

  try {
    InputStream instream = socket.getInputStream();
    int bytesRead = -1;

    while (mListening) {
      bytesRead = instream.read(buffer);
```

```
      if (bytesRead != -1) {
        while ((bytesRead == bufferSize) &&
               (buffer[bufferSize-1] != 0)) {
          result = result + new String(buffer, 0, bytesRead - 1);
          bytesRead = instream.read(buffer);
        }
        result = result + new String(buffer, 0, bytesRead - 1);
        incoming.append(result);
      }
    }
  } catch (IOException e) {
    Log.e(TAG, "Message receive failed.", e);
  }
  return result;
}
```

Bluetooth Profiles

In addition to the generic approach described in the previous section, the Bluetooth API also includes *profiles*. Profiles provide a specialized interface for communicating between devices of specific types and purposes. The Android Bluetooth API includes support for the following profiles:

➤ **Headset**—Facilitates communication between the host device and Bluetooth headsets via the `BluetoothHeadset` class.

➤ **A2DP**—The Advanced Audio Distribution Profile (A2DP) profile facilitates the streaming of high-quality audio between devices via the `BluetoothA2dp` class.

➤ **Health Device**—The Bluetooth Health Device Profile (HDP) lets you communicate with health devices such as heart-rate monitors.

To utilize a profile within your app, call `getProfileProxy` on your Bluetooth Adapter, passing in a `BluetoothProfile.ServiceListener` implementation. When the corresponding remote device connects, the Service Listener's `onServiceConnected` handler will be triggered, providing a proxy object that can be used to interact with the remote device:

```
private BluetoothAdapter mBluetooth;
private BluetoothHeadset mBluetoothHeadset;

private BluetoothProfile.ServiceListener mProfileListener =
  new BluetoothProfile.ServiceListener() {

  public void onServiceConnected(int profile, BluetoothProfile proxy) {
    if (profile == BluetoothProfile.HEADSET) {
      mBluetoothHeadset = (BluetoothHeadset) proxy;
      // TODO Utilize proxy to interact with the remote headset.
    }
  }

  public void onServiceDisconnected(int profile) {
    if (profile == BluetoothProfile.HEADSET) {
      // TODO Stop using proxy to interact with remote headset.
      mBluetoothHeadset = null;
```

```
      }
    }
  };

  private void connectHeadsetProfile () {
    // Get the default adapter
    mBluetooth = BluetoothAdapter.getDefaultAdapter();

    // Establish connection to the proxy.
    mBluetooth.getProfileProxy(this, mProfileListener,
                               BluetoothProfile.HEADSET);
  }

  private void closeHeadsetProxy() {
    // Close proxy connection after use.
    mBluetooth.closeProfileProxy(BluetoothProfile.HEADSET, mBluetoothHeadset);
  }
```

Once connected, you can utilize vendor-specific AT commends to control the remote device, and correspondingly register to receive system broadcasts of vendor-specific AT commands sent by the device.

Additional detail on how to utilize each of these profiles with different hardware implementations are beyond the scope of this book.

Bluetooth Low Energy

Bluetooth Low Energy (BLE) is designed to provide similar functionality to regular Bluetooth, but with significantly less power consumption. BLE is optimized for transferring small amounts of data between nearby devices, making it ideal for interaction between an Android device and low-power devices such as proximity sensors, heart-rate monitors, and fitness devices.

Unlike classic Bluetooth, where each device can be considered a peer, BLE connections are based around a central device that looks for peripheral devices, and the peripherals that advertise their existence.

As a result, peripheral devices require a central device to communicate with—they can't communicate with each other directly.

To connect your device to BLE peripherals, the BLE APIs use the same Bluetooth Adapter described in the previous sections for classic Bluetooth communications. To search for peripherals, use getBluetoothLeScanner to receive a BluetoothLeScanner object, and begin a scan for BLE devices by calling startScan, passing in a ScanCallback implementation:

```
  private void leScan() {
    mBluetooth.getBluetoothLeScanner().startScan(scanCallback);
  }

  // Device scan callback.
  private ScanCallback scanCallback =
    new ScanCallback() {
```

```
      @Override
      public void onScanResult(int callbackType, ScanResult result) {
        BluetoothDevice device = result.getDevice();
      }
    };
```

The onScanResult handler receives a ScanResult object that can be queried for the Bluetooth Device object you'll use to interact with the discovered remote BLE peripheral.

Once you've discovered peripherals, connections and communications are coordinated through the use of Generic Attribute Profiles (GATT). The Bluetooth SIG defines many profiles for Low Energy devices, where each profile specifies how each device works to fulfill a profile's requirements.

As such, each GATT profile defines a specification for sending and receiving *attributes* between BLE devices. Each attribute is optimized for size, and is formatted as *characteristics* and *services*.

Each *characteristic* is a single value with optional descriptors that describe a characteristic value (such as by providing a description, acceptable range, or a unit of measure) that is specific to a characteristic's value.

A *service* is a collection of one or more characteristics that fully describe the functionality provided by the peripheral device—for example, a "Heart Rate Monitor" service would include a "heart rate measurement" characteristic.

A comprehensive list of existing GATT-based profiles and services is available at www.bluetooth .com/specifications/gatt/services.

To connect to a discovered peripheral, call connectGatt passing in a BluetoothGattCallback implementation:

```
BluetoothGatt mBluetoothGatt;

private void connectToGattServer(BluetoothDevice device) {
  mBluetoothGatt = device.connectGatt(this, false, mGattCallback);
}

private final BluetoothGattCallback mGattCallback =
  new BluetoothGattCallback() {
};
```

The returned BluetoothGatt instance can be used to execute GATT operations on the peripheral device, while overriding the onConnectionStateChanged handler allows you to track when the connection has successfully been made, at which point you can use the discoverServices method to query the device for available GATT services:

```
@Override
public void onConnectionStateChange(BluetoothGatt gatt,
                                    int status, int newState) {
  super.onConnectionStateChange(gatt, status, newState);
  if (newState == BluetoothProfile.STATE_CONNECTED) {
    mBluetoothGatt.discoverServices();
  } else if (newState == BluetoothProfile.STATE_DISCONNECTED) {
    Log.d(TAG, "Disconnected from GATT server.");
  }
}
```

The services query is returned through the `onServicesDiscovered` handler:

```
@Override
public void onServicesDiscovered(BluetoothGatt gatt, int status) {
  super.onServicesDiscovered(gatt, status);
  for (BluetoothGattService service: gatt.getServices()) {
   Log.d(TAG, "Service: " + service.getUuid());
    for (BluetoothGattCharacteristic characteristic :
          service.getCharacteristics()) {
      Log.d(TAG, "Value: " + characteristic.getValue());
      for (BluetoothGattDescriptor descriptor :
            characteristic.getDescriptors()) {
        Log.d(TAG, descriptor.getValue().toString());
      }
    }
  }
  // TODO New services have been discovered.
}
```

The preceding snippet iterates over each of the characteristics for each service available on the BLE peripheral. For most peripherals, the values for each characteristic are likely to change over time; rather than poll each value, it's good practice to request notification when a particular characteristic changes using the `setCharacteristicNotification` method on the Bluetooth Gatt proxy object, passing in the characteristic to be monitored:

```
mBluetoothGatt.setCharacteristicNotification(characteristic, enabled);
```

Notifications for modified values are delivered to the `onCharacteristicChanged` callback within your Bluetooth Gatt Callback:

```
@Override
public void onCharacteristicChanged(BluetoothGatt gatt,
              BluetoothGattCharacteristic characteristic) {
  super.onCharacteristicChanged(gatt, characteristic);
  // TODO An updated value has been received for a characteristic.
}
```

Once your app has finished interacting with a BLE device, call `close` on its Bluetooth Gatt proxy object to allow the system to recover its resources:

```
mBluetoothGatt.close();
```

TRANSFERRING DATA USING WI-FI PEER-TO-PEER

Wi-Fi Peer-to-Peer (P2P), compatible with the Wi-Fi Direct communications protocol, is designed for medium-range, high-bandwidth peer-to-peer communications via Wi-Fi without an intermediate access point. Compared to Bluetooth, Wi-Fi Peer-to-Peer is faster, more reliable, and works over greater distances.

Using the Wi-Fi P2P APIs, you can search for, and connect to, other Wi-Fi P2P devices within range. By initiating a communications link using sockets, you can then transmit and receive streams of data between supported devices (including some printers, scanners, cameras, and televisions) and between instances of your application running on different devices without needing to connect to the same network.

As a high-bandwidth alternative to Bluetooth, Wi-Fi P2P is particularly suitable for operations such as media sharing and live media streaming.

Initializing the Wi-Fi Peer-to-Peer Framework

To use Wi-Fi P2P, your application requires the following manifest permissions:

```
<uses-permission android:name="android.permission.CHANGE_NETWORK_STATE" />
<uses-permission android:name="android.permission.ACCESS_NETWORK_STATE" />
<uses-permission android:name="android.permission.ACCESS_WIFI_STATE"/>
<uses-permission android:name="android.permission.CHANGE_WIFI_STATE"/>
<uses-permission android:name="android.permission.INTERNET"/>
```

Wi-Fi Direct connections are initiated and managed using the `WifiP2pManager` system service:

```
wifiP2pManager =
  (WifiP2pManager)getSystemService(Context.WIFI_P2P_SERVICE);
```

Before you can use the Wi-Fi P2P Manager, you must create a channel to the Wi-Fi Direct framework using the Wi-Fi P2P Manager's `initialize` method. Pass in the current Context, the Looper on which to receive Wi-Fi Direct events, and a `ChannelListener` to listen for the loss of your channel connection, as shown in Listing 18-9.

LISTING 18-9: Initializing Wi-Fi Direct

```
private WifiP2pManager mWifiP2pManager;
private WifiP2pManager.Channel mWifiDirectChannel;

private void initializeWiFiDirect() {
  mWifiP2pManager
    = (WifiP2pManager)getSystemService(Context.WIFI_P2P_SERVICE);

  mWifiDirectChannel = mWifiP2pManager.initialize(this, getMainLooper(),
    new WifiP2pManager.ChannelListener() {
      public void onChannelDisconnected() {
        Log.d(TAG, "Wi-Fi P2P channel disconnected.");
      }
    }
  );
}
```

You will use the returned Wi-Fi P2P Channel whenever you interact with the Wi-Fi P2P framework, so initializing the Wi-Fi P2P Manager is done within the `onCreate` handler of your Activity.

Most actions performed using the Wi-Fi P2P Manager (such as peer discovery and connection attempts) will immediately indicate their success (or failure) using an `ActionListener`, as shown in Listing 18-10. When successful, the return values associated with those actions are obtained by receiving Broadcast Intents, as described in the following sections.

LISTING 18-10: Creating a Wi-Fi P2P Manager Action Listener

```
private ActionListener actionListener = new ActionListener() {
  public void onFailure(int reason) {
    String errorMessage = "WiFi Direct Failed: ";
    switch (reason) {
      case WifiP2pManager.BUSY :
        errorMessage += "Framework busy."; break;
      case WifiP2pManager.ERROR :
        errorMessage += "Internal error."; break;
      case WifiP2pManager.P2P_UNSUPPORTED :
        errorMessage += "Unsupported."; break;
      default:
        errorMessage += "Unknown error."; break;
    }
    Log.e(TAG, errorMessage);
  }

  public void onSuccess() {
    // Success!
    // Return values will be returned using a Broadcast Intent
  }
};
```

You can monitor the Wi-Fi P2P status by registering a Broadcast Receiver that receives the
`WifiP2pManager.WIFI_P2P_STATE_CHANGED_ACTION` action:

```
IntentFilter p2pEnabledFilter = new
    IntentFilter(WifiP2pManager.WIFI_P2P_STATE_CHANGED_ACTION);

registerReceiver(p2pStatusReceiver, p2pEnabledFilter);
```

The Intent received by the associated Broadcast Receiver, as shown in Listing 18-11, will include a
`WifiP2pManager.EXTRA_WIFI_STATE` extra that will be set to either `WIFI_P2P_STATE_ENABLED` or
`WIFI_P2P_STATE_DISABLED`.

LISTING 18-11: Receiving a Wi-Fi Direct status change

```
BroadcastReceiver p2pStatusReceiver = new BroadcastReceiver() {
  @Override
  public void onReceive(Context context, Intent intent) {
    int state = intent.getIntExtra(
      WifiP2pManager.EXTRA_WIFI_STATE,
      WifiP2pManager.WIFI_P2P_STATE_DISABLED);

    switch (state) {
      case (WifiP2pManager.WIFI_P2P_STATE_ENABLED):
        // TODO Enable discovery option in the UI.
        buttonDiscover.setEnabled(true);
```

```
            break;
        default:
            // TODO Disable discovery option in the UI.
            buttonDiscover.setEnabled(false);
        }
    }
};
```

Within the `onReceive` handler, you can modify your UI accordingly based on the change in state.

After creating a channel to the Wi-Fi P2P framework and enabling Wi-Fi P2P on the host and its peer device(s), you can begin the process of discovering and connecting to peers.

Discovering Peers

To initiate a scan for peers, call the Wi-Fi P2P Manager's `discoverPeers` method, passing in the active channel and an Action Listener. Changes to the peer list will be broadcast as Intents using the `WifiP2pManager.WIFI_P2P_PEERS_CHANGED_ACTION` action. Peer discovery will remain active until a connection is established or peer discovery is cancelled.

When you receive an Intent notifying you of a change to the peer list, you can request the current list of discovered peers using the `WifiP2pManager.requestPeers` method, as shown in Listing 18-12.

LISTING 18-12: Discovering Wi-Fi Direct peers

```
private void discoverPeers() {
  IntentFilter intentFilter
    = new IntentFilter(WifiP2pManager.WIFI_P2P_PEERS_CHANGED_ACTION);
  registerReceiver(peerDiscoveryReceiver, intentFilter);
  mWifiP2pManager.discoverPeers(mWifiDirectChannel, actionListener);
}

BroadcastReceiver peerDiscoveryReceiver = new BroadcastReceiver() {
  @Override
  public void onReceive(Context context, Intent intent) {
    mWifiP2pManager.requestPeers(mWifiDirectChannel,
      new WifiP2pManager.PeerListListener() {
        public void onPeersAvailable(WifiP2pDeviceList peers) {
          // TODO Update UI with new list of peers.
        }
      });
  }
};
```

The `requestPeers` method accepts a `PeerListListener` whose `onPeersAvailable` handler will execute when the peer list has been retrieved. The list of peers will be available as a `WifiP2pDeviceList`, which you can then query to find the name and address of all the available peer devices.

Connecting with Peers

To form a Wi-Fi P2P connection with a peer device, use the Wi-Fi P2P Manager's `connect` method, passing in the active channel, an Action Listener, and a `WifiP2pConfig` object that specifies the address of a peer from our Wi-Fi P2P Device List to connect to, as shown in Listing 18-13.

LISTING 18-13: Requesting a connection to a Wi-Fi Direct peer

```
private void connectTo(WifiP2pDevice peerDevice) {
  WifiP2pConfig config = new WifiP2pConfig();
  config.deviceAddress = peerDevice.deviceAddress;

  mWifiP2pManager.connect(mWifiDirectChannel, config, actionListener);
}
```

When you attempt to establish a connection, the remote device will be prompted to accept it. On Android devices this requires the user to manually accept the connection request using the dialog shown in Figure 18-4.

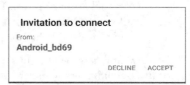

FIGURE 18-4

If the device accepts the connection request, the successful connection is broadcast on *both* devices using the `WifiP2pManager` `.WIFI_P2P_CONNECTION_CHANGED_ACTION` Intent action.

The Broadcast Intent will include a `NetworkInfo` object parceled within the `WifiP2pManager` `.EXTRA_NETWORK_INFO` extra. You can query the Network Info to confirm whether the change in connection status represents a new connection or a disconnection:

```
NetworkInfo networkInfo
  = (NetworkInfo)intent.getParcelableExtra(WifiP2pManager.EXTRA_NETWORK_INFO);
boolean connected = networkInfo.isConnected();
```

In the former case, you can request further details on the connection using the `WifiP2pManager` `.requestConnectionInfo` method, passing in the active channel and a `ConnectionInfoListener`, as shown in Listing 18-14.

LISTING 18-14: Connecting to a Wi-Fi Direct peer

```
BroadcastReceiver connectionChangedReceiver = new BroadcastReceiver() {
  @Override
  public void onReceive(Context context, Intent intent) {
    // Extract the NetworkInfo
    String extraKey = WifiP2pManager.EXTRA_NETWORK_INFO;
    NetworkInfo networkInfo =
      (NetworkInfo)intent.getParcelableExtra(extraKey);

    // Check if we're connected
    if (networkInfo.isConnected()) {
```

```
mWifiP2pManager.requestConnectionInfo(mWifiDirectChannel,
  new WifiP2pManager.ConnectionInfoListener() {
    public void onConnectionInfoAvailable(WifiP2pInfo info) {
      // If the connection is established
      if (info.groupFormed) {
        // If we're the server
        if (info.isGroupOwner) {
          // TODO Initiate server socket.
        }
        // If we're the client
        else if (info.groupFormed) {
          // TODO Initiate client socket.
        }
      }
    }
  });
} else {
  Log.d(TAG, "Wi-Fi Direct Disconnected.");
}
}
};
```

The `ConnectionInfoListener` will fire its `onConnectionInfoAvailable` handler when the connection details become available, passing in a `WifiP2pInfo` object that includes those details.

When a collection is established, a group consisting of the peers connected is formed. The initiator of the connection will be returned as the group owner and would typically (but not necessarily) take on the role of server for further communications.

> **NOTE** *Each P2P connection is regarded as a group, even if that connection is exclusively between two peers.*

Having established a connection, you can use standard TCP/IP sockets to transmit data between devices.

Transferring Data Between Peers

Although the specifics of any particular data transfer implementation is beyond the scope of this book, this section describes the basic process of transmitting data between connected devices using Sockets.

To establish a Socket connection, one device must create a `ServerSocket` that listens for connection requests, and the other device must create a client `Socket` that makes connection requests. This distinction is relevant only in terms of establishing the connection—after that connection is established, the data can flow in either direction.

Create a new server-side socket using the `ServerSocket` class, specifying a port on which to listen for requests. Call its `accept` method asynchronously, to listen for incoming requests, as shown in Listing 18-15.

LISTING 18-15: Creating a server Socket

```
Socket mServerClient;
int port = 8666;

private void startWifiDirectServer() {
  try {
    ServerSocket serverSocket = new ServerSocket(port);
    mServerClient = serverSocket.accept();
    // TODO Once connected, use mServerClient to send messages.
  } catch (IOException e) {
    Log.e(TAG, e.getMessage(), e);
  }
}
```

To request a connection from the client device, create a new `Socket` and asynchronously use its connect method, specifying the host address of the target device, a port to connect on, and a timeout for the connection request, as shown in Listing 18-16.

LISTING 18-16: Creating a client Socket

```
int timeout = 10000;
int port = 8666;

private void startWifiDirectClient(String hostAddress) {
  Socket socket = new Socket();

  InetSocketAddress socketAddress
    = new InetSocketAddress(hostAddress, port);

  try {
    socket.bind(null);
    socket.connect(socketAddress, timeout);
    listenForWiFiMessages(socket);
  } catch (IOException e) {
    Log.e(TAG, "IO Exception.", e);
  }
}
```

Like the Server Socket call to `accept`, the call to `connect` is a blocking call that will return after the Socket connection has been established, so both must always be called from background Threads.

After the sockets have been established, you can create Input Streams and Output Streams on either the server- or client-side Sockets to transmit and receive data bidirectionally.

> **NOTE** *Network communications such as those described here should always be handled on a background thread to avoid blocking the UI thread. This is particularly the case when establishing the network connection because both the server- and client-side logic includes blocking calls that will disrupt the UI.*

USING NEAR FIELD COMMUNICATION

NFC is a contactless technology used to transmit small amounts of data across very short distances (typically less than 4 centimeters).

NFC transfers can occur between two NFC-enabled devices, or between a device and an NFC "tag." Tags can range from passive tags that transmit a URL when scanned, to complex systems such as those used in NFC payment solutions, such as Google Pay.

NFC messages in Android are handled using the NFC Data Exchange Format (NDEF).

To read, write, or broadcast NFC messages, your application requires the NFC manifest permission:

```
<uses-permission android:name="android.permission.NFC" />
```

Reading NFC Tags

When an Android device is used to scan an NFC tag, the system will decode the incoming payload using its own tag dispatch system, which analyzes the tag, categorizes the data, and uses an Intent to launch an application to receive the data.

For an application to receive NFC data, you need to add an Activity Intent Filter that listens for one of the following Intent actions:

➤ `NfcAdapter.ACTION_NDEF_DISCOVERED`—The highest priority, and most specific, of the NFC messages. Intents using this action include MIME types and/or URI data. It's best practice to listen for this broadcast whenever possible because the extra data allows you to be more specific in defining which tags to respond to.

➤ `NfcAdapter.ACTION_TECH_DISCOVERED`—This action is broadcast when the NFC technology is known but the tag contains no data—or contains data that can't be mapped to a MIME type or URI.

➤ `NfcAdapter.ACTION_TAG_DISCOVERED`—If a tag is received from an unknown technology, it will be broadcast using this action.

Listing 18-17 shows how to register an Activity that will respond only to NFC tags that correspond to a URI that points to my blog.

LISTING 18-17: Listening for NFC tags

```
<activity android:name=".BlogViewer">
  <intent-filter>
    <action android:name="android.nfc.action.NDEF_DISCOVERED"/>
    <category android:name="android.intent.category.DEFAULT"/>
    <data android:scheme="http"
          android:host="blog.radioactiveyak.com"/>
  </intent-filter>
</activity>
```

It's good practice to make your NFC Intent Filters as specific as possible to minimize the number of applications available to respond to a given NFC tag and provide the best, fastest user experience.

In many cases the Intent data/URI and MIME type are sufficient for your application to respond accordingly. However, if required, the payload delivered from an NFC message is available through extras within the Intent that started your Activity.

The NfcAdapter.EXTRA_TAG extra includes a raw Tag object that represents the scanned tag. The NfcAdapter.EXTRA_TNDEF_MESSAGES extra contains an array of NDEF Messages, as shown in Listing 18-18.

LISTING 18-18: Extracting NFC tag payloads

```
String action = getIntent().getAction();

if (NfcAdapter.ACTION_NDEF_DISCOVERED.equals(action)) {
  Parcelable[] messages
    = getIntent().getParcelableArrayExtra(NfcAdapter.EXTRA_NDEF_MESSAGES);

  if (messages != null) {
    for (Parcelable eachMessage : messages) {
      NdefMessage message = (NdefMessage) eachMessage;
      NdefRecord[] records = message.getRecords();

      if (records != null) {
        for (NdefRecord record : records) {
          String payload = new String(record.getPayload());
          Log.d(TAG, payload);
        }
      }
    }
  }
}
```

Using the Foreground Dispatch System

By default, the tag dispatch system will determine which application should receive a particular tag based on the standard process of Intent resolution. In that process, the foreground Activity has no priority over other applications; so, if several applications are all registered to receive a tag of the type scanned, the user will be prompted to select which to use, even if your application is in the foreground at the time.

Using the foreground dispatch system, you can specify a particular Activity as having priority, allowing it to become the default receiver when it is in the foreground. Foreground dispatching can be toggled using the enable/disableForegroundDispatch methods on the NFC Adapter.

Foreground dispatching can be used only while an Activity is in the foreground, so it should be enabled and disabled from within your onResume and onPause handlers, respectively, as shown in Listing 18-19. The parameters to enableForegroundDispatch are described following the example.

LISTING 18-19: Enabling and disabling the foreground dispatch system

```
NfcAdapter mNFCAdapter;

@Override
protected void onNewIntent(Intent intent) {
  super.onNewIntent(intent);

  setIntent(intent);
  processIntent(intent);
}

@Override
public void onPause() {
  super.onPause();
  mNFCAdapter.disableForegroundDispatch(this);
}

@Override
public void onResume() {
  super.onResume();
  mNFCAdapter.enableForegroundDispatch(
    this,
    // Intent that will be used to package the Tag Intent.
    nfcPendingIntent,
    // Array of Intent Filters used to declare the Intents you
    // wish to intercept.
    intentFiltersArray,
    // Array of Tag technologies you wish to handle.
    techListsArray);
}
```

The Intent Filters array should declare the URIs or MIME types you want to intercept—any received tags that don't match these criteria will be handled using the standard tag dispatching system. To ensure a good user experience, it's important that you specify only the tag content your application handles.

You can further refine the tags you receive by explicitly indicating the technologies you want to handle—typically represented by adding the NfcF class.

Finally, the Pending Intent will be populated by the NFC Adapter to transmit the received tag directly to your application.

Listing 18-20 shows the Pending Intent, MIME type array, and technologies array used to enable the foreground dispatching in Listing 18-19.

LISTING 18-20: Configuring foreground dispatching parameters

```
private NfcAdapter mNFCAdapter;

private int NFC_REQUEST_CODE = 0;
```

LISTING 18-20 *(continued)*

```
private PendingIntent mNFCPendingIntent;
private IntentFilter[] mIntentFiltersArray;
private String[][] mTechListsArray;

@Override
protected void onCreate(Bundle savedInstanceState) {
  super.onCreate(savedInstanceState);
  setContentView(R.layout.activity_main);

  // Get the NFC Adapter.
  NfcManager nfcManager = (NfcManager)getSystemService(Context.NFC_SERVICE);
  mNFCAdapter = nfcManager.getDefaultAdapter();

  // Create the Pending Intent.
  int flags = 0;
  Intent nfcIntent = new Intent(this, getClass());
  nfcIntent.addFlags(Intent.FLAG_ACTIVITY_SINGLE_TOP);

  mNFCPendingIntent =
    PendingIntent.getActivity(this, NFC_REQUEST_CODE, nfcIntent, flags);

  // Create an Intent Filter limited to the URI or MIME type to
  // intercept TAG scans from.
  IntentFilter tagIntentFilter =
    new IntentFilter(NfcAdapter.ACTION_NDEF_DISCOVERED);
  tagIntentFilter.addDataScheme("http");
  tagIntentFilter.addDataAuthority("blog.radioactiveyak.com", null);
  mIntentFiltersArray = new IntentFilter[] { tagIntentFilter };

  // Create an array of technologies to handle.
  mTechListsArray = new String[][] {
    new String[] {
      NfcF.class.getName()
    }
  };


  // Process the Intent used to start the Activity/
  String action = getIntent().getAction();
  if (NfcAdapter.ACTION_NDEF_DISCOVERED.equals(action))
    processIntent(getIntent());
}
```

USING ANDROID BEAM

Android Beam provides a simple API for an application to transmit data between two Android devices using NFC, simply by placing them back-to-back. For example, the native contacts, browser, and YouTube applications use Android Beam to share the currently viewed contact, web page, and video, respectively.

> **NOTE** *To beam messages, your application must be in the foreground and the device receiving the data must not be locked.*
>
> *Android Beam is initiated by tapping two NFC-enabled Android devices together. Users are presented with a "touch to beam" UI, at which point they can choose to "beam" the foreground application to the other device.*

By enabling Android Beam within your application, you can define the payload of the beamed message. If you don't customize the message, the default action for your application will be to launch it on the target device. If your application isn't installed on the target device, the Google Play Store will launch and display your application's details page.

To define the message your application beams, you need to request the NFC permission in the manifest:

```
<uses-permission android:name="android.permission.NFC"/>
```

The process to define your own custom payload is described as follows:

1. Create an `NdefMessage` object that contains an `NdefRecord` that contains your message payload.
2. Assign your Ndef Message to the NFC Adapter as your Android Beam payload.
3. Configure your application to listen for incoming Android Beam messages.

Creating Android Beam Messages

To create a new Ndef Message, create a new `NdefMessage` object that contains at least one `NdefRecord` containing the payload you want to beam to your application on the target device.

When creating a new Ndef Record, you must specify the type of record it represents, a MIME type, an ID, and a payload. You can use several common types of Ndef Record to transmit data using Android Beam; note that they should always be the first record added to each beamed message.

Using the `NdefRecord.TNF_MIME_MEDIA` type, you can transmit an absolute URI:

```
NdefRecord uriRecord = new NdefRecord(
  NdefRecord.TNF_ABSOLUTE_URI,
  "http://blog.radioactiveyak.com".getBytes(Charset.forName("US-ASCII")),
  new byte[0], new byte[0]);
```

This is the most common Ndef Record transmitted using Android Beam because the received Intent will be of the same form as any Intent used to start an Activity. The Intent Filter used to decide which NFC messages a particular Activity should receive can use the `scheme`, `host`, and `pathPrefix` attributes.

If you need to transmit messages that contain information that can't be easily interpreted as a URI, the `NdefRecord.TNF_MIME_MEDIA` type supports the creation of an application-specific MIME type and the inclusion of associated payload data:

```
String mimeType = "application/com.professionalandroid.apps.nfcbeam";
String payload = "Not a URI";
byte[] tagId = new byte[0];
```

```
NdefRecord mimeRecord
    = new NdefRecord(NdefRecord.TNF_MIME_MEDIA,
                     mimeType.getBytes(Charset.forName("US-ASCII")),
                     tagId,
                     payload.getBytes(Charset.forName("US-ASCII")));
```

You can find a more complete examination of the available Ndef Record types and how to use them in the Android Developer Guide at d.android.com/guide/topics/nfc/nfc.html#creating-records.

When constructing your Ndef Message, it's good practice to include an Ndef Record in the form of an Android Application Record (AAR) in addition to your payload record. This guarantees that your application will be launched on the target device, and that if your application isn't installed, the Google Play Store will be launched for the user to install it.

To create an AAR Ndef Record, use the createApplicationRecord static method on the Ndef Record class, specifying the package name of your application:

```
NdefRecord.createApplicationRecord("com.professionalandroid.apps.nfcbeam")
```

When your Ndef Records have been created, create a new Ndef Message, passing in an array of your Ndef Records, as shown in Listing 18-21.

LISTING 18-21: Creating an Android Beam NDEF message

```
String payload = "Two to beam across";
String mimeType = "application/com.professionalandroid.apps.nfcbeam";
byte[] tagId = new byte[0];

NdefMessage nfcMessage = new NdefMessage(new NdefRecord[] {
    // Create the NFC payload.
    new NdefRecord(NdefRecord.TNF_MIME_MEDIA,
                   mimeType.getBytes(Charset.forName("US-ASCII")),
                   tagId,
                   payload.getBytes(Charset.forName("US-ASCII"))),

    // Add the AAR (Android Application Record)
    NdefRecord.createApplicationRecord("com.professionalandroid.apps.nfcbeam")
});
```

Assigning the Android Beam Payload

You specify your Android Beam payload using the NFC adapter. You can access the default NFC adapter using the static getDefaultAdapter method on the NfcAdapter class:

```
NfcAdapter nfcAdapter = NfcAdapter.getDefaultAdapter(this);
```

You have two alternatives for specifying the NDEF Message created in Listing 18-21 as your application's Android Beam payload. The simplest way is to use the `setNdefPushMessage` method to assign a message that should *always* be sent from the current Activity if Android Beam is initiated. You would typically make this assignment once, from within your Activity's `onResume` method:

```
nfcAdapter.setNdefPushMessage(nfcMessage, this);
```

A better alternative is to use the `setNdefPushMessageCallback` method. This handler will fire immediately before your message is beamed, allowing you to dynamically set the payload content based on the application's current context—for example, which video is being watched, which web page is being browsed, or which map coordinates are centered, as shown in Listing 18-22.

LISTING 18-22: Setting your Android Beam message dynamically

```java
private void setBeamMessage() {
  NfcAdapter nfcAdapter = NfcAdapter.getDefaultAdapter(this);
  nfcAdapter.setNdefPushMessageCallback(
    new NfcAdapter.CreateNdefMessageCallback() {

      public NdefMessage createNdefMessage(NfcEvent event) {
        String payload = "Beam me up, Android!\n\n" +
                         "Beam Time: " + System.currentTimeMillis();

        NdefMessage message = createMessage(payload);

        return message;
      }
    }, this);
}

private NdefMessage createMessage(String payload) {
  String mimeType = "application/com.professionalandroid.apps.nfcbeam";
  byte[] tagId = new byte[0];

  NdefMessage nfcMessage = new NdefMessage(new NdefRecord[] {
    // Create the NFC payload.
    new NdefRecord(NdefRecord.TNF_MIME_MEDIA,
                   mimeType.getBytes(Charset.forName("US-ASCII")),
                   tagId,
                   payload.getBytes(Charset.forName("US-ASCII"))),

    // Add the AAR (Android Application Record)
    NdefRecord.createApplicationRecord("com.professionalandroid.apps.nfcbeam")
  });

  return nfcMessage;
}
```

If you set both a static message and a dynamic message using the callback handler, only the latter will be transmitted.

Receiving Android Beam Messages

Android Beam messages are received much like NFC tags, as described earlier in this chapter. To receive the payloads you packaged in Listing 18-21 and Listing 18-22, start by adding a new Intent Filter to your Activity, as shown in Listing 18-23.

LISTING 18-23: Android Beam Intent Filter

```
<intent-filter>
  <action android:name="android.nfc.action.NDEF_DISCOVERED"/>
  <category android:name="android.intent.category.DEFAULT"/>
  <data android:mimeType="application/com.professionalandroid.apps.nfcbeam"/>
</intent-filter>
```

The corresponding Activity will be launched on the recipient device when an Android Beam has been initiated, or, if your application isn't installed, the Google Play Store will be launched to allow the user to download it.

The beam data will be delivered to your Activity using an Intent with the `NfcAdapter.ACTION_NDEF_DISCOVERED` action and the payload available as an array of `NdfMessages` stored against the `NfcAdapter.EXTRA_NDEF_MESSAGES` extra, as shown in Listing 18-24.

LISTING 18-24: Extracting the Android Beam payload

```
Parcelable[] messages
  = getIntent().getParcelableArrayExtra(NfcAdapter.EXTRA_NDEF_MESSAGES);

if (messages != null) {
  NdefMessage message = (NdefMessage) messages[0];
  if (message != null) {
    NdefRecord record = message.getRecords()[0];

    String payload = new String(record.getPayload());
    Log.d(TAG, "Payload: " + payload);
  }
}
```

Typically, the payload string will be in the form of a URI, allowing you to extract and handle it as you would the data encapsulated within an Intent to display the appropriate video, web page, or map coordinates.

19

Invading the Home Screen

WHAT'S IN THIS CHAPTER?

➤ Creating and updating home screen Widgets

➤ Creating and updating collection-based home screen Widgets

➤ Creating Live Wallpaper

➤ Creating static and dynamic App Shortcuts

➤ Updating and removing dynamic App Shortcuts

WROX.COM CODE DOWNLOADS FOR THIS CHAPTER

The code downloads for this chapter are found at www.wrox.com on the Download Code tab. The code for this chapter is divided into the following major examples:

➤ `Snippets_ch19.zip`

➤ `Earthquake_ch19_Part1.zip`

➤ `Earthquake_ch19_Part2.zip`

CUSTOMIZING THE HOME SCREEN

Widgets, Live Wallpaper, and App Shortcuts let you add a piece of your application directly onto the user's device home screen. By incorporating these features into your app:

➤ Users get instant access to priority functionality.

➤ Users can see important information without needing to open an application.

➤ You get an entry point to your applications directly on the home screen.

A useful home screen Widget, Live Wallpaper, or App Shortcut increases user engagement, can decrease the chance that an application will be uninstalled, and increases the likelihood of its being used.

INTRODUCING HOME SCREEN WIDGETS

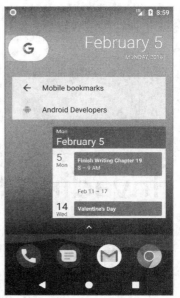

Home screen Widgets, more properly `AppWidgets`, are visual application components that can be added to other applications. The most common feature of App Widgets is that they can be used to enable users to embed an interactive piece of your application directly within the home screen. A good App Widget provides useful, concise, and timely information with minimal battery drain.

Widgets can be standalone applications, but are more commonly a feature of a larger application—such as the Calendar and Gmail App Widgets.

Figure 19-1 shows an example of App Widgets from some of Google's applications, added to the home screen.

FIGURE 19-1

> **NOTE** *The specific process for adding, moving, resizing, and removing App Widgets varies based on type and version of the home screen installed on your device. To add an App Widget to the home screen on the current Pixel and Nexus launchers, long-press a piece of empty space and select Widgets. You will be presented with a list of available Widgets to add to your home screen.*
>
> *After adding a Widget, you can move it by long-pressing it and dragging it around the screen. To resize a Widget, long-press and release; you'll see small indicators along the edges of the Widget that can be dragged to resize.*
>
> *Remove Widgets by dragging them into the garbage can icon or "remove" label at the top or bottom of the screen.*

App Widgets are implemented as Broadcast Receivers. You use `RemoteViews` to modify the Widget UI, which you define within a View hierarchy, that's hosted within another application process.

A new App Widget requires three components:

➤ An XML layout resource to define the UI

➤ An XML file to describe the App Widget meta data

➤ A `BroadcastReceiver` extension to implement the Widget

You can create as many Widgets as you want for a single application, or you can have an application that consists of only one Widget. It's even possible to have an application consisting of no Widgets, which is a particularly simple pattern to implement that we'll leave as an exercise for the reader.

When a Widget is hosted within another application—such as the home screen—it's run within that parent application's process. Widgets will wake the device from low-power sleep mode based on the update rate, to ensure it's up to date when it's next visible. This can have a significant impact on battery life, so as a developer you need to take special care when creating your Widgets to set the update rate as low as possible, and that the code executed within the update method is lightweight and efficient.

Defining the Widget Layout

The first step in creating your Widget is to design and implement its user interface (UI) layout.

UI design guidelines exist for controlling both a Widget's layout size and its visual styling. The former is enforced rigidly, whereas the latter is a guide only. Visually, Widgets are often displayed alongside other native and third-party Widgets, so it's important that yours conform to design standards—particularly because Widgets are most often used on the home screen. You can find the details at the Android Developers Widget Design Guidelines site, at `developer.android.com/guide/practices/ui_guidelines/widget_design.html`, and the material design Widget guidelines at `material.io/design/platform-guidance/android-widget.html#behavior`.

App Widgets fully support transparent backgrounds and allow the use of NinePatches and partially transparent Drawable resources. It's beyond the scope of this book to describe the Widget style promoted by Google in detail, but note the descriptions available at the Widget UI guidelines links provided above.

You construct your Widget's UI as you would other visual components in Android, as described in Chapter 5, "Building User Interfaces," with some restrictions. Best practice is to define your Widget layout using XML as an external layout resource, but it's also possible to lay out your UI programmatically within the Broadcast Receiver's `onCreate` method.

For security and performance reasons, App Widget layouts are inflated in the host Activity as `RemoteViews` that support a limited set of layouts and Views.

Supported layouts are limited to:

- `FrameLayout`
- `LinearLayout`
- `RelativeLayout`
- `GridLayout`

The Views they contain are restricted to the following:

- `Button`
- `Chronometer`
- `ImageButton`

> ImageView

> ProgressBar

> TextView

> ViewFlipper

In the section "Introducing Collection View Widgets" you'll also learn how to use the following collection-based Views within your Widget layouts:

> AdapterViewFlipper

> GridView

> ListView

> StackView

Listing 19-1 shows an XML layout resource used to define the UI of an App Widget. Note that padding is automatically added to your Widget layouts, so you shouldn't add additional padding. Also note that we're setting the width and height of the layout to `match_parent`. You learn how to define the minimum size of your Widget in the following section.

LISTING 19-1: App Widget XML layout resource

```xml
<?xml version="1.0" encoding="utf-8"?>
<LinearLayout
  xmlns:android="http://schemas.android.com/apk/res/android"
  android:orientation="horizontal"
  android:layout_width="match_parent"
  android:layout_height="match_parent">
  <ImageView
    android:id="@+id/widget_image"
    android:layout_width="wrap_content"
    android:layout_height="wrap_content"
    android:src="@drawable/icon"
  />
  <TextView
    android:id="@+id/widget_text"
    android:layout_width="fill_parent"
    android:layout_height="fill_parent"
    android:text="@string/widget_text"
  />
</LinearLayout>
```

Defining Your Widget Size and Other Metadata

The Android home screen is divided into a grid of cells, varying in size and number depending on the device. It's best practice to specify a minimum height and width for your Widget that is required to ensure it is displayed in a good default state.

Where your minimum dimensions don't match the exact dimensions of the home screen cells, your Widget's size will be rounded up to fill the cells into which it extends.

To determine the approximate minimum height and width limits required to ensure your Widget fits within a given number of cells, you can use the following formula:

```
Min height or width = 70dp * (cell count) - 30dp
```

You specify the minimum Widget size, allocate a layout, specify the update rate, and define other Widget settings and metadata in the Widget definition XML resource, stored in the `res/xml` folder of your project.

Use the `appwidget-provider` tag to describe the Widget metadata using the following attributes:

➤ `initialLayout`—The layout resource to use to define the Widget's UI layout.

➤ `minWidth` and `minHeight`—The minimum width and minimum height of the Widget.

➤ `resizeMode`—Setting the resize mode allows you to specify the direction in which the Widget can be resized, using a combination of `horizontal` and `vertical`, or disabling resizing by setting it to `none`. It's best practice to support all resizing modes for your Widget.

➤ `label`—The title used by your Widget in the App Widget picker.

➤ `updatePeriodMillis`—The minimum period between Widget updates in milliseconds. Android will wake the device to update your Widget at this rate, so you should specify at least an hour. The App Widget Manager won't deliver updates more frequently than once every 30 minutes. More details on this and other update techniques are provided later in this chapter.

➤ `configure`—You can optionally specify a fully qualified Activity to be launched when your Widget is added to the home screen. This Activity can be used to specify Widget settings and user preferences. Using a configuration Activity is described in the section "Creating and Using a Widget Configuration Activity."

➤ `icon`—By default Android will use your application's icon when presenting your Widget within the App Widget picker. Specify a Drawable resource to use a different icon.

➤ `previewImage`—A Drawable resource that accurately depicts how your Widget will appear when added to the home screen. This will be displayed by the App Widget picker as a preview.

Listing 19-2 shows the Widget definition resource file for a minimum two-cell-by-two-cell Widget that updates once every hour, and uses the layout resource defined in the previous section.

LISTING 19-2: App Widget Provider definition

```xml
<?xml version="1.0" encoding="utf-8"?>
<appwidget-provider
  xmlns:android="http://schemas.android.com/apk/res/android"
  android:initialLayout="@layout/my_widget_layout"
```

continues

LISTING 19-2 *(continued)*

```
    android:minWidth="110dp"
    android:minHeight="110dp"
    android:label="@string/widget_label"
    android:updatePeriodMillis="360000"
    android:resizeMode="horizontal|vertical"
    android:previewImage="@drawable/widget_preview"
/>
```

Implementing Your Widget

Widgets are implemented as Broadcast Receivers, which specify Intent Filters that listen for the Broadcast Intent actions AppWidget.ACTION_APPWIDGET_[UPDATE, DELETED, ENABLED, and DISABLED] and perform the appropriate actions accordingly.

The AppWidgetProvider class encapsulates the Intent processing and provides you with event handlers for each Intent action, as shown in the skeleton code in Listing 19-3.

LISTING 19-3: App Widget implementation

```java
public class SkeletonAppWidget extends AppWidgetProvider {

  static void updateAppWidget(Context context,
                              AppWidgetManager appWidgetManager,
                              int appWidgetId) {

    // TODO Update indicated app widget UI.
  }

  @Override
  public void onUpdate(Context context,
                       AppWidgetManager appWidgetManager,
                       int[] appWidgetIds) {
    // Iterate through each widget, creating a RemoteViews object and
    // applying the modified RemoteViews to each widget.
    for (int appWidgetId : appWidgetIds)
      updateAppWidget(context, appWidgetManager, appWidgetId);
  }

  @Override
  public void onDeleted(Context context, int[] appWidgetIds) {
    // TODO Handle deletion of the widget.
    super.onDeleted(context, appWidgetIds);
  }

  @Override
  public void onDisabled(Context context) {
    // TODO Widget has been disabled.
    super.onDisabled(context);
  }
```

```
    @Override
    public void onEnabled(Context context) {
        // TODO Widget has been enabled.
        super.onEnabled(context);
    }
}
```

Like all application components, Widgets must be added to the application manifest. As they are implemented as Broadcast Receivers, use the `receiver` tag and add the following two elements, as shown in Listing 19-4:

➤ An Intent Filter for the `android.appwidget.action.APPWIDGET_UPDATE` action

➤ A metadata node associating the `android.appwidget.provider` name with the `appwidget-provider` XML resource file that describes your Widget settings

LISTING 19-4: App Widget manifest node

```
<receiver android:name=".SkeletonAppWidget">
  <intent-filter>
    <action android:name="android.appwidget.action.APPWIDGET_UPDATE" />
  </intent-filter>
  <meta-data
    android:name="android.appwidget.provider"
    android:resource="@xml/widget_settings"
  />
</receiver>
```

Updating the Widget UI Using the App Widget Manager and Remote Views

The `RemoteViews` class is used as a proxy to a View hierarchy hosted within another application's process. This adds a layer of security by letting you change a property or run a method on a View while it's running within another application—but without being able to interact with it directly.

To update the appearance of Views within your Widgets at run time, you must create and modify Remote Views to represent them, and then apply those changes using the `AppWidgetManager`. Supported modifications include changing a View's visibility, text, or image values, and adding Click Listeners.

Creating and Manipulating Remote Views

To create a new Remote Views object, pass the name of your application's package, and the layout resource you plan to manipulate, into the Remote Views constructor, as shown in Listing 19-5.

LISTING 19-5: Creating Remote Views

```
RemoteViews views = new RemoteViews(context.getPackageName(),
                                    R.layout.widget_layout);
```

Remote Views include a series of methods that provide access to many of the properties and methods available on the Views they represent.

The most versatile of these is a collection of `set` methods that let you specify a target method name to execute on a remotely hosted View. These methods support the passing of a single-value parameter, one for each primitive type, including Boolean, integer, byte, char, and float, as well as strings, bitmaps, Bundles, and URI parameters:

```
// Set the image level for an ImageView.
views.setInt(R.id.widget_image_view, "setImageLevel", 2);
// Show the cursor of a TextView.
views.setBoolean(R.id.widget_text_view, "setCursorVisible", true);
// Assign a bitmap to an ImageButton.
views.setBitmap(R.id.widget_image_button, "setImageBitmap", myBitmap);
```

The modifications you apply here will not affect the running instances of your Widgets until you apply them, as described in the following section.

A number of methods specific to certain View classes are also available, including methods to modify Text Views, Image Views, and Progress Bars:

```
// Update a Text View
views.setTextViewText(R.id.widget_text, "Updated Text");
views.setTextColor(R.id.widget_text, Color.BLUE);
// Update an Image View
views.setImageViewResource(R.id.widget_image, R.drawable.icon);
// Update a Progress Bar
views.setProgressBar(R.id.widget_progressbar, 100, 50, false);
```

You can set the visibility of any View hosted within a Remote Views layout by calling `setViewVisibility`:

```
views.setViewVisibility(R.id.widget_text, View.INVISIBLE);
```

So far you have modified the Remote Views object that represents the View hierarchy within the App Widget, but you have not applied it. For your changes to take effect, you must use the App Widget Manager to apply your updates, as shown in the next section.

Applying Remote Views to App Widgets

To apply the changes made to Remote Views to Widgets at runtime, use the App Widget Manager's `updateAppWidget` method, passing in the identifiers of one or more Widgets to update and the Remote View to apply:

```
appWidgetManager.updateAppWidget(appWidgetIds, remoteViews);
```

Override the `onEnabled` handler of your App Widget Provider to apply changes to your Widget UI when it's first instantiated and placed on the user's homescreen, as shown in Listing 19-6.

Similarly, to apply scheduled updates to your Widgets override the `onUpdate` handler; this handler receives the App Widget Manager, and the array of App Widget instance IDs due to be updated, as parameters. It's best practice to iterate over the Widget ID array, enabling you to apply different UI values to each Widget based on its identifier and any associated configuration settings, as shown in the pattern in Listing 19-6.

LISTING 19-6: Applying a Remote View within the App Widget Provider's update handler

```java
static void updateAppWidget(Context context,
                            AppWidgetManager appWidgetManager,
                            int appWidgetId) {

  // Create a Remote View
  RemoteViews views = new RemoteViews(context.getPackageName(),
                                      R.layout.widget_layout);

  // TODO Update the UI.

  // Notify the App Widget Manager to update the widget using
  // the modified remote view.
  appWidgetManager.updateAppWidget(appWidgetId, views);
}

@Override
public void onUpdate(Context context,
                     AppWidgetManager appWidgetManager,
                     int[] appWidgetIds) {
  // Iterate through each widget, creating a RemoteViews object and
  // applying the modified RemoteViews to each widget.
  for (int appWidgetId : appWidgetIds)
    updateAppWidget(context, appWidgetManager, appWidgetId);
}

@Override
public void onEnabled(Context context) {
  AppWidgetManager appWidgetManager =
    AppWidgetManager.getInstance(context);
  ComponentName skeletonAppWidget =
    new ComponentName(context, SkeletonAppWidget.class);
  int[] appWidgetIds =
    appWidgetManager.getAppWidgetIds(skeletonAppWidget);

  updateAppWidgets(context, appWidgetManager, appWidgetIds, pendingResult);
}
```

You can also update your Widgets directly from a Service, Activity, or Broadcast Receiver. To do so, get a reference to the App Widget Manager by calling its static `getInstance` method, passing in the current context:

```java
// Get the App Widget Manager.
AppWidgetManager appWidgetManager
  = AppWidgetManager.getInstance(this);
```

You can then use the `getAppWidgetIds` method on your App Widget Manager instance to find identifiers representing each currently running instance of the specified App Widget:

```java
// Retrieve the identifiers for each instance of your chosen widget.
ComponentName thisWidget = new ComponentName(this, SkeletonAppWidget.class);
int[] appWidgetIds = appWidgetManager.getAppWidgetIds(thisWidget);
```

To update the active Widgets, you can follow the same pattern described in Listing 19-6:

```
// Iterate through each widget, creating a RemoteViews object and
// applying the modified RemoteViews to each widget.
for (int appWidgetId : appWidgetIds)
  SkeletonAppWidget.updateAppWidget(this, appWidgetManager, appWidgetId);
```

Notice that the code used to modify the Widget UI is kept within the `updateAppWidget` method of the Widget implementation. This is done to ensure any manual changes you might apply aren't reverted the next time the Widget is refreshed.

In all cases, it's best practice to have the Widget handle its own UI updates based on changes to underlying data, such as a Room database or Shared Preferences.

Adding Interactivity to Widgets

App Widgets inherit the permissions of the processes within which they run, and most home screen apps run with full permissions, making the potential security risks significant. As a result of these security implications, Widget interactivity is carefully controlled.

Widget interaction is generally limited to the following:

➤ Adding a Click Listener to one or more Views

➤ Changing the UI based on selection changes

➤ Transitioning between Views within a Collection View Widget

> **NOTE** *There is no supported technique for entering text directly into an App Widget. If you need text input from your Widget, best practice is to add a Click Listener to the Widget that starts an Activity to accept input.*

The simplest and most powerful way to add interactivity to your Widget is by adding a Click Listener to its Views. You do this using the `setOnClickPendingIntent` method on the corresponding Remote Views object. Use the App Widget Manager's `updateAppWidget` method to apply the updated Remote Views to your Widgets, as you would for any UI change.

Use this method to specify a Pending Intent that will be fired when the user clicks the specified View, as shown in Listing 19-7.

LISTING 19-7: Adding a Click Listener to an App Widget

```
// Create an Intent to launch an Activity
Intent intent = new Intent(context, MainActivity.class);

// Wrap it in a Pending Intent so another application
// can fire it on your behalf.
PendingIntent pendingIntent =
  PendingIntent.getActivity(context, 0, intent, 0);
```

```
// Assign the Pending Intent to be triggered when
// the assigned View is clicked.
views.setOnClickPendingIntent(R.id.widget_text, pendingIntent);

appWidgetManager.updateAppWidget(appWidgetId, views);
```

Pending Intents (described in more detail in Chapter 6, "Intents and Broadcast Receivers") allow other applications to fire an Intent on your app's behalf. In this case, it allows the host application to start Activities or Services, or to broadcast an Intent as though it was fired from your application directly.

Using this technique you can add Click Listeners to one or more of the Views used within your Widget, potentially providing support for multiple actions.

Forcing Refreshes of Your Widget Data and UI

Widgets are most commonly displayed on the home screen, so it's important that they're kept relevant and up to date. It's just as important to balance that relevance with your Widget's impact on system resources—particularly battery life. Several techniques exist for managing your Widget's refresh rate.

The simplest approach is to set the minimum update rate for a Widget using the updatePeriod-Millis attribute in the Widget's XML appwidget-provider definition. This is demonstrated in Listing 19-8, where the Widget is updated once every hour.

LISTING 19-8: Setting the App Widget minimum update rate

```
<?xml version="1.0" encoding="utf-8"?>
<appwidget-provider
  xmlns:android="http://schemas.android.com/apk/res/android"
  android:initialLayout="@layout/widget_layout"
  android:minWidth="110dp"
  android:minHeight="110dp"
  android:label="@string/widget_label"
  android:resizeMode="horizontal|vertical"
  android:previewImage="@drawable/widget_preview"
  android:updatePeriodMillis="3600000"
/>
```

Setting this value will schedule a repeating Broadcast Intent that will trigger the onUpdate handler of your Widget at the rate specified.

> **NOTE** *The host device will wake up to complete these updates, meaning they are completed even when the device is on low-power standby. This has the potential to be a significant resource drain, so it's very important to consider the implications of your update rate. In most cases the system will not broadcast a minimum update broadcast more frequently than every 30 minutes.*

This technique should be used to define the absolute minimum rate at which your Widget must be updated to remain useful. Generally, the best practice approach is to use a server push—typically initiated through Firebase Cloud Messaging, as described in Chapter 11, "Working in the Background." Where updates are required due to client-side changes or time-based triggers, the update rate should be a minimum of an hour and ideally not more than once or twice a day.

App Widgets are implemented as Broadcast Receivers, so you can trigger updates and UI refreshes by targeting them with explicit Broadcast Intents from within your application. If your Widget requires frequent updates, you should implement an event/Intent-driven model to update it as needed, rather than increasing the minimum polling frequency.

Listing 19-9 creates a new Broadcast Intent that explicitly targets the Widget defined earlier, while including an action that will allow it to understand how to respond.

LISTING 19-9: Sending a Broadcast Intent to an App Widget

```
Intent forceWidgetUpdate = new Intent(this, SkeletonAppWidget.class);
forceWidgetUpdate.setAction(SkeletonAppWidget.FORCE_WIDGET_UPDATE);
sendBroadcast(forceWidgetUpdate);
```

By updating the Widget's `onReceive` method handler, as shown in Listing 19-10, you can listen for this new Broadcast Intent and use it to update your Widget.

LISTING 19-10: Updating App Widgets based on broadcast Intents

```
public static String FORCE_WIDGET_UPDATE =
  "com.paad.mywidget.FORCE_WIDGET_UPDATE";

@Override
public void onReceive(Context context, Intent intent) {
  super.onReceive(context, intent);

  if (FORCE_WIDGET_UPDATE.equals(intent.getAction())) {
    // TODO Update widget
  }
}
```

This approach is particularly useful for reacting to data updates from within your application, or a user action such as clicking buttons on the Widget itself.

In order to refresh the data displayed in your Widget, you may need to asynchronously load data—such as that stored in a SQL or Room database. Because App Widgets are implemented as Broadcast Receivers, you can use the same techniques used to execute Receiver tasks asynchronously to update your Widget.

Specifically, you can call `goAsync` to signal that you will be performing an asynchronous operation, and pass the resulting Pending Result to your static update method, as shown in Listing 19-11.

LISTING 19-11: Updating an App Widget with asynchronously loaded data

```java
@Override
public void onReceive(final Context context, final Intent intent) {
  super.onReceive(context, intent);

  // Indicate an asynchronous operation will take place.
  final PendingResult pendingResult = goAsync();

  if (FORCE_WIDGET_UPDATE.equals(intent.getAction())) {
    AppWidgetManager appWidgetManager =
      AppWidgetManager.getInstance(context);
    ComponentName skeletonAppWidget =
      new ComponentName(context, SkeletonAppWidget.class);
    int[] appWidgetIds =
      appWidgetManager.getAppWidgetIds(skeletonAppWidget);

    updateAppWidgets(context, appWidgetManager, appWidgetIds, pendingResult);
  }
}

static void updateAppWidgets(final Context context,
                             final AppWidgetManager appWidgetManager,
                             final int[] appWidgetIds,
                             final PendingResult pendingResult) {
  // Create a thread to asynchronously load data to show in the widgets.
  Thread thread = new Thread() {
    public void run() {

      // TODO Load data from a database.
      // TODO Update the UI.

      // Update all the added widgets
      for (int appWidgetId : appWidgetIds)
        appWidgetManager.updateAppWidget(appWidgetId, views);

      if (pendingResult != null)
        pendingResult.finish();
    }
  };
  thread.start();
}

@Override
public void onUpdate(Context context,
                     AppWidgetManager appWidgetManager,
                     int[] appWidgetIds) {
  PendingResult pendingResult = goAsync();
  updateAppWidgets(context, appWidgetManager, appWidgetIds, pendingResult);
}
```

continues

LISTING 19-11 *(continued)*

```
@Override
public void onEnabled(Context context) {
  final PendingResult pendingResult = goAsync();

  AppWidgetManager appWidgetManager =
    AppWidgetManager.getInstance(context);
  ComponentName skeletonAppWidget =
    new ComponentName(context, SkeletonAppWidget.class);
  int[] appWidgetIds =
    appWidgetManager.getAppWidgetIds(skeletonAppWidget);

  updateAppWidgets(context, appWidgetManager, appWidgetIds, pendingResult);
}
```

Creating and Using a Widget Configuration Activity

It's often useful to provide users with the opportunity to configure a Widget before adding it to their home screen. Done properly, you can make it possible for users to add multiple instances of the same Widget, each with a slightly different purpose—for example, the weather in different locations or the contents of different e-mail inboxes.

An App Widget configuration Activity is launched immediately when a Widget is added to the home screen. It can be any Activity within your application, provided it has an Intent Filter for the `APPWIDGET_CONFIGURE` action, as shown in Listing 19-12.

LISTING 19-12: App Widget configuration Activity manifest entry

```xml
<activity
  android:name=".MyWidgetConfigurationActivity"
  android:label="@string/title_activity_my_widget_configuration">
  <intent-filter>
    <action android:name="android.appwidget.action.APPWIDGET_CONFIGURE"/>
  </intent-filter>
</activity>
```

To assign a configuration Activity to a Widget, you must add it to the Widget's App Widget Provider settings file using the `configure` tag. The activity must be specified by its fully qualified package name, as shown here:

```xml
<?xml version="1.0" encoding="utf-8"?>
<appwidget-provider
  xmlns:android="http://schemas.android.com/apk/res/android"
  android:initialLayout="@layout/widget_layout"
  android:minWidth="110dp"
  android:minHeight="110dp"
  android:label="@string/widget_label"
  android:updatePeriodMillis="360000"
  android:resizeMode="horizontal|vertical"
  android:previewImage="@mipmap/ic_launcher"
  android:configure=
    "com.professionalandroid.apps.widgetsnippets.MyWidgetConfigurationActivity"
/>
```

The Intent that launches the configuration Activity will include an EXTRA_APPWIDGET_ID extra that provides the ID of the App Widget being configured.

Within the Activity, provide a UI to allow the user to complete the configuration and confirm. At this stage the Activity should set result to RESULT_OK and return an Intent. The returned Intent must include an extra that describes the ID of the Widget being configured using the EXTRA_APPWIDGET_ID constant. This skeleton pattern is shown in Listing 19-13.

LISTING 19-13: Skeleton App Widget configuration Activity

```
private int appWidgetId = AppWidgetManager.INVALID_APPWIDGET_ID;

@Override
public void onCreate(Bundle savedInstanceState) {
  super.onCreate(savedInstanceState);
  setContentView(R.layout.activity_my_widget_configuration);

  Intent intent = getIntent();
  Bundle extras = intent.getExtras();
  if (extras != null) {
    appWidgetId = extras.getInt(
      AppWidgetManager.EXTRA_APPWIDGET_ID,
      AppWidgetManager.INVALID_APPWIDGET_ID);
  }

  // Set the result to canceled in case the user exits
  // the Activity without accepting the configuration
  // changes / settings. The widget will not be placed.
  setResult(RESULT_CANCELED, null);
}

private void completedConfiguration() {
  // Save the configuration settings for the Widget ID

  // Notify the Widget Manager that the configuration has completed.
  Intent result = new Intent();
  result.putExtra(AppWidgetManager.EXTRA_APPWIDGET_ID, appWidgetId);
  setResult(RESULT_OK, result);
  finish();
}
```

It's your responsibility to save the configuration options selected by the user, and apply them based on the Widget ID when updating Widgets.

CREATING AN EARTHQUAKE WIDGET

The following instructions, which extend the Earthquake example, show you how to create a new home screen Widget to display details for the latest earthquake. The UI for this Widget is simple; we leave it as an exercise for the reader to update it to properly conform to the Widget style guidelines.

When completed and added to the home screen, your Widget will appear, as shown in Figure 19-2.

FIGURE 19-2

Using a combination of the update techniques described previously, this Widget listens for broadcast Intents that announce an update has been performed and sets the minimum update rate to ensure it is updated at least once per day.

1. Start by creating new String resources for when no Earthquake is being displayed:

    ```xml
    <resources>
      [... Existing resources ...]
      <string name="widget_blank_magnitude">---</string>
      <string name="widget_blank_details">No Earthquakes</string>
    </resources>
    ```

2. Create a layout for the Widget UI as an XML resource. Save the `quake_widget.xml` file in the `res/layout` folder. Use a Linear Layout to configure Text Views that display the quake magnitude and location:

    ```xml
    <?xml version="1.0" encoding="utf-8"?>
    <LinearLayout
      xmlns:android="http://schemas.android.com/apk/res/android"
      android:orientation="horizontal"
      android:layout_width="match_parent"
      android:layout_height="match_parent"
      android:background="@color/colorPrimaryDark">
      <TextView
        android:id="@+id/widget_magnitude"
    ```

```
        android:text="@string/widget_blank_magnitude"
        android:textColor="#FFFFFFFF"
        android:layout_width="wrap_content"
        android:layout_height="match_parent"
        android:textSize="24sp"
        android:padding="8dp"
        android:gravity="center_vertical"
        />
    <TextView
        android:id="@+id/widget_details"
        android:layout_width="match_parent"
        android:layout_height="match_parent"
        android:gravity="center_vertical"
        android:padding="8dp"
        android:text="@string/widget_blank_details"
        android:textColor="#FFFFFFFF"
        android:textSize="14sp"
        />
</LinearLayout>
```

3. Create a stub for a new `EarthquakeWidget` class that extends `AppWidgetProvider`. You'll return to this class to update your Widget with the latest quake details:

```
public class EarthquakeWidget extends AppWidgetProvider {
}
```

4. Create a new Widget definition file, `quake_widget_info.xml`, and place it in the `res/xml` folder. Set the minimum update rate to once a day and set the Widget dimensions to two cells wide and one cell high—110dp × 40dp. Use the Widget layout you created in Step 2 for the initial layout:

```
<?xml version="1.0" encoding="utf-8"?>
<appwidget-provider
  xmlns:android="http://schemas.android.com/apk/res/android"
  android:initialLayout="@layout/quake_widget"
  android:minHeight="40dp"
  android:minWidth="110dp"
  android:resizeMode="horizontal|vertical"
  android:updatePeriodMillis="86400000">
</appwidget-provider>
```

5. Add your Widget to the application manifest, including a reference to the Widget definition resource you created in Step 4, and registering an Intent Filter for the App Widget update action:

```
<receiver android:name=".EarthquakeWidget">
  <intent-filter>
    <action android:name="android.appwidget.action.APPWIDGET_UPDATE" />
  </intent-filter>
  <meta-data
    android:name="android.appwidget.provider"
    android:resource="@xml/quake_widget_info"
  />
</receiver>
```

6. Update the `EarthquakeDAO` class, adding a new method to query the Earthquake database for the newest Earthquake:

```
@Query("SELECT * FROM earthquake ORDER BY mDate DESC LIMIT 1")
Earthquake getLatestEarthquake();
```

7. Return to the `EarthquakeWidget` class from Step 2, and create a static `updateAppWidgets` method that will create a background thread to update Widgets using the result from Step 6. Note that we call finish on the `PendingResult` parameter to notify the Receiver that the asynchronous work is complete:

```
static void updateAppWidgets(final Context context,
                            final AppWidgetManager appWidgetManager,
                            final int[] appWidgetIds,
                            final PendingResult pendingResult) {
  Thread thread = new Thread() {
    public void run() {

      Earthquake lastEarthquake
        = EarthquakeDatabaseAccessor.getInstance(context)
            .earthquakeDAO().getLatestEarthquake();

      pendingResult.finish();
    }
  };
  thread.start();
}
```

8. Still within the `updateAppWidget` method, create a new `RemoteViews` object to set the text displayed by the Widget's Text View elements to show the magnitude and location of the latest earthquake. Also use the `setOnClickPendingIntent` method to open the Earthquake Main Activity when the widget is clicked:

```
static void updateAppWidgets(final Context context,
                            final AppWidgetManager appWidgetManager,
                            final int[] appWidgetIds,
                            final PendingResult pendingResult) {
  Thread thread = new Thread() {
    public void run() {

      Earthquake lastEarthquake
        = EarthquakeDatabaseAccessor.getInstance(context)
            .earthquakeDAO().getLatestEarthquake();

      boolean lastEarthquakeExists = lastEarthquake != null;

      String lastMag = lastEarthquakeExists ?
        String.valueOf(lastEarthquake.getMagnitude()) :
        context.getString(R.string.widget_blank_magnitude);

      String details = lastEarthquakeExists ?
        lastEarthquake.getDetails() :
        context.getString(R.string.widget_blank_details);
```

```
        RemoteViews views = new RemoteViews(context.getPackageName(),
                                            R.layout.quake_widget);

        views.setTextViewText(R.id.widget_magnitude, lastMag);
        views.setTextViewText(R.id.widget_details, details);

        // Create a Pending Intent that will open the main Activity.
        Intent intent = new Intent(context, EarthquakeMainActivity.class);
        PendingIntent pendingIntent =
          PendingIntent.getActivity(context, 0, intent, 0);

        views.setOnClickPendingIntent(R.id.widget_magnitude,
                                      pendingIntent);
        views.setOnClickPendingIntent(R.id.widget_details,
                                      pendingIntent);

        // Update all the added widgets
        for (int appWidgetId : appWidgetIds)
          appWidgetManager.updateAppWidget(appWidgetId, views);

      pendingResult.finish();
    }
  };
  thread.start();
}
```

9. Override the onUpdate handler. Use the goAsync method to indicate the updates will be handled asynchronously, and call updateAppWidgets to update each widget that requires an update:

```
@Override
public void onUpdate(Context context,
                     AppWidgetManager appWidgetManager,
                     int[] appWidgetIds) {
  PendingResult pendingResult = goAsync();
  updateAppWidgets(context, appWidgetManager,
                   appWidgetIds, pendingResult);
}
```

10. Also override the onEnabled hander. This will be triggered when the first Widget is added, and subsequently when all available Widgets for an application are enabled after having been disabled. Call goAsync before calling updateAppWidgets, passing in all the currently placed instances of this Widget:

```
@Override
public void onEnabled(Context context) {
  final PendingResult pendingResult = goAsync();

  AppWidgetManager appWidgetManager =
    AppWidgetManager.getInstance(context);
  ComponentName earthquakeWidget =
    new ComponentName(context, EarthquakeWidget.class);
  int[] appWidgetIds =
```

```
        appWidgetManager.getAppWidgetIds(earthquakeWidget);

    updateAppWidgets(context, appWidgetManager,
                     appWidgetIds, pendingResult);
}
```

Your Widget is now ready to be used and will update with new earthquake details when added to the home screen and once every 24 hours thereafter.

11. Further enhance the Widget to update whenever the earthquake database is updated. Still within the `EarthquakeWidget` class, create a new action string that will be used within an Intent to indicate a new earthquake has been added to the database. Override the `onReceive` method to add a check for this action when a new Intent is received, and use `updateApp-Widgets` to update each placed Widget. Be sure to call through to the super class to ensure that the standard Widget event handlers are still triggered:

```
public static final String NEW_QUAKE_BROADCAST =
  "com.paad.earthquake.NEW_QUAKE_BROADCAST";

@Override
public void onReceive(Context context, Intent intent){
  super.onReceive(context, intent);

  if (NEW_QUAKE_BROADCAST.equals(intent.getAction())) {
    PendingResult pendingResult = goAsync();

    AppWidgetManager appWidgetManager =
      AppWidgetManager.getInstance(context);
    ComponentName earthquakeWidget =
      new ComponentName(context, EarthquakeWidget.class);
    int[] appWidgetIds =
      appWidgetManager.getAppWidgetIds(earthquakeWidget);

    updateAppWidgets(context, appWidgetManager,
                     appWidgetIds, pendingResult);
  }
}
```

12. Within the Earthquake Update Job Service, modify the `onRunJob` method to broadcast an Intent to the Earthquake Widget with the action String defined in Step 11. Note that since API 26, a Broadcast Receiver can't register to listen for an implicit Intent within the manifest—so ensure the Intent explicitly targets the `EarthquakeWidget` class, as well as setting the action string:

```
@Override
public int onRunJob(final JobParameters job) {
  // Result ArrayList of parsed earthquakes.
  ArrayList<Earthquake> earthquakes = new ArrayList<>(0);

  URL url;
  try {

    [... Download and parse the earthquake XML feed]
    [... Handle Notifications ...]
```

```
EarthquakeDatabaseAccessor
  .getInstance(getApplicationContext())
  .earthquakeDAO()
  .insertEarthquakes(earthquakes);

// Update the Earthquake Widget
Intent newEarthquake = new Intent(this, EarthquakeWidget.class);
newEarthquake.setAction(EarthquakeWidget.NEW_QUAKE_BROADCAST);
sendBroadcast(newEarthquake);

[ ...Handle future scheduling ... ]

return RESULT_SUCCESS;
  }
  [... Exception Handling ...]
}
```

INTRODUCING COLLECTION VIEW WIDGETS

Collection View Widgets are designed to display collections of data represented as lists, grids, or stacks using one of three supported Views:

➤ `ListView`—A traditional scrolling list of items. Each item in the associated collection is displayed as a row in a vertical list.

➤ `GridView`—A two-dimensional scrolling grid where each item is displayed within a cell. You can control the number of columns, their width, and relevant spacing.

➤ `StackView`—A flip-card style View that displays its child Views as a stack. The stack will automatically rotate through its collection, moving the topmost item to the back to reveal the one beneath it. Users can manually transition between items by swiping up or down to reveal the previous or next items, respectively.

Figure 19-3 shows Widgets added to the home screen.

Each of these Views extends the Adapter View class. As a result, the UI used to display each item in the collection is defined using

FIGURE 19-3

whatever layout you provide; however, the UI for each item is restricted to the same Views and layouts supported by App Widgets:

➤ `FrameLayout`

➤ `LinearLayout`

➤ `RelativeLayout`

➤ Button

➤ ImageButton

➤ ImageView

➤ ProgressBar

➤ TextView

➤ ViewFlipper

Collection View Widgets can be used to display any collection of data, but they're particularly useful for creating dynamic Widgets that display data from a database.

Collection View Widgets are implemented in much the same way as regular App Widgets—using App Widget Provider Info files to configure the Widget settings, `BroadcastReceivers` to define their behavior, and `RemoteViews` to modify the Widgets at run time.

In addition, collection-based App Widgets require the following components:

➤ An additional layout resource that defines the layout for each item displayed within the collection.

➤ A `RemoteViewsFactory` that acts as an Adapter for your Widget by populating the item Views. It creates the Remote Views using the item layout definition and populates its elements using the underlying data you want to display.

➤ A `RemoteViewsService` that instantiates and manages the Remote Views Factory.

Using these components, you can use the Remote Views Factory to create and update each of the Views that will represent the items in your collection. This process is described in the section "Populating Collection View Widgets Using a Remote Views Service."

Creating Collection View Widget Layouts

Collection View Widgets require two layout definitions—one that includes either a Stack, List, or Grid View, and another that describes the layout to be used by each item within the stack, list, or grid.

As with regular App Widgets, it's best practice to define your layouts as external XML layout resources, as shown in Listing 19-14.

LISTING 19-14: Defining the Widget layout with a Stack Widget

```
<?xml version="1.0" encoding="utf-8"?>
<FrameLayout
  xmlns:android="http://schemas.android.com/apk/res/android"
  android:layout_width="match_parent"
  android:layout_height="match_parent">
  <StackView
    android:id="@+id/widget_stack_view"
```

```
        android:layout_width="match_parent"
        android:layout_height="match_parent"
    />
</FrameLayout>
```

Listing 19-15 shows an example layout resource used to describe the UI of each card displayed by the Stack View Widget.

LISTING 19-15: Defining the layout for each item displayed within a Stack View Widget

```xml
<?xml version="1.0" encoding="utf-8"?>
<RelativeLayout
  xmlns:android="http://schemas.android.com/apk/res/android"
  android:layout_width="match_parent"
  android:layout_height="match_parent"
  android:background="#FF555555">
  <TextView
    android:id="@+id/widget_text"
    android:layout_width="fill_parent"
    android:layout_height="wrap_content"
    android:layout_alignParentBottom="true"
    android:gravity="center_horizontal"
    android:text="Place holder text"
  />
  <TextView
    android:id="@+id/widget_title_text"
    android:layout_width="match_parent"
    android:layout_height="match_parent"
    android:layout_above="@id/widget_text"
    android:textSize="30sp"
    android:gravity="center"
   android:text="---"
  />
</RelativeLayout>
```

The Widget layout is used within the App Widget Provider Info resource as it would be for any App Widget. The item layout is used by a Remote Views Factory to create the Views used to represent each item in the underlying collection.

Updating Collection View Items with a Remote Views Factory

The RemoteViewsFactory creates and populates the Views that will be displayed in the Collection View Widget—effectively binding them to the underlying data collection.

To implement your Remote Views Factory, extend the RemoteViewsFactory class.

Your implementation should mirror that of a custom Adapter that will populate the Stack, List, or Grid View. Listing 19-16 shows a simple implementation of a Remote Views Factory that uses a static Array List to populate its Views. Note that the Remote Views Factory doesn't need to know what kind of Collection View Widget will be used to display each item.

LISTING 19-16: Creating a Remote Views Factory

```
class MyRemoteViewsFactory implements RemoteViewsService.RemoteViewsFactory {

  private ArrayList<String> myWidgetText = new ArrayList<String>();
  private Context context;
  private Intent intent;
  private int widgetId;

  public MyRemoteViewsFactory(Context context, Intent intent) {
    // Optional constructor implementation.
    // Useful for getting references to the
    // Context of the calling widget
    this.context = context;
    this.intent = intent;

    widgetId = intent.getIntExtra(AppWidgetManager.EXTRA_APPWIDGET_ID,
      AppWidgetManager.INVALID_APPWIDGET_ID);
  }

  // Set up any connections / cursors to your data source.
  // Heavy lifting, like downloading data should be
  // deferred to onDataSetChanged()or getViewAt().
  // Taking more than 20 seconds in this call will result
  // in an ANR.
  public void onCreate() {
    myWidgetText.add("The");
    myWidgetText.add("quick");
    myWidgetText.add("brown");
    myWidgetText.add("fox");
    myWidgetText.add("jumps");
    myWidgetText.add("over");
    myWidgetText.add("the");
    myWidgetText.add("lazy");
    myWidgetText.add("droid");
  }

  // Called when the underlying data collection being displayed is
  // modified. You can use the AppWidgetManager's
  // notifyAppWidgetViewDataChanged method to trigger this handler.
  public void onDataSetChanged() {
    // TODO Processing when underlying data has changed.
  }

  // Return the number of items in the collection being displayed.
  public int getCount() {
    return myWidgetText.size();
  }

  // Return true if the unique IDs provided by each item are stable --
  // that is, they don't change at run time.
  public boolean hasStableIds() {
    return false;
  }
```

```java
  // Return the unique ID associated with the item at a given index.
  public long getItemId(int index) {
    return index;
  }

  // The number of different view definitions. Usually 1.
  public int getViewTypeCount() {
    return 1;
  }

  // Optionally specify a "loading" view to display before onDataSetChanged
  // has been called and returned. Return null to use the default.
  public RemoteViews getLoadingView() {
    return null;
  }

  // Create and populate the View to display at the given index.
  public RemoteViews getViewAt(int index) {
    // Create a view to display at the required index.
    RemoteViews rv = new RemoteViews(context.getPackageName(),
                              R.layout.widget_collection_item_layout);

    // Populate the view from the underlying data.
    rv.setTextViewText(R.id.widget_title_text,
                       myWidgetText.get(index));
    rv.setTextViewText(R.id.widget_text, "View Number: " +
                                    String.valueOf(index));

    // Create an item-specific fill-in Intent that will populate
    // the Pending Intent template created in the App Widget Provider.
    Intent fillInIntent = new Intent();
    fillInIntent.putExtra(Intent.EXTRA_TEXT, myWidgetText.get(index));
    rv.setOnClickFillInIntent(R.id.widget_title_text, fillInIntent);

    return rv;
  }

  // Close connections, cursors, or any other persistent state you
  // created in onCreate.
  public void onDestroy() {
    myWidgetText.clear();
  }
}
```

Updating Collection View Items with a Remote Views Service

The Remote Views Service is used as a wrapper that instantiates and manages your Remote Views Factory, which, in turn, is used to supply each of the Views displayed within the Collection View Widget as described in the previous section.

To create a Remote Views Service, extend the RemoteViewsService class and override the onGetViewFactory handler to return a new instance of a Remote Views Factory, as shown in Listing 19-17.

LISTING 19-17: Creating a Remote Views Service

```
public class MyRemoteViewsService extends RemoteViewsService {

  @Override
  public RemoteViewsFactory onGetViewFactory(Intent intent) {
    return new MyRemoteViewsFactory(getApplicationContext(), intent);
  }

}
```

As with any Service, you'll need to add your Remote Views Service to your application manifest using a `service` tag. To prevent other applications from accessing your Widgets, you must specify the `android.permission.BIND_REMOTEVIEWS` permission, as shown in Listing 19-18.

LISTING 19-18: Adding a Remote Views Service to the manifest

```
<service
  android:name=".MyRemoteViewsService"
  android:permission="android.permission.BIND_REMOTEVIEWS">
</service>
```

Populating Collection View Widgets Using a Remote Views Service

With your Remote Views Factory and Remote Views Service complete, all that remains is to bind the List, Grid, or Stack View within your App Widget Layout to the Remote Views Service. You do this using a Remote View, typically within a static *update* method that's called from within the `onUpdate` and `onEnabled` handlers of your App Widget implementation.

Create a new Remote View instance as you would when updating the UI of a standard App Widget. Use the `setRemoteAdapter` method to bind your Remote Views Service to the particular List, Grid, or Stack View within the Widget layout.

The Remote Views Service is specified using an Intent that includes an extra value that defines the ID of the Widget to which it is being associated:

```
Intent intent = new Intent(context, MyRemoteViewsService.class);
intent.putExtra(AppWidgetManager.EXTRA_APPWIDGET_ID, appWidgetId);

views.setRemoteAdapter(R.id.widget_stack_view, intent);
```

This Intent is received by the `onGetViewFactory` handler within the Remote Views Service, enabling you to pass additional parameters into the Service and the Factory it contains.

The `setEmptyView` method provides a means of specifying a View that should be displayed in place of the Collection View if (and only if) the underlying data collection is empty:

```
views.setEmptyView(R.id.widget_stack_view, R.id.widget_empty_text);
```

After completing the binding process, use the App Widget Manager's `updateAppWidget` method to apply the binding to the specified Widget. Listing 19-19 shows the standard pattern for binding a Widget to a Remote Views Service.

LISTING 19-19: Binding a Remove Views Service to a Widget

```
static void updateAppWidget(Context context,
                           AppWidgetManager appWidgetManager,
                           int appWidgetId) {

  // Create a Remote View.
  RemoteViews views = new RemoteViews(context.getPackageName(),
                                      R.layout.widget_collection_layout);

  // Bind this widget to a Remote Views Service.
  Intent intent = new Intent(context, MyRemoteViewsService.class);
  intent.putExtra(AppWidgetManager.EXTRA_APPWIDGET_ID, appWidgetId);
  views.setRemoteAdapter(R.id.widget_stack_view, intent);

  // Specify a View within the Widget layout hierarchy to display
  // when the bound collection is empty.
  views.setEmptyView(R.id.widget_stack_view, R.id.widget_empty_text);

  // TODO Customize this Widgets UI based on configuration
  // settings etc.

  // Notify the App Widget Manager to update the widget using
  // the modified remote view.
  appWidgetManager.updateAppWidget(appWidgetId, views);
}
```

Adding Interactivity to the Items Within a Collection View Widget

For efficiency reasons, it's not possible to assign a unique `onClickPendingIntent` to each item displayed as part of a Collection View Widget. Instead, use the `setPendingIntentTemplate` to assign a template Intent to your Widget when updating the Remote Views, as shown in Listing 19-20.

LISTING 19-20: Adding a Click Listener to individual items within a Collection View Widget using a Pending Intent

```
Intent templateIntent = new Intent(context, MainActivity.class);

templateIntent.putExtra(AppWidgetManager.EXTRA_APPWIDGET_ID, appWidgetId);

PendingIntent templatePendingIntent = PendingIntent.getActivity(
  context, 0, templateIntent, PendingIntent.FLAG_UPDATE_CURRENT);

views.setPendingIntentTemplate(R.id.widget_stack_view,
                               templatePendingIntent);

appWidgetManager.updateAppWidget(appWidgetId, views);
```

This Pending Intent can then be "filled-in" within the `getViewAt` handler of your Remote Views Service implementation using the `setOnClickFillInIntent` method of your Remote Views object, as shown in Listing 19-21.

LISTING 19-21: Filling in a Pending Intent template for each item displayed in your Collection View Widget

```
// Create the item-specific fill-in Intent that will populate
// the Pending Intent template created in the App Widget Provider.
Intent fillInIntent = new Intent();
fillInIntent.putExtra(Intent.EXTRA_TEXT, myWidgetText.get(index));
rv.setOnClickFillInIntent(R.id.widget_title_text, fillInIntent);
```

The fill-in Intent is applied to the template Intent using the `Intent.fillIn` method. It copies the contents of the fill-in Intent into the template Intent, replacing any undefined fields with those defined by the fill-in Intent. Fields with existing data will *not* be overridden.

The resulting Pending Intent will be broadcast when a user clicks that particular item from within your collection Widget.

Refreshing Your Collection View Widgets

The App Widget Manager includes the `notifyAppWidgetViewDataChanged` method, which allows you to specify a Widget ID (or array of IDs) to update, along with the resource identifier for the collection View within that Widget whose underlying data source has changed:

```
appWidgetManager.notifyAppWidgetViewDataChanged(appWidgetIds,
    R.id.widget_stack_view);
```

This will cause the `onDataSetChanged` handler within the associated Remote Views Factory to be executed, followed by the meta-data calls, including `getCount`, before each of the Views is re-created.

Creating an Earthquake Collection View Widget

In this example you add a second Widget to the Earthquake application. This one uses a ListView-based Collection View Widget to display a list of the recent earthquakes.

1. Start by creating a layout for the Collection View Widget UI as an XML resource. Save the `quake_collection_widget.xml` file in the `res/layout` folder. Use a Frame Layout that includes the List View for displaying the earthquakes and a Text View to display when the collection is empty:

    ```
    <?xml version="1.0" encoding="utf-8"?>
    <FrameLayout
      xmlns:android="http://schemas.android.com/apk/res/android"
      android:layout_width="match_parent"
      android:layout_height="match_parent">
      <ListView
    ```

```
        android:id="@+id/widget_list_view"
        android:layout_width="match_parent"
        android:layout_height="match_parent"
    />
    <TextView
        android:id="@+id/widget_empty_text"
        android:layout_width="match_parent"
        android:layout_height="match_parent"
        android:gravity="center"
        android:text="@string/widget_blank_details"
    />
</FrameLayout>
```

2. Create a new `EarthquakeListWidget` class that extends `AppWidgetProvider` and implements the standard pattern for enabling and updating Widgets. You'll return to this class to bind your Widget to the Remote Views Service that will provide the Views that display each earthquake:

```
public class EarthquakeListWidget extends AppWidgetProvider {

  @Override
  public void onUpdate(Context context,
                       AppWidgetManager appWidgetManager,
                       int[] appWidgetIds) {
    PendingResult pendingResult = goAsync();
    updateAppWidgets(context, appWidgetManager,
                     appWidgetIds, pendingResult);
  }

  @Override
  public void onEnabled(Context context) {
    final PendingResult pendingResult = goAsync();

    AppWidgetManager appWidgetManager =
      AppWidgetManager.getInstance(context);
    ComponentName earthquakeListWidget =
      new ComponentName(context, EarthquakeListWidget.class);
    int[] appWidgetIds =
      appWidgetManager.getAppWidgetIds(earthquakeListWidget);

    updateAppWidgets(context, appWidgetManager,
                     appWidgetIds, pendingResult);
  }

  static void updateAppWidgets(final Context context,
                               final AppWidgetManager appWidgetManager,
                               final int[] appWidgetIds,
                               final PendingResult pendingResult) {
    Thread thread = new Thread() {
      public void run() {

        // TODO Set Widget Remote Views
```

```
              if (pendingResult != null)
                pendingResult.finish();
          }
        };
        thread.start();
      }
    }
```

3. Create a new Widget definition file, `quake_list_widget_info.xml`, in the `res/xml` folder. Set the minimum update rate to once a day, set the Widget dimensions to two cells wide and one cell high (110dp × 40dp), and make it resizable. Use the Widget layout you created in Step 1 for the initial layout:

```xml
<?xml version="1.0" encoding="utf-8"?>
<appwidget-provider
  xmlns:android="http://schemas.android.com/apk/res/android"
  android:initialLayout="@layout/quake_collection_widget"
  android:minWidth="110dp"
  android:minHeight="40dp"
  android:updatePeriodMillis="8640000"
  android:resizeMode="vertical|horizontal"
/>
```

4. Add your Widget to the application manifest, including a reference to the Widget definition resource you created in Step 3. It should also include an Intent Filter for the App Widget update action:

```xml
<receiver
  android:name=".EarthquakeListWidget"
  android:label="Earthquake List">
  <intent-filter>
    <action android:name="android.appwidget.action.APPWIDGET_UPDATE" />
  </intent-filter>
  <meta-data
    android:name="android.appwidget.provider"
    android:resource="@xml/quake_list_widget_info"
  />
</receiver>
```

5. Create a new `EarthquakeRemoteViewsService` class that extends `RemoteViewsService`. It should include an internal `EarthquakeRemoteViewsFactory` class that extends `RemoteViewsFactory`, which should be returned from the Earthquake Remote Views Service's `onGetViewFactory` handler:

```java
public class EarthquakeRemoteViewsService extends RemoteViewsService {

  @Override
  public RemoteViewsFactory onGetViewFactory(Intent intent) {
    return new EarthquakeRemoteViewsFactory(this);
  }

  class EarthquakeRemoteViewsFactory implements RemoteViewsFactory {

    private Context mContext;
```

```java
    public EarthquakeRemoteViewsFactory(Context context) {
      mContext = context;
    }

    public void onCreate() {
    }

    public void onDataSetChanged() {
    }

    public int getCount() {
      return 0;
    }

    public long getItemId(int index) {
      return index;
    }

    public RemoteViews getViewAt(int index) {
      return null;
    }

    public int getViewTypeCount() {
      return 1;
    }

    public boolean hasStableIds() {
      return true;
    }

    public RemoteViews getLoadingView() {
      return null;
    }

    public void onDestroy() {
    }
  }
}
```

6. Update the `onDataSetChanged` handler to query the database:

```java
    private List<Earthquake> mEarthquakes;

    public void onDataSetChanged() {
      mEarthquakes = EarthquakeDatabaseAccessor.getInstance(mContext)
                    .earthquakeDAO().loadAllEarthquakesBlocking();
    }
```

7. The Earthquake Remote Views Factory supplies the Views that represent each Earthquake in the Widget's List View. Populate each of the method stubs to use the data from the Earthquake List to populate the View that represent each item.

7.1 Start by updating the `getCount` and `getItemId` methods to return the number of Earthquakes in the List, and a unique numeric identifier associated with each Earthquake, respectively:

```
public int getCount() {
  if (mEarthquakes == null) return 0;
  return mEarthquakes.size();
}

public long getItemId(int index) {
  if (mEarthquakes == null) return index;
  return mEarthquakes.get(index).getDate().getTime();
}
```

7.2   Then update the getViewAt method. This is where the Views used to represent each Earthquake in the List View are created and populated. Create a new Remote Views object using the layout definition you created for the previous Earthquake Widget, and populate it with data from the specified Earthquake:

```
public RemoteViews getViewAt(int index) {
  if (mEarthquakes != null) {
    // Extract the requested Earthquake.
    Earthquake earthquake = mEarthquakes.get(index);

    // Extract the values to be displayed.
    String id = earthquake.getId();
    String magnitude = String.valueOf(earthquake.getMagnitude());
    String details = earthquake.getDetails();

    // Create a new Remote Views object and use it to populate the
    // layout used to represent each earthquake in the list.
    RemoteViews rv = new RemoteViews(mContext.getPackageName(),
                                     R.layout.quake_widget);

    rv.setTextViewText(R.id.widget_magnitude, magnitude);
    rv.setTextViewText(R.id.widget_details, details);

    // Create a Pending Intent that will open the main Activity.
    Intent intent = new Intent(mContext, EarthquakeMainActivity.class);
    PendingIntent pendingIntent =
      PendingIntent.getActivity(mContext, 0, intent, 0);

    rv.setOnClickPendingIntent(R.id.widget_magnitude, pendingIntent);
    rv.setOnClickPendingIntent(R.id.widget_details, pendingIntent);

    return rv;
  } else {
    return null;
  }
}
```

8.   Add the Earthquake Remote Views Service to your application manifest, including a requirement for the BIND_REMOTEVIEWS permission:

```
<service
  android:name=".EarthquakeRemoteViewsService"
  android:permission="android.permission.BIND_REMOTEVIEWS">
</service>
```

9. Return to the Earthquake List Widget class and override the `updateAppWidgets` method to attach the Earthquake Remote Views Service to each Widget:

```java
static void updateAppWidgets(final Context context,
                            final AppWidgetManager appWidgetManager,
                            final int[] appWidgetIds,
                            final PendingResult pendingResult) {
  Thread thread = new Thread() {
    public void run() {
      for (int appWidgetId: appWidgetIds) {
        // Set up the intent that starts the Earthquake
        // Remote Views Service, which will supply the views
        // shown in the List View.
        Intent intent =
          new Intent(context, EarthquakeRemoteViewsService.class);

        // Add the app widget ID to the intent extras.
        intent.putExtra(AppWidgetManager.EXTRA_APPWIDGET_ID,
                        appWidgetId);

        // Instantiate the RemoteViews object for the App Widget layout.
        RemoteViews views
          = new RemoteViews(context.getPackageName(),
                            R.layout.quake_collection_widget);

        // Set up the RemoteViews object to use a RemoteViews adapter.
        views.setRemoteAdapter(R.id.widget_list_view, intent);

        // The empty view is displayed when the collection has no items.
        views.setEmptyView(R.id.widget_list_view,
                           R.id.widget_empty_text);

        // Notify the App Widget Manager to update the widget using
        // the modified remote view.
        appWidgetManager.updateAppWidget(appWidgetId, views);
      }
      if (pendingResult != null)
        pendingResult.finish();
    }
  };
  thread.start();
}
```

10. As a final step, enhance the Widget to update whenever a new Earthquake is added to the database. Within the Earthquake Update Job Service, modify the `onRunJob` method to broadcast an Intent to the new Widget:

```java
@Override
public int onRunJob(final JobParameters job) {
  // Result ArrayList of parsed earthquakes.
  ArrayList<Earthquake> earthquakes = new ArrayList<>(0);

  URL url;
  try {
```

```
[... Download and parse the earthquake XML feed]
[... Handle Notifications ...]

EarthquakeDatabaseAccessor
  .getInstance(getApplicationContext())
  .earthquakeDAO()
  .insertEarthquakes(earthquakes);

// Update the Earthquake Widget
Intent newEarthquake = new Intent(this, EarthquakeWidget.class);
newEarthquake.setAction(EarthquakeWidget.NEW_QUAKE_BROADCAST);
sendBroadcast(newEarthquake);

// Update the Earthquake List Widget
Intent newListEarthquake = new Intent(this,
                                      EarthquakeListWidget.class);
newListEarthquake.setAction(EarthquakeWidget.NEW_QUAKE_BROADCAST);
sendBroadcast(newListEarthquake);

[ ...Handle future scheduling ... ]

return RESULT_SUCCESS;
}
[... Exception Handling ...]
}
```

11. Then override the OnReceive handler within the Earthquake List Widget to listen
     for the update-request Intent, and use the App Widget Manager's notifyAppWiget-
     ViewDataChanged method to trigger an update of the List View:

```
@Override
public void onReceive(final Context context, final Intent intent) {
  super.onReceive(context, intent);

  if (EarthquakeWidget.NEW_QUAKE_BROADCAST.equals(intent.getAction())) {
    AppWidgetManager appWidgetManager =
      AppWidgetManager.getInstance(context);
    ComponentName earthquakeListWidget =
      new ComponentName(context, EarthquakeListWidget.class);
    int[] appWidgetIds =
      appWidgetManager.getAppWidgetIds(earthquakeListWidget);

    // Notify the Earthquake List Widget that it should be refreshed.
    final PendingResult pendingResult = goAsync();
    appWidgetManager.notifyAppWidgetViewDataChanged(appWidgetIds,
      R.id.widget_list_view);
  }
}
```

Figure 19-4 shows the Earthquake Collection View Widget added to the home screen.

FIGURE 19-4

CREATING LIVE WALLPAPER

Live Wallpaper enables you to create dynamic, interactive home screen backgrounds. Live Wallpapers use a Surface View to render a dynamic display that changes, and can be interacted with, in real time. Your Live Wallpaper can listen for, and react to, screen touch events—letting users engage directly with the background of their home screen.

To create a new Live Wallpaper, you need the following three components:

➤ An XML resource that describes the metadata associated with the Live Wallpaper—specifically its author, description, and a thumbnail used to represent it from the Live Wallpaper picker.

➤ A Wallpaper Service implementation that will wrap, instantiate, and manage your Wallpaper Service Engine.

➤ A Wallpaper Service Engine implementation (returned through the Wallpaper Service) that defines the UI and interactive behavior of your Live Wallpaper. The Wallpaper Service Engine is where the bulk of your Live Wallpaper implementation will live.

Creating a Live Wallpaper Definition Resource

The Live Wallpaper resource definition is an XML file stored in the `res/xml` folder. Its resource identifier is its filename without the XML extension. Use attributes within a `wallpaper` tag to define the author name, description, and thumbnail to display in the Live Wallpaper gallery.

Listing 19-22 shows a sample Live Wallpaper resource definition.

LISTING 19-22: Live Wallpaper resource definition

```
<wallpaper xmlns:android="http://schemas.android.com/apk/res/android"
  android:author="@string/author"
  android:description="@string/description"
  android:thumbnail="@drawable/wallpapericon"
/>
```

Note that you *must* use references to string resources for the `author` and `description` attribute values. String literals are not valid.

You can also use the `settingsActivity` tag to specify an Activity that should be launched to configure the Live Wallpaper's settings, much like the configuration Activity used to configure App Widget settings:

```
<wallpaper xmlns:android="http://schemas.android.com/apk/res/android"
  android:author="@string/author"
  android:description="@string/description"
  android:thumbnail="@drawable/wallpapericon"
  android:settingsActivity="com.paad.mylivewallpaper.WallpaperSettings"
/>
```

This Activity will be launched immediately before the Live Wallpaper is added to the home screen, allowing the user to configure the Wallpaper settings.

Creating a Wallpaper Service Engine

The `WallpaperService.Engine` class is where you define the behavior of your Live Wallpaper. The Wallpaper Service Engine includes a Surface View onto which you will draw your Live Wallpaper, and handlers notifying you of touch events and home screen offset changes.

The Surface View is a specialized drawing canvas that supports updates from background threads, making it ideal for creating smooth, dynamic, and interactive graphics.

To implement your own Wallpaper Service Engine, extend the `WallpaperService.Engine` class, as shown in the skeleton code in Listing 19-23. Note that it must be implemented within the scope of a `WallpaperService` class. We'll explore the Wallpaper Service in more detail in the following section.

LISTING 19-23: Wallpaper Service Engine skeleton code

```java
public class MyWallpaperService extends WallpaperService {

  @Override
  public Engine onCreateEngine() {
    return new MyWallpaperServiceEngine();
  }

  public class MyWallpaperServiceEngine extends WallpaperService.Engine {

    private static final int FPS = 30;
    private final Handler handler = new Handler();

    @Override
    public void onCreate(SurfaceHolder surfaceHolder) {
      super.onCreate(surfaceHolder);
      // TODO Handle initialization.
    }

    @Override
    public void onOffsetsChanged(float xOffset, float yOffset,
                                 float xOffsetStep, float yOffsetStep,
                                 int xPixelOffset, int yPixelOffset) {
      super.onOffsetsChanged(xOffset, yOffset, xOffsetStep, yOffsetStep,
                             xPixelOffset, yPixelOffset);
      // Triggered whenever the user swipes between multiple
      // home-screen panels.
    }

    @Override
    public void onTouchEvent(MotionEvent event) {
      super.onTouchEvent(event);
      // Triggered when the Live Wallpaper receives a touch event
    }

    @Override
    public void onSurfaceCreated(SurfaceHolder holder) {
      super.onSurfaceCreated(holder);
      // TODO Surface has been created, begin the update loop that will
      // update the Live Wallpaper.
      drawFrame();
    }

    @Override
    public void onSurfaceDestroyed(SurfaceHolder holder) {
      handler.removeCallbacks(drawSurface);
      super.onSurfaceDestroyed(holder);
    }
```

continues

LISTING 19-23 *(continued)*

```
    private synchronized void drawFrame() {
      final SurfaceHolder holder = getSurfaceHolder();

      if (holder != null && holder.getSurface().isValid()) {
        Canvas canvas = null;
        try {
          canvas = holder.lockCanvas();
          if (canvas != null) {
            // Draw on the Canvas!
          }
        } finally {
          if (canvas != null && holder != null)
            holder.unlockCanvasAndPost(canvas);
        }

        // Schedule the next frame
        handler.removeCallbacks(drawSurface);
      }
      handler.postDelayed(drawSurface, 1000 / FPS);
    }

    // Runnable used to allow you to schedule frame draws.
    private final Runnable drawSurface = new Runnable() {
      public void run() {
        drawFrame();
      }
    };
  }
}
```

You must wait for the Surface to complete its initialization—indicated by the `onSurfaceCreated` handler being called—before you can begin drawing on it.

After the Surface has been created, you can begin the drawing loop that updates the Live Wallpaper's UI. The code in Listing 19-23 does this by scheduling a new frame to be drawn at the completion of the drawing of the previous frame. The rate of redraws in this example is determined by the specified frame rate.

You can also override the `onTouchEvent` and the `onOffsetsChanged` handlers to add interactivity to your Live Wallpapers.

Creating a Wallpaper Service

While all the drawing and interaction for Live Wallpaper is handled in the Wallpaper Service Engine, the `WallpaperService` class is used to instantiate, host, and manage that Engine.

Extend the `WallpaperService` class, and override the `onCreateEngine` handler to return a new instance of your custom Wallpaper Service Engine, as shown in Listing 19-24.

LISTING 19-24: Creating a Wallpaper Service

```java
public class MyWallpaperService extends WallpaperService {

  @Override
  public Engine onCreateEngine() {
    return new MyWallpaperServiceEngine();
  }

  [... Wallpaper Engine Implementation ...]

}
```

After creating the Wallpaper Service, add it to your application manifest using a `service` tag.

A Wallpaper Service must include an Intent Filter to listen for the `android.service.wallpaper` `.WallpaperService` action and a `meta-data` node that specifies `android.service.wallpaper` as the name attribute and associates it with the resource file described in the previous section using a `resource` attribute.

A Wallpaper Service must also include the `android.permission.BIND_WALLPAPER` permission. Listing 19-35 shows how to add the Wallpaper Service from Listing 19-34 to the manifest.

LISTING 19-25: Adding a Wallpaper Service to the manifest

```xml
<service
  android:name=".MyWallpaperService"
  android:permission="android.permission.BIND_WALLPAPER">
  <intent-filter>
    <action android:name=
      "android.service.wallpaper.WallpaperService" />
  </intent-filter>
  <meta-data
    android:name="android.service.wallpaper"
    android:resource="@xml/mylivewallpaper"
  />
</service>
```

CREATING APP SHORTCUTS

Introduced in Android 7.1 Nougat (API Level 25), App Shortcuts allow you to create shortcuts that link directly from the home screen or app launcher to functionality within your application.

When supported and available for a given app, App Shortcuts are revealed by long-pressing the app icon in the launcher or home screen; they appear, as shown in Figure 19-5.

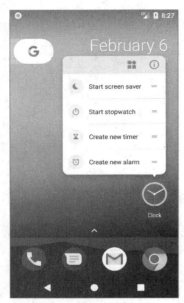

FIGURE 19-5

Once visible, a user can "pin" an App Shortcut directly to the home screen by long pressing, dragging, and then dropping a specific shortcut.

Selecting an App Shortcut will launch its associated Intent, effectively becoming a shortcut to a task, action, or functionality within your application. Each application can offer up to five shortcuts at any given time, though the design guidelines strongly recommend offering only four.

By providing an easily discoverable shortcut to important app functionality, App Shortcuts are a powerful technique for increasing user engagement. When creating shortcuts, you should focus on exposing your app's key functionality—particularly actions that might require complex, multiple steps, or that are time sensitive.

For example, Google offers App Shortcuts within its own apps for sending a new text message, navigating to work/home, taking a selfie, and calling a specific contact.

App Shortcuts are displayed within the launcher and home screen, alongside the icons and App Shortcuts of the system and other third-party apps. As a result, it's important to follow the design guidelines to ensure the icons used by your Shortcuts are visually consistent with other Shortcuts. You can find Google's App Shortcut design guidelines at `commondatastorage.googleapis.com/androiddevelopers/shareables/design/app-shortcuts-design-guidelines.pdf`.

Android supports two alternatives for defining App Shortcuts: static and dynamic, which are described in the following sections.

Static Shortcuts

Static Shortcuts are used to provide links to generic, core functionality that is always relevant—such as composing a new message or remotely arming an alarm. As the name suggests, static Shortcuts can't be modified from within your app at run time. Given the limited number of App Shortcuts available, you should ensure your static Shortcuts are always useful and relevant, and consider using dynamic Shortcuts if that's not the case.

Static App Shortcuts are defined as resources, stored as XML files. By convention, this resource is named `shortcuts.xml`. App Shortcuts were introduced at API Level 25, so it's good practice to store them in the `res/xml-v25` folder.

Create your App Shortcuts using the `shortcuts` tag as the root node, with one or more `shortcut` tags, each specifying a static App Shortcut.

As shown in Listing 19-26, this includes a unique Shortcut identifier, icon, labels, a disabled message, and the Intent to launch when the Shortcut is selected. Note that you must also specify a category—at the time of writing only one category, conversation, was valid.

LISTING 19-26: Defining your static App Shortcuts

```xml
<?xml version="1.0" encoding="utf-8"?>
<shortcuts xmlns:android="http://schemas.android.com/apk/res/android">
  <shortcut
    android:shortcutId="orbitnuke"
    android:enabled="true"
    android:icon="@drawable/nuke_icon"
    android:shortcutShortLabel="@string/orbitnuke_shortcut_short_label"
    android:shortcutLongLabel="@string/orbitnuke_shortcut_long_label"
    android:shortcutDisabledMessage="@string/orbitnuke_shortcut_disabled">
    <intent
      android:action="android.intent.action.VIEW"
      android:targetPackage="com.professionalandroid.apps.aliens"
      android:targetClass="com.professionalandroid.apps.aliens.NukeActivity"/>
    <categories android:name="android.shortcut.conversation" />
  </shortcut>
</shortcuts>
```

The icon and labels are displayed by the launcher to represent each available Shortcut, as shown previously in Figure 19-5. The short title should be approximately 10 characters, while the long title can be up to 25 characters. The long title is displayed when there is enough space.

If a static Shortcut is pinned, and then subsequently removed from the app in a later version of your app, any pinned instances of your static Shortcuts will remain on the desktop, but it will be automatically disabled with the specified disabled message displayed.

Once you've defined your App Shortcuts resource, you must add them to your application by associating the App Shortcuts resource to your launch Activity using a `meta-data` tag with the `android.app.shortcuts` name, as shown in Listing 19-27.

LISTING 19-27: Adding the Shortcuts Resource to the application manifest

```
<activity
  android:name=".MainActivity">
  <intent-filter>
    <action android:name="android.intent.action.MAIN"/>
    <category android:name="android.intent.category.LAUNCHER"/>
  </intent-filter>
  <meta-data
    android:name="android.app.shortcuts"
    android:resource="@xml/shortcuts"
  />
</activity>
```

Dynamic Shortcuts

Dynamic Shortcuts can be generated, modified, and removed at run time using the `ShortcutManager` system Service:

```
ShortcutManager shortcutManager = getSystemService(ShortcutManager.class);
```

You should ensure your dynamic Shortcuts represent the most likely useful piece of functionality given the current context, such as calling a specific contact or navigating to a particular location.

To alter the list of available dynamic App Shortcuts at run time, use the following Shortcut Manager methods:

➤ `setDynamicShortcuts`—Replace the existing List of dynamic App Shortcuts with a new Shortcut List.

➤ `addDynamicShortcuts`—Add one or more new dynamic Shortcuts to the existing List.

➤ `updateShortcuts`—Update the dynamic Shortcuts in the existing List, based on the identifiers of the passed in List.

➤ `removeDynamicShortcuts`—Remove the dynamic Shortcuts in the existing List, corresponding to the passed-in List of identifiers.

➤ `removeAllDynamicShortcuts`—Remove all currently set dynamic App Shortcuts.

To create a new Shortcut to add or update, use the `ShortcutInfo.Builder`, as shown in Listing 19-28, to specify the icon, labels, and launch Intent. Note that the launch Intent must include an action, but can use Intent resolution rather than targeting a specific Activity.

LISTING 19-28: Creating and adding dynamic App Shortcuts

```
ShortcutManager shortcutManager
  = (ShortcutManager) getSystemService(Context.SHORTCUT_SERVICE);
Intent navIntent = new Intent(this, MainActivity.class);
navIntent.setAction(Intent.ACTION_VIEW);
```

```
navIntent.putExtra(DESTINATION_EXTRA, destination);

String id = "dynamicDest" + destination;

ShortcutInfo shortcut =
  new ShortcutInfo.Builder(this, id)
  .setShortLabel(destination)
  .setLongLabel("Navigate to " + destination)
  .setDisabledMessage("Navigation Shortcut Disabled")
  .setIcon(Icon.createWithResource(this, R.mipmap.ic_launcher))
  .setIntent(navIntent)
  .build();

shortcutManager.setDynamicShortcuts(Arrays.asList(shortcut));
```

If you pass a Shortcut to the set or add dynamic Shortcuts method that already exists in the active list, it will be updated accordingly.

When updating dynamic Shortcuts it's important to ensure that the semantic meaning of the Shortcut is maintained. For example, if your Shortcut sends a message to a specific person, it could be updated to reflect an updated profile image for that person, but not to send a message to a different person. If the semantic meaning changes, you should instead remove the previous Shortcut and add a new one with a new unique identifier.

This process is important, because while you can only have five Shortcuts available for users to select at any given time, users can pin Shortcuts to their desktop, as shown in Figure 19-6.

Users can add as many pinned Shortcuts to their desktops as they want, and you can't remove them programmatically. Once pinned, a Shortcut will continue to look and behave as originally defined, even if you remove it from the dynamic list at run time; however, a call to `updateShortcuts` can still be used to modify a pinned Shortcut even if it's no longer available from the dynamic list.

FIGURE 19-6

While you can't remove a pinned Shortcut for users, in circumstances where a previously pinned Shortcut is no longer valid—for example, if the Shortcut's target functionality or associated content has been removed from your app—you can disable it using the `disableShortcuts` method, passing in a List of identifiers to disable, and optionally a disables message to be displayed:

```
shortcutManager.disableShortcuts(Arrays.asList("Id1", "Id2"),
                                 "Functionality Removed");
```

Tracking App Shortcut Use

The order, and in some cases availability, of your App Shortcuts can vary based on the launcher or home screen's prediction of which Shortcuts are most likely to be used at a given time.

These predictions are based on the usage history of each Shortcut, or the underlying functionality they provide a shortcut to.

Use the Shortcut Manager's `reportShortcutUsed` method, passing in the relevant Shortcut ID, to indicate that the user has manually initiated an action that is also represented by a Shortcut:

```
shortcutManager.reportShortcutUsed("Id1");
```

You should make this call no matter how the action was initiated, to ensure the prediction-engine has a full record of the usage pattern of actions for which there are shortcuts, allowing it to promote and display the most appropriate Shortcuts at the right time.

20

Advanced Android Development

WROX.COM CODE DOWNLOADS FOR THIS CHAPTER

The code downloads for this chapter are found at www.wrox.com. The code for this chapter is divided into the following major examples:

➤ `Snippets_ch20.zip`

➤ `Emergency_Responder.zip`

ADVANCED ANDROID

This chapter returns to some of the possibilities touched on in previous chapters and introduces some of the more advanced options available for Android developers.

The chapter starts by taking a closer look at security—in particular, how permissions work and how to define your own permissions and use them to secure your own applications and the data they contain.

Next, the chapter examines how to build applications that are backward and forward compatible across a range of hardware and software platforms, as well as investigating the use of Strict Mode for discovering inefficiencies within your applications.

You are also introduced to Android's telephony APIs and learn to use them to make outgoing calls, monitor phone state, and receive broadcast Intents for incoming calls. Finally, you explore Android's SMS functionality, which enables you to send and receive SMS messages from within your applications. Using the Android APIs, you can create your own SMS client application to replace the native clients available as part of the software stack. Alternatively, you can incorporate the messaging functionality within your own applications.

PARANOID ANDROID

Much of Android's security is supplied by its underlying Linux kernel. Application files and resources are sandboxed to their owners, making them inaccessible by other applications. Android uses Intents, Services, and Content Providers to let you relax these strict process boundaries, using permissions to maintain application-level security.

You've already used the permission system to request access to native system services—including location-based services, native Content Providers, and the camera—using `uses-permission` manifest tags and runtime permission requests.

The following sections provide a more detailed look at the Linux security model and the Android permission system. For a comprehensive view, the Android documentation provides an excellent resource that describes the security features in depth: `d.android.com/training/articles/security-tips.html`.

Linux Kernel Security

Each Android package has a unique Linux user ID assigned to it during installation. This has the effect of sandboxing the process and the resources it creates, so that it can't affect (or be affected by) other applications.

Because of this kernel-level security, you need to take additional steps to communicate between applications, or access the files and resources they contain. Content Providers, Intents, Services, and AIDL interfaces are designed to open tunnels through which information can flow between applications. To ensure information doesn't "leak" beyond the intended recipients, you can use Android permissions to act as border guards at either end to control the traffic flow.

Re-introducing Permissions

Permissions are an application-level security mechanism that lets you restrict access to application components. Permissions are used to prevent malicious applications from corrupting data, gaining access to sensitive information, or making excessive (or unauthorized) use of hardware resources or external communication channels.

As you learned in earlier chapters, many of Android's native components have permission requirements. The native permission strings used by native Android Activities and Services can be found as static constants in the `android.Manifest.permission` class.

To use permission-protected components, you need to add `uses-permission` tags to your application manifest, specifying the permission strings your application requires.

When a package is installed, the permissions requested in its manifest are analyzed and granted (or denied) by checks with trusted authorities and user feedback.

In Android 6.0 Marshmallow (API Level 23), an additional requirement was added for permissions marked as *dangerous*—including those that guard access to potentially sensitive information such as PII (personally identifiable information) and location data.

Dangerous permissions require explicit approval by way of runtime permission requests accepted by the user when first accessed by your app.

Each time you attempt to access information protected by a dangerous permission, you must use the `ActivityCompat.checkSelfPermission` method, passing in the appropriate permission constant to determine if access has been granted. It will return `PERMISSION_GRANTED` if user permission is granted, or `PERMISSION_DENIED` if the user has declined (or not yet granted) access:

```
int permission = ActivityCompat.checkSelfPermission(this,
                  Manifest.permission.READ_CONTACTS);

if (permission==PERMISSION_GRANTED) {
  // Access the Content Provider
} else {
  // Request the permission or
  // display a dialog showing why the function is unavailable.
}
```

To display the system's runtime permission request dialog, call the `ActivityCompat.requestPermission` method, specifying the required permissions:

```
ActivityCompat.requestPermissions(this,
    new String[]{Manifest.permission.READ_CONTACTS},
    CONTACTS_PERMISSION_REQUEST);
```

This function displays a standard Android dialog that can't be customized. You will receive a callback when the user has either accepted or denied your runtime request, returned to the `onRequestPermissionsResult` handler:

```
@Override
public void onRequestPermissionsResult(int requestCode,
                                       @NonNull String[] permissions,
                                       @NonNull int[] grantResults) {
```

```
    super.onRequestPermissionsResult(requestCode, permissions, grantResults);
    // TODO React to granted / denied permissions.
}
```

Declaring and Enforcing Permissions

It's also possible for you to define your own permissions and assign them to protect your own application components.

Before you can assign a new permission to an application component, you need to define it within your manifest using the permission tag, as shown in the Listing 20-1.

LISTING 20-1: Declaring a new permission

```
<permission
  android:name="com.professionalandroid.DETONATE_DEVICE"
  android:protectionLevel="dangerous"
  android:label="Self Destruct"
  android:description="@string/detonate_description">
</permission>
```

Within the permission tag, you can specify the level of access that the permission will permit:

normal—Can be granted at installation time when included in a uses-permission node within an application's manifest

dangerous—Must be explicitly granted by the user the first time it's used within an application

signature—Can only be granted to an application signed with the same signing certificate

You can also supply a label, and an external resource containing the description that explains the risks of granting this permission.

To define custom permissions for components within your application, add a permission attribute to their manifest nodes. Permission constraints can be enforced throughout your application, most usefully at application interface boundaries—for example:

➤ **Activities**—Add a permission to limit the ability of other applications to launch a particular Activity.

➤ **Broadcast Receivers**—Add a permission to control which applications can send Intents to your Receiver.

➤ **Intents**—Add a permission to control which Broadcast Receivers can receive a particular Intent.

➤ **Content Providers**—Add a permission to limit read access and/or write operations on your Content Providers.

➤ **Services**—Add a permission to limit the ability of other applications to start or bind to a Service.

In each case, you can add a `permission` attribute to the application component in the manifest, specifying a required permission string to access each component. Listing 20-2 shows a manifest excerpt that requires the permission defined in Listing 20-1 to start an Activity, Service, and Broadcast Receiver.

LISTING 20-2: Enforcing a permission requirements

```
<activity
  android:name=".MyActivity"
  android:label="@string/app_name"
  android:permission="com.professionalandroid.DETONATE_DEVICE">
</activity>

<service
  android:name=".MyService"
  android:permission="com.professionalandroid.DETONATE_DEVICE">
</service>

<receiver
  android:name=".MyReceiver"
  android:permission="com.professionalandroid.DETONATE_DEVICE">
</receiver>
```

Content Providers let you set `readPermission` and `writePermission` attributes to offer more granular control over read/write access:

```
<provider
  android:name=".HitListProvider"
  android:authorities="com.professionalandroid.hitlistprovider"
  android:writePermission="com.professionalandroid.ASSIGN_KILLER"
  android:readPermission="com.professionalandroid.LICENSED_TO_KILL"
/>
```

Enforcing Permissions when Broadcasting Intents

In addition to requiring permissions for Intents to be received by your Broadcast Receivers, you can attach a permission requirement to each Intent you broadcast. This is good practice when broadcasting Intents that contain sensitive information.

In such cases it's best practice to require a `signature` permission to ensure that only applications signed with the same signature as the host application can receive the broadcast:

```
<permission
  android:name="com.professionalandroid.SECRET_DATA"
  android:protectionLevel="signature"
  android:label="Secret Data Transfer"
  android:description="@string/secret_data_description">
</permission>
```

When calling `sendBroadcast`, you can supply the permission string required for a Broadcast Receivers to receive the Intent:

```
sendBroadcast(myIntent, "com.professionalandroid.SECRET_DATA");
```

Storing Keys in the Android Keystore

The Android Keystore system provides a container in which applications can safely store sensitive cryptographic keys, protecting them from unauthorized access and use. The keystore is designed to prevent the extraction of keys from application processes, and from the Android device.

As a further protection against the potential for unauthorized use of keys, apps are required to specify the authorized uses of keys stored in the keystore including requirements for cryptography, limited times during which a key is authorized, and requiring that a user has been recently authenticated before providing access.

Access to the Android Keystore is provided via two APIs: the Keychain API and Android Keystore Provider. The Keychain API is designed to support the storage and access of system-wide credentials, allowing multiple applications to use the same set of credentials with user consent.

Alternatively, the Android Keystore Provider is designed for applications to store their own credentials, limiting access to the app storing the key. Unlike the Keychain API, apps using the Keystore Provider don't require user interaction to retrieve the credentials they've stored.

Details for creating, storing, and retrieving keys to be stored in the Android Keystore are beyond the scope of this book. You can find more details on these topics and the Android Keystore system at `d.android.com/training/articles/keystore.html`.

Using the Fingerprint Sensor

Android 6.0 Marshmallow (API Level 23) introduced a new API to support user authentication using on-device fingerprint scanners.

To include fingerprint authentication within your app, you must first add the `USE_FINGERPRINT` permission to your manifest:

```
<uses-permission android:name="android.permission.USE_FINGERPRINT"/>
```

Within your application, get an instance of the `FingerprintManager` class using the `getSystemService` method, passing in `FingerPrintManager.class`.

Alternatively, you can use the `FingerprintManagerCompat` class to provide backward-compatible support, using its `from` method to retrieve an instance based on a Context:

```
mFingerprintManager = FingerprintManagerCompat.from(this);
```

Use the Fingerprint Manager to authenticate users with the authenticate method, passing in optional Crypto Object and Cancellation Signal objects along with an Authentication Callback implementation:

```
mFingerprintManager.authenticate(
  null, /* or mCryptoObject*/
  0,    /* flags */
  null, /* or mCancellationSignal */
  mAuthenticationCallback,
  null);
```

A Cancellation Signal can be provided to support cancellation of an ongoing authentication. A Crypto Object can be passed in, if you wish to use fingerprint authentication to mark the related keystore key as authenticated. If a Crypto Object parameter is provided, it will be authenticated and returned within the Authentication Result of the Authentication Callback.

The results will be returned to an implementation of the FingerprintManagerCompat .AuthenticationCallback class using the onAuthenticationError, onAuthenticationHelp, onAuthenticationFailed, and onAuthenticationSucceeded handlers:

```java
FingerprintManagerCompat.AuthenticationCallback mAuthenticationCallback
  = new FingerprintManagerCompat.AuthenticationCallback() {

  @Override
  public void onAuthenticationError(int errMsgId, CharSequence errString) {
    // TODO Handle authentication error.
    Log.e(TAG, "Fingerprint authentication error: " + errString);
  }

  @Override
  public void onAuthenticationHelp(int helpMsgId, CharSequence helpString) {
    // TODO Handle authentication help.
    Log.d(TAG, "Fingerprint authentication help required: " + helpString);
  }

  @Override
  public void onAuthenticationFailed() {
    // TODO Handle authentication failure.
    Log.d(TAG, "Fingerprint authentication failed.");
  }

  @Override
  public void onAuthenticationSucceeded(
                FingerprintManagerCompat.AuthenticationResult result) {
    super.onAuthenticationSucceeded(result);
    // TODO Handle authentication success.
    Log.d(TAG, "Fingerprint authentication succeeded.");
  }
};
```

Your application must implement the UI for fingerprint authentication using the standard Android fingerprint icon.

A complete example of using the Fingerprint API to authenticate a purchase flow, including the Android fingerprint icon (ic_fp_40px.png), is available as the Fingerprint Dialog sample at github.com/googlesamples/android-FingerprintDialog/.

DEALING WITH DIFFERENT HARDWARE AND SOFTWARE AVAILABILITY

From smartphones and tablets to wearables and televisions, Android is now being used on an increasingly diverse collection of hardware. Each new device potentially represents a variation in hardware configuration or software platform. This flexibility is a significant factor in Android's success, but as a result, you can't make assumptions regarding the hardware or software available on the device on which your app is installed and running.

To mitigate this, Android platform releases are forward compatible—meaning that in many cases applications designed before a particular hardware or software innovation is available will still be able to take advantage of it, without requiring changes.

Android platform releases are also backward compatible, meaning your application will continue to work on new hardware and platform releases—again without you needing to upgrade it each time.

By combining forward and backward compatibility, your Android application will continue to work, and even potentially take advantage of new hardware and software features, as the platform evolves.

That said, each platform release includes new APIs and platform features. Similarly, new hardware may become available. Either advance could provide features that might improve the features and user experience of your application.

To take advantage of these new features without losing support for hardware running earlier platforms, you need to ensure your *application* is also backward compatible.

Similarly, the wide range of different Android device hardware platforms means that you can't make assumptions over what hardware might be available.

The following sections explain how to specify certain hardware as required, check for hardware availability at run time, and build applications that are backward compatible.

Specifying Required Hardware

Application hardware requirements generally fall into two categories: hardware that is required for your application to have utility, and hardware that is useful if it is available but isn't strictly necessary. The former accounts for applications built around a particular piece of hardware—for example, a replacement camera application isn't useful on a device without a camera.

To specify a particular hardware feature as a requirement to install your application, add a `uses-feature` node to its manifest:

```
<uses-feature android:name="android.hardware.sensor.compass"/>
<uses-feature android:name="android.hardware.camera"/>
```

This can also be used for applications that don't necessarily require a particular piece of hardware, but which haven't been designed to support certain hardware configurations—for example, a game that requires tilt sensors or a touch screen to control.

> **NOTE** *The more hardware restrictions you place on your applications, the smaller the potential target audience becomes, so it's good practice to limit your hardware restrictions to those required to support core functionality.*

Confirming Hardware Availability

For hardware that would be useful but isn't necessary, you need to query the host hardware platform at run time to determine what hardware is available. The Package Manager includes a hasSystemFeature method that accepts `PackageManager.FEATURE_` static constants:

```
PackageManager pm = getPackageManager();
pm.hasSystemFeature(PackageManager.FEATURE_SENSOR_COMPASS);
```

The Package Manager includes a constant for every piece of optional hardware, making it possible to customize your UI and functionality based on the hardware available.

Building Backward-Compatible Applications

Each new Android SDK release brings with it a new hardware support, APIs, bug fixes, and performance improvements. It's best practice to update your applications as soon as possible following a new SDK release in order to take advantage of these new features and ensure the best possible user experience for new Android-device owners.

At the same time, ensuring your applications are backward compatible is critical to ensure users of devices running earlier Android platform versions can continue to use them—particularly as this is likely to be a significantly larger share of the market than that held by brand new devices.

Many of the Android APIs—particularly convenience classes and UI classes—are distributed within the standalone Android support and Android Architecture Components libraries or, in some cases, the Google Play services APIs. Where features aren't available as part of a standalone library, you'll need to incorporate new features using the techniques described here to support multiple platform versions within the same package.

For each technique described, it's important to know the API level associated with the underlying platform.

> **WARNING** *Importing a class or attempting to call a method not available in the underlying platform will cause a runtime exception when the enclosing class is instantiated or the method is called.*

To find this at run time, you can use the `android.os.Build.VERSION.SDK_INT` constant:

```
private static boolean nfc_beam_supported =
    android.os.Build.VERSION.SDK_INT > 14;
```

The easiest way to determine which API level is required for a given class or method is to progressively lower your project's build target and note which classes break the build.

Parallel Activities

The simplest, though least efficient, alternative for ensuring backward compatibility is to create separate sets of parallel Activities, Services, and Broadcast Receivers, based on a base class compatible with the minimum Android platform version you support.

When using explicit Intents to start Services or Activities, you can select the right set of components at run time by checking the platform version and targeting the appropriate Services and Activities accordingly:

```
private static boolean nfc_beam_supported =
  android.os.Build.VERSION.SDK_INT > 14;

Intent startActivityIntent = null;

if (nfc_beam_supported)
  startActivityIntent = new Intent(this, NFCBeamActivity.class);
else
  startActivityIntent = new Intent(this, NonNFCBeamActivity.class);

startActivity(startActivityIntent);
```

In the case of implicit Intents and Broadcast Receivers, you can add an `android:enabled` tag to their manifest entries that refers to a Boolean resource:

```
<receiver
  android:name=".MediaControlReceiver"
  android:enabled="@bool/supports_remote_media_controller">
  <intent-filter>
    <action android:name="android.intent.action.MEDIA_BUTTON"/>
  </intent-filter>
</receiver>
```

You can then create alternative resource entries based on API level:

```
res/values/bool.xml
  <bool name="supports_remote_media_controller">false</bool>

res/values-v14/bool.xml
  <bool name="supports_remote_media_controller">true</bool>
```

Interfaces and Fragments

Interfaces are the traditional way to support multiple implementations of the same functionality. For functionality that you want to implement differently based on newly available APIs, create an interface that defines the action to be performed, and then create API level–specific implementations.

At run time, check the current platform version and instantiate the appropriate class and use its methods:

```
IP2PDataXfer dataTransfer;

if (android.os.Build.VERSION.SDK_INT > 14)
  dataTransfer = new NFCBeamP2PDataXfer();
else
```

```
        dataTransfer = new NonNFCBeamP2PDataXfer();

    dataTransfer.initiateP2PDataXfer();
```

Fragments provide a more encapsulated alternative to parallelized components. Rather than duplicating Activities, use Fragments—combined with the resource hierarchy—to create a consistent UI that's optimized for different platform releases and hardware configurations.

Most of the UI logic for your Activities should be contained within individual Fragments rather than the Activity itself. As a result, you need only create alternative Fragments to expose and utilize different functionality and inflate different versions of the same layout stored within their respective `res/layout-v[API level]` folders.

Interaction between and within Fragments is usually maintained within each Fragment, so only code related to missing APIs will need to be changed within the Activity. If each variation of a Fragment implements the same interface definition and ID, you shouldn't need to create multiple Activities to support multiple layouts and Fragment definitions.

OPTIMIZING UI PERFORMANCE WITH STRICT MODE

The resource-constrained nature of mobile devices amplifies the effect of performing time-consuming operations on the main application thread. Accessing network resources, reading or writing files, or accessing databases while blocking the UI thread can have a dramatic impact on the user experience, causing your application to become less smooth, more laggy, and, in the most extreme case, unresponsive.

You learned how to move such time-consuming operations onto background threads in Chapter 11. Strict Mode is a tool that helps you identify cases you may have missed.

Using the Strict Mode APIs, you can assign a set of policies that monitor actions within your application and define how you should be alerted. You can define policies related to either the current application thread or to your application's virtual machine (VM) process. The former is perfect for detecting slow operations being performed on the UI thread, whereas the latter helps you detect memory and Context leaks.

To use Strict Mode, create a new `ThreadPolicy` class and a new `VmPolicy` class, using their static builder classes with the `detect` methods to define the actions to monitor. The corresponding `penalty` methods control how the system should react to detecting those actions.

The Thread Policy can be used to detect disk reads/writes and network access, whereas the Vm Policy can monitor your application for Activity, SQLite, and closeable object leaks.

The penalties available to both policies include logging or application death, while the Thread Policy also supports displaying an on-screen dialog or flashing screen border.

Both builder classes also include a `detectAll` method that includes all the possible monitoring options supported by the host platform. You can also use the `StrictMode.enableDefaults` method to apply the default monitoring and penalty options.

To enable Strict Mode across your entire application, you should extend the Application class, as shown in Listing 20-3.

```java
public class MyApplication extends Application {

  public static final boolean DEVELOPER_MODE = true;

  @Override
  public final void onCreate() {
    super.onCreate();

    if (DEVELOPER_MODE) {
      StrictMode.enableDefaults();
    }
  }
}
```

To enable Strict Mode (or customize its settings) for a particular Activity, Service, or other application component, simply use the same pattern within that component's onCreate method.

TELEPHONY AND SMS

Android includes telephony communication APIs, which enable you to monitor phone state and phone calls, as well as to initiate calls and monitor incoming call details.

Android also offers a full suite of SMS functionality, letting you send and receive SMS messages from within your applications. Using the Android APIs, you can create your own SMS client application to replace the native clients available as part of the software stack. Alternatively, you can incorporate some SMS messaging functionality within your own applications.

With the arrival of Wi-Fi-only Android devices, you can no longer assume that telephony hardware will be available on every device on which your application may be available.

Some applications don't make sense on devices that don't have telephony support. An application that provides reverse-number lookup for incoming calls or a replacement SMS client simply won't work on a Wi-Fi-only device.

To specify that your application requires telephony support to function, you can add a uses-feature node to your application manifest:

```xml
<uses-feature android:name="android.hardware.telephony"
              android:required="true"/>
```

> **NOTE** *As described in the previous section, marking telephony as a required feature prevents your application from being found on Google Play using a device without telephony hardware. It also prevents your application from being installed on such devices from the Google Play website.*

If you use telephony APIs but they aren't strictly necessary for your application to be used, you can check for the existence of telephony hardware before attempting to make use of the related APIs.

Use the Package Manager's `hasSystemFeature` method, specifying the `PackageManager.FEATURE_TELEPHONY` String. The Package Manager also includes constants to query the existence of CDMA- and GSM-specific hardware.

```
PackageManager pm = getPackageManager();

boolean telephonySupported =
  pm.hasSystemFeature(PackageManager.FEATURE_TELEPHONY);
boolean gsmSupported =
  pm.hasSystemFeature(PackageManager.FEATURE_TELEPHONY_CDMA);
boolean cdmaSupported =
  pm.hasSystemFeature(PackageManager.FEATURE_TELEPHONY_GSM);
```

Telephony

The Android telephony APIs let your applications access the underlying telephone hardware stack, making it possible to create your own dialer—or integrate call handling and phone state monitoring into your applications.

> **NOTE** *Because of security concerns, the current Android SDK does not allow you to create your own in-call Activity—the screen that is displayed when an incoming call is received or an outgoing call has been placed.*

Initiating Phone Calls Using Intents

Best practice for initiating phone calls is to use an `Intent.ACTION_DIAL` Intent, specifying the number to dial by setting the Intents data using a `tel:` schema:

```
Intent whoyougonnacall = new Intent(Intent.ACTION_DIAL,
                                    Uri.parse("tel:555-2368"));
startActivity(whoyougonnacall);
```

This will start a dialer Activity that will be pre-populated with the number you specified as the Intent data. The default dialer Activity allows the user to change the number before explicitly initiating the call. As a result, using the `ACTION_DIAL` Intent action doesn't require any special permissions.

By using an Intent to announce your intention to dial a number, your application stays decoupled from the dialer implementation used to initiate the call. For example, if users have installed a new dialer that supports IP-based telephony, using Intents to dial a number from your application lets users use this new dialer to place the call.

Creating a New Phone Dialer

Creating a new dialer application, potentially to replace the native phone dialer app, involves two steps. Your app must:

1.   Intercept Intents serviced by the native dialer.

2.   Initiate and manage outgoing calls.

The native dialer application responds to Intent actions corresponding to a user pressing a hardware call button, asking to view data using the `tel:` schema, or making an `ACTION_DIAL` request using the `tel:` schema, as shown in the previous section.

To intercept these requests, include `intent-filter` tags on the manifest entries for your replacement dialer Activity that listens for the following actions:

➤   `Intent.ACTION_CALL_BUTTON`—This action is broadcast when the device's hardware call button is pressed. Create an Intent Filter that listens for this action as a default action.

➤   `Intent.ACTION_DIAL`—This Intent action, described in the previous section, is used by applications that want to initiate a phone call. The Intent Filter used to capture this action should be both default and browsable (to support dial requests from the browser) and must specify the `tel:` schema to replace existing dialer functionality (though it can support additional schemes).

➤   `Intent.ACTION_VIEW`—The view action is used by applications wanting to view a piece of data. Ensure that the Intent Filter specifies the `tel:` schema to allow your new Activity to be used to view telephone numbers.

The manifest snippet in Listing 20-4 shows an Activity with Intent Filters that will capture each of these actions.

LISTING 20-4: Manifest entry for a replacement dialer Activity

```xml
<activity
  android:name=".MyDialerActivity"
  android:label="@string/app_name">
  <intent-filter>
    <action android:name="android.intent.action.CALL_BUTTON" />
    <category android:name="android.intent.category.DEFAULT" />
  </intent-filter>
  <intent-filter>
    <action android:name="android.intent.action.VIEW" />
    <action android:name="android.intent.action.DIAL" />
    <category android:name="android.intent.category.DEFAULT" />
    <category android:name="android.intent.category.BROWSABLE" />
    <data android:scheme="tel" />
```

```
        </intent-filter>
    </activity>
```

After your Activity has been started, it should provide a UI that allows users to enter or modify the number to dial and to initiate the outgoing call. At that point you need to place the call—using either the existing telephony stack or your own alternative.

The simplest technique is to use the existing telephony stack using the `Intent.ACTION_CALL` action. This will initiate a call using the system in-call Activity and will let the system manage the dialing, connection, and voice handling.

To use this action, your application must request the `CALL_PHONE` uses-permission:

```
<uses-permission android:name="android.permission.CALL_PHONE"/>
```

As a dangerous permission, you must also request—and check for acceptance—at runtime as shown in Listing 20-5.

LISTING 20-5: Initiating a call using the system telephony stack

```
int permission = ActivityCompat.checkSelfPermission(this,
                   android.Manifest.permission.CALL_PHONE);

if (permission == PackageManager.PERMISSION_GRANTED) {

  Intent whoyougonnacall = new Intent(Intent.ACTION_CALL,
                                  Uri.parse("tel:555-2368"));
  startActivity(whoyougonnacall);

// If permission hasn't been granted, request it.
} else {
  if (ActivityCompat.shouldShowRequestPermissionRationale(
        this, android.Manifest.permission.CALL_PHONE)) {
    // TODO Display additional rationale for the requested permission.
  }
  ActivityCompat.requestPermissions(this,
    new String[]{android.Manifest.permission.CALL_PHONE},
    CALL_PHONE_PERMISSION_REQUEST);
}
```

Alternatively, you can completely replace the outgoing telephony stack by implementing your own dialing and voice-handling framework. This is the perfect alternative if you are implementing a VOIP (voice over IP) application.

Accessing Telephony Properties and Phone State

Access to the telephony APIs is managed by the Telephony Manager, accessible using the `getSystemService` method:

```
String srvcName = Context.TELEPHONY_SERVICE;
TelephonyManager telephonyManager =
  (TelephonyManager)getSystemService(srvcName);
```

The Telephony Manager provides direct access to many of the phone properties, including device, network, subscriber identity module (SIM), and data state details. You can also access some connectivity status information, although this is usually done using the Connectivity Manager, as described in Chapter 18, "Bluetooth, NFC, Networks, and Wi-Fi."

Almost all Telephony Manager methods require the READ_PHONE_STATE uses-permission be included in the application manifest:

```
<uses-permission android:name="android.permission.READ_PHONE_STATE"/>
```

The READ_PHONE_STATE permission is also marked as dangerous, so you need to check / request the runtime user permission before you can receive phone state detail results, as shown in Listing 20-6.

Android Lollipop (API Level 22) added support for multiple telephony subscriptions (such as dual SIM devices that support multiple active SIM cards). To access the list of active subscriptions, use the Subscription Manager's getActiveSubscriptionInfoList method. Note that like the Telephony Manager, all Subscription Manager methods require the READ_PHONE_STATE permission:

```
SubscriptionManager subscriptionManager = (SubscriptionManager)
  getSystemService(Context.TELEPHONY_SUBSCRIPTION_SERVICE);

List<SubscriptionInfo> subscriptionInfos
  = subscriptionManager.getActiveSubscriptionInfoList();
```

By default, the Telephony Manager methods will return properties related to the default subscriber. Android Nougat (API Level 24) introduced the createForSubscriptionId method to the Telephone Manager, which returns a new Telephony Manager corresponding to the specified subscription Id:

```
for (SubscriptionInfo subscriptionInfo : subscriptionInfos) {
  int id = subscriptionInfo.getSubscriptionId();
  TelephonyManager manager = telephonyManager.createForSubscriptionId(subId);
  [ ... Query properties ...]
}
```

Once you have a Telephony Manager, you can obtain the phone type (GSM CDMA, or SIP), unique ID (IMEI or MEID), software version, and the phone's phone number as shown in Listing 20-6.

LISTING 20-6: Accessing phone-type and the device's phone number

```
String phoneTypeStr = "unknown";

int phoneType = telephonyManager.getPhoneType();
switch (phoneType) {
  case (TelephonyManager.PHONE_TYPE_CDMA):
    phoneTypeStr = "CDMA";
    break;
  case (TelephonyManager.PHONE_TYPE_GSM) :
    phoneTypeStr = "GSM";
    break;
  case (TelephonyManager.PHONE_TYPE_SIP):
    phoneTypeStr = "SIP";
    break;
```

```
    case (TelephonyManager.PHONE_TYPE_NONE):
      phoneTypeStr = "None";
      break;
    default: break;
}

Log.d(TAG, phoneTypeStr);

// -- These require READ_PHONE_STATE uses-permission --
int permission = ActivityCompat.checkSelfPermission(this,
                    android.Manifest.permission.READ_PHONE_STATE);

if (permission == PackageManager.PERMISSION_GRANTED) {
  // Read the IMEI for GSM or MEID for CDMA
  String deviceId = telephonyManager.getDeviceId();
  // Read the software version on the phone (note -- not the SDK version)
  String softwareVersion = telephonyManager.getDeviceSoftwareVersion();
  // Get the phone's number (if available)
  String phoneNumber = telephonyManager.getLine1Number();
// If permission hasn't been granted, request it.
} else {
  if (ActivityCompat.shouldShowRequestPermissionRationale(
        this, android.Manifest.permission.READ_PHONE_STATE)) {
    // TODO Display additional rationale for the requested permission.
  }

  ActivityCompat.requestPermissions(this,
    new String[]{android.Manifest.permission.READ_PHONE_STATE},
    PHONE_STATE_PERMISSION_REQUEST);
}
```

When your device is connected to a network, you can use the Telephony Manager to read the Mobile Country Code and Mobile Network Code (MCC+MNC), the country ISO code, the network operator name, and the type of network you're connected to using the getNetworkOperator, getNetworkCountryIso, getNetworkOperatorName, and getNetworkType methods.

These commands work only when you are connected to a mobile network and can be unreliable if it is a CDMA network. Use the getPhoneType method to determine which phone type is being used.

Monitoring Changes in Phone State Using the Phone State Listener

The Android telephony APIs let you monitor changes to phone state and associated details such as incoming phone numbers. Changes to the phone state are monitored using the PhoneStateListener class, with some state changes also broadcast as Intents.

To monitor and manage phone state, your application must specify the READ_PHONE_STATE uses-permission, including runtime permission checks as described in the previous section.

Create a new class that extends the abstract Phone State Listener class to monitor, and respond to, phone state change events, including call state (ringing, off hook, and so on), cell location changes, voice-mail and call-forwarding status, phone service changes, and changes in mobile signal strength.

> **NOTE** *Your Phone State Listener will receive phone state change notifications only while your application is running.*

Within your Phone State Listener implementation, override the event handlers of the events you want to react to. Each handler receives parameters that indicate the new phone state, such as the current cell location, call state, or signal strength:

```
PhoneStateListener phoneStateListener = new PhoneStateListener() {
  public void onCallForwardingIndicatorChanged(boolean cfi){}
  public void onCallStateChanged(int state, String incomingNumber){}
  public void onCellInfoChanged(List<CellInfo> cellInfo){}
  public void onCellLocationChanged(CellLocation location){}
  public void onDataActivity(int direction){}
  public void onDataConnectionStateChanged(int state, int networkType){}
  public void onMessageWaitingIndicatorChanged(boolean mwi){}
  public void onServiceStateChanged(ServiceState serviceState){}
  public void onSignalStrengthsChanged(SignalStrength signalStrength) {}
};
```

After creating your own Phone State Listener, register it with the Telephony Manager using a bitmask to indicate the events you want to listen for:

```
telephonyManager.listen(phoneStateListener,
                PhoneStateListener.LISTEN_CALL_FORWARDING_INDICATOR|
                PhoneStateListener.LISTEN_CALL_STATE |
                PhoneStateListener.LISTEN_CELL_LOCATION |
                PhoneStateListener.LISTEN_DATA_ACTIVITY |
                PhoneStateListener.LISTEN_DATA_CONNECTION_STATE |
                PhoneStateListener.LISTEN_MESSAGE_WAITING_INDICATOR |
                PhoneStateListener.LISTEN_SERVICE_STATE |
                PhoneStateListener.LISTEN_SIGNAL_STRENGTHS);
```

To unregister a listener, call `listen` and pass in `PhoneStateListener.LISTEN_NONE` as the bitmask parameter:

```
telephonyManager.listen(phoneStateListener,
                PhoneStateListener.LISTEN_NONE);
```

For example, if you want your application to respond to incoming phone calls, you can override the `onCallStateChanged` method in your Phone State Listener implementation, and register it to receive notifications when the call state changes:

```
PhoneStateListener callStateListener = new PhoneStateListener() {
  public void onCallStateChanged(int state, String incomingNumber) {
    String callStateStr = "Unknown";

    switch (state) {
      case TelephonyManager.CALL_STATE_IDLE :
        callStateStr = "Idle"; break;
      case TelephonyManager.CALL_STATE_OFFHOOK :
```

```
        callStateStr = "Offhook (In Call)"; break;
      case TelephonyManager.CALL_STATE_RINGING :
        callStateStr = "Ringing. Incoming number is: "
        + incomingNumber;
        break;
      default : break;
    }

    Toast.makeText(MyActivity.this,
      callStateStr, Toast.LENGTH_LONG).show();
  }
};

telephonyManager.listen(callStateListener,
                  PhoneStateListener.LISTEN_CALL_STATE);
```

The `onCallStateChanged` handler receives the phone number associated with incoming calls, and the `state` parameter represents the current call state as one of the following three values:

➤ `TelephonyManager.CALL_STATE_IDLE`—When the phone is neither ringing nor in a call

➤ `TelephonyManager.CALL_STATE_RINGING`—When the phone is ringing

➤ `TelephonyManager.CALL_STATE_OFFHOOK`—When the phone is currently in a call

Note that as soon as the state changes to `CALL_STATE_RINGING`, the system will display the incoming call screen or notification, asking users if they want to answer the call.

Using Intent Receivers to Monitor Incoming Phone Calls

The Phone State Listener in the previous section is only active while your Activity is running. If you wish to monitor all incoming calls, you can use an Intent Receiver.

When the phone state changes as a result of an incoming, accepted, or terminated phone call, the Telephony Manager will broadcast an `ACTION_PHONE_STATE_CHANGED` Intent.

By registering a manifest Intent Receiver that listens for this Broadcast Intent, as shown in the snippet below, you can listen for incoming phone calls at any time, even if your application isn't running. Note that your application needs to request the `READ_PHONE_STATE` permission in the manifest, and again at runtime, before it can receive the phone state Broadcast Intent.

```
<receiver android:name="PhoneStateChangedReceiver">
  <intent-filter>
    <action android:name="android.intent.action.PHONE_STATE"/>
  </intent-filter>
</receiver>
```

The Phone State Changed Broadcast Intent includes up to two extras. All such broadcasts will include the `EXTRA_STATE` extra, whose value will be one of the `TelephonyManager.CALL_STATE_` actions described earlier to indicate the new phone state. If the state is ringing, the Broadcast Intent will also include the `EXTRA_INCOMING_NUMBER` extra, whose value represents the incoming call number.

The following skeleton code can be used to extract the current phone state and incoming call number where it exists:

```java
public class PhoneStateChangedReceiver extends BroadcastReceiver {
  @Override
  public void onReceive(Context context, Intent intent) {
    String phoneState = intent.getStringExtra(TelephonyManager.EXTRA_STATE);
    if (phoneState.equals(TelephonyManager.EXTRA_STATE_RINGING)) {
      String phoneNumber =
        intent.getStringExtra(TelephonyManager.EXTRA_INCOMING_NUMBER);
      Toast.makeText(context,
        "Incoming Call From: " + phoneNumber,
        Toast.LENGTH_LONG).show();
    }
  }
}
```

> **NOTE** *Before your Broadcast Receiver can receive the phone state change Intent, the user must first explicitly accept the runtime phone state permission. Until they do so, your Receiver will not receive the related broadcasts.*

Sending and Receiving SMS Messages

SMS technology is designed to send short text messages between mobile phones via the carrier network. It provides support for sending both text messages (designed to be read by people) and data messages (meant to be consumed by applications). Multimedia messaging service (MMS) messages allow users to send and receive messages that include multimedia attachments such as photos, videos, and audio.

Android introduced properly supported APIs for SMS messaging in Android 4.4 KitKat (API Level 19).

Because SMS and MMS are mature mobile technologies, there's a lot of information out there that describes the technical details of how an SMS or MMS message is constructed and transmitted over the air. Rather than rehash that information here, the following sections focus on the practicalities of sending and receiving text messages from within Android applications.

Android provides support for sending both SMS messages using a messaging application installed on the device with the SEND and SEND_TO Broadcast Intents.

Android also supports full SMS functionality within your applications through the SmsManager class. Using the SMS Manager, you can replace the native SMS application to send text messages and react to incoming texts.

Android 5.0 Lollipop (API Level 22) added support for multiple telephony subscriptions (such as dual SIM devices that support multiple active SIM cards). As a result, you can choose which cell subscription to use when sending SMS messages. Refer to the earlier section, "Accessing Telephony Properties and Phone State" for details on determining the available subscriptions.

Sending SMS Messages Using Intents

It's best practice to use an Intent to send SMS (and MMS) messages using another application—typically the native SMS application—rather than implementing a full SMS client yourself.

To do so, call `startActivity` with an `Intent.ACTION_SENDTO` action Intent, specifying a target number using `sms:` schema notation as the Intent data. Include the message you want to send within the Intent payload using an `sms_body` extra:

```
Intent smsIntent = new Intent(Intent.ACTION_SENDTO,
                              Uri.parse("sms:55512345"));
smsIntent.putExtra("sms_body", "Press send to send me");
startActivity(smsIntent);
```

The currently selected default SMS app will receive this Intent and display a pre-populated Activity that will allow you to send the message you specify to the contact you indicated.

Creating a New Default SMS App to Send and Receive SMS Messages

On each Android device, only one app can be the *default* SMS App at any given time. Users can modify the default SMS app from the system settings, as shown in Figure 20-1.

FIGURE 20-1

Only the current default SMS app receives the `SMS_DELIVER_ACTION` Intent when a new SMS message arrives, the `WAP_PUSH_DELIVER_ACTION` Intent when a new MMS arrives, and has the ability to write new SMS messages to the SMS Content Provider.

It's also possible to for your app to send and receive SMS messages, and read the SMS Content Provider *without* being selected as the default SMS app as described in later sections. Note that in that case, the default SMS app (and any other app listening for the broadcast) will also still receive each message.

If you wish to create a new default SMS app, you must provide the same functionality as provided by the bundled SMS application. Specifically, that includes the following Manifest entries and associated components:

➤ A Broadcast Receiver with an Intent Filter for the `android.provider.Telephony.SMS_DELIVER` action, and which requires the `BROADCAST_SMS` permission. This Receiver will be triggered whenever a new SMS message is received:

```
<receiver android:name=".MySmsReceiver"
          android:permission="android.permission.BROADCAST_SMS">
  <intent-filter>
    <action android:name="android.provider.Telephony.SMS_DELIVER"/>
  </intent-filter>
</receiver>
```

➤ A Broadcast Receiver with an Intent Filter for the `android.provider.Telephony.WAP_PUSH_DELIVER` action along with the MIME type `application/vnd.wap.mms-message`, and which requires the `BROADCAST_WAP_PUSH` permission. This Receiver will be triggered whenever a new MMS message is received:

```
<receiver android:name=".MyMmsReceiver"
          android:permission="android.permission.BROADCAST_WAP_PUSH">
  <intent-filter>
    <action android:name="android.provider.Telephony.WAP_PUSH_DELIVER" />
    <data android:mimeType="application/vnd.wap.mms-message" />
  </intent-filter>
</receiver>
```

➤ An Activity that allows users to send SMS and MMS messages, which includes an Intent Filter for the `android.intent.action.SEND` and `android.intent.action.SENDTO` actions, supporting the schemes `sms:`, `smsto:`, `mms:`, and `mmsto:`. Your Activity should listen for Intents of this form and fulfill any requests from other apps using the form described in the earlier section, "Sending SMS Messages Using Intents":

```
<activity android:name=".MySendSmsActivity" >
  <intent-filter>
    <action android:name="android.intent.action.SEND" />
    <action android:name="android.intent.action.SENDTO" />
    <category android:name="android.intent.category.DEFAULT" />
    <category android:name="android.intent.category.BROWSABLE" />
    <data android:scheme="sms" />
    <data android:scheme="smsto" />
    <data android:scheme="mms" />
    <data android:scheme="mmsto" />
  </intent-filter>
</activity>
```

➤ A Service that includes an Intent Filter for the `android.intent.action.RESPOND_VIA_MESSAGE` action that supports the schemes, `sms:`, `smsto:`, `mms:`, and `mmsto:`, and which requires the `SEND_RESPOND_VIA_MESSAGE` permission. This Service implementation should allow users to send SMS messages in response to incoming phone calls. The received Intent data contains a URI where the scheme describes the transport type, and the path contains the recipient's phone number (Eg. smsto:3055551234). The message text is stored in the EXTRA_TEXT extra, and the message subject in EXTRA_SUBJECT.

```
<service android:name=".MySmsResponseService"
        android:permission=
           "android.permission.SEND_RESPOND_VIA_MESSAGE"
        android:exported="true" >
  <intent-filter>
    <action android:name="android.intent.action.RESPOND_VIA_MESSAGE" />
    <category android:name="android.intent.category.DEFAULT" />
    <data android:scheme="sms" />
    <data android:scheme="smsto" />
    <data android:scheme="mms" />
    <data android:scheme="mmsto" />
  </intent-filter>
</service>
```

If your app is not set to the default SSM app, its functionality may be limited. You can check if your app is the default SMS app using the Telephony.Sms.getDefaultSmsPackage method, which returns the package name of the current default SMS app.

```
String myPackageName = getPackageName();
boolean isDefault =
  Telephony.Sms.getDefaultSmsPackage(this).equals(myPackageName);
```

You can display a system dialog to prompt the user to select your app as the default SMS app using the Telephony.Sms.Intents.ACTION_CHANGE_DEFAULT Intent, including an extra with the Sms.Intents.EXTRA_PACKAGE_NAME key and your package name as the string value:

```
Intent intent = new Intent(Telephony.Sms.Intents.ACTION_CHANGE_DEFAULT);
intent.putExtra(Telephony.Sms.Intents.EXTRA_PACKAGE_NAME, myPackageName);
startActivity(intent);
```

The following sections describe how to send and receive SMS messages; note that much of this functionality is available to apps that don't provide the full suite of functionality provided by an SMS app.

Sending SMS Messages

SMS messaging in Android is handled by the SmsManager class. You can get a reference to the SMS Manager using the static SmsManager.getDefault method:

```
SmsManager smsManager = SmsManager.getDefault();
```

To send SMS messages, your application must specify the SEND_SMS and READ_PHONE_STATE uses-permission in your manifest:

```
<uses-permission android:name="android.permission.SEND_SMS"/>
<uses-permission android:name="android.permission.READ_PHONE_STATE"/>
```

Note that the SEND_SMS is a dangerous permission, so you must also perform a runtime permission check before attempting to send an SMS message.

To send a text message, use `sendTextMessage` from the SMS Manager, passing in the address (phone number) of your recipient and the text message you want to send:

```
// Check runtime permissions.
int send_sms_permission = ActivityCompat.checkSelfPermission(this,
  Manifest.permission.SEND_SMS);
int phone_state_permission = ActivityCompat.checkSelfPermission(this,
  Manifest.permission.READ_PHONE_STATE);

if (send_sms_permission == PackageManager.PERMISSION_GRANTED &&
    phone_state_permission == PackageManager.PERMISSION_GRANTED) {

  // Send the SMS Message
  SmsManager smsManager = SmsManager.getDefault();

  String sendTo = "5551234";
  String myMessage = "Android supports programmatic SMS messaging!";

  smsManager.sendTextMessage(sendTo, null, myMessage, null, null);

} else {
  if (ActivityCompat.shouldShowRequestPermissionRationale(
    this, Manifest.permission.SEND_SMS)) {
    // TODO Display additional rationale for the requested permission.
  }

  ActivityCompat.requestPermissions(this,
    new String[]{Manifest.permission.SEND_SMS,
                 Manifest.permission.READ_PHONE_STATE},
    SMS_RECEIVE_PERMISSION_REQUEST);
}
```

If your app is set to be the default SMS app, you must also write all sent messages to the SMS Content Provider:

```
ContentValues values = new ContentValues();

values.put(Telephony.Sms.ADDRESS, sendTo);
values.put(Telephony.Sms.BODY, myMessage);
values.put(Telephony.Sms.READ, 1);
values.put(Telephony.Sms.DATE, sentTime);
values.put(Telephony.Sms.TYPE, Telephony.Sms.MESSAGE_TYPE_SENT);

getContentResolver().insert(Telephony.Sms.Sent.CONTENT_URI, values);
```

Note that this requires the `WRITE_SMS` and `READ_SMS` manifest and runtime permissions:

```
<uses-permission android:name="android.permission.WRITE_SMS"/>
<uses-permission android:name="android.permission.READ_SMS"/>
```

Alternatively, if your app is *not* currently selected as the default SMS app, Android will automatically write any messages sent using the SMS Manager to the SMS Provider.

When sending an SMS using `sendTextMessage`, the second parameter can be used to specify the SMS service center to use. If you enter `null`, the default service center for the device's carrier will be used.

> **NOTE** *The Android debugging bridge supports sending SMS messages among multiple emulator instances. To send an SMS from one emulator to another, specify the port number of the target emulator as the "to" address when sending a new message. Android will route your message to the target emulator instance, where it will be received as a normal SMS.*

The final two parameters let you specify Intents to track the transmission and successful delivery of your messages by implementing and registering Broadcast Receivers that listen for the actions you specify when creating the corresponding Pending Intents.

The first Pending Intent parameter is fired when the message is either successfully sent or fails to send. The result code for the Broadcast Receiver that receives this Intent will be one of the following:

➤ `Activity.RESULT_OK`—To indicate a successful transmission

➤ `SmsManager.RESULT_ERROR_GENERIC_FAILURE`—To indicate a nonspecific failure

➤ `SmsManager.RESULT_ERROR_RADIO_OFF`—To indicate the phone radio is turned off

➤ `SmsManager.RESULT_ERROR_NULL_PDU`—To indicate a PDU (protocol description unit) failure

➤ `SmsManager.RESULT_ERROR_NO_SERVICE`—To indicate that no cellular service is currently available

The second Pending Intent parameter is fired only after the recipient receives your SMS message.

The following code snippet shows the typical pattern for sending an SMS and monitoring the success of its transmission and delivery. Note that if your app is the default SMS app, you should also add the message to the SMS Provider when it is first created, and modify its entry to reflect the success or failure of transmission:

```
String SENT_SMS_ACTION = "com.professionalandroid.SENT_SMS_ACTION";
String DELIVERED_SMS_ACTION = " com.professionalandroid.DELIVERED_SMS_ACTION";

// Create the sentIntent parameter
Intent sentIntent = new Intent(SENT_SMS_ACTION);
PendingIntent sentPI = PendingIntent.getBroadcast(getApplicationContext(),
                                                  0,
                                                  sentIntent,

PendingIntent.FLAG_UPDATE_CURRENT);
```

```java
// Create the deliveryIntent parameter
Intent deliveryIntent = new Intent(DELIVERED_SMS_ACTION);
PendingIntent deliverPI =
  PendingIntent.getBroadcast(getApplicationContext(),
                             0,
                             deliveryIntent,
                             PendingIntent.FLAG_UPDATE_CURRENT);

// Register the Broadcast Receivers
registerReceiver(new BroadcastReceiver() {
                 @Override
                 public void onReceive(Context _context, Intent _intent)
                 {
                   String resultText = "UNKNOWN";

                   switch (getResultCode()) {
                     case Activity.RESULT_OK:
                       resultText = "Transmission successful"; break;
                     case SmsManager.RESULT_ERROR_GENERIC_FAILURE:
                       resultText = "Transmission failed"; break;
                     case SmsManager.RESULT_ERROR_RADIO_OFF:
                       resultText = "Transmission failed: Radio is off";
                       break;
                     case SmsManager.RESULT_ERROR_NULL_PDU:
                       resultText = "Transmission Failed: No PDU specified";
                       break;
                     case SmsManager.RESULT_ERROR_NO_SERVICE:
                       resultText = "Transmission Failed: No service";
                       break;
                   }
                   Toast.makeText(_context, resultText,
                                  Toast.LENGTH_LONG).show();
                 }
               },
               new IntentFilter(SENT_SMS_ACTION));

registerReceiver(new BroadcastReceiver() {
                 @Override
                 public void onReceive(Context _context, Intent _intent)
                 {
                   Toast.makeText(_context, "SMS Delivered",
                                  Toast.LENGTH_LONG).show();
                 }
               },
               new IntentFilter(DELIVERED_SMS_ACTION));

// Send the message
SmsManager smsManager = SmsManager.getDefault();
String sendTo = "5551234";
String myMessage = "Android supports programmatic SMS messaging!";

smsManager.sendTextMessage(sendTo, null, myMessage, sentPI, deliverPI);
```

The maximum length of each SMS text message can vary by carrier, but are typically limited to 160 characters. As a result longer messages need to be broken into a series of smaller parts. The SMS Manager includes the `divideMessage` method, which accepts a string as an input and breaks it into an Array List of messages, wherein each is less than the maximum allowable size.

You can then use the `sendMultipartTextMessage` method on the SMS Manager to transmit the array of messages:

```
ArrayList<String> messageArray = smsManager.divideMessage(myMessage);
ArrayList<PendingIntent> sentIntents = new ArrayList<PendingIntent>();
for (int i = 0; i < messageArray.size(); i++)
  sentIntents.add(sentPI);

smsManager.sendMultipartTextMessage(sendTo,
                                    null,
                                    messageArray,
                                    sentIntents, null);
```

The `sentIntent` and `deliveryIntent` parameters in the `sendMultipartTextMessage` method are Array Lists that can be used to specify different Pending Intents to fire for each message part.

To send multimedia MMS messages, use the SMS Manager's `sendMultimediaMessage` method, passing in multimedia to transmit. A fully worked example of sending multimedia MMS messages is beyond the scope of this book, but is available an Android API demo at: `android.googlesource .com/platform/development/+/69291d6/samples/ApiDemos/src/com/example/android/ apis/os/MmsMessagingDemo.java`.

Handling Incoming SMS Messages

For an application to listen for any SMS Broadcast Intents, it needs to specify the `RECEIVE_SMS` manifest and runtime permission:

```
<uses-permission
  android:name="android.permission.RECEIVE_SMS"
/>
```

The `RECEIVE_SMS` permission is marked dangerous, so your app must also request this permission at runtime, otherwise the SMS Broadcast Intents will not be received:

```
ActivityCompat.requestPermissions(this,
  new String[]{Manifest.permission.RECEIVE_SMS},
  SMS_RECEIVE_PERMISSION_REQUEST);
```

When a device receives a new SMS message, the default SMS app will receive a new Broadcast Intent with the `android.provider.Telephony.SMS_DELIVER` action. If your app should still receive SMS messages when it isn't the default SMS app—for example if you're listening for confirmation SMS messages—you can listen for an `android.provider.Telephony.SMS_RECEIVED_ACTION` Intent.

Both broadcast Intents include the incoming SMS details. To extract the array of `SmsMessage` objects packaged within the SMS Intent bundle, use the `getMessagesFromIntent` method:

```
Bundle bundle = intent.getExtras();
if (bundle != null)
  SmsMessage[] messages = getMessagesFromIntent(intent);
```

Each `SmsMessage` contains the SMS message details, including the originating address (phone number), timestamp, and the message body, which can be extracted using the `getOriginatingAddress`, `getTimestampMillis`, and `getMessageBody` methods, respectively:

```
SmsMessage[] messages = getMessagesFromIntent(intent);

for (SmsMessage message : messages) {
  String msg = message.getMessageBody();
  long when = message.getTimestampMillis();
  String from = message.getOriginatingAddress();
}
```

As with outgoing messages, any messages you receive while your app is the default SMS app must be written to the SMS Provider:

```
ContentValues values = new ContentValues();

values.put(Telephony.Sms.ADDRESS, message.getOriginatingAddress());
values.put(Telephony.Sms.BODY, message.getMessageBody());
values.put(Telephony.SMS.DATE, message.getTimestampMillis);
values.put(Telephony.Sms.READ, 0);
values.put(Telephony.Sms.TYPE, Telephony.Sms.MESSAGE_TYPE_INBOX);


context.getApplicationContext().getContentResolver()
  .insert(Telephony.Sms.Sent.CONTENT_URI, values);
```

Once created, remember to register your SMS Broadcast Receiver using the appropriate Intent Filter—either `SMS_DELIVER` if your app should function as a default SMS app, or `SMS_RECEIVED` if not:

```
<receiver android:name=".MySMSReceiver">
  <intent-filter>
    <action android:name="android.provider.Telephony.SMS_RECEIVED"/>
  </intent-filter>
</receiver>
```

Emergency Responder SMS Example

In this example, you'll create an SMS application that turns an Android phone into an emergency response beacon. The robustness of SMS network infrastructure makes SMS an excellent option for applications like this, where reliability is critical.

1. Start by creating a new `EmergencyResponder` project that features a backward-compatible blank `EmergencyResponderMainActivity` Activity. Set the minimum API to 19 (the first Android release to fully support SMS APIs).

2. Add permissions for sending and receiving incoming SMS messages and making phone calls, to the manifest:

```
<?xml version="1.0" encoding="utf-8"?>
<manifest xmlns:android="http://schemas.android.com/apk/res/android"
          package="com.professionalandroid.apps.emergencyresponder">
```

```
<uses-permission android:name="android.permission.RECEIVE_SMS"/>
<uses-permission android:name="android.permission.SEND_SMS"/>
<uses-permission android:name="android.permission.READ_PHONE_STATE"/>

[... Application Node ...]
</manifest>
```

3. Update the res/values/strings.xml resource to include the text to display within the *all clear* and *request help* buttons, as well as their associated default response messages. You should also define an incoming message text that the application will use to detect requests for a status response:

```
<resources>
  <string name="app_name">EmergencyResponder</string>
  <string name="allClearButtonText">Signal All Clear</string>
  <string name="maydayButtonText">Request Help</string>
  <string name="allClearText">I am safe and well. Worry not!</string>
  <string name="maydayText">Tell my mother I love her.</string>
  <string name="querystring">are you OK?</string>
  <string name="querylistprompt">People who want to know if you\'re
ok</string>
</resources>
```

4. Add the Recycler View to the dependencies node within the app module build.gradle file:

```
dependencies {
  [... Existing dependencies ...]
  implementation 'com.android.support:recyclerview-v7:27.1.1'
}
```

5. Modify the main_activity_responder_activity.xml layout resource. Include a RecyclerView to display the list of people requesting a status update, and a series of Buttons that will allow the user to send response SMS messages. The specific layout doesn't matter, provided you include each of the Buttons and the Recycler View using the specified IDs:

```
<?xml version="1.0" encoding="utf-8"?>
<android.support.constraint.ConstraintLayout
  xmlns:android="http://schemas.android.com/apk/res/android"
  xmlns:app="http://schemas.android.com/apk/res-auto"
  xmlns:tools="http://schemas.android.com/tools"
  android:layout_width="match_parent"
  android:layout_height="match_parent"
  <TextView
    android:id="@+id/textView"
    android:layout_width="wrap_content"
    android:layout_height="18dp"
    android:layout_marginEnd="8dp"
    android:layout_marginStart="8dp"
    android:layout_marginTop="16dp"
    android:text="@string/querylistprompt"
    app:layout_constraintEnd_toEndOf="parent"
    app:layout_constraintHorizontal_bias="0.063"
    app:layout_constraintLeft_toLeftOf="parent"
    app:layout_constraintStart_toStartOf="parent"
```

```
        app:layout_constraintTop_toTopOf="parent"/>

    <Button
        android:id="@+id/okButton"
        android:layout_width="0dp"
        android:layout_height="wrap_content"
        android:layout_marginBottom="8dp"
        android:layout_marginEnd="8dp"
        android:layout_marginStart="8dp"
        android:text="@string/allClearButtonText"
        app:layout_constraintBottom_toTopOf="@+id/notOkButton"
        app:layout_constraintEnd_toEndOf="parent"
        app:layout_constraintHorizontal_bias="0.6"
        app:layout_constraintStart_toStartOf="parent"/>

    <Button
        android:id="@+id/notOkButton"
        android:layout_width="0dp"
        android:layout_height="wrap_content"
        android:layout_marginBottom="8dp"
        android:layout_marginEnd="8dp"
        android:layout_marginStart="8dp"
        android:text="@string/maydayButtonText"
        app:layout_constraintBottom_toBottomOf="parent"
        app:layout_constraintEnd_toEndOf="parent"
        app:layout_constraintHorizontal_bias="0.53"
        app:layout_constraintStart_toStartOf="parent"/>

    <android.support.v7.widget.RecyclerView
        android:id="@+id/requesterRecyclerListView"
        android:layout_width="0dp"
        android:layout_height="0dp"
        android:layout_marginBottom="8dp"
        android:layout_marginEnd="8dp"
        android:layout_marginStart="8dp"
        android:layout_marginTop="8dp"
        app:layout_constraintBottom_toTopOf="@+id/okButton"
        app:layout_constraintEnd_toEndOf="parent"
        app:layout_constraintStart_toStartOf="parent"
        app:layout_constraintTop_toBottomOf="@+id/textView"/>

</android.support.constraint.ConstraintLayout>
```

At this point, the GUI will be complete, so starting the application should show you the screen in Figure 20-2.

FIGURE 20-2

6. Create a new Array List of Strings within the Activity to store the phone numbers of the incoming requests for your status, and create a new ReentrantLock object to support thread-safe handling of the Array List. Take this opportunity to get Click Listeners for each Button; both response Buttons should call the respond method.

```java
public class EmergencyResponderMainActivity extends AppCompatActivity {

    ReentrantLock lock;
    ArrayList<String> requesters = new ArrayList<String>();

    @Override
    protected void onCreate(Bundle savedInstanceState) {
        super.onCreate(savedInstanceState);
        setContentView(R.layout.activity_emergency_responder_main);

        lock = new ReentrantLock();
        wireUpButtons();
    }
```

```
      private void wireUpButtons() {
        Button okButton = findViewById(R.id.okButton);
        okButton.setOnClickListener(new View.OnClickListener() {
          public void onClick(View view) {
            respond(true);
          }
        });

        Button notOkButton = findViewById(R.id.notOkButton);
        notOkButton.setOnClickListener(new View.OnClickListener() {
          public void onClick(View view) {
            respond(false);
          }
        });
      }

      public void respond(boolean ok) {}
    }
```

7. Create a new `list_item_requester.xml` layout resource in the `res/layout` folder. This will be used to display each person who requests your status, within the Recycler View. You can use a simple `TextView` with the Android framework's list item text appearance:

```xml
<?xml version="1.0" encoding="utf-8"?>
<FrameLayout
  xmlns:android="http://schemas.android.com/apk/res/android"
  android:layout_width="match_parent"
  android:layout_height="wrap_content">
  <TextView
    android:id="@+id/list_item_requester"
    android:layout_width="match_parent"
    android:layout_height="wrap_content"
    android:textAppearance="?attr/textAppearanceListItem"/>
</FrameLayout>
```

8. Create a new `RequesterRecyclerViewAdapter` class that extends `RecyclerView.Adapter`, and within it create a new `ViewHolder` class that extends `RecyclerView.ViewHolder`. The Adapter should store a list of phone numbers requesting your status, and the View Holder should bind those numbers to the Recycler View List Item layout defined in Step 7:

```java
public class RequesterRecyclerViewAdapter extends
  RecyclerView.Adapter<RequesterRecyclerViewAdapter.ViewHolder> {

  private List<String> mNumbers;

  public RequesterRecyclerViewAdapter(List<String> numbers ) {
    mNumbers = numbers;
  }

  @Override
  public ViewHolder onCreateViewHolder(ViewGroup parent, int viewType) {
    View view = LayoutInflater.from(parent.getContext())
```

```
                    .inflate(R.layout.list_item_requester,
                        parent, false);
        return new ViewHolder(view);
    }

    @Override
    public void onBindViewHolder(final ViewHolder holder, int position) {
        holder.number = mNumbers.get(position);
        holder.numberView.setText(mNumbers.get(position));
    }

    @Override
    public int getItemCount() {
        if (mNumbers != null)
            return mNumbers.size();
        return 0;
    }

    public class ViewHolder extends RecyclerView.ViewHolder {
        public final TextView numberView;
        public String number;

        public ViewHolder(View view) {
            super(view);
            numberView = view.findViewById(R.id.list_item_requester);
        }

        @Override
        public String toString() {
            return number;
        }
    }
}
```

9. Return to the Activity and update `onCreate` to get a reference to the Recycler View, and assign the Adapter from Step 8 to it. Take this opportunity to request runtime permission for receiving and sending SMS messages:

```
private static final int SMS_RECEIVE_PERMISSION_REQUEST = 1;

private RequesterRecyclerViewAdapter mRequesterAdapter =
    new RequesterRecyclerViewAdapter(requesters);

@Override
protected void onCreate(Bundle savedInstanceState) {
    super.onCreate(savedInstanceState);
    setContentView(R.layout.activity_emergency_responder_main);

    lock = new ReentrantLock();
    wireUpButtons();

    ActivityCompat.requestPermissions(this,
        new String[]{Manifest.permission.RECEIVE_SMS,
```

```
                 Manifest.permission.SEND_SMS,
                 Manifest.permission.READ_PHONE_STATE},
    SMS_RECEIVE_PERMISSION_REQUEST);

  RecyclerView recyclerView =
    findViewById(R.id.requesterRecyclerListView);

  // Set the Recycler View adapter
  recyclerView.setLayoutManager(new LinearLayoutManager(this));
  recyclerView.setAdapter(mRequesterAdapter);
}
```

10. Within your Activity, create a new Broadcast Receiver that will listen for incoming SMS messages. The receiver should listen for incoming SMS messages and call the requestReceived method when it sees SMS messages containing the incoming request String you defined in Step 3:

```
BroadcastReceiver emergencyResponseRequestReceiver =
  new BroadcastReceiver() {
    @Override
    public void onReceive(Context context, Intent intent) {
      if (intent.getAction()
             .equals(Telephony.Sms.Intents.SMS_RECEIVED_ACTION )) {
        String queryString = getString(R.string.querystring)
                                   .toLowerCase();

        Bundle bundle = intent.getExtras();
        if (bundle != null) {
          SmsMessage[] messages = getMessagesFromIntent(intent);

          for (SmsMessage message : messages) {
            if (message.getMessageBody()
                   .toLowerCase().contains(queryString))
              requestReceived(message.getOriginatingAddress());
          }
        }
      }
    }
  };

public void requestReceived(String from) {}
```

11. Override the Activity's onResume and onPause methods to register and unregister the Broadcast Receiver created in Step 10 when the Activity resumes and pauses, respectively:

```
@Override
public void onResume() {
  super.onResume();
  IntentFilter filter =
    new IntentFilter(Telephony.Sms.Intents.SMS_RECEIVED_ACTION);
  registerReceiver(emergencyResponseRequestReceiver, filter);
}

@Override
public void onPause() {
```

```
        super.onPause();
        unregisterReceiver(emergencyResponseRequestReceiver);
    }
```

12. Update the `requestReceived` method stub so that it adds the originating number of each status request's SMS to the Array List:

```
public void requestReceived(String from) {
  if (!requesters.contains(from)) {
    lock.lock();
    requesters.add(from);
    mRequesterAdapter.notifyDataSetChanged();
    lock.unlock();
  }
}
```

13. The Emergency Responder Activity should now be listening for status request SMS messages and adding them to the List View as they arrive. Start the application and send SMS messages to the device or emulator on which it's running. When they've arrived, they should be displayed as shown in Figure 20-3. Note that the default SMS app will also receive these incoming messages and will likely display a corresponding Notification.

FIGURE 20-3

14. Update the Activity to let users respond to these status requests. Start by completing the `respond` method stub you created in Step 6. It should iterate over the Array List of status requesters and send a new SMS message to each. The SMS message text should be based on the response strings you defined as resources in Step 3. Send the SMS using the `sendResponse` method (which you'll complete in the next step):

```
public void respond(boolean ok) {
  String okString = getString(R.string.allClearText);
  String notOkString = getString(R.string.maydayText);
  String outString = ok ? okString : notOkString;

  ArrayList<String> requestersCopy =
    (ArrayList<String>)requesters.clone();

  for (String to : requestersCopy)
    sendResponse(to, outString);
}

private void sendResponse(String to, String response) {}
```

15. Complete the `sendResponse` method to handle sending of each response SMS. Start by removing each potential recipient from the "requesters" Array List before sending the SMS:

```
public void sendResponse(String to, String response) {
  // Check runtime permissions.
  int send_sms_permission = ActivityCompat.checkSelfPermission(this,
    Manifest.permission.SEND_SMS);
  int phone_state_permission = ActivityCompat.checkSelfPermission(this,
    Manifest.permission.READ_PHONE_STATE);

  if (send_sms_permission == PackageManager.PERMISSION_GRANTED &&
      phone_state_permission == PackageManager.PERMISSION_GRANTED) {

    // Remove the target from the list of people we
    // need to respond to.
    lock.lock();
    requesters.remove(to);
    mRequesterAdapter.notifyDataSetChanged();
    lock.unlock();

    // Send the message
    SmsManager sms = SmsManager.getDefault();
    sms.sendTextMessage(to, null, response, null, null);

  } else {
    if (ActivityCompat.shouldShowRequestPermissionRationale(
      this, Manifest.permission.SEND_SMS)) {
      // TODO Display additional rationale for the requested permission.
    }

    ActivityCompat.requestPermissions(this,
      new String[]{Manifest.permission.SEND_SMS,
        Manifest.permission.READ_PHONE_STATE},
      SMS_RECEIVE_PERMISSION_REQUEST);
  }
}
```

16. In emergencies it's important that messages get out. Improve the robustness of the application by including auto-retry functionality. Monitor the success of your SMS messaging so that you can resend a message if it isn't successfully sent.

16.1 Start by creating a new public static String in the Activity to be used within Broadcast Intents to indicate the SMS has been sent.

```
public static final String SENT_SMS =
  "com.professionalandroid.emergencyresponder.SMS_SENT";
```

16.2 Update the sendResponse method to include a new PendingIntent that broadcasts the action created in the previous step when the SMS transmission has completed. The packaged Intent should include the intended recipient's number as an extra.

```
public void sendResponse(String to, String response) {
  // Check runtime permissions.
  int send_sms_permission = ActivityCompat.checkSelfPermission(this,
    Manifest.permission.SEND_SMS);
  int phone_state_permission = ActivityCompat.checkSelfPermission(this,
    Manifest.permission.READ_PHONE_STATE);

  if (send_sms_permission == PackageManager.PERMISSION_GRANTED &&
      phone_state_permission == PackageManager.PERMISSION_GRANTED) {

    // Remove the target from the list of people we
    // need to respond to.
    lock.lock();
    requesters.remove(to);
    mRequesterAdapter.notifyDataSetChanged();
    lock.unlock();

    Intent intent = new Intent(SENT_SMS);
    intent.putExtra("recipient", to);
    PendingIntent sentPI =
      PendingIntent.getBroadcast(getApplicationContext(),
        0, intent, 0);

    // Send the message
    SmsManager sms = SmsManager.getDefault();
    sms.sendTextMessage(to, null, response, sentPI, null);

  } else {
    if (ActivityCompat.shouldShowRequestPermissionRationale(
      this, Manifest.permission.SEND_SMS)) {
      // TODO Display additional rationale for the requested permission.
    }

    ActivityCompat.requestPermissions(this,
      new String[]{Manifest.permission.SEND_SMS,
        Manifest.permission.READ_PHONE_STATE},
      SMS_RECEIVE_PERMISSION_REQUEST);
  }
}
```

16.3 Implement a new Broadcast Receiver to listen for this Broadcast Intent. Override its onReceive handler to confirm that the SMS was successfully delivered; if it wasn't, put the intended recipient back onto the requester Array List.

```
        private BroadcastReceiver attemptedSendReceiver
          = new BroadcastReceiver() {
          @Override
          public void onReceive(Context context, Intent intent) {
            if (intent.getAction().equals(SENT_SMS)) {
              if (getResultCode() != Activity.RESULT_OK) {
                String recipient = intent.getStringExtra("recipient");
                requestReceived(recipient);
              }
            }
          }
        };
```

16.4 Finally, register and unregister the new Broadcast Receiver by updating the onResume and onPause handlers of the Activity:

```
@Override
public void onResume() {
  super.onResume();
  IntentFilter filter =
    new IntentFilter(Telephony.Sms.Intents.SMS_RECEIVED_ACTION);
  registerReceiver(emergencyResponseRequestReceiver, filter);

  IntentFilter attemptedDeliveryFilter = new IntentFilter(SENT_SMS);
  registerReceiver(attemptedSendReceiver, attemptedDeliveryFilter);
}

@Override
public void onPause() {
  super.onPause();
  unregisterReceiver(emergencyResponseRequestReceiver);
  unregisterReceiver(attemptedSendReceiver);
}
```

The purpose of this example is to demonstrate the process of listening for SMS messages, and sending them from within your application. Keen-eyed observers should have noticed several areas where it could be improved:

➤ The list of people requesting a response needs to be persisted to a database.

➤ The Broadcast Receiver would be better registered within the manifest to allow the application to respond to incoming SMS messages even when it isn't running.

➤ The parsing of the incoming SMS messages should be moved into Job Scheduler or Work Manager, and executed on a background thread, as should sending the response SMS messages.

➤ Adding the ability to send your current location using the location based services APIs would make the app much more useful in an emergency.

The implementation of these improvements is left as an exercise for the reader.

21

Releasing, Distributing, and Monitoring Applications

Having created a compelling new Android application, the next step is to share it with the world. In this final chapter, you learn how to prepare your app for release, and how to create and use a signing certificate to sign your applications before you distribute them.

You'll be introduced to the Google Play Store, learn how to create a developer profile, and how to create your application listing. You'll also learn how to use the Alpha and Beta release channels to test your app, before using staged rollouts to ensure updates are rolled out in a way to minimize the risk of distributing an update with critical bugs.

The Google Play Store includes a number of tools to monitor your apps in production. You'll learn how to use the statistics, vitals, user acquisition, and user feedback pages to better understand how your app is performing on real devices for real users.

An introduction to the options for marketing, monetizing, and promoting your app will help ensure you have a successful launch.

Finally, an introduction to Firebase, and a deep dive into Firebase Analytics and Firebase Performance Monitoring will help you gain critical insight into the demographics of your users and the performance of your app in real-world scenarios.

PREPARING FOR RELEASE

Before building and publishing the production release of your application, you should take several steps to prepare your application for distribution.

These preparation steps apply to all applications, irrespective of how they are distributed, and can generally be divided into two halves: preparing support material related to publishing your application, and preparing your code for a release build.

Preparing Release Support Material

Start by reviewing your application's launcher icon, and ensure it meets the recommended icon guidelines available at `material.io/guidelines/style/icons.html`.

Your icon should promote your brand and help users discover your app, both within app listings on Google Play and within the app launcher on Android devices.

The first impression of your app for potential users is through the app icon, so its quality is often considered a strong signal for the quality of your app. Great app icons are simple, unique, and memorable. They use a color scheme that's consistent with your brand and avoid including text—particularly the application name.

Once your app is installed, its launcher icon will be used in many situations, so ensure it looks good on a wide variety of backgrounds and has a unique silhouette to make it easier to identify.

Within your project, include density-specific icons for all generalized screen densities, from low-through to xxx-high-density to ensure they look good and crisp across all possible devices.

> **NOTE** *It's best practice to place your launcher icons in the* `res/mipmap` *folders rather than the* `res/drawable` *folders to ensure the system has access to higher resolutions than the device's current density. You can find more details on creating resources for different screen densities in Chapter 4, "Defining the Android Manifest and Gradle Build Files, and Externalizing Resources."*

In addition to the application resources, Google Play requires a high-resolution (512x512 pixel) variation of your launcher icon for use in application listings.

You should also consider preparing an End User License Agreement (EULA) to help protect you, your organization, and your intellectual property, and a Privacy Policy to describe your commitment to protecting user privacy and providing a safe and secure environment for your users. You can find more details regarding privacy and security at `play.google.com/about/ privacy-security-deception`.

Finally, prepare promotional and marketing materials to publicize your app. At a minimum this will include an application name, summary, and description that will be used to describe your app on distribution platforms including the Google Play Store.

It's important to provide high-quality, descriptive titles and application descriptions without spelling or grammatical errors to make it easy for users to find your application and make an informed choice on its suitability. Similar to your application icon, the quality of your descriptions are a strong signal for the quality of your application.

You should also create representative screen captures for each supported device type—such as phone, tablet, and TV—and videos to help describe and promote your app. More details on the particular promotional material required by Google Play are described later in this chapter.

Preparing Your Code for a Release Build

The following recommendations are optional, but they are considered good coding practice to ensure high-quality release builds prior to distribution:

➤ **Choose a good package name**—Once deployed your app's package name cannot be changed, so take care to select a package name that will be suitable for the lifetime of your application. Be sure not to use other companies' names or trademarks, and use language that reflects quality and professionalism.

➤ **Deactivate logging**—To improve efficiency, remove all calls to `Log` and debug tracing calls such as `startMethodTracing` and `stopMethodTracing`.

➤ **Disable debugging**—Remove, or set to false, the `android:debuggable` attribute in your application manifest. If your app uses a Web View to display paid-for content or is using JavaScript interfaces, use the Web View's `setWebContentsDebuggingEnabled` method to disable debugging. This is important because enabled debugging will allow users to inject scripts and extract content using Chrome DevTools.

➤ **Review project code folder contents**—Check the `jni/` and `src/` directories to ensure they contain only source files associated with your application, and that the `lib/` directory contains only third-party or private library files. The `src/` directory should not contain any `.jar` files.

➤ **Review project resource folder contents**—Double-check for any private or proprietary data files that aren't required for deployment, review all the resource folders for files that you are no longer using, and check for asset and static files that should be updated or removed prior to release.

➤ **Review your manifest file**—Verify that your application manifest and Gradle build files are configured to define the correct app version, installation requirements, and permissions, as described in the following section.

UPDATING APPLICATION METADATA IN YOUR APPLICATION MANIFEST

Prior to publishing your application, it's important to review your application's metadata, as defined within your application manifest and Gradle build files and described in more detail in Chapter 4.

In this section we will review some of the nodes unique to production builds and application distribution.

Reviewing Application Installation Restrictions

Review the `uses-permission` nodes within the application manifest. Ensure that only permissions that are relevant and required for your application to function are included. The required permissions will be displayed to users at installation time, so including over-broad or unnecessary permission requirements risks users choosing not to install your application.

Also within the application manifest, review the `uses-feature` nodes. As described in Chapter 4, these nodes are used to specify hardware and/or software features that are strictly required for your application to function.

The inclusion of any `uses-feature` nodes will prevent your application from being installed on any devices that do not support a specified feature. For example, an application that includes the following snippet can't be installed on any Android device that doesn't include NFC support (such as an Android TV):

```
<uses-feature android:name="android.hardware.nfc" />
```

Use this node *only* if you want to prevent your app being installed on devices that don't include certain features. If your app can use particular hardware, but that hardware is not a strict requirement, check the host device for support at runtime rather than including a `uses-feature` node.

Within the Gradle app module, set your app's configuration settings to define the minimum and target SDK versions:

```
defaultConfig {
  applicationId "com.professionalandroid.apps.earthquake"
  minSdkVersion 16
  targetSdkVersion 27
  versionCode 1
  versionName "1.0"
  testInstrumentationRunner "android.support.test.runner.AndroidJUnitRunner"
}
```

Note that it's possible to define different values for minimum and target SDKs using different build flavors within your Gradle builds:

```
defaultConfig {
  applicationId "com.professionalandroid.apps.earthquake"
  minSdkVersion 16
  targetSdkVersion 27
  versionCode 1
  versionName "1.0"
  testInstrumentationRunner "android.support.test.runner.AndroidJUnitRunner"
}

flavorDimensions "apilevel"

productFlavors {
  legacy {
    applicationId "com.professionalandroid.apps.earthquake.legacy"
    minSdkVersion 14
    targetSdkVersion 15
    versionName "1.0 - Legacy"
  }
}
```

This allows you to generate multiple SDKs with different requirements. More details on creating and using build flavors are available in Chapter 4.

The minimum SDK value defines the lowest version of the Android framework onto which your application can be installed. The Android OS enforces system version compatibility, meaning that it will reject any attempt to install an app whose minimum SDK is higher than the current operating system.

The target SDK value indicates the Android platform version against which you did your development and testing. This is used by the system to determine which (if any) forward- or backward-compatibility changes to apply to support your app. It's considered good practice to always target the latest platform release after you've tested your app on it.

Also within the Gradle build file, review the dependencies node to ensure that only relevant, required dependencies are included:

```
dependencies {
  implementation 'com.android.support:recyclerview-v7:27.1.1'
  implementation fileTree(dir: 'libs', include: ['*.jar'])
  implementation 'com.android.support:appcompat-v7:27.1.1'
  implementation 'com.android.support:support-v4:27.1.1'
  implementation 'com.android.support.constraint:constraint-layout:1.1.2'
  testImplementation 'junit:junit:4.12'
  androidTestImplementation 'com.android.support.test:runner:1.0.2'
  androidTestImplementation 'com.android.support.test.espresso:espresso-core:3.0.2'
}
```

Application Versioning

Versioning is an important consideration when deploying your application, critical in ensuring an orderly app upgrade and maintenance strategy.

An orderly versioning system ensures users will find information specific to their app version, and publishing services such as Google Play can properly determine compatibility, and establish upgrade/downgrade relationships. On each device, the Android system uses your app's version information to enforce protection against downgrades.

Your application version is defined within your Gradle build file using two values:

> **versionCode**—An integer defining the current version number, which increases with each new released version. It's used by Google Play and the Android OS to determine whether one version of your app is more recent than another. Typically your first release will be numbered 1, and with each subsequent release the version code is monotonically increased. Note that the highest allowed version code value is 2,100,000,000.

> **versionName**—A string displayed to users as the visible version number. As a string, you can choose to describe the app version as a <major>.<minor>.<point> string, or as any other type of absolute or relative version identifier. The version name has no purpose other than to be displayed to users.

You can define both version code and name in the `defaultconfig`, and override either value within a product flavor block:

```
defaultConfig {
  applicationId "com.professionalandroid.apps.earthquake"
  minSdkVersion 16
  targetSdkVersion 27
  versionCode 1
  versionName "1.0"
  testInstrumentationRunner "android.support.test.runner.AndroidJUnitRunner"
}

flavorDimensions "apilevel"

productFlavors {
  bleedingedge {
  }
  legacy {
    applicationId "com.professionalandroid.apps.earthquake.legacy"
    versionName "1.0 - Legacy"
  }
}
```

SIGNING PRODUCTION BUILDS OF YOUR APPLICATION

Android applications are distributed as Android package files (.APK). To be installed on a device or emulator, Android packages need to be signed.

During development, your applications will be signed using a debug key that is automatically generated by Android Studio. Before distributing your application beyond your testing environment, you must compile it as a release build and sign it using a private release key—typically using a self-signed certificate.

To apply an upgrade to an installed application, it must be signed with the same key, so you must always sign an application using the same release key.

The importance of maintaining the security of your signing certificate can't be overstated. Android uses this certificate as the means of identifying the authenticity of application updates, and applying inter-process security boundaries between installed applications.

Using a stolen key, a third party could sign and distribute applications that maliciously replace your authentic applications.

Similarly, your key is the only way you can upgrade your applications. If you lose your certificate, it is impossible to perform a seamless update on a device or from within Google Play. In the latter case, you would need to create a new listing, losing all the reviews, ratings, and comments associated with your previous package, as well as making it impossible to provide updates to the existing users of your application.

> **NOTE** *If you plan to distribute your applications exclusively through Google Play, you can take advantage of Google Play App Signing—an optional program described later in this chapter—that exists to help you securely manage your signing key.*
>
> *When using Google Play App Signing, Google Play creates, stores, and applies a private release key for your app. You will still create a private key and use it to sign your app as described in this section, however this will become an upload key—used only to identify you as the uploader—that will be removed by Google Play and replaced with the managed private key before being distributed to end users.*
>
> *In addition to the security advantages of using Google to secure your release key, the upload key can be reset by Google, minimizing the risk associated with losing your local signing key.*

The Android guidelines suggest that you sign all your applications using the same certificate, because applications signed with the same certificate can be configured to run in the same process, and signature-based permissions can be used to expose functionality between trusted applications signed with the same certificate.

The JDK includes the `Keytool` and `Jarsigner` command-line tools necessary to create a new keystore/signing certificate, and to sign your APK, respectively. Alternatively, you can use dialogs within Android Studio as described in the next section.

Creating a Keystore and Signing Key with Android Studio

To create a new keystore, and a *release* or *upload* signing key for your app, within Android Studio navigate to the Build ⇨ Generate Signed APK menu item. The resulting dialog will prompt you to either select a new keystore or create one, as shown in Figure 21-1.

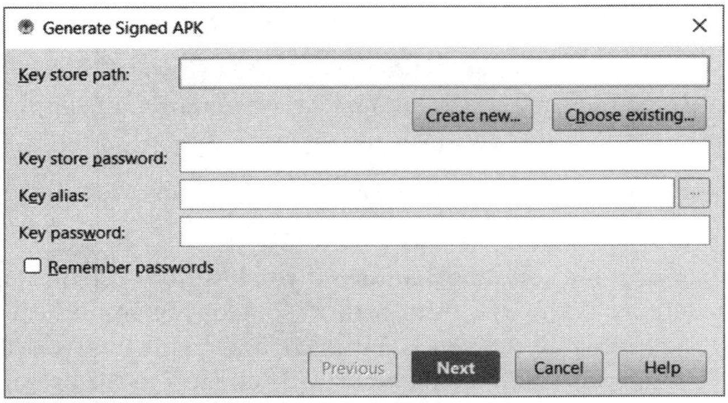

FIGURE 21-1

Click the Create New button and enter a filename and location for your keystore along with a password to secure it. You should then create a new key, or *signing certificate*, by filling in the dialog shown in Figure 21-2.

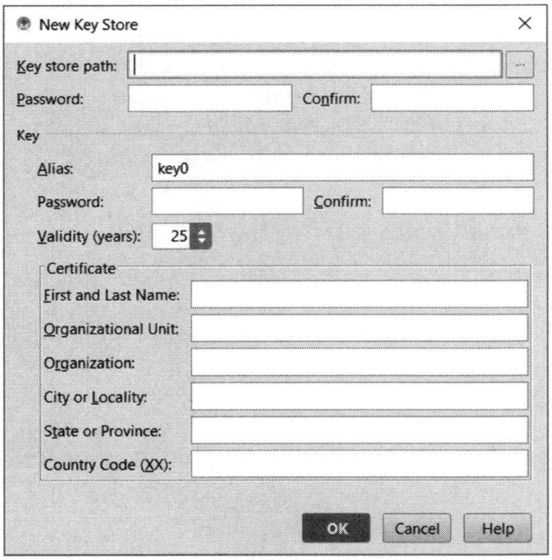

FIGURE 21-2

Applications published on Google Play require a certificate with a validity period ending after October 22, 2033. More generally, your certificate will be used through the lifetime of your application and is necessary to perform upgrades, so you should ensure your signing certificate will outlast your application.

The security of your keystore is extremely important, so be sure to use a strong password to secure it and ensure it is backed up securely.

Obtaining API Keys Based on Your Private Release Key

To prevent unauthorized use and quota theft many third-party libraries—including Google Play services—require you to generate an API key based on the release key used to sign your application.

These API keys will typically require your app's unique package name, and the SHA-1 signing-certificate fingerprint from your release key.

If you are using your own release key, you can obtain its SHA-1 fingerprint using the following command-line command, where `mystore.keystore` represents the full path to your keystore as defined in the previous section:

```
keytool -list -v -keystore mystore.keystore
```

If you are managing your key using Google Play App Signing, as described later in this chapter, you won't have local access to your app's final signing certificate. However, you can obtain the SHA-1, SHA-256, or MD5 fingerprints on the Google Play Console at `play.google.com/apps/publish/` by selecting your app and navigating to the App Signing tab, as shown in Figure 21-3.

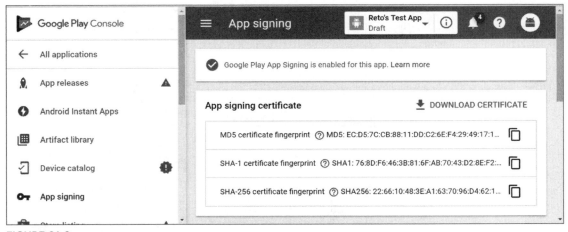

FIGURE 21-3

The Google Play console and Google Play App Signing are covered in more detail later in this chapter in the section, "Distributing Applications on Google Play."

Building and Signing a Production Release

Once you have prepared your project for release, updated its metadata, and created a keystore and private signing key, you're ready to build and sign your app for upload and distribution.

A release build contains the same components as a debug build, but it's also optimized using zipalign and signed with your release certificate. To build your release APK, you can use a simple Android Studio wizard by selecting the Build ⇨ Generate Signed APK menu item.

In the resulting dialog, select your keystore, provide a password, and select a signing key and associated password, as shown in Figure 21-4.

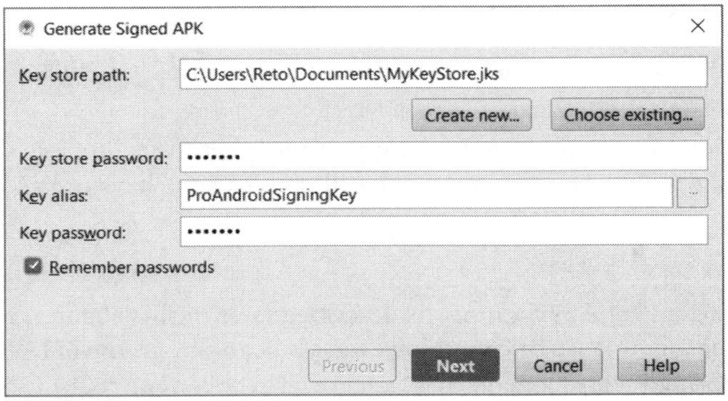

FIGURE 21-4

Click Next to continue to the final wizard dialog shown in Figure 21-5.

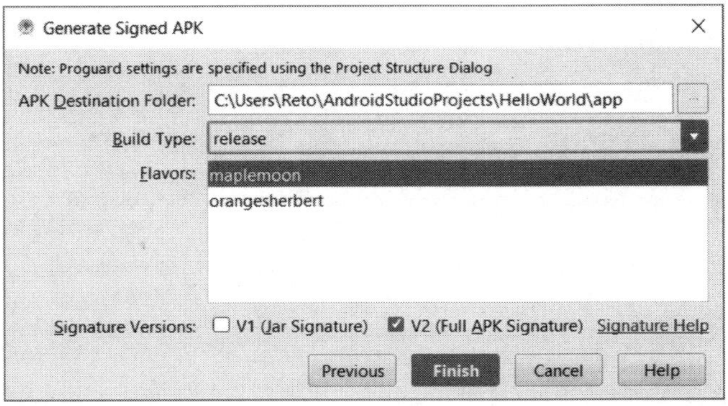

FIGURE 21-5

Select an output location for the final signed APK and select "release" from the build-type drop-down. If you have defined different product flavors, select the flavors to build.

Note that you can choose to apply either of two APK signature schemes. Historically, all Android APKs are signed using v1 (JAR signature); however, Android 7.0 introduced v2 (full APK signature), which offers faster app install times and more protection against unauthorized alterations. Google Play requires at least v1 signing, and it's generally recommended to also use the v2 signature schema if doing so doesn't cause any issues when building your app.

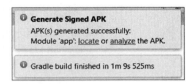

Click Finish and your application will be built, zipaligned, and signed. The indicator shown in Figure 21-6 will notify you of completion, and offers a shortcut to the location of the resulting APK.

FIGURE 21-6

It's also possible to configure the Gradle build files to perform the same actions performed by the wizard when called from the command line. For more details about using the Gradle build files, refer to `d.android.com/studio/build/build-variants.html#signing`.

DISTRIBUTING YOUR APPLICATION ON THE GOOGLE PLAY STORE

One of the advantages of Android's open ecosystem is the freedom to publish and distribute your applications however, and wherever, you choose. The most common and popular distribution channel is Google Play; however, you are free to distribute your applications using alternative markets, your own website, e-mail, social media, or any other distribution channel.

When distributing your application, it's important to note that application package names are used as unique identifiers for each application. As a result, each application—including variations that you plan to distribute separately—must each have a unique package name. Also note that the filename of your APK does not have to be unique—it will be discarded during the installation process (only the package name is used).

Introducing the Google Play Store

The Google Play Store is the largest and most popular Android application distribution platform. At the time of writing this book, it has been reported that in excess of 2.7 million applications are available, with more than 80 billion application downloads from users in over 145 countries.

The Google Play Store is a marketplace—that is, Google Play acts as a mechanism for you to sell and distribute your application rather than as a merchant reselling it on your behalf. That means far fewer controls restricting what you distribute and how you choose to promote, monetize, and distribute it. Those restrictions are detailed within the Google Play Developer Distribution Agreement (DDA) (`play.google.com/about/developer-distribution-agreement.html`) and the Google Play Developer Program Policies (DPP) (`play.google.com/about/developer-content-policy/`).

Applications that are suspected of breaching the DDA or DPP are reviewed, and if found to have breached those agreements and policies, are suspended and the developer notified. In extreme cases of malware, the Google Play Store can remotely uninstall malicious applications from devices.

> **WARNING** *Before publishing your applications, it's important to carefully review the DDA and DPP to ensure your application is compliant. Applications that are in breach of these policies will be suspended, and multiple infringements can result in the suspension or banning of your developer account.*
>
> *If your application isn't eligible to be distributed through Google Play, you can still distribute it using an alternative distribution platform or mechanism.*

Google Play provides all the tools and mechanisms required to handle application distribution, updates, sales (domestic and international), and promotion. Once listed, your application will begin to appear in search results and category lists, as well as potentially within promotional categories.

The full scope of features provided by the Google Play Store is beyond the scope of this book, however we will cover the core functionality that enables you to publish your application.

Getting Started with the Google Play Store

To publish on the Google Play Store, create a developer account at `play.google.com/apps/publish/signup`, as shown in Figure 21-7.

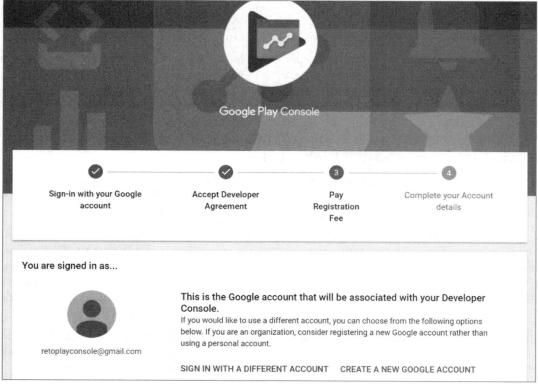

FIGURE 21-7

> **NOTE** *Your Android Developer Profile will be associated with whichever Google account (if any) you are currently signed in to. It's common that multiple people will need access to this account, particularly if you're distributing applications on behalf of a company.*
>
> *It's good practice to create a new Google account specifically for your Android Developer Profile rather than using your personal Google account.*

Ensure you're signed in with the Google account you wish to associate with this developer account, and review and accept the developer distribution agreement before completing the registration process by paying a US $25.00 fee.

You'll then have the opportunity to complete your developer profile. Provide a "Developer Name"—typically your company name—that will be used within Google Play to identify the developer of your applications. Note that it is not a requirement that the developer name used here represent the company or individual who actually wrote the code—it simply identifies the company or individual distributing it.

You should also provide contact details in the form of a physical address, e-mail address, website, and phone number. Note that by providing your e-mail or postal address information, you confirm that you consent to Google publicly displaying or disclosing that information in connection with your apps. Here again, it's good practice to create an email account specifically for app feedback purposes, rather than sharing your personal email account.

Creating an Application on the Google Play Store

After creating your Android Developer Profile, you are ready to create a new application, upload your APK as an app release, and complete your store listing.

Before you begin the process of uploading and distributing your new application, you should thoroughly test the release version on at least one target handset device and one target tablet device.

When you're ready to distribute, start by creating a new app listing on Google Play. Click the Create Application button on the main "All applications" tab, as shown in Figure 21-8.

In the resulting dialog, select the default language, provide your application's title as shown in Figure 21-9, and click Create.

With your app created, you can now complete the store listing details and upload APKs to be used as App Releases, as described in the following sections.

You will create a new App Release each time you wish to distribute an updated APK, while the app listing will contain all the details necessary to promote your app on Google Play. It's important that you supply all the possible content and assets—even those that may be listed as optional. Each asset is used throughout Google Play, including the website, Google Play Store clients, and promotional campaigns. Not including some assets may prevent your application from being featured or promoted.

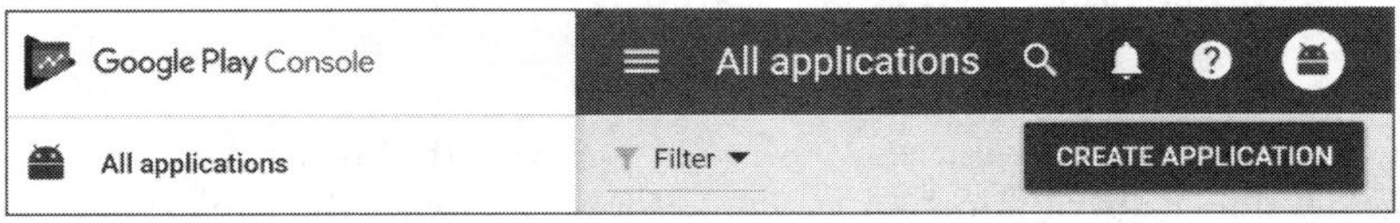

FIGURE 21-8

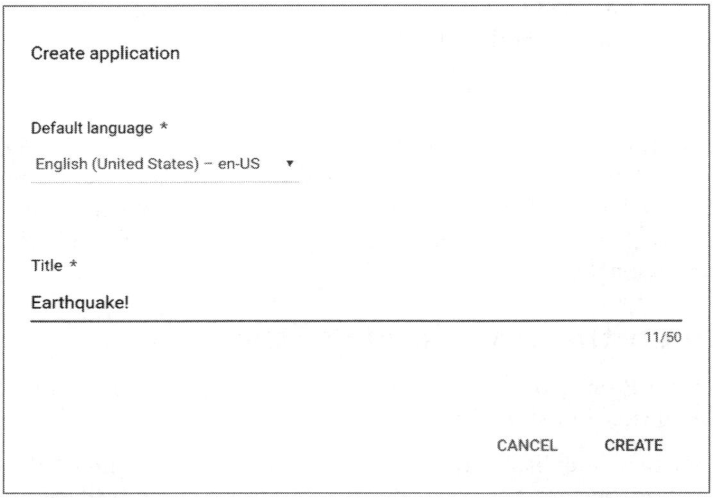

FIGURE 21-9

Uploading a New App Release APK

To upload your APK, select the App Releases option on the sidebar to display the App Releases view, as shown in Figure 21-10. You can choose to publish your application to Alpha, Beta, or Production.

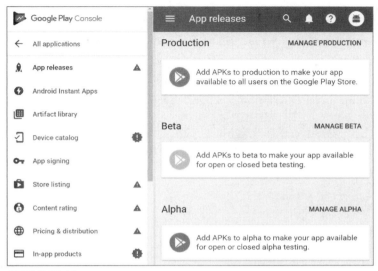

FIGURE 21-10

The Alpha and Beta channels allow you to make the app available to a small group of testers prior to making your app generally available to all users, as described in detail in the "Publishing Your Application" section.

Click the "Manage [channel]" button for the release channel you wish to publish, and click the Create Release button.

You will then have the opportunity to enroll in Google Play App Signing, upload an APK, provide a release name, and complete the release notes.

The first section at the top of the page displays your Google Play App Signing selection—allowing you to enroll, as described in the following section, "Managing Your Private Release Key using Google Play App Signing."

The next section is where you select or upload your signed release package, as shown in Figure 21-11.

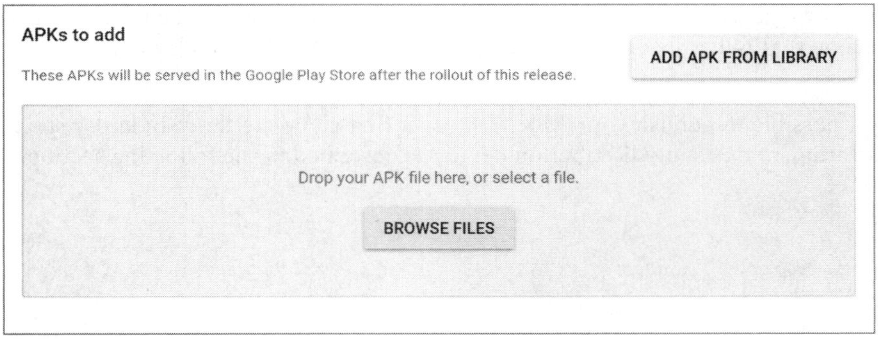

APKs to add

These APKs will be served in the Google Play Store after the rollout of this release.

ADD APK FROM LIBRARY

Drop your APK file here, or select a file.

BROWSE FILES

FIGURE 21-11

> **NOTE** *The package name (not the filename) must be unique. Google Play uses application package names as unique identifiers and will not allow you to upload a duplicate package name.*

You must then enter a Release Name and a description of what's new in this release, as shown in Figure 21-12.

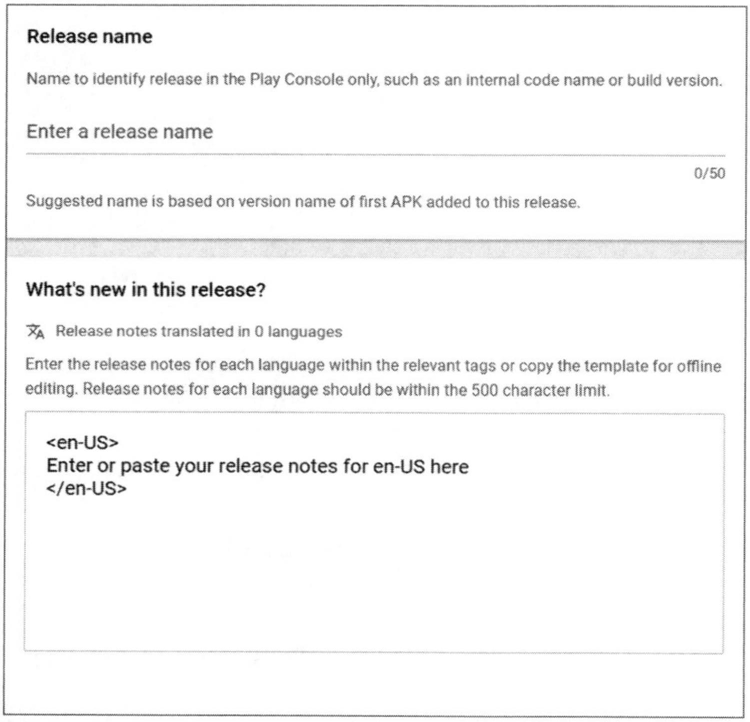

Release name

Name to identify release in the Play Console only, such as an internal code name or build version.

Enter a release name

0/50

Suggested name is based on version name of first APK added to this release.

What's new in this release?

文A Release notes translated in 0 languages

Enter the release notes for each language within the relevant tags or copy the template for offline editing. Release notes for each language should be within the 500 character limit.

```
<en-US>
Enter or paste your release notes for en-US here
</en-US>
```

FIGURE 21-12

The release notes will be displayed with your application on Google Play, while the release name is an internal codename that will only ever be shown to you within the Google Play management console.

Note that it's not yet possible to publish your APK. You must first complete the mandatory store listing details, content rating, and pricing/distribution details as described in the following sections.

Managing Your Private Release Key Using Google Play App Signing

Google Play App Signing is an optional program that exists to help you securely manage your signing key using the same secure infrastructure Google uses to store its own keys.

When you opt-in to Google Play App Signing, rather than signing each app with your key directly you sign your app with an upload key. Should you lose your upload key, you can request a copy from Google—decreasing the risk of losing your key.

When you upload new apps signed with your upload key to the Play Console, Google verifies and removes the upload key signature before re-signing the app with the original app signing key.

> **WARNING** *Once you've enrolled your app in Google Play App Signing, withdrawal is not supported. To preserve the security of your app signing keys, we don't have the ability to remove keys from the secure server. However, opt-in is app-specific, meaning you can choose not to opt-in for future applications.*

You can opt-in to Google Play App Signing when creating a new app release, by clicking the Continue button, as shown in Figure 21-13.

FIGURE 21-13

Alternatively, you can reuse the same Google Play–managed key as your other applications by clicking Reuse Signing Key, as shown in Figure 21-14. The Android guidelines suggest that you sign all your applications using the same certificate.

If you have an existing application being distributed on Google Play, it's possible to opt-in to Google Play App Signing by uploading your existing signing certificate.

Creating a New Application Listing

With your signed APK uploaded, you must prepare your Google Play Store listing. Click the "Store listing" option on the sidebar to display the store listing options, the first of which is shown in Figure 21-15.

Begin by providing a high-quality, descriptive title and description to make it easier for users to discover your application and make an informed choice on its suitability. Don't engage in keyword stuffing or other SEO spam in your title or description, as doing so will likely result in your application being suspended. Refer to `play.google.com/about/storelisting-promotional/metadata/` for more details on Google Play's metadata policy.

Within this section you can also provide video and graphic assets to be used within your application's listing. That includes a link to a promotional video on YouTube, multiple representative screen shots for phone, tablet (7 and 10 inch), TV, and Wear devices, as well as specialized graphics used within Google Play including a high-res application icon, feature and promo graphics, a TV banner, and 360 degree stereoscopic banner for Daydream. You can find full details on the graphic assets and how they are used within Google Play at `support.google.com/googleplay/android-developer/answer/1078870`.

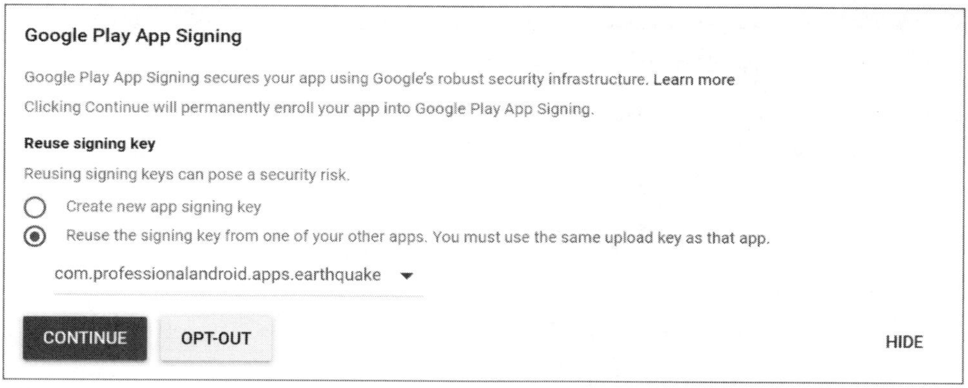

FIGURE 21-14

The application type allows you to indicate if your application is an "app" or a "game," while the category drop-down allows you to specify which category your application should be displayed in within Google Play.

Each application must also receive a content rating, which will be used to inform consumers about the age appropriateness of your app, block or filter your content in certain territories or to specific users where legally required, and to evaluate your app's eligibility for special developer programs.

To determine your app's content rating, click the "Content rating" link—either on the "Store listing" page, or via the left navigation bar. This will display the content rating questionnaire, the start of which is shown in Figure 21-16.

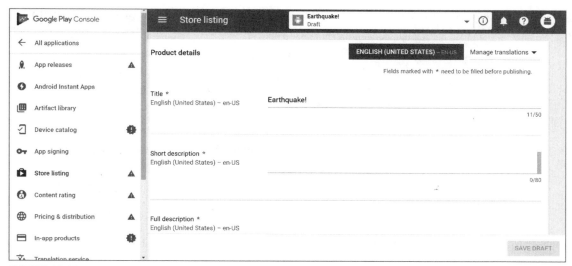

FIGURE 21-15

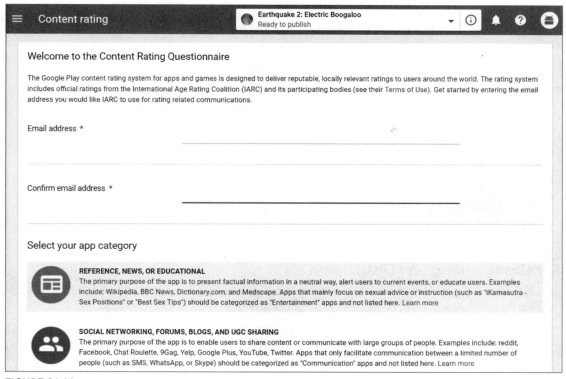

FIGURE 21-16

You must complete the questionnaire for each app, and whenever you distribute an update that changes the app content or features in a way that would affect your responses to the questionnaire.

> **WARNING** *It's important to provide accurate responses to the content rating questionnaire because misrepresentation of your app's content may result in removal or suspension from Google Play.*

Finally, you can supply application-specific contact details for users of your applications, as shown in Figure 21-17.

Contact details

Website

http://...

Email *

Please provide an email address where you may be contacted. This address will be publicly displayed with your app.

Phone

FIGURE 21-17

These details will be published alongside your application's listing in Google Play, so the e-mail and phone number provided should point to a managed support queue rather than to your personal e-mail address.

Specifying Pricing and Distribution

Click "Pricing & distribution" on the left navigation to select the countries and devices you wish to distribute to, as well as the cost (if any) to consumers who wish to use your app.

Start by determining if your app will be free or paid. Details on creating a merchant account and configuring your app for paid distribution is beyond the scope of this book; you can find details at `support.google.com/googleplay/android-developer/#topic=3452890`.

You can then select from which counties your app should be made available, including (in some cases) which carrier networks within those countries, as shown in Figure 21-18.

The Google Play Store allows you to opt-in to a number of special programs designed to distribute your app to specific groups including "Designed for Families"—a program for apps and games designed specifically for kids and family audiences and "Google for Education." The "Pricing & distribution" page provides details on the available programs and their requirements.

Similarly, you can submit your app for review for inclusion in special device categories, including Android Wear, Android TV, Android Auto, and Daydream. These device types require apps to adhere to specific app quality and distribution guidelines (linked to from the Store listing page) before the apps are made available for download to those devices.

	Status ?	Unavailable	Available	
Ukraine	Available (Production, Beta, and Alpha)	◯	◉	
United Arab Emirates	Available (Production, Beta, and Alpha)	◯	◉	
United Kingdom	Available (Production, Beta, and Alpha)	◯	◉	Carrier options
United States		◯	◉	Hide options

Pricing & distribution — Earthquake! Draft

Limit distribution to these carriers:
- ☐ AGMS
- ☐ Aio

FIGURE 21-18

Finally, you must confirm your app conforms to the Android Content Guidelines and acknowledge that your app may be subject to United States export laws.

When you have completed the "Pricing & distribution" section, be sure to click "Save Draft" button.

Publishing Your Application

When you have completed the creation of your store listing, defined the pricing and distribution, and uploaded your APK, you are ready to push your application to production and make it available to customers. This process is commonly known as *release management*.

Your application is ready for publishing when all the gray ticks in the left navigation of the Google Play console have turned green, as shown in Figure 21-19.

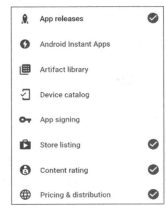

- 🗂 App releases ✓
- ⚡ Android Instant Apps
- 🗄 Artifact library
- 🗂 Device catalog
- 🔑 App signing
- 📱 Store listing ✓
- 🔖 Content rating ✓
- 🌐 Pricing & distribution ✓

FIGURE 21-19

When all issues have been resolved, navigate to "App releases" in the left navigation and select the release channel you wish to publish to. To make your application generally available, use the production channel. The Alpha and Beta channels are described in more detail in the following section.

Click the Review button to confirm that the release details are correct, and click the "Start rollout to production" button to make your app available to users.

You will later use the same process to distribute *updates* to your application; however, for updates you also have the ability to specify a proportion of your existing users who should receive the update—a process known as *staged rollouts*, which is described in more detail in the following sections.

Using the Alpha and Beta Channels

Publishing your application to production makes it available for download by any customer in a country you have selected for distribution, who's using a supported device.

No matter how thoroughly you test your app prior to release, there's no substitute for the testing performed by having real users download and try your application. With a potential audience in the billions, it's good practice to use the Alpha and Beta release channels to make your application available to small, targeted groups to get early feedback and detect potential issues before making your app available to everyone.

This is particularly important because the ratings and reviews provided by your first users can have a dramatic impact on the overall success and popularity of your application. Users of Alpha or Beta releases can't submit public reviews and are aware of, and accustomed to, potential issues in "pre-release" apps. As a result they are likely to provide you with constructive feedback to improve your app prior to general release.

As shown in Figure 21-20, Google Play offers two pre-release channels: Alpha and Beta. There is no functional difference between them, but by convention an Alpha will be used first, and will generally be available to a smaller group than the Beta.

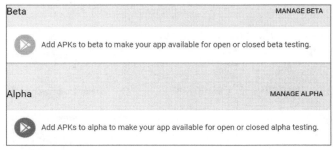

FIGURE 21-20

Either channel allows you to select between an open or closed pre-release. An open Beta (or Alpha) is visible on the Google Play Store, and is available as a download, or update, for anyone who wants to join—though you can restrict the total number of users who can enroll.

Alternatively, a closed Beta (or Alpha) isn't visible in the Google Play Store, except to a restricted group of known users that you specify. You can define this group by e-mail addresses, or select the Alpha / Beta Testing Using Google Groups or Google+ Communities option to supply a corresponding URL; in the latter case, members of the Google Group or Google+ community will have access to the closed Beta (or Alpha). This option is a hybrid of open and closed, and while the listing won't be visible in Google Play for all users, it's possible to configure both Groups and Communities to allow people to join.

In all cases, you must specify a feedback channel that customers can use to provide constructive feedback during the Alpha/Beta testing period.

Once enabled and published, you'll be provided with an opt-in link that you can share with your testers to enable them to join your testing program. Figure 21-21 shows the Manage Testers dialog for a closed Beta.

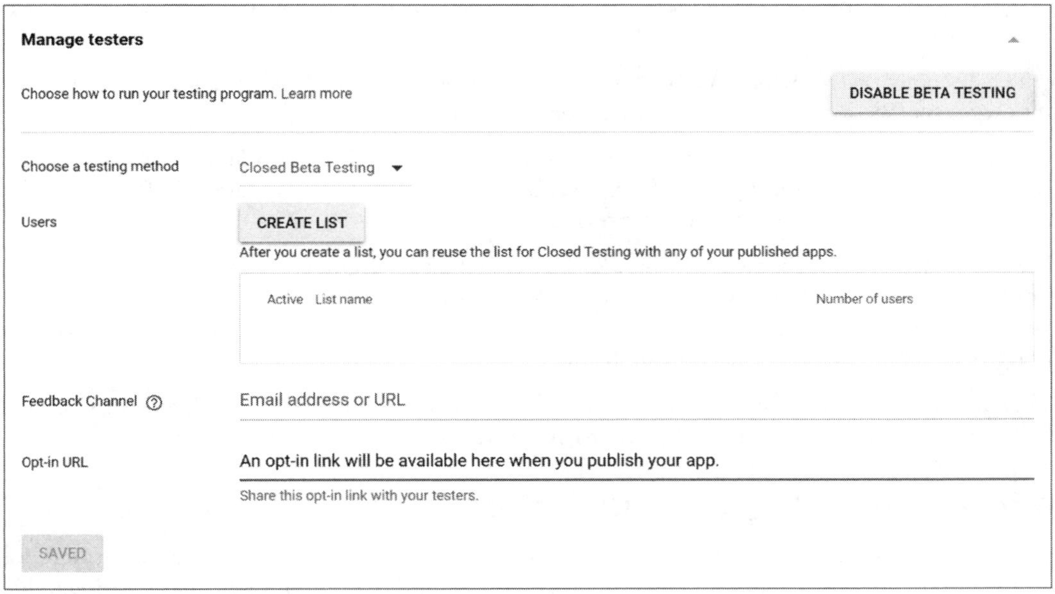

Manage testers

Choose how to run your testing program. Learn more

DISABLE BETA TESTING

Choose a testing method   Closed Beta Testing ▾

Users   CREATE LIST

After you create a list, you can reuse the list for Closed Testing with any of your published apps.

Active   List name   Number of users

Feedback Channel ⑦   Email address or URL

Opt-in URL   An opt-in link will be available here when you publish your app.

Share this opt-in link with your testers.

SAVED

FIGURE 21-21

It's good practice to run a closed Alpha with a known group of testers, followed by an open Beta to solicit feedback, prior to publishing to production. Note that if you run an open Alpha you can't run a Beta test simultaneously.

After Alpha or Beta users follow your opt-in link, they will receive an explanation of what it means to be a tester and a link to opt-in

In addition to the link or e-mail address you provide for feedback, open Alpha or Beta tests allow your testers to provide you with private feedback through the Google Play Store.

The testing process assumes that new APKs will progress from Alpha, to Beta, and finally production; accordingly, your Alpha test APK should have the highest version code.

To join your Alpha or Beta test channel, potential users need a Google or G Suite account. Note that it may take a few hours for the link to your Alpha or Beta app to propagate across Google's servers and become available for testers to use. The same is true for new APKs distributed through these channels.

Staged Rollouts

Alpha and Beta testing allows you to get feedback from a select group of real users prior to a production release. When you're ready to push to production, you should consider a staged rollout—making the update available to a percentage of your existing and new users—to further minimize the chance of introducing significant bugs or crashes.

While the first production version of your application must be made available to all potential users at the same time, updates can be applied in stages, defined as a percentage of the total audience of existing and newly added users.

You can specify the percentage of users to receive the new APK in the "Manage production releases" form.

The target percentage is achieved from a random selection of new and existing users, meaning you can't target specific users, devices, countries, or OS versions.

If you detect potential issues with a release, you can pause the rollout. While it's not possible to revert to a previous release, if you perform a staged rollout for a new—updated—APK, it will first be offered to the users who received the previous update.

Once you're happy with the results from a given percentage of users, you can increase the staged rollout percentage from the "Manage production releases" page. To minimize risk, it's generally good practice to begin very small, targeting 1–2 percent of users, and gradually increasing that percentage over time—carefully monitoring feedback, analytics, and crash reports.

If your app update requires changes to the store listing, it's good practice to update your store listing only when your release has been rolled out to 100 percent of users.

Monitoring Your Application in Production

Once your applications are published, your "All applications" page will list each application, along with the number of active users and installations, average rating and total number of ratings, the last update date, and each app's status, as shown in Figure 21-22.

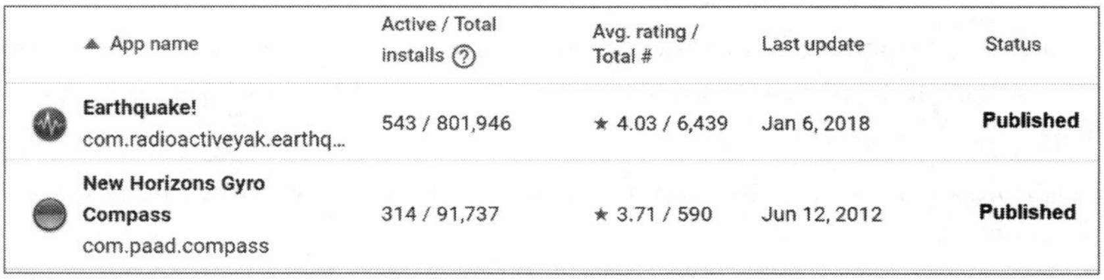

▲ App name	Active / Total installs ⑦	Avg. rating / Total #	Last update	Status
Earthquake! com.radioactiveyak.earthq…	543 / 801,946	★ 4.03 / 6,439	Jan 6, 2018	**Published**
New Horizons Gyro Compass com.paad.compass	314 / 91,737	★ 3.71 / 590	Jun 12, 2012	**Published**

FIGURE 21-22

Using the left navigation you can select the following pages to learn more about how your app is behaving in production. Each page is described in more detail within this section:

➤ **Statistics**—Provides access to a detailed breakdown of your application's installation statistics, including a graph-based timeline of the application's installs, ratings, and crashes.

➤ **Android vitals**—Provides technical performance details and anonymous error reports and stack traces received from users who have opted in to automatically share usage and diagnostics data.

➤ **User acquisition**—Provides a detailed breakdown of the acquisition channels used by customers installing your application from Google Play.

➤ **User feedback**—Provides rating trends and access to, and dynamic analysis of, user reviews.

Application Metrics with Google Play Statistics

The Google Play Statistics page allows you to generate reports that offer a detailed breakdown of your application's installation statistics, including daily updated values for installs, uninstalls, and upgrades, average and cumulative average ratings, and the number of crashes and freezes.

These metrics can be measured across a number of dimensions to provide analytical insight into your users, including breakdowns based on:

➤ The app version

➤ Android platform release

➤ Hardware device

➤ Country and language

➤ Carrier

These reports can be downloaded or displayed as a timeline graph, as shown in Figure 21-23.

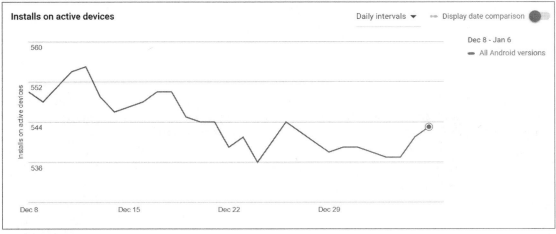

FIGURE 21-23

This information can be extremely useful for deciding where to allocate your resources, which versions of the Android platform you want to support, and in which countries your application is underperforming.

Monitoring Your Application with Android Vitals

The Android Vitals page provides insights into app technical performance in terms of stability, battery, and render times, and anonymous error logging and stack traces collected from Android devices whose users have opted in to automatically share usage and diagnostics data.

The Overview page allows you to view time series graphs for daily rates of freezes, crashes, slow rendering, frozen frames, stuck wake locks, and excessive wakeups. These metrics can be measured across app version, device, or Android OS version.

The "ANRs & crashes" page shows you a summary of ANR (Application Not Responding) freezes and crashes, as shown in Figure 21-24.

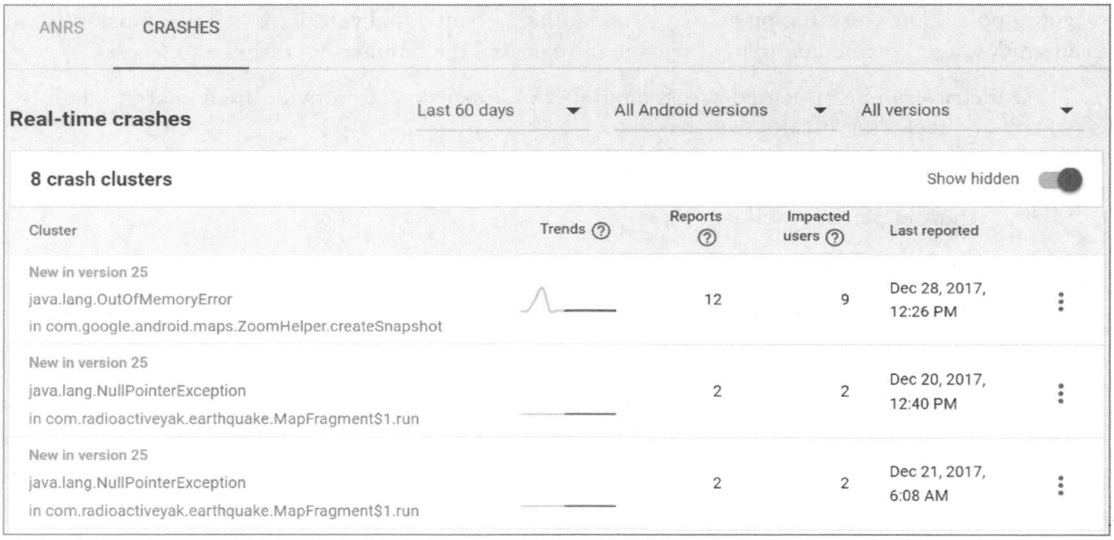

FIGURE 21-24

You can drill down into freezes/crashes to get further details on each error, as shown in Figure 21-25. Each error is described in terms of the exception at the head of the stack, along with the class that threw it and the number/frequency of reports that match those criteria.

FIGURE 21-25

The same page displays a line graph displaying the frequency of reports for this error between a specified date range, along with the distribution of devices on which the errors occurred, and the full stack trace for each error.

These error reports are invaluable for debugging your application in the wild. With hundreds of different Android devices being used in dozens of countries and languages, it's impossible to test every variation. These error reports make it possible for you to determine which edge cases you've missed and rectify them as quickly as possible.

User Acquisition Reports

The "User acquisition" page allows you to generate reports that provide insight into how users find and interact with your Google Play Store listing. By clicking the Retained Installers tab, you can see the unique users who visited your app's store listing, then installed your app and kept your app installed for at least 30 days.

If your application offers in-app purchases or subscriptions, you can select the Buyers tab to generate reports on how your acquisition channels perform in terms of converting users to buyers and repeat buyers, split by country.

It's possible to compare buyer data between acquisition channels or between countries, to investigate which channels/countries attract the highest value users.

Analyzing User Feedback

The User Feedback page allows you to analyze your app's ratings and reviews.

The Ratings page displays your current average rating, the total number of ratings (and reviews), and a histogram of user ratings by number of stars given, as shown in Figure 21-26.

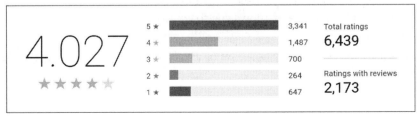

FIGURE 21-26

A time series graph displays the trend in your app on a daily, weekly, or monthly basis either per period or cumulatively. You can also drill-down across a number of dimensions, including breakdowns based on:

➤ The app version

➤ Android platform release

➤ Hardware device

➤ Country and language

➤ Carrier

The Reviews page provides direct access to all user-provided reviews and allows you to compose replies. Each review includes contextual information about the device and user, including:

➤ Application version code

➤ Application version name

➤ Hardware device

➤ Hardware device manufacturer

➤ Device Type (phone, tablet, and so on)

➤ Language

➤ CPU make and model

➤ Native platform

➤ Device RAM

➤ Device screen size and density

➤ OpenGL ES version

➤ Android OS version.

You can search for specific text, or filter reviews based on the preceding criteria.

The Reviews Analysis page provides analytical insight into reader comments. The Updated Ratings section allows you to track ratings and reviews that have been changed, making it possible to see the impact of your replies or app updates.

The Benchmarks section shows your app's ratings for a pre-determined set of topics for apps within the same category on the Google Play Store, and allows you to compare your ratings with similar apps in the same category.

Finally, the Topics section shows ratings for a dynamic set of words mentioned in your app's reviews in English, Spanish, and Japanese.

Note that while direct feedback from users is invaluable, such feedback can be unreliable and contradictory. It's good practice to also use app analytics to reconcile user comments with statistical analysis.

AN INTRODUCTION TO MONETIZING APPLICATIONS

As an open ecosystem, Android enables you to monetize your applications using whatever mechanism you choose. If you choose to distribute and monetize your applications using Google Play, four options typically are available:

➤ **Paid applications**—Charge users an upfront fee before they download and install your application.

➤ **Free applications with In-App Billing (IAB)**—Make the download and installation of the application free, but charge within the application for virtual goods, upgrades, and other value-adds.

➤ **Free applications with Subscriptions**—Make the download and installation of the application free, but charge within the application for a subscription to virtual goods, content, and other value-adds.

➤ **Advertising-supported applications**—Make the download and installation of the application free, and monetize it by displaying advertising.

If you choose to charge for your applications on Google Play, either through upfront charges or IAB/subscriptions, the revenue is split between you and Google Play in the form of a transaction fee. At the time of writing this book, that revenue split is set at 70 percent for the developer.

To use either approach, you must first create a Google Checkout Merchant Account—you can do this from your Android publisher account. Your application listings will then include the option to set a price for the application and the items sold using IAB.

In each case you are the application distributor and merchant of record, so you are responsible for any legal or taxation obligations associated with the sale of your application, subject to the terms described in the DDA.

You can also monetize your application using in-app advertising. The specific process required to set up advertising within your application will vary depending on the ads provider you choose.

It's beyond the scope of this book to describe the setup process for any particular advertising API; however, the general process could be described as follows:

1. Create a publisher account.
2. Download and install the associated ads SDK.
3. Update your Fragment or Activity layouts to include an ad banner.

It's important to ensure that any ads included within your application are as unobtrusive as possible and don't detract significantly from the user experience of your application. It's also important to ensure that your user interaction model doesn't encourage accidental clicks on the ad banner.

In many cases, developers have chosen to offer a paid alternative (either using upfront payment or IAB) to allow users to eliminate ad banners from their applications.

APPLICATION MARKETING, PROMOTION, AND DISTRIBUTION STRATEGIES

The first step in effectively marketing and promoting your application is ensuring that you provide the full set of high-quality assets for your Google Play Store listing.

Several promotional opportunities are available within Google Play; however, with more than 2.7 million other applications available, it's important that you consider alternative avenues for marketing and promotion rather than simply launching your application and crossing your fingers.

While your marketing and promotion strategies will vary widely depending on your goals and budget, the following list details some of the most effective techniques to consider:

➤ **Offline cross promotion**—If you have a significant offline presence (such as stores or branches), or a large media presence (such as within newspapers, magazines, or on TV), cross promoting your application through those channels can be a particularly effective way to increase awareness and help to ensure users trust the download. Traditional advertising techniques such as TV and newspaper advertisements can be extremely effective in raising awareness of your application.

➤ **Online cross promotion**—If you have a significant web presence, promoting your application through direct links to Google Play can be an effective way to drive downloads. If your application provides a better user experience than your mobile website, you can detect browser visitors from Android devices and direct them to Google Play to download your native app.

➤ **Third-party promotion**—Distributing a promotional video on YouTube and leveraging social networks, blogs, press releases, and online review sites can help provide positive word of mouth.

➤ **Online advertising**—Online advertising using in-app ad networks (such as AdMob) or traditional search-based advertising (such as Google AdWords) can drive significant impressions and downloads for your application.

Application Launch Strategies

Ratings and reviews can have a significant impact on your application's ranking in category lists and within Google Play search results. As a result, it can be difficult to recover from a poor launch. The following list describes some of the strategies you can use to ensure a successful launch:

➤ **Use closed Alphas, open Betas, and Staged Rollouts**—Make your application available to small, targeted groups to get early feedback and detect potential issues before making your app available to everyone. Users of Alpha or Beta releases can't submit public reviews and are aware of, and accustomed to, potential issues in "pre-release" apps. As a result they are likely to provide you with constructive feedback to improve your app prior to general release.

➤ **Iterate on features not quality**—A poorly implemented but feature-rich application will receive worse reviews than a well-polished application that doesn't do everything. If you are using an agile approach of releasing early and often, ensure each release is of the same high quality, adding new features as part of each release. Similarly, each release should be more polished and stable than the last.

➤ **Create high-quality Google Play assets**—The first impression your application makes is through its appearance in Google Play. Maximize the likelihood of that impression resulting in an installation by creating assets that represent the quality of your application.

➤ **Be honest and descriptive**—Disappointed users who find your application is not as it was described are likely to uninstall it, rate it poorly, and leave negative comments.

Internationalization

At the time of writing, Google Play was available in more than 190 countries. While the exact breakdown varies by application category, in most cases more than 50 percent of application installations are downloaded from countries outside the United States on devices whose language is set to non-English.

Japan and South Korea represent the two largest consumers of applications outside the United States, while on a per-capita basis South Korea, Taiwan, and Hong Kong represent the most voracious consumers of Android applications.

Externalizing all your application's string (and where appropriate, image) resources, as described in Chapter 4, makes it easy to localize your applications by providing alternative translated resources.

In addition to the application itself, Google Play provides support for adding local language titles and descriptions for your applications, as shown in Figure 21-27.

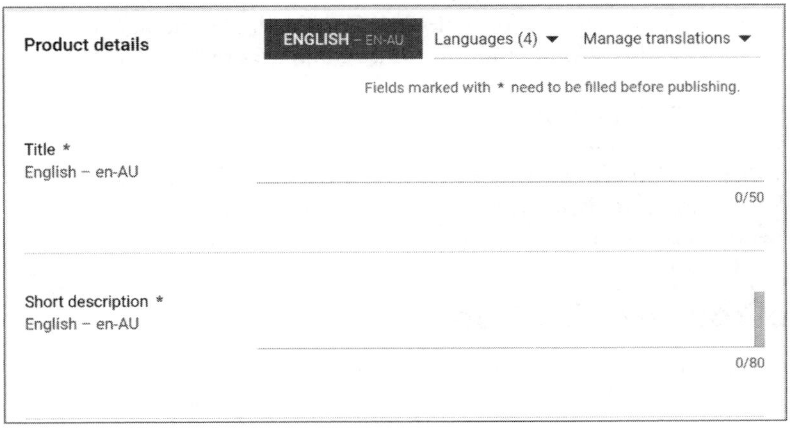

Product details

ENGLISH – EN-AU   Languages (4) ▼   Manage translations ▼

Fields marked with * need to be filled before publishing.

Title *
English – en-AU

0/50

Short description *
English – en-AU

0/80

FIGURE 21-27

While nonnative speakers may be able to use your applications, there is a very good chance that they'll search and browse Google Play using *their* native language. To maximize the discoverability of your application, it's good practice to invest in creating translations for at least the title and description of your application.

> **NOTE** *The process of providing fully localized translations for your application can be expensive and time-consuming, so it's often useful to use the Android Developer Console statistics to prioritize the languages to localize for.*
>
> *Anecdotally, it has been found by many developers that bad translations are considered worse than no translation.*

USING FIREBASE TO MONITOR YOUR APPLICATION

Google's Firebase SDK includes a variety of tools that can help you monitor your application after launch to ensure you're providing the best possible user experience, including:

- ➤ **Firebase Analytics**—Analyze users and user behavior to better understand who is using your application and how they are using it.

- ➤ **Firebase Performance Monitoring**—Provides tools to monitor app performance and diagnose performance issues.

- ➤ **Firebase Crash Reporting**—Allows you to receive detailed reports from app crashes, and to use the Firebase Crash dashboard to monitor your app's overall health.

- ➤ **Firebase Test Lab**—Provides physical and virtual devices you can use to run tests that simulate actual usage environments.

The Firebase SDK interacts with the Google Play services application, and requires the Google Play services SDK to be installed. You can find more information on Google Play services, and how to install the SDK, in Chapter 15, "Location, Contextual Awareness, and Mapping."

> **NOTE** *Due to Firebase's dependency on the Google Play Store, if you plan to release via other distribution channels you may need to include alternative implementations for functionality that depend on Google Play services.*

Adding Firebase to Your Application

To add any of the Firebase monitoring tools described in this section, you must first install the Firebase SDK, which requires Android 4.0 Ice Cream Sandwich (API Level 14) and Google Play services version 10.2.6 or higher.

Android Studio includes a Firebase Assistant to simplify adding Firebase components to your app. To use it, select Tools ➪ Firebase to display the assistant window.

Selecting any Firebase tool you wish to add to your application, such as Analytics, will display a wizard that allows you to "Connect to Firebase."

If this is the first time you've added a Firebase component to an app in Android Studio, you'll be prompted to select a Google account to connect to, and a series of permissions to accept.

Once you're signed into Firebase, return to Android Studio and you'll see a dialog that allows you to create a new Firebase project, or select an existing one to use for your app.

With your app connected, you can return to the wizard. The next step adds the relevant Firebase tool to your project, by adding Firebase Gradle build script dependency to your project-level `build. gradle` file, adding the Firebase plug-in for Gradle, and a dependency for the Firebase tool to your `build.gradle` file.

Using Firebase Analytics

Mobile application analytics packages, such as Firebase Analytics, are effective tools for better understanding who is using your application and how they are using it. Understanding this information can help you make objective decisions on where to focus your development resources.

While the statistics provided by the Google Play Console (described earlier in this chapter) offer valuable insight into your users' language, country, and handsets, using detailed analytics can provide a much richer source of information, from which you can discover bugs, prioritize your feature list, and decide where best to allocate your development resources.

> **NOTE** *There are no restrictions on which analytics packages you can use within your Android applications. Although this section describes the process for configuring and using Firebase Analytics specifically, the same general process is applicable for most alternatives.*

If you're using the Firebase wizard in Android Studio, following the steps described in the previous section will add Firebase to your application and apply the necessary changes to you app module Gradle build file. Note that Firebase Analytics requires only the Firebase-core library as a dependency:

```
compile 'com.google.firebase:firebase-core:10.0.1'
```

To start tracking app analytics, open the launch Activity and declare the `com.google.firebase. analytics.FirebaseAnalytics` object as a member variable, and initialize it within the `onCreate` handler:

```
private FirebaseAnalytics mFirebaseAnalytics;

@Override
protected void onCreate(Bundle savedInstanceState) {
  super.onCreate(savedInstanceState);

  // Obtain the FirebaseAnalytics instance.
  mFirebaseAnalytics = FirebaseAnalytics.getInstance(this);
}
```

Once you've added and initialized the Firebase SDK, you will automatically begin receiving a number of user properties and events.

> **NOTE** *To ensure user privacy, minimum thresholds are applied to all data when viewed in the Firebase Analytics console to prevent viewing reports that could be used to infer the demographics of individual users.*

The user properties available include your users' age, gender, country, language, and interests; the device category, brand, model, and OS version; the store from which the app was installed; the current app version; if the user is new or established; and when the user first opened the app.

The automatically recorded events include the first time the app is launched after installation, the completion of any in-app purchases, user engagement, session starts, app updates, app removal, OS updates, exceptions, and app data resets.

You can learn more about the automatically collected user properties and events here: `support` `.google.com/firebase/answer/6317485`.

You can also use the `FirebaseAnalytics` instance to log predefined or custom events using the `logEvent` method. Pass in the type of event that occurred using a static constant from the `FirebaseAnalytics.Event` class, or a custom event, and a Bundle that uses `FirebaseAnalytics` `.Param` constants to provide the relevant parameters for that type:

```
Bundle bundle = new Bundle();
bundle.putString(FirebaseAnalytics.Param.SEARCH_TERM, searchTermString);

mFirebaseAnalytics.logEvent(FirebaseAnalytics.Event.SEARCH, bundle);
```

Standard event types include joining a group, logging in, presenting an offer, searching, selecting content, sharing, signing up, spending virtual currency, and beginning and ending a tutorial.

A full list of the predefined events appropriate for all apps, and links to event types for apps in the retail/e-commerce; jobs, education, local deals, and real estate; travel; and games categories are available at `support.google.com/firebase/answer/6317498?` `ref_topic=6317484`.

You can see the corresponding predefined parameters at `firebase.google.com/docs/reference/` `android/com/google/firebase/analytics/FirebaseAnalytics.Param`.

Alternatively, you can generate custom events with custom parameters:

```
Bundle bundle = new Bundle();
bundle.putString(MISSILE_NAME, name);
bundle.putInt(MISSILE_RANGE, range);

mFirebaseAnalytics.logEvent(LAUNCHED_MISSILE, bundle);
```

Integrating analytics into your app is critical to understanding the way your application is being used, and will help you to optimize your workflows in the same way you would a website. As such, it can be useful to log events that move users from one Activity to another.

Taken one step further, you can record any action—which options were changed, which menu items or Action Bar actions were selected, which popup menus were displayed, if a Widget was added, and which buttons were pressed. Using this information, you can determine exactly how your application is being used, allowing you to better understand how well the assumptions you made during design match actual usage.

When building games, you can use the same process to gain insight into players' progress though the game. You can track how far people progress before quitting, identify levels that are more difficult (or easier) than you expected, and then modify your game accordingly.

Perhaps most usefully, if your app has a commerce component—such as purchasing goods or booking hotels—you can track the paths that led to successful purchases and bookings.

To view and analyze the analytics recorded from your application, navigate to the Firebase console at `console.firebase.google.com`. Select your app, and then choose the Analytics option from the left menu to be presented with the Analytics dashboard shown in part in Figure 21-28.

If you upgrade your Firebase account to the paid "Blaze" plan it's possible to link your Firebase analytics to Google BigQuery, a serverless, petabyte-scale data warehousing and analytics engine. Using BigQuery you can use SQL queries to access your raw, unsampled event data along with all of your parameters and user properties.

Once your Firebase app is linked to a BigQuery project, your event data will be exported to the selected BigQuery dataset each day. You can then query, export, or join your analytics dataset with data from external sources to perform custom analysis.

To join Firebase Analytics to BigQuery, click the cog icon from the left navigation of the Firebase console and click Project Settings. Then click the Account Linking tab followed by the Upgrade Project and Link on the BigQuery card, and then follow the instructions to create a BigQuery dataset.

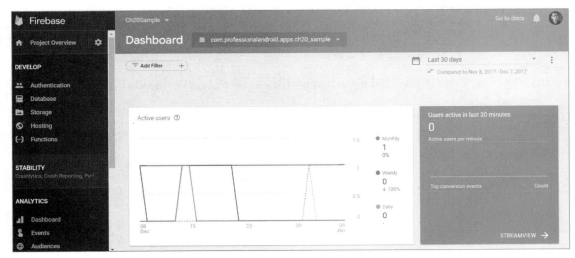

FIGURE 21-28

BigQuery provides 10Gb of free storage and 1Tb of free queries each month, and doesn't charge for ingesting data. You can find more information on BigQuery and its pricing model at `cloud.google` `.com/bigquery/pricing`.

Firebase Performance Monitoring

Firebase Performance Monitoring (FPM) enables you to gain insight into the performance characteristics of your apps. Performance issues are a significant factor in the user experience, but to fix performance issues it's first necessary to understand where and when those issues arise for real users in real-world usage environments.

Firebase Performance Monitoring works by reporting *traces*—reports of performance data captured between two points in time. This includes a number of automatic traces including app startup time, background time, and foreground time, as well as any custom traces you define.

At the time of writing, Firebase Performance Monitoring is in Beta, and is not available within the Android Studio Firebase assistant. Use the technique described in the previous section to connect your app to Firebase, and then use the following steps to add Performance Monitoring to your app.

Within the project-level Gradle build file, ensure `jcenter()` is included in the `buildscript` repositories, and add the `com.google.firebase:firebase-plugins` classpath to the `buildscript` dependencies:

```
buildscript {
  repositories {
    google()
    jcenter()
  }
  dependencies {
    classpath 'com.android.tools.build:gradle:2.3.3'
    classpath 'com.google.gms:google-services:3.0.0'
    classpath ('com.google.firebase:firebase-plugins:1.1.5') {
      exclude group: 'com.google.guava', module: 'guava-jdk5'
    }
  }
}
```

Open the app-level Gradle build file and apply the `com.google.firebase.firebase-perf` plug-in:

```
apply plugin: 'com.android.application'
apply plugin: 'com.google.firebase.firebase-perf'
```

Finally, add the `com.google.firebase:firebase-perf` dependency:

```
dependencies {
    implementation 'com.google.firebase:firebase-core:11.8.0'
    implementation 'com.google.firebase:firebase-perf:11.8.0'
}
```

Once installed, Firebase Performance Monitoring automatically collects traces that measure:

Application startup—The time between when the user opens the app and when the app is responsive.

Time in foreground—The time between when the first foreground Activity calls `onResume` until the last foreground Activity calls `onStop`.

Time in background—The time between the last foreground Activity calls `onStop` until the next Activity to reach the foreground calls `onResume`.

Firebase Performance Metrics will also produce a report on all HTTP/S network requests that captures the response time, payload size, and success rate of each request.

In addition to the automated tracing and monitoring, it's also possible to create your own custom traces, allowing you to measure performance metrics in specific areas of your app.

The simplest way to trace the performance of a given method is to use the `@AddTrace` annotation, providing a string to identify the resulting trace:

```
@AddTrace(name = "onReticulateSplinesTrace", enabled = true)
protected void reticulateSplines() {
  // TODO Method implementation
}
```

This will result in a trace that begins when the method is called, and stops when the method completes.

Alternatively, you can create a custom trace, which allows you to specify traces that include counters, and which span across multiple methods. You can have multiple custom traces in your app, potentially running concurrently.

To create a custom trace, create a new `Trace` object by calling the static `getInstance` method on the `FirebasePerformance` class to return the `FirebasePerformance` instance, then call `newTrace`—specifying a string identifier—to create a new `Trace` object:

```
Trace splineTrace =
  FirebasePerformance.getInstance().newTrace("spline_trace");
```

To begin the trace, call `start` on the `Trace` object:

```
splineTrace.start();
```

While the trace is running, you can add counters for performance-related events using the `incrementCounter` method, specifying a string identifier:

```
if (cacheExpired) {
  splineTrace.incrementCounter("item_cache_expired");
} else {
  splineTrace.incrementCounter("item_cache_hit");
}
```

When the process you're tracing completes, stop the trace by calling its `stop` method:

```
splineTrace.stop();
```

To view the results of Firebase Performance Monitoring, navigate to your app within the Firebase Developer Console, and click the Performance option from the Stability section within the left navigation. The performance page shows each of the tracked performance metrics, all of which can be broken down by dimensions including app version, country, device, and OS version.

INDEX